This Is My Word
A and Ω
The Gospel of Jesus

The Christ-Revelation
Which True Christians The World Over
Have Come to Know

With a brief autobiography of
Gabriele, the prophetess and emissary of God
for our time

D1300933

Fourth Expanded Edition, January 2011
© The Word – The Universal Spirit
in Universal Life
P.O. Box 3549
Woodbridge, CT 06525
USA

Licensed edition
translated from the original German title:
„Das ist Mein Wort.
A und Ω. Das Evangelium Jesu.
Die Christus-Offenbarung, welche inzwischen
Die wahren Christen in aller Welt kennen"

Order No. S 007en

From the Universal Life Series
with the consent of
© Gabriele-Verlag Das Wort GmbH
Max-Braun-Str. 2, 97828 Marktheidenfeld
Germany

With a short autobiography of Gabriele, the
prophetess and emissary of God for our time

The German edition is the work of reference for
all questions regarding meaning of contents.

ISBN: 978-1-890841-38-6

A Short Autobiography

The Prophet –
The Instrument of God
Gabriele Remembers

Gabriele, The Prophetess of God.

The Eternal consents to a charcoal drawing,
but no photograph.

Table of Contents

A Short Autobiography
The Prophet – The Instrument of God
Gabriele Remembers

*The first spiritual instructions
through my spiritual teacher,
brother Emanuel*

Thirty-two years ago, I was about 40 years of age. As I sat one Christmas morning in the living room with my small family, I focused my attention on the Christmas tree because I was a Catholic. Next to the Christmas tree stood a beautiful wooden figurine, a Christmas present. Suddenly I saw how something moved behind the figurine; it was a beautiful being. I saw it and heard in the very depths of my inner being the words: "I am your spiritual teacher, brother Emanuel!" I became frightened, very frightened. What was this all about? I didn't know any brother Emanuel.

One or two days went by and again I heard a message: "I am your spiritual teacher, brother Emanuel, and I will prepare you for the great and mighty 'I Am the I Am from eternity to eternity,' for the prophetic word, that has never dried up."

My fright was great, and I told my family about this. My husband shrugged his shoulders and said,

"What should that mean? I don't understand that." And we left it at that. But this lasted at the most only two more days. Suddenly I heard a mighty voice that roared into me. It was like a blazing fire, on which wood is placed. It said, "I Am the I Am from eternity to eternity. I, the I Am, will have you trained to be my prophetess for this world, for all the nations of this Earth. I have placed my servant at your side, a divine being, the cherub of divine wisdom. He will prepare you and show you how you can receive My word more and more and ever more deeply."

Again, I cringed, because as a spiritual novice, I couldn't begin to deal with that. I was a Catholic Christian, and as such, spiritually ignorant. For this reason, I couldn't make any sense out of it. Even though this message in my heart came with a mighty stream of love, that felt like balm to me, I still didn't understand what was happening.

Some days later my spiritual teacher, brother Emanuel, spoke in my heart again. This is how he introduced himself to the Earth, to this world. Slowly and simply, with words taken from my own plain vocabulary, he explained to me that what I had believed as a Catholic until that moment is not the word of God; it is not the will of God. He explained to me what it means to pray. He explained that prayer comes from the heart, that prayer should become the language of the soul, and that a person who calls himself Christian should also be a follower of Jesus of Nazareth.

Only a few sentences came. At first, they were merely short explanatory teachings that I received in my heart. But soon the word grew deeper, and the spiritual teacher spoke in ever more detail. He explained to me how I was to think and live in the future, because, as he said: "The mighty Spirit, who already speaks into you, Himself, wants to train you to become His prophetess. The word that flows into you comes from heaven. It is God, the Almighty, in Christ, your Redeemer. His word is His message to all people. You went forth for the message from heaven, to give it in the prophetic word."

I must say that I was not a good Catholic, just like many others. Every now and then I went to church, but I couldn't begin to deal with many of the things that Catholicism taught. I had other ideas for my life: I liked sports, I liked going here and there, meeting with acquaintances, I cultivated a social life. My parents were Catholic. And so, I was baptized a Catholic and taught about Catholicism in school.

Now suddenly I heard in me: "In the spirit of love, in the spirit of truth, in the Kingdom of God, there are no ceremonies, there are no rites, there are no dogmas, there are no costumes worn by men." And I knew that the eternal Spirit, in this case, brother Emanuel, the cherub of divine wisdom, wanted to say the following to me: Remain a simple person! Give God alone the honor.

This meant that whoever lives in the spirit of God bows before the eternal Spirit deep in his inner being, for the Spirit dwells in each person, in the soul of every human being. And every person is a temple of the Holy Spirit. For me, as a Catholic, that was new, but this message came over and over again. And over and over again, it said: "The more you believe this and immerse yourself in your innermost being and do the will of God, the more the prophetic Spirit will radiate through, the life."

I thought, well, the prophetic Spirit, but why me in particular? I'm no more than a simple person. I'm not eloquent, so why me, of all people? and the voice came over and over again, speaking in the following sense: "You went out, in order to give the prophetic word. He, the mighty Spirit, will place it on your lips, after a certain training, after a certain spiritual alignment. And you will speak out that which is His will."

The spiritual teacher, the cherub of divine wisdom, said to me: "I will prepare you, and the 'I

Am the I Am' will speak mightily through you."
This kept dismaying me every time anew. Whenever I heard the words "I Am the I Am from eternity to eternity," my heart sank to its lowest point:
I, a small, simple person, unpracticed in free speaking, above all before a lot of people, and not in the
least bit eloquent, should go out in public as a
prophetess? – This seemed impossible to me!

But the prophetic Spirit, here, Brother Emanuel,
did not let up: "If God wants this, it will be done.
And He wants it! And your soul obeys His will!
As a human being, you also have to obey, so that
it will be fulfilled, what the divine being in you,
called a soul in the human being, received from
above, from the Kingdom of God, for the Earth:
the prophetic word for the nations of this Earth."

I still had no idea what all that would mean for
me. The voice of brother Emanuel was, on the
one hand, foreign to me, and on the other hand, it
kept drawing closer to me, because it was loving,
but direct and assertive. He taught me to think away
from Catholicism. I kept hearing from him: "Pray
from your heart, and bow only before Him, by
doing His will. Do not bow before the humanness
of the person. The one who bows before God will
also bow before the innermost part of his neighbor,
because the eternal Spirit is in the soul of every
person and in all things."

He taught me that a large part of Catholicism is the work of human beings and has nothing to do with God's will.

I learned little by little, that God is the greatest, the Almighty. God is the All-One, the All-Law, the eternity and infinity. But He is also the Father of all of His children, whom He loves. He, the mighty Spirit, explained to me that there is no eternal damnation, and that I should not worry about being eternally damned. There is no such thing. God, the love, safeguards all of His children; all will return to Him, to His Father-heart. This is why the Son of God went out, to bring redemption, the light, that is a beacon for every soul on the way to the Father's house.

Hope drew into me, thankfulness and peace. Ever more often, I sat in a corner and prayed the Lord's Prayer. Suddenly, I again heard brother Emanuel in my heart. It was his voice that spoke in my thoughts. I noticed that I couldn't think in any other way; he took over my world of thoughts. Regarding this, he explained to me: "I am the monitor of your thoughts." So I prayed, and he interrupted me over and over again in the Lord's Prayer and taught it to me.

The right kind of prayer
shown with the example of the
Lord's Prayer

As an example, I want to use the Lord's Prayer that many Christians pray, and explain how I was given an understanding of the Lord's Prayer, a Lord's Prayer in the Original Christian meaning.

I had hardly spoken the words: "Our Father who art in heaven, hallowed is Your name!" – when already I heard brother Emanuel. He instructed me to again speak the prayer words that Jesus, the Christ, had given to us people, and to do so slowly and consciously this time. As I did this, my spiritual teacher asked me:

"What do you understand with the words, 'our Father'? Both these words, 'our Father,' show that all people, all souls and all heavenly beings are meant. The Father is the Father of all people, of all beings; He is the Father of love. Remember that He also loves you and will make you His instrument!"

My soul softened, and my heart jubilated. And yet, I couldn't let go of a certain fear. I became apprehensive. Me, a simple, insignificant person, should become a prophetess? All too happily, I withdrew into my old habitual perception of things.

Oh, but I'm secure in my family, and secure at home. I want to continue to serve the family as a mother and wife.

And yet, I continued to pray:

"Our kingdom comes, Your will is done, on Earth as it is in heaven." Again, brother Emanuel spoke up: "What is our kingdom?" He gave the answer in the following sense: "It is the eternal homeland, it is the Father's house, that wants to have all His children back again soon, in the Kingdom of Peace." And he explained to me: "As in heaven, that is how it should be on Earth." Brother Emanuel added the following: "At this moment, you still don't understand what the prophetic message means. But soon you will learn about it."

Again, I prayed: "You give us this day our daily bread. And forgive us our trespasses as we forgive those who trespass against us." Brother Emanuel spoke extensively, in order to explain the law of cause and effect, of sowing and reaping: "To forgive means to develop remorse for what is not in the will of God, and to ask for forgiveness. And if people have done something to *you* that hurt you, forgive them. And if you have recognized a culpability that you can make amends for with works of love, then do it! This is how you free yourself from sin and grow in the spirit of love, also for the prophetic word."

I continued to pray: "You lead us in time of temptation and deliver us from evil." "Well, He delivers all souls and people from evil," said brother Emanuel. "For the redeeming power of the Christ of God is in the soul of every person. The person who repents, clears up his sins and no longer commits them truly feels himself delivered, freed from the evil that he, in the final analysis, imposed upon himself." I began to see the Lord's Prayer with totally different eyes. Reverence rose from my inner being. I gradually began to understand what it means to bow before the Almighty.

I closed the Lord's Prayer: "For ours is the kingdom and the power and the glory from eternity to eternity." In my heart I felt the following: I may very well be a human being, but there is something in me, that is not of this world. What is not of this world I call "soul." But in the very depths, it is a divine being that wants to serve the Eternal. And so now, a great "yes" for the prophetic calling came from the heart of my person. My soul had already long since spoken the "yes." But I, the human being, did not yet grasp what the "yes" of the human being meant for the prophetic calling, much less what it would bring for me.

*The extensive work of the prophet on himself,
in order to become "clean"*

The yes of the prophet has a lot, a lot of content.
I had to learn to recognize and get rid of my all-
too-human aspects, my whole way of thinking and
wanting, that was focused on me, the human being.
As seen from the soul, I had to become clean; I
had to clean my whole person from the top of my
head to the soles of my feet. And so this means,
that I had to accomplish what the Spirit, even today,
teaches over and over again. Everything that we
describe as sin, or as a wrong attitude against the
life, against the law of love and of freedom, I had
to recognize, repent of step by step, clear it up,
and no longer do it. And so, I was no longer allowed
to give free rein to my all-too-human thoughts.

Nevertheless, I could ask questions, ask for
advice of my spiritual teacher: Well, then how
should I think? In this case, he did not tell me how
I should think, instead, he said: "You have the Ten
Commandments and the Sermon on the Mount of
Jesus in front of you – read them. From that,
deduce how you should think."

And so, I began to think, as God wants. And
always, when I was against a person, the voice of
the heart would make itself heard: "Why are you

against him? Why are you upset with him? Why are you negative toward him? What is your concern? When you think that way, what do you want to achieve?"

Brother Emanuel gave me time to be able to explore myself, in terms of why I felt the way I did. I always kept coming back to my all-too-human root: I didn't like this one. I didn't like that one. Because there was something about him that disturbed me. Because there was something about him that I liked or didn't like. *All of this* I had to recognize, and then repent of it and clear it up. And I had to learn to bow, particularly before the innermost part of those people whom I belittled, because the Spirit of God dwells in every person.

And so, in my inner being I bowed before the Spirit in that person. And then I came to realize that in this way I learned to understand my neighbor, whom I had rejected at first. Suddenly I was able to give him a word that rose from the depths of my soul. I looked into the eyes of my neighbor, and his eyes shone. And I felt: His soul accepted this word, because it came from the depths of my soul. This is how I learned to become clean, that is, to become pure. But this meant a constant orientation to the inner light, the inner life.

It was a very powerful and unusually manifold preparation to become a prophet. It's not so easy to simply imagine what it means, when it is said, "God broke into the life of the person in order to make of him His instrument." The prophet, who at first is an unknowing person with many different human programs and patterns of thought, has to clean up his act – and this, in a relatively brief period of time – he has to purify himself, in order to be able to receive this mighty life that is the unity. And so, from the very beginning, he is strictly guided and schooled by the Spirit of God in everything and everywhere. The prophet has to learn about everything, and above all, fulfill – this means, do it himself – whatever he passes on to his fellowman.

A preparation for what awaited me on the way to becoming a prophet

Soon after, the Christ in God, our Father, the mighty Spirit, spoke up again. He explained to me the work of His redemption. He explained to me the divine work for this Earth. And He explained to me, what it means to be prophetess. He explained to me that I would have to orient myself totally and completely to the eternal Spirit in me, that I would have to leave everything that would have a disturbing effect on my mission, on the mission from the heavens. Christ spoke in absolute terms. He explained to me with full authority and in the mighty I Am, that the prophetic word would be strong and mighty and that He would lead me out of the family, to the people of all nations.

Christ also did not keep from me that I would be attacked by the churches. Through His word, I learned that they will not listen to me. They will condemn the prophetic word, as has been done at all times. That the prophets went through very difficult times and He said that I, too, would go through a lot of difficulties. That He will build an Original Christian work, as it is in the Original Christian tradition, where people come together, who step by step live the Lord's Prayer, who fulfill the Sermon on the Mount, who see the Ten Commandments of God as a part of their life. And there will again be Original Christians who live together, who work together, who later would then found Original Christian enterprises. They will work to earn a living in the enterprises, but mainly for building the Kingdom of God on Earth.

Based on my "yes,"
I became a captive of God.
The prophet no longer has free will

I didn't understand it; nevertheless, I had to speak out the words. A pressure came into my consciousness from above with such might and authority, that I could no longer say "no," and I felt how the free will disappeared. Suddenly I saw myself as a captive of the Almighty. Well, I let myself be captured, because even as a human being, I had given my yes. But over and over again, I struggled against it, when I suddenly felt that I could no longer practice any sports, which I wanted, when I could no longer go out into society, which was all-too-human. I felt in my heart that I shouldn't do it and, in the end, it was that I may not.

The prophet is called from above to fulfill God's will. In this way, the prophetic Spirit takes effect in the soul of the person, in the prophet, so that he does what the soul, that is, the divine being, had promised in the homeland: *Your* will is done; on Earth as it is in heaven. The person is simply turned off. What the soul wants, the spirit being from above, is fulfilled. Even when the person still keeps on complaining – the message from above, the message from the heavens, *must* be fulfilled. With this, the will of the person is secondary; it is hardly heeded.

The prophetic Spirit took possession of me and led me to the people. And so, He tore me out of my secureness in the family. He taught me how to receive the word ever more deeply. And, in the end, He spoke with full authority through me. I often didn't even know how it happened to me. My yes was coercion. He forced me to do what He wants.

Many a one is of the opinion that the language of the Almighty has to come in a state of trance. Why should it, if God is *in me*? Why must I fall into a trance, into some kind of nebulous state? The alertness of the human being is a prerequisite for the word of life. The only thing that I had to do, and could not let go of, was to maintain the constant connection to Him, the great Spirit in me. I had to learn how to do this. And it was often very, very difficult, particularly when it became clear that I could no longer return to the family.

Why not in the family? Why no longer with the relatives? The one could accept what I did, the other couldn't understand; and another distracted me with all kinds of situations and thoughts and desires that I should fulfill. And I couldn't do it. I would've gotten out from under God's control. As a result of this, He took me out of the family, out of the society I was in, out of the midst of my relatives, and placed me in the middle of this world as a simple, plain woman, who often had a difficult time speaking with people. I was, and am, shy, very reserved, but very alert, when it has to do with justice or with the truth.

One thing was very odd to me. When I spoke with people, I often made a mistake and didn't know what I should say. But when the Almighty went to work, then all barriers were suddenly wiped away. He placed His word on my lips, and I had to speak out what was and is His will. I saw, and heard at the same time, what God's will was, and this, right up to this very day.

The prophet no longer has free will. God's will – His law, His plan – is the determining factor. To accept this was often very, very difficult for me, particularly, when I was attacked by the churches, by the sect commissioners, who wanted to destroy Original Christianity via radio and television.

The divine message of unity.
Why live as a vegetarian?

Despite all these inner and outer demands, the Spirit began to teach, teach and teach again. He first taught about the message of unity, the message of love. He taught people who came to Him what it means to live in unity. He taught us people what peace means. He taught us the love of enemy. He taught us the love for God and for neighbor. He taught us how we should behave toward the animals and toward the Mother Earth. He taught us how we could become vegetarian. He taught us that creation is the omnipresent life, because He, God, is in all things.

God is present in all things. He is the Creator-God, the mighty light, the Christ of God, who is in all things, in nature, in the plants, in the animals, in the minerals. This mighty Spirit taught me to walk over the Earth attentively, because the light, the All-power, God, is in all things. And He taught me that He, the Creator, the mighty Spirit, is the life in the animals, in the plants and in the stones.

"Life is a revelation," this is how He spoke to me. "If you are for life, then you are linked in unity and in love with the innermost part of your neighbor, and also with the love in the animals, in the plants and in the minerals." He taught me the fine and subtle language of light of the animals, of the plants and of the stones. And I became clean in myself: I respected the animals. I began to love the animals, just as God, the great Spirit, the Creator of life, had led me to understand it. I came to understand the Mother Earth, who breathes a sign of relieve with every step that we take in the awareness that under our feet is the Spirit, the life. He taught me to kick no stone away from me deliberately, but to respect the life.

In this way, the Eternal Spirit made me aware of what it means to live as a vegetarian. For the life is in all things. The animal receives from the Earth; the human being receives from the Earth; so we should take the food for ourselves that the Earth gives us.

At first, I rebelled and protested: "Animals, though, eat other animals!" The voice of the spiritual teacher explained to me: "That is so because man does it. People eat animals. For this reason, animals also eat animals. Why? Because killing draws through the atmosphere and the behavior of the animals is a certain deformation, a spawn of the thoughts of man. If the human being returned to vegetarianism, if he were to eat from what the

Mother Earth gives to him, then the animals, in time, would do the same thing."

The symbol of the resurrection of life:
The cross without a corpse

Every time the Spirit of God shone the light of truth very sternly on the evil and unlawfulness in the sphere of the churches, it became very difficult for me to speak out the word of God. My heart then became heavy. Because when God, for example, spoke against the splendorous works of the Catholic Church, or against the exorbitant wealth, against all these machinations, I could not understand much of it; it was incomprehensible to me. Today it is different. Today, the Catholic and Lutheran Churches themselves expose what they truly are. Back then, on the other hand, I had to speak out something that I did not understand. I simply had to do it; I was absolutely subject to the compulsion of prophecy.

It was only later that I experienced more and more how the Catholic and Lutheran Churches, well, in the end, everything that turns to without – whether they are called churches or whatever they call themselves – are not in the will of God. For God does not dwell in churches built of stone. God does not want all the external, showy pageantry. God does not want all the magic that is built up around Him. But God does not want the so-called crucifix either, for the eternal Father had His Son resurrected! Christ brought redemption. The symbol of the resurrection of life is the cross without the corpse. Whoever carries the symbol with the corpse wants to demonstrate the "defeat" of the Lord and wants to raise himself.

"As a person, I did not want
the prophetic word..." The prophet gives God
the honor, not himself

Now, after 32 years, I can say that right up until today, everything has been fulfilled that the Eternal brought me to understand at the very beginning of the prophetic word. His work, which I was privileged to establish with His power, His love, with His wisdom and greatness, has grown and is known worldwide. He told me and explained to me over and over again: People come, and people go; people reject the word, people accept the word – and there will be Original Christians who will acknowledge Him as the prophetic Spirit and will gather around the prophetic Spirit.

Let it be understood: They do not gather around me as the prophetess of God, instead they gather around the prophetic Spirit, around the Christ of God! For I was and am a simple woman, who gives Him the honor and not herself.

As a person, I did not want the prophetic word, but my soul carried it in itself. As a person, I wanted to live in my family, simply and plainly. As a person, I wanted to be active in sports, to live a social life, to go out among my relatives. As a person, I wanted nothing more than to live a withdrawn life in peace. Exactly the opposite, however, was predetermined and granted, for the mission of the prophetic word, of the office of prophet, does, after all, come from above.

To be a prophet does not mean that God suddenly speaks through a person. Instead, the prophetic Spirit, God, the Almighty, in Christ, His Son, our Redeemer, first takes the prophet in hand and teaches him so that he may learn everything – and above all, do it! – that he will then teach others. And so, the prophetic Spirit does not simply start speaking through the prophet – first, the prophet has to do what God wants. Whatever the prophet passes on to his fellowman, he has to first have learned on himself. Then he becomes cleansed and is constantly connected to the prophetic stream, which is the Original Christian stream.

During the approximately 30 years since, thousands of revelations have flowed, and the Spirit gave, in detailed form, the lawful principles of life, the Inner Path. He taught how people should behave, in order to draw closer to Christ in their inner being. He taught how Christ can take a person by the hand, in order to lead him to the Father.

For many years, He taught this mighty event: "Christ in you – Christ with you – and Christ with you to the Father." This is how Original Christianity expanded more and more; just as it was 2000 years ago, it is similar today.

Whoever cleanses his soul does not become a prophet through this

Often, I am asked if every person who takes up the purification of his soul will become a prophet. That's not how it works. The prophetic mission is a so-called office that comes from above. The soul has brought this mission, this prophetic office, from heaven with itself to the Earth. So, not every person who strives toward God becomes a prophet.

But a person who purifies himself gains little by little a higher quality of life. He senses the eternal Spirit. He senses the life in him. He gains experience of God. Suddenly, from within, he becomes aware of what he has to do in a given situation. And if he takes what he has recognized and measures it against the commandments of God, then he knows that it was a hint from God for him.

Whoever has taken a number of steps on the Inner Path, the path to the cosmic consciousness, and has found his way to the inner life, experiences God in many situations of his daily life. He feels the guidance of God. He can pray from his heart. Prayer is no longer something he has to force himself to do; instead, it is a living communication with Christ, a fulfillment of life. He bows before the great Spirit and, in his heart, is happy to be so near to Him.

Experiences of God are given in nature. Suddenly, you feel that a plant bows before your innermost being. And a mighty tree, which is shaken by the wind, whispers to you: "See how firmly rooted I am in the Mother Earth! – Be this way, too, firmly grounded in the Creator!" Such fine and subtle impulses come from the soul. It is the love of God, who shows Himself and always gives impulses to the one who does His will.

The divine stream is in every person, but with the prophet, it is a calling that comes from above.

The calling from above is a spiritual channel of light, which, in soul and person, opens for the eternal Spirit, which makes use of the person from then on. For this, there is no need for a state of trance or any other kind of provisions. No! He speaks His word in that moment when I say: Lord, You will is done. – And then, His will is done!

Meanwhile, it has become practically a matter of course for me that the person no longer rebels, that the person does what God wills, and so I can receive God's word at any moment. There is no need for ceremony; there is no need for any special kind of act of devotion; instead, you must be one with Him. I had to learn this, often under the most difficult conditions: to become one with Him, the law of the universe, the primordial stream of infinity, the Eternal, who is in all things. So it can be said that my soul has become one with the Eternal, and the person does what God wills.

Here is
the mighty work of revelation of Christ,
This Is My Word
A and Ω
The Gospel of Jesus
The Christ-Revelation
which true Christians the world over
have come to know

The Life in God
is eternally flowing energy.
Just as it flows from the eternal source
to the human child,
our sister Gabriele,
is it gradually given to us.

Christ,
the Redeemer of all men and souls,
the ruler of the Kingdom of Peace,
conveys His word to us, so that in it
we may recognize our life and
fashion it in such a way that
it is pleasing to God.

This Is My Word

A and Ω

The Gospel of Jesus

The Christ-Revelation Which True Christians the World Over Have Come to Know

Christ,
The Son of God,
The Co-Regent of the Heavens,
The Redeemer of all men and souls
The builder and ruler
Of the Kingdom of God on Earth,
Gives a revelation about
His life, His thinking and His work,
As Jesus of Nazareth

through the prophetess of God
Gabriele of Würzburg

Table of Contents *

---

*   *The headings of the chapters of "The Gospel of Jesus" are in medium-bold italics; the sub-headings in normal italics refer to the explanations, corrections and deepenings of "The Gospel of Jesus" by Christ today [1989]. The numbers in parentheses indicate the respective verses of "The Gospel of Jesus" to which Christ's explanations, corrections and deepenings refer.*

His omnipotence through all the forms of life (6).
Reprimanding out of love and earnestness (8).
Respect for the life of plants and animals (9). The
responsibility of one who was healed (10)

*20. **The Return of the Seventy-two** – Success or*
failure of those sent out by Christ – Refinement of
matter – Earth spots, the remainders of negative
energies: the base for the last rebellion of the
demons at the end of the Kingdom of Peace – The
release of the Earth's soul – About "spirits" (3).
The "wise" of the world do not recognize the
powers of the universe; they are controlled and
fight against the light (4). Christ reveals His own
position and His relationship to God, the Fall
event and His deed of redemption (5). Christ in the
earthly garment could, and His messengers can,
be recognized only by those who have developed
the inner vision and hearing – The divine law un-
veils itself to the one who hears and actualizes the
commandments of Christ, and he lives in Him (6).
The mighty radiation of the eternal truth through
the Wisdom at the turn of time (7)

*21. **Jesus Reproves Cruelty to a Horse** – The*
selfish, egocentric man dominates and tortures
the animals – The one who lives in God is one
with all creatures (2-4). The human being violates
and destroys the life on Earth – The extinction of

11

souls in the Absolute Law of God – The peace-makers have peace in themselves – The fight of the pioneers on several fronts – Churchmen, Pharisees, wolves in sheep's clothing – A battle-field behind the wall of fog – Pray for the unen-lightened souls (2-4). Earthly wealth as obliga-tion and task – The abuse of wealth has severe consequences – A warning to those who scorn – Wealthy people, rulers, false prophets, flatterers, sham Christians: instruments of Satan (5). The righteous are the salt of the Earth who bring in-justice to light (6). The calling and mission of the prophetess and emissary of God – The activities of the pioneers under direct schooling and guid-ance – The New Jerusalem (7). Liberation, through Christ, from the law of sowing and reap-ing; becoming bound to the law of the Fall through denominations and dogmas – Today, Christ leads into the whole truth (8). False and true teachers (9). Salvation only by faith and ac-tualization (10). Christ transforms sins freely handed over to Him (11). Clearing up, before a severe karma emerges – The seeming enemy, your mirror (12-13). Everyone receives what he himself has sown (14). Give love selflessly (15). Personal wishes lead to becoming bound to peo-ple and things – "Life in a stagnant pool" (16). Winged seeds onto the field of your neighbor's soul – The pioneers' path of purification to the Kingdom of Peace (17-18)

The path to the Kingdom of Peace: The fight and sacrifice of the just (5). The one who aligns with God receives the power of life (6). Redemption and grace are in Christ – Illness, suffering and fate are the guilt that has become visible – The Day of Judgment (7). The human eye sees only the earthly shell which perishes – The spirit body slips in and steps out of the earthly body – The way of the cross of the prophetess of God at the turn of time – The development of externalized Christianity (8-10)

*31. **The Bread of Life – The Testimony of Peter – The Camel Driver** – The spiritually dead – There are no masks in the realms of the souls – Words are only symbols and guides – Castigation is repression – Every person has free will: A good seed brings a good harvest – God admonishes, He does not punish (1-3). The wandering of Moses through the wilderness with the people of Israel: A parable for the journey of mankind – The people of today are no different than the people of Israel – The path into the Kingdom of Peace (4). The one who loves God more than this world lives in God – The one who is of the truth receives from the truth (5-6). To the people in the Kingdom of Peace – The evolution of the people and of the Earth toward the fine-material – Change in measuring time – Earth spots, the reserves of the demons – The guiding back of the*

19

principle – All Being is based on polarity (4-11).
The tri-unity: spirit, soul and man – When will
the Kingdom of God come to Earth? (12-13)   721

*67. **Entry into Jerusalem – The Last Judgment** –*
Hosanna – Crucify Him: The one who thinks only
of his own welfare is inconsistent – For the past
2000 years, the Jews have been reaping their
sowing – Man should respect God in every cre-
ated form and, therefore, in his neighbor, too;
otherwise he will stand to the left of Christ (1-10).
The expiation and purification of the most heavily
burdened souls (11). What you have not done to
one of the least of My own you have not done to
Me, either (12-14). The path of evolution of the
most heavily burdened souls (15)   728

*68. **Parables of Divine Judgment** – "The King-*
dom of God will be taken from you and given to
another people which brings forth its fruits"
(1-7). The fight against the messengers of God
who also live what they teach (8-10). I came in
Jesus and come as Christ (11). Inner and outer
dignity – The earthly rulers will be broken on the
cornerstone, Christ, who will become the cap-
stone (12-14). Turn back in time, before fate takes
its course – Human words, terms, standards and
their meaning are but guides to the truth (15-
20)   737

Only the meaning of the word vivifies (5-7). Every person marks himself (8-11)

72. **Jesus' Words of Farewell** – *The image of the Father (1-3). They will do greater works than I as Jesus (4). I will grant the one who serves self-lessly what he asks for (5). The one who keeps the temple sacred lives in Me (6-7). Selfless love is communication with God (8). The meaning of the words, "The Father is greater than I" (9-11)*

73. **The True Vine** – *Each branch of vine in Me bears fruit (1-2). The one who does not abide in Me sins (3). To live in Christ (4). The clear eye of the soul attains the gift to discern between truth and error (5). The faithful bear good fruits in My name (6-8). The one who perceives is no longer blind (9). Why Christ reveals Himself again today (10-11). The knowledge of the laws obligates you to actualize (12). No man will be able to say, "I did not know anything about Christ" (13)*

74. **Jesus Prepares His Disciples for the Coming Events** – *The fight in the name of Christ against Christ (1). The Work of Redemption is fulfilled (2-3). Today the truth flows as a great stream (4-5)*

75. **The Last Passover Supper** – *Become pure in heart (1-2). About the betrayal – Tolerance and understanding towards the ignorant (3-6). In the*

New Era of Christ, there is no more bloodshed
(7-9). The purified Earth gives in abundance (10).
To live in Christ leads to the nobility of the soul
and to true freedom (11-12). The law of life, the
commandment of love – The one who scorns his
neighbor does not find his way to Christ, to the
truth, into the eternal Being – Every person
judges himself (13-16). The New Israel and the
New Jerusalem (17). From all nations and
tribes, those who do the works of God will join in
brotherhood (18)

76. **Washing the Feet of the Disciples – The Last
Supper** – The development of the seven basic
powers of the soul begins with order (1-3). The
one who loves selflessly fulfills the law and perceives God in everything (4-5). The true fighters
for Christ are pure in heart (6). The goal and the
task of the soul: to become the law again (7). The
meaning of incense (8). About the Last Supper –
Not a ceremony, but a symbol (9). The prayer of
Jesus for His own. Fulfill the word of God and
the commandment of love; let flow what God
gives you (10-19). The prayer of unity (20-21).
Bread and wine (22). The spiritual substance in
the gifts of nature (23-25). Concessions by Moses
became unlawful customs and habits (26-28). The
betrayal of Christ – Why Jesus could be captured
and was crucified – The deed of Christ for the
lineage of David (29-30)

33

*94. **The Regulations for the Community (Part 4)** – About the burial of the dead – Conscious living – The spiritually dead – God does not want repeated incarnations (1-4). The one who has found his way to his inner God needs no earthly leaders – Criteria for the genuineness of those responsible: Selfless service – About clothing: Inner beauty becomes visible on the outside (5-7). Growth and livelihood of the community, a task in common (8-10)* 989

*95. **The Ascension** – The resurrected One teaches His disciples about the fulfillment of the Redeemer-mission and about the influence of negative powers – In the mighty memory bank of the All, as well as in the atmospheric chronicle, the work of leading-back and the Kingdom of God on Earth are stored as positive energy and build up more and more (1). The earthly rule in the name of Christ through the tools of the demons (2-3). This mighty turn of time allows for all negativities to become visible – The darkness in its effects and self-created chains (4). The promise of the Holy Spirit (5). Bear Christ within you (6). I return in all glory (7). Selfless love is a bond that cannot be severed (8). As human being, Jesus experienced and suffered what it means to be a human being (9-10)* 1003

*96. **The Outpouring of the Holy Spirit** – About the tasks and status of the disciples (1-3). The one*

Remarks concerning the translation of this book
into the English language

Aside from the usual difficulties associated with correctly translating one language into another, in this particular translation many of the expressions used in the original German text are not generally used in the German language either. Today's language is poor in spiritual terminology.

Therefore, we have had to coin and introduce a few new words in English – such as the "All," "Being," etc. The frequency of capitalization, which is not common in English, may also seem strange to the reader. In this connection, we have adhered to the way the "I Am," and the possessive pronouns and other terms which relate to God, Christ and the divine are written in the original text.

In the German language, the "being" (Wesen) and the "Being" (Sein) are two different words. In English there is only one word for "Sein" and "Wesen." Therefore, it was necessary to write "Being" with a capital letter in expressions like "the eternal Being" in order to differentiate between this expression of the pure Being, which is heaven, all the way to the heart of God, and, on the other hand, the spirit beings, nature beings, etc.

Since it is the Spirit of the Christ of God who reveals Himself in this work, we have tried to give a true rendering of the original German text in the English version. This has sometimes led to compromises in style and rhythm and in the very character of the English language.

For this reason, we would like to point out that in the case of a misunderstanding of the text, of possible ambiguities or doubts, etc., please refer to the original German text which was used as the basis for the English translation.

And, particularly in reading this text, let us keep in mind that it is always the meaning of the words that is important to understand. For "...the one who takes the words literally that I spoke as Jesus of Nazareth will still go astray today, for words were and are just symbols and guides to inner truth. ... The meaning of the words of life can be grasped and correctly interpreted only by those people who long for the truth and also strive for it." (pp. 408-409)

The translators, Original Christians in Universal Life
Würzburg, 2010

Preface

by Brother Emanuel
the cherub of divine wisdom

For many a reader it is difficult to understand that Christ, the Son of God, refers to a relatively unknown gospel, and not only builds on it, but also explains, corrects and deepens, that is, supplements, it.

The reason for this is the following:

Christian denominations and communities, as well as many Biblical scholars, have made "their Bible," which they consider as the whole and pure truth, into their own property. They are mistakenly convinced that the word of God was given in their Bible once and for all time and that is the end of it. For this reason, it was not possible for Christ, the Redeemer of all souls and men, to explain, correct and deepen their book, their Bible, within the existing Christian denominations and the communities that bind people to them.

Therefore, Christ used other possibilities; He has, and is, revealing the truth outside the Christian denominations and the communities that bind. For all beings and men should know about God, the eternal light, the unlimited truth. Everyone is given the free will to accept or reject it.

Christ, the Son of the living God, the Redeemer of all men and souls, is the One who gives the inspiration in His Work of Redemption, Universal Life – from which the Kingdom of Peace of Jesus Christ emerges. At the beginning of this decade [1980], He asked a few brothers – all of whom, except one, were Biblical scholars – to put in writing the essence of the truth from the Old Testament as well as from the New Testament.

Christ's desire was and is that the facts about His life and thinking as Jesus of Nazareth be recorded, so that they are available at a later time as a historic report for those who live in the Kingdom of Peace of Jesus Christ and who will have reached perfection through Him, for the most part.

In His revelation, He spoke to these brothers in the following sense:

Take the Biblical texts that I will lead to you and let your spiritual consciousness glide over the texts. This means, read with the eyes of truth – not with the mind, for it clouds the eye and the sense for truth. The eye of truth will then fall upon those passages in the text that contain the truth, which is important for the present and the coming time, for I will place it in your heart. I will then explain and deepen it through you. It is the words of God, which great prophets and enlightened people have received from the Spirit of truth as a preview for the present and coming time.

His motive was and is that His own who live in the present and the nearly perfect people of the coming time in the Kingdom of Peace could read and comprehend what He brought to mankind as Jesus of Nazareth, and who He was and is in the spirit. When the Kingdom of Peace of Jesus Christ has encompassed the Earth, then the redemption of mankind is finished; for in the Kingdom of Peace, only those souls that are mostly perfect will incarnate.

In the Kingdom of Peace of Jesus Christ, spiritual knowledge has become insignificant because the nearly perfect human beings are close to the divine, because they possess wisdom and no longer have to find their way to wisdom through spiritual knowledge. And the numerous versions of the Bible, on which the denominations still rely at this time [1989], will then be insignificant. For the one who has attained divine wisdom has opened his spiritual consciousness; and his pure spirit body, in which the essence of infinity is fully effective, will then be the book of divine wisdom for him. When the Kingdom of Peace of Jesus Christ encompasses the Earth, no work of man will then exist anymore. The denominations and their Bibles are also works of man, into which they have inserted a great deal at their own discretion and from which they have taught whatever seemed necessary to them from their denominational point of view.

Many spirit beings incarnated for the Work of Redemption. It is like a large mosaic, in which all four purification levels, including the Earth, are contained. Each of these spirit beings has taken on a task in the Work of Redemption and, as its share of the task, took one or more of the "mosaic pieces" into its spirit body so that in its earthly existence it could fulfill what it had taken on as a task. This share of the task is thereby engraved in the soul and must be fulfilled.

Some spirit beings took on various possibilities in their mosaic pieces. This means that if the task for which a spirit being incarnated has not been fulfilled, then the "debit" which is thereby engraved in his spirit body has to be fulfilled by him in another way – either in a further incarnation or in the spheres of purification.

However, when the time has come for this mosaic piece of the task to be put into use on Earth, then other incarnated spirit beings take over what their neighbors did not fulfill in the mission because of a burden or a temptation by the satan of the senses. This mosaic piece, which has now been fulfilled by other incarnated spirit beings, that is, by human beings, is then erased in the mission-potential for the Earth. But the spirit being concerned, which failed to accomplish its part in the Mission of Redemption in time, will have to make amends for it in some other way.

If here and there doors thus remain closed to Christ, then He takes other paths, as happened, for example, with the present book "This Is My Word."

When the Lord addresses the spiritual gifts in a person, for instance, when He reminds these brothers of their spiritual task, then the prince of this world, too, has the opportunity to put them to the test and perhaps to tempt them – this also applies to those who live as men among men, in order to bring truth and peace into the world. In the Kingdom of Light they had decided to fulfill the works of God while in the earthly garment and to serve Christ and their neighbor in the world, which is the territory of the darkness. At every moment, however, each person stands at the crossroads, before the decision "for" or "against" God.

The brothers who incarnated with the spiritual task of writing a work that is important now and in the future, succumbed to human weakness. They could not fulfill what they had entered in their spirit body, according to plan. And so, another way was taken, that is, another possibility opened up: the path through our sister, the prophetess and emissary of God. For the writing of the book "This Is My Word" is an essential component in the work of the Lord, the Universal Life, because it will have its significance predominantly in the Kingdom of Peace of Jesus Christ. It contains all the important events that Christ, the ruler of the Kingdom of Peace, lived and suffered through as Jesus of Nazareth. For He brought redemption to mankind through His life and thinking and through His love for mankind.

Only through His act of redemption will His Kingdom of Peace emerge on Earth. Blessed, hence, nearly perfect, men will then live on Earth and possess it more and more, because the reign of the darkness is coming to its end. For since His "It is finished" on the cross, all that is satanic binds itself more and more. Once the Kingdom of Peace has encompassed the Earth, the satanic will be bound. This has become possible only through the deed of redemption.

Christ, the Redeemer of all men and souls, thus has many ways to accomplish that which is important for the present time [1989] and particularly for the New Era.

The book "This Is My Word" was not part of the direct task of our sister, the prophetess and emissary of God. She accepted the possibility of using the book, "The Gospel of Jesus"* as the basis for the work of revelation, "This Is My Word." Christ accommodated her with this book, since the task to receive such a work for the present and the future was not directly a part of her mission. Among other things He said to her, Christ spoke to our sister in the following sense:

Since another way has to be taken now, and you, however, are destined for the spiritual tasks of your direct assignment, I want to oblige you as far as it is possible on Earth with this written work. So that you can fulfill your direct tasks for this earthly life and since the time for this is valuable, I will take the book, "The Gospel of Jesus," and build on it with My explanations, corrections and deepenings.

The book that men call "The Gospel of Jesus" contains – despite the translations and despite the words which have different meanings at the present time [1989] – deep insights into what took place during My earthly life as Jesus of Nazareth.

You live in the earthly garment. For this reason, it is not necessary to write a completely new work with much effort, as this would hinder you for a fairly long

---

* *Das Evangelium Jesu. Was war vor 2000 Jahren? (Rottweil, 1986) From here on, referred to in short as "The Gospel of Jesus."*

time from keeping up with the tasks of your direct assignment and accomplishing them.

This is why Christ builds upon the truth at hand in the book, "The Gospel of Jesus." He explains, corrects and deepens it, and fulfills thereby, through our sister, the task contained in the Work of Redemption: to bring out a historic work for the Kingdom of Peace of Jesus Christ, the work, "This Is My Word."*

Since the will of our sister rests in the will of God that she fulfills, the work "This Is My Word" grew out of the book "The Gospel of Jesus."

This work will first reach its full significance in the Kingdom of Peace of Jesus Christ.

Whether it will be read by mankind during the present time or in the future – up to the complete unfoldment of the Kingdom of Peace – Christ is and remains the same: the Co-Regent of the heavens; and we are with Him as brothers and sisters from eternity to eternity.

As long as I teach through our sister, the prophetess and emissary of God, I will call myself Brother Emanuel for mankind. In the Spirit of God, I am the cherub of divine wisdom, the responsible one in the Work of Redemption of Jesus Christ.

In the Kingdom of Peace, only the eternal law of love will then apply. Then, no teachings or explanations of the eternal law will be necessary any longer.

---

* *This work contains the original text, written in italics, from the book "The Gospel of Jesus," as well as the text revealed anew by Christ for the individual passages – the latter is printed in normal type.*

I am and remain the angel of the law of God, the guardian of the divine wisdom.

Peace!

I Am

My speech as Jesus of Nazareth was not the murmuring of the Pharisees and scribes who flattered the people in order to receive recognition, praise and reward. My speech as Jesus of Nazareth was clear and unmistakable – just like My speech as Christ flows through My instrument, through My prophetess, the ray of divine wisdom.

Only the sinners, those who wanted to persist in their sins, said to Me as Jesus of Nazareth, "Your speech is harsh. Who can listen to it?" The eternal law is absolute. And the one who hears it realises that it demands decision and resoluteness – either for or against God. However, the one who does not want to make a decision – because he himself is the cream on the milk – so that he can skim the milk himself, that is, get something out of everything, in order to benefit from it, speaks about the harshness of the eternal law.

I am the law, the absoluteness. The undecided one is harsh against his fellow man, but soft as butter when it comes to his personal concerns, to himself. He just wants to move on the surface – like the cream on the milk – and not explore the depth and the truth, because the eternal law requires resoluteness from him.

The one who reads My words and turns away from them with the arguments of the former scribes and Pharisees and their adherents – "His speech is harsh.

Who can listen to it?" – should leave it until he recognizes himself as the Pharisees and scribes of today who again do not want to accept the Christ, who I Am, because he does not want to decide for the truth.

My words are the All-law, the eternal law; they require the decision for or against Me. May he who can grasp it, grasp it. May he who wants to leave it, leave it. Everyone bears what he is – and for that which he is, he bears the responsibility before the All-law, God.

You are your sensation, your thought, your word and your deed. Measure yourself by this!

This Is
My Word
A and Ω

The Gospel of Jesus

The Christ-Revelation
Which True Christians the World Over
Have Come to Know

In the Name of the Most Holy
Amen

Here begins the Gospel of Jesus, the Christ, the descendant of David through Joseph and Mary in the flesh, and the Son of God through divine love and wisdom in the spirit.

Prologue

From eternity to eternity
is the eternal thought,
and the eternal thought is the word,

the word of God is eternal primordial sensation;[*]
it is light and power –

and the word is the deed,
and these three are one in the eternal law;
and the law is with God,
and the law emanates from God.

God is the eternal law.
It emanates from the Primordial Central Sun
throughout the realms of infinity
and through all pure beings,
through all pure Being.

---

[*] *With the text in normal type, Christ explains, corrects and deepens the corresponding passages from the book "The Gospel of Jesus," which are in italics here.*

*Everything is created through the law
and without it nothing is created
that exists.*

*In the word is life and substance,
is the fire and the light.*

The word of God is life and substance,
is fire and light.

*The love and the wisdom
are one for the redemption of all.*

From the love, therefore, came the wisdom
and dwells among men,
so that they may receive
what God, the love and wisdom,
has to say to them –
today [1989] in the great time
of liberation of the generations
from a life of restriction and affliction.

*And the light shines in the darkness
and the darkness does not conceal it.*

The light is the strength,
the power and the might.

*The word is the one life-giving fire
and, shining into the world,*

it becomes the fire and light in every soul
that enters into the world.

I Am in the world,
and the world is in Me;
and the world does not know it.

I Am in the world,
and I radiate throughout the world –
but the world does not know it.

I come to my own house,
and My friends do not receive Me.
But to all who receive and obey
is given the power
to become the sons and daughters of God,
and also to those who believe in the holy name,
who are born not of the will of flesh and blood,
but of God.

I come to My own house,
to all souls and men,
and My friends do not receive Me.
But all those who receive Me
and obey Me
are given the power
to consciously become the sons and daughters of God,
as well as those
who believe in the holy name
and live accordingly,

who do not succumb to the will of flesh
and blood,
but fulfill the will of God.
They are born consciously of God.

And the word became flesh and dwells amongst us,
and we beheld His glory full of grace.

Behold the goodness and the truth
and the beauty of GOD!

CHAPTER 1

The Announcement of the Birth of John the Baptist

*John the Baptist; his parentage
and task in the Work of Redemption (4-6). Explanation of
the muteness of Zacharias (8)*

1. There was in the days of Herod, the king of Judea, a priest named Zacharias, from the tribe of Abia, and his wife, one of the daughters of Aaron, called Elizabeth.

2. They were both devout before God and lived blamelessly all the commandments and laws of the Lord. And they had no child; for Elizabeth was barren and both were well on in years.

3. And it so happened that, according to the order of his service, he had to perform the priest's office. According to the custom of the priest's office, his lot was to burn incense when he went into the temple of Jehovah. And the whole multitude of the people were outside and prayed at the time of the offering of incense.

4. And there appeared unto him an angel of the Lord, standing over the altar of incense. And when Zacharias saw him he was startled, and fear fell upon him. But the angel said unto him, "Fear not, Zacharias, for your prayer is heard; and your wife Elizabeth will bear you a son, and you shall call him John.

5. And you will be full of joy and bliss, and many will rejoice at his birth. For he will be great in the sight of the Lord and will neither eat meat nor drink strong drinks and will be filled with the Holy Spirit, while still in his mother's womb.

6. And he will convert many of the children of Israel to God, their Lord. And he will go before Him in the spirit and power of Elijah, to turn the hearts of the fathers to the children and the disobedient to the wisdom of the just, to make ready a people prepared for the Lord." (Chap. 1:1-6)

I, Christ, explain, correct
and deepen the word:

Zacharias heard the meaning of these words in his heart. For God and His angels do not have the language of man.

The cherub of divine will, named Elijah on Earth, was not incarnated in John, but the spirit of Elijah illuminated John.

The being which was incarnated in John is, in the spirit, a direct descendant of the cherub of divine will.

John, too, had already received the task from God to call and teach the children of Israel. They were to convert and become one people, in order to accept Me and receive Me, when I would come in the flesh as Christ in Jesus. For I wanted to fulfill the Mission of Redemption together with them. I fulfilled the Work of Redemption –

not, however, with the people of Israel, but alone in God.

Since the children of Israel did not listen, the plan of God was delayed. Nevertheless it is being fulfilled, for God knows no time. He continues to call until the children of God become one people and fulfill the will of God. Then Israel and Jerusalem will be there, where men do the will of God.

7. *And Zacharias said unto the angel, "How shall I know that? For I am old and my wife is well on in years." The angel answered and said to him, "I am Gabriel, who stands in the presence of God, and I am sent to speak to you, and to bring to you these glad tidings.*

8. *And behold, you will be dumb and will not be able to speak until the day when these things will happen; then your tongue shall be loosened, so that you may believe my words which will be fulfilled in their time."* (Chap. 1:7-8)

I, Christ, explain, correct
and deepen the word:

The angel Gabriel is the cherub of divine mercy. It was not the angel of the Lord who deprived Zacharias of his speech, but it was the fear of the mighty light of the angel and the doubt about what he saw and heard that paralyzed the vocal chords of Zacharias. The law of God does not bind. It inflicts neither punishment nor misery on souls and men. These are the effects of causes which were created by the person himself.

9. *And the people waited for Zacharias, and were astonished that he tarried so long in the temple. And when he came out, he could not speak to them, and they realized that he had seen a vision in the temple; for he made signs to them and remained speechless.*

10. *And so it happened that, when the time of his service was over, he went home to his house. And after those days, his wife Elizabeth conceived and hid herself five months, and she said, "Thus has the Lord dealt with me in the days when He looked upon me, to take away my disgrace among men." (Chap. 1:9-10)*

CHAPTER 2

The Pure Begetting of Jesus Christ

1. *And in the sixth month, the angel Gabriel was sent by God into a city of Galilee, named Nazareth, to a virgin betrothed to a man called Joseph, of the house of David; and the virgin's name was Mary.*

2. *Joseph was a just and sensible man, and he was skilled in every kind of work in wood and in stone. And Mary was a sensitive and discerning soul, and she wove veils for the temple. And they were both pure before God. And from them both was Jesus-Maria who is called the Christ.*

3. *And the angel came to her and said, "Hail, Mary, you have found favor, for the motherhood of God is with you. Blessed are you among women and blessed is the fruit of your womb."*

4. *And when she saw him, she was confused about his saying and reflected to herself what meaning this greeting could have. And the angel said to her, "Fear not, Mary, for you have found favor with God. Behold,*

you will conceive in your womb and will give birth to a son who will be great and will be called a Son of the Highest.

5. And God, the Lord, will give Him the throne of His father David, and He will reign over the house of Jacob forever, and there will be no end to His Kingdom."

6. Then Mary said to the angel, "How shall this happen, when I know no man?" ... (Chap. 2:1-6)

I, Christ, explain, correct
and deepen the word:

David is the progenitor in the flesh of all beings of light who are engaged in the Mission of Redemption. They will found the Kingdom of Peace of Jesus Christ together with Me and will build it up over long periods of time. At the same time, coarse matter will gradually be refined until it becomes – in the final stage of the Kingdom of Peace of Jesus Christ – a finer light-material substance. For this reason it is said: And God, the Lord, will give Him the throne of His progenitor on Earth, David.

The meaning behind the words, "How should this happen, when I know no man?" is: How should this happen, when I am only betrothed to a man?

... And the angel answered and said to her, "The Holy Spirit will come upon Joseph, your promised one,

and the power of the Highest will overshadow you, O Mary; therefore, also the holy One who will be born of you will be called Christ, the Son of God, and His name on Earth shall be Jesus-Maria; for He shall redeem men from their sins, whenever they show repentance and obey His law. (Chap. 2:6)

I, Christ, explain, correct
and deepen the word:

And so it happened. I have accomplished it.

My light of redemption burns in all souls up to the fourth purification plane – whether they are in the flesh or in the realm of the souls.

Every one – whether soul or person – will attain liberation from sin and guilt only when he repents and keeps the eternal laws.

The sin of the person and of the soul has its effects in soul and person. The guilt is equal to the sin. It often binds several people to each other, who together have caused the same or like thing, so that they forgive one another and clear up with one another what brought them together.

7. *Therefore, you shall eat no flesh, nor drink strong drinks; for the child shall be consecrated to God from His mother's womb, and neither flesh nor strong drink shall He take, nor shall a razor ever touch His head.*

*8. And behold, your cousin Elizabeth is also preg-
nant with a son in her old age and this is the sixth
month for her, who was called barren. For with God
nothing is impossible." And Mary said, "Behold, I am
the handmaid of the Lord; be it unto me according to
your words." And the angel departed from her.
(Chap. 2:7-8)*

I, Christ, explain, correct
and deepen the word:

The angel of the Lord spoke to Mary in the language
of the heavens, in the language of light, which flows
into the pure soul. He simply alluded to what had happened to Elizabeth, but did not speak about the month
or her infertility.

*9. And the same day, the angel Gabriel appeared to
Joseph in a dream and said to him, "Hail, Joseph, you
have been chosen, for the fatherhood of God is with
you. Blessed are you among men and blessed the fruit
of your loins."*

*10. And as Joseph reflected on the words, he was
confused. And the angel of the Lord said to him, "Fear
not, Joseph, son of David; for you have found favor
with God, and behold you will beget a child, and you
shall give Him the name Jesus-Maria, for He shall save
His people from their sins."*

11. Now all this was done so that what the Lord has said through the prophets would be fulfilled, namely, "Behold, a maiden will conceive and will be pregnant and will give birth to a Son, and will give Him the name Emmanuel*, which has the meaning, God in us."

12. When Joseph awoke, he did as the angel had bidden him, and went to Mary, his betrothed, and she conceived the Lord in her womb. (Chap. 2:9-12)

I, Christ, explain, correct
and deepen the word:

And so, they were united as man and wife before God. Their union was blessed by God.

13. And Mary arose in those days and went with haste into the hill country to a city of Judea and entered into the house of Zacharias and greeted Elizabeth.

14. And it so happened that when Elizabeth heard the greeting of Mary, the child leaped in her womb. And Elizabeth was filled with the power of the Holy Spirit and said in a clear voice, "Blessed are you among women, and blessed is the fruit of your womb.

15. And how is it that the mother of my Lord comes to me? See, as soon as I heard the voice of your greeting, the child in my womb leaped for joy. And blessed is she

---

* *In the Lord's work it is revealed, "Immanuel" is God, and "Emanuel" is His servant. Emmanuel actually means Immanuel.*

who has believed. For what was told her from the holy One shall be accomplished."

16. And Mary said, "My soul glorifies You, the Eternal, and my spirit rejoices in God, my Savior. For He has seen the humbleness of His handmaiden; for behold, henceforth all generations will call me blessed.

17. For You who are mighty have done great things to me, and holy is Your name. And Your mercy is forever and ever with those who fear You. (Chap. 2:13-17)

I, Christ, explain, correct
and deepen the word:

Mary attributed her bliss mainly to her innermost being, to her awakened soul – not to her person. She is and remains the pure, selfless being in God, His servant and the servant of mankind. She meant that blessed is the soul of the person who fulfills the will of God.

The Old Covenant is a point of transition from the belief in many gods, the belief in a world of gods, to the belief in the one true One, who is from eternity to eternity. This is why the idea of a punishing and chastising God, whom man should fear, comes up again and again. But I say to you that man should be respectful before God by conscientiously fulfilling the commandments of God. The true eternal One is love. He does not punish nor chastise. The person who violates God's commandments inflicts punishment and chastisement upon himself, thus receiving what he has sown, unless he repents in time and clears up what he has caused. I, Christ in Jesus, revealed and impressed upon men the one God and Father of love, who is the truth and the life from eternity to eternity.

18. You have used power with Your arm, You have scattered those who are arrogant in the illusion of their hearts.

19. You have toppled the mighty from their seats and have exalted the humble and the meek. You fill the hungry with good things and send the rich away empty.

20. You help Your servant Israel in remembrance of Your mercy, as You have spoken to our forefathers, to Abraham and his descendants for all times." And Mary stayed with her three months and then returned home.

21. And these are the words that Joseph spoke, "Blessed are You, God of our fathers and our mothers in Israel; for You have heard me at the right time and have helped me on the day of salvation.

22. For You said: I will keep you and make with you a covenant with the people, in order to renew the face of the Earth and set the desolate places free from the hands of the spoiler.

23. That You may say to the captives, "Go forth and be free," and to those who walk in darkness, "Show yourselves in the light." And they shall feed on the paths of joy and never again shall they hunt or kill the creatures which I have created to rejoice before Me.

24. They shall not suffer hunger nor thirst any longer, neither shall the heat smite them nor the cold destroy them. And I will make on all My mountains a way for travelers; and My high places shall be exalted.

25. Sing, you heavens, and rejoice, you Earth; O you deserts, echo with song! For You, O God, help Your people and comfort those who have suffered wrong." (Chap. 2:18-25)

I, Christ, explain, correct
and deepen the word:

The people of Israel remained deaf. They did not accept the gifts of grace of the Christ of God.

Now a new era has come; love and wisdom are active in the plan of redemption. God, the righteous All-One, revoked [1988] the covenant with the old Israel and formed a New Covenant with those who serve on Earth in My Work of Redemption. And it will then be the New Israel and the New Jerusalem on Earth. In the course of its evolution, the Kingdom of Peace of Jesus Christ will emerge from this people and it will be as it is written in the following sense, "Go forth and be free".

And those who have walked in the darkness until then will walk the path to the light and will bear witness of the light. And they will feed on the paths of joy, and never again will they hunt or kill the creatures which the Eternal has created. They will no longer hunger nor thirst nor suffer, neither will the heat smite them nor the cold destroy them. For in the Kingdom of Peace, another sun will shine and the elements will no longer be in conflict with the streaming love. Sing, you heavens, and rejoice, you Earth – for everything will be fruitful, including the deserts. For You, O God, help Your people and comfort with the gift of inner life those who have suffered unjustly.

CHAPTER 3

The Birth and Naming of John the Baptist

The true prophets (5)

1. When the time came for Elizabeth to deliver, she gave birth to a son. And her neighbors and relatives heard how the Lord had shown great mercy upon her; and they rejoiced with her.

2. And it happened that on the eighth day they came to circumcise the child; and they called the boy Zacharias, after his father. But his mother answered, saying, "Not so, for he shall be called John." And they said to her, "But there is none in your family called by that name."

3. And they made signs to his father, how he would have him called. And he asked for a writing tablet and wrote, saying at the same time: His name is John. And they all marveled; for his mouth suddenly opened and his tongue loosened, and he spoke and praised God. (Chap. 3:1-3)

I, Christ, explain, correct
and deepen the word:

Zacharias's acceptance of what was announced to him by the angel and his joy about the child, which he faithfully named John, dissolved in him what he had caused.

4. *And great awe came upon all who were nearby; and this happening was made known throughout the hill country of Judea. And all those who heard it took it to heart, saying, "What kind of child might this be?" And the hand of Jehovah was with him.*

5. *And his father Zacharias was filled with the Holy Spirit, and prophesied, saying, "Glory be to You, O God of Israel; for You have accepted and redeemed Your people, and have raised a horn of salvation for us in the house of Your servant David, as You spoke through the mouth of Your holy prophets who have existed since the world began. (Chap. 3:4-5)*

I, Christ, explain, correct
and deepen the word:

Words often have many different meanings. It depends on the feeling which the person puts in the word. And so it was with the words "Your holy prophets," which did not mean only the prophets recorded in the books of the so-called Old Testament.

Only one is holy: God, the Eternal.

Blessed were and are the prophets sent by God, who fulfilled His will, giving the word of God from their own fulfilled lives, and admonishing people to accept it and actualize it. These are the genuine prophets.

6. That we should be saved from our enemies and from the hand of all those who hate us. That You show the mercy which You promised to our forefathers and remember Your holy covenant,

7. the oath which You have sworn to our father Abraham that You would grant to us, that being delivered out of the hand of our enemies, we can serve You without fear, in holiness and righteousness all the days of our lives.

8. And this child will be called the prophet of the Highest; for he will go before Your face, O God, to prepare Your ways and to bring the knowledge of salvation to Your people through the forgiveness of their sins.

9. Through the loving mercy of our God, through which the sunrise from on high has visited us, so that He may give light to those who sit in darkness and in the shadow of death, and may guide our feet on the path of peace."

10. And the child grew and became strong in spirit, and his mission remained hidden till the day of his appearance before the people of Israel. (Chap. 3:6-10)

CHAPTER 4

The Birth of Jesus Christ

The people of Israel have failed – The reign of Christ in the Kingdom of Peace is being prepared by the incarnated sons and daughters of God from the tribe of David (5). The "visions of angels" of the shepherds were inner processes (6-9). Acknowledgment of the earthly laws as long as they do not oppose the divine laws (12)

1. *The birth of Jesus, the Christ, took place in this way: In those days it happened that Caesar Augustus issued a decree that a census of the whole world should be taken. Everyone in Syria went to his hometown to be registered; it was midwinter.*

2. *And Joseph with Mary also went up from Galilee, out of the city of Nazareth into the land of Judea, unto the city of David, which is called Bethlehem – because he was of the house and lineage of David – in order to be registered with Mary, his betrothed, who was great with child.*

3. *While they were there, the time came for her to deliver. And she gave birth to her first Son in a cave and wrapped Him in swaddling clothes and laid Him in a manger which was in the cave, because there was no room for them in the inn. And behold, the cave was filled with light and radiated like the sun in its splendor.*

4. *And in the cave there were an ox, a horse, a donkey and a sheep, and beside the manger lay a cat with her little ones; and there were also doves over them, and each animal had its mate, a male or a female.*

5. *Thus, it came to pass that He was born in the midst of the animals. For He came to free them, too, from their suffering. He came to liberate men from their ignorance and selfishness and to reveal to them that they are sons and daughters of God. (Chap. 4:1-5)*

I, Christ, explain, correct
and deepen the word:

As Jesus, I revealed the Kingdom of God and lived and taught His laws. With the sons and daughters of Israel from the tribe of David, and with all the sons and daughters of God who fulfill the will of the Eternal, I wanted to found and build up the Kingdom of God in Israel. And after My return into the glory of My Father, I wanted to come again in the spirit and continue to expand it with the people of Israel, and to rule over the Kingdom of Peace, which will reach its pinnacle on fine matter. But the sons and daughters of God and of Israel were blinded by sin.

Throughout the centuries following My deed of redemption, God, the Eternal, repeatedly called the sons and daughters from the lineage of David and from other lineages who fulfill His will so that they would recognize what their mission is.

Now [1989] a new era has dawned: It is the turn of time from the old world to the new world, the world of Christ. I am preparing for My coming in the spirit – again through the sons and daughters of the tribe of David and other sons and daughters of the Eternal from other lineages who fulfill the will of God. Through the incarnate divine wisdom, I instruct them as well as all those who follow Me, so that they may become conscious sons and daughters of God who fulfill the will of God.

What is revealed will then be carried out: I will come in the spirit. Then all people will live in peace, and the animals, too, will be freed from their slavery and suffering through Me, the Christ of God. For the one who places his life in the sonship and daughterhood of God will not kill – neither men nor animals.

6. *And in the same area, there were shepherds in the field, watching over their flock by night. And behold, the angel of God appeared to them, and the glory of the Highest shone around them, and they were much afraid.*

7. *And the angel said to them, "Fear not, for behold, I bring you good tidings of great joy which will come to all people; for unto you is born this day, in the city of David, the Savior, who is Christ, the holy One of God. And this shall be a sign for you: You will find the infant wrapped in swaddling clothes, lying in a manger."*

8. And suddenly there was a multitude of the heavenly host with the angel, praising God and saying, "Glory to God in the highest, and peace on Earth to all who are of good will."

9. And as the angels ascended into heaven, the shepherds said to one another, "Let us go now to Bethlehem and see what has happened, which our God has made known to us." (Chap. 4:6-9)

I, Christ, explain, correct
and deepen the word:

The angel spoke to the shepherds. However, they did not see him with human eyes and did not hear him with human ears. Nor did they see or hear with human eyes and ears the heavenly host, praising and glorifying God. Some of the shepherds perceived the light in their inner being, while others heard the praise of God in their hearts. For that which does not wear the garment of the flesh does not have the word of the flesh nor the sound of the word. The word of God and that of the beings of God is perceived in the innermost being of a person.

The angel of the Lord did not stand before them like a human being. They were standing by the fire warming themselves. They saw how the pillar of fire leapt up. And in the fire they thought they saw the figure of an angel, which some of them perceived in their hearts. The shepherds were not of one mind about what they saw and heard. Those, however, who felt the meaning of the tidings in their hearts set off for Bethlehem.

Just like in those days, the angels of God are announcing today, too: Prepare the way for the Lord. Christ, the Redeemer, is coming in the spirit – and He will be the Shepherd of one flock, which is the people of God on Earth. He will reign over them in His kingdom on Earth, and they will be with Him in the spirit, because they keep the laws of God.

10. And they came in haste and found Mary and Joseph in the cave and the child lying in the manger. And when they had seen them, they spread the words which were told them concerning the child.

11. And all those who heard this wondered at what the shepherds had told them. But Mary kept all this and treasured it in her heart. And the shepherds returned, glorifying and praising God for all they had heard and seen.

12. And when the eight days were over and the child was circumcised, He was named Jesus-Maria, as was said by the angel before He was conceived in the womb. And when, according to the law of Moses, the days of her purification were over, they brought the child to Jerusalem, to present Him to God. (As it is written in the law of Moses, that all that is male which opens the mother's womb shall be consecrated to the Lord.) (Chap. 4:10-12)

I, Christ, explain, correct
and deepen the word:

Circumcision is the law of the Jews. Since it does not oppose the eternal law, this earthly law is tolerated by God – exclusively for human beings. When a being from God becomes man by way of incarnation, then the human being is subject to the laws of nature and has to abide by the worldly laws, as long as these do not oppose the laws of God.

13. And behold, there was a man in Jerusalem, whose name was Simeon, and he was just and devout, waiting for the consolation of Israel; and the Holy Spirit fell upon him. And it was revealed to him that he should not see death before he had seen the Christ of God.

14. And, inspired by the Spirit, he came into the temple. And when the parents brought in the child Jesus, to do as prescribed by the law, he perceived the child as if He were a pillar of light. Then he took Him in his arms, praised God and said:

15. "Now You let Your servant depart in peace, according to Your word. For my eyes have seen Your Savior, whom You have prepared to be a light before the face of all peoples, to enlighten the Gentiles and for the glory of Your people Israel." And His parents marveled at all that was spoken of Him.

16. And Simeon blessed them and said to Mary, His mother, "Behold, this child is set for the fall and rise of many in Israel and for a sign which will be spoken against (and verily a sword shall pierce through your own soul, too), so that the thoughts of many hearts may be revealed."

17. And there was Anna, a prophetess, the daughter of Phanuel, of the tribe of Aser, who was advanced in years and never left the temple, but served God with fasting and praying night and day.

18. And coming in at this hour, she praised the Lord and spoke of Him to all those who were waiting for redemption in Jerusalem. And when they had accomplished all things according to the law of the Lord, they returned into Galilee, to their hometown Nazareth. (Chap. 4:13-18)

CHAPTER 5

The Worship of the Wise Men and Herod

*The significance of the six rays
of the star of Bethlehem (5). The messages of God and of
His angels are indications, but not direct statements about
what is possible – Indirect guidance (13)*

1. When Jesus was born in Bethlehem in the land of
Judea, in the days of King Herod, behold, some wise
men from the East came to Jerusalem. They had purified themselves and had tasted neither flesh nor strong
drink, so that they might find the Christ whom they
sought. And they said, "Where is the new-born king of
the Jews? For we have seen His star in the East and
have come to worship Him."

2. When King Herod heard this, he was troubled and
all Jerusalem with him. And he called all the high
priests and scribes of the people together and demanded of them to know where the Christ should be
born.

3. And they said to him, "In Bethlehem, in the land of
Judea; for thus it is written by the prophet: And you,
Bethlehem, in the land of Judea, are not the least
among the princes of Judah, for out of you shall come
forth the ruler who shall rule My people, Israel."

4. Then Herod secretly sent for the wise men and in-
quired of them precisely when the star had appeared.
And he sent them to Bethlehem and said, "Go and

search diligently for the infant; and when you have found Him, bring me word again, so that I may come and worship Him, too."

5. When they had heard the king, they departed; and behold, the star that the wise men of the East had seen and the angel of the star went before them, till the star came and stood over the place where the infant was. And it shone with six rays. (Chap. 5:1-5)

I, Christ, explain, correct
and deepen the word:

What does the symbol of the six rays mean? The Son of God brings the law of God, the seven basic rays of the heavens, to this Earth. In spirit, six rays radiate down upon Him – the seventh ray, mercy, dwells among men: The Son of the Most High in the earthly garment, the Christ of God in Jesus. Mary also bore a part of the ray of mercy for, in the Spirit of the Lord, she is united with the cherub of divine mercy.

6. They went their way with their camels and donkeys laden with gifts. And while looking intently at the star in the sky in search of the child, they forgot for a while their weary animals, which had borne the burdens and the heat of the day and were thirsty and exhausted. And the star disappeared from their sight.

7. In vain they stood and gazed and looked at each other in dismay. Then they remembered their camels and donkeys and hastened to unload them, so that they might have rest.

8. Now there was near Bethlehem a well by the wayside. And as they stooped over it to draw water for their animals, behold, the star, which they had lost, reflected on the still surface of the water.

9. And when they saw it, they were filled with great joy.

10. And they praised God who had shown them mercy at the very moment they had shown mercy to their thirsty animals.

11. And when they entered the house, they found the infant with Mary, His mother, and they fell down and worshipped Him. They opened their treasures and displayed their gifts before Him: gold, frankincense and myrrh.

12. And having been warned by God in a dream not to return to Herod, they went back to their homeland by another way. And they kindled a fire according to their custom and worshipped God in the flame.

13. When they had departed, behold, the angel of the Lord appeared to Joseph in a dream, saying, "Arise and take the infant and His mother and flee to Egypt, and remain there until I tell you more, for Herod seeks to kill Him." (Chap. 5:6-13)

I, Christ, explain, correct
and deepen the word:

It is written, "... for Herod seeks to kill Him." The words of the angel and the inspiration from the Spirit said in the following sense, "Now flee with the infant and His mother to Egypt and remain there for the time being." The tidings that Herod wanted to kill the infant came to Joseph, who associated them with the statement of the angel, from other sources.

Because the people of the New Era know freedom in the law of life, through the actualization and fulfillment of the eternal laws, they will doubt this statement or similar ones, "Herod seeks to kill Him." For they know that God and His angels do not make such or similar direct statements, for they would thus affirm something which is still hanging in the balance.

For this reason I, Christ, explain, correct and deepen this statement and other ones, so that this book may be a work of recognition for many.

God allows messages to be conveyed to people via other sources, that is, indirectly – when a person's intention has already been spoken out by himself and can be conveyed by a second or third person who has heard it. When it is of significance, it will then reach the person concerned indirectly. In this way, God guides indirectly, in the law of sowing and reaping.

14. He arose and took the infant and His mother by night and escaped to Egypt and remained there for about seven years until the death of Herod; so that it might be fulfilled what the Lord had spoken through the prophet who said, "Out of Egypt have I called My Son."

15. *Elizabeth, too, when she heard this, took her infant son and went up into the mountains with him and hid him there. And Herod sent his men to Zacharias in the temple to ask him, "Where is your child?" And he answered, "I am a servant of God and am always in the temple. I do not know where he is."*

16. *And again he sent them to him, to ask, "Tell me honestly, where is your son, do you not know that your life is in my hands?" Zacharias answered, "God is witness: If you shed my blood, God will receive my soul, for you shed the blood of an innocent."*

17. *And they slew Zacharias in the temple between the holy of holies and the altar; and the people knew of it through a voice which cried out, "Zacharias has been slain, and his blood shall not be washed away until the avenger has come." And after some time the priests cast lots, and the lot fell to Simeon, who took his place.*

18. *Then Herod, seeing that he had been deceived by the wise men, became exceedingly enraged and sent out his people and had all children slain in and around Bethlehem who were two years of age and younger, according to the time of which he had learned from the wise men.*

19. *Thus was fulfilled what was said by Jeremiah, the prophet, "In Rama a voice was heard weeping – lamentations and great mourning. Rachel, weeping for her children, will not be comforted, because they are no more."*

20. *But when Herod had died, behold, the angel of the Lord appeared in a dream to Joseph in Egypt, say-*

ing, "Arise and take the child and His mother and return into the land of Israel, for those who sought the child's life are dead."

21. And he arose and took the child and His mother and returned into the land of Israel. And they dwelt in a city called Nazareth and He was called the Nazarene. (Chap. 5:14-21)

CHAPTER 6

The Childhood and Youth of Jesus

The temple of the inner being (4). Christ, the bridegroom, and the bride (5). Matrimony as a covenant of fidelity before God – The experience of the female nature for Jesus of Nazareth – The suffering and death on the cross should not have been (10). A correct understanding of the text – The wisdom of the Egyptians (11). A short report about the life of Jesus before He began His teaching activity (12). Jesus lived and gave from the omnipotence and love of God and fulfilled the commandment "pray and work" (14). The last covenant, made with the Original Community New Jerusalem – The darkness has lost – The purification process of the Earth (17)

1. Now Joseph and Mary, His parents, went up to Jerusalem every year for the feast of the Passover; they celebrated the feast according to the custom of their brethren, who abstained from bloodshed and the eating of flesh and from strong drink. When Jesus was twelve years old, He went up to Jerusalem with them, according to the custom of the feast. (Chap. 6:1)

I, Christ, explain, correct
and deepen the word:

Thus it is revealed that God, the Lord, does not interfere in the laws of men, as long as they are customs that are not contrary to the heavenly law. Even the person Jesus kept the custom, and the Lord accompanied Him with His Spirit.

2. *And when the days came to an end and they returned, the child Jesus stayed behind in Jerusalem; and His parents did not know it. They thought He was in the group with them and went a day's journey. Then they sought Him among friends and acquaintances. And when they did not find Him, they turned back to Jerusalem and looked for Him there.*

3. *And it came to pass that after three days they found Him in the temple in the midst of the scholars. He was sitting, listening to them and asking them questions. And all those who heard Him were astonished at His understanding and His answers.*

4. *When His parents saw Him, they were filled with consternation. And His mother said to Him, "My Son, why did you do this to us? Behold, Your father and I have sought You full of worry." And He said to them, "Why did you seek Me? Don't you know that I must be in My Father's house?" ... (Chap. 6:2-4)*

I, Christ, explain, correct
and deepen the word:

With the words "... that I must be in My Father's house," the boy did not mean the house, the temple made of stone, but the house made of flesh and bone – the

85

human being in whom dwells the Spirit of God, who spoke through the boy, Jesus. Jesus meant, I must rest within Myself, in the temple of the inner being, in order to give to the people – and to answer those who have asked Me.

Every person is a temple of God. The one who keeps this temple pure also senses, thinks, speaks and acts purely and, through this, lives in the consciousness of God. In the temple of Jerusalem, Jesus taught from this "temple of the inner being" to those who wanted to hear Him in the temple made of stone.

... And they did not understand the words which He said to them. But His mother kept all these words in her heart.

5. And a prophet who saw Him said to Him, "Behold, the love and the wisdom of God are united in You, therefore in the age to come You shall be called Jesus; for through the Christ, God will redeem mankind which today is verily like the bitter sea; but this bitterness will be turned into sweetness. However, the bride will not yet be manifest to this generation, nor yet in the age to come." (Chap. 6:4-5)

I, Christ, explain, correct
and deepen the word:

The prophet prophesied from the Spirit. Meanwhile, ages have passed. But the bridegroom, the Spirit of

Christ, who I Am, has now set out to call the people who believe in Me and fulfill the will of the Father, in order to lead them into the land of peace. Like a bride arrayed with the adornment and virtue of inner life, many souls and people are coming to meet Me, and there will be more and more people who turn from bitterness to sweetness and who appear at My right side.

6. *And He went down with them and came to Nazareth and was obedient to them. And He made wheels and yokes and also tables with great skill. And Jesus increased in stature and also in favor before God and man.*

7. *And on a certain day, the boy Jesus came to a place where a snare was set for birds and there were some boys there. And Jesus said to them, "Who has set this snare for the innocent creatures of God? Behold, they will likewise be caught in a snare." And He beheld twelve sparrows that appeared to be dead.*

8. *And He moved His hands over them and said to them, "Fly away and, as long as you live, remember Me." And they rose and flew away with cries. The Jews who saw this were very astonished and told it to the priests.*

9. *And the child did other wonders, and flowers were seen to spring up from beneath His feet, there where nothing but barren ground had been before. And His companions stood in awe of Him.*

10. And in the eighteenth year of His life, Jesus was married to Miriam, a virgin of the tribe of Judah, with whom He lived seven years. And she died; for God took her, so that He might go on to the higher tasks that He had to accomplish and suffer for all the sons and daughters of man. (Chap. 6:6-10)

I, Christ, explain, correct
and deepen the word:

I was never married. In this generation [1989] the word "married" has another meaning. For people of this time, it means a wedding at the registry office and possibly a ceremony in a church on the Earth before and with a priest.

The word "matrimony," too, has, in the Spirit, another meaning than "marriage." Matrimony in the Spirit of God means that two people enter into a covenant with God and endeavor to become one in God. Marriage is a decision according to the laws of this world. Matrimony, on the other hand, is a covenant of fidelity with one's neighbor before God, wherein two persons decide to actualize the divine laws and to lead a pure, God-filled life together.

In this book, the word "married" means to be united through God's love.

Jesus was united in spirit with all men and beings, with all Being – just as I Am, as Christ.

As Jesus – that is, as the Son of Man – I also had to experience this union with the female sex, in order to understand it and be able to help it. As Jesus of Nazareth, I had a deep, pure union with this woman, who was very close to My nature. The law reads: Like attracts like. This woman had some aspects in her being that vibrated similarly to those in My soul. Through these aspects, we were in deep communication. I sensed Myself in her and she sensed herself in Me. Thus, I experienced the world of sensations of the female principle in the earthly garment and through this also understood the many women who were with Me in the years of My teaching activity.

Just before My years of teaching, the time on Earth for this woman came to an end. God, our eternal Father, took her back, as He later took back many men and women who followed Me. For in this world, the coming and going of the soul is a lawful process which is not subject to choice, but to the course of events in the law of sowing and reaping or in the law of light of God.

My task as Jesus of Nazareth, the Christ of God, was to embed the spark of redemption in the souls of human beings. My suffering and physical death showed the stubbornness of man. Had the sons and daughters of God from the lineage of David allowed themselves to be called by John and Me, and had they faithfully followed the Christ in Jesus, then further sons and daughters of God from other lineages would have joined them, in order to follow Me faithfully. This would have resulted in a people which could have consciously been the people of David for the Kingdom of Peace of Jesus Christ. Because the lineage of David, which is in the mission of the Work of Redemption, remained in sin, I enveloped Myself with a part of its guilt, as well as with parts of the guilt of individuals from other lineages. This is why I could be taken captive. And thus, the suffering began.

Had the lineage of David not remained in sin, then I would have brought the spark of redemption to all souls and men, but without having to endure the suffering and physical death on the cross. So I suffered for the sons and daughters of man, because they did not consciously become the sons and daughters of God, by fulfilling the will of God.

Had the lineage of David stood by Me, all of the events together would have taken another turn. And had the Jewish people in its entirety, including its scribes and Pharisees, accepted and received the Son of God by fulfilling the laws of God, then the part-power would have remained in the primordial power. For the one who fulfills the eternal law needs no support.

11. *And when He had finished His study of the law, Jesus went down to Egypt again, so that He might learn the wisdom of the Egyptians, as Moses had done. ... (Chap. 6:11)*

I, Christ, explain, correct
and deepen the word:

Since many passages in this book are understood not according to their meaning, but literally, some things have to be repeatedly explained and corrected.

I have already revealed that when this book was written, some words had a different meaning than what they have today [1989]. Besides, the man who, at that time, received the word and wrote it down had a certain vocabulary; only this could be used. The translators, too, had their own vocabulary for the translation. For this reason, everything given from the divine in words should be understood in its essence. Where it is absolutely necessary to explain, correct or deepen, I will act again and again through My instrument of the present time [1989], and explain, correct or deepen.

In this text I also correct the words, "... went down to Egypt again, so that He might learn the wisdom of the Egyptians, as Moses had done." This meant that He repeatedly met with Egyptians in order to speak with them about the wisdom of God. However, I did not go to Egypt in order to learn the wisdom of God from the Egyptians. As a child I was in Egypt with My earthly parents, but even then it was not to learn the divine wisdom.

Furthermore, I repeatedly met with men and women in the desert, in order to pray and to speak with them about the eternal truth. Among them were often many

Egyptians. Even as the boy Jesus, the wisdom of God was already manifest in Me; it also spoke through Me. And so, already as the boy Jesus, I spoke out of the wisdom of God to the so-called scholars in the temple. The wisdom of God was therefore active in Me. So why learn it?

... And going into the desert, He meditated, fasted and prayed, and He received the authority of the holy name, by which He worked many miracles.

12. And for seven years He spoke face to face with God, and He learned the language of the birds and animals, and the healing powers of the trees, herbs and flowers, and the hidden powers of precious stones, and also learned the movements of the sun and the moon and the stars, and the power of letters, the mysteries of the square and the circle and the transmutation of things and forms, of numbers and signs. From there, He returned to Nazareth to visit His parents, and He taught there and in Jerusalem as an accepted Rabbi, even in the temple, none hindering Him.
(Chap. 6:11-12)

I, Christ, explain, correct
and deepen the word:

Everything that God created and maintains lies in the soul of man. The one who lives in God, receives from

God, and – even as a human being – is taught by God. As Jesus of Nazareth, I lived in God and received from God, My Father, with whom I was in constant communication.

The divine wisdom flowed from the inner being of Jesus, and He spoke with the animals in the water, in the air and in and on the Earth. And Jesus, in whom I lived, experienced the life of plants and stones within Himself.

As Jesus, I experienced from My inner being the movement of the stars and planets, about which I spoke at length with the Egyptians, among whom were truly wise men.

Because I, as Jesus, taught in the temple, many people called Me Rabbi. But I was a prophet and the Son of God – the Son of Man in the earthly garment, who taught and lived the laws of God and sacrificed Himself, so that redemption could enter the souls of men and the souls which lived in the spheres of the Fall.

13. *After some time, He went to Assyria and India and to Persia and into the land of the Chaldeans. And He visited their temples and spoke with their priests and their wise men for many years, and He did many wonderful works and healed the sick, as He journeyed through the countries.*

14. *And the animals of the field felt reverence toward Him, and the birds had no fear of Him, for He did not frighten them. Even the wild animals of the desert felt*

the power of God in Him and served Him willingly, carrying Him from place to place. (Chap. 6:13-14)

I, Christ, explain, correct
and deepen the word:

As Jesus, I met with many people from different backgrounds and of various languages and spoke with Assyrians, Indians, Persians, Chaldeans, Israelites and with other men and women from various tribes. Yet I did not go to their countries or to others in order to learn the wisdom of God. I went into several countries and came to several borders. Language was often a hindrance. However, when we spoke about the laws of love, everyone knew what the other wanted to say. The language of the heart knows no boundaries – not even today, in the time which is close to the year two thousand.

Out of the love for man, the power of healing also broke through – in order to help people and to bear witness of what dwelt in Me, the Jesus: the omnipotence of God.

The technology which still exists today [1989] makes it possible for My word to be translated and transmitted more quickly, so that the people's hearts awaken and they learn the language of love; it is understood by all those who think with the heart.

Many people are of the opinion that I travelled for years in order to gather wisdom and do works of love. As Jesus of Nazareth, I did travel a great deal in order to teach and to do works of love and mercy. I did not, however, fail to observe the commandment "pray and work."

Just like Joseph and My own brothers, I actualized, as a carpenter, what God commanded of mankind, "pray and work."

The meaning behind the statement "carrying Him from place to place" is that many animals travelled a long distance with Me, and some of them, from place to place. The one who loves God loves the nature kingdoms, too. And the nature kingdoms serve the one who loves God. For all Being is the life that comes from God – and the one who loves God is served by all Being.

15. *For the spirit of divine humanity filled Him and thus all things around Him and made all things subject to Him; and thus the words of the prophets have been fulfilled, "The lion shall lie down by the calf, and the leopard by the kid, and the wolf by the lamb, and the bear by the donkey, and the owl by the dove. And a child shall lead them.*

16. *And none shall hurt or kill on My holy mountain; for the Earth shall be filled with the knowledge of the holy One, just as the waters cover the bed of the sea. And in these days I will again make a covenant with the animals of the Earth and the birds of the air, with the fishes of the sea and with all the creatures of the Earth. And I will break the bow and also the sword, and I will banish all the instruments of warfare from the Earth; and they shall lie down in safety and live without fear.*

17. And I will betroth Myself to you forever in righteousness and in peace and in kindness of heart, and you shall recognize your God, and the Earth shall bring forth the grain and the wine and the oil, and I will say to those who are not My people: You are My people; and they will say to Me: You are our God." (Chap. 6:15-17)

I, Christ, explain, correct
and deepen the word:

This has happened.

Since the Israelites did not accept or receive Me, Christ, as their Redeemer, the Eternal and I, Christ, are gathering the sons and daughters of God on another continent. "Israel" is now there, and the new "Jerusalem"* is also there. For God does not bind Himself to one place or to promises from people who do not keep their promise, who do not fulfill what He has commanded them.

Another people stand in the covenant. It is My people, and I will be their Shepherd. The first stirrings of the Kingdom of Peace will now rise from there.

---

* cf. *"Der Bund mit Gott für das Friedensreich Jesu Christi. Christus ruft alle geistigen Gruppen, Konfessionen und Religionen"; Würzburg 1989, 2nd enlarged edition. ("The Covenant with God for the Kingdom of Peace of Jesus Christ. Christ calls all spiritual groups, denominations and religions.") Available in German only.*

God revoked the covenant with the people of Israel and made a New Covenant – the last covenant – with this other people, with people who strive to fulfill the will of God. They are from the great lineage of David and from other lineages that keep the commandments of life.

The Eternal and I, Christ, have called and call into this world through the mouth of a prophet and gather all willing sons and daughters of God. The small people already in existence will grow into a mighty people of God.

The final covenant is made and is valid. It brings much help from the law of God to those who keep it. I, Christ, Am at the head of the people of God and have no human being as a representative. The original community New Jerusalem, which became the Covenant Community, is this people of God. It is the central light in Universal Life.

The people of God will still have many a hurdle to overcome. However, the Spirit of truth and life is with them, and all those who are in the covenant with honest heart will be the founders and builders of the Kingdom of God on Earth. At this time – close to the year two thousand – what was written, as follows, is becoming manifest: I, your Lord and God, will make the covenant with another people.

The darkness has lost; the covenant is made; the Earth is purifying itself – just as it was prophesied.

The Earth will tremble and open and devour many people. But before all this occurs, illness, affliction, blows of fate and much more will come over mankind. The angel of death goes forth and sweeps away more and more people. All that is impure will pass away. The seas will overflow their basins and will cover all negativity, and the heavenly bodies will purify the Earth with their rays. Then the sword and all instruments of war will be broken. The Kingdom of Peace will then emerge all over the Earth, and people who fulfill the will of God will live on Earth. And there will be peace. For what is written will be fulfilled:

"The lion shall lie down by the calf, and the leopard by the kid, and the wolf by the lamb, and the bear by the donkey, and the owl by the dove. And a child shall lead them." All this will happen.

18. And one day He was walking on a mountain path along the edge of the desert; He met a lion being pursued by many men who wanted to kill it with stones and javelins.

19. But Jesus rebuked them, saying, "Why do you hunt the creatures of God, which are more noble than you? Through the cruelties of many generations, they were made the enemies of men, whereas they should have been their friends.

20. Just as the might of God is visible in them, so is His patience and His compassion. Stop persecuting this creature! It does not want to harm you. Don't you see how it flees from you and is terrified by your violence?" (Chap. 6:18-20)

I, Christ, explain, correct
and deepen the word:

The word "compassion" means God's help. I have brought redemption for all men and souls. The liberation of animals is also a part of redemption. For through redemption, everything will be raised in the process of evolution, to unity, into the light of God, which is unity, life, substance and power.

21. And the lion came and lay at the feet of Jesus, and showed Him its love. And the people were very astonished and said, "See, this man loves all creatures and He has power even over the animals of the desert, and they obey Him." (Chap. 6:21)

CHAPTER 7

John's Sermon of Penitence

*The significance of symbols
and ceremonies (4). The judgment: The law of sowing and
reaping – Purification of the soul (10)*

1. Now in the fifteenth year of the reign of Caesar Tiberius, Pontius Pilate being governor of Judea and Herod being tetrarch of Galilee (Caiaphas being the high priest and Annas the chief of the Sanhedrim), the word of God came to John, the son of Zacharias, in the wilderness.

2. And John came into the countryside on the Jordan and preached the baptism of penitence for the forgiveness of sins. As it is written in the prophets, "Behold, I send My messenger ahead of You, to prepare Your way before You. It is the voice of one calling in the wilderness: Prepare the way for the holy One and level the paths for the anointed.

3. All valleys shall be filled in and all mountains and hills shall be leveled; and the crooked shall be made straight, and rough ways shall be made smooth. And all flesh shall see the salvation of God."

4. John had his raiment of camel hair and a girdle of the same about his loins; and his food was the fruit of the locust tree and wild honey. And the people of Jerusalem and all of Judea and the region along the Jordan went to him and were baptized by him in the Jordan and confessed their sins. (Chap. 7:1-4)

I, Christ, explain, correct
and deepen the word:

Even in this report, man recognizes that God allows habits and customs which are not against the eternal, holy law. In this case it is baptism by water.

God leaves it up to His human children whether they still wish to keep water as a symbol of purification, until they are baptized with the Spirit of life.

However, the one who has developed love for God and for his neighbor is raised by the Spirit of God, that is, he is imbued with the Spirit of truth.

The one who is spiritually mature needs fewer and fewer symbols and ceremonies. He lives in the inner being, just as it is in heaven: pure! The pure one is filled with the Spirit of truth and imbued with the Spirit of life: He is thus baptized by the Spirit of God.

5. And he said to the people who came forth to be baptized by him, "O you disobedient generation! Who has warned you to flee from the wrath which will come? Bring forth therefore honest fruits of penitence and do not begin to say of yourselves: We have Abraham as father.

6. For I say to you: From these stones God can bring forth children for Abraham. And the axe is already laid at the root of the trees, and every tree which does not bring forth good fruits will be hewn down and cast into the fire."

7. And the rich ones asked him, saying, "What shall we do then?" He answered and said to them, "The one who has two coats shall give to him who has none; and the one who has food shall do likewise."

8. Some tax collectors also came to be baptized and said to him, "Master, what shall we do?" And he said to them, "Do not demand more than what is prescribed to you, and be lenient, according to your discretion."

9. The soldiers likewise asked him, "What shall we do?" And he said to them, "Do not do violence or injustice to anyone and be content with your wages."

10. And to all he spoke, saying, "Keep yourselves from the blood of the strangled and from the carcasses of birds and animals and guard against all cruelty and all injustice. Do you think that the blood of animals and birds can wash away sin? I tell you: No! Speak the truth. Be just, be merciful to your neighbor and to all creatures that live, and walk humbly with your God." (Chap. 7:5-10)

I, Christ, explain, correct
and deepen the word:

The word "wrath" means the judgment which will befall him who does not change in time: The one who disregards the divine law will suffer what he has sown. No person can flee from his own judgment, from the effects of his own causes. Only by his repenting, asking for forgiveness, forgiving and making amends – as long as this is still possible – cleanse the soul of sin. The human being carries with himself what he has entered into his soul, light and shadow, until the latter is erased. At whatever time and in whichever place he is, he carries with him the shadows which he, himself, has entered into his soul – until these are erased.

The words, "And the axe is already laid at the root of the trees, and every tree which does not bring forth good fruits will be hewn down and cast into the fire" mean: Every cause not atoned for will have to be borne. The axe is the law of sowing and reaping. The tree is the human being who does not repent of his sins and does not make amends for what he has caused. The fire symbolizes the purification of the soul; it is the active effect of the deed which was committed and not atoned for, the cause.

The one who is able to grasp the meaning of what is written realizes that the soul and the person will become pure only when they recognize their mistakes and sins, repent, forgive, ask for forgiveness and atone – that is, when they make amends and no longer do the same or a similar thing.

Recognize: All of nature, the animals, plants and stones are God's garden, His work of creation. The one who disregards this commits a sin – and he will be confronted with his sins again and again until he recognizes, repents and atones. And if he sins no longer and keeps the commandments, he will live in Me, and I will live consciously through him.

The one who loves his neighbor selflessly will neither kill nor consume animals anymore. Such a person becomes pure in his soul, and the fruits which he brings forth will be the life in Me.

11. And the people were in expectation, and all thought in their heart and wondered whether John was the Christ or not. John answered, saying to them all, "I baptize you with water; but a mightier One will come after me, whose shoe-straps I am not worthy to loosen.

12. He will baptize you with water and with fire. In His hand is the shovel and He will cleanse His threshing floor and will gather the wheat into His barn; and He will burn the chaff with unquenchable fire." And he said many other things to the people in his sermon of penitence. (Chap. 7:11-12)

CHAPTER 8

The Baptism of Jesus, the Christ

Today, God and Christ reveal the entire truth
through the seraph of divine wisdom – The tribe of David
prepares the Kingdom of Peace with Christ (3)

1. And it was midsummer, in the tenth month. Then Jesus went from Galilee to the Jordan unto John, to be baptized by him. But John forbade Him, saying, "I have need to be baptized by You, and You come to me?" Jesus answered him, saying, "Let it be so now, for we ought to fulfill all righteousness." So he consented.

2. And when Jesus was baptized, He stepped immediately out of the water; and behold, the heavens opened above Him, and a shining cloud stood over Him, and from behind the cloud twelve rays of light, and out of it, the Spirit of God descended upon Him, like a dove, and shone around Him. And behold, a voice from heaven spoke, "This is My beloved Son, in whom I am well pleased. And on this day I have begotten Him." (Chap. 8:1-2)

I, Christ, explain, correct
and deepen the word:

Water symbolizes the purification of the soul and of the body. Water is flowing; Spirit is flowing.

105

The event which took place after the baptism of Jesus and which is reported here happened in the spirit. Within himself, John saw it in these symbols. The word "begotten" should mean "called." Through this calling by the Eternal, I, the Christ, accomplished what was becoming more and more manifest in Jesus.

3. And John gave witness of Him, saying, "This was He of whom I spoke, He will come after me and is placed before me, for He was earlier than I. And all of us have received from His fullness, grace upon grace. For the law was partly given through Moses, but the grace and truth came in fullness through Jesus Christ.
(Chap. 8:3)

I, Christ, explain, correct
and deepen the word:

The eternal truth now radiates into this world in countless facets. In many generations, the Eternal always gave – from the eternal truth, which He is – those facets of the truth which men striving towards God could understand and live by. So, through Moses, He gave those facets of the truth appropriate for the generations of that time. I, Christ in Jesus, gave the fullness from the truth. However, only a few could understand Me.

Now [1989] the time has come, in which I reveal all facets of the truth. May he who can grasp it, grasp it!

Recognize: The eternal truth will now spread over the entire world, and all untruth will fall prey to the fire, so that the fullness, the entire truth, becomes manifest. I have chosen the divine wisdom as the progenitress, in the Spirit, of the Kingdom of Peace of Jesus Christ. The female ray, the seraph from the wisdom of God, is in the flesh today and is active for the Eternal and for Me, as prophetess and emissary of God. Through her, the Eternal and I, Christ, have called and are calling into this world and are bringing the entire truth to all willing people – as long as this is possible in words.

According to the will of God, David, from whom the lineage of David came, is the progenitor, in the flesh, of the Kingdom of Peace of Jesus Christ. For he brought the seed into this world, and from it the genes which form the tribe of David.

Beings from God incarnate in those human beings in whom the genes of David are active. They stand together with further sons and daughters from other lineages in the Mission of Redemption, in My work, the Universal Life.

David is therefore the progenitor, in the flesh, of the Kingdom of Peace of Jesus Christ, and the ray of the divine wisdom is the progenitress, in the Spirit.

So it was David who brought the seed and the genes for God's people as seen from the flesh; the divine wisdom brings the entire truth in human words through its incarnated part-ray, the seraph of divine wisdom.

The souls in the flesh are called.

Souls and men receive from Me, the Christ, in the revealed word, the entire truth through the prophetess and emissary of God. The incarnated part-ray of divine wisdom also teaches the eternal laws in all their details and shows all those who are willing how these can be fulfilled in the world.

The time has come. The world is moving towards the year two thousand. I prepare My coming as Christ through the chosen people of God, with whom the Eternal and I, Christ, have made the last covenant in the omnipotence, God. Only those souls and those people who know the entire truth, and also fulfill it, will stand at My right side.

4. *No man has ever seen God. God is revealed solely in the only begotten One, who comes from the bosom of the Eternal." And this is the statement of John, when the Jews sent priests and Levites from Jerusalem to ask him, "Who are you?" And he denied not, but confessed, "I am not Christ."*

5. *And they asked him, "Who then? Are you Elijah?" And He said, "I am not." "Are you the prophet of whom Moses spoke?" And he answered, "No." Then they said to him, "Who are you then? So that we may give an answer to those who have sent us. What do you say of yourself?" And he said, "I am the voice of a caller in the wilderness. Prepare the way for the holy One, as the prophet Isaiah has said."*

6. And those who had been sent were of the Pharisees, and they asked him, "Why do you baptize then, if you are not Christ, nor Elijah, nor the prophet of whom Moses spoke?"

7. John answered them, saying, "I baptize with water; but among you stands the One whom you do not know. He will baptize with water and with fire. He is the One who will come after me, yet who will go ahead of me; I am not worthy to loosen His shoe-straps."

8. This took place in Bethabara, beyond the Jordan, where John was baptizing. And Jesus was thirty years of age at this time, being indeed the son of Joseph and Mary according to the flesh, but according to the Spirit, Christ, the Son of God, the eternal Father, as was announced with might by the Spirit of holiness.

9. And Joseph was the son of Jacob and Elisheba, and Mary was the daughter of Eli (called Joachim) and Anna, who were the children of David and Bathsheba, of Judah and Shela, of Jacob and Leah, of Isaac and Rebecca, of Abraham and Sarah, of Seth and Maat, of Adam and Eve, who were the children of God.

(Chap. 8:4-9)

CHAPTER 9

The Four Temptations

The darkness may measure itself against the light (1).
The one who lives in God is united with all Being
and is never lonely (5)

1. Jesus was led by the Spirit into the desert, to be tempted by the devil. And the wild animals of the desert were around Him and served Him. And since He had fasted forty days and forty nights, He was hungry. (Chap. 9:1)

I, Christ, explain, correct
and deepen the word:

Satan was allowed to try Jesus. The Spirit of My eternal Father allowed the test to happen. Thereby, even Satan should be able to recognize and measure himself, in order to learn that those who live in God are stronger than the power of the darkness.

It is a law from God's love and grace that, when people have acquired knowledge and wisdom from God, the darkness may measure itself against them. Even the soul which has fallen the furthest is thereby given the possibility of self-recognition: In its defeat, it may learn that the one who lives in God is superior to

Satan; purity serves him. The one who has not yet unfolded God's Spirit in his inner being is inferior to Satan, for he serves the latter in many aspects of his earthly life.

The word "fasting" means to partake of little food.

2. *And the tempter came to Him, saying, "If You are the Son of God, command that these stones be turned into bread; for it is written: I will feed you with the finest of wheat, and with honey of the rock will I satisfy you."*

3. *But He answered and said to him, "It is written: Man shall not live by bread alone, but by each and every word that comes from the mouth of God."*

4. *Then the devil placed before Him a woman of remarkable beauty and grace and of subtle wit and versatile mind, and he said to Him, "Take her, if You wish, for her desire is for You, and You will enjoy love and happiness all Your life and will see Your children's children. For is it not written, it is not good for man to be alone?"*

5. *And Jesus said, "Get thee behind Me! For it is written: Do not let yourself be seduced by the beauty of a woman, for all flesh is like grass and the flowers of the field; the grass withers and the flowers fade away, but the word of the Eternal lasts forever. My task is to teach and heal the children of man, and the one who is born of God keeps his seed within him." (Chap. 9:2-5)*

I, Christ, explain, correct
and deepen the word:

The meaning of the words "keeps his seed within him" is that men in God will not squander their strength on pleasures or enticements. The one who lives in God loves the inner values of man, inner beauty and virtue. The one who loves the inner being of man is linked with all people and beings. He will never be alone or lonely, because he keeps the good of his neighbor in himself. The commandment, "It is not good for man to be alone" is fulfilled only in this way.

God is unity – and the one who lives in God lives in communion with all Being. And all Being, all that is pure, is with him and works through him.

Only the person who rejects and belittles his fellow man is lonely.

6. *And the devil led Him into the holy city and set Him on a pinnacle of the temple. And he said to Him, "If You are the Son of God, cast Yourself down; for it is written: He will order His angels to protect You and to carry You in their hands, so that You do not dash Your foot against a stone."*

7. *And Jesus answered and said to him, "It is also written: You shall not tempt the Lord, your God."*

8. *Then the devil took Him up on a very high mountain in the midst of a great plain and around the mountain were twelve towns with their inhabitants. From*

there, in one moment, he showed Him all the kingdoms of the world. And the devil said to Him, "I will give You all this power and their glory, for this has been delivered unto me. And I will give it to whomever I will; for it is written: You shall rule from sea to sea; You shall govern Your people with righteousness and the poor with mercy and shall put an end to all oppression. If You will worship me now, all this shall be Yours."

9. *And Jesus answered and said to him, "Get thee behind Me, Satan; for it is written: You shall worship God and Him only shall you serve. Without the power of God, the end of evil cannot come."*

10. *Then the devil, having offered all the temptations he had, left Him for some time. And behold, angels of God came and served Him. (Chap. 9:6-10)*

CHAPTER 10

Joseph and Mary
Prepare a Feast for Jesus –
Andrew and Peter Find Jesus

To the people of the New Era:
Do not forget the deed of redemption of Jesus (2). Character-
ization of the followers of Jesus of Nazareth – Giving a name
in human terms and the radiation name
of the soul (10)

1. The same day, when Jesus had returned from the desert, His parents prepared a feast for Him. They gave Him the gifts which the wise men had presented Him in His infancy. And Mary said, "We have kept these gifts for You to this day." And they gave Him the gold, the frankincense and the myrrh. And He took of the frankincense, but He gave the gold to His parents and the poor, and of the myrrh He gave to Mary, called Magdalene.

2. Now this Mary was from the city of Magdala in Galilee. And she was a great sinner, having seduced many by her beauty and charm. And she came to Jesus by night and confessed her sins to Him, and Jesus extended His hand and healed her. And He cast seven demons out of her, and said to her, "Go in peace, for your sins are forgiven." And she rose and left everything and followed Him and served Him with her possessions, as long as He was active in Israel. (Chap. 10:1-2)

I, Christ, explain, correct
and deepen the word:

For better understanding, so that the eternal law may be recognized: It was Mary, called Magdalene, who spoke of the seven demons which, she said, are supposed to have left her. She was of the opinion that this is what had happened. An enlightened one does not speak of such things. He helps and heals, as it is good for the soul.

This explanation is given above all for the people of the present time [1989] and for the people at the onset of the New Era, who know the laws of God.

The book "This Is My Word" is particularly significant for the people of the New Era. For they experience Christ as the ruler of the world and no longer as the Redeemer. Therefore, this book will be a historic work for them.

The people of the New Era should not forget the foundation upon which the Kingdom of Peace of Jesus Christ was built, the redemption. The way of thinking and living, the work and the suffering of the Son of God in Jesus of Nazareth, who is now the ruler of the Earth and the directing power of the Kingdom of God on Earth, should be kept in the memory of the people of the New Era.

3. *The next day John saw Jesus coming towards him and said, "Behold the lamb of God, who takes away the sins of the world through righteousness. This is He of*

whom I spoke: He was before me. And I did not know Him; but so that He would become known in Israel, I have come to baptize with water."

4. And John gave witness, saying, "I saw the Spirit descending from heaven like a dove, and it stayed on Him. And I did not know Him; but the One who sent me to baptize with water spoke to me: The One upon whom you will see the Spirit descend and stay is the One who will baptize with water and with fire and with the Spirit. And I saw it, and give witness that this was the Son of God."

5. The day after, John stood by the Jordan with two of his disciples. And as he saw Jesus walking, he said, "Behold the Christ, the lamb of God." And the two disciples heard him and followed Jesus.

6. Jesus turned and saw them following and said to them, "What do you seek?" But they said to Him, "Rabbi (this means, Master), where do You dwell?" He said to them, "Come and see." They came and saw where He dwelt, and stayed with Him that day; for it was about the tenth hour.

7. One of the two who heard John and followed Jesus was Andrew, Simon Peter's brother. He found his brother Simon and said to him, "We have found the Messiah (which means, the Christ)." And he brought him to Jesus. And when Jesus beheld him, He said, "You are Simon Bar Jona, you shall be called Kephas (this means, a rock)."

8. The following day, Jesus went to Galilee and found Philip and said to him, "Follow Me." Now Philip was from Bethsaida, the city of Andrew and Peter. Philip found Nathanael, called Bar Tholmai, and said to him, "We have found Him of whom Moses, in the law, and the prophets, have written, Jesus of Nazareth, the son of Joseph and Mary." And Nathanael said to him, "Can anything good come out of Nazareth?" Philip said to him, "Come and see."

9. Jesus saw Nathanael coming to Him and said of him, "Behold, a true Israelite in whom is no guile." Nathanael said to Him, "Whence do You know me?" Jesus answered and said to him, "Before Philip called you, when you were under the fig tree, I saw you." Nathanael answered and said to him, "Rabbi, You are the Son of God; You are the king of Israel. Yea, under the fig tree did I find You."

10. Jesus answered and said to him, "Nathanael Bar Tholmai, do you believe because I said to you that I saw you under the fig tree? You will see greater things than these." And He said to him, "Verily, verily, I say to you, from now on you will see heaven open and the angels of God ascending and descending upon the Son of Man." (Chap. 10:3-10)

I, Christ, explain, correct
and deepen the word:

In many cases, the meaning of what was written down in this book a long time ago corresponds to the actual events. For this reason, each statement should

117

not be understood literally, but according to its meaning.

There was great dissension amongst those who believed in Me and followed Me – whether they are quoted by name or not. It was often questions of belief or situations in life which inflamed their temper. The one believed immediately in My mission, the other doubted it, because he was not able to understand much of what I said to him and to his neighbor. The one wanted to follow Me, the other still had worldly interests which were more important to him. Still others wanted to take all their possessions with them on their travels, in order to increase them in suitable places. Their concepts and interests were manifold and their way of thinking was as varied as the people themselves. With many there was a lengthy back and forth, and ifs and buts. The indecision was, for many, their undoing. They remained for some time – then they parted from Me again. It was a small, colorful group of believers, doubters, interested ones and those who wanted to make a profit through Me, through My way of thinking and living as Jesus of Nazareth.

Those who decided with their heart and actualized My teachings stood at My right side and remained at My right side. Even today, they stand at My right side in the spirit. The righteous beheld the angels who served the Son of Man. Many of them are active in the spirit for the great whole. Some came and come repeatedly into the earthly garment – each person according to his spiritual mission – in order to prepare My coming in the great totality of the process of evolution.

Every person has a first name and a surname, which are given to him at his earthly birth. This first name and surname correspond to the vibration of the soul at the moment of incarnation. When, in the course of their earthly years, people have worked through a spiritual phase of development, the radiation of their soul also changes. In the cosmic process of evolution the radiation name of the soul then also changes.

When, for example, something is cleared up between people – as between parents and child – then the radiation name of the soul also changes. This happens in the evolutionary process of the person, as well as of the soul in the spheres of purification and in the spheres of preparation, until the spirit being bears once again its original name from God, because it has once again become pure.

Thus, the radiation names of the person change according to the development of the soul. In the spheres of purification, the soul is conscious of this as it goes from one evolutionary level to another.

In many cases, rigid forms apply on Earth. The person maintains his first and family names as identification, so to speak, during his entire earthly existence. According to worldly law, this rigid form of giving names stays the same in marriage, too. In some peoples, the wife then bears the surname of the husband, which can be of a positive or negative significance for her life.

In still others, people change their names according to their own self-appointed criteria and rituals.

Many human aspects can cling to a name given at birth – such as old traditions or incidents which happened a long time before – but which still accompany the name in the form of memories. For this reason, to some who wanted to follow Me, I gave names which corresponded to the radiation of their soul at that time and also to their new sphere of activity.

If the worldly law would take into consideration the evolutionary path of the soul and person, many worldly names could be changed according to the degree of maturity of the soul. Then the danger would no longer be so great that new correspondences could develop from memories, from what has been put aside.

CHAPTER 11

The Anointing of Jesus by Mary Magdalene

Judging by worldly standards (6).
The enlightened one perceives (10)

1. *And one of the Pharisees invited Him to eat with him. And He went to the Pharisee's house and sat down to eat.*

2. *And behold, a woman of Magdala, who was reputed to be a sinner, was in the city. When she heard that Jesus was at the Pharisee's house for a meal, she brought an alabaster vessel of ointment and stepped behind Him. Weeping, she covered His feet with tears, dried them with the hair of her head, kissed His feet and anointed them with ointment.*

3. *Now when the Pharisee who had invited Him to his home saw this, he thought to himself, "If this man were a prophet, He would know who and what kind of woman touches Him, for she is a sinner."*

4. *Jesus said to him, "Simon, I have something to say to you." He said, "Master speak."*

5. *"There was a creditor who had two debtors. The one owed five hundred pence, the other fifty. And as they could not pay, he forgave them both their debt. Tell me now, which of them will love him most?"*

6. *Simon answered, "I think, he to whom he forgave the most." And He said to him, "You have rightly judged." (Chap. 11:1-6)*

I, Christ, explain, correct
and deepen the word:

"You have rightly judged" means: You have judged according to worldly standards.

Recognize: Every judgment is a condemnation and gives evidence of spiritual ignorance. Even though the debtor who was excused from the greater debt loves the creditor more, it is not God who applies these standards. He loves all equally. The one who is nearer to God loves Him more.

7. *And he said to Simon, "Do you see this woman? I have come to your house, and you have given Me no water for My feet; but she has covered My feet with tears and has dried them with the hair of her head. You have given Me no kiss, but this woman has not ceased to kiss My feet since the time I came in. You have not anointed My head with oil, but she anointed My feet with ointment.*

8. *Therefore, I say to you: She has been forgiven many sins; for she has loved much, not only people, but also the animals and the birds of the air, yea, even the fishes of the sea. But to whom little is forgiven, the same loves little."*

9. *And He said to her, "Your sins are forgiven." And those who were sitting with Him at the table began to say to themselves, "Who is this one who even forgives sins?"*

10. For He did not say, I forgive you, but your sins are forgiven you; for He discerned true faith and penitence in her heart. Jesus did not need that anyone testify for another one, for He knew what is in man. (Chap. 11:7-10)

I, Christ, explain, correct
and deepen the word:

The enlightened one perceives the soul and the person. He perceives the honesty and the sincerity and sees the sin and the atonement, too. He sees the dishonesty and the hypocrisy. He also addresses them impersonally, as it is good for the soul and the person. When the person sincerely repents and no longer falls into the same sin, it is forgiven by the eternal Father, too, provided his neighbor against whom he committed the sin has also forgiven him. The one to whom God has granted remission of the greatest sin, has settled it in God, and thus, it is forgiven him.

CHAPTER 12

The Wedding in Cana –
The Healing in Capernaum

The incarnated spirit beings and their mission in the Work of Redemption (9). God is love, He does not damn – People far from God create avenging gods – Idolatry is also the veneration of worldly powers and rulers – "Eternal damnation" is a mockery of God (11). Heaven and hell are in man himself – The atmospheric chronicle (12). Living in the truth – The three steps towards the truth (16)

1. *And the next day there was a wedding in Cana of Galilee, and the mother of Jesus was there. And Jesus and Mary Magdalene were there, and His disciples also came to the wedding.*

2. *And as the wine ran short, the mother of Jesus said to Him, "They have no wine." Jesus said to her, "Woman, what is that to you and Me? My hour has not yet come." And His mother said to the servants, "Whatever He says to you, do it."*

3. *And six earthenware water jugs were set up, according to the custom of Jewish purification; these contained two or three portions for each one. And Jesus said to them, "Fill the water jugs with water." And they filled them to the brim. And He said to them, "Dip some out now and bring it to the kitchen master." And they brought it to him.*

4. When the kitchen master tasted the water, it had become wine. He did not know where it came from and called the bridegroom and said to him, "Everyone gives good wine at the beginning, and when the guests have drunk much, they are then served the inferior wine. But you have kept the good wine for the end."

5. With this Jesus began His miracles in Cana of Galilee and revealed His glory. And many of His disciples believed in Him.

6. After this He went down to Capernaum, He, His mother and Mary Magdalene, His brothers and His disciples, and they stayed there for many days.

7. And a question about purification arose between some of John's disciples and the Jews. And they came to John and said to him, "Master, the one who was with you beyond the Jordan, to whom you bore witness, behold, He baptizes and everyone goes to Him."

8. John answered, "A man can receive nothing, unless it is given him from heaven. You, yourselves, are witness to what I said: I am not the Christ, but I have been sent before Him.

9. The one who has the bride is the bridegroom. But the friend of the bridegroom, who stands by Him and hears Him, rejoices greatly at the bridegroom's voice. This joy of mine is thus fulfilled. He must increase; but I must decrease. The one who is of the Earth is earthly and speaks of earthly matters. The one who comes from heaven is above all." (Chap. 12:1-9)

I, Christ, explain, correct
and deepen the word:

Many spirit beings came from the heavens. They were born and are being born into the lineage of David and other lineages. However, those beings who are from the lineage of David, as seen from the flesh, bear the responsibility for the formation of the Kingdom of Peace of Jesus Christ, because they are in the mission, in the Work of Redemption. These and other messengers of God came to Earth from heaven for that purpose.

Those who have come into the flesh for Me are not of this Earth. They bring the powers of the heavens. In their souls, they bring from heaven what is given to the Earth by God, the Eternal. They are called to bring to people the path to the heart of God, to found and build up the Kingdom of Peace of Jesus Christ and to raise the Earth into the light of God more and more. The messengers of God will be active until their substance has become fine-material and is able to enter into the life which lasts eternally, from eternity to eternity. My kingdom on Earth will also be their kingdom; for the one who comes from heaven stands above all humanness and has the powers of the All-One, which he puts to use for heaven on Earth. These are the selfless ones around the year two thousand, and all the people in the Kingdom of Peace, as well.

My Work of Redemption came to this Earth in order to save souls and men. And all those who are redeemed will raise the Earth with Me and will bring it into a higher radiation, so that the old world will pass away and a new world, that of the Christ, will emerge. And the one who follows the law of love, which I revealed and am revealing to him through the divine wisdom, will be the son and the daughter of God who goes before Me, to prepare the way for Me.

10. And some of the Pharisees came and questioned Jesus, saying, "How did You say that? That God will damn the world?" Jesus answered, saying, "God so loved the world, that He gave His only-begotten Son and sent Him into the world, so that all who believe in Him do not perish, but have everlasting life. For God did not send His Son into the world to damn the world, but so that the world may be saved through Him.

11. Those who believe in Him will not be damned, but those who do not believe are already damned, for they have not believed in the name of the only-begotten Son of God. And this is the damnation: that the light has come into the world, and men loved the darkness more than the light, because their deeds were evil.
(Chap. 12:10-11)

I, Christ, explain, correct
and deepen the word:

God is love.

God does not damn. However, the person who thinks, speaks and acts against the divine law subjects himself to his own judgment and calls this damnation.

The words "damn" and "damnation" arose from the fear of God and from the belief in avenging gods. Avenging gods are nothing but human conceptions, that is, idols which man himself created, because he became poor in energy through his thoughts and actions that are far from God, thus distancing himself from the true, the One, the Eternal. The negative thoughts caused him pangs of conscience; for deep within he realized that the unlawful, what is far from God, is not his true life. Since his spiritual heritage – the divine law – could no longer be effective through him because of his sins, he became frightened, because he no longer had command over the elements, instead it was the elements that had command over him. From this he deduced that those who ruled the elements were gods, to whom he had to offer sacrifices so that they would be well-disposed towards him.

In the times that followed, men raised themselves to be gods, acquired riches and prestige and built up power, in order to thus dominate entire nations. In the end, riches, prestige and power became the idols of many people. Secular power and ecclesiastic authority are also idols of this world, which the people still venerate at the present time [1989]. Their office holders have great wealth, prestige and influence at their disposal, and with this, they exercise power over the people. The one who reveres them makes himself dependent on them and raises them to be idols, for binding oneself to people, to human tendencies and concepts, is idolatry.

When the effects come to a person, the causes of which the person himself has created by his thinking and acting that are far from God he becomes frightened and accuses God and calls Him an avenging God, who damns and punishes.

However, you should not fear your heavenly Father, for He loves you. Fear your human thoughts, your words and your unlawful actions, because they can lead you into a long "damnation." God is love. Do not fear God, therefore, but venerate God and honor Him in everything, in your thinking, speaking and acting – but not a human being. You should respect people, your fellow men, but not honor them; for honor is due to God alone, the Eternal, the All-One.

God is the light of love, and all in His light – all that is, is even those who, through their sins against the law of life, "damn" themselves. Every form of idolatry, including honoring the human ego, will fade away, for nothing that is not of God will last. The numerous religions and denominations that still cling to the conception of an avenging God and infer eternal damnation from this will also fade away.

Only the person who keeps the laws of God experiences in himself the one, eternal God. He experiences the God who never punishes or chastises, the God who, out of love, allows each person the freedom to decide – for or against Him. He experiences the God of love, who does not damn any of His creatures. For him, "eternal damnation" is a mockery of God. He experiences the God who speaks to man about the law of sowing and reaping, according to which the person reaps what he himself has sown. For man himself is the one who sows his good, less good and bad deeds. He harvests what he has sown. Each seed already bears its fruit within itself, and the one who has brought the seed into the acre of life will harvest the fruit.

The time is at hand when the sinful life will pass and the people will bring a good seed into the field of life. The fruit is then the law of life, which they fulfill – and which fulfills them. Then, only the love of God will remain among men, because they will live the selfless love towards Him and towards their fellowmen. It is from this that the Kingdom of Peace of Jesus Christ, of which I Am the ruler, will arise.

12. *All those who do evil hate the light and do not come to the light, so that their deeds may not be condemned. But those who do what is right come to the light, so that their deeds may be made manifest, for they are done in God." (Chap. 12:12)*

I, Christ, explain, correct
and deepen the word:

All those who deliberately act against the law are against the light of the Father and also do not want to come to the light, since they think that – in so doing they would not be judged. In reality they bear their own judgment within themselves, for heaven and hell are in man himself. But all men who fulfill the law stand in the light and their deeds are manifest, for they are done in God.

Redeemed* is the person who repented, asked for forgiveness, forgave and atoned, and no longer does what he had caused; then everything has been resolved. Because I, Christ, have come to free and solve and not to bind.

In the mighty turn of time, which is becoming manifest today [1989], the atmospheric chronicle is also gradually being purified. Everything sinful that is still recorded there is gradually passing on to those who caused the sin, to the souls in the spheres of purification as well as to the human beings. Everything unlawful – even the unlawful intentions of individuals, that which people still plan for the Earth and have already fed into the atmospheric chronicle through their thoughts – is being erased or is coming back to its originators, depending on the decision of the person's soul in the further course of events: for or against God. Furthermore, all knowledge – from books and the Bible – is fading from the atmospheric chronicle; only the truth that has been lived remains manifest for souls and men.

---

* *Redeemed means: to have reached perfection for the most part. Redemption is the Redeemer-light of the soul, which leads the soul to perfection.*

13. And there was a nobleman whose son lay sick at Capernaum. When he heard that Jesus had come into Galilee, he went to Him and asked Him if he would come down and heal his son; for he was at the point of death.

14. And Jesus said to him, "Unless you see signs and wonders, you will not believe." The nobleman said to Him, "Lord, come down before my child dies."

15. Jesus said to him, "Go your way, your son lives." And the man believed the word that Jesus had spoken to him and went his way. While he was going down, his servants met him and said, "Your son lives."

16. Then he asked them the hour when he began to get better. And they said to him, "Yesterday at the seventh hour the fever left him." Thus, the father knew that it was at the same hour when Jesus had said to him, "Your son lives." And so he believed, and his whole household with him. (Chap. 12:13-16)

I, Christ, explain, correct
and deepen the word:

Faith moves mountains and makes men healthy if it is good for their souls.

When men live the eternal truth, the law of life, they bring heaven to this Earth. The one who lives in the truth is the voice of the truth, the divine law. He is free from all evil. For those who live in the truth stand in the light of the truth, and their deeds are the deeds of God.

The coming Kingdom of God on Earth, the Kingdom of Peace, which, from epoch to epoch, is becoming refined – that is, more light-filled – is in the light of Christ and is the light of Christ. Those who live in the truth will consciously be called the sons and daughters of God. The one who lives in the truth will neither feel nor taste death. He will help all those who believe in the life and do the deeds of selfless love to attain the life.

From the very beginning, many people have clung only to the word "faith." They are of the opinion that this would be enough. But the one who clings exclusively to the word "faith" remains blind in his heart, because he takes no further step beyond faith.

The first step towards the truth is faith. Yet it still keeps man blind. The second step is trust in God, which allows man to become alert in regard to his lawful or unlawful thinking, speaking and acting. When faith and trust unite, the third step follows: the actualization of the divine laws. Thus, the person becomes one who perceives. The one who is able to perceive the truth in his spiritual body is the pure one: Everything is manifest to him.

CHAPTER 13

The First Sermon in the Synagogue

The gospel of love, the path into inner freedom (2).
Faith, trust and actualization as a basis for help and healing
from the Spirit (4)

1. *And Jesus came to Nazareth, where He had grown up, and, as was His custom, He went into the synagogue on the Sabbath day and stood up to read. There the scroll of the prophet Isaiah was presented to Him.*

2. *When He had opened the scroll, He found the place where it was written, "The Spirit of the Lord is with me, because He has anointed me to proclaim the gospel to the poor; He has sent me to heal the broken-hearted, to preach to the captives that they should be free, to restore sight to the blind and to set free those who are bound; to announce the year of grace of the Lord." (Chap. 13:1-2)*

I, Christ, explain, correct
and deepen the word:

As Jesus of Nazareth, I deepened what Isaiah had said and accomplished.

In today's time, in this great turn of time [1989], in which the tide is turning from the old sinful world to the new world, to the Era of Light, the Kingdom of Peace is rising more and more in the hearts of the faithful ones who keep the laws of God; it is also becoming visible in the world. Despite the growing light of grace, there are more and more sick and suffering people, because in this time of radical change from the old sinful life to the new pure life, everything not yet atoned for is coming toward man at shorter intervals.

However, the one who believes and trusts will walk the path within and will recognize the free life in Christ, which makes him truly rich. The one who lives in Me will no longer look to the perishable body, because he has found the kingdom of the inner being, his true heritage. When the soul is imbued with the light of Christ, the body, too, is healthy.

For this reason, until I have taken over the rulership of the Earth, the following holds true: Repent, forgive, ask for forgiveness and sin no more! Then you will recognize and experience in yourself that I have served you through your living faith in Me. For I, the Redeemer and Savior of all men, have proclaimed, as Jesus of Nazareth, the gospel of love, which makes man free. I am proclaiming it again, as Christ, through those who fulfill the will of God. On the path within, which I have brought and bring to My own, everyone can find Me.

The meaning behind the words ."... to proclaim the gospel to the poor" is that I brought and bring the gospel to the poor in spirit and the poor of the Earth, for all people should become rich in their heart, so that on

Earth they may also possess what they need, in order to live as children of God.

"... to heal the broken-hearted" means to bring to all people comfort, help and the Spirit of truth, so that their faith and trust in God may grow and they may become peaceful.

"... to preach to the captives" means to give all people an understanding of the divine law of freedom, so that they can gradually let go of their opinions and concepts, which make them captives of their own ego, and so that they may awaken in the divine truth, which makes them free.

"... to restore sight to the blind" means to give again to soul and person the sight, the true vision, the perception which they gain by following the laws of life, of selfless love.

3. *And He closed the scroll, gave it back to the attendant and sat down. And the eyes of all those who were in the synagogue were directed to Him. And He began to speak to them, "Today this scripture is fulfilled in your hearing." And they bore witness of this and wondered at the loving words which came out of His mouth. They said, "Isn't this the son of Joseph?"*

4. *And some brought to Him a blind man, in order to test His power, and said, "Master, here is a son of Abraham, blind from birth. Heal him as You have healed Gentiles in Egypt." And He, looking at him, noted his unbelief and that of those who had brought*

him, and their desire to ensnare Him. And He could do no mighty work in that place because of their unbelief. (Chap. 13:3-4)

I, Christ, explain, correct
and deepen the word:

"Today this scripture is fulfilled in your hearing" means that Isaiah, a prophet sent by God, announced My coming: the Redeemer and Messiah, who would free the people from their bondage. The word of Isaiah has been fulfilled: The word was followed by the deeds of Christ. I fulfilled and fulfill what the Eternal had revealed through Isaiah.

The one who doubts and just wishes to put his neighbor to the test cannot receive from the Spirit; for he does not believe, but is only testing. His doubts, which go before him, are a hindrance to healing and help.

The one who wants to put Me to the test does not receive. For this reason I, as Jesus of Nazareth, could not accomplish deeds where unbelief prevailed. Where the basis of faith and trust is lacking, where doubt and egocentricity shape the person, neither do the words of truth fall into the heart, nor can the person obtain help and healing from the Spirit. For this reason, the teachings from the truth are required first. When a person has received and actualized the teachings from the eternal truth, he has established the true basis of faith and trust and can become whole in body and soul through the power of the Spirit.

Whether someone calls his neighbor gentile or orthodox is not something the truly wise man pays attention to. The person who is not able to look into the heart of his neighbor sees only the outer and hears only the word. He does not look more deeply. But the one who looks deeper into the heart of his neighbor perceives how he really is. He then speaks no longer of a gentile because this one may still have gentile customs; he gives to the one who keeps his heart open to God – whether people still call him gentile or orthodox. This is how I acted as Jesus, and this is what I maintain as Christ.

5. *And they said to Him, "Whatever we have heard about Your deeds in Egypt, do them here in Your own country, too." And He said, "Verily, I say to you, no prophet is recognized at home or in his own country; just as little as a physician can heal those who know him. (Chap. 13:5)*

I, Christ, explain, correct
and deepen the word:

The meaning is not, "about Your deeds in Egypt," but "about the deeds among the Egyptians." Verily, the prophet is not honored, neither in his earthly family nor in his own country. For people see only the person who once lived and is living with them, yet in his heart did not think as they did, when it concerned human matters.

6. *But I tell you a true story: There were many widows in Israel in the days of Elijah, when heaven was closed three years and six months and a great famine prevailed throughout the country. But Elijah was sent only to Sarepta, a city of Sidon, to a woman who was a widow.*

7. *And many lepers were in Israel in the time of Elisha, the prophet; and none of them was cleansed except Naaman, the Syrian."*

8. *And all those who were in the synagogue, when they heard that, were filled with wrath. They rose up and thrust Him out of the city and led Him to the edge of the hill whereon their city was built, in order to push Him off. But He, passing through the midst of them, went His way and escaped. (Chap. 13:6-8)*

CHAPTER 14

The Calling of Andrew and Peter –
The Dog-trainer – The Rich Ones

The path into the following of Christ is taken only after putting all of one's human relationships and affairs into order(1-3). Prerequisites for healing (4). Sinning against creation, by despising and killing fellow creatures, and the consequences – In the time of radical change, the causes take effect more quickly – The possibility to incarnate decreases with the refinement of the Earth – The time of radical change is the time of disasters – Christ protects His own – Life on the purified Earth (6-7). External and inner riches (11-12)

1. Now Herod, the tetrarch, added one more to all the evils which he had already done: He had John the Baptist thrown into prison after John reproved him because of Herodias, his brother Philip's wife.

2. Jesus began to preach and said, "Repent, for the Kingdom of Heaven is at hand." And as He was walking by the Sea of Galilee, He saw Simon, called Peter, and Andrew, his brother, casting a net into the sea; for they were fishermen. And He said to them, "Follow Me, and I will make you fishers of men." And they abandoned their nets and followed Him.

3. And continuing on, He met two other brothers, James, the son of Zebedee, and John, his brother, in a boat with Zebedee, their father, mending their

nets; and He called them. And they immediately left their nets, the boat and their father, and followed Him. (Chap. 14:1-3)

I, Christ, explain, correct
and deepen the word:

In all things, the meaning of what is said should be recognized, also in what was written: "And they immediately left their nets, the boat and their father, and followed Him." This should mean as follows: They gave up fishing, put their family affairs in order and followed Him.

Until they entered My following, many suggestions and explanations were necessary, including for their families and relatives who did not readily let them go. Much had first to be prepared, arranged and cleared up in the house, on the farm, in the field and at their place of work, so that those left behind would not have to suffer sorrow or want because of the change of attitude of those who followed My call.

The law is: The path to the eternal truth can be walked only of one's own free will. Therefore, the person who walks the path of truth of his own free will and for the sake of truth will leave everything behind in good order and duly arranged. For in the following of the Christ of God man shall take along neither dispute nor enmity nor disorder. When a person parts from his neighbor in dispute and enmity, then dispute and enmity will also go with him. The person takes along what is not cleared up before the law of God, regardless of the place or country he travels to or the person he walks with. What is unresolved remains and clings to him.

4. And Jesus went through all of Galilee, teaching in the synagogues and preaching the gospel of the Kingdom of God and healing all kinds of pestilence and many diseases among the people. And the fame of His miracles spread throughout all of Syria, and they brought to Him many sick people afflicted with all kinds of diseases, infirmities and torments. And there were lunatics and those sick with palsy, and He healed them all. (Chap. 14:4)

I, Christ, explain, correct
and deepen the word:

I could not help everybody, nor could I heal each one. The law of the Eternal reads: Believe, for you will be given according to your faith. Ask for forgiveness and forgive and make amends for what you have caused, then go forth and sin no more! And so only those became healthy who were filled with faith in the life and in whose life-radiation one could read that they would henceforth strive to sin no more.

5. *And there followed Him great multitudes of people from Galilee, from the ten cities and from Jerusalem, from Judea and from the land of Jordan.*

6. *As Jesus went with some of His disciples, He met a man who trained dogs to hunt other animals. And He said to the man, "Why do you do this?" And the man answered, "Because I live from this. What sort of use have these animals? These animals are weak, but the dogs are strong." And Jesus said to him, "You lack wisdom and love. Behold, every creature that God has created has its meaning and purpose. And who can say what good there is in it or what use it is to you or to mankind?*

7. *And for your living, behold the fields, how they grow and are fertile, and the fruit-bearing trees and the herbs. What more do you want than what the honest work of your hands will give you? Woe to the strong who misuse their strength. Woe to the crafty who hurt the creatures of God! Woe to the hunters! For they themselves shall be hunted." (Chap. 14:5-7)*

I, Christ, explain, correct
and deepen the word:

I Am the truth! The one who acts against life is also against himself, since he, too, is the life. For all the forces of life are active in him – including the life of animals and plants. For everything is the life that flows from the one primordial source, from God.

143

Man will suffer for as long as he inflicts suffering on his neighbor – be it human beings, animals or plants. In the past two thousand years, My words to the people about the law of sowing and reaping have been fulfilled, and they will continue to be fulfilled until the law of sowing and reaping has been transformed because all people have come to love one another selflessly.

The Kingdom of God comes to the Earth! In the course of further epochs, great areas all over the Earth will become refined. Light-filled people will live on them. They will be with the animals and the animals with them. The lamb will lie by the lion, and they will understand each other because people will be free from sin for the most part.

Many animals adopt the vibrations of people and behave like people. If human beings change and live in accordance with the divine law, then animals, too, will again become trusting and will be the friends of humans.

Until the sinful world has changed into the world of God, many human beings, animals and plants will still have to suffer from the unbending will of the domineering man who opposes God's creation.

However, all might and glory has been given by the Father to the Christ of God and never to the person who disregards the laws of God. Woe to the hunters, and woe to those who crave for meat! Both the hunters and those who, like cannibals, greedily consume the flesh of animals will be tormented and pursued by the anguish, suffering and pain of the animals. The same applies to those who violate the plant and mineral kingdoms. They, too, will suffer because of their sinful deeds. The person will harvest what he sows, either in his earthly life or as a soul in the spheres of purification. Therefore, watch your thoughts, words and deeds, for they can become your undoing.

My kingdom on Earth will be a kingdom of unity and peace, as was revealed: Man and animal will live with one another in peace, because the souls of people will be pure for the most part.

Now, during this time of powerful radical change, where the consequences of existing causes are taking place more quickly, I, the Christ of God, also work more comprehensively in this world and through those who strive to fulfill the will of God, so that many more people may recognize themselves, and consequently repent of their sins and no longer commit them.

Recognize that the souls of many people who continue to create what is negative despite knowing better will press again and again towards the Earth. After their physical death, the causes they have not atoned for will remain in the atmospheric chronicle. In a further incarnation, these souls will call up what is stored there and will live again in an earthly garment with the same inclinations and desires.

But now, during the turn of time, the atmospheric chronicle is being cleansed of all human conceptions, inclinations, opinions, desires and all that has not been accomplished. For this reason, according to the law of cause and effect, everything that was caused, that is, that was not atoned for, and which vibrates in the atmospheric chronicle, will fall back upon people and souls more quickly. For human beings as well as souls this will be hard to bear. For some souls, this can be the so-called hell.

Over great periods of time, the materialistic world is gradually going under. At the same time, the Kingdom of God on this Earth is emerging in evolutionary cycles. For the heavily burdened souls, this means that when the Earth becomes more light filled, they will not be able to return to Earth. For the heavily burdened souls, the paths from the planets to the Earth will be limited more and more and will finally be cut off by the spiritual layer, the universal atmosphere, the Christ-layer, which will envelop the Kingdom of God on Earth with its radiation. One day, only largely pure souls will be born into the Kingdom of Peace of Jesus Christ, because the new purified Earth will also have a purified atmosphere.

In this mighty time of radical change, epidemics, diseases and Earth disasters will fall upon the entire Earth. However, all this is not yet the end of this human era. As long as man wants to rule over the Earth, it will shake and open up.

In this turn of time, the eternal Spirit radiates more intensely into all material suns and heavenly bodies, and the light, similar to a fire, radiates more intensely from the universe. It brings the seas into stronger movement, so that they overflow their basins, flooding and covering over low-lying regions. And the stars and planets will transform the impure into the pure.

As a result of these effects of the light of God and of the stars and planets upon the seas and upon the Earth, the planet Earth will then become fertile again.

All of this will still happen before the tide has completely turned. The one who remains faithful to God despite these effects that are falling upon mankind, who praises and glorifies Him is saved and will uplift and give life to the new Earth with his sowing and the seed of love.

In this time of radical change from the old sinful world to the world of the Spirit, I know how to protect My faithful. I will also preserve their establishments for the Kingdom of Peace of Jesus Christ. The Spirit of God will envelop the people who stand in the light of truth, that is, who fulfill the law of God, and will keep everything negative away from them. They have been given the strength by Me to cultivate the purified land, to found communities in My Spirit, thus subduing the Earth in love. Then the Earth and all that the Earth bears – stones, plants, animals – will serve them. And, last but not least, the angels of the heavens will live and work with their light-filled human brothers and sisters for the Kingdom of God on Earth.

The man in My Spirit will bear good seed and the womb of the spiritual woman will conceive lovingly; and the man and woman who unite in God will keep the covenant with God; and their children, who are the children of the Father-Mother-God, will bear the light of divinity. In their souls, redemption has already been accomplished since the souls come from higher levels of light. These souls are attracted according to the light-filled soul of the man – who begets the earthly body – and the light-filled soul of the woman – who is with child and gives birth. For the cosmic law reads: like attracts like.

8. *And the man was very astonished and stopped training the dogs to hunt; and he taught them to save life, not to destroy it. And he embraced the teachings of Jesus and became His disciple.*

9. *And behold, two rich men came to Him and one said to Him, "Good Master." But He said to him, "Do not call Me good, for only One is the all-good and that One is God."*

10. *And the other said to Him, "Master, what good work shall I do so that I live?" And Jesus said, "Follow the law and the prophets." He answered, "I have followed them." Jesus answered, "Go, sell all that you have, divide it with the poor and follow Me." But these words did not please him.*

11. *And the Lord said to him, "Why do you say that you have followed the law and the prophets? Behold, many of your brethren are clad with filthy rags, dying from hunger, and your house is full of many goods, and they receive nothing from it."*

12. And He said to Simon, "It is hard for the rich to enter the Kingdom of Heaven, for the rich take care of themselves and despise the others who have nothing." (Chap. 14:8-12)

I, Christ, explain, correct
and deepen the word:

I Am the truth and the life. Outer riches harden the soul and impoverish it. A life in material wealth is not the life in Me, but is merely an outer show; it concerns the garments of the soul, not the true being. People whose wealth is solely in the possessions of this world, the outer things, keep themselves from uniting with their neighbors. At the same time, they separate themselves from God through this, thus becoming poor in their souls. Only the one is truly rich who is able to enrich his neighbor through acts of selfless love. He remains in unity with his neighbor and is thereby also in unity with God; for God is in everyone, and every one is a part of God. The one who separates himself from his neighbor separates himself from God, because God's love is active in his neighbor.

CHAPTER 15

The Healing of a Leper, a Paralyzed Man and a Deaf Man

The people in the Spirit of the Lord

1. And it came to pass, when Jesus was in a city, that a leper threw himself at His feet and said to Him, "Lord, if it is Your will, You can cleanse me." And Jesus put forth His hand and touched him, saying, "Blessed are you who believe; it is My will, be cleansed." And immediately the leprosy left him.

2. And Jesus charged him, saying, "Tell no man, but go and show yourself to the priest, and make an offering for your cleansing, as Moses has commanded, as a testimony for him." But His fame spread more and more, and great multitudes came to Him, in order to hear Him and to be healed of their infirmities. He withdrew into the desert and prayed.

3. And one day it came to pass, as He was teaching, that there were Pharisees and scribes sitting by, in order to observe Him. People had come from every town, from Galilee and Judea, and from Jerusalem; and the power of God was present and healed them.

4. And behold, they brought a man on a bed, who was paralyzed, and they tried to bring him in and to lay him before Him. And when they could find no way to bring him in, because of the great number of people, they climbed onto the housetop. They lowered him with

his bed down through the roof and into their midst, before Jesus. And when He saw their faith, He said to him, "Man, your sins are forgiven you."

5. And the scribes and the Pharisees began to reflect and said, "Who is this who speaks such blasphemies? Who can forgive sins, but God alone?" But as Jesus perceived their thoughts, He answered them, saying, "What are you thinking in your hearts? Can even God ever forgive sins, if man does not repent of them? Who said: I forgive you your sins? Did I not rather say: Your sins are forgiven you?

6. Which is easier to say: Your sins are forgiven you; or to say: Rise up and walk? But so that you may know that the Son of Man has power upon Earth to discern and to declare the forgiveness of sins" – He said to the paralyzed man, "I say to you, stand up, take your bed and go home."

7. And immediately he stood up before them and took up the bed on which he had lain and went home, and praised God. And they were all amazed and praised God and were filled with reverence, and said, "We have seen amazing things today."

8. As Jesus came to a village, He was met by a man who was deaf from birth. And he did not believe in the sound of rushing wind or the thunder or the cries of the animals or the voices of the birds crying with hunger or because they were wounded, or that others heard these things.

9. And Jesus breathed into his ears, and they were opened, and he heard. And he enjoyed with infinite glad-

ness the sounds he had denied before. And he said, "Now I hear everything."

10. But Jesus said to him, "Why do you say that you hear everything? Can you hear the sighing of the prisoners or the language of the birds or the animals when they speak with each other, or the voices of the angels and the spirits? Think how much you cannot hear, and be humble in your lack of knowledge." (Chap. 15:1-10)

I, Christ, explain, correct
and deepen the word:

Those who live in the truth fulfill the will of God. They are the pure ones, who, already in today's time, hear the angels of the heavens and behold life in its abundance. They read the thoughts of men and hear their sighs and see their suffering. In My name and from My Spirit, they help and serve their neighbors.

People who are in the Spirit of the Lord also understand the language of animals. In the rushing of the wind, in lightning and thunder, they recognize the all-ruling law, God. The one who lives in this high divine consciousness is truly a son and a daughter of God. They are My faithful ones.

In this mighty turn of time [1989], the first steps are being taken on the path towards the Kingdom of Peace of Jesus Christ, which is gradually emerging. The primordial power is guiding ever more people onto the path within, towards the Kingdom of God, which is within each person. People who draw nearer to the consciousness of Christ on the path of evolution find their way back to the original language of love. The language of the universe becomes accessible to them again.

CHAPTER 16

The Calling of Matthew –
New Wine in Old Skins

The possibility of reincarnation and expiation is limited

1. And then He went on and saw a tax collector, named Levi, sitting at the collection of taxes. And He said to him, "Follow me." And he left everything, stood up and followed Him. (Chap. 16:1)

I, Christ, explain, correct
and deepen the word:

And Levi, so named, also followed Me, Jesus, but only after he had settled everything in his family and at his place of work and had taken care of his neighbors, whom he left only externally, in order to serve the truth.

2. And Levi prepared a great feast for Him in his house. There was a great company of tax collectors and others, who sat at the table with Him. But the scribes and Pharisees grumbled and said to His disciples, "Why do you eat and drink with publicans and sinners?"

3. And Jesus answered and said to them, "Healthy people do not need a physician, but the sick ones do. I did not come to call the righteous to repentance, but the sinners."

4. And they said to Him, "Why do the disciples of John fast so often and pray so much, and likewise the disciples of the Pharisees; but Your disciples eat and drink?"

5. And He said to them, "With what shall I compare the men of this generation, and what are they like? Are they not like children, sitting in the market place, calling to one another, saying: We have piped before you and you have not danced, we have mourned before you, and you have not lamented?

6. For John the Baptist came, and he neither ate nor drank, and you said: He is possessed by the devil. The Son of Man comes, and He eats and drinks the fruits of the Earth and the milk of the flocks and the fruit of the vine and you say: Behold, what a glutton and drunkard, a friend of publicans and sinners.

7. Would you have allowed the wedding guests to fast, while the bridegroom is with them? But the time will come, when the bridegroom will be taken away from them. Then they will fast in those days." (Chap. 16:2-7)

I, Christ, explain, correct
and deepen the word:

The bridegroom is the Christ of God in Jesus. And the bridegroom will leave them. The one who does not keep Him in his heart will not fulfill the works of love either. On the day of horror which will come upon mankind; he will have to fast, for the Earth, which is purifying itself from human wheeling and dealing, will no longer give bread to those who have contributed to the dissolution of the atmospheric layers and to the contamination of the Earth and its waters.

8. *And He spoke this parable to them, "No one patches a piece of new cloth on an old garment. For then the new does not suit the old, and the garment is made worse by so doing.*

9. *And no one puts new wine into old skins; for the new wine will split the skins and be spilled, and the skins will be damaged. But new wine should be put into new skins; thus, both are preserved.*

10. *And there is no one who, having drunk old wine, immediately desires new wine. For he says, the old is better. But the time will come when the new will have become old, and then the new will be desired. For as one changes old garments for new ones, so do they also change the dead body for the living body, and what is past for what is coming." (Chap. 16:8-10)*

I, Christ, explain, correct
and deepen the word:

As long as the sinful world exists and souls live within the wheel of reincarnation, the incarnation of

156

Earth-bound souls will still be possible. They lay aside their old garments, the old bodies, and slip once more into new garments, into newborn bodies. However, they repeatedly bring with them into the new garment the sins which they did not clear up in previous incarnations nor in the spheres of purification. A soul cannot enter higher and more light-filled spheres until it has settled – through repenting, forgiving, asking for forgiveness and clearing things up – what it has inflicted upon itself.

When, in the course of the turn of time – which extends over great periods of time – a soul has not cleared up in the earthly garment what it has inflicted upon itself, it will no longer be able to incarnate after that. It will then have to endure as a soul, in the spheres of the souls, what it could have cleared up, possibly in years, while in the earthly garment. For it will no longer be assigned a new body, because the light will then dwell on the Earth and, for the time being, the shadows will no longer have access there.

CHAPTER 17

Jesus Sends Out the Twelve

The progress of the Work of Redemption depends on the faithfulness and development of those entrusted with it (3). Baptism with the Spirit of truth (6). Healing of the sick and raising of the dead – Collective guilt – Casting out of demons – Gifts of love should not be imposed (7). Hell is not a place, but a condition of the soul (10). Nothing is concealed from God – Only the one who lives in the light of truth knows the word of truth (13). The one who is against Christ is against his neighbor (14)

1. *And Jesus went onto a mountain to pray. And, having called His twelve disciples, He gave them power to cast out unclean spirits and to heal all kinds of diseases and pestilences. And the names of the twelve apostles who stood for the twelve tribes of Israel were:*

2. *Peter, called Cephas for the tribe of Reuben; James, for the tribe of Naphtali; Thomas, called Dydimus, for the tribe of Zebulun; Matthew, called Levi, for the tribe of Gad; John, for the tribe of Ephraim; Simon, for the tribe of Issachar.*

3. *Andrew, for the tribe of Joseph; Nathanael, for the tribe of Simeon; Thadaeus, for the tribe of Zebulun**;*

---

* *The repeated name of this tribe goes back to a mistake in the passed-down text of the "Gospel of Jesus."*

Jacob, for the tribe of Benjamin; Jude, for the tribe of Dan; Philip, for the tribe of Asher. And Judas Iscariot, a Levite, who betrayed Him, was also among them (but he was not of them). And Matthias and Barsabbas were also present with them. (Chap. 17:1-3)

I, Christ, explain, correct
and deepen the word:

The words "unclean spirits" mean the impure souls, which often cling to human beings in clusters.

As Jesus of Nazareth, I already indicated what was to come, by entrusting the twelve disciples with building twelve communities. Because they, too, just like people in further generations, could hardly grasp the depth of inner life which says "fulfill the laws and then act," they were unable to fulfill many things which I had entrusted to them. I had entrusted these things to them because they had heard much divine wisdom, and it would have been time to give it a material form. Despite everything, ever further evolutionary steps of the Kingdom of Peace of Jesus Christ took place from one epoch to another.

At the present time [1989] as well, in which the first foundations of the Kingdom of Peace of Jesus Christ are becoming visible, many of My faithful from the tribe of David and from other lineages are active in My Work of Redemption. The faithful are with Me, and I work through them. As in those days, so today, there are a few among them who do not gather, but scatter. They repeatedly create points of access for the darkness through which it can attack. For that reason, the faithful have great difficulties.

Nevertheless, with them, I Am the victor over the Earth and over the spheres of purification. Just as I sent the apostles into the world at that time, so will I gradually send My own, who fulfill the law of life, into the world as spiritual teachers. Through My own, I will found new first communities in Me, Christ, the Universal Spirit, so that many people find their way, via these stations of communities, to the central light, to the New Jerusalem on this Earth with its twelve gates.

4. *And in like manner, He called twelve others to be prophets, to be men of light with the apostles, and He showed them the secrets of God. And their names were: Hermes, Aristobulus, Selenius, Nereus, Apollos and Barsabbas; Andronicus, Lucius, Apelles, Zachaeus, Urbanus and Clementos. And then He selected twelve more to be evangelists and twelve to be pastors. He called four times twelve and sent them out to the twelve tribes of Israel, four to each tribe.*

5. *And they stood around the Master, clad in white linen raiments, called to form a holy priesthood of God in service of the twelve tribes to which they would be sent. (Chap. 17:4-5)*

I, Christ, explain, correct
and deepen the word:

As Jesus of Nazareth in the earthly garment, I acted
in a way similar to how I taught and teach [1989] the
prophets and spiritual teachers and all sons and daughters of God from the lineage of David and from other
lineages, via the prophetic word through the incarnated
part-ray of divine wisdom, sending them into the world
according to their actualization.

I taught the faithful ones and instructed them in the
actualization of the laws of God. A few of them began
to speak prophetically. Others, who are called evangelists and pastors in this book, were the spiritual teachers
and elders, who were to co-found the communities and
look after them.
The word "priesthood" has the following meaning:
They are people who strive only to fulfill the will of
God, without ceremonies or rites.

6. *Jesus sent out these four times twelve and charged
them, saying, "With your companions, I want you to be
My twelve apostles, a testimony to Israel. Go into the
cities of Israel and to the lost sheep of Israel. And when
you go there, preach and say: The Kingdom of Heaven
is at hand. As I have baptized you with water, so baptize all those who believe. (Chap. 17:6)*

I, Christ, explain, correct
and deepen the word:

In the book it is written, "As I have baptized you with water ..." This means the following: Just as you were baptized with water, so will I, as the Christ of God, baptize with the Spirit of truth all those whom you have taught according to the laws of life and who have actualized them. And they will speak henceforth from the Spirit of truth.

7. *Anoint and heal the sick, cleanse the lepers, raise the dead, cast out the demons. Freely you have received it, freely give it. You shall not provide yourselves with gold, nor silver, nor copper money in your purses, nor a bag for your journey, nor two coats, nor shoes, not even a staff. For a workman is worthy of his food. And eat what is set before you; but do not touch what was taken at the cost of life, for it is not lawful for you. (Chap. 17:7)*

I, Christ, explain, correct
and deepen the word:

"Anoint and heal the sick" means: Cleanse and heal the sick and lepers and anoint them with the Spirit, by instructing them in the laws of life and helping them to recognize these laws and to actualize them, that is, to clear things up and no longer do what is sinful.

I spoke from the "supreme law," the Absolute Law, which is above all humanness: "... raise the dead, cast out the demons." Raising the dead is possible only when the soul is not burdened with grave causes and collective guilt. I did, indeed, entrust this assignment to My apostles and disciples. However, at the same time, I also said that this is possible only for the one who lives in the Absolute Law and who works from the Absolute Law.

Raising the dead was possible at My time as Jesus of Nazareth, because then, the poor seldom had to expiate a collective guilt. At the present time [1989], most people bear part of a collective guilt, so that raising the dead in this sinful world is hardly possible.

A collective guilt comes into being when together, people kill human beings or animals and violate the plant and mineral kingdoms.

The soul of a so-called dead person can be called back into the body only if it is spiritually awakened and freely decides to return. Otherwise, the raising of a deceased person would be against the law of free will of the soul, because when its spiritual eyes are clouded by sin, it cannot freely decide. Furthermore, the soul can return only as long as it is still connected with the body through the information cord.

"Casting out demons" means driving earth-bound, benighted souls from the temple, from the human be-ing. This is possible only for the one who fulfills the laws of God and speaks with authority – and at that, only when the human being who attracted the earth-bound soul no longer holds on to it through the thoughts, words and actions that attracted it in the first place.

The statement "You shall not provide yourselves with gold, nor silver, nor copper money in your purses, nor a bag for your journey, nor two coats, nor shoes, not even a staff" means that you should not surround yourselves with the burdensome weights of this world, nor laboriously bear what is unnecessary to you, for the paths are stony and you walk on them with your feet. Everything that is unnecessary is useless weight, and only delays you on your journey.

8. *And into whatever city you will enter, inquire whether there is someone who is worthy. And stay there until you leave. Whenever you come into a house, greet it. And if the house is worthy, let your peace come upon it; but if it is not worthy, let your peace return to you.* (*Chap. 17:8*)

I, Christ, explain, correct
and deepen the word:

"... but if it is not worthy, let your peace return to you" means to bring love and peace into every house. Do not impose the gifts of heaven upon the one who does not want them. And when you are not received, do not be annoyed. Then the peace which you have expressed toward the house and its dwellers will be with you again.

9. *Be wise as serpents and harmless as doves. Be innocent and pure. The Son of Man has not come to destroy, but to save, neither to take life, but to give life to the body as well as to the soul.*

10. *And do not fear those who kill the body, but are not able to kill the soul. Rather, fear him who is able to destroy both soul and body in hell. (Chap. 17:9-10)*

I, Christ, explain, correct
and deepen the word:

It is only the person himself who destroys his soul and his body through his human thinking, speaking and acting, whereby he establishes contact with the darkling. What is against the divine law brings destruction to man. Therefore, fear solely your own offences, for what man sows he will reap. And recognize: Hell is no place, but the condition of a soul which has given itself into the hands of the unlawful, of the "prince of darkness."

11. *Are not two sparrows sold for a farthing? Yet none of them falls to the ground without the will of the Most High. Verily, even all the hairs on your head are*

numbered. Therefore, do not be afraid. If God cares for the sparrows, should He not care for you, too?

12. It is enough for disciples to be as their master and the servants as their lord. If they have called the master of the house Beelzebub, how much more will they call his household! Therefore, fear them not. Nothing is concealed that will not become revealed, and nothing is secret that will not be known.

13. When the time comes for it, bring to light what I tell you in secret. And preach on the housetops what you hear in your ear. Therefore, whosoever will confess the truth before men, him will I also confess before My Father who is in heaven. But whosoever will deny the truth before men, him will I also deny before My Father who is in heaven. (Chap. 17:11-13)

I, Christ, explain, correct
and deepen the word:

God is omnipresent. And He knows everything that is, for He is the life and the power in everything. His power is in every animal, and so the animal is life from Him. The power of God, His life, is in each hair. He is. And since He is and is in all things, He also knows everything and knows about everything. All the more does the eternal Father know His child, whom He has created in His image. Nothing is concealed from Him, the Eternal. Even when a person has secrets from others, these seemingly secret things are not concealed

166

from Him. When the time has come, everything will be disclosed, the good and the less good.

A person should therefore fear only his humanness, because this is his seed. When this begins to sprout and grow, it will become apparent and visible to the person who has sown it, himself, as well as to the one who is involved or who was innocently despised because of it.

Therefore, be careful to sow only good seeds, so that your harvest will be the inner maturity. The truth should be voiced. It is the light of the soul. And the one who lives in the light of truth knows the word of truth. He will neither judge nor condemn, but will accept and receive his neighbor in his heart and will thus be with Me, the Christ.

Again and again, you should become conscious of the fact that human words can have different meanings. The one who lives in the Spirit of truth does not repudiate his neighbor. The one who repudiates him has banished him from his heart. For this reason, the words "... him will I also deny before My Father who is in heaven" mean that I cannot lead to My Father the one who does not live the law, the truth, and He cannot raise him into heaven – for heaven is the truth, and the truth is the law.

Recognize: The one who rejects the truth because he does not want to accept and actualize it from the commandments, does not know himself as a being of light. The one who does not know himself is also unable to enter heaven, which is his real home. Only after the purification of his soul, will he know himself and enter heaven.

The pure one is from the truth and speaks from the truth. The one who does not live the truth denies the truth, which is God, to whom everything is revealed. Since God is manifest truth, nothing remains hidden, nor anything secret.

14. *Verily, I have come to send peace to Earth. But behold, when I speak, a sword follows. I have come to unite; but behold, a son will be against his father and a daughter against her mother and a daughter-in-law against her mother-in-law. And a man's enemies will be of his own household. For the unjust cannot be together with the just. (Chap. 17:14)*

I, Christ, explain, correct
and deepen the word:

"But behold, when I speak, a sword follows" means that the one who hears the word of the truth and does not follow it and only speaks of it acts against the truth and therefore, against the Holy Spirit. He creates the sword himself, which is also called the cause. And thus, My words, which are the truth, are the sword for those who do not actualize them.

"I have come to unite" means to bring all men and nations together, to be *one* people of God.

The one who acts against the law of life, of unity, is also against God, who is the unity, and against His Son, Christ, who I Am. The one who thinks, speaks and acts against God and My work on this Earth scatters and does not unite. He does not follow the laws of life.

The one who is not for Me is against Me. The one who is against Me, the life, is also against his neighbor. Thus, what is written takes place, "... a son will be against his father and a daughter against her mother and a daughter-in-law against her mother-in-law. And a man's enemies will be of his own household. For the unjust cannot be together with the just." The law of God says: Like attracts like; the unjust are drawn to the unjust, the just to the just.

15. *And those who do not take up their cross and follow Me are not worthy of Me. The one who finds his life will lose it; and the one who loses his life for My sake will find it." (Chap. 17:15)*

I, Christ, explain, correct
and deepen the word:

"The one who finds his life will lose it; and the one who loses his life for My sake will find it." The meaning of these words is that the one who considers his earthly life to be his real life will lose it and will not know himself as a soul and will not find his home. The one who values his earthly life, but places his spiritual life above everything, will also find it within himself. And he will also know his home, for he is consciously a son or a daughter of God in the kingdom of life.

CHAPTER 18

Sending Out the Seventy-two

About passing on the truth (3).
Conduct befitting a guest (6). Criteria for people to live
together; the aim: selfless love (10-12)

1. *Afterwards, the Lord called seventy-two additional disciples and sent them, two by two, before Him into every city and place of the tribes where He Himself wanted to go.*

2. *Therefore, He said to them, "The harvest is truly great, but the laborers are few. Therefore, ask the Lord of the harvest to send laborers into His harvest.*

3. *Go your ways, behold, I send you forth as sheep among wolves. Carry neither purse, nor bag, nor shoes and greet no man on the way." (Chap. 18:1-3)*

I, Christ, explain, correct
and deepen the word:

In the time when I, Christ, went over this Earth as Jesus, the simple people used to walk; they neither rode nor drove. The feet carried the body from place to place. The one who carried along a lot of weight progressed but slowly. The words, "Carry neither purse, nor bag, nor shoes and greet no man on the way" mean to take only so much along on your travels that you may

171

go forward on the path and reach those who already bear spiritual fruits and also those whose soul's soil is yet to be tilled. Even the thieves will then see that there is nothing to be gained from you and will not waylay you.

"... and greet no man on the way" means not to hold useless conversations, but to bring the salvation of life, the truth, to the people. Keep going, conscious of the goal, for the time in which I will abide among men is limited.

4. *And whenever you enter into a house, say first: Peace be in this house. And if a spirit of peace is there, your peace will rest upon it; if not, it will return to you again. (Chap. 18:4)*

I, Christ, explain, correct
and deepen the word:

Enter a house only when you yourselves have peace. Thus, carry your peace from house to house. Where it is not accepted, it leaves with you again. Wherever peace, the truth of life, is not accepted, peace and truth should also no longer be spoken about. Everyone has his free will to accept or reject the peace from God, the truth. For this reason, do not argue about the truth. Bring it! When peace, the truth, is not accepted, then carry the gifts of salvation to another house. Thus, you maintain peace within yourselves.

5. And whatever city you enter, and they receive you therein, eat what is set before you, but not what was alive. And heal the sick who are there and say to them: The Kingdom of God has come near.

6. And remain in this house, eat and drink what they set before you without the shedding of blood; for the laborer is worthy of his hire. Do not go from one house to another. (Chap. 18:5-6)

I, Christ, explain, correct
and deepen the word:

"... eat what is set before you, but not what was alive," "... eat and drink what they set before you without the shedding of blood" – in both statements lies the following meaning: When they shed the blood of an animal for you, then refuse it in time, before it is led to the slaughterhouse for you; for no animal shall be sacrificed – neither for God nor for men. Human and animal sacrifices are an abomination before God. God, the One, spoke against animal and human sacrifices in the Old Covenant as well as in the New Covenant.

However, when a meal which contains meat and fish is served to you, and when the food was already prepared before your coming, then eat of it and offer these few bites in prayer to the Father-Mother-God. His power then transforms the lower into the higher. Remember: It is what comes out of the mouth that can become a sin, not what goes into the mouth and is given to the body in the awareness of the life from God.

7. But whenever you enter into a city and they do not receive you, go your way through the streets saying, "We shake off on you even the very dust of your city which has clung to us; however, be sure that the Kingdom of God has come near to you. (Chap. 18:7)

I Christ, explain, correct
and deepen the word:

Words are symbols. For this reason, I also want to correct the words written in the book called "The Gospel of Jesus" as they should be understood at the present time [1989], for words have different meanings from generation to generation.

The one who is not well received in the town should shake the dust off his feet. That is, he should go on and nevertheless leave behind the blessing of God. For the positive powers of positive people continue to be effective in those people, places and towns to which they were brought. And thus, many a one who is spiritually mature will receive the fruit, the truth. It flows, so to speak, to those who are from the truth. For the eternal truth is the Kingdom of God, which comes to those who long for the Kingdom of God and fulfill the laws of life.

8. Woe to you, Chorazin! Woe to you, Bethsaida! For if such mighty works had happened in Tyre and Sidon as those which have happened to you, they would have repented a long time ago in sackcloth and ashes. But the sentence shall be better for them on the Day of Judgment than for you.

9. And you, Capernaum, which are exalted to heaven, you will be thrust down to hell. Those who hear you hear Me, too. And those who despise you despise Me, too, and Him who has sent Me. But let everyone realize this in his own mind."

10. And again Jesus said to them, "Be merciful, so that you receive mercy. Forgive others and you will be forgiven. You will be measured by the same standards you use to measure others.

11. And as you do unto others, so will it be done unto you. And as you give, so will it be given unto you. And as you judge, so will you be judged. And as you serve others, so will you be served.

12. For God is just and rewards each one according to his works. You will reap what you sow."
(Chap. 18:8-12)

I, Christ, explain, correct
and deepen the word:

Take care that you do not fall into temptation! Cherish Me in your hearts, then you will give from the eternal truth. For I have come to teach people the truth and to prepare them, so that they can actualize the law of God, which alone is the life, the truth. The truth is the life. God is the truth, the life. His law, the truth, the life, is selfless love. Heed this, and you will not fall into temptation.

Now about the words which are in the book called "The Gospel of Jesus:"

"Those who hear you hear Me, too. And those who despise you despise Me, too, and Him who has sent Me. But let everyone realize this in his own mind. … Be merciful, so that you receive mercy. Forgive others and you will be forgiven. You will be measured by the same standards you use to measure others. And as you do unto others, so will it be done unto you. And as you give, so will it be given to you. And as you judge, so will you be judged. And as you serve others, so will you be served. For God is just and rewards every one according to his works. You will reap what you sow."

These indications, and admonishments hold true for all people from generation to generation, until that human race has emerged which lives the law of selfless love. Then these indications and admonishments will no longer be necessary.

However, until this generation of inner life has grown away from the dark and stands in the light of truth, these indications and admonishments will continue to hold true. They lead to the law of selfless love, to the truth, to the light that radiates in and through the people in the Kingdom of Peace of Jesus Christ. It is the light of the truth, which I Am, Christ.

CHAPTER 19

Jesus Teaches How to Pray

*Correct and incorrect prayer (2-4). The essence of all
being is in the innermost part of every soul – The one who
consciously lives in unity with God is served by His omnipotence through all the forms of life (6). Reprimanding out
of love and earnestness (8). Respect for the life of plants and
animals (9). The responsibility of one
who was healed (10)*

1. As Jesus was praying on a mountain, some of His
disciples came to Him, and one of them said, *"Lord
teach us how we should pray."* And Jesus said to him,
*"When you pray, go into your quiet chamber. And when
you have closed the door, pray to the Father who is
above you and within you. And your Father, who also
sees the outermost, will answer you openly.*

2. *But when you are gathered and pray together, do
not use vain repetitions, for your heavenly Father
knows what you need before you have asked Him.
Therefore, you should pray like this:*

3. *Our Father, You who are above us and within us,
hallowed be Your name. May your kingdom come to all
in wisdom, love and justice. Your will be done, as in
heaven so on Earth. Let us partake day by day of Your
holy bread and give us the fruit of the living vine. And
as You forgive us our trespasses, so may we forgive all
those who trespass against us. Shower Your goodness*

upon us, so that we may do the same to others. In the hour of temptation, deliver us from evil.

4. For Yours is the kingdom, the power and the glory: From eternity to eternity. Now and forever. Amen." (Chap. 19:1-4)

I, Christ, explain, correct
and deepen the word:

Formulated prayers, which are only repeated word for word, have little power, for they come from the mind and not from the heart. Casually spoken words are uninspired. They do not reach God in the innermost of the person, because he has not vivified them with a life from God. Intellectual prayers may lead the person even more astray, who has already lost his way through his incorrect way of thinking and living. The one who prays but behaves differently than what he says in prayer falls into more burdens.

Therefore, you should pray from the heart. And when you say your prayers aloud, they should be vivified by the inner life, which I Am. This is why it is important to pray from the heart only, and not just speak the words. Therefore, you should not repeat formulated prayers word for word. Even the prayer written here should not be understood literally or repeated mechanically. Every prayer should be understood according to its essence, since the language of the heart is the language of the sensations of the soul. However, if the sensations of the heart, which are clothed in words, are taken literally by one's neighbor, they lose in meaning.

My own, who faithfully follow Me, will find their way into the perfection of life more and more. Their prayers will then be the life in Me, that is, the fulfillment of the eternal law. The Kingdom of God, the life, has also come to the one who has opened the Kingdom of God within himself and henceforth lives the life from God.

"Let us partake day by day of Your holy bread and give us the fruit of the living vine." These words mean the inner life, the Spirit, which also maintains the material body in the material substance.

The meaning of the statement, "In the hour of temptation, deliver us from evil" is: Lord, You lead us in time of temptation, so that we can find our way out of the labyrinth of the human ego, and no longer be in bondage to the tempter, the evil.

5. *And wherever there are seven gathered in My name, there I Am in the midst of them; yes, even if there are only three or two. And even when there is but one who prays in the stillness, I Am with that one.*

6. *Raise the stone, and you will find Me. Split the wood, and I Am there. For in the fire and in the water, as well as in every form of life, God is manifest as its life and its substance. (Chap. 19:5-6)*

I, Christ, explain, correct
and deepen the word:

Respect, cherish and honor the creative power in all Being! Behold: In the innermost part of his soul, every person bears all that is power and light. The spiritual body in the human being is the substance of all Being, because God, the eternal Father, has given every single one of His children everything as essence, as heritage. The eternal Spirit is in all forms of life, and it also streams from all forms of life.

When the person has consciously become the child of God, the omnipotence of God serves him through all forms of life, through stone, wood, fire and water, through flowers, grasses, plants and animals. All heavenly bodies serve the one who lives in Me, the Spirit of truth. When the Creator-power is able to permeate the created one, because his soul is full of light and power, then he is again consciously the child, the son or daughter, of infinity and has once again taken up the heritage, the All-power.

Each earthly day is a gift to the person, so that he may recognize and find himself in it. The nature kingdoms offer themselves to man. Fire and water serve him, and the heavenly bodies, too, by day and by night. Realize how rich the day is for each individual! Every person who develops the inner wealth is rich. The one who is in communication with the Almighty, thus becoming the All-power once again, is truly rich. God is omnipotent because He is omnipresent, and the pure being is the All-power from Him. It is divine.

7. *And the Lord said, "If your brother has sinned in words seven times a day and has repented seven times a day, receive him." Then Simon asked Him, "Seven times a day?"*

8. *The Lord answered and said to him, "And I say to you, also seven times seven, for expressions of sin were found even in the prophets after they were anointed by the Holy Spirit. (Chap. 19:7-8)*

I, Christ, explain, correct
and deepen the word:

Every emotion or expression that is supposed to show a person his limits, but does not flow from the fire of the Holy Spirit and therefore does not come from God's love, earnestness and power, is not in and from the Spirit but from the human being and is sin.

Therefore, watch that what you say flows from the fire of the Holy Spirit. And even though what you say is earnest and shakes up the person, it still has to be spoken out of selfless love and divine earnestness. Everything else is against the Holy Spirit. This applies to all men, whether they strive towards God or not, or even when they have been called, like the prophets, for example.

And may the following also be said to you: If a true prophet who has been called by God and has submitted to His will is tormented and involved in activities by his fellow man until the substance of his inner strength is affected, he receives additional energy from God. If, in this situation, he becomes annoyed about the non-actualization or non-fulfillment or negative actions of his fellow man, which took place despite his knowing better, then he receives this additional energy, which neutralizes in him what had happened out of this annoyance. For this did not come from a correspondence, but he had been drained of his strength.

9. *Therefore be considerate, kind, sympathetic and friendly not only to your own kind, but also to every creature which is within your care, for you are as gods to them, whom they look up to in their need. Beware of anger, for many sin in anger and repent of it when their anger is past." (Chap. 19:9)*

I, Christ, explain, correct
and deepen the word:

The child of God is in the image of God-Father and is therefore in itself eternally creating power, for it bears in itself all the substances of the eternal power. They are all perfectly developed in it. For this reason, animals, plants and stones look up to the image of God and want the unity with the fully matured beings from God, into whom the life that has taken on more and more form is spiritually developing higher.

Therefore, feel the unity with each creature and with all stones and plants and protect the life that is entrusted to you. Flowers and grasses are offerings from the hand of God. For this reason, take them for your own use only when their outer life is withering. And be careful to leave the roots in the ground. Take what sprouts from the roots, but only when the time has come for this form of life. And if you remove it with the roots, leave it lying in a shaded place, so that the life may gradually withdraw, in order to return to the primordial substance where all powers are united. Do everything in the right kind of love and with understanding, for everything lives.

Never slaughter an animal for your personal use. Behold, nature, the life of creation, provides for you. The fruits of the fields, of the gardens and the forests should be sufficient for you. And never trample on life intentionally, neither that of the animals nor that of the plants. The one who intentionally tramples on life creates causes. It is as if he tramples on his own life, and he will suffer from it.

10. *A man whose hand was withered came to Jesus and said, "Lord, I was a mason and earned my living with my hands. I implore You, restore my health to me, so that I may not have to beg so shamefully for my*

bread." And Jesus healed him, saying, "There is a house made without hands, see that you, too, dwell therein." (Chap. 19:10)

I, Christ, explain, correct
and deepen the word:

The man whose hand was withered in compliance with the law of sowing and reaping, received back the life in his hand, in order to be able to earn his living again. However, I gave him this lesson for his path through life: Enter into the house that is not built by human hands – into your inner being, for it is the temple of God. When a person does this, the power that he received from Me continues to operate in him. If he does not do so, then what I granted him – the life in his hand – is given to him only temporarily. The one who continues to sin in spite of this gift of life takes back what I had removed, for then, it was only postponed.

God gives. What the person then makes of it is at the discretion of the soul and person alone. The person received from the eternal law the advice to sin no more and to enter into the temple of his inner being. And so, he is no longer unknowing. The knowing person then bears responsibility for what he knows.

CHAPTER 20

The Return of the Seventy-two

Success or failure of those sent out by Christ – Refinement of matter – Earth spots, the remainders of negative energies: the base for the last rebellion of the demons at the end of the Kingdom of Peace – The release of the Earth's soul – About "spirits" (3). The "wise" of the world do not recognize the powers of the universe; they are controlled and fight against the light (4). Christ reveals His own position and His relationship to God, the Fall event and His deed of redemption (5). Christ in the earthly garment could, and His messengers can, be recognized only by those who have developed the inner vision and hearing – The divine law unveils itself to the one who hears and actualizes the commandments of Christ, and he lives in Him (6). The mighty radiation of the eternal truth through the Wisdom at the turn of time (7)

1. The seventy-two returned joyfully after some time, saying, "Lord, even the devils are subject to us in Your name."

2. And He said to them, "I saw Satan fall from heaven like lightning.

3. Behold, I have given you power to tread on serpents and scorpions and over all the power of the enemy; and nothing will harm you. However, do not rejoice that the spirits are subject to you. But rather rejoice that your names are written in heaven." (Chap. 20:1-3)

I, Christ, explain, correct
and deepen the word:

Not all men and women whom I referred to as disciples in the sense of the word remained faithful to the law of God. Some succumbed to the temptations of this world. They returned with empty hands. You should not cling to the number seventy-two either. See this number as a term that means there were many. All those whom I sent out and who returned again were once among My followers. All those who remained in the Spirit of truth worked from the Spirit of the Father and defeated the satan of the senses in many people, thus leading them to a higher life. With the words "even the devils are subject to us in Your name," they meant the satan of the senses, for many to whom they brought the teaching of life accepted it and also complied with it.

So it was, as I walked in the earthly garment over this Earth: Those whom I had sent out and who lived in Me, the life, put an end to the unlawfulness. Their so-called enemies had no power over them; for they were protected by the law of life, because they complied with it. So it is at the present time [1989]: All those who resist the satanic will consciously be the children of God who possess the Earth. Their names are already now written in heaven. Through My power, they will attain what is still unimaginable for many people: the transformation of their human ego and the transformation of this world from the satanic to the divine. Everything will serve them – the Earth and all that is on the Earth. For it is they who possess the Earth in My name.

After some epochs have passed in the Kingdom of Peace, the people in the Kingdom of God will be of one spirit, because they have overcome the satanic in their souls and live consciously in Me, the Christ. Through them I will accomplish more works of love on Earth.

Although the mantle and the atmosphere of the Earth will be mostly cleansed by the heavenly bodies and the seas, some regions of the Earth called Earth spots, which are of coarser substance, will still remain. They are consolidated centers of negative energies. These still existing negative energies are remainders from past ages in which the darkness operated on the Earth and remainders of the atomic processing, remainders of chemical substances and all other negativities that man inflicted upon the Earth. These energies will remain inactive for a long time because they will be covered over by lava.

In the new atmosphere, too, regions will remain in which aspects of human and animal suffering are still stored. These regions will remain inactive for just as long as the Earth spots on Earth are inactive.

At the end of the Kingdom of Peace, with its finer matter – before this transformation of the Earth takes place – Satan, that is, the demonic powers, with the help of these remaining negative energies, will be allowed once more to measure himself against man and against the Earth. Once more, the Eternal in Me, Christ, will give the adversary the opportunity to recognize himself, before he puts himself in chains in the spiritual fields of evolution. The demonic beings will fight until the end to save their territory. God-Father in Me, the Christ, will also give these, His children, once more the chance for self-recognition and change. Those souls which do not use this last opportunity will have to build themselves up again in the spiritual fields of evolution, because the particle structure of their spiritual body will have been damaged. Such a deformed soul-body thus needs regeneration through the spiritual forces of consciousness of the animals, plants or even minerals.

The soul of the Earth will also release itself from the Earth – however, only after many energetic light years. This will take place in a similar way as when the soul of man leaves the material body and goes into the fine-material realms. Man calls this process the death of the body.

When the soul of the Earth frees itself from the Earth's mantle, the latter will burst apart; that will then be the dissolution of the Earth. However, until this all-powerful process of transformation takes place, the Earth will still have much to bear. Man as well as the Earth will experience still many things.

In the statement, "However, do not rejoice that the spirits are subject to you," I want to correct the word "spirits."

Two thousand years ago and in later centuries, too, burdened souls were called "spirits." Nature beings and inexplicable phenomena were also described as "spirits." However, these are energies that have taken spiritual form, which are invisible to man.

Reality is the eternal Spirit, the all-permeating life from which the substances come forth, the beings that have taken form, such as spirit beings, nature beings, animals, plants, minerals. The Spirit is the eternal, pure, all-permeating life, which sustains spirit beings, human beings, animals, plants, minerals, yes, everything.

4. *In that hour, Jesus rejoiced in spirit and said, "I thank You, Holy Father of heaven and Earth, that You have hidden these things from the wise and clever, and have revealed them to the unknowing. Yes, All-Holy One, for so it seems good in Your eyes.*
(Chap. 20:4)

I, Christ, explain, correct
and deepen the word:

In this context, the word "wise" means those people who deem themselves to be clever, on the sole basis of their intellect, that is, of their intellectual knowledge. Truly wise, however, is only the person who fulfills the laws of God.

Many who consider themselves "wise" and clever because of their intellect have made a wasteland of the Earth. They do not yet recognize the powers of the

Father and His Son, Christ, who I Am – those powers which are becoming more and more effective through sons and daughters of God in the earthly garment and which are changing the world. These forces of the universe are still hidden from those who keep their heart closed to the meaning of life. They still think that they have to accomplish what corresponds to their mental faculties and which they therefore hold to be correct and essential. In so doing, they believe that they have to give expression to their wisdom and cleverness.

You people in the emerging and growing Kingdom of Peace of Jesus Christ, who will possess the Earth ever more in the coming generations, recognize: Up until the full unfoldment of the Kingdom of Peace, worldly-oriented people will eagerly join forces again and again, in order to fight against the works of the Lord. Many of them do not realize that they are already irradiated, that is, blinded, by the light of the truth. Unconsciously and seized by slavish zeal, they react as the demons inspire them to do and fight against the light.

To My own of the present time [1989], who strive for the path to the true wisdom of God, I say: Remain true! For the time has dawned in which I, Christ, with divine love and wisdom, pour ever more, through people who are of good will and make them into true instruments of God.

The path to the heart of God, which I set forth in the Sermon on the Mount and explained, supplemented and deepened in many revelations, is the path to the love and wisdom of God, to the true humanity. Do grasp this in today's time [1989]!

The people in all the developmental stages of the Kingdom of Peace, the Kingdom of God on Earth, should also know this, so that they can realize that, already in today's time [1989], I was with My own more intensely, that I schooled and guided them.

5. *Everything is entrusted to Me by My Father. And no one but the Father knows the Son, and no one but the Son and the one to whom the Son will reveal it know who the Father is." (Chap. 20:5)*

I, Christ, explain, correct
and deepen the word:

"Everything is entrusted to Me by My Father." I Am the Father's first-beheld and firstborn Son, the Co-Regent of the heavens. I Am omnipresent in the four powers of creation, the four natures of God – order, will, wisdom and earnestness. My spiritual heritage flows in these four nature-streams. In the four powers of creation, it is the radiation of omnipresence in the primordial principle, God.

Thus, I Am God in the Creation-Spirit of the Father in the four natures – order, will, wisdom and earnestness. The three natures and attributes of God – patience, love and mercy – are the filiation attributes. In them, I

Am the Son among all the sons and daughters of God. God means: Highest, omnipresent energy, which brought and brings forth everything and which is from eternity to eternity.

From this omnipresent energy, the eternally flowing primordial potential, the Spirit, I removed a great part of My spiritual heritage and implanted it as sparks into the souls that had burdened themselves by disregarding the law in the three attributes and in the four natures of God – which, when considered as a whole, are the seven basic powers of creation. The life force of these burdened souls has thus been transformed down to the four lower Fall domains. These four lower Fall domains became planes of purification after My "It is finished." Since the "It is finished," the spark of redemption is security and support for the fallen souls, so that their spirit substance does not dissolve into the eternal flowing Spirit.

For in the first Fall-thought lay the desire to dissolve all spiritual forms. With this the unlawful beings wanted to bring about a new beginning of creation. The eternal Father, whose Son I Am, entrusted Me with the power to accomplish what lies in His will, in the eternal law: to maintain all Being as a whole. Through the Redeemer-deed, each heavily burdened soul received the spark of redemption. With it the soul is supported, thus excluding the possibility that it would dissolve in the omnipresent Spirit, the stream of God, and would merge into it as flowing energy. Through redemption, the soul becomes the spirit being once again and remains the child of God in spirit form. Had I not removed My heritage and given it to the children of the Fall, as support and power of development, many spirit bodies would have dissolved as a result of the increasingly growing burdens. Thus, the equilibrium of creation would have come out of balance and the dissolution of all spiritual forms would have been the inevitable result.

And so, it is given to Me by the Father to act as Redeemer for all deeply fallen souls and people and to lead these, His children, back to His heart again. I remain, therefore, the Redeemer for each soul until it has overcome the four planes of purification. When the soul has activated these four divine rays of consciousness, it will be attracted by the three planes of attributes, the planes of preparation – also called planes of unfoldment to the Absolute – which are the filiation powers of the Father-Mother-Principle. In these three planes of attributes, the spirit being in coming activates again the entire radiation law, the eternal primordial law. When the entire primordial law is again active in the spirit body, the pure being enters again into the Absoluteness, into the eternal Being.

When the soul on the path to perfection has developed the fourth plane of purification, the consciousness of divine earnestness, redemption is accomplished in that soul. The part of My heritage which, as spark of redemption, has supported, upheld and guided the soul then returns to the primordial power, to the All-power. On the path to the Absoluteness through the three planes of preparation, the spirit being in coming then accepts consciously the filiation of God once again.

As Jesus of Nazareth, I could not yet teach in all its details about the Redeemer-deed, about the outflow of My heritage, because I had not yet accomplished the Work of Redemption. My heritage was still in the primordial law. At My baptism in the Jordan River by John the Baptist, when the Spirit came over Me in the symbol of the dove, My heritage in the primordial law became more strongly active. On Golgotha, with My words "It is finished" it flowed out and divided into spiritual sparks. Every deeply fallen soul received from it the support, the spark of redemption.

The meaning of the statement "... no one but the Father knows the Son" is the following: The person whose thinking is only human and who regards and acknowledges matter as the only reality does not feel the Spirit of the eternal Father in himself. Only the one who knows himself as a child of God, because he fulfills the laws of love, also feels the Father, the life, in himself. Thus, the Father can be felt only by those who actualize the law of love, which I taught as Jesus of Nazareth and reveal and teach as the Christ of God to those who love God more than this world.

6. And He turned towards His disciples and said to them in confidence, "Blessed are the eyes which see what you see. For I tell you: Many prophets and kings

wanted to see what you see and have not seen it, and wanted to hear what you hear and have not heard it. (Chap. 20:6)

I, Christ, explain, correct
and deepen the word:

I Am in God, your Father and Mine, the Son of God and God in the eternal four powers of creation.

The words "Blessed are the eyes which see what you see" mean that I, the Son of God, the Co-Regent of the heavens, was in the earthly garment among the people. Blessed was the soul in an earthly garment that recognized Me, the Son of God, in the earthly garment. The person saw Me only as I was, as a man among men. The souls of the blessed ones recognized in Me the image of the eternal Father. Many who came to this Earth after My physical death heard Me through the mouths of prophets. However, I no longer spoke directly to them; for the one who no longer has a physical body, no longer has a human voice either. Then there is a need to transmit the word of God through prophets.

The inner vision, too, is only indirect and not direct; it is as people see it in the three-dimensional world. After My physical death as well as at the present time [1989], I gave and give the word of life through the mouths of prophets, so that My own can find their way to Me and attain bliss and, behold the Father face to face after their physical body passes away.

And so, the one who fulfills the words of Life will, after his physical death, behold the Father and know Him. He will be in Him consciously, just as I know Him and Am in Him. But the one who only hears or reads My words and does not integrate them into his life will neither feel the Father within himself nor behold Him after his physical death and will not know Him either. For the Eternal is the law of life. The one who does not keep it is spiritually dead. Only that soul and that person who accept My word and live accordingly are consciously in the Father. They will become His image again.

As it was at the time of My earthly life, so is it also at the present time [1989]. During My earthly life, I, the Christ in Jesus, physically stood before My apostles and disciples as the image of the Father. But most of those who followed Me and saw Me did not recognize Me. Only a few of the apostles and disciples perceived Me, the Christ, in Jesus. As it was at that time, so is it also in this era: Christ can be seen only to those who have opened their spiritual eyes through a life according to the eternal law of love.

To many people I brought the message of the heavens and spoke to them about My coming as Christ. However, only a few understood the message of salvation. Among other things, they wanted no Messiah in the person of a simple man, of Jesus of Nazareth, who was a son of the carpenter, Joseph. For they wanted a king on Earth who would relieve them of their burdens, without their doing anything for it. Many people heard Me, the Nazarene, speak – and yet they did not hear Me because they saw only the Nazarene and heard only the words of the Nazarene. They did not grasp the word of God that spoke through Me, the Nazarene, because they heard only Jesus, the Nazarene – and not God through His Son in the garment of the Earth.

In this era, too, My word flows in the fullness through the incarnated part-ray of divine wisdom – a human child among the people, who bears in herself the closeness to God. The unity with the eternal Father in her is recognized just as little as I, too, the Son of Man among the people, was once recognized.

It is an old concept of man that each of his fellow men should be just as he, himself, is. Thus, many people make differences only between outer wealth and poverty, but not between inner wealth and poverty of the soul. They cannot recognize or distinguish inner processes. For this reason, they see every person from the perspective of their human ego. To them, their fellow man has only the significance which their ego attaches to him. This is why the emissaries of God in the earthly garment are not recognized, and the words of life that flow through them are accepted by only a few as being the word of God, the law of life.

Thus the word of the Eternal through the emissaries of God in an earthly garment is for many people only the word of man – and yet it is and remains the word of God, sent to man through His emissaries.

7. Blessed are you in the inner circle, who hear My word and to whom the mysteries are revealed, who do not imprison or kill any innocent creature, but seek the good in all, for to such belongs eternal life.
(Chap. 20:7)

I, Christ, explain, correct
and deepen the word:

I explain the statement, "Blessed are you in the inner circle, who hear My word and to whom the mysteries are revealed." The one who knew how to listen to the word of the Father through Me, His Son in the earthly garment, Jesus, also lived accordingly. He was truly blessed and entered the inner circle of My flock and was in Me consciously, and I in him, as the light of the world. Verily, the blessing flowed in abundance through Me, Jesus, to many people and to My apostles and disciples.

In a similar way, the blessing, the word of the I Am, flows at the present time [1989] through the part-ray of the incarnated divine wisdom. It is given to all people and flows again today in the inner circle to those who gather around My holy word. I give it through the person being in whom the being of light is incarnated, whom I have sent to the people in today's time, at the beginning of the mighty turn of time, so that they may hear My word through her and live accordingly. And as they actualize My holy word, which I teach them once more, and keep My commandment to love one another selflessly – as I, as Christ, love them, – they will again be My true disciples, the sons and daughters of God, who consciously prepare My coming.

As Jesus of Nazareth, I taught the eternal laws to My apostles and disciples. The so-called "mysteries" were revealed to the one among them who actualized My teaching, because the veils of the human ego fell from him and he thereby lived in the truth. In a similar way, I, as Christ, now teach again the law of love through the incarnated part-ray of divine wisdom. The one who actualizes it uncovers the eternal law. His veils of ego-centricity dissolve, and soul and man then stand in the light of the truth.

Everything is made manifest to people in the Spirit, because they fulfill the law of life. Today [1989], I teach the path to selfless love in all its details and lead all willing people who are ready to let go of their human ego, in order to become divine, into the Kingdom of God that is in every human being.

Only the soul and the person who are filled with My Spirit keep what I have commanded them. People of the Spirit will not take or hold captive innocent creatures, much less kill them. The one who lives in the truth knows that the infinite love prevails and is effective in every creature. People in the Spirit of truth live with nature and all its creatures.

On the path to the heart of My Father, I teach [1989] people to recognize themselves, to accept themselves as beings from God and to find the good in all people and in everything that comes toward them. The one who recognizes his true being keeps the commandment of commandments, "Love one another selflessly, as I have loved you as Jesus and love you as Christ." My teaching is the law of life. The one who actualizes it is filled by the Spirit of the Father and lives in Me, the Christ. All those who keep the commandment of commandments live in Me and I act through them. For through them I fulfill what is revealed: the Kingdom of God on this Earth.

Mankind stands in a great turn of time. I, Christ, prepare My coming and pass on My message through sons and daughters of God who are in the mission of a task in My redemption, so that many may find their way to Me and become one under the outspread mantle of Universal Life – for God is universal life, universal Being.

8. *Blessed shall be those who abstain from all things received through bloodshed and killing, and practice justice and righteousness. Blessed are you, for you will attain bliss." (Chap. 20:8)*

I, Christ, explain, correct
and deepen the word:

At the turning point from the old time to the New Era, from the time under the influence of the causal law to the Era of Light, I give My revelations from all seven basic rays of God through the part-ray of divine wisdom. A mighty ray-band of the eternal truth flows through the divine wisdom to the people. Once more, My thinking and living as Jesus of Nazareth is given to them to understand. I also teach again the laws of life and their lawful application to all those who build upon Me, the Christ. The one who actualizes them begins to have a fulfilled life and is a fellow builder of the Kingdom of Peace of Jesus Christ, which was announced by prophets and enlightened ones in past epochs.

Verily, verily, blessed are those who follow Me, Christ, by fulfilling the commandment of commandments. They will neither bind nor kill. They will practice justice and righteousness, so that peace will be among men. For the time has come [1989], in which I gather from all four winds those who strive to keep what I have commanded them.

Know that despite My instructions and teachings, still many people will destroy themselves through their causes, which they repeatedly create despite knowing better. Yet, their souls remain preserved by Me, the Redeemer. All those who, despite knowing better, disregard the commandments of life will remain at My left side until they have accepted Me and received Me, the Redeemer, and find and keep peace and love within themselves, thus becoming the law of love. Then they will change from the left to the right side and will be with Me until all souls, whom I will bring back to the Father as the image of God, stand at My right side.

CHAPTER 21

Jesus Reproves Cruelty to a Horse

*The selfish, egocentric man dominates
and tortures the animals – The one who lives in God is one
with all creatures (2-4). The human being violates and destroys the life on Earth – The extinction of many species of
animals – The importance of many animals for the ecological balance – The law of sowing and reaping holds true
also in dealing with creation (5). Selfless love, the key to
understanding and helping one's neighbor and to the insight
into the causal law and overcoming it – The soul's hunger
and thirst for the inner source (7). Killing animals, even as
a sacrifice, is an abomination before God – Each person
should voluntarily sacrifice his ego – A false image of God
– The correct understanding of "An eye for an eye, a tooth
for a tooth" (8) and "So will I cast you out" – Passing on
and interpreting biblical words (10). Worldly wealth and
inner wealth (11). Outer wealth is just a loan to be used for
many (12-13). The law of God is absolute and will be fulfilled – Baptism with water, a symbol – The "It is finished"
– Christ now teaches the entire truth (14). The planning and
preparation of the Redeemer's mission and of the Work of
Redemption – Many spirit beings are on assignment until all
the beings of the Fall have returned (16)*

1. And it came to pass that the Lord departed from
the city and went into the mountains with His disciples.

And they came to a mountain with very steep paths.
There they met a man with a beast of burden.

2. But the horse had collapsed, for it was overladen.
The man struck it till the blood flowed. And Jesus went
to him saying, "You son of cruelty, why do you strike
your animal? Do you not see that it is much too weak
for its burden and do you not know that it suffers?"

3. But the man retorted, "What have You to do there-
with? I may strike my animal as much as it pleases me,
for it belongs to me; and I bought it with a goodly sum
of money. Ask those who are with You, for they are
from my neighborhood and know thereof."

4. And some of the disciples answered, saying, "Yes,
Lord, it is as he said, we were there when he bought the
horse." And the Lord rejoined, "Do you not see then
how it is bleeding, and do you not hear how it wails
and laments?" But they answered saying, "No, Lord,
we do not hear that it wails or laments."
(Chap. 21:1-4)

I, Christ, explain, correct
and deepen the word:

Even when a person has acquired an animal, nevertheless, it is not his property. Just as the spiritual body,
the soul in the human being, is part of the eternal Being
– because the Eternal has created the spiritual body, and
the spirit being lives, through the Eternal, in the eternal
Being – so was the animal created by the eternal Cre-

203

ator-Spirit and is part of the life which is and lasts eternally – God.

The whole of infinity is serving love, serving life. Man, too, is called by Me, Christ, to serve his neighbor in a selfless way. This also includes his second neighbor. For the animal, too, is endowed with the gifts of selfless serving and serves gladly and readily the person who loves it.

When a person does not selflessly love his neighbor, that is, his fellow man, he will not serve him selflessly either. He then transmits his selfishness also to the worlds of animals, plants and minerals.

An animal cannot speak. It suffers and endures silently and can hardly express its pain and grief. Only the one who selflessly loves people, animals, plants and stones perceives the pain and agony endured by the animal.

The egocentric person, the domineering person, expects his fellow man to serve him. He also demands that an animal serve him beyond its capacity and strength. He gives orders – and does not serve. For this reason, he inflicts unspeakable torment on people and animals. If a person makes his fellow men dependent on him – as if they were slaves – he will also subjugate the animals. The one who no longer listens to his conscience becomes hard-hearted towards man and animal. He cares solely for his own interests, his self-serving interests. He is full of self-importance and, in this, forgets that his neighbor and his second neighbor, the animal, suffer under his egocentric dominance. Nor does he sense anymore what his neighbor and the animal need. When a person's senses have become brutal, the whole person is poor in feeling. However, he reacts all the more sensitively when his own ego is addressed and his actions are questioned.

Recognize that the one who is solely with this world also looks at just the small, limited world of his ego. He thereby becomes numbed to the law of life, thus becoming a spiritually dead person. Spiritually dead people are deaf and dumb to the true life. They will be again born into matter, as long as this is still possible according to the laws of incarnation, so that in the course of their changing fate, they will learn and experience that their neighbor, who stands beside them, as well as the animal feel and suffer – particularly since all of them receive their life from God.

Happy are those who recognize that their further existence can mean torment or freedom, because man reaps what he sows.

The time has drawn close when the heavily burdened souls will no longer be able to enter the temporal, because the light will then dwell on Earth. The shadows of the human ego will then no longer be able to rule the world, because the will of God is lived and becomes visible.

The one who has consecrated his life to God has become selfless. His life is then one of selfless service to his neighbor. The person in the Spirit of the Lord no longer speaks of thine and mine. He lives in the fullness of God from eternity to eternity, in what God has bequeathed to him: all the Being, the eternity.

Therefore, the one who truly lives beholds what the spiritually dead do not see and hears what the spiritually dead cannot hear: it is the life, that flows from human being, animal, plant and stone, from all of infinity. For the one who lives in Me is one with all people, beings, animals, plants, stones and with all of infinity. He understands the language of love.

5. *And the Lord became sad and said, "Woe to you; because of the dullness of your heart, you do not hear how it laments and cries to its heavenly Creator for pity; but thrice woe to the one against whom it cries and wails in its torment!" (Chap. 21:5)*

I, Christ, explain, correct
and deepen the word:

Woe to those who sin against man, animal, plant, stone and against everything God has given them for a life in Him! Many people have become numbed in their very nature. Their human ego strives solely for its own benefit. In so doing, the selfish person deals unfairly with his fellow man and exploits the nature kingdoms, as well. The human being of this time [1989] has laid hands on the great earth-man, the Earth, and is still doing so today. He pollutes the Earth, violates the life on it and interferes in the atmosphere through his use of nuclear power, as well as of chemicals and other things. Thus, he violates the Earth and all that lives on it, and destroys its atmospheric mantle, which provides it and all earthly life with protection.

Especially in this turn of time, the turning point from the old sinful time to the Era of Light, animal and plant species are calling out – with the forces of their sensations, with the language of their consciousness – to their Creator for help and rescue. Animals and plants are suffering unimaginably from the excesses of the human ego, of human selfishness. The oppressed life calls for mercy and deliverance.

God, My Father, the Creator of all life-forms, has heard the oppressed creatures. Many animal species are dying out because of man's unlawful conduct. Their spiritual forces either return to the soul of the Earth or go into the pure spheres of the eternal Being. For many, this is a deliverance. Many of them, however, will come back when the light dwells on the Earth, because people will then live in unity with God.

Know that every misdeed and every ill-treatment that has not been atoned for – whether toward humans, animals, plants or even stones, that is, toward the whole Earth and the atmosphere – falls back upon the originator. Recognize that many animals are given to man so that they may serve him. Many are given to maintain the ecological balance. However, a right kind of serving, a reciprocal serving, can exist only when man has unfolded the filiation-love that comes from the Father-

Mother-God and when he has unfolded the Creator-love which is effective in the animal, in plants and stones. Then he can also communicate with all Being.

Wherever there is pure communication, the eternal, cosmic energy also flows. But where the forces of love are bound, there, hard-heartedness, selfishness and slavery is found. There, neither understanding nor tolerance is found; there, only taking is found and no flowing that comes from giving and receiving.

It is the law: What man does unto the least of My brothers, unto his fellow man, that he has done unto Me, the Christ – and in the final analysis, also unto himself; for what man sows, he will reap. The harvest always corresponds to the seed. When a person violates the eternal law of selfless love, he turns away from the eternal energies that he needs for a healthy life, for the well-being of his soul and of his body, as well. Therefore, the one who turns to the world and its shadows turns away from Me, the light. And the one who turns away from Me steps into the shadows of the human ego. The one who stands in the shadows suffers and wastes away and becomes the slave of his own ego and, in turn, makes of his neighbor a slave.

Recognize that only the person allows himself to become the slave of the domineering man who himself stands in the shadows and is thereby already enslaved. He then sells himself to the domineering man for a few pieces of silver, thereby betraying his true Lord. This happens towards humans, animals, plants, the Earth and the atmosphere.

6. *And He went forward and touched the horse, and the animal stood up, and its wounds were healed. But He said to the man, "Go on your way now and henceforth strike it no more, if you, too, hope to find mercy."*

7. *And seeing the people come to Him, Jesus said to His disciples, "Because of the sick, I Am sick; because of the hungry, I go hungry; because of the thirsty, I suffer thirst." (Chap. 21:6-7)*

I, Christ, explain, correct
and deepen the word:

"Because of the sick, I Am sick" means that the one who selflessly loves is open for his neighbor and can also feel and empathize in his heart with the anguish, the suffering and the sickness of his fellow man. People who are there selflessly for their neighbor receive from Me the strength to give the sick person comfort and help. People in My Spirit serve their neighbor selflessly, if he wants it.

Recognize that every person has his free will, and no one should force himself upon his neighbor. For this reason, a person should give help only when it is wanted.

The Spirit of love flows through selflessly serving people to many of His human children, bestowing help upon them. God helps His human children in every situation – also through people whose heart beats selflessly for God and for their fellow man. The one who loves selflessly also serves selflessly. Through this, the good comes into this world: God.

The one who recognizes his own causes is also aware of the chains of causes that take their course in this world, and whose effects have led and lead to manifold diseases, afflictions and torment. The one who has insight into the law of sowing and reaping also knows the way out of the turmoil and entanglement of the human ego. And the one who takes the path out of suffering, torment, sickness and lingering infirmity will create less and less causes. Thus, the bad seed in the soil of life decreases. The good seed, the life in Me, the Christ, then sprouts in him.

"... because of the hungry, I go hungry; because of the thirsty, I suffer thirst" means that as Jesus of Nazareth I sensed and as Christ I know why many of My human children lack nourishment and why they thirst. As Jesus I saw the deficiencies and as Christ I know them. The deficiencies are the lack of light in the soul. The awakened soul hungers and thirsts for Me, the Christ. A soul that has awakened in Me will not rest until the person recognizes why it hungers and thirsts. If the person has recognized the need of the soul and with My power clears up what he has recognized, what had led to the lack of light in the soul, then the soul breathes a sigh of relief, and the person becomes healthy.

Recognize that the soul lives solely by the light of God. If the soul has too little of this light, the body becomes sick, or the person has to hunger and thirst, depending on the kind of seed he has sown in the soil, in his soul.

Every thirsty person yearns for the wellspring, for water. When the wellspring of inner life flows but sparsely in the person because he has turned away from the source, the wellspring, then soul and person suffer. The one who lives in God senses the suffering of his neighbor and will not rest until all souls and people have reached the wellspring of life and the souls have united with the origin of the wellspring, in order to be again the wellspring itself.

Until all men and souls live in this spiritual consciousness, I will be with the people and souls as their Redeemer and feel with them their illness, their hunger and their thirst, and I will still their hunger and quench their thirst – until all humanness has been dissolved and the soul is again the wellspring from God, Himself, the spirit being of the heavens, the image of God.

8. *And He also said, "I have come to put an end to the sacrifices and feasts of blood. If you do not cease to offer and consume the flesh and blood of animals, the wrath of God will not cease to come upon you, just as it came upon your ancestors in the wilderness, who indulged in the consumption of flesh and were filled with rottenness and consumed by pestilence. (Chap. 21:8)*

I, Christ, explain, correct
and deepen the word:

"I have come to put an end to the sacrifices and feasts of blood" means that I have come to teach you the Gospel, the law of love, and to live it as an example for you, so that you may recognize that only the person who keeps the laws of God is rich in spiritual power in his inner being. People who have the inner values will not lack in anything. For the one who is rich in his heart is with his neighbor, not against him, thus being for God, the life, which is the fullness. People who have inner values are also with the world of animals and plants and are not against the creation of God. The one who is against his neighbor will fight against him and kill him. And whoever is against his neighbor will not be for other forms of life – neither for the life of animals nor of plants or stones.

The one who is against the life in Me, the Christ, hungers and thirsts for success, wealth, power and prestige. For his feasts and for the lusts of his palate, he kills animals and consumes their flesh. Thus, he demonstrates that he is far from God.

Animal sacrifices, too, are an abomination before God, the Eternal. He does not want animals to be sacrificed or consecrated to Him. God has given the life to all forms of Being and thus to animals as well. Why should they be sacrificed to Him, since He Himself, the life, dwells in them?

However, if man were to sacrifice his human ego, his passions and cravings to Me, the Christ, and were to strive for and lead a life that is pleasing to God, that is, devoted to Him, this would contribute to the unity of all life-forms. God is the spirit of love and freedom. For this reason, every human being should voluntarily sacrifice his ego. Only then will he become meek and humble of heart and will find his way to the great unity: God. This development of man towards Him is what God loves in His children.

And the one who devotes himself to the eternal Father-Mother-God, by transforming his humanness into the divine, will not slaughter animals or consume their flesh, nor will he deliberately kill any animal. Such people will also treat the plant world with selfless love, as this, too, is a gift of creation from God to His human children. The plants and the fruits of the field and forest willingly give themselves to man and want to serve him as nourishment and as remedy for his sick body.

The "wrath of God" comes from the heathen world of conceptions which was still very much alive in the Old Covenant. It was believed that the "gods" would take revenge on people. It would be good if the sinful person were to recognize that it is he himself who has created the so-called "wrath of God." The "wrathful God" is the human ego, which takes revenge for what it itself has caused, for man will reap what he sows.

The words "an eye for an eye, a tooth for a tooth" also were and still are wrongly interpreted. Man should not take revenge on his neighbor and give tit for tat. He is called upon to forgive his neighbor, to ask him for forgiveness and to no longer do the same or similar thing. The one who does not follow this commandment subjects himself to the law of expiation. It reads, "an eye for an eye, a tooth for a tooth." Then he will reap – "an eye for an eye, a tooth for a tooth" – what he has sown.

Recognize that sooner or later, the wrathful, dominating ego, the ego-god of man, will collapse at the latest, when the causes that man has sown flow out of his soul.

Furthermore, recognize that the suffering of animals and the consumed flesh of the animals that have been deliberately killed gnaw, in turn, at the flesh of the person. The consequences are disease and pestilence. They are the effects of these and similar causes.

9. *And I say to you, even when you are gathered in My bosom, but do not keep My commandments, I will cast you out. For if you do not want to keep the lesser mysteries, how shall I give you the greater ones?*

10. *The one who is faithful in the smallest way will also be faithful in a large way; and the one who is unjust in the smallest way will also be unjust in a large way. (Chap. 21:9-10)*

I, Christ, explain, correct
and deepen the word:

"And I say to you, even when you are gathered in My bosom, but do not keep My commandments, I will cast you out" should mean: Even when the person calls out "Lord, Lord!" and speaks much about Me and about the gospel of love, but does not actualize and follow in his own life what he talks about, through his human ego, he will cast himself out. He thereby withdraws from the law of love and creates causes whose effects will break in over him if he does not recognize them in time, if he does not repent and stop doing such things. It is not the I Am, God, who casts out the soul and the human being. The person himself turns away from the law of love and life, thus creating his own law, from which he then suffers. For man will receive what he has sown. Therefore, strive to remain in My bosom through a life in Me, the Christ, through selfless love and selfless deeds.

The statement "I will cast you out" never comes from the Spirit of God, who I Am. The meaning of this statement is that through your own small ego, you cast your soul into the valley of causes, under which you will then suffer. For it is only the ego of the human being that builds up the law of sowing and reaping in the soul and in the physical body.

Idiomatic expressions from the time before and after the Old Covenant slipped into many of the old texts that were given in earlier times and were repeatedly edited and translated. If those who edited and translated these texts still clung to this world of conceptions, then they also used these terms again and adopted them into the new versions of the text – believing that they had correctly understood the text in hand and therefore had also edited and translated it correctly.

In your so-called Bibles, too, such old terms were repeatedly adopted. This happens even today [1989]. This is also why many Bible experts and theologians are not able to understand My revealed word for the present time and for the New Era, the Era of Light. Much that was the work of man came into the Bibles through the rigid use of such terms. It was not always deliberately interpreted into the texts; it often flowed in unconsciously out of human conviction. But the old forms of speech and the old terms which were used to render the divine truth into human words often have other implications and meanings at the present time [1989].

Had mankind listened to the prophets sent by God – also within the church institutions – and had it fulfilled what God taught through His instruments; and had mankind also listened to what I, as Jesus of Nazareth, had taught and lived as an example, then this epoch would be full of light, that is, full of truth – and there would be no need for further prophets.

Recognize that the one who does not fulfill the least commandment, namely to practice understanding and tolerance towards his fellow man and to respect his free will, cannot fulfill the greatest commandment either, the commandment of love. How can a person who does not acknowledge the law of sowing and reaping and therefore condemns his neighbor as guilty receive greater things, the law of love, the true life?

Knowledge is not wisdom. Divine wisdom remains veiled to the one who just collects knowledge.

Whoever is faithful, sincere and honest towards himself in the smallest things is the same towards his neighbor. Such people will then also accomplish great things that are lasting, because they live in My will. On the other hand, the one who is covetous, envious, jealous and greedy in the smallest things will think, speak and act accordingly, in greater things and matters as well.

Know that war, murder, destruction and estrangement between peoples rose out of envy, jealousy, greed and dispute.

Speaking to the people in the light-filled Kingdom of Peace: It was still this way during the epoch in which I revealed this work through the incarnated part-ray of divine wisdom, at the beginning of the mighty turn of time.

11. And if you have not been faithful in the sinful worldly possessions, who will entrust you with the true riches? And if you have not been faithful in what is another man's, who will give you your own?
(Chap. 21:11)

I, Christ, explain, correct
and deepen the word:

When you consider your earthly goods as your own
and are concerned solely with increasing them for your
own purposes, you are impoverished in your innermost
being, because you do not administer the possessions
lawfully – for the good of many. God will then not entrust you with the true riches: to carry the law of life into
this world. For the one who does not fulfill the law of love
and of life is spiritually impoverished. And if you have
taken advantage of your neighbor, that is, if you have
not remained true to the law of life and of love, how
can you attain the Kingdom of Heaven, the selfless life?

The one who wishes to enter into heaven must be
rich in his inner being – rich in inner values and divinity. The one who has acquired riches for himself on
Earth and considers them to be his own is poor in the
Spirit of life. For what is given to him in external
wealth has only been entrusted to him so that with it he
may further the common good on Earth. This means:
One for all, and all for One.

The one who considers earthly riches to be his property and to his merit is no better than the person who
envies his neighbor for his belongings and seeks to take
them away from him or wants to enrich himself with
them.

However, the one who strives first for the Kingdom
of Heaven has recognized the eternal life in himself and
has consciously accepted and received it.

The one who develops inner wealth will also lack nothing as a human being. For God, the Father-Mother-God, cares for His earthly children, so that they do not suffer want. However, when men live in want and suffer hunger, then, in former lives, they have refused bread and help to their human brothers and sisters or, as knowing ones, have often not guided them lawfully according to the commandment of "pray and work."

God entrusted external wealth to many people, so that they use it for the common good and increase it in the right way for the good of all. The one who suffers and lives in want should be comforted and helped by those to whom God has given the gifts so that they distribute them correctly among His needy and hungry children. However, they should be distributed lawfully according to the commandment of "pray and work."

12. *No one can serve two masters. For either he will hate the one and love the other; or he will hold to the one and despise the other. You cannot serve God and mammon at the same time." And the Pharisees, who were covetous, heard all these things and derided Him.*

13. *And He said to them, "You are those who justify themselves before men; but God knows your hearts. For what is highly esteemed among men is an abomination in the sight of God. (Chap. 21:12-13)*

I, Christ, explain, correct
and deepen the word:

No one can serve two masters. But the one who entrusts himself to the one Lord, the Father-Mother-God, by fulfilling the will of God, will also serve God in his neighbor and will not value himself more highly than his neighbor. However, the one who calls external riches his own will look down upon his neighbor and denigrate him. Such people are often selfish, apprehensive and narrow-minded and are suspicious and mistrustful towards their neighbor; for they are of the opinion that their neighbor could take advantage of them and take away the wealth which, according to the law of life, they do not even possess – which is only lent to them so that they may use it correctly for many. Such people love only themselves and their seeming wealth and oppose all those whom they think want to rob them.

At all times there were and still are Pharisees, who give fine speeches and have many arguments and excuses, in order to keep what they have acquired as their seeming property.

Recognize: Everyone who defends and justifies himself is accusing himself and bears witness of who he is. God knows all His children. He does not look upon the speeches of the individuals, but into their hearts. Nothing is concealed from the Eternal. When it is time, He lets everything be revealed, so that each sinner may recognize himself, in order to repent, ask for forgiveness, forgive, make amends and no longer do the same, so that he find himself again in God.

For this, I, Christ, am teaching once more the inner path in this era [1989], so that all people who are of good will may recognize themselves and find their way to God again and attain unity with Him and with their neighbor through the Son, who I Am.

14. The law and the prophets were valid until John. And since that time, the Kingdom of God has been preached, and everyone enters into it. But it is easier for heaven and Earth to pass away than that one iota of the law be not fulfilled." (Chap. 21:14)

I, Christ, explain, correct
and deepen the word:

"The law and the prophets were valid until the time of John" means that the law which the prophets taught became manifest up till the appearance of John. What the prophets taught from the law of God in addition, I, as Jesus, deepened and lived as an example to the people. As Jesus, I built upon this and began to proclaim the Kingdom of God and its laws, which the prophets before John had already announced. Every soul that actualizes and keeps the laws of life enters the Kingdom of God.

The law of God is absolute. Not one iota of it can be removed. The law of the Eternal will be fulfilled in all facets of life on and in the Earth and in the spheres of purification. I came as Jesus of Nazareth in order to fulfill the law of God, and the one who follows in My footsteps will do as I have taught, lived and thus commanded.

In this era [1989], I, Christ, teach the eternal law once more through My prophetess and emissary and lead My own into the kingdom of the inner being. I also teach them again the eternal laws for the Kingdom of God on this Earth. The one who walks in My footsteps, in those of the Nazarene, is the co-founder and fellow builder of the Kingdom of Peace of Jesus Christ on Earth.

And so, I, Christ, came as Jesus into this world to proclaim the Kingdom of God on Earth and to teach the laws of the Kingdom of God.

With the words "teach and then baptize," I meant baptism by the Holy Spirit, because the one who has received and fulfilled the teachings of the Spirit is the spiritually baptized one; he no longer needs baptism by water. Baptism by water can now be seen merely as a symbol, because every person who actualizes the laws of God is baptized by the Spirit of life and can enter heaven because he fulfills the law of life, God in Me, the Christ.

I, Jesus, received from John the baptism by water as a symbol and from then on I began to preach and to teach and to give people an understanding of the Kingdom of God. At the same time, the part-power from the primordial power, the light-potential in the Primordial Central Sun for all fallen and burdened souls; came into action more and more. And just as I preached the Kingdom of God as Jesus of Nazareth, and taught and lived the path as an example to it, to the law of love, so did all other prophets whom I sent after My "It is finished" – and so will I also continue until many people live in the fulfillment of the eternal laws.

Recognize that with the "It is finished," the evolutionary path into the eternal heavens is predetermined for each soul. No soul will be left behind, because the light of redemption is in all souls, yes, even in the demon; it is the lighting of the soul that keeps it from dissolution.

Only the one who has again become the absolute law of love, the spirit being, will return to the dwelling places which the eternal Father holds in readiness for him. For each soul that has become pure again must fulfill the law of God totally; not one iota of the law may remain unfulfilled.

I, Christ, reveal Myself again in this turn of time [1989], which leads to the New Era, to the Kingdom of Peace of Jesus Christ. By way of the divine wisdom, the all-encompassing law of God in all its details comes once more to this Earth. All those who are of good will not only find their way out of the law of sowing and reaping, but also receive teachings and instructions as to how they can comprehensively apply the eternal law of life on this Earth.

And so, I, Christ, teach the whole truth in this epoch. The one who is from the truth understands the meaning of what is revealed by Me in the spoken word and in writing, for people who draw closer to the Eternal no longer cling to the word nor to the letter. Words and letters are merely symbols.

People who consciously walk the inner path of love step by step will no longer ask about what is behind the so-called mysteries of God. Everything will be manifest to them, because the person who draws nearer to the inner life opens his spiritual consciousness, that is, he immerses into the eternal law, God, which is closed only to those who do not actualize and keep it.

Even now, the people are rich in the Spirit of life who walk the path of love and keep the community with their neighbor are rich in the Spirit of life. They can be certain that they are standing at My right side, even now.

I repeat: I, Christ, explain and correct the text in hand from the book, "The Gospel of Jesus," insofar as the terms and words of that time no longer correspond with those of the present time, because another meaning is attached to them. I also correct significant unlawful interpretations which flowed in – also through translations. I also deepen the explanations and add further aspects of the law. Thus, all those who will live in the Kingdom of Peace of Jesus Christ should gain insight not only into what took place during My time as Jesus of Nazareth, but also into what took place until the awakening Kingdom of Peace of Jesus Christ came into being.

15. And some women came to Him and brought to Him their infants, which they had at their breast, so that He would bless them. But some said, "Why do you bother the Master?"

16. But Jesus reprimanded them, saying, "From these will come those who will proclaim Me before the people." And He took them in His arms and blessed them. (Chap. 21:15-16)

I, Christ, explain, correct
and deepen the word:

With the words "From these will come those who will proclaim Me before the people," I alluded to the coming of those who are with Me in the mission of the Father-Mother-God, which is to lead all fallen and burdened souls and men back to the heart of love.

In the eternal Being, in the eternal city of Jerusalem, the Mission of Redemption was planned and prepared in all its details in the presence of the eternal Father. Every being who decided for this mission brought one or more building blocks from the great mosaic of the plan of redemption – as its potential of love and help for the fallen and burdened souls – into the Primordial Central Sun and into the prism suns, that is, into the suns of the natures and attributes. Starting from the Primordial Central Sun and the suns of the natures and attributes, which are the basic powers of infinity, the mission for the redemption radiated into all Fall worlds and into the atmosphere of this Earth.

During this mighty event, the sons and daughters of God also absorbed their share in the Work of Redemption, into their spirit body.

Many sons and daughters of God decided to carry out the Work of Redemption with Me, Christ, until the last soul is once more in the eternal Being. But not every spirit being that is in the Mission of Redemption will be active with Me, Christ, to the very end, that is, until all beings have again attained purity. This mighty rescue action – until the last soul has returned home – is incumbent upon those beings who have committed themselves to it and who come mostly from the centre of all Being, from the Sanctum, where the Fall began. They are those who came into this world via the lineage of David and who will keep on coming to the Earth again and again, until the Kingdom of Peace of Jesus Christ has reached its high point. They will remain with Me in the Mission of Redemption to the very end and are, with Me, Christ, those who have the main responsibility in My Work of Redemption.

Each spirit being which took on a share of the responsibility for the Work of Redemption contributed the corresponding spiritual potential from the endowment of its spiritual mentality. This spiritual potential that was contributed by the sons and daughters of God prepared the way for Me, Christ, and for themselves through the Fall realms, which became the purification planes after the "It is finished." Their contributed spiritual potential is their different spiritual mentalities with which, in the human garment, they develop the corresponding abilities for the Kingdom of Peace of Jesus Christ.

And so, many sons and daughters of God, who are in the Mission of Redemption, brought into this mission a part of their spiritual potential for leading home all children of God, and are now active in the Work of Redemption. The awakened souls that decided for Me in their earthly garment are taking their places in the great whole according to their task and serve in the Work of Redemption, which is also their work. They bear in themselves the radiating mission of leading all souls and beings home to the great eternal primordial light, God.

The lineage of David and the sons and daughters of God from other lineages form a great, mighty people, the people of God on this Earth. Some of them have burdened themselves over incarnations and cannot yet be addressed by Me, the Christ of God, because their heart is still far from Me. Others among the sons and daughters of God who are in the mission are still on the way to fulfill the part of the task incumbent upon them. Some of them returned to the "world" again, for they were still too entrapped by the world. Their souls, however, have heard My call and, in the due course of time, will return to their task in the Work of Redemption. Their return need not be in this incarnation, in this earthly existence [1989]. It can still take place in later incarnations, for My Kingdom of Peace on this Earth is only now being built.

Still other sons and daughters of God are gradually growing into their task and accept their assignment consciously.

Others are already completely in the mission, and are fulfilling what they have entered into the Primordial Central Sun as spiritual potential to that end, into the seven basic powers of creation, into the Fall worlds and into the atmosphere.

Many sons and daughters of God who are in the mission and other children of love who have awakened in the Spirit of life will proclaim the Son of God as the Redeemer of all souls and men until all souls have consciously accepted redemption and have set out on the path to perfection.

The sons and daughters of God who came and come into the world via the lineage of David will remain in the Mission of Redemption until everything is accomplished. I already indicated this as Jesus of Nazareth, when some women brought their children to Me so that I would bless them. From the radiation of the children, I recognized which soul was part of the Mission of Redemption. Every being that is in the Mission of Redemption has a radiation seal in its spirit body. This radiates through the physical body, too, through the Christ-center that is active near the heart.

CHAPTER 22

The Raising of the Daughter of Jairus

Prerequisites for healing the body – The Christ is in you (2-5). The raising of the "dead" (6-12)

1. And behold, there came one of the wardens of the synagogue, Jairus by name. And when he saw Him, he fell at His feet and implored Him, saying, "My little daughter is at the point of death. I beg You, come and lay Your hands on her, so that she may be healed and live." And Jesus went with him, and many people joined Him and crowded around Him.

2. And there was a woman who had been bleeding for twelve years and had suffered much at the hands of many physicians and had spent all that she had for this purpose; and nothing had improved, but rather grew worse.

3. As she had heard of Jesus, she pushed her way behind Him and touched His garment. For she said to herself, "If I only touch His garment, I will get well." And immediately the blood stopped flowing. And she felt in her body that she was healed of her plague.

4. And Jesus, Himself, immediately felt that a power had gone out of Him, and turned to the people crowded around Him, saying, "Who touched my garment?" And His disciples said to Him, "You see that the crowd is pushing and ask: Who touched Me?"

5. *And He looked around to see the one who had done this. But the woman, fearing and trembling – as she knew what had happened in her – came and fell before Him and told Him the whole truth. But He said to her, "My daughter, your faith has made you whole. Go in peace, and be healed of your disease."*
(Chap. 22:1-5)

I, Christ, explain, correct
and deepen the word:

What happened then can also happen today. For behold, you who read My words, the Christ no longer walks in Jesus over this Earth – the Christ, O human child, is in you! And wherever you are, wherever you go: I Am the power of redemption in you, which also brings about the healing of your body if this is good for your soul. You, O man, need not seek Me – you find Me in you! You need not go here or there – I Am in you! And wherever you are, I Am there. Withdraw to a quiet chamber and go into the little chamber of your heart in order to pray from your heart. In prayer, bring your heart's concerns to Me, who has taken up dwelling in you, and believe that I can do everything.

And if you allow no doubt into your faith in Me, what is good for you and serves the salvation of your soul will happen. Just as then, the law "your faith has helped you" applies today as well. And if you no longer sin – by striving to keep the commandments of life – your request is already answered in your soul. Salvation will then become effective in your soul and on your body, if it serves the further development of your soul.

6. *While He was still speaking, some servants of the synagogue warden came and said, "Your daughter has died. Why do you trouble the Master further?"*

7. *As soon as Jesus heard the words that were spoken, He said to the warden of the synagogue, "Be not afraid, but just believe." And He let no one follow Him, except Peter, James and John, the brother of James.*

8. *And He came into the house of the warden of the synagogue and saw the crowd and the minstrels of the temple, and they were all weeping and wailing loudly.*

9. *And when He had come in, He said to them, "Why are you making this noise and weeping so? The girl has not died, she is just sleeping." And they laughed at Him; for they thought she was dead, and they did not believe Him. But after He had driven them all out, He took two of His disciples with Him and entered into the room where the girl was lying.*

10. *And He grasped the girl by the hand and said to her, "Talitha cumi!" This means something like, "Girl, I say to you, get up!"*

11. *And straightaway the girl arose and walked around. She was twelve years old. And they were exceedingly amazed.*

12. *And He strictly ordered them that nobody should make it known, and commanded that she should be given something to eat. (Chap. 22:6-12)*

I, Christ, explain, correct
and deepen the word:

Recognize My deeds in the depths of your heart, not only as Jesus of Nazareth, but also as the Christ of God. For I Am come again to you in the spirit of love, in order to help and serve you.

As long as the silver cord – also called the information cord – that joins soul and body is not yet severed from the body, the spiritual circulation still exists and the life forces still flow from the incorruptible nucleus of the soul, God, into the soul, from the soul into the body and from the body back to the soul and to the nucleus of the soul, God. I saw this in the girl and first spoke silently with the power of My Father in Me, the indwelling I Am. Then I established a spiritual connection with the soul of the child and through it increased the flow of cosmic energies to the silver cord. Via the nucleus of the soul, this enhanced life force then flowed into the soul and, via the soul, into the brain cells and the organism of the child. This is how I raised the human being from so-called death.

In this way, I brought back into the flesh all those whose time in the earthly garment had not yet expired. They would have left the Earth only because of external circumstances that deprived the soul of its support and thereby would have driven it out of the body earlier than was predetermined for it according to the cosmic laws.

It is written in the law of life that a certain earthly life cycle is predetermined for each soul in the earthly garment. This cycle includes the possibility of an earlier or a later death of the earthly garment. The earthly death can also occur within this timespan. As Jesus of Nazareth, and with the power of the Spirit, I could, during this timespan, call the souls back to their earthly existence.

I accomplished these works of love when it was good for the soul and person. From the consciousness radiation of the soul, I recognized whether soul and person would burden themselves anew during their extended earthly existence or would strengthen their faith in the Eternal by forgiving, asking for forgiveness and by making amends.

The commandment for all human beings is: If your faith is as great as a mustard seed, then many things can happen in and to you out of the works of divine love.

CHAPTER 23

Jesus and the Samaritan Woman

The water of life, the truth,
an eternally flowing power (3-7). The one who seeks ear-
nestly finds the truth – Examine those who talk about the
truth – About the value of external forms of worship – Who
are the people of Israel today? – The New Jerusalem – The
last covenant (16)

1. Jesus came into a city of Samaria called Sychar,
near the field that Jacob had given to his son Joseph.

2. Jacob's well was there. As Jesus was tired from
His journey, He sat on the edge of the well. It was
about the sixth hour.

3. And a woman of Samaria comes to draw water.
Jesus says to her, "Give me to drink." (For His disciples had gone to the city in order to buy food.)

4. And the Samaritan woman says to Him, "How is it
that You, a Jew, ask for a drink of me, a woman of Samaria?" (For the Jews do not associate with the
Samaritans.)

5. Jesus answered, saying to her, "If you knew the
gift of God and who says to you, 'Give Me to drink,'
you would have asked God who would have given you
living water."

6. And the woman says to Him, "Sir, you have nothing to draw with and the well is deep; from where then
have You that living water? Are you then greater than

our father Jacob, who gave us this well and drank from it, he and his children and his camels and oxen and sheep?"

7. Jesus answered, saying to her, "The one who drinks of this water will thirst again. But the one who drinks of the water that I will give him will never thirst again, for the water that I will give him will spring up in him like a well of water into everlasting life."
(Chap. 23:1-7)

I, Christ, explain, correct
and deepen the word:

The water of life flows more strongly into this world since My deeds as Jesus of Nazareth – and even stronger since My "It is finished."

The one who drinks from the water of life draws from the wellspring of eternal truth, because he has returned to the primordial source of all Being. He will never thirst again, nor will he ever lack anything. He has what he needs and beyond that.

People in the spirit of truth are themselves the spiritual fountain of truth. They give and give – and never go dry because the Spirit of God, which is active through them, is eternally flowing power, the origin of the wellspring and the wellspring itself, the truth.

Recognize: I Am the water of life. The one who makes My life as Jesus of Nazareth his life, by keeping what I have commanded him, will live in Me, the living water, and will be a fountain of living salvation from which the water of life flows unceasingly. Only then can he offer the true, fresh drink of living water to many people. Henceforth, they will no longer seek the truth, since they will have found the truth, the I Am. They will no longer thirst, for they drink from the eternal wellspring of truth.

The one who receives from the water of life does not remain a loner; nor does he swim with the tide of the old sinful time. He rows against it, by no longer promoting his human aspects, but by dissolving them through the power of love. This is how he finds in himself the eternity, the life, the truth, the primordial source, God.

In this way, the Era of Light and a new human race in me, the Christ, gradually emerge – people who will build and maintain the Kingdom of Peace, since they themselves are peaceful.

8. *Then the woman says to Him, "Sir, give me this water, so that I do not thirst, nor have to come here to draw." Jesus says to her, "Go, call your husband and come here." The woman answered, "I have no husband."*

9. *Jesus, looking upon her, says to her, "You have said correctly: 'I have no husband.' You have had five husbands and the one whom you now have is not your husband. You have spoken the truth."*

10. Then the woman said to Him, "Sir, I recognize that You are a prophet. Our forefathers have prayed on this mountain and You say that Jerusalem is the place where men ought to worship."

11. Jesus says to her, "Woman, believe Me, the time will come when you will worship God neither on this mountain nor in Jerusalem. You do not know what you worship; but we know what we worship. For salvation comes from Israel.

12. But the time will come, and is already there, when the true worshippers will worship the All-Father in the spirit and in the truth. For the All-Holy wants to have such worshippers. God is Spirit and those who worship Him must worship Him in the spirit and in the truth."

13. Then the woman says to Him, "I know that the Messiah who is called Christ will come. When He comes, He will tell us everything." Jesus says to her, "I Am the One who speaks to you."

14. And meanwhile His disciples came and were surprised that He talked with the woman. Yet no one asked, "What do you seek?" Or, "Why do You talk with her?"

15. Then the woman left her jug, went her way into the city and said to the people, "Come and see a man who has told me all that I have ever done. Is this One not the Christ?"

16. Then they went out and came to Him, and many of the Samaritans believed in Him and asked Him to stay with them. And He stayed there two days.
(Chap. 23:8-16)

I, Christ, explain, correct
and deepen the word:

The one who speaks from the truth, his words are eternal life. They are imbued with the life and the power which I Am in the Father-Mother-God. The one who earnestly seeks the water of life, the truth, finds his way to the person who is able to show him the path to the origin of the wellspring, and finds the life, the truth, in his innermost being.

Words of life are words of truth. Whoever lives according to the meaning of the living word fulfills the law of life and dwells in the spirit of truth. Therefore, examine the people who speak of the wellspring of living salvation, whether they bring the water of life, the truth, or whether they only stand at the well of truth.

Recognize that where the light is, that is where those who strive toward the light gather. However, there are also many among them who only speak about truth while having dark intentions. Therefore, use the measure of your own honesty in order to examine and recognize their deeds. Do not look to or listen to those who make impure speeches – not even when they call themselves "Rabbi." Examine the meaning of their words and their behavior towards their fellow man – and they will be an open book for you. People of the Spirit are modest, humble and meek, yet their being is irradiated and illuminated by the One, who I Am, Christ, the living water.

The one who lives in the truth lives from the truth, and perceives the truth and also sees the untrue. As Jesus of Nazareth, I saw the woman at the well with the eyes of truth. I saw her past and present life. On that basis, I addressed what could have served for her recognition on that day.

At all times and still in today's time [1989], people created and create for themselves outer signs and symbols, in order to worship These outer pictures, signs and symbols for worship, such as statues, synagogues, churches, squares, high places, mountains, as well as rites and ceremonies will be created by man for himself until he acknowledges God, the spirit of truth, within himself and keeps the "temple-order," the commandments of life.

Every human being is a temple of God. Therefore, a place to worship God is not needed. Worship God in the "holy of holies" of your inner being, and keep your temple pure with noble thoughts, with God-filled words and deeds; then you are keeping the "temple-order" – and God will answer your prayers, because you are in communication with Him.

In today's time [1989], too, many people do not yet know whom or what they are worshipping. They are imitators of those who have created and uphold the cults, because they are still impoverished in their heart. Because the true, almighty God, the God of the inner being, is foreign to them, they need an outer god. However, the outer god is never the God of truth, but an idol.

I explain the words, "For salvation comes from Israel." Israel is where people fulfill God's will.

Today's Israel is no longer the Israel where I lived as Jesus of Nazareth. It is nothing more than the name which this country still bears. A great many of the Israelites did not keep the covenant with God, nor did they accept Me as their Redeemer. For this reason, God, the Eternal, has renewed the covenant with some of the people who were once incarnated in ancient Israel and who today are incarnated in another country and are still in the mission.

God, the Eternal, has now [1989] also made the covenant with those who were not incarnated in Israel at the time of My earthly existence, but have gone into the earthly garment again and again over the past centuries and have prepared the work of homebringing. These, too, are in the Mission of Redemption. He also made the covenant with those people who, in the Work of Redemption, work for the salvation of their fellow man, thus also taking part in the mission of homebringing.

And so, Israel is there, where the people are incarnated who are in the Mission of Redemption and are willing to fulfill the will of God.

Many spirit beings from the great mission-potential for redemption were incarnated at the time of Moses and also at the time of My sojourn on Earth in old Israel. Sin has scattered many people to the four winds, who are in the mission of the Work of Redemption. But now, I gather them once more in another country. It is there that the New Israel will be.

Even now [1989], many brothers and sisters are gathering in the country where the incarnated part-ray of divine wisdom teaches and is active: in the New Jerusalem. The Eternal has now made the last covenant with the brothers and sisters in New Jerusalem, in the emerging Israel.

The people of God on this Earth will become a mighty people. For this reason, more and more people are coming to make the eternal covenant with God. For I, Christ, call them – and they come. They gather to work for the New Era, the Era of Light. They no longer worship the Eternal in front of monuments and statues. They have no outer churches. They do not go on mountains to seek the Eternal, believing to find Him there. They have no ceremonies or rites. They worship the Eternal in their temple, in their inner being; for there dwells the one Eternal One, the God of Abraham, Isaac and Jacob, the spirit of the eternal Father, whose children are all spirit beings, men and souls. Although they meet in places, it is not to seek God there, but to experience unity with one another and to pray together to the One who is the life: God, the spirit of truth, who dwells in every spirit being, in every soul and in every human being.

God is also the Creator-Spirit who has created all Being, who lives in every plant, in every stone, in every animal, in every atom – in all Being. God is spirit, and those who truly worship Him do so in the spirit and in the truth, and they keep the laws.

Verily, I say to you: As Jesus I went away from you; as Christ, the risen One, I came to you, so that you may resurrect in Me, the Redeemer, in order to return again to God, the primordial stream.

Know that as Jesus, I stayed with the people a considerable length of time; as the Christ of God I dwell in you. And I remain eternally in you; for I Am in the eternal Father, and the Father is in Me, and We are the one spirit of truth, which dwells in all people.

CHAPTER 24

Jesus Condemns Cruelty –
He Heals the Sick and Casts Out the Demons

All violations of the law of life fall back on man; nature and the creatures on Earth are gifts of God for the well-being of men (1). Explanation of the "withered arm" (3). Salvation and healing for the body, if it is good for the soul (7). Pharisees yesterday and today – The fight against the growing light on Earth and in the spheres of purification, still in the time of the Kingdom of Peace – At the turn of time, the foundation of the Kingdom of Peace will be laid and will take form – A reminder to the people in the Kingdom of Peace: Do not forget the pioneers and the incarnated seraph of divine wisdom, My prophetess and emissary – The fight behind the wall of fog continues (8). Explanation of the "miracle of the food" (12-13)

1. *As Jesus passed through a village, He saw a group of idlers. They were tormenting a cat which they had found and ill-treated it shamefully. And Jesus commanded them to stop and began to reproach them; but they disregarded His words and reviled Him. (Chap. 24:1)*

I, Christ, explain, correct
and deepen the word:

The one who torments and ill-treats people and animals will one day experience torment and ill-treatment on his own body. The same applies to offences against the plant and mineral kingdoms. For what is manifest in matter as a life-form also exists in the soul as spirit-substance. Therefore, the one who violates life passes judgment on himself, because he burdens a part of his spiritual heritage. For everything that comes from God also exists as essence in the soul of man.

Recognize that the Earth brings forth food for the people. People also need shelter and clothing, because they cannot create their food, shelter and clothing like the angels in heaven. The Earth is the bearer of life for all things. It should neither be violated nor exploited. The Earth and everything that lives on it, animals, plants and minerals, want to serve the people. The prerequisite for this is that man accept and receive his Earth, that is, that he care for it, for the Earth is a great living organism.

God, the Eternal, gave man the animals and plants and granted him fruits, vegetables and grain from the earth. He gave these to man and said, "Make the Earth subject to you," which means in its correct implication: Respect and care for the life in all living forms, and they will serve you.

Recognize: The pure life-forms of the animals are created by God, and each plant belongs to God, the great potential of creation, which continues to develop in the evolutionary cycle. Thus, every life-form is a part of the great whole.

Man is commanded by God to treasure and love life and to keep the commandment "pray and work." For this reason, the life of so-called idlers is a waste of the energies of the day. They are people who steal God's energy. The one who does not use the day, but only abuses it in order to exploit his fellow man or to do violence to animals and plants, acts against the law of life.

People who think only of their own welfare will torment the animals and exploit the Earth and poison the life on it, because their thoughts are poisoned by greed and envy. For the people who do not know themselves torment people and animals and are against nature. They do solely what their egoistic thinking urges them to do. They themselves are driven, and therefore, want to drive away everything that is around them, because everything that does not fit their conceptions disturbs them. Their human ego makes such people act as if they were of unsound mind.

They do not know the commandment of asking for forgiveness, of forgiving and of making amends. They get even with their neighbor: an eye for an eye, a tooth for a tooth. But in so doing, they burden their own soul with what they inflict upon their neighbor. For what man does to his neighbor – and to the animal, to the plant, indeed, to the entire organism of the Earth – is what he inflicts upon himself. So it was and still is in today's sinful time [1989]. Yet a new generation is rising and strides into the new era, into a life with each other and with God.

2. *Then He made a whip of knotted cords and drove them away, saying, "This Earth, which My Father created for happiness and gladness, you have made into the lowest hell with your deeds of violence and cruelty." And they fled before His face. (Chap. 24:2)*

I, Christ, explain, correct
and deepen the word:

The whip symbolizes the law of cause and effect. The one who despises and tortures his neighbors and his second neighbors as well, the one who commits violence and cruelty against man and animal, against plants and minerals and against other life-forms in and on the Earth will experience the effects of his causes – unless he repents in time.

Like a whip, the law of cause and effect will lash all those who have ill-treated and still ill-treat life – in whatever form and in whatever state of consciousness it appears. The Earth is given to the people, so that they become conscious again that they are children of God, that their life – as all life – is from God, so that they learn to cherish and love life. In whatever form and in whatever state of consciousness life comes towards the person and manifests itself: in everything is God – the life.

Everything pure wants to serve selflessly, including the Earth with its nature kingdoms. The one who recognizes that his life is from God and lives accordingly, keeps peace with all creatures, with everything that is given out of the bosom of God for the joy and well-being of man. God wishes for peaceful and joyful children. However, the one who does not want to recognize God nor to accept His ruling hand is against Him and against everything given to man from His hands, thus becoming bad-tempered, unhappy, worried and ill.

3. But someone even worse than the rest returned and threatened Him. And Jesus extended His hand, and the young man's arm withered. And great fear came upon all. And one said, "He is a sorcerer." (Chap. 24:3)

I, Christ, explain, correct
and deepen the word:

"And Jesus extended His hand, and the young man's arm withered." This action was misunderstood and therefore was passed on in this way. A person who lives in the law of God never interferes in the law of cause and effect in order to speed up and bring about what a wrongdoer causes and determines for himself.

The one who commits violence will reap the same or similar thing. Had I caused the arm to wither, as is written, I would have interfered in the law of sowing and reaping. The incident occurred in compliance with the law of sowing and reaping: While ill-treating the animal, the wrongdoer had hit his arm on a hard, rough object. The blood congealed, the arm turned blue and then hung limp. I stretched out My hand and pointed out the effect, in order to explain to him the cause. Since the people of those days knew of the law of sowing and reaping only in the form of the words "an eye for an eye, a tooth for a tooth" and, what is more, misinterpreted it, they believed that I had conjured this up and was a sorcerer.

In this way, I repeatedly showed the people that they will reap what they sow: The one who brings bad seed into the field of life will also have a bad harvest, for the fruit already lies in the seed.

However, the one who recognizes his faults in time, repents and does not repeat them, accepts the law of God and gradually learns to love all life-forms. He then receives from the hands of grace of the Eternal, and his soul and body will attain light, salvation and healing.

Recognize that the seed does not always immediately yield the harvest. What man sows in this earthly life, that is, what he causes – also to the animal and plant kingdoms – is what he will reap, if not in this earthly existence then in a future life on Earth or as a soul in the spheres of purification.

Therefore, live each day consciously. For each day shows every person what is good and less good about himself and what he can make amends for today, on this day.

4. The next day, the mother of the young man came to Jesus, and asked that He heal his arm again. And Jesus spoke to them of the law of love and the unity of all life in the one family of God. And thereafter He said, "As you do in this life to your fellow creatures, so shall it be done to you in the life to come."

5. And the young man believed and confessed his sins. And Jesus stretched out His hand, and the withered arm became as whole as the other. And the people praised God that He had given such power to a man.

6. And behold, as Jesus went His way, two blind people followed Him. They cried out, saying, "Lord, You son of David, have mercy on us." And when He came into the house, the blind ones came to Him, and Jesus said to them, "Do you believe that I Am able to do this?"

7. And they said to Him, "Yes, Lord." And Jesus touched their eyes, saying, "Let it be done unto you according to your faith." And soon after their eyes were opened again. But Jesus commanded them strictly, "See that you tell no man." But, after they had left, they spread His fame in all the land. (Chap. 24:4-7)

I, Christ, explain, correct
and deepen the word:

It is given to the one who believes!

Healings from the spirit of life are no miracles, but principles of the law.

249

God's love and grace stand by His human children. The right faith comes from the heart. People with a deep faith remain steadfast, no matter what comes towards them, and they receive salvation for their soul – for the grace and help of God pour first into the soul. From there, come the salvation and the healing for the body, if it is good for the soul, that is, if the person no longer commits the same sins that led to the suffering or illness of the body in the first place.

"Soon after" means that the healing did not take place directly, but according to the commandment of faith; for I think first of the soul. In it is the law of life, the law, God. If man keeps it, insofar as he is aware of it, then he attains salvation and healing in and on the body as well.

The gifts of grace for the soul in this earthly existence do not always have their effect in and on the body. They can also develop in the soul realms – when the soul is discarnate – or in another incarnation. When this happens, what is unlawful in the soul is gradually transformed into positive power, which then flows into the body. This means that the soul is freed from it and the body, too, will no longer have to bear what the person once caused.

8. *As they left, behold, they brought to Him a man who was mute and possessed by a demon. And when the demon had been cast out, the mute man spoke. And the people marveled, saying, "Such things have never been*

seen before in Israel." But the Pharisees said, "He casts out the devils by way of the prince of devils." (Chap. 24:8)

I, Christ, explain, correct
and deepen the word:

As Jesus of Nazareth, I was active wherever My Father placed Me. To many people, I could bring relief and healing through the power of the Father, and could also guide them to recognition through the living word.

Not every person who came to Me could I help or serve. I laid My hand on many, but they did not become healthy. Nor did every dark power which I addressed in a person leave him. For the law of life says: It will be given to you according to your faith! And: Henceforth sin no more! Furthermore, the law of life says: Believe even if you do not yet feel on your body what already has been accomplished in the soul. Only those faults and sins the person recognizes and repents of, for which he asks forgiveness and forgives – and which he no longer commits – will become effective in and on the body.

Recognize: Every person who speaks other than he thinks is a Pharisee.

Even today [1989], the Pharisees use the same slanderous speech as when I walked on Earth as Jesus of Nazareth and, to stir up the people, they pour out the same scorn and ridicule. However, the one who is able to look into the hearts of people recognizes that deep down every Pharisee is a person filled with anxiety who is constantly concerned with seeing to it that his structure of lies does not waver. Particularly the Pharisees and the scribes, too, have already planted much untruth in the world and have spread it among the people.

The blinded Pharisees, the leaders of nations and many churchmen say many untruths unintentionally and, in part, deliberately. They deliberately say false things for fear of losing their prestige. They speak false things unintentionally, because they do not examine or control their sensations and thoughts, wasting their earthly days without self-recognition. They do not clear up their wrong behavior and they give vent to their aggressions which are aggravated by their fears.

The Pharisees, many scribes and churchmen accuse their fellow men of untruths and condemn those who speak from the eternal truth. The one who bears false witness against his neighbor is afraid of the eternal truth, which is God.

Many Pharisees wearing clerical vestments are convinced of their competency in questions of faith. They accuse their neighbors of being satanic or of "belonging to the devil," because they themselves more or less serve him in their way of living and thinking. Therefore, beware of those who spurn their neighbors and say evil things about them, for they are, themselves, in alliance with evil.

For the people who will then live in the Kingdom of Peace of Jesus Christ, it is important to know that the battle of the darkness against the light, as it took place at the time of My earthly life as Jesus of Nazareth, continued over the following eras and is escalating once more today [1989].

Everything that I experienced as Jesus of Nazareth was experienced by many faithful men and women in the centuries that followed. They, too, were scorned, ridiculed and slandered for the sake of the truth. And yet, after their physical death, their souls came back into the earthly garment again and again, in order to prepare the Kingdom of God on Earth, and, now [1989], to found and build it.

The first steps into the Era of Light were accomplished – at first invisibly to the people of the world – through acts of neighborly love. Then, in the course of time, the works of God on Earth became more and more visible. People of higher consciousness guided their fellow men, their fellow brothers and sisters, on the path within to Me, the Christ of God. They acquired land and founded Christian establishments, where people began to actualize the Sermon on the Mount, the law of God for this Earth. These establishments were repeatedly destroyed by opposing forces.

What took place during these times of battle, when light and darkness encountered one another on Earth, is still taking place now, while you are living in the Era of Light on Earth on the levels invisible to you, in the spheres of purification. There, many former scribes, Pharisees and churchmen who were in an earthly garment at that time [1989], are still active. They continue to influence the souls of people who were once servile to them, in order to sow discord in the spheres of purification as well.

You, who live in the Era of Light in the Kingdom of God on Earth, should know about what once happened on Earth and is still taking place in the lower soul realms, in the spheres of order. You should be informed about it when you leave this world after your physical death and go through the wall of fog, through which the physical eye is unable to see. For the one who – as a soul – crosses the wall of fog knowing about the causes which are still having their effects will then not be shocked or disheartened, but will immediately begin to teach and instruct the souls that are led to him, so that they may learn about the light of truth which already dwells on earth: the Christ of God, who I Am.

All those who worked and fought and were persecuted for the sake of the Kingdom of God in the period of almost two thousand years after My life as Jesus of Nazareth are, to you who live in the Kingdom of Peace of Jesus Christ, the pioneers of the New Era. Great things were accomplished by them. During the various epochs following My life on Earth, they came into the earthly garment again and again and created and increased ever more the spiritual potential for the Kingdom of God on Earth. At first, it was an invisible spiritual potential, which then very gradually became manifest on Earth, above all in the atmosphere. From time to time, some of this was realized, that is, it became visible – there, where people began to live and work according to the Sermon on the Mount.

Then the turn of time dawned, that epoch [1989] which unveiled the Kingdom of Peace of Jesus Christ in all its details. Again, pioneers came to this Earth. They are the incarnated spirit beings who are in the Mission of Redemption and come from the lineage of David and other lineages. Now [1989], they let what they had prepared in past generations become visible.

Here and there, the great family of God became visible on Earth. Many lived in original Christian communities. The central primordial light among them was the Covenant Community New Jerusalem which, already at that time, carried the responsibility for all emerging original communities and for the Kingdom of God in coming on the Earth. In the light-material Kingdom of Peace, as the city of Jerusalem, it now forms the center, from which all original communities are guided.

The original communities in Universal Life, which formed even in the midst of the sinful world, consisted mainly of people of the spirit, who lived more and more in Me, the Christ, and thus, in the law of God. They created community establishments which they, as human beings, needed for living. They acquired and built houses in which they lived in community. They founded artisan enterprises where they actualized the law of "pray and work." Together they founded and built clinics, nursing homes, kindergartens, schools, father-mother-houses, dining halls and everything that is necessary for people to live on this Earth.

There were neither superiors nor subordinates among them. They all consciously felt themselves to be children of God; they affirmed the sonship and daughterhood in our eternal Father. According to their abilities, they worked for the great whole, the common good.

As already revealed, among these pioneers for the New Era in Me, the Christ, there lived a woman, the incarnated seraph of divine wisdom. She worked as prophetess and emissary for Me and, as a shining example, led the way for everyone in fulfilling the eternal laws. I rang in and launched the New Era through her, the incarnated part-ray of divine wisdom, and her spiritual dual, the positive principle of divine wisdom. For the love and wisdom are active in the Work of Redemption and, with them, all beings, all sons and daughters of God who took upon themselves the task of contributing what is given them by God: strength, love and wisdom, order, will, earnestness, patience and mercy – for the New Era.

All incarnated light-beings were active according to their spiritual origin, their spiritual mentalities, which marked their earthly abilities for the Kingdom of God on Earth. These pioneers for the Era of Light also endured humiliation, scorn, and ridicule. They, too, had much evil said of them. However, they strove to live in Me, and I was with them.

So that you may keep it in your heart, I repeat and say to you who now live in the New Era: Again and again, the Pharisees, many scribes and churchmen of that time [1989] fought against the pioneers. Through slander, they incited the people against them. But, just as it was at the time of My life on Earth, so it was in this epoch [1989]: The truth was victorious. Unshakable, no matter what the slanderers said about them, they continued to work in order to pave the way for Me, the Christ, into the Era of Light. They saw to it that what serves the New Era become more and more visible.

Rejoice, you who now live in peace – and fulfill the laws of love thankfully! Remember your brothers and sisters who, as pioneers, prepared the way for Me into the New Era and acquired, founded and built for you what then changed in radiation again and again for the Era of Light – and which you now have in My name.

But do not forget: Behind the wall of fog is not yet the life in Me! There, the fight between the light and the darkness still continues. However, the atmosphere of the Earth protects you from these forces, so that you may live on Earth in peace.

With these words of Mine, you should learn and recognize that redemption is not yet completed in all spheres. In the lower soul realms behind the wall of fog, many of you will encounter things that are similar to what took place on Earth – just as I have revealed it here to you, and as it is recorded as history in this book "This Is My Word." It will be reality for many of you again, when you have laid aside your earthly garment and step behind the wall of fog in your spiritual body. Because after your physical death, you should go forearmed into those realms and help, so that everything that is not yet in accordance with the divine order is put in order and everything that is still bound is released.

9. *And Jesus went to all cities and villages, taught in their synagogues, preached the gospel of the Kingdom of God and healed every plague and all illness in the people. (Chap. 24:9)*

I, Christ, explain, correct
and deepen the word:

I healed many plagues and diseases, but I could not remove "every plague and all illness," because many people thought only of their body. They were not willing to think of their soul first. Many of the suffering people were intent on only saving their earthly body. The one who thought in this way was unable to receive. He attained neither help nor healing – neither for his soul nor for his body. For this reason, many went from them disappointed, because nothing happened in and to them. They then spoke against Me, while flattering the Pharisees and scribes. And because of such talk by those who were disappointed, the Pharisees and many of the scribes were encouraged to proceed against Me, the Christ in Jesus.

10. But when He saw the multitudes, He was moved to compassion; for they were lethargic and scattered like the sheep which have no shepherd. (Chap. 24:10)

I, Christ, explain, correct
and deepen the word:

"Compassion" means to suffer with them: I perceived their suffering and their misery and suffered with them. To perceive suffering out of mercy means to have mercy and to help where help is appropriate.

11. And He said to His disciples, "The harvest is truly plentiful, but the laborers are few. Therefore, ask the Lord of the harvest to send laborers into His harvest."

12. And His disciples brought Him two small baskets of bread and fruits, and a pitcher of water. And Jesus placed the bread and the fruits in front of them and also the water. And they all ate and drank and were filled.

13. And they marveled; for each one of them had enough and even some left-over, even though there were four thousand. And they went their ways and praised God for all they had heard and seen.
(Chap. 24:11-13)

I, Christ, explain, correct
and deepen the word:

There were many people, almost four thousand.
They all heard the words of the Almighty through Me,
Jesus. The word of God is substance and power. Many
of them took the word of God as nourishment from the
heavens. They decided to eat more of this bread and of
these fruits everyday – that is, to devote their life to
God, the law of life. In this way, positive energies were
set free.

I took a part of these positive energies – which arose
from the desire and the will of many who were present
to actualize ever more in themselves the spiritual bread
and spiritual fruits each day – and condensed the spiritual energies, which then, for the hungry multitude,
became bread, fruit, water and also fish, the staple food
of these people. The condensation of the spiritual
energy was a manifestation of light from the Spirit of
God. It bore solely the spiritual life in the bread as well
as in the fruit, in the water and in the fish. What is
manifested from the Spirit is not pure material substance. It does not bear in itself the earthly life and thus,
nor the earthly process of growth. Manifested spiritual
substance cannot be killed.

The people present were in a raised vibration. They
saw the full baskets, the full water vessels, they saw the
bread, the fruit, the water in front of them and took the
gifts of life from the baskets and vessels – and yet everything took place in and from themselves. They drew

these gifts from within because they had developed the higher energies for this – through their good will to devote their life to God, the law, and to increase the powers of God within themselves. They were satisfied and their thirst was quenched.

Because the multitude was in a state of raised consciousness, I, Christ in Jesus, was able to undertake this manifestation of the light.

CHAPTER 25

Sermon on the Mount
(Part 1)

*The Sermon on the Mount, the Inner Path to perfection –
The blessed – The "poor" – Bear your suffering in the right
way – Meekness, a quality of those who love selflessly – The
Ten Commandments and the Sermon on the Mount as the
path to truth and justice – Mercy, the gate to the eternal
Being – The pure souls in the Absolute Law of God – The
peacemakers have peace in themselves – The fight of the
pioneers on several fronts – Churchmen, Pharisees, wolves
in sheep's clothing – A battlefield behind the wall of fog –
Pray for the unenlightened souls (2-4). Earthly wealth as
obligation and task – The abuse of wealth has severe consequences – A warning to those who scorn – Wealthy people,
rulers, false prophets, flatterers, sham Christians: instruments of Satan (5). The righteous are the salt of the Earth
who bring injustice to light (6). The calling and mission of
the prophetess and emissary of God – The activities of the
pioneers under direct schooling and guidance – The New
Jerusalem (7). Liberation, through Christ, from the law of
sowing and reaping; becoming bound to the law of the Fall
through denominations and dogmas – Today, Christ leads
into the whole truth (8). False and true teachers (9). Salvation
only by faith and actualization (10). Christ transforms sins
freely handed over to Him (11). Clearing up, before a severe
karma emerges – The seeming enemy, your mirror (12-13).
Everyone receives what he himself has sown (14). Give love*

selflessly (15). Personal wishes lead to becoming bound to people and things – "Life in a stagnant pool" (16). Winged seeds onto the field of your neighbor's soul – The pioneers' path of purification to the Kingdom of Peace (17-18)

1. When Jesus saw the multitudes, He went on a mountain. And when He had sat down, the twelve came to Him. He looked up at His disciples, saying:

2. "Blessed in the spirit are the poor, for theirs is the Kingdom of Heaven. Blessed are those who grieve, for they shall be comforted. Blessed are the meek, for they will possess the Earth. Blessed are those who hunger and thirst for righteousness, for they shall be satisfied.

3. Blessed are the merciful, for they will attain mercy. Blessed are the pure in heart, for they will behold God. Blessed are the peacemakers, for they will be called children of God. Blessed are those who are persecuted for righteousness' sake, for theirs is the Kingdom of God.

4. Blessed are you, when men will hate you and exclude you from their company and speak all sorts of evil against you and outlaw your names, for the sake of the Son of Man. Rejoice in that day and leap with joy, for behold, your reward is great in heaven. For their forefathers did the same to the prophets. (Chap. 25:1-4)

I, Christ, explain, correct
and deepen the word:

The Sermon on the Mount is the Inner Path to the heart of God, which leads to perfection.

The blessed ones will behold the Christ and, in all meekness and humility, will possess the Earth with Me, the Christ. Happy the one who beholds the glory of the Father-Mother-God in all things! He has become the living example for many.

I guide My own to the recognition of the truth.

The one who is of the truth hears My voice, because he is the truth and thus hears and perceives the truth as well.

The blessed ones are fearless and joyful; for they perceive and hear what those do not see and hear, who still hide behind their human ego, holding on to it with utmost effort so that they are not recognized.

However, the blessed ones look into the prison of the human ego and recognize the most deeply hidden thoughts of their fellow men. With the power of their light-filled consciousness, they shine into it and call out to their fellow men:

"Blessed in the spirit are the poor, for theirs is the Kingdom of Heaven."

The words "the poor" do not mean material poverty. It is not this that brings bliss in the spirit, but the devotion to God, out of which the person fulfills what is the will of God. This is inner wealth.

The words "the poor" mean all those who do not strive for personal possessions and do not hoard goods. Their thinking and striving aim at the community life in which they administer the goods that God has given to everyone in a lawful way. They do not set their minds and aspire to have worldly things. They serve the common good and extend their arms to God and consciously walk the path to the inner life. Their goal is the Kingdom of God in their inner being, which they want to proclaim and bring to all people who are of good will. Their inner wealth is the life in God, for God and for their neighbor. They live the commandment "pray and work."

They strive towards the Spirit of God and receive from God what they need for their earthly life and even more. These are the blessed in the Spirit of God.

"Blessed are those who grieve, for they shall be comforted."

The grief of man does not come from God, but it is either the grieving one who himself has caused it – or his soul has taken over a part of the debt of a brother or sister soul in the realm of the souls, to pay off that debt in the earthly existence, so that the brother or sister soul can enter higher spheres of inner life.

God's mercy will be granted to the one who bears his grief without accusing his neighbor and who recognizes his faults and weaknesses in the grief, repents of them, asks for forgiveness and forgives. For God, the Eternal, wants to comfort His children and to take away from them what is not good and beneficial for their soul. For when the grief leaves the soul, that is, when the causes which became effective in the soul are settled, man finds his way closer to God.

"Bear your grief" means: Do not complain about it; do not accuse God or your neighbor. In your grief, find your sinful behavior that led to this grief.

Repent, forgive and ask for forgiveness, and no longer do what you have recognized as sin. Then the debt of the soul can be erased by God and thereupon you receive increased strength, love and wisdom from Him.

If you meet a grieving and sorely afflicted person and he asks you for help, then support him and help him as far as it is possible for you and as far as it is good for his soul. And when you see that your neighbor thankfully accepts the help and builds himself up with it, then give him even more, if it is possible for you.

However, you who give help, do it selflessly. If you do it only as an outer obligation, you will receive no spiritual reward – and you will render no service to the soul of the person who is suffering and is sorely afflicted, but only to his body, to the vehicle of the soul.

"Blessed are the meek, for they will possess the Earth."

Meekness, humility, love and kindness go hand in hand. The one who has become selfless love is also meek, humble and kind. He is filled with wisdom and strength.

People in My Spirit, the selflessly loving ones, will possess the Earth. Oh see, the path to the heart of God is the path into the heart of selfless love. The peace of God flows out of selfless love.

The people who journey toward the heart of God and the people who already live in God work for the New Era, by teaching all willing people the path to God. In this way, they take more and more possession of the Earth in My Spirit.

Those who love selflessly are the ones who will live in the Kingdom of God on Earth, in the Kingdom of Peace. Rejoice that already now [1989] you are walking the path to the heart of God! In Me, you are the trailblazers and pioneers for the New Era. Many of you will be born in the New Era, in the kingdom of light, and will bring with you the fulfillment in God, because already now you are walking the path which leads there. Rejoice and be grateful for the purification and cleansing of your souls, for you will then behold Me and will consciously live and be in and with Me.

"Blessed are those who hunger and thirst for righteousness, for they shall be satisfied."

The one who hungers and thirsts for the righteousness of God is a seeker of truth, who longs for the life in and with God. He shall be satisfied.

My brother, My sister, you, who long for righteousness, for the life in and with God, take heart and raise yourself out of the sinful human ego! Rejoice, for the time has come in which the Kingdom of God draws closer to those people who endeavor to keep the commandments of life.

Behold, I, your Redeemer, Am the truth in you. And so, in you, I Am the way, the truth and the life.

The truth is the law of love and of life. In the Ten Commandments, which are excerpts from the all-encompassing law of God, you find the mnemonic phrases for the path to the truth. Keep the Ten Commandments and you will draw ever more onto the path of the Sermon on the Mount, on which the path to the truth is fundamentally worked out.

The path to the truth is the path to the heart of God, to the eternal life, which is selfless love. The Sermon on the Mount is the path into the Kingdom of God, into the laws for the Kingdom of Peace of Jesus Christ. When you delve deeper into them and fulfill them, you will attain divine wisdom.

You have already read that the part-ray of divine wisdom is in an earthly garment [1989], in order to give the word of God and to interpret the laws of God. Through this, My instrument, I now reveal the Sermon on the Mount in all details and guide and accompany the willing ones on the Inner Path, with teachings and lessons which, if they are actualized, lead to the Father, to the eternal light. Moreover, I teach the Absolute Law, the law of eternity, through My instrument.

Recognize that no one should hunger or thirst for righteousness. Take the first step toward the kingdom of love by first being righteous to yourself. Practice a positive way of living and thinking and you will very gradually become a righteous person. Then you will bring the righteousness of God into this world; and you will also represent this because you fulfill the will of God, the Lord, out of His love and wisdom.

Recognize: The time is near when what was prophesied takes place. The lion will lie by the lamb, because the people have gained victory over themselves – through Me, their Redeemer. They will form a great family in God and will live in unity with all animals and with all of nature.

Be glad, for the Kingdom of God has drawn close – and, with the Kingdom of God, I, too, your Redeemer and bringer of peace, the ruler of the Kingdom of Peace, of the World Kingdom of Jesus Christ.

"Blessed are the merciful, for they will attain mercy."

The mercy of God corresponds to the gentleness and goodness of God and is, for all souls, the gate to the perfection of life. The people who have unfolded in their souls all seven basic powers of life – the law, from order to mercy – through Me, the Christ, who lives in the Father-Mother-God, will, as pure spirit beings, again enter the selfless love, through the gate of mercy. They will go into the Kingdom of God, into the heavens, and will live in peace. The seventh basic power, the mercy – called kindness and gentleness in the Spirit of God – is the gate to the eternal Being. All people who practice being merciful will also attain mercy and will stand by those who are on the way to mercy.

Recognize that the path to the heart of God is the path of the individual in community with those of like mind. For God is unity, and unity in God is community in and with God and with one's neighbor.

The one who has taken the first steps on the path to perfection will fulfill the commandment of unity: One for all, Christ – and all for One, Christ.

As revealed, the Sermon on the Mount is, the path of evolution toward the inner life. All those who are further ahead on this path of unfoldment towards the heart of God help, in turn, those who are only starting the path. In and over all, shines the Christ, who I Am.

"Blessed are the pure in heart, for they will behold God."

The pure heart is the pure soul which has risen once again to be an absolute spirit being through Me, the Christ in the Father-Mother-God.

The pure souls that have again become beings of the heavens are then the image of the eternal Father once more, and behold the Eternal face to face again. At the same time, they see, live and hear the law of the eternal Father, because they have again become spirit of His Spirit – the eternal law itself.

As long as people and souls still have to listen for the Spirit of God in themselves, they are not yet spirit of His Spirit, not yet the law of love and of life itself.

However, the one who has again become the law of love and life beholds the eternal Father face to face and is in constant conscious communication with Him. He also perceives the law of God, the life from God, as a whole, because he himself is the life and the love, and moves in them. Whoever moves in the Absolute Law of

God has also opened it up completely – from order all the way to mercy. All the seven basic powers of infinity serve him, because he is in absolute unity and harmony with all Being.

"Blessed are the peacemakers, for they will be called children of God."

According to their sense, these words mean: Blessed are those who keep peace. They will also bring true peace to this Earth, because they have become peaceful within themselves. They are consciously the children of God.

Many of the sons and daughters of God who bear peace in themselves and bring it into the world are the incarnated beings who are in the mission of God, fighting for the New Era, so that the spiritual humanity may emerge which lives in the Kingdom of Peace of Jesus Christ, in the Era of Light.

Words from the ruler of the Kingdom of Peace on Earth to the people of the New Era:

You people in the New Era, in the ever more light-filled Kingdom of Peace of Jesus Christ in coming, you who read this book, "This Is My Word," realize that the pioneers of Christ had to fight against the satanic on several fronts at the same time, in order to help the proclaimed Kingdom of God on Earth to make its breakthrough.

And so, you are living in peace, in Me, the Christ, your divine brother, the ruler of the Kingdom of Peace.

But those souls which did not let themselves be grasped by the Sermon on the Mount, the path into the inner life, are living and acting behind the wall of fog. They still live in the prison of their human ego. As human beings, they did not want to hear the call of the pilgrims to the heart of God. They kept their ears and their hearts closed to the truth and hid themselves behind their human ego, behind their concepts, opinions and theological views. Even during the period of preparation from the old to the New Era, the Era of Light, they remained Pharisees, hypocrites, persecutors and slanderers.

Know that the light of redemption shines in all souls up to the fourth level of purification. So these souls, too, are not lost. Many pure spirit beings are active behind the wall of fog in the name of the Lord. Among them are also many sons and daughters of God who, in different earthly garments and at various epochs, paved the way on Earth for Me, the Christ, into the increasingly light-filled Kingdom of Peace in coming. There, in the soul realms, they continue to act in selfless service for their neighbors. The righteous men and women who brought the law of love and of life into this world had a very difficult time during that epoch [1989].

Recognize, you brothers and sisters who are now living in the Kingdom of God on earth: The pioneers of Christ for the New Era also took a stand against the satanic and demonic powers during that great turn of time from the old era, characterized by materialism, to the New Era, the Era of Light.

"Blessed are those who suffer persecution for righteousness' sake, for theirs is the Kingdom of God."

What else happened during that period of preparation [1989]? The pioneers of Christ for the New Era suffered persecution for the sake of the Kingdom of God on Earth. They were despised and slandered by Pharisees and scribes, by churchmen and all those servile to the churchmen. The truth was deliberately placed in a false light and distorted. Those who faithfully fought for the truth were ridiculed for the sake of the truth. People who had Me, Christ, only on their lips, but not in their hearts, preached against them in their churches and outside the church walls as well, they slandered and discriminated against them. They were insulted and accused of false teachings.

Because they themselves did not live what I had commanded them as Jesus of Nazareth, the sham Christians denied that the true followers of Christ were Christians. Just as it was during My time as Jesus, they may have very well preached from their Bibles and piously affected a belief in Me before the people – and were, however, the wolves in sheep's clothing. For they did not do what I commanded the people: to love one another selflessly, as I love them; that is why they are Pharisees and hypocrites. And whoever disregards the commandment to love one's enemy disregards the Christ, who I Am.

May the one who reads this later remember the pioneers of Christ, who prepared the Earth and the atmosphere of the Earth for the New Era. They brought a part of the eternal law of radiation to the Earth and into its atmosphere. Remember them in love, because many of them will no longer go into the earthly garment, to live and be active in the Kingdom of Peace on Earth. They continue to fight in the spheres of purification. They struggle for the souls, so that these, too, can become free from their sins and can enter into the glory, which I Am in the Father.

Recognize that what the souls on Earth did not clear up they take with them behind the wall of fog. There, they must recognize and expiate what they had caused in the earthly garment. The soul which, as a human being, did not attain self-recognition, and therefore did not atone, continues, as a soul, to vegetate in a somnambulistic state, as it were, behind the wall of fog, just as it did in the earthly garment – which it called life. Many who were once hypocrites and Pharisees in an earthly garment again slander their fellow brothers and sisters in the soul realms; there, too, they ridicule them and deny that they are Christians, thus wanting to place themselves in a good light. This will take place until they recognize – most probably under the greatest suffering and pain – what they had caused and in whose hearts Christ truly is risen.

According to the cosmic law of attraction, the soul will experience on its soul body what it has caused in its earthly garment to its fellow man and did not clear up. The soul sees its sins in the form of pictures and, at the same time, experiences in its own soul body the suffering and torment of its neighbors, which it had inflicted upon them as a human being. The sins now active in the soul will keep affecting it, until the soul repents from the heart, asks for forgiveness and is willing to forgive its neighbor. Only then, is the sinful energy transformed into divine power and the soul becomes more light-filled and pure.

Pray for those who continue acting behind the wall of fog as they once did in the earthly garment on earth! Pray that they recognize themselves and atone. Many of the slanderers will have to recognize, experience and possibly endure in their souls the suffering and pain of the pioneers until it has become a certainty to them that I, Christ, was with the pioneers, with My brothers and sisters, and that now I Am with them as their divine brother.

Pray that they recognize and feel in time that they were servile to the dark forces in the unlawful and power-hungry world! The darkness even abused My name in vain, in order to lead the people astray and make the work of the pioneers difficult, the work of the sons and daughters of God on Earth, in the vineyard of the Lord.

Recognize that the one who followed Me was not respected by the worldlings, because I, too, as Jesus, was held in disdain by them. At all times, people who stepped into the true following of the Nazarene had to endure and suffer a great deal.

However, many of the pioneers for the New Era unshakably led the way and stayed in My footsteps. Remember those courageous men and women who waged a righteous battle for the New Era with an unshakable faith in Me.

Rejoice, you, who live in the New Era, in the Kingdom of Peace, that becomes of ever lighter substance. You are united with them. In the great turn of time, many of you were as pioneers in the earthly garment, to attain the breakthrough for the Kingdom of God. The fight and the victory for Me, the Christ, remained in your souls as memory. Some of you intuitively sense that you participated as pioneers in that epoch. You also sense that, at that time, the causes became effective more quickly and the positive, the Era of Light rose mightily – the era of Christ in which you are now living again in a garment of finer substance.

5. *Woe unto you who are rich! For you have received your consolation in this life. Woe unto you who are sated, for you will hunger. Woe unto you who laugh now, for you will mourn and weep. Woe unto you when all men speak well of you, for so did their forefathers with the false prophets.* (Chap. 25:5)

I, Christ, explain, correct
and deepen the word:

"Woe unto you who are rich, for you have received your consolation in this life."

People who look upon their wealth as their property are poor in spirit. Many who are rich in earthly goods were given in the cradle the spiritual task for their earthly life, to be an example to those rich people who tie themselves to their wealth with hardened, relentless hearts and whose sole thinking and striving consist in increasing this wealth for themselves. A person who is rich in earthly goods and has recognized that his wealth is a gift – which he has received from God only to bring it into the great whole for the well-being of everyone and to administer it in the right way for all – is the one who actualizes the law of equality, freedom, unity and brotherhood. He contributes as a selfless giver so that the poor do not live in privation and the rich in luxury.

In this way, a balance will gradually be established, an upper middle class for all those who are willing to selflessly fulfill the law "pray and work." Thus, very gradually the true humanity of a community arises, whose members do not collect personal earthly riches, but rather consider everything to be common property given to them by God.

If a rich person considers money and property as his own and is esteemed in the world because of his wealth, then – as the effect of his causes – he will live in poor countries in subsequent earthly lives and there, he will beg for the bread that, as a rich man, he once denied the poor. This will happen as long as such incarnations are still possible.

The soul of such a rich person will also find no rest in the spheres of purification. The souls that are poor in light and had to endure suffering and hunger in the earthly garment because of him will recognize him again as the one who denied them what could have helped them out of the entanglement of the human ego. Many will accuse him and then his soul itself will feel how they suffered and hungered. In this way, a soul that was rich and esteemed as a human being in the earthly garment may suffer great need; this need is much greater than if it had had to beg for bread in the earthly garment.

Recognize that according to the laws of the Eternal, everyone who selflessly keeps the commandment "pray and work" is due the same; for God gives everyone what he needs and beyond that. However, as long as this commandment is not yet observed by all people, there will be the so-called rich on Earth. It is their task to divide their accumulated wealth and to live just as those who selflessly fulfill the commandment "pray and work." If in this way, they think of the welfare of all and not of their own, the inner wealth will gradually turn without and no person will hunger or live in want.

Woe to you, you rich ones, you who call your money and property your own and make your neighbor work so that your wealth may increase! I say to you, that you will not behold the throne of God, but will continue to live where the feet of God are – on Earth, again and again in earthly garments, as long as this is still possible. Even if you promote social service establishments, but you yourselves are so much wealthier than those who are supported thereby, then you are nevertheless servile to the satan of the senses, who wants the differences between rich and poor.

Through these differences, power and subservience, envy and hatred emerge. These give rise to dispute and wars. For this reason those who cling to their wealth, even though they now and then think of the social good, serve the satan of the senses and act against the law of life: against equality, freedom, unity and brotherliness.

The one who considers money and property as his own and hoards them for himself, instead of letting these material energies flow, is, according to the law of life, a thief, for he denies his neighbors a part of their spiritual heritage. For everything is energy. The one who ties it up through "me" and "mine" acts against the law, which is flowing energy.

"Woe unto you who are sated, for you will hunger."

The wealthy, sated man who fills only "his" barns is empty at heart. He knows only the mine and thine. His senses and thoughts revolve around "my" property, "my" possessions, "my" bread, "my" food. "All this belongs to me" – this is his world. Such a person will one day hunger and live in want until he realizes that everything is the Being. Everything belongs to God and to all people who strive to do the works of God: to fulfill selfless love and the law of life for the Earth, "pray and work."

People who speak only of mine and thine are light-poor people who already in this incarnation are preparing another sojourn on Earth or a long pilgrimage of their soul in the realm of the souls and, in both cases, in the garment of a beggar.

The soul that is dazzled by material things unconsciously hungers for light, because it is poor in light. It compulsively tries to compensate for this with outer things, such as earthly wealth, greed, gluttony, alcoholism or other cravings and pleasures. It is insatiable.

"Woe unto you who laugh now, for you will mourn and weep."

The one who laughs and mocks his neighbor will one day be very sad and will cry over himself – because he failed to acknowledge those whom he made fun of and mocked. He will have to recognize that, in the end, he had laughed at, scorned and ridiculed himself. For the one who judges and condemns his neighbor, who laughs at him, who scorns and ridicules him, judges, condemns, laughs at, scorns and ridicules Me, the Christ.

Recognize that whoever sins against the least of My brothers sins against the law of life and will have to suffer under this. At the same time, he has bound himself to the one he held in disdain. Therefore, be on your guard and practice self-control. It is not what enters through your mouth that soils your soul, rather it is what goes out from your mouth that burdens soul and person.

"Woe unto you when all men speak well of you, for so did their forefathers with the false prophets."

If you flatter your fellow man, so that he praises you and holds you in esteem, then you are like the counterfeiters who, for the sake of their own advantage, pay with false money .

It was and is similar with the false prophets, as well. They were and are esteemed by the people because they flattered the people and because those of high standing among the people were in league with them, having promised themselves personal profit and gain through this.

Recognize, you people in the Kingdom of Peace, that in the sinful world many righteous prophets and enlightened men and women, as well, were slandered and persecuted by the rich and the powerful of this world, by church leaders and their adherents, and many of them were tortured and killed. At all times, the satanic used as tools those who wanted to keep and increase their earthly wealth for themselves, who strove for power and those who were servile to the rich and powerful, as well.

You should know this, so that you can understand why the old sinful world perished in such a terrible way.

In addition, false prophets were also those who may very well have preached the gospel of love, but themselves did not live accordingly. And they were also all those who called themselves "Christian" and behaved in an un-christian way in their life. They were often lauded for their eloquence and were honored and praised because of their wealth and prestige.

Oh see, nevertheless and in the course of time, all true prophets and enlightened ones contributed to the fact that the crystal of inner life, with its many facets of eternal truth, sparkled and shone more and more. In this way, the Kingdom of God on Earth was very gradually built up.

It is up to you, dear brothers and sisters in the Kingdom of Peace, to cherish, guard and preserve this now perfect, sparkling and shining crystal, the inner life, like a precious flower. It is the law of love and wisdom of God, His order, His will, His wisdom, His earnestness, His kindness, His infinite love-radiation, and His gentleness.

6. *You are the salt of the Earth, for every sacrifice must be salted with salt, but if the salt has lost its taste, with what shall one salt? Henceforth, it is good for nothing, but to be poured out and trodden underfoot. (Chap. 25:6)*

I, Christ, explain, correct
and deepen the word:

The righteous are the salt of the Earth.

They will repeatedly point out the deplorable state of affairs of this world and lay their finger on wounds of

282

sin. For much damage has been and is being done in this still sinful world – and many people became victims for the sake of the gospel.

The righteous who became victims shall be rehabilitated by righteous men and women, for everything shall become manifest through the salt of the Earth. Now, in this time of radical change from the old sinful world to the New Era, the Era of Light, the righteous will bring injustice to light and will cause it to become evident, so that those who have done wrong may recognize themselves and atone for it.

However, you righteous ones, who are the salt of the Earth, beware that the salt does not lose its taste, that you therefore remain in righteousness and do not let yourselves be led astray. For who shall bring righteousness into this world, and who shall point out the deplorable state of affairs and sins that people have created? Surely, only those who know My name and are recorded in the book of the lamb.

The one who is no longer the salt of the Earth falls among those who have and are abusing My name for their own purposes and have persecuted, slandered and killed the righteous.

When the salt of the Earth loses its taste and the person disregards his neighbor, he will succumb to his own causes; figuratively speaking, he will trample himself underfoot. His un-expiated causes will then bring about illness, infirmity and grief. The light-poor soul will live in want and will feel on its own soul body what it has caused to its neighbor.

7. You are the light of the world. The city that is built on a hill cannot be concealed. Neither does one light a candle and put it under a bushel, but on a candlestick; and it gives light to all who are in the house. Let your light so shine before the people, that they may see your good works and praise your Father who is in heaven. (Chap. 25:7)

I, Christ, explain, correct
and deepen the word:

I Am the light of the world.

Through My faithful ones, through men and women who fulfill the will of the Eternal, it now radiates more intensely into this world.

I have put My light on the lighting of divine wisdom and justice, so that it may shine for all those who are of good will.

My brothers and sisters in the Kingdom of Peace of Jesus Christ, it is important for you to know the following: I very gradually brought My light to shine in the incarnated part-ray of divine wisdom. I called the human child in whom the female principle of the cherub of divine wisdom was incarnated, and informed her of her spiritual mission, which then became more and more manifest in her soul.

Know that when the spiritual mission begins to pulsate in the incarnated soul, the law wants the human being's attention to be drawn to the mission and to be asked whether he accepts what is active in his soul.

The human child accepted it in the following sense: Eternal One, I am Your handmaid; Your will be done in me.

Thereupon, the great all-encompassing spiritual mission began for her, to be My prophetess and emissary for the whole Earth. My light became ever brighter and more powerful in her soul, until it totally irradiated the person. When the person was also fortified enough to give My holy, eternal word, I sent her into this world. Guided by My Spirit, she visited countries and cities on several continents. Through her, I gave My holy word in countless revelations.

In many facets of the eternal truth, My light radiated into this world, onto this Earth. It is the wisdom from God.

In the mighty turn of time, more and more hearts were kindled by My light. The people recognized the eternal truth in My words. Ever more people walked the Inner Path and accepted the gift of life, the teachings and lessons from the eternal truth, in order to draw closer to God, the eternal Being.

Many men and women became My faithful ones, for they fulfilled the will of God. They became brothers and sisters in My Spirit and became the pioneers for the New Era, who laid the foundation of the Kingdom of God on Earth and began to build upon it.

Ever more people became seekers of light. On the path to inner life, they kindled their inner flame with My light more and more and united with the pioneers, in order to work with them for the New Era.

Furthermore, know that from the deep teachings which I gave through the incarnated divine wisdom, they recognized the eternal laws and abided more and more in the righteousness of God.

At all times, the pioneers also had some defeats to overcome. However, in each defeat they recognized their own weakness and then conquered it with Me, the Christ. They repented of their unlawful behavior, praised and glorified God for His untiring guidance – also out of their defeats. In this way, the men and women became stronger in Me, the Christ.

The victory in Me, the Christ, they did not count as their victory. They thanked, praised and glorified the eternal name and rejoiced that the Eternal through Me, and I through and with them, could accomplish what needed to be done for the Era of Light in which you now live.

Through the actualization of the eternal laws, the faithful men and women drew nearer and nearer to Me and became aware of My guidance. Through the incarnated part-ray of divine wisdom, the Eternal, God, the Father of us all, and I, Christ, spoke to them. We admonished the pioneers over and over again to overcome their still existing faults. At the same time, My Father and I, Christ, led them to self-recognition – in accordance with the law of free will – by bringing it to their attention as soon as they had violated the eternal law. We explained to them how they could make amends for their faults. In all essential questions and situations the

Eternal and I, Christ, revealed ourselves and guided them to the law-abiding answer and solution. They cleared up immediately what needed to be dealt with, so that what was not in accordance with the eternal law could be cancelled.

The time of the pioneers was a great time, for the pioneers spoke with God, who gave His revelations to them through the great light of divine wisdom. Through this deep link with the Father-Mother-God and with Me, their Redeemer and divine brother, they increased in strength in their inner being. They became ever more filled with love and wisdom.

What I reveal here in this book "This Is My Word" took place in an evolutionary process over generations. The first pioneers for the New Era did not yet recognize the great light that lived among them, because the incarnated part-ray of divine wisdom behaved as a sister among brothers and sisters, without distinguishing herself. This modest sisterliness, which sprang from great humility and reverence before God, then also brought about true brotherliness and sisterliness among some of the pioneers. For them, the high bearer of light was a sister who could advise them in every situation and circumstance of life, because her spiritual body was one with God, the life.

You, who live in the New Era, recognize that all this, and much more that was not recorded, had to happen, so that My light could shine more and more brightly in this world. It shone mightily into the turn of time and prepared the New Era through My faithful ones.

The pioneers in Me were the spiritual task force that fought according to the law of life, of love and of free will.

After making the covenant with God, the Eternal, they lived and were active out of the central primordial light of the Covenant Community New Jerusalem in the emerging New Israel. In the course of further generations, emerged, from the Covenant Community New Jerusalem, the mighty city of Jerusalem on the Earth, the substance of which was becoming ever finer.

The city of New Jerusalem that is built on the hills cannot be concealed. It shines and radiates as the central primordial light for all the Earth.

From the city that is built on the hills, from the New Jerusalem, impulses are given for the entire World Kingdom of Jesus Christ. The city of New Jerusalem is the central coordinating point for the Kingdom of Peace of Jesus Christ. So it was revealed – and so it is.

8. You should not think that I Am come to destroy the law or the prophets; I Am not come to destroy, but to fulfill. For verily, I say to you: Till heaven and Earth pass away, not the smallest letter nor one dot will pass away from the law or the prophets until all that is fulfilled. But behold, One greater than Moses is here, and He will give you the higher law, even the perfect law, and you shall obey this law. (Chap. 25:8)

I, Christ, explain, correct
and deepen the word:

As Jesus of Nazareth, I taught parts from the perfect law, from the Absolute Law, to the men and women who followed Me and all those who listened to Me. I also explained to them that the Absolute Law of love radiates into the law of sowing and reaping; for the Spirit is omnipresent and is also active in the law of sowing and reaping, the law of the Fall.

Through Me as Jesus of Nazareth, the incarnated Christ, and through all the true prophets of God that followed, the Eternal taught and admonished His children in the imperfect spheres that the law of the Fall, the law of sowing and reaping, is constantly active. The one who does not stop and think it over and does not turn back in time will have to bear his causes as effects. The Eternal was and is making every effort, also in today's time [1989], to lead His human children and all souls to His heart, to the law of eternal love, before the harvest – the effects of the causes created by them – falls upon them. The Eternal led and leads them to self-recognition through Me, Christ. He gave and gives them the strength to clear up what they recognized and recognize as a sin and shortcoming.

In Jesus of Nazareth, the Christ, who I Am, came to this Earth, into this world, to teach, as the Son of Man, the eternal law to the people and to live it as an example. This was done so that the people would recognize the path to the eternal Father and fulfill His law – and

289

thus enter again into the eternal homes that He keeps ready for all His children.

The people who followed My example during My lifetime on Earth and who actualized the eternal laws, were My true followers.

In the generations that followed, there existed a Christianity and a sham Christianity: the true followers who freely followed Me, the Christ, by keeping the laws of the Sermon on the Mount – and the sham Christians who just talked about Me, the Christ, but acted against the laws. In addition, there was the so-called coerced following of Christ: This resulted from the forced Christianization of the masses carried out by the churches.

Recognize that there is no coercion in the eternal law. God, the Eternal, has given all His children free will. The one who freely decides has, through his free decision, the strength for what characterizes true Christianity: equality, freedom, unity, brotherliness and justice. All coercion originates from the law of sowing and reaping, also called the law of the Fall. It is given to man to freely choose his spiritual path. I, Christ, offered and offer the path to the heart of God, but I force no man to walk it. Whoever forces his neighbor lives himself under the coercion of the law of the Fall and personifies the Fall thought.

Several so-called Christian denominations force their faithful into baptism with water. Even the little children whose free will is not yet developed and who therefore cannot yet decide for themselves are forced, through baptism by water, into the membership of a church and thereby induced to participate in its other rituals.

This is an infringement of the individual's free will and, a forced Christianization, so to speak. These are things that take place within the law of the Fall.

People who do not freely accept and receive Me, Christ, in themselves out of the deepest inner conviction, often have great difficulties in correctly understanding and accepting the Ten Commandments, the excerpts from the eternal laws. This is because these have been pushed into the background through many externalizations, dogmatic ceremonies, rites, customs and cults. Within the denominations, these externalizations became the most important thing, yet, they have nothing in common with inner Christianity, the Inner Religion, but originated, in part, directly from the times of polytheism and idolatry, and thereby from the region of the Fall planes.

Only when people freely break away from the dogmas and rigid ceremonies that have been forced upon them, from rites and cults, as well as from their own concepts of God, can they gradually be guided into their inner being, into their true being. There, in their inner being, they then discover themselves as true beings in God and as inhabitants of the Kingdom of God, which is within, in every person. This inner life is the true religion, the inner religion.

Recognize that the eternal, all-embracing, universal law, the law of the heavens, is irrevocable. It is the law of all pure Being. The law of sowing and reaping emerged through the Fall and can be dissolved only through the actualization of the eternal laws. However, it cannot be evaded. The law of sowing and reaping remains active in each soul, until the sins are recognized, cleared up, atoned for and given over to Me, the Christ of God. The Fall law in the soul is then cancelled. The soul is then freed from its impurity for the most part. It becomes again the pure being in God that lives the Absolute Law, since it strives again towards the absolute, all-ruling law of love and of life.

The law of sowing and reaping is valid until all that is unlawful is settled and transformed into positive energy. and every being lives again in God, out of which it came forth. To the same degree in which all beings from God have again been received into the heart of God, into the Absolute Law, so will all purification planes – all part-material and material planes, including the Earth – transform into cosmic energy and again vibrate in the Absolute Law. The Fall law is then abolished, and the love of God is conscious and all-prevailing in all Being, in every being.

Not one "dot" will be removed from the eternal law, which the true prophets brought before and after Me, and which I, as Jesus of Nazareth, lived as an example.

When it says "not the smallest letter," then it is referring to a single aspect of the eternal truth, not the letter and the word of human beings as such. Human words are often only symbols that conceal what is deep within. Only when the person is able to feel into the language of symbols does he recognize the truth and the meaning of life, which lies deeply hidden in human words.

"The higher law" is the step into the perfect law. This will be taught – to the mostly pure beings, that have come from Earth and the soul realms – in the preparation planes, which are situated before the gate of heaven. The higher law is the last level of instruction before the gate of heaven. It shows the mostly pure beings how the lawful radiation is reactivated in the spirit body, so that it can be applied in infinity.

As Jesus of Nazareth, I taught parts of the perfect law, the Absolute Law. The whole truth still had to remain concealed from the people in those days, because they were still too attached to their belief in gods and too oriented towards the various trends of belief of that time. For that reason, I spoke in the following sense: When the time has come, I, the Spirit of truth, will lead you into all truth.

On the hill of Golgotha – this means, the place of the skulls – I was crucified by the Romans, because the Jewish people had not accepted and received Me as the Messiah. Although I preached, taught, healed and gave many signs of My deity, up and down the valley of the Jordan, the stubborn Jewish people remained submissive to the ministers of the temple, thus becoming partly responsible for the death of Jesus of Nazareth.

With the words in the sense of "It is finished," the spark of redemption entered all burdened and fallen souls. Thus, I became and I Am the Redeemer of all men and souls.

As the Christ of God, I acted and continue to act. In all generations up to the present time [1989], I gave and give My revelations through true instruments of God, through people whose souls are for the most part purified.

During this mighty turn of time, in which the Era of Light draws ever closer to man, I teach the eternal law in all its facets, and ever more people walk the path within, to the love of God.

Now the time is come, which I announced as Jesus of Nazareth: "Today you are not yet able to bear it, that is, to grasp it; yet when the Spirit of truth comes, He will guide you into all truth." Now, in spirit, I Am among My own, the faithful pilgrims to the eternal Being, to the consciousness of My Father; and I teach them the absolute, eternal law, so that also those who will live in the Kingdom of Peace may fulfill it and thereby live in Me and I through them.

My words are life, the eternal law. They are preserved in the pilgrims to the eternal life and in many written records as well – as it is with this book – for the Kingdom of Peace of Jesus Christ.

Recognize that only the eternal law of love makes people free – not the law of sowing and reaping. This brings them only suffering, illness, misery and infirmity.

9. The one who breaks one of these commandments, which He gives, and teaches the people to do the same will be called the least in the Kingdom of Heaven. But the one who keeps and teaches them, the same will be called great in the Kingdom of Heaven. (Chap. 25:9)

I, Christ, explain, correct
and deepen the word:

The Ten Commandments that God gave to His human children through Moses are excerpts from the eternal law of life and of love. Whoever violates these commandments, who only teaches them to his fellow man but does not keep them himself, is a false teacher. He sins against the Holy Spirit. This is the greatest sin. This counterfeiter uses the love of God, the law of life, for his own purpose. Thereby, he misuses the eternal law. Every misuse is robbery; and every robber is a hunted and hounded person who, sooner or later, is caught and convicted by his own deeds, by his own causes. For God is a just God; everything will be revealed through Him, the good as well as the less good and the evil.

However, the one who keeps the law of love and of life, that is, who fulfills it in his daily life, and teaches people what he himself has actualized is a true spiritual teacher. He offers the bread of the heavens to the people and will thus satisfy many. The one who gives out of his own fulfillment is filled by divine wisdom and strength and, when the time has come, will shine like a star in heaven. For the God-filled person draws from the stream of salvation and selflessly gives to those who hunger and thirst for righteousness.

Recognize: Through such righteous men and women, the eternal law of love and of life comes into this world. And so, the one who keeps and teaches the eternal law will be called great in the Kingdom of Heaven; this means that he will harvest a rich reward in heaven.

10. Verily, those who believe and obey will save their souls, and those who do not obey will lose them. For I say to you: If your righteousness is not greater than that of the scribes and Pharisees, you will not enter the Kingdom of Heaven. (Chap. 25:10)

I, Christ, explain, correct
and deepen the word:

The statement, "... those who believe and obey will save their souls, and those who do not obey will lose them" means that the one who believes and follows the laws of God will deliver his soul from the wheel of reincarnation, which will continue to draw him into the flesh until he has atoned for all that repeatedly drew him into incarnation.

Recognize that the mere belief in the law of life is not enough. Only the belief in the life and the actualization of the laws of life lead man and soul out of the wheel of reincarnation.

The one who does not keep the laws of God betrays God and sells his soul to the darkness. Thereby, he covers the light of his soul, his true life. This person then lives in sin and his soul lives in the slumber of this world. The law of incarnation, the wheel of reincarnation which draws the soul into incarnation, will still be in effect for some time, so that the incarnated soul may recognize that it is not of this world, but is in the earthly garment to discard what is human – and to uncover what is divine: its true eternal life.

Not all who know the written characters interpret them solely according to the letter – but according to the meaning. For this reason, it should say: If your righteousness is not greater than that of the many scribes – who pretend to be righteous and teach My law, but do not keep it themselves – you will not enter the Kingdom of Heaven.

Therefore, do not tie yourselves to the opinions and views of people. Actualize what you have recognized from the law of life; then you will recognize the further steps to the higher spiritual principles.

Recognize that the justice of God is the love and wisdom of God. The one who does not bring them to unfoldment in himself does not radiate them; he neither perceives the depth of eternal Being nor fathoms his true life. His earthly life is in a state of vegetation. Vegetating, he passes by the true life. On this side of life as well as in the beyond, he is the spiritually dead one. Neither in this earthly existence nor in the life beyond does he have the right orientation, because he did not live according to the laws of life. He is not wise, but only passes on the knowledge he has stored. Thus, he becomes an adherent of sin and finally, a sinner. He acts against the eternal law and in this way falls deeper and deeper into the law of sowing and reaping.

11. Therefore, when you offer your gift on the altar and remember that your brother has something against you, leave your gift before the altar, go there first and reconcile with your brother, and then come and offer your gift. (Chap 25:11)

I, Christ, explain, correct
and deepen the word:

"... when you offer your gift on the altar and remember that your brother has something against you, leave your gift before the altar, go there first and reconcile with your brother, and then come and offer your gift" means: When you devote your life to Me, the Christ, and want to relinquish your faults and sins to Me, and you recognize that you have not yet reconciled with your neighbor, then leave your sin lying before the inner altar for the moment. Go to your neighbor and reconcile with him – and, if you no longer want to do the same or similar thing which led to the sin, then lay your sin upon the altar. The altar is in the innermost part of your temple of flesh and bone. The spirit of love and life will then transform the sin into strength and life. For you will attain liberation from that which you freely, willingly and without pressure give over to Me, thus no longer doing the same or similar thing. Your soul will then increasingly receive the light from Me.

Take heed of the following lawful principle: When you have sinned against your neighbor exclusively in thoughts, through unloving, envious, revengeful, jealous or hate-filled thoughts, then do not go to him to talk about it. Know that your neighbor does not know your world of thoughts. If you let it become manifest in words, he will think about it. Come solely to Me, the Christ, who I Am in your inner being, and repent of your thoughts and send at the same time positive, selfless thoughts to the soul of your neighbor, thoughts of asking for forgiveness and thoughts of inner unity. Then I will undo what was caused in thoughts. And if you no longer think the same or similar thing, then it is already forgiven you.

Recognize that if you speak to your neighbor of your human thoughts, you might possibly stir up in him some human aspect that is just in the process of transformation. It could then break out once more in your neighbor. He then begins to think and speak negatively again and burdens himself anew.

The law says that through your wrong behavior not only the one who is stimulated to think about it again burdens himself, but you, too, burden yourself when you express your thoughts and, through this, activate in your neighbor the humanness that was in the process of transformation.

However, if unlawful things leave your mouth in that you accuse and insult your neighbor and speak ill of him – even if he hears it from a second or third party – then go to him and ask him for forgiveness. If he has forgiven you, so has the eternal heavenly Father in Me, the Christ, also forgiven you. But if he has not forgiven you, then your heavenly Father in Me, the Christ, will not be able to forgive you either. However, the love of the Father-Mother-God will touch the still rigid heart more and more, so that the person think things over sooner and forgive you, and so that God in Me, the Christ, can also forgive you; then all that was once unlawful is annulled and transformed.

Beware of your own tongue! For the unlawful things that leave your mouth can do much greater harm to your neighbor and to yourself than your thoughts, which you have recognized and relinquished to Me, the Christ in you, in time – before they have taken effect.

Recognize a further spiritual principle: You cannot see nor hear thoughts – and yet they are there. They vibrate in the atmosphere and can influence the one who thinks the same or like things. If you relinquish them to Me in time, they are cancelled – unless the soul of your neighbor has already registered them in itself. Then you will be guided in such a way that you will be able to do good to the person of whom you thought negatively. And if you do good selflessly, without expressing your earlier thoughts, then what you unlawfully thought about your neighbor and which he already had absorbed into his soul will be erased there. And what your soul had radiated is erased in you, as well.

12. Reach agreement with your adversary quickly, while you are still on your way with him, lest one day your adversary hand you over to the judge, and the judge hand you over to the guard, and you will not come out until you have paid the last penny.

13. You have heard that it has been said: You shall love your neighbor and hate your enemy. But I say to you who listen: Love your enemies, do good to those who hate you. (Chap. 25:12-13)

I, Christ, explain, correct
and deepen the word:

"Reach agreement with your adversary quickly, while you are still on your way with him" means: Do not let the sin that you have committed against your neighbor linger. Clear it up as quickly as possible, for he is still with you on your path through life in the earthly existence. If his soul has left the Earth, you may have to wait until you can meet him again and can ask him for forgiveness.

Recognize: The judge is the law of sowing and reaping. If it becomes effective, the person will not come out from under it until he has paid the "last penny" – that is, until everything is atoned for that he caused and did not repent of in time .

For this reason, use the chance to ask your neighbor for forgiveness and to forgive him as long as you are still on your way, walking over the Earth with him and the sin has not yet engraved itself into the soul and become a cause. The one who does not forgive nor asks for forgiveness has to bear the effect until he has "paid the last penny."

Therefore, become one with your neighbor as quickly as possible. If the causes – for example, quarrel, resentment or envy – have already taken root in your soul, and if the same has also taken place in the neighbor, whom you are against, then it is possible that your neighbor will not forgive you so quickly – not even when you have recognized your sin and repented. For the guilt complex may have hardened in his soul through the same or a similar way of thinking that you triggered in him. Through your sinful behavior that you nurtured over a longer period of time, he also nursed a grudge against you in his soul – and, like you, too, has thus created an extensive negative energy field, a guilt complex, that now has to be worked on by both of you. Clearing this up can still take place during this earthly existence or even later in the realms of the souls or in further incarnations.

Recognize that before a blow of fate strikes a person, he is admonished by the spirit of life, which is also the life of the soul, and also by his guardian spirit or by people. The admonishments from the spirit are the finest sensations that flow out of the soul or that the guardian spirit lets flow into the person's world of sensations or thoughts. They admonish the person to change his way of thinking or to clear up what he has caused. The eternal spirit of life and the guardian spirit may also stimulate people to go to the one who is on the verge of being struck by a blow of fate. They will then approach the person concerned and will enter a conversation which will spontaneously refer to the matter in question. From this conversation, the cause of the looming fate may be recognized and cleared up.

And so, you can see that the eternal light gives admonishments and indications in manifold ways and means – both to your neighbors with whom you have created causes, as well as to you, yourselves.

Also through impulses by way of the day's events, the person is admonished in time, before what was caused by him breaks in over him as fate.

Anyone who takes such hints seriously and clears up what he recognized as sin, by repenting, forgiving, asking for forgiveness and making amends, need not bear what was caused by him. If the sin is great, then it is possible that he has to bear a part of what wanted to break out of the soul, but not all of it. However, the one who overlooks and fails to heed all the admonishments, because he numbs himself with human things, will have to bear his self-created causes until "the last penny is paid."

The commandment of life reads, "Love your enemies, do good to those who hate you."

Every person should see in every one of his fellow men his neighbor, his brother and his sister. Even in your seeming enemy, you should recognize your neighbor and strive to love him selflessly.

The seeming enemy can even be a good mirror for your self-recognition when you become upset because of the hostility, which may have many faces; for when something on your neighbor upsets you, the same or similar thing exists in you, as well.

However, if you are able to forgive your neighbor who has blamed and accused you without being unduly agitated, no correspondence is in you; that is, you do not have the same or similar thing in you and thus, no resonance for this in your soul. It is possible that, in a former life, you already cleared up and atoned for what you were accused of – or even that you never built it up in your soul. Then, it was only in the soul of the one who thought and spoke against you and accused you. Therefore, if no emotion reverberates in you, if no echo comes from your soul, then you were a mirror for him. Whether he looks into this mirror for his human ego or not – leave that to God and to him, His child.

Recognize that even the mere sight of you stirs his conscience and reflects to him that, for example, he once thought and spoke unlawfully about you. Now he has the chance to clear it up. If he does this, by repenting and henceforth no longer thinking or doing the same or similar thing, then it is removed, that is, transformed, in his soul. Only then will he see you with the eyes of the inner light.

A sign that the unlawful has been transformed into the positive in a soul is the good will and understanding towards one's neighbor.

14. Bless those who curse you and pray for those who abuse you out of wickedness, so that you may be children of your Father who is in heaven and who lets the sun rise on the evil and the good and sends rain on the just and the unjust. (Chap. 25:14)

I, Christ, explain, correct
and deepen the word:

The one who keeps these commandments is just towards his fellow man and, through his life in God, will guide many people to the life in God. God does not punish and chastise His children. This is already said by the words, "... who lets the sun rise on the evil and the good and sends rain on the just and the unjust."

God is the giver of life, because He is the life, Himself. From the eternal law of life, God gave human beings the free will to decide freely for or against Him. Whoever is for Him keeps the eternal laws of love and of life and will also receive the gifts of love and of life from the eternal law. The one who feels, thinks and acts

305

against the eternal law receives what he has sown, that is, what he felt, thought, spoke and did.

Therefore, everyone receives what he himself has sown. The one who sows good seed, that is, who fulfills the laws of God, will also reap good fruits. The one who sows human seeds, which he brings into the field of his soul as human sensations, thoughts, words and deeds, will also harvest the corresponding fruits.

From this, you can see that God does not intervene in the will of man. He is the giver, helper, admonisher, leader and protector of those who endeavor to do His will, because they turn to Him. The one who turns away from Him, by creating his own human law, will also be controlled by his own human "ego-law."

And so, God does not interfere in the law of sowing and reaping. In manifold ways, God offers His help to His children; and those who sincerely pray to Him from their heart and fulfill what I, the Christ in God, My Father, have commanded them – to love one another selflessly – are in God, and God is active through them.

15. *For if you love those who love you, what reward will you have? For sinners also love those who love them. And if you do good to those who do good to you, what reward will you have? For even sinners do the same. And if you greet only your brethren, what more are you doing than the others? Do not even the tax collectors do so? (Chap. 25:15)*

I, Christ, explain, correct
and deepen the word:

Therefore, accept and receive your neighbor in your heart, even if he does not love you, even when he does not stand by you and ignores you, by refusing to greet you. Do love him! Do stand by him selflessly and do greet him – even if it is only in thought, when he does not wish to be greeted with words. Even a greeting from the heart, which is given in thought, enters the soul and brings good fruit at the right time.

Make sure that you act like the sun that gives – whether the person wants to see it or not, whether he wishes for rain or storm, whether he wants the cold or the warmth.

Give selfless love, as the sun gives to the Earth, and respect all people, all Being. Then you will receive your reward in heaven.

Do not flatter people. Do not discriminate, like people who associate only with those who think and act the same way and condemn those who think and act otherwise.

16. *And if you desire something as much as your life, but it leads you away from the truth, let go of it, for it is better to enter life possessing the truth than to lose life and be cast into outer darkness. (Chap. 25:16)*

I, Christ, explain, correct
and deepen the word:

What the person craves for himself personally concerns his person, his base ego. All this is binding. A binding means to be tied to people and things. The one who ties himself to people and things, that is, who is bound to something, reduces the flow of cosmic energies.

If you tie a person to yourself only for your advantage, then, with your self-will, you pursue interests which lead you away from the life in Me, the Christ. You thereby forsake the impersonal selfless life, you entangle yourself in wanting to possess, to be and to have, and become impoverished of the spiritual life in your inner being. If you do not desist in time from wanting to possess, to be and to have, you will lose everything one day.

If you do not recognize yourself in the effects – for example, through the loss of all your worldly goods or in illness or in misery and in suffering – and then do not repent and make amends either, you will wander in the darkness as a soul and as a human being, because you were concerned solely about yourself, about your own personal well-being.

Therefore, recognize yourself every day anew and actualize the laws of God daily, and stop desiring something for your personal ego. Remain truthful – and thus, faithful to the law of God. Then you will enter the life which is your true being – and you will be rich in yourself, because you have opened heaven within you.

The truth which is impersonal cannot flow into the one who is not a vessel of the truth. Such a person is concerned only about himself and accumulates things only for himself. This behavior leads to his turning away from God's eternally flowing power and to the life of a "stagnant pool": Only the unlawful flows into the pool and little flows out. This means that he will feel in his own body what he has accumulated in his stagnant pool.

On the other hand, the eternal truth streams into and through the person who is a vessel of the truth. He receives from God and gives from God and thus becomes the wellspring of life for many. The cosmic energy of life, the source of all Being, streams through all forms of Being and through those human beings and souls who have turned towards God, that is, who have become the vessel of God.

Recognize: The eternally flowing power streams only through the person and the soul who do not accumulate for selfish purposes, but give selflessly. Only through the one who gives selflessly does the stream of God flow unceasingly! If God can flow unhindered through the person, then this person lives in the truth, in God, in the life that lasts eternally. Only such people give from Me, the life, because they are in Me, the life and the truth.

17. And if you desire something which causes an-other pain and sorrow, tear it out of your heart. Only in this way will you attain peace. For it is better to endure sorrow than to inflict it on those who are weaker than you.

18. Be therefore perfect, as your Father in heaven is perfect." (Chap. 25:17-18)

I, Christ, explain, correct
and deepen the word:

Everything that goes out from you and is not divine – like unlawful thoughts, words and deeds – can cause pain and sorrow not only to your neighbor, but also to you, yourself. For what the person sows, he will reap.

The harvest corresponds to the seed. It is always harvested by the one who has sown – not by his neighbor. Your neighbor did not sow your seed, and neither will he reap your harvest.

However, your seeds can have wings – like the seeds of different types of flowers, which, after blooming, are carried away by the wind and take root where they are able to hold fast. So can your thoughts, words and deeds also fall like winged seeds on the field of your neighbor's soul and sprout, if they find the same or si-milar conditions there.

The same or similar thing to what is in you is also in him, if he becomes upset and angry by the words and deeds with which you caused him sorrow. Stimulated by your winged seeds, he thinks, speaks and does the same or similar thing. You, however, you have triggered it and can be called to account for it in the law of sowing and reaping. You are commanded to love your neighbor selflessly and to serve and help him – and not to cause him pain and sorrow by your behavior.

If your neighbor then burdens himself because of your unlawful behavior, because you penetrated the field of his soul and brought causes into vibration, which he later has to bear and from which he has to suffer greatly, then you are bound to him. And if he, too, reacts unlawfully to your behavior, he is, in turn, bound to you. In this or another form of existence, you will have to clear this up together.

Recognize that a small insignificant winged seed of human ego can create a great cause, which already bears its effect in itself.

And so, recognize that every cause must be removed!

A further example: If you send out your negative thoughts, words and deeds like winged seeds and your neighbor hears what you say about him but takes no notice of it, because he has no correspondence to it in the field of his soul, then only you will burden yourself; and you are bound to him – not he to you. Your neighbor can enter heaven because he has not accepted and received your negative seeds, since he did not think or speak the same or similar as you. However, if by your wrong behavior you have set causes into motion in your neighbor that would not have had to come into effect in him, because he would have been able to clear them up later without pain and sorrow, then you are the one who bears the greater guilt and have to bear that part which you have caused to your neighbor.

If, therefore, you have to endure pain and sorrow, do not blame your neighbor for your condition. You yourself are the instigator – and not your neighbor. Your pain and your sorrow are the seeds in your soul that have sprouted – and also show themselves in or on your body as harvest.

Only I, Christ, your Redeemer, can free you from this – and only when you repent and no longer do the same or similar thing. Then the burden is taken from your soul and things will be better for you.

Recognize that the one who realizes that his pain and his sorrow are his own seed and accepts his suffering shows true inner greatness. This is a sign of spiritual growth; spiritual growth gradually leads to perfection.

The pure being is perfect; it is the image of the Father-Mother-God. It lives in God, and God lives through the pure being.

Blessed are those who are pure in heart; for they will behold God – because they have again become images of the heavenly Father. From a pure, devoted heart, flows meekness and humility.

I, Christ, the Redeemer of mankind, lead the ever growing people of God on Earth towards inner purity. The people of God consists [1989] of men and women who resolutely walk the path of love within, and thus follow Me, Christ, the one and only Shepherd. Not all of them will incarnate again in the generations to come, but many will live in the spirit of love and will work in the spirit for the great whole and for the Kingdom of Peace of Jesus Christ.

Oh recognize, you who live in the Kingdom of Peace: Many of you were already there as human beings, in the time of the pioneers. And as pioneers, many a one of you maintained the unity in God with the pioneers and walked, together with them, the path within. By so doing, you set aside much humanness, whereby your souls became more and more imbued with the light of truth. Upon disincarnating, your souls then took this light of truth into the higher planes of light. From there, you then returned with the light of truth, in order to live and be active in the earthly garment, in the Kingdom of Peace of Jesus Christ.

The light of truth now radiates once more through your new earthly bodies. In this earthly existence you are now fulfilling what you acquired in previous existences: the light of My light and the power of My power – the law of life. Filled with the spirit of God, your soul is now active through its new earthly garment in the Kingdom of Peace of Jesus Christ, in which I Am the ruler and the life.

CHAPTER 26

Sermon on the Mount
(Part 2)

The first steps on the Inner Path,
a process of evolution into selflessness (2). Prayer as self-
display or inspired prayer (4). Truly wise ones rest in them-
selves and do not argue (5). About the Lord's Prayer (6).
Forgiving and asking for forgiveness; the justice and grace
of God (7-9). The earthly death – The consciousness of the
soul afterwards – The mourners – Re-embodiment – Bind-
ings between human beings and souls – The correct attitude
(10-11). Collecting treasures – The end of incarnations in
the New Era (12-14). Worrying about oneself, planning with
confidence in God – The right way of praying and working –
All Being is in God's keeping (15-18)

1. "Take heed that you do not give your alms before
people, in order to be seen by them. Otherwise you
have no reward from your Father in heaven. When you
give alms, you should not sound a trumpet before you,
as the hypocrites do in the synagogues and in the
streets, so that they may be praised by the people. Verily, I say to you, they already have their reward.

2. But when you give alms, do not let your left hand
know what your right hand is doing, so that your alms
remain secret; and the One who sees into the secret will
publicly acknowledge it. (Chap. 26:1-2)

I, Christ, explain, correct
and deepen the word:

The Sermon on the Mount that is lived is the inner path to the heart of God. What a person does not do selflessly, he does for himself. Selflessness is the love for God. Self-interest is human love. The one who does good for his neighbor only when the latter thanks him for it and praises his good deeds has not done it for his neighbor, but for himself. The gratitude and the praise are then his reward. He is thus already rewarded and will receive no further reward from God. Only selflessness will be rewarded by God. Selflessness grows and matures only in the person who has taken the first steps towards the kingdom of the inner being, that is, who has actualized.

The first steps towards this are to monitor and control one's thoughts: Replace egocentric, negative, brooding or passionate thoughts with positive, helpful, joyful, noble thoughts and with thoughts about the good in a person and in all that you encounter. Then you will gradually bring your senses under control. You will then also no longer want anything from your neighbor and will no longer expect anything from him. In the further course of the Inner Path, you will speak only what is positive and essential. Thereby, you gain control over your human ego because you have learned to rest in yourself. Then your soul becomes more and more light-filled and you find in everything that comes towards you the good that you are then able to address and express in the right way. If you have learned this, then you will also address negative matters lawfully. In this way, uprightness and honesty awaken in you and you remain faithful to God in all things.

This spiritual evolutionary process towards selflessness is the Inner Path to the heart of God. Everything that you do out of selflessness brings you manifold fruits.

Therefore, if your sensations are without expectations and your thoughts are noble and good, then the power of God is in your words and in your deeds. This power is My energy of life. It goes into the soul of your neighbor and causes your neighbor to also become selfless. For, sooner or later, what goes out of your light-filled soul enters your neighbor's soul and his nature, too, depending on when he opens himself for it.

The one who gives selflessly does not ask whether his neighbor knows what he has given. The selfless person gives! He knows that God, the eternal Father, sees into the heart of all His children and that the Eternal, whose Spirit dwells in every human being, rewards the selfless one when the time for this has come. This alone is important.

Recognize that all good works, that is, selfless ones, become manifest in the right time, so that those who should see them may recognize them, so as to also, become selfless, in that they, too, accept and strive for the life in Me, and do what I have commanded them: to love one another selflessly, as I, the Christ, love them.

3. And when you pray, you should not be like the hypocrites who like to pray in the synagogues and on the corners of the streets, so that they may be seen by the people. Verily, I say to you, they already have their reward.

4. But when you pray, go into your chamber and when you have shut the door, pray to your heavenly Father who is hidden away; and the hidden One, who sees into that which is hidden, will publicly acknowledge it. (Chap. 26:3-4)

I, Christ, explain, correct
and deepen the word:

When you pray, withdraw into a quiet chamber and immerse deeply into your inner being; for the spirit of the Father, whose temple you are, dwells in you.

If you pray just to be seen or so that your neighbor may think you are pious and devout, then I say to you that this is not devoutness, but false piety; it is hypocrisy. Such externalized prayers are without power. The one who prays just from his lips or in order to be seen sins against the Holy Spirit, for he misuses holy words for his own self-interest.

Recognize that if you address God in prayer and do not fulfill in your life what you have prayed for, that is, if your prayers are only a display of your ego and do not come from the depths of your soul and are not inspired by the love for God, then you sin against the Holy Spirit. This is the greatest sin.

When your prayers do not flow selflessly from your heart, it would be better not to pray and to first become aware of your thoughts and human wishes and to gradually give them over to Me – so that the selfless love which is in you will grow and you will be able to pray from the heart. Then your prayers will be inspired more and more and imbued with the love for God and for your neighbor.

"... and the hidden One, who sees into what is hidden, will publicly acknowledge it" means that your thoughts of light and your power-filled prayers, which are inspired by the love for God, will one day bear fruit in this world. You will be allowed to recognize your seed of love and many will also recognize you as a source of love.

5. *And when you pray together, do not use empty repetitions, as the heathens do; for they think that they will be heard when they make many words. Therefore, you should not do the same as they; for your Father in heaven knows what you need before you ask ...*
(Chap. 26:5)

I, Christ, explain, correct
and deepen the word:

Only the person who has actualized very little of the law of truth uses many words and empty, uninspired repetitions in prayer and in daily life.

The one who speaks much about the law of truth and of life, thus using many words for it, cannot fill them with power and life, because he himself is not filled with the law of God. Such words are egocentric and, for that reason, without love, even though they are chosen as if they were carried by love. Uninspired speech does not reach the innermost recesses of your neighbor's soul, and thus finds no echo in the person who lets the love of God prevail in and through him. The one who speaks without inspiration about the law of truth and of life, which, however, he himself does not actualize, merely stimulates a person, who hears this and likewise is still oriented to outer things, to engage in arguing.

Recognize that the one who argues about spiritual laws does not know the laws of God. Everyone who wants to argue is convinced that he knows better than his neighbor and wants to confirm this to himself. The one who argues only gives evidence of himself, namely, that he knows nothing and is unsure. This is why he argues.

However, the one who has found the truth does not argue about the truth, not even about what belief is. The word "belief" also implies lack of knowledge: In the end, the person believes what he does not know or cannot prove. The one who believes in the truth has not yet found the eternal truth. Nor does he move in the stream of the eternal truth, yet. Therefore, belief is still blindness.

However, the one who has found the eternal truth no longer has to believe in the truth – he knows the truth, because he moves in the stream of truth. This is the true wise man, who has raised the treasure of truth in himself. The true wise ones rest in themselves. This is inner confidence and stability. They do not argue about belief, because they have found their way from belief to wisdom, which is the truth.

Therefore, the one who only believes in God without knowing the depth of the eternal truth, the eternal law, uses many words about his belief.

Even in prayer, he will behave in a similar way: He uses many words, because he does not inspire his words with selfless love. He is of the opinion that with many words he is able to convince God or even persuade Him. He thinks he has to make himself understood before God, for he assumes that God could understand his prayers in a different way than what he meant. Pagans think and pray in a similar way.

Recognize that the deeper the person immerses himself into the divine wisdom, the fewer words he also uses in prayer. His prayers are short yet powerful, because the word radiates the power that is lived.

... Therefore, when you are gathered together you should pray in this manner:

6. Our Father, who are in heaven, hallowed be Your name. Your kingdom come. Your will be done on Earth, as it is in heaven. Give us day by day our daily bread and the fruit of the living vine. And as You forgive us our sins, so may we also forgive the sins of others.

Leave us not in temptation. Deliver us from evil. For Yours is the kingdom and the power and the glory in all eternity. Amen. (Chap. 26:5-6)

I, Christ, explain, correct
and deepen the word:

The community prayer, the Lord's Prayer, is prayed with different words and contents, because every community prays it according to the potential of love of the community.

As Jesus of Nazareth, I taught the community prayer, the Lord's Prayer, in My mother tongue, that is, with other words, and thus with another content than as was prayed in later times and in other languages.

The words as such are unessential. What is important is that the person actualize what he prays. Then every word that comes out of his mouth is inspired with love, power and wisdom.

You should not pray according to the letter nor strive to pray, word for word, the Lord's Prayer, which I taught My own. What is essential is that you inspire the words of your prayers with the love for the Eternal and for your neighbor, and that the contents of your prayers correspond to your life.

People who are filled by the eternal truth, the love and wisdom of God, will, in turn, pray in another way than those who pray only because it was thus taught to them or because they belong to a denomination where the prayers are spoken according to the consciousness of the denomination.

People who are on the path to their divine origin pray freely, that is, with self-chosen words that are vivified with love and power.

People who live in My Spirit, who are imbued with the love and wisdom of God, who thus actualize the laws of God in their daily life will, above all, thank God for their life and for everything. They will praise and glorify Him and devote their life more and more to Him – in sensations, thoughts, words and deeds – because they have become life of His life.

People in the spirit of the Lord live their prayer. This means that they fulfill the laws of the Eternal more and more, and have themselves become the prayer, which is an adoration of God.

Therefore, the one who fulfills the will of God lives in adoration of God more and more. Such people not only keep the laws of God, but they have mostly become the law of love and wisdom.

In the maturing Kingdom of Peace of Jesus Christ that is coming into its own, in which I Am the ruler and the life, the people will keep the law of God more and more. Many of them will have become the law – and thus, God-men who personify the life, God, in all that they think, speak and do. Their prayers are the life in Me, the fulfillment of the eternal law. With their life, which is the law of God, they thank God for the life.

And so, the gratefulness to God is the life in God. Their life, which is a single act of giving thanks, streams into the Kingdom of Peace.

They pray according to the following words which they fulfill in daily life:

Our Father, Your spirit is in us,
and we are in Your spirit.
Hallowed is Your eternal name in us
and through us.
You are the spirit of life,
You are our Ur-Father.
We bear our eternal names from you.
You, eternal One, have given them to us
and have placed in our names all the
fullness of infinity.
Our names, which You have breathed into us,
are the love and wisdom –
the fullness out of You,
the law in us and through us.
Our eternal kingdom is the infinity –
the power and the glory, in and from You.
We are heirs to the eternal kingdom.
Therefore, we are the kingdom itself,
the eternal homeland.
It is in us and is active through us.
Your infinite, glorious will is in us
and is active through us.
The power of Your will is our strength of will.
It is active in us and through us,

for we are spirit of Your Spirit.
Heaven is not space and time –
heaven and Earth are one,
because we are united in You.
The love and power in us and through us
is our daily bread.
You, O eternal, glorious Father,
have brought forth in us everything
which vibrates in infinity.
Through us, You create
in heaven and on Earth.
We are in You, and You prevail
in us and through us.
We are filled in Your Spirit,
for we are spirit
of Your Spirit.
We are rich in You,
for we live our heritage,
the infinity, out of You.
Our eternal heritage,
spirit of Your Spirit,
brings forth that which we need
as human beings in the Kingdom of Peace.
We live in You and from You.
Life streams and gives itself.
We live in the fullness of God,
because we ourselves are the fullness.
The Earth is heaven
and the Kingdom of Peace
is the wealth of the Earth,

in which we live and are –
spirit of Your Spirit.
We live in the inner kingdom –
and yet are human beings who personify externally
that which radiates in the inner being.
Praised is the name of the Lord,
He is the life in and through us.
The name of God is the law of love
and of freedom that is lived.
Sin is transformed –
The light is come.
We live from His light
and live in and from His Spirit,
for we are spirit of His Spirit.
In God everything has been cleared.
His name has made everything pure.
The glory of God be praised!
God's will, love and wisdom
permeate the earth and the land.
We ourselves are earth and land –
will, love and wisdom.
In us is the goodness of God –
the good from God.
We are in God and act out of God.
The Earth is the Lord's –
it is the kingdom of love.
It is active in us and through us.
The life, the glory of the Father,
is active in us and through us –
from eternity to eternity.

In its essence, this glorification is the life of those who live in the Kingdom of Peace of Jesus Christ. They live in Me, the Christ, and I live through them; and together we live in the Father-Mother-God, and the Father lives through us from eternity to eternity.

7. *For if you forgive men their trespasses, your heavenly Father will also forgive you. But if you do not forgive men their trespasses, your Father in heaven will not forgive you your trespasses.*

8. *And when you fast, do not look downcast like the hypocrites. For they disguise their faces, in order to appear as men who fast. Verily, I say to you, they already have their reward.*

9. *And I say to you, you will never find the Kingdom of Heaven unless you protect yourself from the world and its evil ways. And you will never see the Father in heaven, unless you keep the Sabbath and cease your haste to gather riches. But when you fast, anoint your head and wash your face, so that you do not display yourself before the people with your fasting. And the holy One, who sees into that which is hidden, will publicly acknowledge it. (Chap. 26:7-9)*

I, Christ, explain, correct
and deepen the word:

The commandment to forgive and ask for forgiveness holds true until all that is not in accordance with the eternal laws is atoned for and cleared up. The commandment to forgive and ask for forgiveness is a part of the law of sowing and reaping. It will be rescinded when all humanness has been cleared and every soul has become a pure, immaculate spirit being.

And so until then, the commandment holds true: Forgive and you will receive forgiveness. If you ask for forgiveness and your neighbor forgives you, then your Father in heaven has also forgiven you. But if you ask for forgiveness and your neighbor does not yet forgive you because he is not yet ready to do so, then your eternal Father will not forgive you either. The one who has sinned against his neighbor must also receive forgiveness from his neighbor. Only then does God take away the sin.

The eternally just One loves all His children – including those who do not yet have the strength to forgive. If He were to forgive only the one who caused a sin to be committed and were not to forgive the one who was led by the former into sin and cannot yet forgive – where would the justice of God then be? Both of them can enter heaven only when their sins are cleared up.

For this reason, be careful of what goes out of your mouth and pay heed to your deeds, whether they are in accordance with the eternal law, that is, whether they are selfless! Something negative is said or done very quickly – but it can take a long time before it is forgiven.

If you have asked for forgiveness and your neighbor is not yet ready to forgive you, then the grace of God will become stronger in you; it will envelop you and carry you – however, He will not take away from you what has not yet been cleared up. God's mercy will then become stronger in your neighbor, too, and, while taking into consideration his free will, will lead him in such a way that he may more promptly recognize his faults, repent and forgive you. Only when all those against whom you have sinned have forgiven you – that is, when everything has been cleared up – can you enter the heavens, because God will have then transformed all humanness into divine power.

God is omnipresent. Thus, He is also effective in the law of sowing and reaping. In everything negative is also the positive, God, the eternal law. When a person recognizes and repents his sins and faults, the positive powers will then become active in them and will strengthen the person, who has come to know his guilt, to clear up his sins with Christ's strength.

Recognize the law of God; it is eternal life from eternity to eternity – everything in all things: Everything is contained in everything, the smallest in the large and the large in the smallest, the strength to forgive in the sin, and the ascent to the inner life, to the eternal Being, in the power that is set free through forgiveness.

Therefore, the divine can also be effective in the negative when the person asks for forgiveness from his heart, forgives and sins no more. However, the person must take the first step towards the inner life.

Recognize that everything you do – be it praying, fasting or giving alms – if you do not do it selflessly, but to be seen by your fellow man, then you have already received your reward from the people. God will not reward you then. And if you fast only because of your corpulence, you will not increase the Spirit of your Father in you. However, the person who takes in nourishment in the name of the Most High and exercises moderation, fasting from time to time, in order to relax and purify his body so that the power of God can maintain all cells and organs in the right way, is the one who sincerely practices accepting and receiving in himself the life from God, in order to live in this life. And at the same time, he will dedicate his life to God, the Eternal, in prayer, in order to gradually become the prayer that is lived.

10. You should do likewise when you mourn for the dead and are sad, for your loss is their gain. Do not act like those who mourn before the people and make loud lamentation and rend their garments, so that others may see their sadness. For all souls are in the hands of God and all those who have done good will rest with their ancestors in the bosom of the Eternal.

11. Pray, rather, for their rest and ascent, and consider that they are in the land of rest, which the Eternal has prepared for them, and will receive just reward for their deeds, and do not murmur like hopeless people. (Chap. 26:10-11)

I, Christ, explain, correct
and deepen the word:

The one who mourns for the dead is still far from eternal life, because he sees death as the end of life. He has not yet reached the resurrection in Me, the Christ. He is counted among the spiritually dead.

Do not mourn your dead! For the one who mourns the loss of a person does not consider the gain of the soul, which – if it has lived in Me, the Christ – enters into higher consciousness spheres of life. For if its life in its earthly existence was in God, then it will also be in God in another form of existence.

Recognize that the temporal life, the life in the body, is not the life of the soul. The soul has taken on the flesh for just a short period of life, in order to clear up and settle in the temporal what it has inflicted upon itself in different earthly garments. The Earth is to be seen as a mere transit station in which the souls in earthly garment can clear up in a short time what they cannot overcome so quickly beyond the veils of consciousness – also called the walls of fog.

When a soul leaves its earthly garment, a person cries only for the garment of the soul, not thinking of the soul that has slipped out of the garment.

After laying aside its earthly body, a light-filled soul will be led by light-filled beings, invisible to man, into that plane of consciousness which corresponds to the way of thinking and living of the person in whom this soul was incarnated.

Recognize that every soul that has left its body still is drawn for some time to the people with whom it lived together as a human being. Should it learn that its former earthly relatives mourn for its shell, this is very painful for the soul. The soul which is still close to Earth recognizes very well why its relatives grieve only over its human shell and why it is ignored as a soul by the mourners. A soul which has to recognize this then feels the first deep soul-pain after laying aside its physical body; for it learns of why the person mourns instead of thinking of it with love and unity. With this, it perceives many a self-interested thought from its former earthly relatives. It cannot draw their attention to itself, because it is not perceived by them. What it says the person does not hear, and what it can see he does not see. But the soul perceives a lot.

I encourage you to think about this: Do you grieve when the snake sheds its skin, when it leaves its skin behind and slithers away?

It is similar with the soul. It leaves its perishable body, its shell, and travels on. Therefore, you are grieving the loss of the shell, and are not thinking of the soul. The person who thinks of the soul thanks God who called the soul back to His bosom, if the soul made use of its life in God, in the earthly garment, and thereby drew closer to Him. Remember that for a light-filled soul, putting aside the body is a gain.

And if you mourn the loss of a person just in front of people, you are playing the hypocrite. In reality, you think neither of the person nor of the soul. You think only of yourself. The soul which registers this recognizes that it has not been loved selflessly, that possibly it was there just for its neighbor's self-interest.

Many souls have to recognize that, while in the earthly garment, their earthly relatives and acquaintances lived through them. This means that, as human beings, they could not develop themselves and live according to their own characteristics, because they had to do the will of those who demanded of them what was advantageous to the former. Many of these souls perceive what they missed in their earthly existence and, for this reason, return once more into the earthly existence. Through the veils of consciousness, they return to the Earth and, as souls, stay again among those who had lived through them. Still others seek to live on Earth what they were unable to develop as human beings.

As long as people are tied to people or things – like possessions, wealth and power – their souls return to Earth and slip once more into new earthly garments. There are manifold causes and reasons for souls to reincarnate. If a soul recognizes, for example, that it is chained to its relatives through sin, then it often becomes resigned and gives in to the wish to take on a new body. Inspired by this wish, it lives on the plane of consciousness that corresponds to its spiritual condition and is taught there. Among other things, it is made to understand the pros and cons of a new incarnation. It then goes into incarnation when the stars in which its pros and cons are stored – and thereby, its pathway to Earth as well – show the way to matter; and when on

Earth an earthly body is conceived which corresponds to its spiritual level of consciousness. It then slips into this human shell at its birth.

The man who begot the body and the woman in whom the embryo grew attracted that soul with which they still have something to clear up together – or in order to walk the path of the Lord together, in selfless service to their neighbor.

The person should not look just to his body, but above all to the incarnated being within him, and should strive to do the will of God and not allow the human will of a second or third person to be imposed on him.

Recognize that even if you say, "I do the will of my neighbor, in order to keep outer peace," you prevent your soul and also your neighbor's soul from developing and unfolding as it is good for both. You prevent yourself and your neighbor from fulfilling the tasks which your souls have brought with them into the earthly existence: to purify themselves and to free themselves from the burden of sin, which perhaps was brought along into this incarnation from previous incarnations. The one who allows his fellow man to lead him by the nose – thus doing what others say although he recognizes that this is not his way – is lived and his own actual earthly existence passes him by. He does not use the days; he is used by those to whom he is servile and therefore does not know his own path over this Earth as a human being.

The one who binds his fellow man, by forcing his will upon him, is comparable to a vampire who sucks the energy from his fellow man. He does not know himself and at the same time ties himself to his victim – and vice versa, the victim who lets himself be drained also ties himself to the former. Both will be brought together again, in one of their lives, either in an earthly garment or as souls in the spheres beyond – and this, so often and for so long, until the one has forgiven the other.

If two people tie themselves to each other – no matter whether the one has done the binding or let himself be bound – both of them have burdened themselves and both must clear things up together, so that love and unity can be re-established between them.

No one can say, "I did not know about the laws of life." I say to you that Moses brought you excerpts from the eternal laws, the Ten Commandments. And if you keep these, then you will not tie yourselves to each other, but will live in peace with one another.

Recognize that only love and unity among one another show souls and men the pathways to the higher life.

God, the eternally gracious One, offers His hand to each soul and to each person. The one who takes it uses his earthly life. He treasures the days and is also able to live them according to the commandments, by clearing up what the day shows him. As soul, he will one day walk and rest in God, together with all those who likewise have used their earthly existence in that they have, day after day, recognized and overcome with Me, the

Christ, what the day brought them and showed them – joy and suffering.

And when you do not mourn the mortal shell which your neighbor laid aside for your own sake, but rejoice in spirit that the soul in earthly garment has recognized its spiritual life and has prepared itself for it, then you will pray joyfully for your neighbor to the Father, through Me, the Christ. You will send powers of love to the soul that is now closer to God, so that it goes on to higher planes in order to unite with God more and more.

The soul feels the joy and suffering of its relatives. The souls which have passed away in Me, the Christ, feel linked through Me, Christ, with all those who still walk in the earthly garment. The joy of the soul for being remembered with love by its relatives fills it with strength.

Recognize that selfless, loving prayers give power and strength to the soul that walks on its path towards the divine. It feels the unity in your selfless prayers and receives increased strength. Through this, it will more quickly lay aside the humanness that still clings to it and thus become free for Him, who is freedom and love – God, the life. The reward from God is great for every soul that earnestly strives to fulfill the will of God.

Recognize that only the one is without hope who merely speaks about his faith, but does not live what he appears to believe. In the last analysis, the doubter does not believe in what he pretends to believe. From this, hopelessness develops.

12. You should also not gather for yourselves trea-sures on Earth, which the moths and rust consume and which thieves dig up and steal. But gather for your-selves treasures in heaven, where neither moths nor rust consume them and where thieves neither dig up nor steal. For where your treasure is, there is also your heart.

13. The eyes are the lamps of the body. So if you see clearly, your whole body will be full of light. But if your eyes are lacking or if they are dull, your whole body will be dark. Now if the light that is in you is darkness, how great the darkness will be!

14. No one can serve two masters. Either he will hate the one and love the other, or he will be devoted to the one and despise the other. You cannot serve God and the mammon at the same time. (Chap. 26:12-14)

I, Christ, explain, correct
and deepen the word:

Only the person who does not believe in God, in His love, wisdom and goodness, collects treasures on Earth. Many people pretend to believe in God; however, you will recognize them by their works. Many people speak about the love and the works of God – by their deeds alone, will you recognize them.

Many people speak about the inner kingdom and about the inner wealth, and yet gather in the barns for themselves personally and accumulate worldly riches for themselves personally, so as to be held in high esteem by the people.

The one who is concerned only about his personal well-being does not yet sense the bird of prey that has already raised its wings to destroy the nest and steal the wealth, which the rich man, the builder of the nest, calls his personal property.

However, the one who strives first for the Kingdom of God gathers inner values, inner treasures. He will also receive all that he needs and beyond, in the temporal.

The one who is rich in his inner being will not live in want externally. But the one who is externally rich and hoards his wealth will live in want some day. The one who gathers treasures on Earth, will find them taken away from him so that he may reflect upon the treasure of the inner being and be able to enter the life, the inner wealth.

The soul will lack divine light until it strives first for the Kingdom of God. And as long as it is still possible on Earth, a light-poor soul will again be born into a light-poor body and will possibly live in poverty among the poor. The recognition will come that the treasure, the wealth, is in God alone.

The one whose heart is with God will be rich in inner values and will enter into the Kingdom of Peace.

I, Christ, give you a criterion, so that you may recognize where you stand – either in the light or in the shadow, "For where your treasure is, there is also your heart," and there will your soul be one day.

Take heed! The one who reads these words and stands at the turning-point of the old to the New Era should hasten, so that he can still find his spiritual life! For when the New Era, the era of Christ, is manifest over the whole Earth and the inner life is lived, there will no longer be incarnations for those who strive for external values. Then, too, there will be no more incarnations for the worldly rich, so that they may atone, as the poorest among the poor, for what they neglected to do as the rich.

When the Kingdom of Peace of Jesus Christ has taken further evolutionary steps, there will be neither poor nor rich. All people will then be rich in My Spirit, for they will have opened the inner kingdom. They will also live accordingly on the new Earth, under another heaven.

For this reason, be prepared to serve God and to serve your fellow man as well, out of love for God.

Recognize: No one can serve two masters, God and mammon. Only selfless love unites all people and nations. Both the human being on Earth and the soul in the spheres of purification will one day be led to the decision: to serve God or mammon, to be for God or against God. There is nothing in between: either for God, or for the satanic.

15. Therefore, I say to you: Do not be anxious for your life, what you will eat and drink; not even for your body, for what you will put on. Is not life more than food and the body more than clothing? And what shall it profit a man, if he would gain the whole world but lose his life?

16. Look at the birds in the air: they neither sow nor reap, nor gather into barns, and yet your heavenly Father nourishes them. Are you not looked after much better than they? But who among you could add one cubit to his life span, if he wanted to? And why are you so concerned about your clothing? Consider the lilies of the field, how they grow; they neither toil nor spin. And yet, I say to you, even Solomon in all his splendor and glory was not arrayed like one of these.

17. But if God so clothes the grass of the field, which today is alive and tomorrow is burnt in the oven, why should He not much more clothe you, O you men of little faith?

18. Therefore, you should not be anxious and ask: What will we eat? What will we drink? or: What will we wear? (As the Gentiles do.) For your heavenly Father knows that you need all that. But seek first the Kingdom of God and His righteousness, and all these things will be added to you. Therefore, do not be concerned about the evil of tomorrow. It is enough that each day has its own evil." (Chap. 26:15-18)

I, Christ, explain, correct
and deepen the word:

The person who worries about his personal life, about his well-being – for example, what he will eat and drink or clothe himself with tomorrow – is a poor planner; for he thus thinks only about himself, about his own well-being and about his possessions. With this, at the same time, he also plans in his pain and woe.

On the other hand, the one who fulfills the will of God is a good planner. He will plan both his days and his future. However, he knows that his planning is only a guideline that rests in the hands of God.

He lays his plan in the hands of God, works with the powers of God and lets himself be guided by God during the events of the day. For he knows that God is the all-knowing Spirit and the wealth of his soul. The one who entrusts himself to God, who places his day's work in the light of God and who fulfills the law "pray and work" will receive his just reward. He will have everything that he needs.

If God, the Eternal, adorns nature and clothes the lilies of the field, how much more will He feed and clothe His child who fulfills His will! Therefore, do not worry about tomorrow, but plan and commit your plan to the will of God – and God, who knows your plan, will fulfill for you what is good for you.

I give you an example: A good architect will carefully plan a house and pay attention to all the details. Once he has finished his plan, he will check it once more and will then submit it to the client who commissioned the building for examination. If the latter agrees to the plan, then the workmen will work according to the plan. The architect and his client will supervise the execution of the plan and will interfere only when something does not conform to the planning.

You should lead your life in a similar way. Plan each day and plan well! Allow yourselves time for some reflection, too, in which you can find inner stillness and think over your life and your planning again and again. God will also penetrate with His will a carefully made plan of the day that has been placed in His will. The one who carries out his plan in this way need not worry about tomorrow. His belief in the guidance of God consists of positive thoughts; from these emerge positive words and law-abiding actions. Positive thoughts, words and actions are the best tools, because the will of God is active in them. This means that the will of God, His Spirit, is at work in every positive thought, in every selfless word, in every selfless gesture and deed. God will give the good planner all that he needs and beyond that.

Only the one who does not entrust himself to God, who lets the days slip by and does not use them, worries about tomorrow. The person who lives from day to day and then blames his neighbor when he fails in many things, when he is sick, when he goes hungry, when he cannot acquire what he needs for his daily life – is not a good planner. He is an anxious and egocentric person who attracts what he does not want and what he fears. The person who does not plan the hours, days and months with God's help and does not place his plan and himself in the will of God cannot be guided by God. Only the one who entrusts his daily work to God and conscientiously fulfills the commandment "pray and work" can be guided by God and is fulfilled by Him – he is filled with love, wisdom and power. This means that his vessel, his life, is filled with trust and faith in God.

People in the Spirit of God will not live in want. They are good planners, they are strong in faith and work with the powers of the Spirit. Only the anxious person is concerned about himself, about his small ego. He worries about tomorrow, because he is not steadfast in God and does not believe in God's wisdom and love. With this, he unconsciously opens the barn for the thieves who come and steal. He will lose what he has taken and hoarded for himself personally.

From the hands of God, man receives food, shelter and clothing. The one who places his life, his thinking and his work in the hands of God does not need to worry about tomorrow. He will have what he needs to-day, tomorrow and in the future – and beyond that.

And so, the one who lives in the inner kingdom will not live externally in want either. However the one who is poor in his inner being will live externally in want. If today he lives externally and increases worldly wealth for himself and keeps it for himself personally, then he is poor in his inner being and will live in want, that is, he will be poor in another earthly garment.

Therefore, strive first for the Kingdom of God and His justice, then everything you need and beyond that, will be given to you by God. Look at the birds of the air. They do not sow or reap, nor gather into barns; and yet your heavenly Father feeds them. "Consider the lilies of the field, how they grow; they neither toil nor spin." Nature in all its diversity is clad more beautifully than the richest of the rich. The one who thinks only about his well-being and his full barns will earn his bread by the sweat of his brow, either in this earthly existence or in another incarnation – as long as this is still possible.

The right "pray and work" means to work for oneself and for the common good. Recognize that the lilies of the field – all of nature – are there for all people and give themselves to them in the most manifold ways. The one who is able to grasp and appreciate this will not have to earn his bread by the sweat of his brow. He will fulfill the law "pray and work" – for himself and for his neighbor.

And when it is written, "they neither toil nor spin," this means that a person should not think solely of himself and work only to gain profit for himself alone, in order to adorn and display himself with it.

Recognize that all Being is in the care of God. Animals, trees, plants, grasses and stones are in the care of God. They are in the life of evolution which is guided by the eternal Creator-God. Since all life comes from God, the animals, trees, plants, grasses and stones also sense and feel. They experience within themselves the Creator's power of evolution that vivifies them and leads them to further unfoldment in the cycle of divine eons. The power of the Creator, the eternal Being, gives the nature kingdoms what they need. The gifts of life flow to the life-forms to the same extent as these are spiritually developed.

The eternal Father remembers every blade of grass. How much more does the Eternal remember His children who have already developed in themselves the evolutionary steps of the mineral, plant and animal kingdoms! The children of God bear in themselves the microcosm from the macrocosm and are thus in communication with all of infinity.

But how poor is the person who worries about tomorrow! He himself shows that he has not yet mastered yesterday, since he is unable to live in today, in the now, that is, in God.

The inner being of a person, the pure being, is the essence of infinity. The one who grasps this as a human being looks within and unfolds the laws of life, so that he may perceive everything external in the light of truth.

Recognize that infinity serves the person who thinks and lives in an all-encompassing way – that is, without limitation. People in the Spirit of love are not self-centered, but all-conscious. They are in constant communication with the powers of God in all Being. Whatever they do, they do from within, with the power of love. They plan and work according to the commandment "pray and work" and do not waste the day. They know how precious is the day, the hours and the minutes, and make use of the time.

Therefore, the one who truly lives does not worry about tomorrow; already today, he receives what he will have tomorrow. For the one who lives in God will not be in want, neither today nor tomorrow. But the one who stays anxious and clings to his possessions will be poor tomorrow.

However, the one who sees himself as a cosmic being, who fulfills the will of God without reservation, acquires wisdom and strength. The life of the person who is filled with love and wisdom is permeated with the power of God. He will lack nothing. But who ever worries about tomorrow and sees the future as gloomy attracts evil; and he will have his burden every day.

Therefore, do not think anxiously about tomorrow! Plan with God's strength – and let the Eternal work through you. Then your thoughts are positive magnets that attract, in their turn, what is positive and constructive. For thoughts, words and deeds are magnets. According to their kind, they attract, in turn, the same or something similar.

CHAPTER 27

Sermon on the Mount
(Part 3)

*Your negative thoughts, words and deeds are
your own judges (1). Splinter and beam – The need for self-
recognition (2). Proselytizing is wanting to convince – Live
the truth and be an example (3). Asking, seeking, knocking;
the inner gate does not open for the intellect (4). What you
demand of your neighbor is what you yourself do not have
in your heart; an attitude of expectation leads to binding
(6). The fight on the narrow path to life (7). Distinguishing
between good and bad fruits (8-9). Take in the word of
life with your heart – "This Is My Word. Alpha and Omega.
The Gospel of Jesus. The Christ-revelation which true
Christians the world over have come to know:" A work of
life and of love (13)*

1. *"Do not judge, so that you will not be judged. For
you will be judged in the same way you judge others;
and with whatever measure you measure, you will be
measured again in turn. And as you do to others, so
will it be done to you. (Chap. 27:1)*

I, Christ, explain, correct
and deepen the word:

You have read that thoughts, words and deeds are
magnets. The one who judges and condemns his neigh-

bor in thoughts and with words will experience the same or similar things on himself.

Recognize that your negative thoughts, words and deeds are your own judges. "With whatever measure you measure" – whether in thoughts or in words and actions – so will you yourself be measured. Just as you denigrate your neighbor, in order to exalt yourself, so will you be valued: You will know and suffer your own worth. And if you say, "What the one has is enough for him – the other one should receive more," then one day you will have only as much or even less than the one to whom you have conceded less. Just as you treat your neighbor in thoughts, words and deeds, so will you fare yourself some day.

2. *How is it that you see the splinter in your brother's eye and are not aware of the beam in your own eye? Or how can you say to your brother that you want to take the splinter out of his eye? And see, a beam is in your eye. You hypocrite, first take the beam out of your own eye; only then will you see clearly, in order to be able to take the splinter out of your brother's eye. (Chap. 27:2)*

I, Christ, explain, correct
and deepen the word:

Only that person talks constantly about the splinter in his neighbor's eye who is not aware of the beam in his own eye. Only the one busies himself with wanting to extricate the splinter from the eye of his brother who does not know his own way of thinking and living. Who ever does not know himself nor his beam – the sins of his soul which are reflected in his own eyes – has no eye for the truth. His eye is clouded by sin. He then sees in his neighbor just what he himself still is: a sinner. Only the one who works on the beam in his own eye perceives increasingly more clearly. Then, he will be able to recognize the splinter in his brother's eye ever more clearly and will help him remove it, according to the law of love of neighbor.

And so, whoever speaks negatively about his fellow men, who denigrates and slanders them, does not know his own faults.

You shall recognize them by their fruits! Each one, himself, shows who he is, that is, his fruit. Whoever gets upset about his fellow men and makes fun of them shows who he truly is.

The one who first discards his own faults is also able to help his neighbor. This is why each one who speaks disparagingly about his brother's faults – and in so doing does not notice the beam in his own eye – is a hypocrite.

3. *You should not give what is holy to the dogs nor cast your pearls before the swine, lest they trample them with their feet, turn round and rend you. (Chap. 27:3)*

I, Christ, explain, correct
and deepen the word:

It is not in accordance with the eternal law of free will that you go with the words of truth from place to place, from house to house, using your skills to persuade and convince, proselytizing to every one you get hold of.

For that would mean that you do not hold the truth sacred, and do as it is figuratively written, "You should not give what is holy to the dogs nor cast your pearls before the swine." This means, you should not impose the word of God upon your neighbor. The person who thinks that his neighbor should believe and accept what he thinks he is convinced of still has doubt himself and questions his own belief.

To proselytize means to want to convince. The one who wants to convince is himself not convinced in his own inner being of what he extols.

So, be good examples in your belief and not ones to proselytize. You can offer the content of your faith and leave everyone the option, to believe in it or not, to go along with you or not.

The freedom in God is an aspect of the eternal law. When your neighbor approaches you of his own free will and asks you about your belief, he is taking the first step towards you; and the one who is firm in his faith will then go towards his neighbor and answer him.

The one who is in divine communication with his neighbor will not tie him to his faith – but will communicate to him only as much as he himself has recognized and actualized. Only the person who has developed little selfless love will want to tie his neighbor to his belief.

Therefore, beware of the overly zealous, who want to convince you of their belief. Offer the eternal truth in the spoken and written word – and live accordingly yourselves; then, those who have recognized the life in themselves will approach you.

4. Ask, and it will be given to you; seek, and you will find. Knock, and it will be opened to you; for every one who asks will receive and the one who seeks will find, and to those who knock it will be opened. (Chap. 27:4)

I, Christ, explain, correct
and deepen the word:

Only the person who has not yet entered his inner being, the kingdom of love, asks, seeks and knocks at the gate to the inner life. The Kingdom of God is within, in the soul of every person.

The first step on the path to inner life, on the way to the gate of salvation, is to ask God for help and support. The next step is to search for the love and justice of God. The pilgrim finds the life, God's love and justice, in the commandments of life, which are signposts on the way within.

A further step is to knock at the inner door, in the little chamber of one's own heart. This gateway to the heart of God opens itself only to the one who has sincerely prayed, searched and knocked. The inner door does not open to the intellectual who seeks only external values and ideals. Those who doubt will not be received either.

Therefore, the one who asks, seeks and knocks must do so out of love for God and not in order to test the love of God.

Recognize that whoever just wants to test whether God's love really exists will himself be put to the test very quickly. The heart's gateway stands open to the one who lives in God. He need not ask anymore; he has already received, for God knows His children. The one who has entered the heart of God has already received in his soul. This means that the wealth from God shines more intensively in his soul and radiates through him, the person. Whoever has entered his inner being no longer needs to seek – he is at home in the kingdom of the inner being. And whoever has consciously taken up dwelling in Him no longer needs to knock; he has already entered and lives in God, and God lives through him.

Only those will ask, seek and knock who still stand on the outside and do not yet know that, deep within their soul, they bear what makes them truly rich: God's love and wisdom.

5. *Which man among you here gives a stone when his child asks for bread, or a serpent when he asks for a fish? If you, who are evil, can nevertheless give good gifts to your children, how much more will your Father in heaven give good things to those who ask Him.*

6. *Whatever you want that people should do to you, do it likewise to them, and whatever you do not want them to do to you, do not do it to them either; for this is the law and the prophets. (Chap. 27:5-6)*

I, Christ, explain, correct
and deepen the word:

Recognize that you should not demand from your fellow man what you yourself are not willing to give.

When you expect your neighbor to do something for you, ask yourself the question: Why do you not do it yourself? The person, for example, who expects money and property from his neighbor so that, in his laziness, he will not have to work himself, or the person who expects faithfulness from his neighbor while he is not faithful himself, or the person who wants to be accepted and received by his neighbor, yet neither accepts nor receives his fellow man – that person is selfish and poor in spirit.

Whatsoever you demand of your neighbor is what you do not have in your heart yourself.

It is unlawful – out of an attitude of expectation – to force your fellow man into acts, statements or ways of behaving, which, of himself, he would not be willing to do.

If, in wanting something from your neighbor, you have recognized your expectant attitude turn back quickly and do first what you demand of your neighbor.

All coercion is the application of pressure, which produces, in turn, coercion and counter-pressure. Through such extortionate behavior towards your fellow man, you bind yourself to him and turn yourself – as well as the one who lets himself be blackmailed – into a slave to a baser nature. Coercive methods such as "I expect of you and you expect of me or each gives to the other what the other demands of the former" lead to binding.

What is bound has no place in heaven. Both who are tied to one another will meet again one day, either in the fine-material life or in further incarnations.

This form of binding does not apply to one's place of work. When, in your professional life, you have freely taken a position in a certain field of work, and the responsible person gives you duties that you should carry out within the framework of your job, you have already given your consent to that upon joining the enterprise. You have freely taken your place in the field of work and on the work team, in order to do what is assigned to you. So, when you choose a job, you should also carry out what is assigned to you, according to the field of work you have chosen yourself. The statement "Whatever you want that people should do to you, do it likewise to them ..." therefore, does not apply to a self-chosen profession or field of work.

"Whatever you do not want them [the people] to do to you, do not do it to them either" means: If you do not want to be laughed at and ridiculed, or you do not want to be robbed or lied to, or you do not want to be deprived of your belongings, or you do not want to be led by the nose, or you do not want to be robbed of your free will, or you do not want to be beaten or insulted, then do not do it to your fellow man. For what you do to the least of your brothers, this you do to Me – and to yourself. What you do not want to be done to you, you should not do to any of your neighbors either – for everything that goes out from you returns to you. Therefore, examine your thoughts and guard your tongue!

7. *Enter by the strait gate. For narrow is the way and strait is the gate that leads to life, and few are those who find it. But wide is the gate and broad is the road that leads to ruin, and there are many who walk on it. (Chap. 27:7)*

I, Christ, explain, correct
and deepen the word:

"... narrow is the path and strait is the gate that leads to life" means that in each one who endeavors to walk the narrow path to life the darkling makes himself known and shows him – as he showed Me, as Jesus of Nazareth – the treasures and comforts of this world.

Each day anew, the satanic should be resisted and opposed. Whoever is not watchful will be servile to him.

Recognize that every person who takes the first steps towards the life at first feels confined and restricted, until he has made a final decision. For now he should cease to do those things which he thought and did in human terms until now.

The first steps lead into the unknown – they are called belief and trust. Until the first steps are taken, the path to life is strait and narrow. The first hurdles that should be overcome on the path to the heart of God are called: Change your way of thinking and cease your old human habits! Repent, forgive, ask for forgiveness and sin no more! For every individual this means a personal effort and a readjustment of everything that until now was customary to him.

However, the one who perseveres with My strength will leave the narrow path and reach the great road of light into the kingdom of the inner being, on which he will strive toward the door to absoluteness, to the life in God, with those who journey into the light.

The person is tested each day: for or against God.

The one who decides against Me, by keeping all human comforts and everything that makes him human, will not be led into temptation on the wide dark road, since he has given himself up to the tempter. Many, indeed, follow this road to ruin. They are not tested like those who walk the narrow path to life.

The one who has given himself up to the tempter thereby also gives his unrestricted assent to what he has to harvest on account of his seed.

8. *Beware of false prophets, who come to you in sheep's clothing, but are inwardly ravenous wolves. You will know them by their fruits. Can one gather grapes from thorns or figs from thistles?*

9. *Likewise, every good tree brings forth good fruit, but a bad tree brings forth bad fruit. Every tree that does not bring forth good fruit is only fit to be cut down and thrown into the fire. This is why, you should distinguish the good from the bad by their fruits.*
(Chap. 27:8-9)

I, Christ, explain, correct
and deepen the word:

At the end of the days of materialism, of the "time of avarice and greed," many false prophets will appear. They will talk much about the love of God – and yet their works are works of men. Not the one who speaks of the love of God is a true prophet and a spiritually wise man, but solely the one whose works are good.

The gift of discernment, however, is given only to the one who first examines his own cast of mind: whether he truly believes in the gospel of selfless love himself and fulfills what is meant by it, and, what he has already actualized, himself, in selfless love towards his neighbor.

You can recognize your fellow man and sense the difference between the good, the less good and the bad, only when you have attained a certain degree of spiritual maturity.

The one who still condemns his neighbor and thinks and speaks negatively about him cannot yet examine his fellow man. He lacks the gift of discernment. He only passes judgment and does not look more deeply.

If you are still a bad fruit, yourself, how can you recognize the good fruit? The one who does not actualize the laws of God thus lacks the gift to discern between what is good, less good and bad.

And so, the one who wants to examine his neighbor should first examine himself to see whether he possesses the gift of discernment between the just and the unjust.

A good fruit can be discarded very quickly and the bad one approved, when the rotten fruit makes a show of itself with much talking and acts with a lot of seemingly convincing words and gestures.

Recognize that like attracts like. The rotten fruits are closer than the good fruits to the one who is himself still a rotten fruit. But the one who is selfless is a good fruit and the good, the selfless, is also close to him.

The one who is selfless also has the gift to discern between the good, the less good and the bad fruits. And so, the one who wants to differentiate between the good and bad fruits must first be a good fruit himself. Only the good fruit can recognize the bad. The bad fruit seeks like-minded bad fruits again and again, in order to act against the good ones. The bad fruits condemn, discard, judge and bind.

The good, ripe fruits are understanding, benevolent and tolerant, and are kind toward their neighbor. They may very well address the wrongs, but they keep their neighbor in their heart. This means that they no longer judge, condemn or convict.

I repeat: You shall recognize them by their fruits.

The good fruit knows the bad fruit, yet the bad fruit does not recognize the good fruit. The good fruit looks only upon the good, the bad fruit only upon the bad. The person thinks, speaks and acts accordingly.

10. Not all who say to Me: Lord! Lord! will enter the Kingdom of Heaven, but those who do the will of My Father who is in heaven. Many will say to Me on that day: Lord, Lord, have we not prophesied in Your name? Have we not cast out devils in Your name? Have we not done many wonderful works in Your name? Then I will declare to them: I have never known you; depart from Me, you evil-doers. (Chap. 27:10)

I, Christ, explain, correct
and deepen the word:

The one who only calls on My name and does not fulfill the will of My Father is poor in spirit, despite his seemingly spiritually effective speech and his seemingly courteous words, and will not enter into the Kingdom of Heaven.

But the one who accomplishes selfless deeds without expecting reward or acknowledgment is the one who does the will of My Father, for he acts as he thinks and speaks.

Selfless deeds result only from God-filled sensations and thoughts. If a person's thoughts are impure, then his words are empty and his deeds egocentric.

Recognize that the one who appears to speak from the I Am, that is, who seems to speak My word and appears to accomplish deeds in My name, living well from this, has already received his reward. He will receive no further reward in heaven. The one who does selfless works of love and works for his earthly bread will receive the just reward in heaven.

Recognize that the spiritual bread is the spiritual nourishment for the soul. The bread for the body should be earned according to the law of "pray and work."

The spiritual bread comes from heaven and will be offered to those who keep the law of love and of life and also fulfill the commandment "pray and work."

God gives men the earthly food through the Earth. The fruits of the Earth require preparation through the work of the hands. Thus, the worker is worthy of his wage.

Recognize the difference between the bread for the soul and the bread for the earthly body! Both may flow from one source, yet the one is spiritual and is offered to the soul, and the other is condensed substance, matter, and is given to the physical body. What the great Spirit, God, gives man for his physical body requires human work; for example, it must be sown, cultivated, harvested and processed. For this, man should also be paid by man.

Only the one who does everything out of love for God and man will be received into the Kingdom of God.

11. Therefore, I compare the one who hears these words of Mine and follows them with a wise man who built his house solidly upon a rock. And the rain fell and the floods came and the winds blew about this house. And it did not fall in, for it was founded upon a rock.

12. And the one who hears these words of Mine and does not follow them should be compared with a foolish man who built his house upon sand. And the rain fell and the floods came and the winds blew and beat against that house and it fell in, and great was its collapse. But a city which is built solidly, walled solidly in a circle or on the top of a hill and founded upon a rock can never fall nor be hidden."

13. And it happened that when Jesus had ended these sayings, the people were astonished at His teaching. For He addressed the head and the heart when He taught and did not speak like the scribes who taught only by the authority of their office. (Chap. 27:11-13)

I, Christ, explain, correct
and deepen the word:

The one who hears and follows My word develops his spiritual life. He founds his life on Me, the rock. He will then stand firm against all storms and floods. After this earthly life, his soul will consciously enter the spiritual life and will be no stranger there, because while on Earth the human being already lived in the kingdom of the inner being.

The prophetic spirit is the fire in the prophet and in all enlightened ones. God did not and does not speak through them as those "who taught only by the authority of their office." The prophets and enlightened ones spoke and speak with the full authority of the Eternal, the speaking God, whether people want to admit it or not.

It is written, "He addressed the head and the heart." What the intellect, the head, absorbs is talked over and argued by the "head-thinkers." Despite this, many a tiny seed falls into their heart. The one who receives the word of life with his heart also moves it in his heart, causing the good seed, the life, to sprout immediately.

But the one who wants to grasp the word of God with his intellect alone will have to later recognize – perhaps only after some blows of fate – what it is he rejected through his doubt and intellectual arrogance. He will have to recognize that the seed, the word of God that was given from the horn of plenty of life through prophets and enlightened ones, would have spared him much.

The book "This Is My Word" will be effective into the New Era, into the time of Christ. My life once, as Jesus of Nazareth, and My word as Christ today [1989] are the foundation.

The way I thought, taught and lived as Jesus of Nazareth will be the standard for the way of living and thinking of the people of the New Era in the Kingdom of Peace of Jesus Christ. In this way, I Am very close to them. They will greet Me in the spirit as their brother and will accept and receive Me as the ruler of the Kingdom of God on Earth.

This book is a work of love and of life. From it, the people in the Kingdom of Peace will also learn how I initiated and built up the Era of Light on Earth. They will learn that I worked through many faithful ones who fought and suffered with Me for the New Era. Therefore, this book "This Is My Word" is a historic document. It will be read now – in the declining old world – as well as then – in the ever more dawning New Era.

The people will also recognize from it the fulfillment of the divine Mission of Redemption, which started with My work as Jesus of Nazareth and then as the Redeemer, as the Christ of God – and now as the builder of the New Era, in which I prepare My coming as the ruler of the Kingdom of Peace, in which I Am brother to those who live in the brotherhood of Christ with Me and with the many whose hearts are pure.

CHAPTER 28

Jesus Frees the Animals and Confirms John the Baptist

The Fall: The condensation of energy all the way to matter – The spirit body in the human body – Man becomes brutish – Abuse of the creatures and of creation – The domineering man – Superstition, punishing gods, blood sacrifice – God's admonishers point the way – Animal experiments are an abomination before God (1-3). The pure recognize the pure – Food, a gift of God (4). The fight of the darkness against God's plan and His just prophets – Tools of the darkness – False prophets are not opposed by the darkness (16)

1. And it happened one day, after Jesus had finished His speaking, that, in a place near Tiberias where there are seven wells, a young man brought Him live rabbits and doves, that He might consume them with His disciples.

2. And Jesus looked at the young man lovingly and said to him, "You have a good heart and God will enlighten you; but do you not know that in the beginning God gave man the fruits of the Earth for food and by this did not make him lower than the apes, or the oxen, or the horse or the sheep, that he may kill his fellow creatures and consume their flesh and blood?

3. You believe that Moses rightfully commanded such creatures to be offered in sacrifice and consumed and *so you do this in the temple; but see, One greater than Moses is here and He comes to abolish the blood sacrifices of the law and the orgies and to restore the pure offering and the bloodless sacrifice as it was in the beginning, namely, the grains and the fruits of the Earth. (Chap. 28:1-3)*

I, Christ, explain, correct
and deepen the word:

I came into this world as Jesus of Nazareth, in order to bear witness of God, My Father, and of all that God has created.

Out of the first Fall-thought – wanting to be like God – emerged the Fall. The Fall-beings and, with them, all the children of God who let themselves be led astray by enticements and promises, received parts of spiritual suns and spiritual planets from the kind hands of the Eternal – who loves all His children and sees them eternally in Himself as pure beings. These parts of spiritual suns and planets fell with the Fall-beings and gradually became matter – over the infinite periods of time of the descent from the fine-material to ever coarser condensation. They also contained spiritual kingdoms of minerals, plants and animals, which went through the same process of development into matter. This means that the light decreased in the spiritual forms more and more. As it decreased, the spiritual bodies of the children of

God became smaller: They contracted more and more into themselves. At the same time, the human being gradually took form – the outer shell, which then enclosed the light-poor and reduced spiritual body.

Know that the spiritual body consists of spiritual particles. In them are the spiritual atoms, in which the forces of the spiritual natures and attributes of God are stored. As the light decreased, many particles began to encase themselves in each other, in that one particle took another into itself.

The negative sensations, thoughts and actions of the Fall-children and of those whom they led astray thus caused the transformation of the cosmic energies from fine-material to coarse-material. The more the Fall-beings and those they led astray turned away from God through their negative thoughts, wishes and actions, the more the condensation increased, so that the fine-material body became even smaller and the coarse-material one became even denser.

Thus, the Fall caused a kind of mutation; a part of the pure spiritual forces of the body transformed into low-vibrating energies, out of which the human body then gradually emerged. In the course of these periods of time, the spirit body in the human body became a bearer of spiritual energy for the human organism. The contracted – that is, encased – spirit body, remained in the shell, man, and is the transformer of the life force for the human being. Thus, without this spiritual body, the soul, the human being cannot live.

The mineral and plant kingdoms of this Earth receive their life force from the primordial power, the All-Spirit, through the spiritual part-planet in the Earth which is enclosed by matter, the Earth. The animals of the Earth, which also emerged in the course of the condensation, were and are contributing to the balance of energies in nature. Some animal species which do not yet have a part-soul also receive their life force from the spiritual part-planet in the Earth. Animal species which already have part-souls – that is, potentiated spiritual particles – are vivified directly by the primordial power without the intermediate function of the spiritual part-planet in the Earth.

God, the Eternal, gave everything to His human children – the Earth with its plants, fruits, seeds and sources of water – so that they could also nourish their physical body. The first human beings subsisted on plants, fruits and seeds and drank spring water. The animals were their friends and helpers. During this process of development, procreation for human bodies emerged.

In the course of time, the human race became more and more brutish. Desires, the wanting to possess, to be and to have grew, and with this lusts and cravings also grew. The human beings transformed the gifts of God with an increasingly undue amount of effort in their preparation and thus increased their cravings and the gratification thereof. Men began to desire women and took several women. The "lusts of the flesh," for the woman's body, increased. More and more, the lusting of the senses and their gratification took precedence over the begetting of a child.

As the lusting of the senses increased, man's cravings also turned towards the animal. It was hunted and slaughtered and its flesh prepared and consumed. Man then behaved like a cannibal. The animals became the enemies of man, because they were hunted and thus frightened by man.

Through all this, the human races fell away from God more and more. Men then considered the gifts of God – not only the plants and animals, but also the Earth and their fellow men – as their property. They were no longer brothers and sisters among each other, but subjugated their equals and called them their slaves. They made them work like animals under the yoke and in servitude and even traded them as goods. In this way, the domineering man emerged.

The domineering men divided the Earth into plots which they considered their own and confined themselves in "mine and thine." The one who did not misappropriate any piece of the great cake Earth or owned just a tiny piece of land was the vassal, the maid or the slave of the master. The latter made his fellow men work for him and exploited people and animals, that is, his slaves. Many of the slaves fell dead from exhaustion. Their lives were of no value to the domineering man – unless it was a female slave whom he took to gratify his sensual desires and held captive like a bird in a cage.

The domineering man robbed his brothers and sisters, by withholding a part of the Earth from them.

Later, the Earth was divided into countries, and borders came into being.

As a result of the brutalization of mankind, the Earth began to defend itself: Natural occurrences rose to the level of disasters – they are the consequences of man's violation of the law. Mankind was then helplessly at the mercy of natural forces and, again and again, human beings fell victim to disasters.

Since people lacked insight into this development, they imagined the natural forces to be gods who were arbitrarily well or ill-disposed towards them and who sent them the disasters. With this, the people turned more and more away from the one God of love and of truth, the Creator of the heavens and the Earth, forgetting Him and worshipping their gods.

And so superstitions began. The domineering man who disrespected life, who gave little importance to animals and human beings whom he called his slaves, offered human beings and animals as sacrifices to these gods, so that they would be well-disposed towards him. Recognize: All of this is an outrage and a sin against mankind and the nature kingdoms – and against God, the law of life.

With the prophets of God and many enlightened men and women who brought the truth to mankind once again, the return to the one God began quite gradually.

From the one, eternal God of love and truth, Moses brought the Ten Commandments. He ordered the Israelites not to kill nor consume the creatures of God. The

Israelites did not always obey Moses. Especially when their own causes broke in over them as effects, they thought again of their gods and resumed the old rituals of sacrifice.

Again and again, the admonishers of God came forth. Over and over again, the people were given an understanding of the one God. The great prophet Isaiah, the bearer of divine wisdom in heaven, announced the Messiah, the bringer of life and of light for all souls and men.

The prophesy was fulfilled: I, Christ, came to mankind in Jesus and became the Son of Man. I came in order to show the people the way out of sin and slavery. As Jesus of Nazareth, I taught the laws of God and lived them as an example for the people. Mankind, however, did not recognize Me.

I taught the people to love one another, to love the animals, to respect nature, to acknowledge the Earth as the mother in whose bosom the human children live and work. I taught the people equality, freedom, unity, brotherliness and justice; I taught that they should not divide the Earth, but should share everything with each other in a brotherly way.

With this, evolution began, that is, people gradually turned towards God again.

At first, the belief in many gods was abolished, then the sacrifice of human beings and, in the further course of time, the sacrifice of animals. Today, in the turn of time from the old to the New Era, I will put an end to the cruel animal experiments, the slaughtering of animals and the consumption of their flesh. Oh recognize: It is a time of evolution – the overturn of the old, so that spirituality may come forth.

Oh grasp that I came as Jesus of Nazareth. I interpreted the laws for the people and also set an example of a life in the law of God for the people. On Golgotha, I became the Redeemer of all souls and human beings.

Your Redeemer is now also your leader into the New Era, into the time of Christ, who I Am. More and more people are turning away from the slaughter and consumption of animals. More and more people see the Earth as a whole, as their nourisher, as a part of their life. They nourish themselves with what the Earth gives them and prepare it in a lawful way, too. In the course of generations, the human race, which knows the laws of God, which keeps them and nourishes itself accordingly will quite gradually emerge.

I Am come as Jesus of Nazareth to teach the laws and live them as an example and, in this way, also to abolish the blood sacrifices and the consumption of animals and to do away with revelries. I Am come to create a new human race which fulfills the will of the eternal Father, who is the one God, from eternity to eternity.

4. You should eat of what you offer to God in purity, but you should not eat of what you do not offer in purity; for the hour will come when your bloody sacrifices and feasts will cease and you will adore God with holy veneration and pure offering. (Chap. 28:4)

I, Christ, explain, correct
and deepen the word:

The one who is pure in heart lives from what the Earth gives him. He thanks and honors God in everything. He also offers up his food to God out of a pure heart. He partakes only of that nourishment which God gives him through the Mother Earth. The pure one recognizes the pure and lives in and with it.

The impure one knows only the impure and in this way creates further filth and lives in it.

My coming has been revealed. Prepare in yourselves the path for Me, the Christ of God, for the Kingdom of God from which I come is within you.

Prepare yourselves for My coming and examine your life day by day, whether it is in the will of God. If you recognize that your sensations, thoughts, words and actions are not in conformity with the will of God, change them immediately. You should observe this when you eat and drink, too.

You should gratefully accept the gifts from God and eat that food which is in keeping with the divine law. Dedicate your pure heart to God, so that you may be the consecrated ones of life, who keep the laws of God.

The hour is drawing near, when every one will have to answer for what he has done to human beings, to nature and to animals. The New Era is dawning, in which the bloody sacrifices and animal experiments will cease, and the slaughter and consumption of animals, too, for these are the second neighbors of man. The Earth is cleansing itself from all that is base. All that is unlawful is being replaced by the higher life, in which the will of God will be fulfilled more and more.

People in the New Era will not just worship God, but will keep His laws.

5. *Therefore, let the creatures go free, that they may rejoice in God and bring no guilt to man." And the young man set them free and Jesus tore apart their cages and their fetters.*

6. *But see, they were afraid to be taken captive once more and did not want to leave Him. But He spoke to them and sent them away and they obeyed His words and departed full of joy.*

7. *As they sat by the middle one of the seven wells, Jesus stood up and called out, "Let those who thirst come to Me and drink, for I will give them of the water of life.*

8. *Rivers of water will flow out of the hearts of those who believe in Me, and they shall speak what is given to them with authority, and their teaching will be like living water.*

9. *(This is what He said of the spirit which should be attained by those who believed in Him; for the fullness of the Spirit had not been poured out, since Jesus had not yet been transfigured.)*

10. *The one who drinks of the water that I shall give will never thirst; for the water that comes from God*

shall be in him like a spring, gushing forth into eternal life."

11. In those days, John sent two disciples to ask Him, "Are You the One who shall come or shall we wait for another One?" And in this hour, He healed many sicknesses and infirmities and cast out evil spirits and gave the blind their sight.

12. Jesus answered and said to them, "Go back and report to John what you have seen and heard: That the blind see, the lame walk, the lepers are cleansed, the deaf hear, the dead are raised and the gospel is preached to the poor. And blessed is the one who does not become angry with Me."

13. And when John's messengers had departed, Jesus began to speak to the people about John. "What did you want to see when you went out into the desert? A reed that the wind blows back and forth, or a man clothed in soft garments? Behold, those who are richly clothed and live comfortably are in the courts of the kings.

14. Or what have you gone out to see? A prophet? Yes, I say to you, and he is the greatest of the prophets.

15. This is he, of whom it is written: Behold, I send My messenger before You, who will prepare Your way for You. For I say to you: Of all those born of women, there is not a greater prophet than John the Baptist."

16. And all the people and the tax gatherers who heard Him praised God and let themselves be baptized with the baptism of John. But, the Pharisees and lawyers rejected God's plan for them, and did not let themselves be baptized by him. (Chap. 28:5-16)

I, Christ, explain, correct
and deepen the word:

At all times, the Pharisees, the scribes and the sticklers for the letter of the law were the enemies of the
righteous prophets. Their preconceived opinions and
their striving for prestige, the obsession for knowing
better than their fellow men, called them up to fight
against the messengers of God again and again. The
Pharisees, the scribes and the sticklers for the letter of
the law were and are the ones who, again and again,
were and are anxious about their position and their
prestige.

The darkling knows the concern of God and senses
the power which comes from the true prophets and enlightened ones. In the sight and mind of those who have
appropriated some of the mighty potential of the Earth,
the great prophets and the enlightened ones are their
enemies, who want to take from them what, in the last
analysis, does not belong to them. This is why they
fought and are still fighting in today's time [1989]
against the just prophets and the enlightened ones, despising them and persecuting them, ridiculing them and
pouring scorn and derision upon them.

The darkling knows the message and the origin of all
great prophets and enlightened ones and also knows
whose blood flows in their veins. In all great prophets
and enlightened ones, from Abraham through Moses,
Daniel, Isaiah, up to the great teaching prophetess of
God today [1989] the same power is active: It is God's

primordial being, the light from the Sanctum of God. Many men and women and I, too, as Jesus of Nazareth, came and come, as seen from the flesh, from the lineage of David. This Christ-David-lineage has its roots in the Sanctum of God and its spiritual mission in Me, the Christ of God, namely, to set free, with Me, all that is bound.

A sign of the authenticity of a true, great prophet is that he is persecuted, slandered, despised, ridiculed and mocked by the means and methods available during his particular time.

That happened in past times, in the Old Covenant; that happened to Me when I walked the Earth as Jesus of Nazareth – and it is happening again today [1989] to the prophetess of God. Again and again, the past becomes the present, because, again and again, those souls incarnate who, already in former existences as human beings, have persecuted and killed the prophets. Their assignment to do so comes from the regions below.

Recognize that when the sinful world passes away in the last days and the new humanity emerges, many so-called prophets will appear. The one who only talks and passes himself off as a prophet, but does not reveal the depth of the word, is not a prophet. He will also not be attacked, doubted nor persecuted by the Pharisees, scribes and sticklers for the letter of the law, since he tells them what they want to hear.

Such so-called prophets are even supported by the darkness, because they lead the people astray through their "spiritual" speeches that are not imbued with the fire of the Holy Spirit. The words of the one who speaks only for his own sake are not vivified by the Spirit of truth. Neither does a vivifying spark inspire the listeners, and thus no movement towards the spiritual takes place in them, either.

Therefore, examine!

For all true prophets and enlightened ones and for all those who actualize the word of God, His holy law, My words hold true, "If they have persecuted Me, they will also persecute you."

CHAPTER 29

The Feeding of the Five Thousand –
Jesus Walks on Water

*The part-power of the primordial power
in Jesus of Nazareth, the Christ – Explanation of the multiplication of the fishes – Living and dead food – Castigation
and fanaticism – The transformation of negative habits on
the path to a higher life (4-7). Fear is doubt in the power
and love of God (12-13). There are no coincidences – The
transformation of man into the divine only by working on
himself (14). Not everyone receives help
and healing (15-18)*

1. The Passover feast came and the apostles and those who accompanied them gathered around Jesus and told Him everything that they had done and taught. And He said to them, "Come and let us go to a secluded place and rest a little." For many people came and went and they could not even eat in peace.

2. And they took a boat and secretly sailed to a lonely place. But the people saw them sailing away. Many knew Him and ran there on foot from all the cities. They arrived there first and met together close by Him.

3. And as Jesus got out of the boat, He saw many people; and He was moved to compassion, for they were like sheep who had no shepherd.

377

4. As the day was almost over, the disciples came to Him and said, "This is a secluded place and the time is almost over. Send them away, so that they may go into the nearby villages in order to buy bread; for they have nothing to eat."

5. But Jesus answered, saying to them, "Give them something to eat!" And they said to Him, "Should we go and buy bread for two hundred pennies and give them something to eat?"

6. But He said to them, "How much bread do you have? Go and see." And when they knew, they said, "Six loaves of bread and seven clusters of grapes." And He told them all to sit down on the grass in groups of fifty. And they sat down in rows of hundreds and of fifties.

7. And as He took the six loaves of bread and the seven clusters of grapes, He looked up to heaven, blessed and broke the bread and did the same with the grapes, and gave them to His disciples so that they could serve them to the people, and they distributed everything among the people. (Chap. 29:1-7)

I, Christ, explain, correct
and deepen the word:

I, Christ, worked in Jesus with the full authority of the Father; for in Jesus I was the Christ, the I Am, from eternity to eternity, the Co-Regent of the heavens.

As the part-power of the primordial power, I brought in Jesus the decisive turn in the Fall event: The part-power of the primordial power became the redeeming power and is the support for all souls and people, and is effective as the energy of evolution for all souls and people.

My heritage, the part-power of the primordial power, flowed in Me, the Jesus, and worked through Me. And so I linked with My mighty heritage and with this power I could accomplish the great so-called miracles and healings.

My task also encompassed helping, healing and raising the dead. This I did with the full authority of My Father in connection with My heritage, the part-power of the primordial power, and with this, I showed the people the power of the Christ of God on Earth. With the multiplication of the bread, the fruit and also the fish, I showed them that no person has to hunger nor be in want, if he fulfills the laws of God.

In this so-called miracle of the multiplication, it was revealed that man could live in the fullness, if he fulfilled the will of God; because the universal law is inexhaustible for spirit beings and for the souls and human beings who do the will of My Father, who is also their Father.

My disciples brought Me bread and grapes to be multiplied. On that day, dead fish were also offered to Me in order to be multiplied. As I took this dead substance into My hands, I explained to the people that the power-potential of the Father, the high power of life, was gone from it for the most part and that I would not create live fish so that they be killed again.

I explained to the people that life is in all forms of life and that man should not kill them deliberately. The people, especially the children, looked at Me very sadly. They could not understand Me, because they lived for the most part on fish, bread and little else. And then I spoke to them in the following sense: The energies of the Earth are still maintaining the dead fish. And so I will not give you living fish from the Spirit of the Father; but – from the energy of the Earth – I will create for you fish that are dead, that is, poor in vibration. They will never bear life and cannot be killed. I will show you how living things – bread and fruits – taste, and in comparison with them, the taste of the dead food.

And from the energies of the Earth, I created for them fish which bore little spirit substance. I gave them the dead fish and, at the same time, I told them to eat bread and fruits, so that they could recognize the difference between living and dead nourishment, between highly-vibrating and low-vibrating food.

In this and similar ways, I taught the people. Furthermore, I showed them – and with this I also show you who read My words – that every abrupt break with old habits is fanaticism. In the one who lets go of his old habits from one minute to the next, an abrupt break takes place and not a transformation. In this abrupt break, there lies the seed for a renewed outbreak of the old suppressed habits, which could then come out more persistently and be more difficult to put away than before the time of castigation.

Thus, old habits should not be abruptly stopped, but it should be a gradual letting go that leads to a transformation in which the person turns to higher goals and values. This is a spiritual departure to new shores.

Fanaticism lies in every castigation. In feelings and thoughts, a fanatic condemns his neighbors who still have the same or like things as what he has suppressed. In this way, he nourishes what is suppressed.

Recognize that the man of habit must be granted some humanness, until he himself recognizes his mistakes and, through self-recognition and self-experience – or through suffering – lets go of the old in order to mature spiritually. This is then the correct understanding and law-abiding guidance.

And so, with the multiplication of the fishes, I showed that man should transform and not castigate himself. Every transformation is accomplished in a law-abiding way; it is the complete change from a lower to a higher life. Just as a stone cannot turn into a flower from one day to the next, but only in the process of evolution, in the same way, the one whose habits lie in his blood and in his soul cannot change into an absolutely spiritual person from one hour to the next. Just as the stone changes in the course of evolution, the human being changes from the lower to the higher.

Thus, transformation is the change from what is human to what is spiritual. In this lies the gradual letting go of humanness and at the same time the awakening of spiritual divineness.

8. *And they all ate and were satisfied. And they gathered twelve baskets of pieces that were left over. There were five thousand men, women and children who ate from the bread and the fruits; and He taught them many things.*

9. *And when the people had seen and heard, they were filled with joy and they said, "Truly this is the prophet, the prophet who should come into the world." And as He perceived that they were determined to make a king of Him, He urged His disciples to get into the boat and go ahead of Him to the other shore, to Bethsaida, until He had sent away the crowd.*

10. *And when He had sent them away, He went up on a mountain in order to pray. When the evening had come, He was there alone, but the boat was in the middle of the sea and was tossed back and forth on the waves, for the wind was against them.*

11. *And around the third night watch, Jesus came to them; He walked on the sea. And when the disciples saw Him walking on the sea they were frightened and said, it is a ghost, and cried out in fear. But Jesus spoke to them immediately, saying, "Be of good courage. It is I, be not afraid!"*

12. *And Peter answered Him, saying, "Lord, if it is You, then let me come over the water to You." And He said, "Come!" And when Peter had stepped out of the*

boat, he walked on the water toward Jesus. But as the wind was stormy, he became afraid and, when he began to sink, he cried out, "Lord! Save me!"

13. At that very moment, Jesus reached out His hand, caught him and said to him, "O you of little faith, why do you doubt? For have I not called you?"
(Chap. 29:8-13)

I, Christ, explain, correct
and deepen the word:

Recognize that every fear is doubt in God's power and love.

God is the supporting and maintaining life. The one who doubts in this goes under. This is why every doubt in God is a falling away from God, a sinking into the floods of humanness.

Many people disregard the laws of God; they mistrust God through their fear, thus opening themselves to the promptings of the satanic. Every sensation, every thought, every word and every deed directed against the divine law of the supporting and maintaining all-harmony is a letting go of the hand of God and a sinking into the floods of the world.

Therefore, be attentive and practice recognizing and fulfilling the will of God. If you do not yet know the law of God in all details, then take the Ten Commandments in hand. They are excerpts from the powerful and all-encompassing law of God. Strive to recognize their meaning and to live accordingly, and gradually you will experience the whole law of God. For it is given today [1989] by Me through the prophetess of God, who is at the same time the teaching prophetess and emissary for the New Era.

The one who keeps the law of God is under His direct guidance.

14. *And He went to them in the boat and the wind abated. And they were amazed and marveled beyond all measure. Because they had not gained more insight through the miracle of the bread and fruits; for their hearts were hardened. (Chap. 29:14)*

I, Christ, explain, correct
and deepen the word:

And as it was at that time, when I, in Jesus of Nazareth, abided among My own, so it is still today. Every day, so-called miracles happen. Man takes them for granted, as so-called coincidences or strokes of luck which, he believes, occur from time to time, but for which there is no explanation.

Recognize that there are no coincidences. Everything is either based on the law of sowing and reaping - or it is guidance and providence through the law of love.

The power of Christ, which I Am, which once was personified in Jesus of Nazareth, continues to be active in space and time. Many people are healed through My Spirit and many are protected from bad accidents. And many a person will be led in such a way that he will be able to avoid severe problems and physical suffering. The one who believes in Me and keeps the commandment of forgiving and of asking for forgiveness and does not commit the same or similar sins anymore orients himself to My helping and healing power and receives.

All this is the so-called miracles.

My apostles and disciples were around Me daily and were witness to how the sick became healthy and how those who were believed to be dead were awakened once again to life. In spite of these experiences, the hearts of many remained cold. They were indeed amazed with these events, but it stayed at that. They could not grasp the great working of the cosmic powers, because the world still held their thoughts and senses captive.

Although I taught them the laws of God and their application, many of them remained captive in the law of sowing and reaping and were amazed at such power each day anew.

Not all of them understood that the law of God lived in them, too, and wanted to work through them in a similar way as through their master and teacher, the Son of God in Jesus of Nazareth. They were preoccupied again and again with the same questions: Why and how come was this one and not that one helped?

Since I lived and worked in the law of My Father, I was able to bring help and healing to many people. Many others, however, I could not help, because they had not brought with them the prerequisites for this in their souls. Not every one of My apostles and disciples could understand this. Again and again, a few of them began to doubt in Me and to weigh the "for and against."

In prayer, I spoke to God, My Father, again and again: How long must I still remain among these unrelenting and stubborn people?

Recognize that the one who only listens to the law of love and does not actualize it in his life can be around an enlightened person day after day, hour after hour; yet he remains the sinner that he was and is. The transformation of a person from the sinful to the divine happens through actualization, through working on oneself.

Thus, the transformation to the divine requires working on oneself beforehand. Act by transforming with Me, the Christ, your sensations, thoughts, words and actions into positive powers and then you will attain enlightenment! And then much will be possible for you through the power of the Holy Spirit. For the one who truly follows Me will do similar things as I have done.

15. *And when they got into the boat, there was a great calm. And they came to Him and paid homage to Him saying, "Truly, You are the Son of God."*

16. When they crossed over, they came into the area of Gennesaret and landed at the shore. And when they got out of the boat, He was recognized immediately. And they went about the whole surrounding countryside and when the people heard He was there, they began to bring the sick in their beds.

17. And wherever He came into villages or cities or into the countryside, they laid the sick at the roadside and asked Him that they be allowed to touch only the hem of His garment; and all those who touched Him became well.

18. And after that, Jesus came to Judea with His disciples, and He remained there and baptized many who came to Him and accepted His teachings.
(Chap. 29:15-18)

I, Christ, explain, correct
and deepen the word:

Many people came to Me in Jesus of Nazareth; yet not every one of them received what he had asked for. Many came and wanted help only for their bodies, so that they could live in the flesh again, as they had formerly: in sin. Many touched the hem of My garment, yet not all of them received help and healing. Help and healing were given to those who touched the hem of My garment and believed in the love of God and continued to maintain the good in their hearts. The one who touched the hem of My garment and thought only of his body, who kept sin in his heart and continued to sin in the following earthly years, received neither help nor healing.

It is written, "... and He remained there and baptized many." The word "baptism" means the blessing of the heart, of the inner being, through the Holy Spirit. I saw into the hearts of My own and recognized that those who lived in the actualization of the laws of God increased the light and the power of God in themselves every day. My blessing caused further seeds of inner life to grow in them and caused them to strive towards perfection in order to pass on to the people what they actualized in and on themselves, in their present earthly life and in further incarnations.

CHAPTER 30

The Bread of Life
and the Living Vine

Christ gives spiritual bread for the inner life –
The path to the Kingdom of Peace: The fight and sacrifice of
the just (5). The one who aligns with God receives the power
of life (6). Redemption and grace are in Christ – Illness,
suffering and fate are the guilt that has become visible –
The Day of Judgment (7). The human eye sees only the
earthly shell which perishes – The spirit body slips in and
steps out of the earthly body – The way of the cross of the
prophetess of God at the turn of time — The development
of externalized Christianity (8-10)

1. *On the following day, the people who stood on the*
other side of the sea saw that there was no other boat
there than the one which His disciples stepped into, and
that Jesus was not in the boat with them, but that the
disciples departed alone. And as the people saw that
Jesus was not there, nor His disciples, they also took a
boat and went to Capernaum, looking for Jesus.

2. *As they found Him on the other side of the sea,*
they said to Him, "Rabbi, how did you get here?" Jesus
answered them, saying, "Verily, I say to you, you look
for Me not because you saw miracles, but because you
ate of the bread and the fruits and were satisfied. Do
not labor for the food which is perishable, but for the

food that endures unto everlasting life which is given to you by the Son of Man, who is also the child of God; for God, the All-Father, sent Him."

3. Then they asked Him, "What shall we do so that we do the work of God?" Jesus answered, saying to them, "This is the work of God, that you believe in Him whom He has sent and who gives you truth and life."

4. They then said to Him, "What sign do You give so that we can see and believe You? What do you bring about? Our forefathers have eaten manna in the desert, as it is written: He gave them bread from heaven to eat."

5. Then Jesus said to them, "Verily, verily, I say to you, not Moses gave you the true bread from heaven, but My Father gave you the true bread from heaven and the fruit of the living vine. For this is the food of God, which comes from heaven and gives life to this world." (Chap. 30:1-5)

I, Christ, explain, correct
and deepen the word:

Verily, God, My Father, the great All-One, appointed Me, His first-beheld and firstborn Son, as Co-Regent of the heavens and gave Me the omnipresent power in His four natures. They are the steps of evolution towards the filiation in God.

Thus, My omnipresent power is also the energy of evolution. A part of this energy of evolution became the power of redemption for all fallen and burdened souls and human beings.

Redemption is evolution; it is also the support, liberation and guidance for all souls and men back to the Father-Mother-God; for all spirit beings, souls and men are His children.

I became a human being in order to show the people the path into the Father's house. I came into the earthly existence and gave evidence of the inner power with which man is capable of everything if he enters the inner life. I multiplied bread, fruits and fishes. I transformed water into wine; I helped and I healed many people; I awakened many a one from so-called death, if the spiritual information cord, which connects soul and body, was not yet severed from the body. I taught the people that they can live in the world in fullness only if they also fulfill the law of God in daily life; for the law of God is the fullness.

Many did not want to understand Me, for they were concerned only with their body and its well-being. This is why they could not, or did not want to understand Me when I spoke about the spiritual bread for the inner life. They did not long for the bread that comes from heaven and which is the only food for the soul. They wanted to remain as sinful as they were, and wanted the earthly bread for their material bodies and further comforts for their earthly existence.

God, My Father, the Father-Mother-God of all His children, appointed Me in heaven as Co-Regent of the entire creation and sent Me to all souls and people as Redeemer. The one who comes to Me and accepts and receives Me, his Redeemer, who returns to the inner kingdom is also rich in his inner being; he will neither hunger nor thirst. He will receive that which his soul has opened up as light and power. He will have food and drink in the earthly existence and will receive what he needs for his body: clothing and shelter – and beyond that. Therefore, the one who strives first towards the Kingdom of God will not live in want as a human being.

I spoke to the people about the Kingdom of God which is within them. With the power of this inner kingdom, I helped them within as well as without. Most people, however, wanted a miracle-worker who would make their earthly life comfortable for them. They wanted a king for an earthly kingdom and not the inner king, the Co-Regent of the heavens.

My brothers and sisters, you who are living in another time, in the Era of Light, can hardly understand what is written here. And yet, the Earth, the soil on which you live in earthly garment, was bought with My blood and with the blood and the body and the sacrifice of many just prophets and just men and women. Every humiliation they endured and every drop of blood that flowed for justice was for the redemption of all.

The Earth, the seat of the darkness, was conquered by the light through these selfless deeds and divine works, and the demonic was bound. Over many generations, blood flowed and people sacrificed themselves for justice and helped the plan of God, redemption, to break through.

They were the pioneers for the New Era in ever new incarnations. Again and again, they were persecuted, even as these words were being written down [1989].

From generation to generation, the light on Earth increased through those people who fulfilled the laws of God more and more. Out of the chaos of the human ego, the light streamed and took form and shape on Earth.

With My power and in My name, the pioneers for the New Era bound the satanic.

The Earth has been won back by brothers and sisters from the lineage of David, the tribe for the Kingdom of Peace of Jesus Christ, and by many righteous men and women from other lineages. Satan, the demonic, is bound. The men and women who suffered unimaginably much in the earthly garment now stand in their spiritual garment at My right side and shine like the stars in heaven.

6. *And they said to Him, "Lord, give us such bread and such fruits forever." And Jesus said to them, "I am the true bread and the living vine and the one who comes to Me will never hunger and the one who believes in Me will never thirst. And verily, I say to you, unless you eat the flesh and drink the blood of God, you will not have the life. However, you have seen Me and do not believe. (Chap. 30:6)*

I, Christ, explain, correct
and deepen the word:

"... you eat the flesh and drink the blood of God"
means that you eat the food of heaven, thus receiving
the energy of God, and drink from the source of life,
from the Spirit of God.

Recognize that God provided the Earth with fruits,
herbs and water for the well-being of the human body.
The one who accepts the gifts of God thankfully by fulfilling the law of God not only satisfies his body, but
also nourishes his soul. In every earthly gift of God is
also the power of God, the bread of heaven and the
water of life.

The bread and the fruits of the Earth nourish all people only when people do not consider them as their personal property, but regard the gifts of God as His gift
for all people. But the prerequisite for this is that the
person not only think about the satisfaction of the body,
but cause the source of the soul to flow: the Spirit of
God, which is the living bread and the living fruit. The
one who comes to the Spirit of God in Me, to the Christ
of God, to the Redeemer of all souls and men, will
receive from the eternal bread and will neither hunger
nor thirst.

For the bread and the fruit of the earth, also grow
only through the life in and out of God. Nothing comes
from itself. Everything that is good comes from God.
The one who does not believe in God will not receive

from God in the long run, because he does not align himself with the inner life, with the giving God.

Many people saw and heard Me as Jesus of Nazareth and yet did not believe in the power of life, about which I taught and which I personified.

7. All those whom My Father has given to Me will come to Me, and I will not cast out the one who comes to Me. For I came down from heaven, to do not My will, but the will of God who has sent Me. However, this is the will of God who has sent Me, that I not lose any of those who were given to Me, but that I raise them again on the Day of Judgment." (Chap. 30:7)

I, Christ, explain, correct
and deepen the word:

My Father, who is also your Father, sent Me to the people. I became a human being in order to dwell among men and to make known, in the language of man, what eternal life is.

The Son of God who, as human being, became the Son of Man, came from heaven to bring redemption. Since God, My Father, loves all children in the same way, He also gave Me the authority and the power to lead all souls home to His heart. I came from heaven to reveal the will of God to the people and to fulfill His will among the people.

No man and no soul will be cast out by Me, for I have brought redemption for all. Only the person who rejects the will of God and continues to live in his own self-will, in sin, casts himself into his own fate. In spite of everything, he bears redemption in himself and, at My hand, he will one day find his way back, and I will lead him to the Father, for all souls and men are redeemed in and through Me.

The one who devotes himself to Me, the Christ, does not have to bear every sin that he committed. For the one who, from his heart, comes to Me, the Christ, also strives to recognize and fulfill the will of God in every situation. And the one who honestly strives to do the will of God has already received from God.

To come to Me means not only to pray to Me, but also to actualize the laws of life on oneself and in relation to one's neighbor. The one who heeds the laws of God has turned towards Me, the Christ of God. He will not have to harvest his human sowing.

The one who turns towards Me experiences in and around himself the grace of the Most High. It supports each person in every situation of life. It builds up the person, strengthens him and helps him to recognize the sins and to clear them up before they manifest themselves on the physical body.

Sins formerly committed become visible on the body when the person is unreasonable and deliberately overlooks the many admonishments and hints. If the sin has become visible on the body through illness, grief or fate, then it should also be borne by the person.

However, do not despair! Pray to God and place yourselves in His holy will. Then the love and grace of God can become active, remove the illness or give you strength, so that you are able to bear the sin which has flowed out.

Every sin which has become visible can be compared to a birth: The sin shows itself in the body as the offspring of what the soul has carried. The stubbornness of the person is the midwife who delivers the sin from the soul. The person makes room for the sin to spread itself out in the body.

The "Day of Judgment" for the soul is not the hour of death of the person, nor a predetermined time, but is the awakening of the soul to the divine and the entering into higher, more light-filled spheres of life, all the way to the Father-Mother-God, who is the absolute life.

All people, souls and beings, as well as I, Christ, the Redeemer, are children of the eternal life. As the Son of God and as the Redeemer, I Am the omnipresent life in God, My Father. Through His power, I lead every soul into the consciousness of the unity with and in God, into the eternal life.

8. *Then the Jews grumbled that He said, "I Am the bread which has come down from heaven." And they said, "Is this not Jesus, the son of Joseph and Mary, whose parents we know? How can He now say, I Am come down from heaven?"*

9. *Jesus answered, saying to them, "Do not grumble among yourselves. No one can come to Me unless holy love and wisdom draws him, and they shall resurrect on the Day of Judgment. And it is written in the prophets: They shall all be taught by God. Each one who has heard and grasped the truth comes to Me.*

10. *Not that anyone has seen the Holiest at any time, except those who are of the Holiest, they alone see the Holiest. Verily, verily, I say to you, the one who believes in the truth has everlasting life."(Chap. 30:8-10)*

I, Christ, explain, correct
and deepen the word:

The words "I Am the bread which has come down from heaven" mean that only the life in and with God is the true life. Everything else is human conceptions of life or projections of wishes and longings.

The bread, which I, as Jesus of Nazareth, brought to mankind is the Spirit of God, the nourishment of the soul – the life that I Am in the Father. The one who has become the truth is the truth and lives in the truth. He will never live in want, for the truth is God and God is the fullness.

I Am the truth and the bread of the soul. The eternal heavens are the law of truth. I came from the truth and I Am the truth.

Jesus was the flesh that came from the material substance – the earthly body which, as an instrument, served the truth. This alone is what the people saw and expressed as follows, "Is this not Jesus, the son of Joseph and Mary, whose parents we know?"

The man begets the body, and the woman carries it under her heart and gives birth to the outer life, the form in which the being from God, the soul, dwells.

The human eye looks only at the flesh and the human mouth speaks of the flesh. The human eye does not perceive the inner being which is enclosed by the shell, the flesh. However, the one who looks to the Spirit of God, by fulfilling the laws of God, perceives the inner being of the person and does not inquire about the reputation and position of the person or about his parents. He perceives what the flesh does not see and knows that it is not the status and prestige in this world that matter, but only the inner being of the person.

Recognize: No awakened soul lives in a rich one who only thinks of possession and prestige and whose heart has become cold. Such a soul is still asleep, dozing unawakened, and, as a result, does not yet grasp its origin either.

But the time to turn back will one day come to the rich one, too, whose only thinking and striving is directed towards possession and prestige; and his soul will be jolted and shaken, so that it may awaken in the Spirit of truth and gradually recognize its origin. For only those who have opened their heart for the love of God and for wisdom can come to God, in the heart of the inner life.

One day, all will accept and receive in themselves the teachings from the Spirit of love and wisdom and walk the path to the Father that I, Christ, Am. I Am the way, the truth and the life. Only the one who accepts and receives Me, the Christ of God, the Redeemer, in himself, finds his way into the very heart of the Eternal.

The one who believes in the truth and fulfills the laws of God consciously possesses the life even now. For him there is no death, which the unaware one calls the end. For the awakened one, death is the gateway to inner life, which he has already unfolded as a human being on the path within.

Know that in the eternal Being, life is the universal power of God. It is the consciousness of the Father-Mother-God, out of which the spirit form came forth. The pure spirit form, the spiritual primordial form, is weightless primordial substance, is it compressed eternal law. It is the spirit being in the heavens. Only when it goes into matter for incarnation does its spiritual body envelop itself with the substances of the purification planes, become a soul and then enter into a body which is subject to decay.

No soul will resurrect with its earthly body, for it has discarded it. And when the soul returns to the flesh again, a new body is begotten and born for it, into which it slips and which it will slip out of again, because no physical body is able to enter the fine-material worlds. There is only the slipping into the body and the stepping out of the flesh.

I came into the flesh in order to live among men and to give them an understanding of the gospel of love in the language of men. It frees the person who lives accordingly and aspires to the love and wisdom of God.

The one who fulfills will be filled with the love and wisdom of God. He has become the truly wise one. He lives consciously in God and God lives through him. Such a person has already reached the spiritual resurrection. In the hour when he leaves his earthly body, his spiritual body will consciously enter the glory of the eternal Father. His spiritual body will behold the eternal Holy One, because the child of God has become the truth. The awakened soul, joined with God, will not seek out an earthly body anymore – unless it still has to fulfill a divine mission for men and souls.

Now I speak to My brothers and sisters in the New Era, in the era of Christ:

My brothers and sisters in Me, Christ, in the book "This Is My Word," you read again and again, that the female principle of divine wisdom was in an earthly garment. The person served Me as an instrument in order to address and express with the language of man – as I did as Jesus – what was of significance at that time [1989]. She came into this world with the mission of preparing the New Era with Me, Christ, and with her spirit-dual who was, as I, active in the Spirit of God and out of the omnipotence of God.

In many situations, the life of the divine wisdom in earthly garment resembled My life as Jesus of Nazareth.

The high being in the earthly garment, the handmaid of God, had to endure similar things as I did, as Jesus of Nazareth. Her life in the service of God for man was a daily way of the cross. She bore the cross of mockery, ridicule, slander and deliberate lies by those who called themselves Christian. Among them were many representatives of the church institutions of that time.

It was an externalized Christianity, a so-called state religion that was split into two main branches, a Catholic and a Protestant church. Both denominations were based on a Bible which contained only parts of the eternal truth. However, this book was not the standard for their lives, although they referred to it as the word of God. They spoke about the Bible and, from it, read the gospel to their believers. And yet, only the fewest of those who called themselves shepherds followed what they expected of their faithful.

Before My time as Jesus of Nazareth and after My earthly life, much was revealed from the eternal truth. Many people wrote down the truth, also in the so-called gospels. What happened? Some scholars appointed by the church institution selected from the numerous existing spiritual writings just a few which they considered to be the truth, and made a book out of them, which they called "Bible." According to their understanding and at their own discretion, they crossed out many truths and inserted untruths.

And so it became a book, like many other books, because it contained only parts of the truth. The one who wanted to find the truth in it would have had to first walk the path of the Sermon on the Mount, the Inner Path. But the result of this would have been that there would no longer have been a hierarchy in the church with power and authority over its fellow man. The representatives of the church would have had to give up their high earthly income and the institutions would have had to forgo their wealth – according to the word, "You should not gather any riches that may be eaten by moths or rust and where the thieves will come and steal it. Gather treasures for yourselves in the Kingdom of God." They would have had to be brothers among brothers and sisters.

The representatives of both denominations also call themselves shepherds of their flocks. Many also used My name, Christ, in order to do business with it and to subjugate, slander, defame and kill their fellow man. Mark My words, they used My name for self-seeking purposes, but not for Me, the Christ.

Many representatives of the church lacked humility; they even distinguished themselves with arrogance and abused the faith of their subjects.

In the course of many centuries, this so-called Christian world gradually dissolved. It disintegrated from within, for I, Christ, could not be with the so-called Christian churches, as they did not want to be with Me. In spite of the opposition of both main church branches, I, Christ, was victorious with the divine wisdom and with many brothers and sisters in the earthly garment and, ahead of all, with those from the lineage of David.

My brothers and sisters in the New Era: The struggle is over – the life out of God is born. You live in the New Era solely with Me, the Christ, and we live in God, our Father, without external religion and dogma. The life is the life out of God; the law of love links and unites us. These words, My words of the Christ, I gave at the turn of the age from the old, sinful world to the New Era, at the beginning of the Kingdom of Peace of Jesus Christ [1989].

I repeat, so that it may be impressed upon you: The seraph of divine wisdom served Me as instrument and took on the flesh for this and other tasks in order to serve God-Father and Me, the Christ, as the handmaid of God. The life of this woman in earthly garment was one great sacrifice. Despite much resistance – especially on the part of the church representatives of that time – and, despite many a defeat, through people who, though having given their yes to Me, sought out the world again, she rose to the fight again and again, picked herself up anew, and fought against all adversity and opposition which was brought against her. Day and night, the darklings lurked around her in order to torment and thus silence her. However, the woman, the high spirit being in earthly garment, the handmaid of God, did not keep silent. After each fight, even though it exhausted her body, she picked herself up and continued to fight for justice, for the Kingdom of God on Earth, the Kingdom of Peace – in which you now live.

I repeat many things when it has to do with the co-bearer of divine wisdom in the earthly garment. You should carry her in your heart; for when you close your physical eyes, you will see a shining crystal before your spiritual eyes. It is the seraph of divine wisdom in the radiant garment of inner life. With you, she will continue to serve the Eternal in the fine-material spheres, in order to bring all souls home to the Father's heart in Me and through Me, Christ, your divine brother.

CHAPTER 31

The Bread of Life –
The Testimony of Peter – The Camel Driver

*The spiritually dead – There are no masks
in the realms of the souls – Words are only symbols and
guides – Castigation is repression – Every person has free
will: A good seed brings a good harvest – God admonishes,
He does not punish (1-3). The wandering of Moses through
the wilderness with the people of Israel: A parable for the
journey of mankind – The people of today are no different
than the people of Israel – The path into the Kingdom of
Peace (4). The one who loves God more than this world
lives in God – The one who is of the truth receives from the
truth (5-6). To the people in the Kingdom of Peace – The
evolution of the people and of the Earth toward the fine-
material – Change in measuring time – Earth spots, the
reserves of the demons – The guiding back of the Fall
realms – The book "This Is My Word" will be raised again
and again toward the light-material – The "for" and
"against" of many people serves the darkness (7-9). Love the
animals, too! (12-16)*

1. And once again Jesus said, "I am the true bread
and the living vine. Your forefathers ate manna in the
wilderness and died. This is the food of God which
comes down from heaven, so that the one who eats of it
will not die. I am the living food which comes down

*from heaven. The one who will eat of this food will live
forever. And the bread that I will give is My truth, and
the wine that I will give is My life."*

*2. Then the Jews quarreled among themselves say-
ing, "How can this man give himself to us as food?"
Jesus said to them, "Do you think that I speak of eating
flesh, as you unknowingly do in the temple of God?*

*3. Verily, My body is divine substance, and this is the
true food; and My blood is the life of God, and this is
the true drink. Not as your ancestors who craved flesh,
and in His wrath God gave them flesh and they ate it in
their depravity until it stank in their nostrils. Thousands
fell to the plague, and their corpses lay in the wilderness.
(Chap. 31:1-3)*

I, Christ, explain, correct
and deepen the word:

The food of heaven is the law of God – the truth.
The drink is the eternally flowing life – God. The one
who accepts and actualizes the law of God will neither
hunger nor live in want, nor will he feel or taste
death.

The one who believes in death is spiritually dead because his soul is blinded by sin. But the one who has
unfolded the life in himself will neither feel nor taste
death, because for him, the direct life in God is without
end.

However, the one who is incorrigible and wastes his earthly days and sees his earthly life alone as the standard for all things will, as a soul, also be what he was as a human being: spiritually dead, blinded by his own sins and incorrigible – until he feels his deeds on his own soul body and has to recognize what grace had been granted the soul in the earthly garment.

Recognize that there are no masks in the realm of the souls. Everything with which the person disguises himself, so that his thoughts and deeds will not be recognized, falls away from him at the moment of physical death. The soul does not take the masks of the human ego with it into the realm of the souls. There, everything is manifest. The soul itself is an open book to all other souls – and to it, too, every other soul is visible in the garment of its deeds.

The one who partakes of the spiritual food, of the eternal truth, by fulfilling the will of God, becomes the living source of true life and will offer, to men as well as to souls, the bread of truth and the drink of the eternally flowing life: Christ. The life that I, as Jesus, brought to man is divine substance, the true food and the divine stream, the drink, the life in and from God.

However, the one who takes the words literally that I spoke as Jesus of Nazareth will still go astray today, for words were and are just symbols and guides to the inner truth.

The one who takes the word literally misunderstands his fellow man and belittles him – just as the Pharisees and the scribes misunderstood My words as Jesus and disparaged Me. The meaning of the words of life can be grasped and correctly interpreted only by those people who long for the truth and also strive for it. But the one who is against his neighbor by disparaging him and treating him without understanding will go astray again and again. The one who rejects his fellow man for whatever reason knows neither his neighbor nor himself.

Some of the Jews, too, lived in this consciousness; for they spoke in the following sense, "How can this man give himself to us as food?" However, I did not speak of the flesh as material substance, but of the divine substance, of the true food and of drink, of the eternally flowing life, the Spirit, God.

The soul of the person who makes of meat and fish his main food gradually is blunted to the fine cosmic vibrations; his physical body becomes coarser in its structure, and he becomes more egocentric and more brutal towards his surroundings.

Recognize that if the body of a person is accustomed to eating meat, he should not stop this from one day to the next. This would be castigation, which, in turn, leads to other excesses. That is why Moses made concessions to the people and I, too, as Jesus of Nazareth – like, for example, the multiplication of the fishes.

It is better for a person to recognize his faults and weaknesses and to outgrow them gradually through the actualization of the eternal laws, than to castigate himself and thereby possibly build up further negativities and immoralities as well.

The human, that is, non-divine, aspects gradually fall away, as if by themselves, from the person who actualizes the laws of God. It is a spiritual principle that when you actualize the commandments of God, your soul becomes more light-filled, your senses become finer and your character becomes selfless. Through castigation, the humanness is only suppressed, but not transformed.

"Verily, My body is divine substance, and this is the true food" means that the spiritual body is divine primordial energy that has taken on form. Through it, the life, the primordial power, flows – it is the food and drink in one.

The words "... in His wrath God gave them ..." are to be understood as follows: God gave free will to all spirit beings as well as to all souls and men. This is why every person also has free will. He can accept and actualize the laws of freedom and of life, or he can disregard them and also act contrary to the laws. For this, he then has to bear what he has sown.

The good seed brings a good harvest, the bad seed, a bad harvest. Every person can freely choose which seed he sows: a good, a less good or a bad one. Each one himself – and not his neighbor – harvests the fruits that come from this; each one harvests only the fruits of his own sowing. Many people who have to bear the effects of their causes do not know that these are the fruits of their own sowing and, as a result, they are of the opinion that the wrath of God has hit them.

God is love and does not get angry.

God takes man's vices from him, but only when he repents of them and gives them over to Him, when he makes amends and no longer indulges in them. God does not punish His children. God admonishes His child in manifold ways to turn back, to refine and to ennoble itself in sensations, thoughts, words and deeds, as well as in its choice of food. God does not punish His child, even if it does not listen to the manifold admonishments and indications. However, according to the law of sowing and reaping, the one who does not want to listen has to bear what he has caused himself. God did not include castigation in the law of sowing and reaping, but the transformation of the base into the higher.

And so, illnesses and epidemics are based on a wrong way of feeling, speaking and acting, and also on a wrong diet and animal-based food. If a person nourishes himself solely with the gifts of nature which the Earth gives to man, but violates the divine law in his feeling, thinking, speaking and acting, then he neutralizes the positive powers in the food, that is, he transforms them down into negative power.

4. *For of this it is written: Before they enter the land of rest, they shall wander in the wilderness forty-nine years until they are cleansed of their cravings; yes, seven times seven years shall they wander; for they have not known My ways, nor followed My commandments. (Chap. 31:4)*

I, Christ, explain, correct
and deepen the word:

Moses received the mission from God to lead the enslaved Israelites out of Egypt and into the promised land, into the land of their forefathers.

A great part of the people which God had entrusted to Moses was stubborn. For this reason, Moses made several concessions to the people, in order to lead many a one, by way of his stubbornness, to recognition and inner maturity. He emphatically taught them that these concessions were not the laws of God, but only aids so that through self-recognition they should find their way onto the path of the commandments.

Some found their way to the commandments and followed them; others remained faithful to the commandments, as did Moses and Aaron; yet many from the people of Israel continued to sin despite knowing better. They continued to eat meat, to drink strong drinks and to pursue their cravings and passions. Many also remained faithful to their idols and clung to the customs of the Egyptians. And so, for a long time, the wandering people remained a multitude of people without inner unity.

What man sows, he will reap. This was also true of the Israelites: By the thousands, they died in the wilderness on their way to the so-called promised land. Their souls left the Earth. Many of them recognized their wrong behavior in the soul realms, atoned and then returned more free and light-filled into a new earthly garment; for the Israelites begot and gave birth on the way to the promised land. In this way, the people multiplied and regenerated. In the alteration of birth and death, more and more Israelites accepted the one God and refined their customs. After seven times seven years, only a few from the first generation were still in the earthly garment and came into the land that was destined for them.

During these forty-nine years, Moses, the prophet, had to endure unimaginably much. He suffered for the sake of the people. He prayed for the people; he pled with God for mercy for the people and asked God again and again that he be allowed to make concessions. The people saw Moses, but in the end did not recognize or grasp who was with them in Moses. Moses brought the Ten Commandments and taught the people how they should keep them. Yet many did not understand him. Many prayed and sinned at the same time. Many spoke of the commandments of God and did not keep them. Many accused Moses because of his leadership, calling him a false prophet or a stubborn wise man, because he did not grant them everything they expected from him. For the same reason, many accused God, yet remained in the flock and, again and again, poisoned the hearts of other Israelites. Many Israelites kept their golden calf. At the very latest, as souls, they had to recognize that they had opposed God and Moses. They repented and returned into the flesh to the children of Israel and were in their ranks again as infants, then as youth and as older ones. When the Israelites entered the seemingly promised land many years later, many could no longer remember the exodus out of Egypt.

I, Christ, the ruler of the Kingdom of Peace, now speak to the people of the New Era who will read My word and think about the people of God which, today [1989], is again being guided out of its enslavement into the New Era, into the time of Christ.

At the time of Moses, the Israelites were not only the slaves of the Egyptians, but were also enslaved by their way of thinking. The other peoples were just as enslaved by their way of thinking as were the Israelites. People thought only of themselves, they were greedy and feuded with their neighbor.

People fought against people with weapons; they were enemies of one another and not brothers. Nation fought against nation. Many people fought against each other with negative thoughts, too. Through hatred, enmity and quarrel against each other, they isolated themselves against each other and created systems of laws which they made into their rules. They also confined themselves in "mine and thine" and thereby made claims of ownership for the individuals and for their people. This is why they drew national borders and checked all those who wanted to cross them. And so, one was against the other. The one who did not heed the rules, the law of the country, who thought or wanted to live differently, was punished according to his offence, either by way of his property, his freedom or even by death.

The excesses of the people were manifold. The peoples of the old, sinful world degenerated more and more. Just as in the time of Noah, they seduced and let themselves be seduced. They were gluttonous and drank strong drinks. They killed animals and consumed them. They violated the plant and animal kingdoms. This continued all over the Earth, also after My life on Earth.

During the turn from the sinful era to the New Era [1989], they modified the plants, animals and human beings and did gene-experiments on them. They created so-called test-tube babies. They destroyed nature with nuclear tests and constructed nuclear reactors to produce energy. They polluted the rivers, lakes and seas with chemical substances and caused the death of earthly life in great stretches of water.

In all nations, many people forgot the existence of God. Their god was self-interest. They calculated in terms of years of life, for they considered the earthly existence as the only possibility of life. This is why they worked solely for their own advantage and went marauding in order to take possession of as much and as fast as possible, so that they could live as seemed comfortable to them; for they considered this to be happiness. They had their idols although they prayed to o n e God. Their idols were money and possessions, prestige, power and high ranking people. What took place in the evolution of mankind over long periods of time showed manifestations that were quite similar to the life of the people of Israel at the time of Moses.

Under the guidance of Moses, the Israelites reached the first station of the promised land. The journey of the people into the promised land continued from the time of Moses onward. Generation after generation wandered through the "wilderness world," that is, their own human morass. In spite of all this, more and more people awoke to spirituality and in this way grew out of the morass of their own ego.

After Moses and after My earthly life as well, God, the Almighty, sent prophets, prophetesses and enlightened men and women over and over again. They all were proclaimers and admonishers to mankind for the Kingdom of God. They taught the path within and interpreted the commandments of the Lord in the language of their respective time.

Many of these admonishers and proclaimers also prepared the way on Earth for the part-ray of divine wisdom, the messenger of God, who worked in the mighty turn of time [1989] and had a similar mission as Moses and as I had at that time, as Jesus of Nazareth.

I, Christ, and the cherub of divine wisdom revealed the eternal laws through the incarnated female principle of divine wisdom and so gathered the people of God, in order to lead it into the inner being, into the Kingdom of God which is within, in every person.

Again, it was similar as in the time of Moses. Those who let themselves be touched by God and could understand the word of God and the guidance through Me, Christ, according to their consciousness, strove to walk the path of God, merely in response to the word. However, at that moment when they should have worked on themselves to really fulfill what I commanded them – to repent, to forgive, to ask for forgiveness and to no longer commit the same faults and sins – many became stubborn; for they did not want to look at their faults and weaknesses and thus, did not want to clear them up, either. They only wanted to hear the word of God and argue about what they heard, while remaining the same. They clung to possessions and property, and placed money and goods before the fullness of God. And so, like the children of Israel, they doubted the word of God and pilloried the prophetess of God.

A further group of people wanted to maintain their base, human aspects and to live accordingly and, at the same time, to aspire to the highest. However, man cannot serve two masters, mammon and God. Great difficulties and discrepancies resulted from this.

Still other people covered up their negative thoughts with hypocritical words, by pretending spirituality. And yet other people spoke about following Christ and did the opposite, by persecuting the true followers.

However, the people of God gradually crystallized out of this colorful conglomeration of human egos, of hypocrites, word-twisters, slanderers, doubters and sanctimonious ones:

Sons and daughters of God consciously entered the following of the Christ. They were mainly from the lineage of David, which became the tribe of David for the Kingdom of Peace. Their mission, to be active, with Me, Christ, in the Work of Redemption, became more and more tangible in them and activated them.

With their sister, the prophetess and emissary of God, they gathered further sons and daughters from the tribe of David and from other lineages.

According to My instructions, they founded – as already revealed – the Inner Spirit-Christ Churches, gathering places for all seeking people. They taught the path to the heart of God which was revealed on My behalf by the cherub of divine wisdom, called Brother Emanuel by the people. In order to be able to fulfill the laws of God in all areas of life, they set up artisan enterprises and acquired farms. They founded kindergartens, father-mother-houses, schools, clinics and homes for the elderly. They thus began building up everything that people needed for the New Era and in the New Era. They placed all the new and developing activities for the Kingdom of God into the law of God which reads: Pray and work, and keep peace with your neighbor.

Through them, I founded the Original Community New Jerusalem, which became the Covenant Community and the central light for all further original communities in Universal Life and in the emerging Kingdom of Peace of Jesus Christ.

The prophetess and emissary of God stood in the midst of this time of setting out and of radical change. She was loved and respected by some people and despised, doubted, slandered and ridiculed by others. As in My time as Jesus of Nazareth, the Pharisees and scribes again incited the people against Me, the Universal Spirit, in order to silence Me. To no avail. They passed away, and the New Era, the Kingdom of Peace of Jesus Christ, emerged.

It is important to record this: My instrument, the incarnated part-ray of divine wisdom, and many sons and daughters of God from the tribe of David and from other lineages who had gathered in the Covenant Community New Jerusalem around the central light, Me, Christ in God, My Father, withstood the enticements and attacks of the satanic. With many righteous men and women, in the midst of the gradual disintegration of the sinful world, they began to found the people of God which, over generations, became a mighty purified people in Christ.

It happened as in the time of Moses: The souls discarded their earthly bodies and slipped once more into newborn bodies. Generations passed and new, more light-filled generations came to the Earth. From them, the purified people of God and the Kingdom of Peace of Jesus Christ gradually emerged. The emerging people of God begot and gave birth to children in which souls came again that had already taken some steps on the path within, in the first and the following generations.

And so, throughout the generations, the Kingdom of Peace of Jesus Christ, the Kingdom of God on the purified, light-filled Earth on which you live, came into being. The demonic is bound. Selfless love radiates in and from the hearts of the blessed ones. Peace and joy are among them.

5. *But the one who eats this flesh and drinks this blood lives in Me and I in him. Just as the living Father, out of whom I live, has sent Me, even they shall live by Me who eat of Me, who Am the truth and the life.*
6. *This is the living bread which has come down from heaven and gives life to the world. Not as your forefathers who ate the manna and died. The one who eats this bread and this fruit will live forever." He said such things in the synagogue as He taught in Capernaum. When many of His disciples heard this, they said, "That is a harsh speech; who can accept it?"(Chap. 31:5-6)*

I, Christ, explain, correct
and deepen the word:

"But, the one who eats this flesh and drinks this blood lives in Me and I in him" has the following meaning:

The one who lives in the Spirit of God, that is, who does the will of God, receives the spiritual gifts. And the one who loves God more than this world lives in God and in Me, the Christ of God. For the Father sent Me, His Son, to the people, so that I might set an example for the people of what makes them rich in heart, and so that I might bring them what raises them once again to be children of God: the redemption and the guidance to the heart of God.

"... even they shall live by Me who eat of Me, who Am the truth and the life" means:

Christ lives through the one who lives in Christ, and the one who lives in Me bears witness of the truth. For the one who is of the truth receives from the truth and will neither hunger nor thirst, for he is in Me the truth and the life. The eternal truth is the eternal love of God, the primordial law.

The one who is imprisoned in egoistic love cannot understand the absolute, consistent, eternal law. His deceitful ego, the egoistic love, then speaks of the harshness of the eternal law, because his human ego does not acknowledge it.

The one who lives in the law of God speaks the truth, because he has become the truth. Only the one who is earnest and righteous towards himself and his neighbor can understand and joyfully accept the truth. But the one who is caught up in his conceptions and opinions speaks about the harshness of the law and about the punishment, because he wants to see and have it differently for himself, personally.

7. *But when Jesus recognized that His disciples were grumbling about it, He said to them, "Does this offend you? How would it be if you were to see the Son of Man ascend to where He has been before? It is the Spirit that gives life; flesh and blood profit nothing. The words which I speak to you are Spirit and are life.*

8. *But there are quite a few among you who do not believe." For Jesus knew from the beginning which ones did not believe and who would betray Him. This is why He said to them, "No one can come to Me unless it is given to him by My Father."*

9. *From then on, many of His disciples left and henceforth walked with Him no more. And so Jesus spoke to the twelve, "Do you, too, want to leave Me?"* (Chap. 31:7-9)

I, Christ, explain, correct
and deepen the word:

My beloved brothers and sisters who live in the Kingdom of Peace of your brother Christ, recognize:

What I experienced and endured as Jesus of Nazareth continued in all generations, until men and the Earth became more light-material.

In this book "This Is My Word," you read about what repeatedly occurred in the old satanic time.

Recognize that the Kingdom of Peace of Jesus Christ was founded and was built up over many generations. Over and over again, people experienced the decline as well as the rise of what had been accomplished in the Spirit of God. However, after each decline, the Kingdom of Peace of Jesus Christ rose more radiant and perfect, more and more world-encompassing in its light-nature. For just as everything is an evolution towards the Eternal, the Kingdom of Peace of Jesus Christ also had its evolution, from the beginning all the way until great areas of the Earth became light-material. Finer matter is light-material. During the first generations of construction after its founding, still in the deepest condensation of matter, the satan of the senses led people astray again and again, in order to lay hands on the part-foundations of the Kingdom of Peace of Jesus Christ.

What is written has been fulfilled: In the course of innumerable generations, expansions and pole-shifts took place on the Earth. Many substances of the Earth thereby refined; they attained an ever higher degree of vibration. Very gradually, a great part of the coarse-material forms was taken away and finer, more subtle forms replaced them. In this way, the nature kingdoms and mankind also gradually changed.

And so over innumerable generations, everything on the Earth was refined until the light-material, finer matter, gradually emerged. All that had first been created on coarse-material matter for the Kingdom of Peace of Jesus Christ and the way in which man and Earth had refined went into the universal atmospheric layer and into the new heaven, which came into being through the change of the planets and their orbits, and into the Earth's soul, as well, thus bringing forth a new Earth, a light-material Earth, a finer matter. It is this Earth, in the garment of light-materiality, on which you now live.

Likewise, many material stars refined in this change of time. As a result of the intense transformation of the whole, from full-matter to the light-materiality of finer matter, even another sun and other stars are shining on the light-material Earth.

You who are in the light-material Kingdom of Peace can hardly feel anymore what these conditions were like. For your earthly garment, that is, your earthly body, no longer consists of coarse-material, highly condensed matter, such as people had at the beginning of the Kingdom of Peace of Jesus Christ, instead, it consists of light-materiality.

I repeat: The light-material is a materially finer, radiating substance. Many a one who reads My words today [1989], in full matter, at the beginning of the Kingdom of Peace of Jesus Christ, thinks it would require endless time until the Kingdom of Peace of Jesus Christ is in full bloom.

You have heard that the stars are changing and also full matter, the earth; for it is written: "A new heaven and a new Earth will come into being." And so, the measurement of time as people in full matter have it will not apply, either. There will be another sun, and transformed stars will encompass the new Earth. This means that the so-called measurement of time will also be different. It will be measured by moons, so that the span of time of light of the so-called earthly years will be completely different. The year will then no longer have the twelve months that it had for the people of the coarse-material time, but much shorter spans of time of light; for, at the end of the Kingdom of Peace, the days will be longer and the nights of the light-material, transparent Earth will be much shorter.

I say to you: Even on the light-material Earth there will still be areas of coarser matter, so-called Earth spots. On some of these, for a period of time, more highly condensed people will still exist, who do not have the same degree of purity as the people under the direct sun of the Kingdom of Peace of Jesus Christ. For, as I have already revealed, My Father, who is also your Father, is grace, love and mercy and allows once again the push of the satanic to conquer the Earth. At the end of the Kingdom of Peace, these Earth spots will extend over the earth; however, they will not encompass all the Earth anymore. On them, the demonic world may once again try its strength against the divine.

Then, the end of the Earth will come. It will break open like a nutshell, and the inner light, the fine-material substance, the spiritual part-planet from the eternal Jerusalem, will strive heavenwards and with it, all those who are imbued with the light of the truth.

Recognize that My word, which flowed through many righteous prophets, aligned not only many souls and men with the inner light, but also parts of the material substance – as a result of the actualization of the eternal law by many people.

From the Fall event on, it took countless spans of light and endless ages, until full matter had crystallized. For it developed in proportion to the hardening of the hearts of the spirit beings and in proportion to the burdens of souls and men.

Recognize, however, that the dissolution of matter and the leading of the Fall realms back to the eternal

Kingdom of God will not take as long as the Fall event once did until the formation of full matter. For from the beginning of the Fall on, the leading back of the Fall beings and of the Fall worlds had already began. So when you think of the overall duration of the leading back, you have to include all spans of light and time in your thinking, because the leading back began already with the beginning of the Fall; that is, it has already been going towards the light and the heavens for count-less spans of time. This means that there will no longer be as many spans of light and time until the light-material Kingdom of Peace of Jesus Christ and then, until the dissolution of matter.

My explanations and statements in the book "This Is My Word" were copied again and again over genera-tions and raised to the language of the respective gen-eration. This happened all the way to light-materiality. My word is truth – and it remains, because it is eternal. However, the language of man changed, and so did the material of books.

In the material time [1989], the material of a book was coarse-material substance – people called it paper. In the era of light, all the way to light-materiality, the material of this book corresponded to the respective light-material substance. In the Kingdom of Peace of Jesus Christ, in the light-materiality, there are other sources of light and material than in full matter and in the beginning of the refinement of matter. My word, however, is and remains the truth.

My brothers and sisters in the Kingdom of Peace of Jesus Christ, you read about My way of thinking and living as Jesus of Nazareth. Again and again you ascertain that each person in each generation has his free will. No person and no soul was or is forced to accept the eternal truth, the living Being. The one who wanted to find his way to the inner truth had to go into his inner being and experience the inner truth in and on himself, and live through it himself. And so I, too, as Jesus of Nazareth, only bore witness of the eternal truth.

In all generations, the people who clearly decided for Me, the truth, also remained with Me, the truth and the life. Those who were neither hot nor cold left Me, because they could not understand My speech. They did not want to actualize the commandments because they were of the opinion that they should be given what their neighbor put into practice every day – selfless love, the law of God, the eternal truth.

Thus, in all generations, people who could not decide for the eternal truth left My flock again and again. Opinion-makers and know-it-alls believed that the truth could be bought or acquired merely by listening.

However, the bread of heaven had to be eaten and digested in the right way; this means that the law of life had to be humbly accepted and actualized. Only in this way, did soul and person find their way to the inner life. The actualization of the eternal laws thus brought spiritual gain only to those who decided for the life in Me, the Christ of God, and did not persist in being "for" and "against," that is, once "cold" and then "hot" again.

Over generations, the law of free will was taught: Man finds his way to God only when he also decides for God, the truth, by constantly striving to do the will of God.

The "for" and "against" of many people who were at one time "hot" and then again "cold" enabled the darkness to break into the rows of the righteous again and again. Again and again, the satanic led the senses of many people astray. They then began to doubt the truth and left the faithful. This "for" and "against" extended throughout the generations, until the time had come when only light-filled souls could incarnate into the Kingdom of Peace. They went into the earthly garment with the goal to continue building and populating the new world. Thus, the Kingdom of Peace of Jesus Christ emerged through a process of evolution. Because the souls came into the earthly garment ever more light-filled and peaceful, each generation became more light-filled and the Kingdom of Peace became larger and more perfect.

Recognize that words change their meaning – yet the truth remains. The word which I spoke as Jesus of Nazareth and revealed as the Christ of God through My instrument is the eternal truth. Only the one grasps the truth who has walked towards the truth – into the Kingdom of God, which is in the innermost recesses of every person.

It is the Spirit of God alone, which brings the word to life, not the human being, the flesh and blood.

At all times and in all generations, the same and similar things occurred as in the time when I, as Jesus, walked in the earthly garment. The one believed in the word of truth, the other, in turn, derided the truth and the one who conveyed it. At all times, people found their way to the truth, and at all times, people turned away from it. And so it was with Me, too, as Jesus of Nazareth. Many people came to Me, they became My disciples – and many of the disciples left Me again.

The one who only listened to the truth and did not incorporate it into his daily life continued to walk in the darkness and the darkness then caught him again.

10. Then Simon Peter answered Him, "Lord, to whom shall we go? You have the words of eternal life. And we have believed and are certain that You are Christ, the Son of the living God."

11. Jesus answered them, "Have I not chosen you twelve? And one among you who is a traitor?" He was speaking of Judas Iscariot, the son of Simon, the Levite; for he was the one who betrayed Him afterwards.

12. Jesus went to Jerusalem and came upon a camel with a heavy burden of wood. The camel could not haul its load up the hill and the driver beat it and treated it cruelly, but could not get the animal to move.

13. And as Jesus saw it, He said to him, "Why do you beat your brother?" And the man retorted, "I did not know that it is my brother. Is it not a beast of burden, made to serve me?"

14. And Jesus said, "Has not the same God created this animal and your children who serve you from the same material and have you not both received the same breath from God?"

15. And the man was very astonished by this talk. He stopped beating the camel and freed it from a part of its burden. And so, the camel went up the hill and Jesus went before it and it no longer stopped until the end of its day's journey.

16. The camel recognized Jesus, for it had felt the love of God in Him. And the man wanted to know more of the teachings and Jesus taught him gladly and he became His follower. (Chap. 31:10-16)

I, Christ, explain, correct
and deepen the word:

Everything is energy. I, the Christ of God in Jesus, recognized from the radiation of the people which ones were striving as human beings to live a life that is righteous before God, and which ones, despite knowing better, violated the law of life.

As Jesus of Nazareth, I spoke to many people about the law of life and thus, about the animals which, like human beings, feel pain, grief and joy. Just as man should not be against, but for his neighbor, so should he also be for the animals and bear responsibility for them, because they serve man. Over and over again, I taught the people that animals, too, are creatures of God, which man should not disregard, but should love. The one who beats and tortures them will one day experience the same or similar thing on his soul and on his body. For, what man does to his fellow men and to his fellow creatures, the animals, he does to himself.

Many people recognized their callousness and began to actualize My teachings. They repented and accepted the animals as their friends. And so, many a one understood My words and followed Me.

CHAPTER 32

God as Food and Drink –
The Meaning of Flesh and Blood

Nourishment and health
according to the will of God (1-6). The coarsening of man,
the harshness of the human ego – The turning back of men
to unity with nature (8-12)

1. And so it happened that, as He sat with His disciples at the time of the evening meal, one of them said to Him, "Master, why did you say that you want to give us your flesh to eat and your blood to drink? For this is hard for many to understand."

2. And Jesus answered, saying, "The words that I spoke to you are Spirit and they are life. For those who are unknowing and carnally minded, they sound like bloodshed and death; but blessed are those who understand.

3. Look at the grain, how it grows to ripeness and is cut down and ground in the mill and baked in the fire to become bread. Of this bread is made My body, which you see. And see the grapes which grow to ripeness on the vine, and are picked and put in the wine press and yield the fruit of the vine. Of this fruit of the vine and of water is My blood made.

4. For I partake of the fruits of the trees and the seed of the plants alone, and these are transformed by the

Spirit into My flesh and into My blood. Of these alone and their like you shall eat, you who believe in Me and are My disciples; for from these, in the spirit, come life, health and healing unto man.

5. Verily, My presence shall be with you in the substance and in the life of God, and shall become visible in this body and in this blood; and of these shall all of you who believe in Me eat and drink.

6. For in all places will I resurrect for the life of the world, as it is written in the prophets. From the rising of the sun to its setting, everywhere a pure offering with incense shall be made in My name. (Chap. 32:1-6)

I, Christ, explain, correct
and deepen the word:

Recognize that the word of God is Spirit and life in the words of people. It is revealed and given to people, so that they may grasp that it is not the word alone that brings salvation, but the meaning of the word that has been given to the people by God and that should be actualized each day.

People in the Spirit of the Eternal know that the substance of life – which maintains the health of the body of a human being, its fleshy substance and blood – is in the fruits of the field and of the forest, but not in animals that are killed and consumed, for meat is dead food. People should neither kill people nor deliberately kill or slaughter animals for consumption; for, as creatures of God, they are his "second neighbor."

When a person dedicates his earthly life to God, then the Spirit of God keeps the body of the person healthy, the substance, the flesh and blood; then his way of feeling, thinking, speaking and acting will also be noble and good. Only from this, do the high ethics and morals come. The ethical moral values of such a person will then be of significance in the choice of food, too. He will refrain from eating meat and fish and also from taking strong drinks.

Then, the presence of God will be visible in and on the body as well as in the blood. The person will be healthy because he thinks and eats in a healthy way. This means that his sensations, thoughts, words and deeds are in the law, just as what he partakes of, as food and drink. The one who believes in Me and does the will of God will live in the works of God and will also eat and drink what nature offers him.

"... in all places will I resurrect for the life of the world" means that in all places of this world, the gospel of love will be proclaimed, and all people who are of good will shall actualize My teachings that I gave as Jesus and that I give again as Christ. They will consciously be children of God; for they will have devoted their life to God and gladly and joyfully sacrifice their still existing humanness, by giving it over to Me, in order to gain the Kingdom of God.

In the word "incense" lies the meaning of a devoted life.

7. *As in the physical, so, too, in the spiritual. My teachings and My life shall be food and drink for you, the bread of life and the wine of redemption.*

8. *Just as the grain and the grapes are transformed into flesh and blood, so, too, must your earthly thoughts be transformed into the spiritual. Strive for the transformation of the physical into the spiritual!*
(Chap. 32:7-8)

I, Christ, explain, correct
and deepen the word:

"Strive for the transformation of the physical into the spiritual!" means: Give over to Me your humanness, your human sensations, thoughts, words, deeds, your stirrings, tendencies and passions. Everything that is human is related to the flesh, that is, to the body. The one who strives for the divine in his inner being is aligned with God, with the law of life. He fulfills the law of selfless love in his way of feeling, thinking, speaking and acting.

9. *Verily, I say to you, in the beginning, all creatures of God found their sustenance in the plants and the fruits of the Earth alone, until the ignorance and self-ishness of man turned many away from that and to-wards what was contrary to the original order of things as given by God. But even those shall return again to*

the natural nourishment, as it is written in the prophets.
For their words shall not be doubted.

10. Verily, God gives eternally from the eternal life
and the eternal substance, so that the forms of the uni-
verse are always renewed. This is why all of you take
part in the flesh and blood and the substance and the
life of the Eternal, and My words are the Spirit and the
life.

11. And if you keep My commandments and lead a
life of righteousness, you will be happy in this life and
in the coming life. Do not be amazed about what I have
said to you. Unless you eat of the flesh and drink of the
blood of God, you will not have the life in you."

12. And the disciples answered, "Lord, give us for-
ever of this bread to eat and of this cup to drink, for
your words are truly food and drink. Through your life
and through your substance, we will live forever."
(Chap. 32:9-12)

I, Christ, explain, correct
and deepen the word:

Verily, to live in God means to fulfill the eternal
laws of God. This also means to live from what nature
gives to man.

Human beings and animals developed very gradually
on this Earth. In the garden of God, both man and animal subsisted on plants. When man fell ever deeper into
sin, he thereby fell into the darkness of ignorance and

lapsed into selfishness. Just as the coarse-material became ever denser, so did man's senses become coarser and with this, his organs, too, changed very gradually.

In his selfishness, man sought all kinds of pleasures and began to crave the spicy, the sour and the animal. The hard shell, the human ego, the coarse senses, gave rise to sensuality, which sought gratification. With this, people tried to compensate for the life force which they spent unlawfully.

The sensualist, whose thoughts became more and more self-centered, then, was driven to the food that corresponded to his way of thinking and acting. Because he distanced himself from God more and more, he became harsher in his speaking and acting. The coarsened senses reflected the harshness of the human ego and, therefore, sought correspondingly pungent spices and foods. When a person failed in something, he reacted with bitterness and his senses sought gratification in ever new pleasures. The tensed nerves of the human being sought relaxation in sensuality.

More and more, the body demanded what the person radiated in his sensations, thoughts, words and actions: sweet and sour, spicy and passionate. This is why he began to change the substances of nature, by dressing them more and more in the sour, the spicy and the sweet.

The result of all this was that human beings began to hunt animals, to kill them and season and consume their flesh. Through this, the human being became a hunter and a poacher. In his sensuality, which was growing stronger and stronger, he craved the "carnal," the male or the female sex.

All this occurred and is still occurring in this generation, too [1989]. Only when man turns back to the Spirit of life by raising his thoughts to God, will he also refine his senses.

I Am come to bring the law of life to man. The one who accepts it and applies it to himself turns back to the life in God. The life in God and with all Being is the highest and finest ethics and morals.

All souls will find their way again to this Being, because they came from God – the eternal Being, the life – and possess the life from God, in themselves, eternally.

The one who keeps the commandments, the excerpts from the eternal law, lives in and out of God and is just towards all forms of life.

Verily, the word of God is food and drink; it is the life. The one who lives in God also lives out of God. He lives in the Being. The Earth is a part of the eternal Being; for this reason, the person who lives consciously will also possess and cultivate it lawfully, because he lives with the Earth and is not against the Earth, nor is he against anything that lives on it.

The soul lives from the purely spiritual substance; the earthly body lives from the life which has become material substance from the spiritual substance. Both the pure spiritual substance and the spiritual-material substance are gifts from God for soul and person. God gave man the fruits and the plants. They are the life for the body. Man will return to nature and will live with nature, because he will recognize that the life and the health of the body are from God alone, from the life that, in nature, gives itself to the children of God.

Nature gives strength to the healthy body and healing to the sick body. The prerequisite is, however, that the person's thoughts, words and actions be wholesome.

In the Kingdom of Peace of Jesus Christ, the children of God live in absolute unity with the nature kingdoms, and God nourishes them with the fruits and the plants, with the life of nature.

CHAPTER 33

About Blood Sacrifice and the Forgiveness of Sins –
The Healing at the Pool of Bethesda

The concessions made by Moses
under the circumstances of that time became law (1-3).
Animal sacrifice and the eating of meat – Human regulations
bind; God is unlimited love and freedom (4-14)

1. *Jesus taught His disciples in the outer court of the temple, and one of them said to Him, "Master, it is said by the priests that without shedding blood there is no forgiveness of sins. Can then the lawful blood sacrifices take away sins?"*

2. *And Jesus answered, "No blood sacrifice of animal or bird or man can take away sins. For how can a guilt be paid off by shedding innocent blood? No, it will increase the guilt.*

3. *The priests indeed receive such offerings as an appeasement from the faithful for the violations against the law of Moses; but for the sins against the law of God, there is no forgiveness except by repentance and a change for the better. (Chap. 33:1-3)*

I, Christ, explain, correct
and deepen the word:

Moses brought the Ten Commandments from God. When he realized that the Israelites could not put the

Ten Commandments into practice in a short time, because most of them had thought and acted against the Ten Commandments for decades, he made some concessions in order to lead them through self-recognition, to the inner experience. However, many of the Israelites disregarded these concessions as well and continued to compulsively indulge in idolatry. After further generations, these concessions were raised to law by the stubborn Israelites.

Animal sacrifices are against the law of God and also against the Ten Commandments.

4. *Is it not written in the prophets: Take your blood sacrifices and your burnt offerings, and do away with them. Stop eating meat; for I did not speak of this to your forefathers, nor have I commanded them to do so when I led them out of Egypt. But this is what I commanded them:*

5. *Obey My voice and walk the paths that I have commanded of you, and you will be My people and things will go well for you. And yet they were not so inclined and did not listen.*

6. *And what did the Eternal command you, other than to practice justice and mercy and to walk humbly with your God? Is it not written that, in the beginning, God ordained the fruits of the trees and the seeds and the plants to be food for all flesh?*

7. *But they have made of the house of prayer a den of thieves and, instead of the pure offering with incense,*

they have stained My altars with blood and have eaten the flesh of slain animals.

8. *But I say to you: Shed no innocent blood and eat no flesh. Be upright, love mercy and do right, and your days will endure in the land for a long time.*

9. *Is not the grain that grows from the earth with the other grains transformed by the Spirit into My flesh? Are not the grapes of the vineyard and the other fruits transformed by the Spirit into My blood? Let these, with your bodies and souls, be your memorial to the Eternal.*

10. *In these, the presence of God is visible as substance and as the life of the world. You should all eat and drink of these for the remission of sins and for the eternal life to all who obey My words."*

11. *Now, there is in Jerusalem a pool which is called Bethesda, by the sheep market. In five galleries, there lay a great multitude of infirm people, blind, lame, and withered, waiting for the moving of the waters.*

12. *For at a certain time, an angel came down into the pool and moved the water. The one who first went in after the water had been moved was healed of whatever disease with which he was afflicted. And a man born lame was also there.*

13. *And Jesus spoke to him, "Do the waters bring you no healing?" He said to Him, "Yes, Lord, but I have no one to put me into the pool when the water is moved. And when I try to get in, another goes in before me." And Jesus said to him, "Get up, take up your bed and walk." And he stood up immediately and walked. And it was the Sabbath on this day.*

14. And the Jews said to him, "Today is the Sabbath, and it is against the law to carry your bed." And the healed one did not know that it was Jesus. And Jesus had left, for there were a lot of people at that place. (Chap. 33:4-14)

I, Christ, explain, correct
and deepen the word:

In the law of God, nothing is written about blood sacrifice nor about burnt offering, nor about the deliberate killing of animals, nor about the consumption of the flesh of animals.

Only the one who obeys the voice of God by fulfilling His laws walks in God and belongs to the people of God. It is a law that man should practice justice and mercy and walk humbly to the Kingdom of God of the inner being, where the true and eternal home of the soul is. The one who keeps the laws of God also nourishes himself from what the law of God brings forth in nature. He will also bring his life, his sensing, thinking, speaking and acting in conformity with the eternal law.

From the beginning, God gave man the fruits, the seeds and the plants for nourishment. This law will hold true until all souls live in the fine-material spheres and no human beings live, who need for their bodies the energy which has taken form, the life from nature.

443

The temple should be a house of prayer, where a person cultivates unity with his neighbor, in prayer and by worshipping God. From this, he gains for his daily life the strength to lead a consecrated, pure life and to live in unity with his neighbor.

In My time as Jesus of Nazareth, people defiled the stone altars in their houses of prayer with blood and then even ate the flesh of the animals they had killed. They defiled their temples of flesh and bone with negative sensations, thoughts, words and actions. Even the people of this time [1989] still do this again and again. And they, too, still defile themselves with the blood of animals which, against their better knowledge, they kill and whose flesh they consume.

Recognize that the law of God is and will be eternally. What was valid in former times is valid today, too, for God is the same law, today, tomorrow and in all eternity.

The one who sheds innocent blood, who consumes flesh is merciless and will have to suffer his own lack of mercy on himself.

A pure soul and a healthy body, which the pure soul keeps healthy, are the memorial to the Eternal.

Natural food contains the substance of God. It is the life of the earthly body.

The one who repents of his sins and does not commit them anymore will also let his sensations, thoughts, words and deeds rest in God and will eat what God has given him.

I correct: It was not an angel who moved the pool, but the elements that moved and move the water. It is not the water that heals, but solely the belief in Him who is, as substance, even in the water.

Just like the Jews, people of all generations kept and keep the Sabbath only externally, because, as such, it is simply a habit for them. But in their daily behavior, they acted and act contrary to what they teach by using only words. Their thoughts were and are impure, as are their deeds which they carry out behind walls, so that these are not seen. They talked and talk of the Sabbath commandments, and yet they themselves did not and do not keep the Sabbath, neither in their sensations nor in their thoughts, their words and their deeds.

Sprinkling yourself with earthly water is only a symbol. The one who believes in God's spiritual stream and consecrates his life to God receives soothing and healing through the life from God, whether he immerses himself in the water, which is only a symbol, or calls out to God with all his heart, no matter where he may be.

God is omnipresent power. God helps, soothes and heals. He does not ask whether it is a workday or the Sabbath. The one who asks with all his heart receives, no matter on which day or at what hour. Only the narrow-minded person has a lot of regulations. He wants to thereby limit the all-encompassing Spirit.

Recognize that God is unlimited love and freedom. The law of unlimited love and freedom does not know the narrowness of the human ego. The human ego is the ego law which man has created for himself. It is the seed, which already bears the fruit in itself. Man himself has put it into the acre of life, into his soul.

CHAPTER 34

The Love of Jesus for All Creatures

*The one through whom God flows
becomes a blessing (2-6). Respect for all that is created;
disrespect is subject to the causal law (7-10)*

1. When Jesus noticed how the Pharisees murmured and took offence that He gained and baptized more disciples than John, He left Judea and went again to Galilee.

2. And Jesus came to a tree, beneath which He dwelt for several days. And Mary Magdalene and other women also came there and served Him with what they had, and every day He taught all who came to Him.

3. And the birds gathered around Him and greeted Him with their singing; and other creatures came to His feet, and He fed them, and they ate from His hand.

4. And when He departed, He blessed the women who had shown Him their love; and He turned towards the fig tree and blessed it, too. And He said, "You gave Me shelter and shade against the burning heat, and moreover you gave Me food.

5. Be blessed, grow and be fruitful and let all who come to you find peace, shade and food, and let the birds of the air find their joy in your branches."

6. And behold, the tree grew and flourished in quite an extraordinary way, and its branches extended more and more upwards and downwards, so that no similar

tree of such beauty and size and none with such an
abundance and such goodness of fruit was to be found.
(Chap. 34:1-6)

I, Christ, explain, correct
and deepen the word:

The one who lets the blessing, the power of God, flow through him is a source of strength for human beings, animals, plants and minerals.

When a person lets God flow through him, he will be a blessing for everyone and everything. The one through whom God streams loves people, animals, plants and minerals selflessly. The one who incorporates people and the nature kingdoms into his life is in communication with the All-life. Life in its diversity thanks him by giving itself in abundance, and it will give to all who come to the source of life.

The one who respects life also knows the eternal homeland. Already on Earth, he lives in the midst of God's paradise, for the nature kingdoms serve him and the elements obey him.

7. *Jesus came into a village and saw there a stray kitten, and it suffered from hunger and cried out to Him. And He picked it up, wrapped it in His robe and let it rest at His breast.*

8. *And when He went through the village, He gave the cat to eat and to drink. And it ate and drank and showed Him its thanks. And He gave it to one of His disciples, a widow called Lorenza, and she took care of it.*

9. *And some of the people said, "This man takes care of all the animals. Are they His brothers and sisters, that He loves them so?" And He said to them, "Verily, these are your fellow brothers from the great family of God, your brothers and sisters who have the same breath of life from the Eternal.*

10. *And whoever cares for the least of them and gives it food and drink in its need does this to Me, and the one who deliberately allows that one of them suffer privation and does not defend it when it is ill-treated allows this evil to happen as if it were done to Me. For just as you have done in this life will it be done to you in the life to come." (Chap. 34:7-10)*

I, Christ, explain, correct
and deepen the word:

Verily, I say to you, the life is the breath of God. Whether it is man or animal, they are all respirated by *one* power, by God.

God is life, and life is breath. The one who deliberately robs his neighbor of his breath by killing him will fall into spiritual death. In the realm of the souls, he will be a stranger; for he does not know his own consciousness and, therefore, does not know whether he lives or is dead. Even if a person deliberately and knowingly allows people and animals to be tortured, neglected and ill-treated, he will experience the same or something similar.

So, what a person does to his neighbor and second neighbor, that is, the animals, plants and stones, he does to Me, and thus to himself.

Recognize that even stones are creation-powers of God, and they, too, should be met with respect.

And so, the seed of man will also be his harvest.

CHAPTER 35

The Parable of the Good Samaritan – Mary and Martha

What you do to your neighbor you do to Christ and to yourself – About your behavior towards your neighbor (1-8). Pray and work; the right measure (9-11). A picture for building the house of God, the New Jerusalem on Earth – The divine wisdom calls the sons and daughters of God; she prepares the Inner Path and brings the all-encompassing divine laws – Those who live in Me will become the living wellspring (12-15)

1. A scribe who wanted to convict Him came up to Him and said, "Master, what must I do in order to gain eternal life?" He said to him, "What is written in the law? How do you read it?"

2. He answered, saying, "You shall not do unto others what you would not have them do unto you. You shall love God, your Lord, with all your heart, with all your soul and with all your mind. You shall do unto others what you would have them do unto you."

3. And Jesus said to him, "You have answered correctly. Do this and you will live. All the laws and the prophets depend on these three commandments, for the one who loves God also loves his neighbor."

4. However, he wanted to defend himself and said to Jesus, "And who is my neighbor?" Jesus answered,

saying, "There was a man who went down from Je-
rusalem to Jericho and he fell among thieves who
stripped him of his raiment, wounded him and walked
away, leaving Him lying half dead.

5. And it came to pass that a priest was coming down
this street; and when he saw him, he passed him by.
Likewise, a Levite, as he came down and saw him,
passed by on the other side.

6. But a Samaritan also came on his journey to
where the man lay and, when he saw him, he had com-
passion on him. He went to him, poured oil and wine on
his wounds and bandaged them. He then sat him on his
own animal and brought him to an inn and took care of
him.

7. The next morning, because he had to continue his
journey, he took out two pence, gave them to the inn-
keeper and said to him, 'Take care of him and, if you
need more, I will repay you when I come back.'

8. Which of these three do you think was a neighbor
to the one who had fallen among the thieves?" He said,
"The one who showed mercy towards him." And Jesus
said to him, "Go and do the same." (Chap. 35:1-8)

I, Christ, explain, correct
and deepen the word:

This statement too, like many others, should go with
you on your earthly journey: "A scribe who wanted to
convict Him came up to Him."

452

Recognize that you should never set a trap for your neighbor, for with this you give the tempter the opportunity to bring about your own downfall.

If you are not watchful, that is, if you do not control your sensations and thoughts, then the tempter will creep in through your own sensations and thoughts, through your human ways, your human ego, and will tempt you to do what corresponds to your human condition at that time.

Recognize the law: What you do to your neighbor, you do to yourself. The effect can come by way of a second or third person, or through the invisible dark power, the tempter.

And "You shall not do unto others what you would not have them do unto you" means to pay attention to every moment of your earthly life. Then you have insight into your world of sensations and thoughts and can give your humanness over to Me, the Christ, in time, before you do to your neighbor what would then fall back on you. What you do to your neighbor, you do also to Me, the Christ – and to yourself, for your neighbor is a part of Me and also a part of you.

The one who loves God with all his heart and all his soul also loves his neighbor selflessly from the depths of his soul and heart. This means that you should do to your neighbor what you want him to do to you. Thus, you should respect your neighbor and do to him what is in accordance with the eternal law – but not the unlawful things which he demands of you.

Furthermore, recognize that you should love and do good not only to those who love you and do the same or similar things to you. Love all your fellow men and do good to all, according to the law of selfless love and of the right way of giving and receiving. Therefore, love also those who do not love you and do good also to those who despise and reject you.

However, in the commandment of giving, take into consideration the free will of your neighbor. If he does not want your selfless help, then do not give it. But if he wants your selfless help in order to become rich through you – for instance, so that he need not work to earn his bread – then offer him your help to find work, so that he can earn what he expected of you.

If it concerns your fellow man, remember in every situation the commandment of unity with all people. Have you practiced selflessness when you love only those who love you and help only those who were or are helpful to you? This is what the Pharisees do.

As you fulfill the commandments of selflessness more and more, you begin to truly live.

The commandments of giving, of freedom of will, of unity and selflessness are basic elements of the eternal law of God. They hold true for all beings and people. The just prophets, too, fulfilled and fulfill them.

Recognize that every one, without exception, is your neighbor.

I have already revealed that, from generation to generation, mankind attributed to many words yet again another purport – that is, another meaning.

And so, the word "compassion" has another meaning in the law of life than what man attributes to it today:

In the law of life, compassion means to feel, to empathize, with the person who is suffering, in order to sense what he needs.

The word "compassion" also means to practice mercy – however, not to join in with the wailing and to deplore and pity your neighbor as a "poor fellow." For the one who acts in this way can thereby awaken self-pity in the one who is suffering, thus contributing to his getting caught up in his own grief, through self-pity.

The person who empathizes with true selflessness senses in his heart the situation of his neighbor. He will help selflessly and will, according to the law of life, do his best possible for his neighbor.

9. *Now it came to pass that on the way they came into a village. A woman called Martha received Him into her house. And she had a sister called Mary; she also sat at Jesus' feet and listened to His word.*

10. *But Martha busied herself with serving Him. And she came to Him, saying, "Lord, don't you care that my sister lets me serve alone? Why don't You tell her that she should help me?"*

11. *And Jesus answered, saying to her, "Martha, Martha, you are concerned and trouble yourself with many things; but only one thing is necessary. And Mary has chosen this good part and it shall not be taken from her." (Chap. 35:9-11)*

I, Christ, explain, correct
and deepen the word:

"And Mary has chosen this good part and it shall not be taken from her" means that not the mere bustling about and serving externally bring spiritual gain to a person, but the right measure in all things. The determining factor is that the person accomplish everything from his heart and with the power of God.

God works through the one who rests in God. His selfless activity is then a blessing for many.

12. *Once again, as Jesus sat for the evening meal with His disciples in a certain city, He said to them, "Like a table on twelve pillars, similarly Am I in your midst.*

13. *Verily, I say to you, wisdom builds her house and hews her twelve pillars. She prepares her bread and her oil and mixes her wine. She arranges her table.*

14. *And she stands on the high places of the city and calls the sons and daughters of man. Whosoever wants, let him be led to this place, let him eat of My bread and take of My oil and drink of My wine.*

15. *Break with the foolish ones and live and walk on the path of insight into all things. The veneration of God is the beginning of wisdom, and the knowledge of the holy One is understanding. Through Me, your days will be multiplied and the years of your life will increase." (Chap. 35:12-15)*

I, Christ, explain, correct
and deepen the word:

"Like a table on twelve pillars, similarly Am I in your midst" means that the table on twelve pillars symbolizes the Sanctum of God in the carrying power of the twelve elders in whose midst I Am, the Christ of God. In the same way, as Jesus of Nazareth, I was in the midst of the twelve apostles who symbolized the twelve elders of the Sanctum.

I Am the way, the truth and the life, the bread, the oil and the wine.

"Verily, I say to you, wisdom builds her house and hews her twelve pillars" means that the wisdom from God – His nature in the angel-prince of the divine wisdom and his spirit-dual in earthly garment – builds the spiritual house, the tent of God among men: The New Jerusalem.

The divine wisdom prepares the path into the inner life, to Me, the Christ of God, the Redeemer of all souls and men, for the people of good will. It is the Inner Path.

With Me, the Christ, she calls the sons and daughters of God from the lineage of David and from other lineages, to found and build the Kingdom of Peace of Jesus Christ. The lineage of David is the same as the tribe of David for My Kingdom of Peace on this Earth.

The divine wisdom, with men and women from the lineage of David and from other lineages, hews the twelve pillars. This means that they create the foundation of the Kingdom of Peace of Jesus Christ, in which the house, the tent of God, the New Jerusalem, is the center, the supporting pillar for the Kingdom of Peace of Jesus Christ. The twelve pillars also symbolize the twelve gates of the eternal city of God and of the New Jerusalem, on the light-filled Earth in the Kingdom of Peace of Jesus Christ.

"She prepares her bread and her oil and mixes her wine" means that the divine wisdom brings to man the all-encompassing laws of God. The one who lives according to the laws of God stands at My right and sits with all righteous men and women at the table of the Christ of God and of the divine wisdom.

The one who sits at the table of life also receives from the table of God. The bread, the oil and the wine symbolize the gifts of life which are offered to all those who live in Me, the Christ of God.

The words "she arranges her table" mean that the divine wisdom invites guests to the Lord's supper in the house of God, the New Jerusalem on Earth. And those of honest heart eat at the table of God with Me, the Christ. They are consciously the carriers of the coming generations.

This table of God in the house of God is already prepared. Those who sit at the table of the Lord are the brothers and sisters of the original community New Jerusalem, who have made the covenant for the Kingdom of Peace of Jesus Christ with the Eternal and with Me, the Christ of God.

As revealed, I, Christ, and the divine wisdom call all sons and daughters of God from the lineage of David and from other lineages.

The table of God is prepared for all people of good will, and they will all come, for they will feel that they are welcome.

I correct the statement: "And she stands on the high places of the city and calls the sons and daughters of man." On the prepared places of many cities and communities, the divine wisdom calls the sons and daughters of man to turn back and to turn within and calls the sons and daughters from the lineage of David and from other lineages, so that they may fulfill their divine mission.

Everyone who is of good will is called. This is the meaning of the words, "Whosoever wants, let him be led to this place, let him eat of My bread and take of My oil and drink of My wine."

The gifts from the origin of the source, God, offered through the divine wisdom, are the fullness from the law of God. The one who fulfills the laws of God lives in God and in His fullness. And he will lack nothing.

"Break with the foolish ones and live and walk on the path of insight into all things" means: Break with the human ego and with all those who want to tie you to themselves through their conceptions and opinions, and with all the foolish ones who, though knowing better, want to stay as they are: foolish and petty. To break with them means to let go externally and to keep them in your inner being.

Walk on the path of insight and you will turn within – to the life which is within, in every person.

The divine wisdom brought the all-embracing Inner Path, so that the true seeker may find himself in Me, the Christ of God, and be able to draw from the inexhaustible source, God. The one who truly walks the Inner Path, which I, the Christ of God, have revealed to man through the divine wisdom, attains true greatness.

He will recognize God in all things, honor Him and live in His holy will. In this way, he will live in the law of selfless love and will recognize and understand all things and all that is, in the light of truth.

In these days and through Me, the people who live in Me, the Christ of God, will become the living wellspring. I will multiply their days because they live in Me and, through Me, bring salvation into this world to their fellow brothers and sisters.

In the course of generations, they will work together during the years of their earthly existence and will be a witness to all those who still live in the materialistic world.

CHAPTER 36

The Adulteress –
The Pharisees and the Tax Collectors

The law of correspondence –
The one who knows himself also knows the adversary –
Temptation through the satan of the senses before and also
after the great turmoil (1-6). Spiritual greatness grows out
of humility (7-10)

1. One day early in the morning, Jesus came into the temple again, and all the people came to Him; and He sat down and taught them.

2. And the scribes and Pharisees brought a woman caught in the act of adultery and put her in the middle and said to Him, "Master, this woman was caught in the act of adultery. Now Moses has commanded us in the law that such a woman should be stoned. What do you say?"

3. But they said this to tempt Him, so that they could find a charge against Him. But Jesus bent down and wrote on the ground with His finger, as if He did not hear them.

4. When they continued to ask Him, He stood up and said to them, "Let the one among you who is without sin throw the first stone at her."

5. And He bent down once more and wrote on the ground. And those who heard this were convicted by their own conscience and went out, one after the other,

461

starting with the elders to the last ones; and Jesus was left alone; only the woman still stood there.

6. When Jesus stood up and saw no one but the woman, He said to her, "Woman, where are they, your accusers? Has no one condemned you?" She said to Him, "No one, O Lord." And Jesus said to her, "So I will not condemn you either. Henceforth, sin no more, and go in peace." (Chap. 36:1-6)

I, Christ, explain, correct
and deepen the word:

The old sinful world with its manifestations and customs still exists [1989]. Many people are still caught up in it. The satan of the senses is still bringing in a harvest among them. For his aim is that people violate the law of God. Again and again, the darkling tries to tempt them, and with iron claws he holds on to those who let themselves be tempted.

As in My time as Jesus of Nazareth, this still happens in the turn of time [1989].

Despite the change from the old and sinful to the New Era, the era of the Spirit, the same sin still prevails: The darkling disguises himself in accusations and slander against his neighbor. However, more and more people recognize the law of correspondence: The one who reproaches his neighbor for a sin and blames and accuses him because of it has the same or a similar sin. The one who accuses his neighbor accuses himself.

The one who has no mercy and no understanding for his neighbor lives in sin. The sinner has mercy and understanding, only for himself, and has many excuses where his human ego is concerned.

Recognize that every person gives witness of who and what he is through his gestures, facial expression, his way of speaking and his behavior. Through this, I recognized the hypocrites and saw through them.

When the Pharisees brought a woman alleged to have been caught in the act of adultery to Me, Jesus, I read from the radiation of their souls, their auras, and from their words, that they had committed the same or similar sins.

That is why I said to them, "Let the one among you who is without sin throw the first stone at her."

Recognize that no truly spiritual, that is, wise, person will accuse and repudiate his neighbor. Nor will he want to lead his fellowman into temptation. The one who himself has overcome the adversary knows him and knows his skills and tactics in temptation. But the person who nourishes his sin knows neither himself nor the adversary who tempts him, and is, so to speak, a glove on his hand.

This is why I teach once again, as the Christ of God, together with the divine wisdom: Recognize yourself! Then you will know through which gateways and channels of your human ego the adversary slips in to lead you astray and win you over for his purposes.

You who live in Me in the Kingdom of Peace of Jesus Christ and read about the truth and the many events which I revealed at the turn of time [1989] through the incarnated female principle of divine wisdom recognize: All that you read about in the book "This Is My Word" and much more took place up to the time of the mighty Earth disasters and world upheavals, and even after that. On some parts of the Earth, the satan of the senses rose over and over again and led astray those who let themselves be led astray. Again and again, they sinned in manifold ways. They seduced each other, let themselves be seduced and committed adultery and sinned – until more pestilence and Earth and world disasters took away the sinfulness more and more.

In every case, what remained was the foundation and the beginnings of the Kingdom of Peace of Jesus Christ, which the pioneers for the New Era had established in the old world through struggle and the willingness to make sacrifices against the darkness. Pioneers for the Era of Light came into the earthly garment again and again. Over many generations, they built on the Kingdom of Peace of Jesus Christ. In this way, My light increased on Earth.

7. *He said this parable to some who considered themselves righteous and disdained others, "Two men went up into the temple to pray, one a rich Pharisee versed in the law, the other a tax collector who was a sinner.*

8. The Pharisee stood and prayed in the following way, 'God, I thank you that I am not like other people, usurers, unjust, adulterers or even like this tax collector. I fast twice a week and give tithes of all that I possess.'

9. And the tax collector stood far away, would not raise his eyes to heaven, but beat his breast saying, 'God, be merciful to me, a sinner.'

10. I say to you: This one went down to his house more justified than the other one. For the one who exalts himself will be abased; and the one who humbles himself will be exalted." (Chap. 36:7-10)

I, Christ, explain, correct
and deepen the word:

The self-satisfied person does not know himself, because he just looks at how he appears to others and does not consider why he wants to give this impression. But the one who recognizes his sins and asks the eternal Father for help, so that he may gain the strength to be able to let go of them, has already received grace and help from the Eternal.

Spiritual greatness grows only out of humility. Arrogance is sin itself, for the small ego places itself above God. And so, arrogance is the basis for further temptations. The one who has inner greatness will struggle with his human ego until his life has become My life, the cosmic consciousness.

The one who has reached inner greatness is no longer satisfied with dipping into the source of knowledge every now and then. He will work on himself until he reaches the origin of the source and lives in God eternally.

CHAPTER 37

The Rebirth of the Soul

Through suffering and atonement to perfection – The grace of the Father works more intensively on the Earth – The end of the chance for heavily burdened souls to incarnate – Reincarnation in the Spirit of God (1-10)

1. Jesus sat at the entryway of the temple and many came in order to learn His teachings. And someone asked Him, "Lord, what do you teach about life?"

2. And He said to them, "Blessed are those who go through many experiences, for they will become perfect through suffering. They will be like the angels of God in heaven and they will no longer die, nor will they be born again; for death and birth have no dominion over them any longer.

3. Those who have suffered and overcome will be made pillars in the temple of My God, and they will never leave it again. Verily, I say to you, if you are not born through water and fire again, you will not see the Kingdom of God."

4. And a Rabbi (Nicodemus) came to Him during the night for fear of the Jews and asked Him, "How can a person be born again when he is old? Can he enter a second time into his mother's womb and be born?"

5. Jesus answered, "Verily, I say to you, unless a person is born again of flesh and of Spirit, he cannot enter the Kingdom of God. The wind blows where it

will and you indeed hear its rushing, but you do not know from where it comes and where it goes.

6. *The light shines from the East to the West; the sun rises from darkness and sets again into darkness. And so it is with man from lifetime to lifetime.*

7. *When the suns comes out of the darkness, so was it there before, and when it again sets into the darkness, so it is that it may rest a little while and afterwards be there again.*

8. *And so you have to go through many changes in order to become perfect; as it is written in the book of Job: I am a pilgrim and I change one place after the other and one house after the other, until I come into the city and into the house which are eternal."*

9. *And Nicodemus asked Him, "How can this happen?" And Jesus answered, saying, "Are you a teacher in Israel and do not understand this? Verily, we speak what we know and bear witness to what we have seen, and you do not accept our testimony.*

10. *If I tell you about earthly things and you do not believe, how would you believe if I told you about heavenly things? No one has ascended into heaven; but the One who is in heaven has descended from heaven, namely, the Son of Man." (Chap. 37:1-10)*

I, Christ, explain, correct
and deepen the word:

"Blessed are those who go through many experiences, for they will become perfect through suffering" means that the person, who accepts his sins – which can also appear in the form of suffering – and recognizes himself as sinful in the sorrow, illness and need, who repents, asks for forgiveness, forgives, makes amends and no longer commits his sins – will grow stronger and more perfect through atonement. Death and birth will hold sway over the sinner only until he has discarded his sins and fulfills the will of God. Then his soul begins to shine. Both soul and person then look towards heaven. And once they have overcome – even if it is through sorrow – the soul will enter the Kingdom of God.

Recognize that when the soul comes from the darkness, that is, when it has burdened itself in its former earthly existences and has not cleared up the sins, it will linger for a while in the realm of the souls and then come again into an earthly existence. It will strive for the flesh, for an earthly garment, until it has cleared up what drew it again and again to the Earth in the earthly garment.

The Earth is thus a magnetic point of attraction for souls until they have atoned for and transformed, on Earth, what has drawn them again and again into an earthly existence. For there are burdens which are "earth-heavy" and which draw the souls to Earth again and again until these burdens have been removed. Many souls do not find peace in the planes of purification until they have overcome this attraction to Earth. On the other hand, those burdens that are not earth-heavy, and which the souls have caused in the earthly garment, can be paid off faster in the beyond.

Happy the souls and human beings who, through the grace of the Father, make amends on Earth for their earthly guilt, for what they have caused; for this grace is more strongly effective on Earth.

Recognize that the time is drawing nearer and nearer, in which heavily burdened souls will no longer be able to seek out the Earth so easily. For the Earth will be cleansed and the whole planet Earth, including the entire solar system, will be raised and will be refined in its structure. Then, the incarnation of heavily burdened souls will no longer be possible. They will feel like prisoners in the purification planes, on those planets which correspond to the state of their soul, that is, to their state of consciousness. There, they will suffer through what they could have expiated on Earth without great anguish.

Rebirth into the Spirit of God is attained by that person's soul which looks toward heaven and which, in its earthly existence, aligns its feeling and thinking with God, hour by hour, day by day, and thereby, becomes attuned to God. The words and actions of such a person are then divine. After the death of the body, this soul will gradually rise to heaven, because it has opened heaven in itself.

The path to the heart of God is selfless love. I and the divine wisdom on Earth teach, through revelation, how it can be attained. The word of truth streams into this world through My instrument [1989]. My word serves all those who walk the path of selfless love, as a help for their salvation and joy.

That which is written explains the coming and going of the souls. No one can ascend to heaven who has not opened heaven in himself.

However, all souls and human beings have come down from heaven and will enter heaven again, because they are from heaven. My mission as the Redeemer is to lead all back to the eternal Father, into the eternal heavens.

CHAPTER 38

About Killing Animals – Raising
the Youth of Nain from the Dead

The one who does not
fulfill the laws of God burdens his soul;
and he cannot teach or explain the law of the heavens –
The chaff will be separated from the wheat (1-2). Jacob's
ladder – With the refinement of thoughts and senses, the
unlawful falls away (3). About the use of violence and the
shedding of blood (4). Having compassion for animals –
Killing animals to deliver them from suffering (5). The one
who recognizes himself and clears things up learns to love
the life (6). The raising from
the dead (8-10)

1. *And some of His disciples came to Him and spoke*
to Him about an Egyptian, a son of Belial, who taught
that it is not against the law to torment animals if their
suffering brings profit to people.

2. *And Jesus said to them, "Verily, I say to you, the*
one who derives benefit from the injustice that is in-
flicted on a creature of God cannot be righteous. Just
as little can those whose hands are stained with blood
or whose mouths are defiled with flesh deal with holy
matters or teach the mysteries of heaven.
(Chap. 38:1-2)

I, Christ, explain, correct
and deepen the word:

Recognize that everything that lives feels. In a way similar to man, all forms of life feel joy and sorrow, whether they be animals, plants or stones. Life is consciousness. The consciousness radiates countless facets of evolution of the I Am. Consciousness is also a process of becoming conscious. People, animals, plants and stones feel according to their consciousness.

Recognize that the one who hunts animals will himself be hunted one day. The one who torments animals will himself be tormented one day. The one who exploits the life of the Earth will become the prey to those who taught him to do this.

Every seed has its harvest. What a person sows goes into the field of his soul; from there it sprouts and grows. In every seed already lies the fruit.

Thus, the one who is against his neighbor and against the nature kingdoms is also against God – for God, the life, is in all Being.

Recognize that the one who does not fulfill the laws of God burdens his soul. The hands of the one who torments or kills animals are stained with blood. The one who consumes the flesh of animals, who pollutes and violates nature is impure. Such people can neither deal with holy matters nor experience the so-called "mysteries" of the heavens, and, thus, not teach or explain the law of the heavens, either.

The one who teaches what is most holy – the laws of the heavens – and instructs his fellowman to keep them, while he himself does not keep them, will reap approval only from those who live and think as he does.

All that is godless does not endure in the long run. It will fade away just as the night recedes before the day. The time has drawn near, in which the light will bring everything out into the light of day, and people will recognize the God-distant life of those who may have taught and told them to keep the laws of life, but who themselves did not keep them, whose hands are stained with blood and whose bodies are defiled by the consumption of meat.

God's mills grind slowly. One day, the chaff will be separated from the wheat, and those who are God-filled will stand at My right side, and the chaff, the godless, will fall victim to purging, according to the law of sowing and reaping.

3. *God gives the grains and the fruits of the Earth as food; and for the righteous man, there is no other lawful nourishment for the body. (Chap. 38:3)*

I, Christ, explain, correct
and deepen the word:

"God gives the grains and the fruits of the Earth as food; and for the righteous man, there is no other lawful nourishment for the body" means that from the bosom of Mother Earth God gives man all that the earthly body needs for living. The one who fulfills the laws of love and life in his way of feeling, thinking, speaking and acting also lives from what Mother Earth gives him.

Indeed, many are standing on Jacob's ladder which leads into the pure temple of life. Many people are still great sinners in their inner being as well as externally, and remain so over decades or even over many incarnations or soul sojourns, until the causes they have built up hit them as an effect.

However, from the temple of love, God extends His hand to everyone, to the greatest sinner, as well. Again and again, the eternal Being, the All-Father, teaches the gospel of love through Me, the Christ. Again and again, souls and men are instructed to live with one another, to develop the sense of community of inner life and also to stop killing animals and eating their flesh. Again and again, souls as well as men are called upon to ennoble their sensations and thoughts, so that their senses may also become refined. For as long as there is still one iota of impurity in the soul, it cannot enter heaven.

It is a spiritual principle that the person who keeps his thoughts and words pure and raises his actions to God refrains more and more from dead food, from eating meat and fish, until he is so purified that he gratefully accepts the gifts from the bosom of Mother Earth.

The impure will not defile the pure one if, for example, he is invited to a meal and partakes of a dish of meat which his hosts offer, having prepared it with much joy and effort. Then, this is a gesture of respect towards the host. Here, the following statement holds true in its meaning: It is not what goes into the mouth – for example, a few bites of meat – that defiles the body, but what comes out of the mouth: loveless, hate-filled and envious feelings, thoughts and words. They defile the soul and the body.

However, the gratification of the craving for fish, meat and alcohol burdens the soul and defiles the body.

In a general conversation with the host, it could then be pointed out that you, the guest, refrain more and more from meat and fish because you have recognized that dead food does not benefit the soul or the body, because the law of God is life. Through such and similar general hints, the host will also come to think about it so that he, too – who also stands on Jacob's ladder – can purify himself and climb, rung for rung.

Every selfless word and every selfless deed serves your neighbor for his salvation. With good, selfless conversations, many a one can recognize what I, Christ, as Jesus, told the people: For selfless, righteous people, there is no other food for the body than the lawful food which nature brings forth – grain and fruit.

Moreover, I told My own not to castigate themselves, but to refine their thoughts and senses. Then, the intake of dead food, too, of fish and meat, will be reduced. With the refinement of soul and person, the unlawful falls away. Then it is not suppressed, but is removed through the life in Me, the Christ.

4. The robber who breaks into a house built by man is guilty; but even the least of those who break into a house built by God are the greater sinners. This is why I say to all who want to become My disciples, keep your hands free from bloodshed and let no meat touch your lips; for God is just and bountiful and has ordained that man shall live by the fruits and seeds of the Earth alone. (Chap. 38:4)

I, Christ, explain, correct
and deepen the word:

The law of life states the following: The one who breaks into a house built by man makes himself guilty before the law of God and before the law of man. Man shall neither steal or plunder. He shall respect the property of his neighbor. The one who falls into need shall ask for help, but shall not steal or plunder. The one who robs his neighbor, even if this one possesses ever so great a wealth, becomes guilty before the spiritual law and the earthly law.

The one who breaks into the house of God, into the temple of the Holy Spirit, is a far greater sinner. The human body and the soul, which is from God and lives in the human body, are the house of God, the temple of the Holy Spirit. Deep in the soul is God's love, wisdom and justice. Thus, God dwells in the soul. Accordingly, the soul and body of the human being are the temple of

God. And so, the one who breaks into the house of flesh and bone, by doing violence to people, by subjugating them, by treating them as slaves, or even killing them, sins against the Holy Spirit. This is the gravest sin.

So keep your hands and your soul pure, not just from theft and robbery. But above all, do not use violence, be it on people or on animals, and beware of shedding their blood.

The one who loves his neighbor selflessly will neither do violence to him, nor kill him. And the one who loves his neighbor selflessly will not deliberately kill animals, either. The one who respects man and animal has no warlike designs, because he respects the laws of God to which belong the laws of nature, too. The one who strives to actualize the laws of God will refrain from eating meat more and more, and will gratefully accept the gifts of the earth, that is, that food which comes from God for His human children.

5. *But if an animal suffers greatly, so that its life is a torment for it, or if it becomes dangerous to you, release it from its life quickly and with as little pain as you can. Send it to the other side in love and mercy and do not torment it, and God, your Father, will show mercy to you, just as you have shown mercy to those who were given into your hands. (Chap. 38:5)*

I, Christ, explain, correct
and deepen the word:

I, Christ, give this, My word of revelation, during this mighty turn of time [1989], in order to point out once again, among other things, that just like the life of human beings, the life of animals, plants, stones and minerals, too, is in the hands of God.

Many people have turned away from the Father-Mother-God and have sold themselves to materialism. As a result of this externalization, the senses of man, as well, become ever coarser. The person thereby loses his fine sensitivity towards his fellow man and also towards nature. He has only an ear, a mind, for himself, for his ego. The result is that he pays attention to himself alone and does his utmost to gratify his own desires, without thinking of how it fares for his neighbor and his second neighbor, the animal, as well.

The animals suffer under domineering people. This is why it cannot readily be said in this time [1989], "But if an animal suffers greatly, so that its life is a torment for it, or if it becomes dangerous to you, release it from its life quickly and with as little pain as you can." For today, many animals constantly suffer torments and pain through the brutality of the human ego. The following does not hold true here: Release these animals by delivering them quickly from their torment and suffering. I, Christ, say to you: Try to experience their torment and suffering in your world of sensations. Feel into their torment and suffering and recognize how they

479

suffer because of your human doings! You are called upon to change by devoting yourselves to God, so that you can feel and understand your neighbor and your second neighbor, the animal, in your inner being.

Recognize that what you do to the animals, you do to Me, the Christ, and to yourselves, as well. The torment and suffering of the animals will one day be your torment and suffering. God, the Eternal, has also given the animals into the hands of man – however, not that he torment them, but that he live with them. Man should be *for* the animal, and then the animal is also *for* man. Then it will also serve him joyfully.

If an animal has to suffer a lot because of an accident or because of its age, then the person should release the spiritual life of the animal, the part-soul or the part-ray, from the earthly body quickly, while inflicting little pain, and should give it over in love and mercy into the hands of the eternal Creator. He, the great All-One, knows each animal. He has created it and lives as power in the part-soul or in the part-ray. The part-soul or the part-ray of the animal is the unfolded powers of consciousness of the All-Spirit, which have become spiritual form.

6. *And whatever you do to the least of My children, you do to Me. For I Am in them and they are in Me. Yes, I Am in all creatures and all creatures are in Me. In all their joys, I, too, rejoice and in all their afflictions, I, too, suffer. This is why I say to you: Be kind to one another and to all the creatures of God." (Chap. 38:6)*

I, Christ, explain, correct
and deepen the word:

What man sows he will reap, also means that what man does to the least of his fellow men – also to animals, plants and stones – he does to Me and to himself.

Each day is given to man for self-recognition; each day, every person can experience what he should recognize in himself and clear up on that day. The one who does this becomes sensitive to life. On himself he experiences what it means to love life.

The one who loves God is consciously in God, and God in him. The days become more light-filled to him as a human being, because his soul becomes freer. Then he also understands the statement, "I Am in all creatures, and all creatures are in Me."

The kind person is the merciful person who lives in harmony with his fellow man, with the animals and all the powers and forms of life.

7. *And it came to pass that on the next day He came into a city called Nain. And many of His disciples and a great multitude went with Him.*

8. *And behold, when He came close to the gate of the city, a dead person, the only son of his mother, was being carried out; she was a widow. And many people from the city went with her.*

9. *And when the Lord saw her, he had compassion for her and said to her, "Weep not! Your son sleeps."*

And He stepped closer and touched the coffin, and those who carried it stopped. He said, "Young man, I say to you, arise!"

10. And the one who was considered dead sat up and began to speak. And Jesus delivered him to his mother. And awe came upon all and they glorified God, saying, "A great prophet is risen among us, and God has come to His people." (Chap. 38:7-10)

I, Christ, explain, correct
and deepen the word:

In this and similar ways, I, the Son of God, the Co-Regent of the heavens, was active in the earthly garment, with My heritage, the part-power of the primordial power.

Many of the so-called dead whom I awakened from deep sleep were not yet in the realm of the souls, but the soul was still connected to the body by the silver cord, also called the spiritual information cord.

Deep sleep is like being unconscious. It occurs before the cord releases itself from the body. People designate it as already being the moment of death.

Only when the information cord is separated from the body is the soul also fully detached from the body. Then, the house of the soul, the body, gradually decomposes into its elements: water and earth.

CHAPTER 39

The Seven Parables from the Kingdom of Heaven

The Path to the Kingdom of God –
The one who wavers in his decision will not find
the treasure in heaven (1-6)

1. Again Jesus was sitting under the fig tree and His disciples around Him, and around them also a great crowd of people who wanted to hear Him. And He said to them, *"With what shall I compare the Kingdom of Heaven?"*

2. And He told this parable, *"The Kingdom of Heaven is like a seed, a small seed, that a person took and sowed in his field. But when it has grown, it becomes a great tree that spreads out its branches, which bow down to the Earth, take root and grow upwards, until the field is covered by the tree. And the birds of the air come and nest in its branches, and the creatures of the Earth find shelter in its shade."*

3. He gave another parable to them, saying, *"The Kingdom of Heaven is like a great treasure that lies buried in a field. A man finds it and hides it and, out of his joy in it, he goes and sells everything he has and buys that field; for he knows how great his wealth will be from it.*

4. In the same way, the Kingdom of Heaven is like a pearl of great value. A merchant found it as he was looking for good pearls. And when he found it, the mer-

chant sold everything that he owned and bought it; for he recognized how much more precious it is than everything that he gave for it."

5. And once again He said, "The Kingdom of Heaven is like a leaven which a woman took and hid in three measures of flour. When the whole was leavened and baked in the fire, it became a loaf of bread. Or again, it is like a man who takes one measure of pure grape juice and pours it into two or four measures of water, until the whole is mixed to become the fruit of vine.

6. The Kingdom of Heaven is like a city which was carefully built on the summit of a high mountain and founded on a rock, surrounded with a strong wall and with towers and gates lying to the north and to the south, to the east and to the west. Such a city will not fall, nor can it remain hidden, and its gates are open to all, and all who have the keys will enter."
(Chap. 39:1-6)

I, Christ, explain, correct
and deepen the word:

The one who loves God does not hoard for himself. In a brotherly way, he shares with his neighbor who has the same goal that he has: to be active for the life from God.

The one who gives up everything in order to reach the Kingdom of Heaven has found the treasure: the Kingdom of God in himself. It radiates from his inner being as selfless love, as virtue and kindness, and gives itself to the one who hungers and thirsts for it. The one who possesses the Kingdom of Heaven receives everything that he needs. The one who does not worry about tomorrow, but plans with God, is in God, and God is active through him for the good of all who aspire to the Kingdom of God with an honest heart.

Recognize that as long as you still cling to this world with just one fiber of your being, you will not find the inner treasure, because your thoughts draw towards this small spark in the world. It is like a straw to which you cling. Only the one who turns inward with all his sensations, thoughts, words and deeds will find the treasure that makes man blessed.

Only in this way will you attain the key which fits the gates of life.

The one who has gained the inner strength opens the gate to heaven and stands, bathed in light, in the eternal homeland, which is already known to him as a human being.

In many parables, man was and is, again and again, led to understand that only the one who decides for God alone can attain the Kingdom of Heaven. Everything else, for example the "for" and "against" – once for God, but then again for the world – is conflicting and is not the path to the Kingdom of God which is within, in every soul. It is the task of all souls and men who have moved away from God through the "for" and "against" – once spirit, then again world – to awaken and open the Kingdom of God in themselves again. Through Me,

Christ, the soul will again enter into heaven, because I Am the way, the truth and the life.

How many detours a person makes and how much pain he will endure, because of his negative and conflicting life, is solely at the discretion of each individual person, for each one has the free will to decide freely when he wants to walk the direct path that leads to liberation and freedom.

7. *And He gave them another parable, saying, "The Kingdom of Heaven is like the good seed that a man sowed in his field. But in the night, as the people slept, his enemy came and sowed weeds among the wheat and left. And when the stalks grew and the ears brought forth fruit, the weeds also became visible.*

8. *And the servants went to the owner of the house and said: Lord, did you not sow good seeds in your field? Then from where does it have the weeds? And he said to them: An enemy did this.*

9. *And the servants said: Do you not want that we go there and weed? He answered: No, so that you do not uproot the good wheat when you tear out the weeds.*

10. *Let both of them grow together until the harvest. And at harvest time, I will say to the reapers: Collect first of all the weeds and bind them in bundles to burn them and enrich the soil; but gather the wheat for me into my barn."*

11. *And He said once again, "The Kingdom of Heaven is like the sowing of the seed. Behold, a sower went*

forth to sow. And while he was sowing, some of the seed fell by the wayside. And the birds came and ate it up.

12. And others fell on rocky ground without much Earth and soon sprouted because they had no depth of Earth. But when the sun shone, they were scorched and, having no roots, they withered away.

13. Some fell among thorns and the thorns grew and choked them. And some fell on good soil, which was well prepared, and bore fruit, some a hundred-fold, some sixty-fold, and some thirty-fold. The one who has ears to hear, let him hear." (Chap. 39:7-13)

CHAPTER 40

Jesus Reveals the Parables of the Kingdom of Heaven

The parable of the Kingdom of Heaven; the good seed; recognizing and removing the weeds at the right time – Through actualization, into the fullness of the Kingdom of God (1-2). The great harvest: Separating the chaff from the wheat; the torments of hell (3-7). The seed on the wayside: To only hear the truth (9)

1. And the disciples came and said to Him, "Why do you speak to the multitude in parables?" He answered and said to them, "Because it is given to you to know the mysteries of the Kingdom of Heaven, but it is not given to them.

2. For it will be given to the one who has, so that he may have more in abundance; but from him who has nothing, even what he seems to have will be taken. (Chap. 40:1-2)

I, Christ, explain, correct
and deepen the word:

As Jesus, I, Christ, gave the good seed from the Kingdom of Heaven into this world and into the souls of all the children of God. The good seed sprouts only in those children of the Kingdom of God who strive day by day. The weed is the seed of evil. It sprouts in those children of this world who do not live in unity with the children who aspire to the Kingdom of Heaven. In the end times, when the materialistic world draws to an end, the all-encompassing harvest will follow. The reapers are the angels and all those people who turn within and endeavor to fulfill the will of God.

You should also reflect in your inner being upon the following parable: The Kingdom of Heaven is the good seed which is given to man. It falls into the field of life, into the soul, in order to prepare it again for the Kingdom of Heaven. Be watchful and look after the good seed! For the darkling, the enemy of the good, strives at all times to sow weeds in the field of life, in the soul, so that the good be overgrown by the weeds. However, do not go and pull out the weeds, unless it is given to you today to recognize the weeds that you should remove. Then you will remove only the weeds, as you have gained a clear eye for this. The good seed is then preserved.

Recognize that each day has its hours, minutes and seconds. If you use the days and are watchful, you will learn, each day, from which field of life you should remove a weed. Then you will not uproot the good seed.

Every day is given to man for recognition, to recognize and to clear up one or several weeds, that is, what is sinful. The one who uses the day to do this will not uproot the good seed, because today he is able to clearly recognize and also to clearly grasp the weed, as it has become ripe for uprooting today.

And if you yourself sow, take care that you sow the good seed, the law of life, on good soil. Then the seed will also bring forth manifold good fruits. The good seed, the law of life, will fall into your neighbor's soul, this means on good soil, only if you yourself have actualized what you sow, that is, what you pass on, having saturated it with your inner life.

I explain the following word, "For it will be given to the one who has, so that he may have more in abundance; but, from him who has nothing, even what he seems to have will be taken from him." To the one who has already actualized much from the law of life and continues to strive for it and to give selflessly will be given even more, so that he may live in spiritual fullness.

The one who owns and hoards only material goods and strives only for them has nothing before the law of life. He is poor in spiritual strength. What he thinks he owns will also be taken from him, so that he may learn to strive for the Kingdom of God.

3. This is why I speak to these in parables, for they do not see and do not hear and do not understand.

4. For in them the prophesy of Isaiah is fulfilled, which says, 'You will hear but will not understand, you will see but will notice nothing; for the heart of this people has become hardened and their ears are hard of hearing, and they have closed their eyes until that time when they will see with their eyes and hear with their ears and understand with their heart and will be converted, and I will heal them.'

5. However, blessed be your eyes because they see, and your ears because they hear and your hearts because they understand. For verily, I say to you: Many prophets and righteous ones have wished to see what you see, and have not seen it, and have wished to hear what you hear, and have not heard it."

6. Then Jesus sent the crowd away, and His disciples came to Him, saying, "Explain to us the parable of the field." And He answered and spoke to them, "The one who sows the good seed is the Son of Man, the field is the world, the good seed is the children of the Kingdom of Heaven, the weed is the children of evil. The enemy who sowed the weeds is the devil. The harvest is the end of the world and the reapers are the angels.

7. Just as the weeds are gathered and burnt in the fire, so will it be at the end of the world. The Son of Man will send out His angels and they will gather all offences and all who do evil from His kingdom and throw them into a burning oven; and those who are not cleansed will be totally consumed. Then the just will shine like the sun in the Kingdom of Heaven.
(Chap. 40:3-7)

I, Christ, explain, correct
and deepen the word:

The word of God for all men should be grasped according to its meaning.

The one who is far from God and sees the truth in the letter is blinded by the truth; for he looks at the truth and yet cannot grasp it, because he acknowledges only the letter. For such people I spoke as Jesus and I speak, as Christ, in parables again and again. This occurs today [1989], as well, through revelations. During this time, too, many people hear My word and do not understand it, because they look only at the letter.

Many recognize the truth, but do not live according to the truth. Many see that the law of God brings fulfillment, and yet do not live according to the law of truth. Many believe in the truth and continue to live in the delusion of the human ego. But the time is near when many willingly accept and actualize what they hear, and move in their heart what they see.

The time is near when all over the Earth, the former seed will be harvested, and the chaff will be separated from the wheat. Then many souls and people will have to endure the burning oven, which is within, in them. The burning oven symbolizes the condition of the burdened souls, which are bound to the world. It is the torments of hell, which the soul has to endure if it did not repent of its sins in time and make amends for what it caused in the earthly garment. And those who act against the law of love and the law of life over and over again, despite knowing better, will one day have to regenerate their spirit body in the spiritual planes of development, since they were no longer able to fully bring the particle structure of their spiritual body to unfoldment. This is the explanation of the words "will be totally consumed."

The just will shine like the suns in the Kingdom of Heaven. However, even the unjust will not have to live forever in their own self-caused torments of hell. One day, they, too, will recognize that they are children of God and will grasp the hand of grace of the Father and will walk the path to Him, who also beheld and created them.

8. Hear, too, the parable of the sower. The seed which fell on the way is like those who hear the word of the Kingdom of Heaven, but do not understand it. Then the wicked enemy comes and steals away what was sown in their heart. They are those who received the seed on the wayside. (Chap. 40:8)

I, Christ, explain, correct
and deepen the word:

The one who only hears the word of God and does not live accordingly himself will not understand it either. Then he also teaches his conceptions or the notions of others.

At all times, many people received the words of truth, which is also the case at the present time [1989].

Many heard and hear the words of truth. They enriched and enrich themselves with it. They taught and teach. They preached and preach the truth, but they did not live, nor do they live in conformity with it and, for this reason, also let themselves be paid for it. The one who lives according to the truth and teaches from his actualization, from his fulfilled heart, receives his reward from the kingdom of truth. Only the person who teaches the truth and does not live accordingly sees to it that his pockets are filled. They are those who stand at the wayside, gather the seeds of life, pass them on and do not fulfill them.

When the seed falls into the heart, it begins to sprout and to grow and also brings forth selfless fruits.

9. And those who have received the seed on stony ground are those who hear the word and immediately receive it with joy. Yet it does not take root in their inner being and does not last long; for as soon as grief and persecution rise because of the word, they will gradually fall away. (Chap. 40:9)

I, Christ, explain, correct
and deepen the word:

Many heard and hear the words of truth, accepted and accept them joyfully. However, the one who only hears the truth and does not live accordingly is and remains a wavering reed in the wind. When he is then called to answer for what he has heard and accepted, he denies the truth and forsakes it. And when he is persecuted for the sake of the gospel, he sets out for the seemingly safe shore. He wants to save himself, by renouncing the truth, seeking out the world again and disappearing into its waters, so as not to be seen and attacked anymore. So the one who only hears the truth just accepts it, but does not receive it in himself.

To receive it means to live accordingly. The one who lives the truth will also be a rock in the surf when the storms of grief and persecution come.

10. And also those who received the seed among the thorns are those who hear the word, and the cares of this world and the deceitfulness of riches choke the word, and they become barren.

11. But those who have received the seed on good soil are those who hear the word and understand it, who bring forth and bear fruits, some thirty-fold, some sixty-fold and some hundred-fold.

12. I explain all this to you who are of the inner circle. But to those on the outside, I say it in parables. Let all those hear who have ears to hear." (Chap. 40:10-12)

CHAPTER 41

The Conversion of the Bird Catcher –
The Healing of a Blind Person

*Dealing in animals; Slave-trade – Keeping the Sabbath –
The penalty for those who are knowing and for those who
are unknowing (1-9). The one who fulfills the law of God
sees into the depths of the Being (10-13)*

1. And as Jesus was going to Jericho, He met a man
with young doves and a cage full of birds which he had
caught. And He saw their misery, as they had lost their
freedom and, furthermore, were suffering hunger and
thirst.

2. And He said to the man, "What are you doing with
these?" And the man answered, "I earn my living by
selling the birds which I have caught."

3. And Jesus said to him, "What would you think, if
someone stronger or more clever than you would capture and shackle you, or would throw your wife or your
children and you into prison, in order to sell you for his
own profit and to earn his living from this?

4. Are these not your fellow creatures, only weaker
than you? And does not the same God, Father and
Mother, care for them as for you? Let these, your little
brothers and sisters, go forth into freedom and see to it
that you never do such a thing again, but that you earn
your bread honestly."

5. *And the man was astounded at these words and His authority, and he let the birds go free. As the birds came out, they flew to Jesus, sat upon His shoulders and sang to Him.*

6. *And the man asked more about His teachings and he went his way and learned basket weaving. He earned his bread from this work and broke his cages and traps and became a disciple of Jesus.*

7. *And Jesus saw a man who was working on the Sabbath and said to him, "Man, if you know what you are doing, then be blessed, for you are not breaking the law in the spirit. But if you do not know it, then you are damned and an offender of the law."*

8. *And Jesus said once again to His disciples, "What should happen to those servants who know the will of their Lord and yet do not prepare themselves for His coming, nor do they act according to His will?*

9. *Verily, I say to you, those who know the will of their master, but do not follow it, shall receive many lashes. But those who do not know the will of their master and therefore do not do it should receive fewer lashes. To whom much has been given, of him much will also be required. And to whom little has been given, of him only little will be required."(Chap. 41:1-9)*

I, Christ, explain, correct
and deepen the word:

The one who makes a profit from his neighbor and his second neighbor, the animal, sins against the law of freedom. When a man offers his wife to another man and when a woman offers her husband to another woman, because both have nothing more in common, then this is like a slave trade. Or when, at their discretion, parents give their children in marriage, or wed their daughter to a man who has given money and goods for her, then this is dealing in people. This is the same as slave trade. And the one who makes money from his second neighbor, the animal, is not much better than the one who gives away his neighbor, no matter for what reason.

According to their state of spiritual consciousness, our fellow creatures, the animals, are the weaker ones, because they do not yet have the developed soul-potential of a filiation-soul, like, for example, the soul in a human being. This is why man should offer protection to the animals and live with them, his fellow creatures, and neither reject them nor make a profit from them.

Just as the person thinks, so is the state of his soul – light or dark. He also behaves accordingly towards his fellow man, the animals and all of nature.

The words "Man, if you know what you are doing, then be blessed, for you are not breaking the law in the spirit. But if you do not know it, then you are damned and an offender of the law" mean:

The one who, on the Sabbath, helps his fellow men selflessly, doing work for them that cannot be postponed – as, for example, for people who, on the Sabbath, are in need or fall ill, or suffer grief and pain – does not violate the law of life.

But when a person desecrates the Sabbath for the sake of his advantage, then he transgresses the law that God has given man: At the end of the week, you shall rest one day and live even more consciously in God, in order to gather strength for the days of work.

The statement "Verily, I say to you, those who know the will of their master, but do not follow it, shall receive many lashes" has the following meaning: The one who knows the laws of God – be it only the Ten Commandments, the excerpts from the law of God – and does not keep them, that is, does not fulfill the will of God, judges himself. His judgment will scourge his body, that is, will strike it with what he has sown and not atoned for. For the one who knowingly acts against the law of God, sins against the Holy Spirit. This is the gravest of sins.

"But those who do not know the will of their master and therefore do not do it should receive fewer lashes" means that, because of their burden, the sin which weakens the soul, they are not yet able to grasp and actualize the laws of God. And yet, they, too, will have to recognize and repent of their sins and make amends for them. And if they do not do this in the time given to them for recognition, they will have to pay them off in full, that is, they, too, will be the beaten ones. However, they, too, will awaken one day and will then be able to grasp much. And then, much will also be demanded of them – to fulfill what they have accepted: the law of life.

The one who actualizes the laws of life becomes rich within. The one who does not actualize remains poor or will become poor. Yet everyone who accepts the law of life will one day have to give an account before the law, for what he accepts from the law obligates him to actualize it.

10. And there was a man who was blind from birth. And he denied that there were such things as the sun, the moon and the stars, or that colors existed. And they tried in vain to convince him that other people saw these things. And they brought him to Jesus, and He anointed his eyes and made him see.

11. And he rejoiced in amazement and awe and declared that before he was blind. "And now, after this," he said, "I see everything, I know everything, I distinguish all things, I am a god."

12. And Jesus said to him, "How can you know everything? You cannot see through the walls of your house, nor read the thoughts of your fellow man, nor understand the language of the birds or of the wild animals. You cannot even recall the events of your former life, of your conception or of your birth.

13. Remember with humility how much remains unknown, yes, invisible, to you. And when you do this, you will see more clearly." (Chap. 41:10-13)

I, Christ, explain, correct
and deepen the word:

Recognize your life in what is written! Though many of you see the sun, the moon, the stars and the colors, nevertheless your eyes are still blind. For as long as man does not fulfill the will of God, he does not behold His glory either. He looks only at the surface of life and does not look into the depths of Being. Only the one who fulfills the law of God becomes clearer and looks into the depths of life and perceives the thoughts of people and understands the language of animals. He also understands the plants which emit their sensations and their energy and thus communicate with him in this way. He knows the paths into infinity and knows the effectiveness of the stars, and he knows which ones serve as stations in order to reach infinity.

The one who fulfills the law of God will see more clearly and the one who has become the law of God is at home in infinity.

CHAPTER 42

Jesus Teaches about Marriage –
The Healing of the Ten Lepers

*The inner union of marriage partners even in outer
separation – Polarity and duality – Inner values (1-5).
The state of celibacy (6-8). Lasting healing only through
the actualization of the eternal laws (13)*

1. *After these sayings, Jesus left Galilee and came to
the shore of the Jordan in Judea. And a great multitude
followed Him, and He healed many there.*

2. *The Pharisees also came to Him in order to tempt
Him, and said to Him, "According to the law, is it right
that a man cast out his wife for any reason?"*

3. *And He answered, saying to them, "Among some
peoples, one man has many wives and casts out whom
he will for a just reason. And among some peoples, the
woman has many husbands and casts out whom she
will, for a just reason. And in other peoples, the man is
joined to one woman in mutual love, and this is the
better and the highest way.*

4. *For have you not read that, in the beginning, God
so created man, that there should be a male and a female, and said: This is why a man or a woman shall
leave father and mother and cleave to his wife or her
husband, and the two shall be one flesh?*

5. *And so they are now no longer two, but one flesh. For what God has joined together, shall no man put asunder." (Chap. 42:1-5)*

I, Christ, explain, correct
and deepen the word:

Verily, I say to you: Even if the reason to cast out your neighbor seems to be justified, no one has the right to exclude his neighbor from his life. May those who are without fault throw the first stone.

Whoever excludes his neighbor from his life locks his heart to God's love.

This is why a person should not cast his neighbor out, not even when there seems to be a reason for this. He should forgive his neighbor and ask him for forgiveness. For there is no discord in which only one is guilty. There are always at least two people involved.

When people separate, no matter for what reasons, then it should only be an outer separation, but not a final break with each other.

The one who unites with his neighbor in his inner being, by clearing up everything that led to the discord, remains linked with him, even when both are externally separated from one another.

A marriage with several women or men, in which a man has several wives or a woman has several husbands, is against the law of divine love.

God created polarity and duality in the pure Being. In the heavens, two divine beings unite in God and love one another in God. This union in God is God's act of creation. It comes from the principle of polarity and of duality. The two divine beings are eternally joined in God as children of God and thereby as brother and sister, as well.

It shall be on Earth as it is in heaven.

When two people promise faithfulness in marriage before God, or when several people join together in a community of brothers and sisters – people who cultivate absolute purity among themselves in order to fulfill common tasks or to fulfill the law – they should also remain faithful to one another. For the one who promises faithfulness before God makes a covenant of faithfulness with God, as well. The one who keeps this covenant of faithfulness will also see his neighbor as the temple of God and will also respect him.

The recognition of the inner values of a person lies in mutual respect. The one who learns to love the inner values in his neighbor also keeps the inner union with his neighbor. And the one who keeps this inner union is also linked with God.

Such a marriage or community of brothers and sisters is lasting in this earthly existence and enters eternity, because God is the law of unity and of communion.

People who are willing to live in the Spirit of the Lord will fashion their earthly lives together, they will support each other and be devoted to one another in trusting, selfless love. Such a marriage or community of brothers and sisters does not lead to bindings, but it is the lived union with one another and with God.

Man and woman in marriage are of one spirit and of one flesh, and yet they are two souls.

After the death of their body, they live as brother and sister and, in the purifying process of evolution, return to their spiritual dual.

Heavenly duals are two beings from God who are eternally united in God. The male is the giving principle and the female is the receiving principle. They are joined in God as a heavenly pair, from eternity to eternity.

Each being and every person has free will to freely decide, for or against the laws of God. It is according to the law of life that partners in the marriages of this world do not separate. However, since each being and every soul – and also every person – has free will, it is up to them, also according to the law of free will, whether they separate or not. In doing so, they mostly look to outer values, orienting themselves to outer things or applying human criteria as their measure. Such a separation brings people into the law of sowing and reaping. The consequences of this human decision have to be borne by both, but the greater part rests on the one who separated from his neighbor for human reasons.

The one who separates from his marriage partner in order to live with someone else in a human way has committed adultery. The so-called partnerships, too, are subject to the same law. For this reason, pay attention to your thinking and acting before you enter into a marriage or partnership and examine yourselves, in terms of the reasons and motives which induce you to do so. Is it your body that desires this? Is it the material goods which bring you together? Or is it selfless love which is active as a seed of inner life in the inner values of both who are striving for higher ideals and goals?

Recognize that on the higher levels of evolution to divine life, higher laws hold true. They also include marriages and families that strive towards higher ideals and values. They orient themselves to the inner values and the steps of evolution of the individual on the path to Me.

6. *And they answered Him, "Then why did Moses command to give a letter of divorce?" And He said to them, "Because of the hardness of your hearts, Moses suffered that you get divorced from your wives, just as he also allowed you to eat meat in many cases; but it was not like this from the beginning.*

7. *And I say to you: Whoever casts his wife out, except that it be for a legitimate reason, and marries another in her place commits adultery." And then the disciples said to Him, "If such is the case for a man with his wife, then it is not good that they marry."*

8. *But He said to them, "Not everyone grasps the words, but only those to whom they are given. For there are celibates who were born as such from their moth-*

*er's womb, and those who are made to be celibate by
people, and those who make themselves celibate for the
sake of the Kingdom of Heaven. May the one who can
grasp it, grasp it." (Chap. 42:6-8)*

I, Christ, explain, correct
and deepen the word:

When a person is celibate, no matter for what reasons, then this lies in the self-chosen path of evolution or perhaps in the law of sowing and reaping. Celibacy can be due to the fact that in previous lives, for example, he caused many a thing which is coming into effect in this earthly existence and which he now has to bear so that his soul may mature.

If a person dissolves his marriage or does not get married, to thereby reach the Kingdom of Heaven, he is subject to deception. He is bound to false conceptions, opinions and precepts. And the one who stays celibate for his own benefit sins against the law of unity.

Verily, I say to you, the union of two beings is instituted by God. In heaven, the union of two spirit beings is called duality. On Earth, the union of two people is called marriage or partnership. The union of two spirit beings or of two human beings is, at the same time, a covenant with God, and means the joint fulfillment of the laws of God, of divine love and purity. The one who disregards this law by violating the unity in God, for example, through infidelity or claim of ownership, opposes the law of selfless love.

The one who thinks he will enter heaven by way of celibacy locks himself off from heaven. He sees marriage as a desecration, because in it he only looks at the humanness, the sinfulness. The one who does not acknowledge the divine law in marriage sees only his own weaknesses and sins, thereby degrading what God has given: the union of two people which should be a covenant in and with God.

Recognize that no one can reach the Kingdom of Heaven who does not work on himself to transform, with Me, the Christ, the humanness into the spiritual-divine. This holds true for marriages and for those unmarried.

9. *Then the little children came to Him, so that He lay His hands on them and bless them. But the disciples warded them off.*

10. *But Jesus said, "Let the little ones come to Me and do not forbid them, for theirs is the Kingdom of Heaven." And He laid His hands on them and blessed them.*

11. *When He came to a city, He was met by ten lepers who were standing at the roadside. And they raised their voices and called, "Jesus, Master, have mercy on us!"*

12. *And when He saw them, He said to them, "Go and show yourselves to the priests." And it happened*

that they were cleansed as they went away. And one of them, when he saw that he was healed, turned back and glorified God with a loud voice and fell on his face before Jesus and thanked Him. And he was a Samaritan.

13. And Jesus said, "But were not ten cleansed? Where are the other nine? These did not turn back and glorify God, as did this stranger." And He said to him, "Arise and go your way. Your faith has made you whole." (Chap. 42:9-13)

I, Christ, explain, correct
and deepen the word:

What happened to those who were healed and did not thank God for it?

Out of the love and grace of God, the Almighty, who acted through Me, Jesus, they attained healing and, with the healing, the possibility to recognize their true being in order to thank God, the Eternal, through the actualization of the eternal laws.

Only the one found God in himself and remained healthy. The others turned to the world again, attracted their former illnesses and fell sick again.

CHAPTER 43

The Rich Man and the Kingdom of Heaven –
The Commandments of Purification

Possessions and the following of Christ (1-4). All things are possible for the one who strives toward the spiritual-divine as his true nature (6). God or mammon – Striving towards the material and its consequences (7). The one who renounces materialism will receive manifoldly in the eternal Being (8-9). Outer cleansing and inner purity – Faithfulness to the letter indicates unfaithfulness towards God (10-16)

1. And behold, someone came to Him and said, "Good Master, what good shall I do so that I attain eternal life?" And He said to him, "Why do you call Me good? No one is good except God. But if you want to enter into life, then keep the commandments." Then he said to Him, "Which are these?"

2. Jesus said, "What does Moses teach? You shall not kill; you shall not commit adultery; you shall not steal; you shall not bear false witness; you shall honor your father and mother; you shall love your neighbor as yourself." Then the young man said to Him, "I have been doing all this since my youth. What do I still lack?"

3. Jesus said to him, "If you want to be perfect, go and sell what you have in abundance and give it to

those who have nothing; thus, you will have a treasure in heaven. Then come and follow Me."

4. *But when the young man heard these words, he went away saddened; for he had great wealth, yes, more than he needed. (Chap. 43:1-4)*

I, Christ, explain, correct
and deepen the word:

The one who seeks earthly goods and considers the money that he possesses to be his property and increases it for his material benefit alone has already been rewarded by the world and can receive no more reward in heaven. Nor can he follow Me, the Christ.

People who live in the "for" and "against" are divided, on the one hand, by considering their possessions and money as their property and, on the other hand, by wanting to follow Me, Christ. On the one hand, their hearts are with their material goods and, on the other, their senses are with the gospel of love. Both cannot be brought into conformity with each other. This behavior only brings difficulties to the person and burdens to the soul. For no one can serve two masters – the Spirit of God and mammon. Each person and each soul is sooner or later led to the decision: to serve either God or mammon.

5. *Thereupon, Jesus said to His disciples, "Verily, I say to you, a rich man will hardly enter the Kingdom of*

Heaven. And, furthermore, I say to you: It is easier for a camel to pass through the gate of the needle's eye than for a rich man to enter the Kingdom of God." (Chap. 43:5)

I, Christ, explain, correct
and deepen the word:

This comparison with the eye of a needle now has a symbolic meaning. It refers to the conditions in Israel at the time when I, Christ, was incarnated in Jesus. In Jerusalem there was a narrow gate like the eye of a needle, through which only one person could barely pass.

6. When His disciples heard this, they were much amazed and said, "Who then can be saved?" But Jesus looked at them and said to them, "For the physical senses, this is impossible, but for the spiritual, all things are possible. (Chap. 43:6)

I, Christ, explain, correct
and deepen the word:

The statement, "For the physical senses, this is impossible, but for the spiritual, all things are possible," refers to the human and the spiritual senses. The human senses aspire to earthly well-being, but the spiritual senses are the fine powers of the soul which are linked with the Eternal.

The one who refines his human senses and turns to God in his inner being attains the right sense for the true life, since he strives for the spiritual-divine as his true being. For the spiritual person who does only the will of God, all things are possible, because he receives from the kingdom of the inner being. The one who lives in the kingdom of the inner being will have all that he needs and beyond that, also externally.

The human being is a child of God and, according to his true being, has the abundance of God in himself. When a person opens this up – by repenting of his recognized sins, by forgiving and asking for forgiveness, by clearing things up and renouncing what is sinful more and more – then the fullness from God radiates out through him, and brings into effect that which contributes to the well-being of the soul and the person.

7. And I say to you, do not make of yourselves friends of the mammon of unrighteousness, so that he does not take you into his earthly abodes when you pass away. Rather make of yourselves friends of the true wealth, which is the wisdom of God, so that you may be received into the everlasting mansions." (Chap. 43:7)

I, Christ, explain, correct
and deepen the word:

The statement "And I say to you, do not make of yourselves friends of the mammon of unrighteousness, so that he does not take you into his earthly abodes when you pass away" means that the one who makes of himself the friend of mammon is also bound to mammon and thus to this world. For the mammon is this earthly world with its riches.

The one who strives for the mammon gradually becomes unjust towards his fellow man and towards what surrounds him, the powers of the Earth and its forms of life. He no longer treasures the life of his neighbor and of the Earth. He thinks solely of his ego, which wants to confirm itself more and more through wealth and prestige.

Wherever the senses of the person go toward, there is his heart, there is his treasure. When the soul of an egocentric person leaves its house, the human body – that is, when the shell, the person, dies – it will be received by those who served this person in his earthly existence. This could have been human beings or souls. Then, the soul of this person will either come together in the realm of the souls with those souls which prepared the way to success for it during its earthly existence, or it will reincarnate with the souls of those people, that is, they will be brought together in new human bodies and will dwell with each other in earthly abodes.

"Rather make of yourselves friends of the true wealth, which is the wisdom of God, so that you may be received into the everlasting mansions" means to devote your living and thinking to the Eternal and, above all, to strive for attaining the Kingdom of God. Then you will become wise and will, already in the earthly garment, live consciously in the kingdom of the inner being. After the death of your body, you will go to the eternal mansions that are your true home. The journey over the Earth in ever new garments, in new earthly bodies, and the journey through the soul realms will come to an end when the soul has found its inner home.

8. *Then Peter said to Him, "Behold, we have forsaken everything and have followed You." And Jesus said to them, "Verily, I say to you that when the Son of Man sits on the throne of His glory, you who have followed Me in the regeneration will also sit on the twelve thrones and judge the twelve tribes of Israel. But it is not My concern to give of the things of this world.*

9. *And the one who forsakes goods, houses or friends for the sake of the Kingdom of Heaven and its righteousness will receive a hundred fold in the life to come and will inherit eternal life. But many that are first will be last, and the last will be first." (Chap. 43:8-9)*

I, Christ, explain, correct
and deepen the word:

I, Christ, say to you: The one who forsakes everything *and* leads a righteous life, by making his feeling, thinking, speaking and acting divine, has been born again in his inner being, for he has attained the rebirth in the Spirit. After the death of its body, his soul will no longer seek out the flesh.

When I come again in the spirit, the righteous will see Me on the throne of eternal glory, for I come in all might and glory; and all those who live in the kingdom of the inner being will be with Me.

The twelve thrones are, among other things, symbols for the twelve tribes of Israel, which spurned the high task of being the people of God. God does not judge. Likewise, all men and beings are called upon not to judge. The one who creates causes is his own judge; he is his own judgment.

"But it is not My concern to give of the things of this world." I Am the light of the world and I bring the light into this world, and not what makes the world poor, the mammon.

The one who renounces materialism, the mammon – that is, who forsakes goods, houses or friends for the sake of the Kingdom of Heaven and its righteousness – will receive in a manifold way in the life to come, in the eternal Being, and will consciously be at home there, too. Therefore, strive first for the Kingdom of God which is the inner life.

10. *And the scribes and Pharisees who had seen one of His disciples eat with unwashed hands came to Him.*

11. *And they were offended at that; for the Jews do not eat without having first washed their hands; moreover, they follow a lot of other customs in the washing of cups, vessels and tables.*

12. And they said, "Why do not all of your disciples follow the traditions of the elders? We saw how they ate with unwashed hands."

13. And Jesus said, "Certainly, Moses commanded you to clean yourselves and to keep your bodies and your vessels clean, but you have added things which often cannot be followed by everybody at all times and in all places.

14. So, listen to Me: It is not only the unclean things which enter into the body that defile man, but much more do the evil and unclean thoughts which pour from his heart defile the inner man and also others. Therefore, heed your thoughts and cleanse your hearts and let your food be pure.

15. You should do these things and not leave the other laws undone. The one who breaks the regulations of cleanliness, because it is inevitable, is free from blame; for he does not do this out of self-will, nor to disrespect the law which is good and just. For cleanliness in all things is a great gain.

16. Do not take on the bad customs of the world, even for the sake of appearances. For many are led to evil through outer appearances and the disguise of evil." (Chap. 43:10-16)

I, Christ, explain, correct
and deepen the word:

The washing of hands and the cleaning of cups, vessels and tables is a necessity in this world; for the Earth is matter made of stones, soil and dust. These and other substances of life are necessary for the human body to live.

Just as the wind and the rain clean the atmosphere and the Earth again and again, so does the earthly body, too, need cleaning, as well as cups, vessels, tables and all other objects. All of these outer things should be taken care of because the cleanliness of the outer life is also an expression of the inner life.

Yet outer cleanliness alone does not bring about the cleansing of the soul. When a person is impure in his inner being through sin, then often he attaches great importance to the regulations of outer cleanliness, in order to hide the impurity of his thoughts, words and actions. However, the one who is pure in his inner being will pay attention to purity and cleanliness in his outer life, too.

Washing one's hands before a meal is not always possible, because of external circumstances. However, that has nothing to do with the impurity of the soul. The one who objects to such external things again and again, especially when there is no possibility for cleansing, has an eye for external things only, because, with him, the inner values are still buried by sin.

Moses commanded the people to stay pure in their inner life and in their outer life. However, the one who has an eye only for the outer, for the world and its practices, also creates only outer regulations and, with that, forgets what it really is all about. The one who cannot grasp the words of righteous men and women cannot interpret them either, and then relates everything to this world and to its establishments, practices and customs.

Beware of considering the word alone, and its literal message to be the truth. Recognize that the truth does lie in the word, but the word is only a symbol and not the truth itself.

The one who looks only at the word and the letter and considers and passes them on as the truth will interpret the word of God at his own discretion and will therefore also add, according to his consciousness, what he thinks to be the truth.

I repeat: The one who looks at the word alone does not find the truth in it.

Those faithful to the letter indicate their disloyalty towards God. The person who does not actualize the laws of God therefore clings to the letter. This literal kind of thinking has led the world into chaos. This happened at all times and in all places and is also happening in today's time [1989].

Note well: It is not the impure – for example, what is still on the hands, the vessels or the food and goes into the mouth – that makes person and soul impure, but it is rather the ugly, the negative, unlawful sensations, thoughts, words and actions that defile soul and person. For they enter the soul of the person and from there go out again. They affect the body, and then the person has to bear what he has sown. For this reason, watch your feeling, thinking, speaking and acting, and partake only of the food that God has given to you. The Eternal offers it to you from nature, and you should keep to this.

Recognize that inner purity is decisive. But at the same time, do not neglect the other laws: selfless love, mercy and kindness, free will and unity with life.

The one who does not keep the laws of outer cleanliness when it is not possible does not thereby burden his soul, for he does not do it in self-will. Self-will disregards the eternal laws.

The law of God commands that one should strive for cleanliness in all things. Man should neglect neither his body, nor his soul, nor his environment; for the life from God is in everything and should be respected in everything.

Do not cling to the customs of the world, not even for the sake of appearance. Keep the justice of God in everything, and you will be open and honest and upright in your outer deeds.

The darkling wraps itself in many robes in order to "shine." Only the one who strives toward the Being, toward the wisdom and justice of God, unfailingly recognizes the "shine." He is not deceived by appearance, by shine.

CHAPTER 44

The Profession of Faith of the Twelve –
The Pillars of the Community

God has no secrets; sin veils the truth (2-3).
True original communities are founded on the rock, Christ
(4). The falsification of the truth by the church – The justice
of God allows each sinner a long time to turn back (7-8).
The law of God comes into this world; the truth becomes
visible (10-12). Mankind will find its way into unity with Me,
the Christ (13-15)

1. Jesus sat once again near the lake in the midst of twelve palm trees, where He often rested. And the twelve and their companions came to Him; they sat in the shade of the trees, and the holy One in their midst taught them.

2. And Jesus said to them, "You have heard what the people say about Me, but who do you say I am?" Peter stood up with his brother Andrew and said, "You are Christ, the Son of the living God, who descended from heaven and dwells in the hearts of those who believe and who obey Him for the sake of righteousness." And the others stood up and spoke, each in his manner, "These words are true, and so do we, too, believe."

3. And Jesus answered them saying, "Blessed are you, My twelve, who believe; for it is not the flesh and blood that revealed this to you, but the Spirit of God

that dwells in you. Verily, I Am the way, the truth and
the life. And the truth knows all things. (Chap. 44 :1-3)

I, Christ, explain, correct
and deepen the word:

The one who is of the truth speaks the word of truth, for he is able to perceive into the depths of truth. God also reveals all seeming mysteries to the one whose heart is with God. For nothing is a secret to the person who lives in God. He knows the laws of God, because he himself has become the law. The one who lives in Me, the Christ, also knows that I came from the heavens in order to announce to the people, as Jesus, the gospel of love, which is the way, the truth and the life.

"And the truth knows all things" means that the soul and the person who live in the truth, in the law of God, also know the truth and about all the things of the truth. Such people are the righteous proclaimers of the truth.

Recognize that many people speak of the "mysteries" of God, because they look at the sin which veils the truth. God has no secrets, neither in heaven nor on Earth. God has given the eternal truth, the divine law, to all His children as heritage. Through this, the child of God became the image of the Father. Only the person who lives in the shadow of sin speaks of the mysteries of God. He looks only at the shadow, the sin, and does not know the truth which is hidden to him behind the veils of his sin. The one who gives his sins over to Me, the Christ, day by day, and repents, forgives, asks for forgiveness and does not commit the sins he has recognized any longer will find his way to the inner truth which sets him free.

When the sins are erased, the light of the soul, the truth, can radiate through the person ever more strongly. Then the person remains faithful to the truth more and more, in feeling, thinking, speaking and acting. The one who lives in the truth knows all things because he remains faithful to the truth, God, in his daily behavior. Only in this way does the soul find its way back to its origin, to its being, which is divine.

And so, God does not hide from people. Man, however, hides from God because of his sin.

There are no mysteries of God. The works of God are mysteries only for those people who do not do the works of God.

4. *All truth is in God, and I bear witness to the truth. I am the true rock and on this rock I will build My community; and the gates of hell shall not prevail against it and, out of this rock, rivers of living water will flow in order to give life to the peoples of this Earth.*

5. *You are My chosen twelve. On Me, the head and the cornerstone, are built the twelve pillars of My house on the rock; and My community shall be built on you in Me, and in truth and righteousness shall My community be established.*

6. And you will sit on twelve thrones and send forth, through the Spirit, light and truth to all twelve tribes of Israel. And I will be with you even unto the end of the world. (Chap. 44:4-6)

I, Christ, explain, correct
and deepen the word:

The faithful apostles are the founders of the original community in Me, the Christ. The communities of Christ that live in Me, the Christ, stand on the rock, Christ.

A community in Christ is formed by people who endeavor to fulfill the will of God. Since My life as Jesus of Nazareth, free original communities, which were formed outside of the church institutions, came into being again and again and at all times.

Many of these original communities – which were founded on Me, the truth and the life, the gospel of selfless love, and in which the Spirit of God, the truth, spoke and acted directly – were again destroyed in their outer establishments by the outer power of satanic rule; but the power that brought them forth was not destroyed.

Recognize that it was only an external destruction of the original communities. In reality, the spiritual potential was invisibly built up more and more. Again and again, this power then came forth from the invisible, and original communities flared up anew in the world. They disappeared again – but in the spirit, the potential of

Christian living grew. These smaller or greater steps of evolution are a part of the first steps for the Kingdom of Peace of Jesus Christ.

In the current setting forth into a new time [1989], a far greater stream of original Christian life is flowing into this world and becoming more and more visible. This inexhaustible divine stream – the Christ-consciousness in connection with the divine wisdom – is gradually taking hold of the whole world, the entire Earth, and is preparing the New Era.

Today [1989], life in the original Christian sense is emerging again. Original communities emerge again; their central point is the Original Community New Jerusalem, which has become the Covenant Community. The prophetic Spirit is active in the original communities and leads people into the New Era, similar to when Moses led the Israelites to the first stopping place in the promised land.

And in today's turn of time, there is still the "for" and "against" of the human ego; for even the people in the developing and growing original communities still show they have humanness in and about them.

Despite all this, more and more people on the Earth are touched by the Spirit of God and many already go the path within, to the inner kingdom, in order to live in Me, the Christ. The humanness is passing away and the will of God is becoming more and more manifest through the stream that gives itself: the Christ in connection with the divine wisdom.

I, Christ, Am the true rock, and all the communities that actualize the laws of God and keep them in their daily life are built on Me, Christ, the true rock. The communities in Me are formed by those people who gather around Me, the life, through the actualization of the eternal laws and who rely only on Me – for I Am the way, the truth and the life and, in the Father, the justice.

In unity with Me, the Christ, people form the communities of Christ. So it was, so it is again, and so it will be in the future on the Earth, which becomes ever more light-filled. People who fulfill the laws of God need no outer leaders. They have Me, Christ, the law of life, and are thus for one another and not against one another. Those who are against one another are against Me and, consequently, are also not My community.

7. But after you, people of perverse mind will come and, out of ignorance or through violence, will suppress much of what I have told you and will attribute words to Me which I have never spoken; and so they sow weeds among the good wheat which I have given you to sow into the world.

8. For the truth of God has to endure the opposition of sinners, for thus it has been and thus it will be. But the time will come when everything they have hidden will be revealed and made known, and the truth will set free all those who were bound. (Chap. 44:7-8)

I, Christ, explain, correct
and deepen the word:

The law of sowing and reaping will stay in effect, until the negative has passed away and the divine dwells on Earth, that is, until all people on the transformed, new Earth fulfill the will of God. Gradually, the time is drawing to a close, in which My word has been twisted and distorted, in order to make it serve the purposes of those who thought they stood above the truth and created underlings for themselves.

Recognize that the weeds were sown by opinion-makers who did not understand My words, My sayings, and who, partly deliberately and also unintentionally, twisted the truth. Many interpreted the truth in their favor. Among other things, this resulted in church institutions marked by dogmas and doctrines, which interpreted and interpret each gospel in such a way that it served and still serves their institution. Only those people who submitted themselves to these dogmas and doctrines had and have access to these institutions. This alone gives insight into what I have just revealed. They have twisted and distorted My word in order to make it serve them.

The truth is the power of infinity and is there for all people. The truth radiates into this world in countless facets. Who claims that the facets of divine truth can be pressed into dogmas and forms?

And so weeds grew among the good seed. Although the weeds overran the good seed in the course of the centuries, the good seed was maintained undetected. The time has come in which the weeds are very gradually removed from the acre of life, so that the good seed may sprout and yield a good harvest. Very gradually and with much effort and patience, the bad seed is taken from the acre of life, so that no kernel of the good seed is lost and thrown into the oven where the weeds burn. This is the justice of God.

Even though many people cannot understand that the transition from the sinful world to the Era of Light spans a very long period of time, this is nevertheless in accordance with justice. For, again and again, God gives every sinner the opportunity to turn back. Each spark of true remorse, no matter how small, is heeded and nourished. That is the love and justice of God. God, the Eternal, is just to every soul and every person.

God's truth may have to endure the dissent of sinners – but not for all eternity. The time has come in which everything that was hidden by the opposing force is exposed and made known, for everything is already manifest in the atmospheric radiation. In this way, the truth becomes free, and it will free all people who let themselves be set free by the truth, by God.

9. One is your Master, and you are all brothers, and no one is greater than the other in the place which I have given you; for you have one Master, namely, Christ, who is over you and with you and in you, and there is no inequality among My twelve or their followers.

10. All are equally near to Me. Therefore, do not strive for first place; for you are all first, because you are the cornerstones and the pillars of the community, which is built on the truth and which is in Me and in you. And for all people you shall establish the truth and the law, as they have been given to you.

11. Verily, when you and your brothers are in agreement to begin something in My name, I will be in your midst and with you.

12. Woe to the time, when the spirit of the world enters into the community and My teachings and commandments are rendered void through the corruption of men and women. Woe to the world, when the light is hidden! Woe to the world, when these things shall be!"
(Chap. 44:9-12)

I, Christ, explain, correct
and deepen the word:

And it happened again and again that the one deemed himself greater than the other, that the one thought he was nearer to God and, out of this vanity, disdained his brother.

I say to you: The law of God is for all, and those who keep it are humble and make no differences. The law of God comes into this world and those who keep it are in and with Me, the Christ. And those who do not keep it will leave this Earth and will find themselves again in the soul realms. For the Earth is cleansing itself from every untruth and from every trifle of this world.

Who wants to resist the truth, the rock, Christ?

The water washes round the rock and the waves cover it for only a short time. Yet the rock, the truth, which I Am, will become visible and come to the fore again and again. And all those who, despite all opposition, hold fast to the rock, to Me, the Christ, will also become strong in Me and form My community, which is built on Me, the rock, through the steadfast faith of innumerable men and women who unshakably believed and believe in the truth and who served and serve the truth.

13. Then Jesus raised His voice, saying, "I thank you, O righteous Father, Creator of heaven and Earth. You have kept all these things hidden from the wise and the prudent, but You reveal it to the children.

14. No one knows You except Your Son, who is the Son of Man. No one knows the Son, except those to whom Christ is revealed.

15. Come to Me all you who are weary and heavy laden, and I will give you peace. Take My yoke upon you and learn from Me; for I am meek and humble at heart, and you will find peace in your souls. For My yoke is equal and easy, and My burden is light and does not weigh upon you unequally."

(Chap. 44:13-15)

I, Christ, explain, correct
and deepen the word:

To the "wise and prudent," that is, to the intellectual and egocentric people, the truth is hidden, because they cover it with their egocentric thinking and acting. But from the Eternal through Me, it is revealed in all its facets to the humble and meek people who strive for the truth – and is made manifest to them for their life in God.

No one knows the Father but the Son who lives in the Father. In Jesus, I, the Son, personified the humanity that will find its way into the sonship and daughterhood, which is a brotherhood, into the unity with Me, the Christ. For the one who has accepted and received in his heart the Son, Me, the Christ of God, also knows the Father who lives in and through the Son – and in those and through all those who live the gospel of love and personify it in their daily life.

The one who comes to Me, the Christ – who dwells in the innermost being of every person – and gives his hardship and burden over to Me and, from then on, lives in Me more and more will attain inner peace through Me and will bring peace into the world. Only the one who comes to Me and abides in Me becomes meek and humble. His yoke is also a part of My yoke; it will then be easier for him to carry, for I Am the supporting power for all souls and men. And his burden, too, becomes light and does not weigh unevenly on him, for I carry the weight for all souls and men.

CHAPTER 45

Looking for Signs – The Impure Spirit –
The Parents and the Brothers and Sisters of Jesus –
Earthly Riches

The "blind one" expects miracles –
The danger of being influenced by negative powers (1-6). To
sin against the Holy Spirit is to act against better knowledge
(7). To be a member in the family of God, or a loner and
advocate for the human ego (8-10). The material riches; the
effects of greed (11-16)

1. *Several scribes and Pharisees said to Him,*
"Master, we would like to see a sign from you." But He
answered, saying to them, "An evil and corrupt gen-
eration looks for a sign and no sign shall be given to it
except the sign of the prophet Jonas.

2. *Yes, just as Jonas was in the belly of the whale for*
three days and three nights, so will the Son of Man be
three days and three nights in the heart of the Earth and
will then rise again.

3. *The men of Nineveh will rise and judge and con-*
demn this generation, because they repented with the
preaching of Jonas; and behold, here is one greater than
Jonas.

4. *The queen of the south will rise and judge and con-*
demn this generation, for she came from the farthest
parts of the Earth to hear the wisdom of Solomon; and
behold, one greater than Solomon is here."

5. And He continued, saying, "When the impure spir-it has gone out of a person, it goes through dry places in order to find rest; and finding none, it says, 'I will return to my house from where I came.' And when it has come there, it finds the house empty, swept and decorated, for they did not ask the good Spirit to dwell therein and be their eternal guest.

6. Then it goes and takes with it seven other spirits who are even more evil than it, and they move in and dwell there, and this last state of all such cases is worse than the first. Even so, shall it be also unto this evil generation which refuses entrance to the Spirit of God. (Chap. 45:1-6)

I, Christ, explain, correct
and deepen the word:

The one who expects signs and miracles from God does not recognize himself as the work of God which He created. May the one who wants to see signs and miracles observe his house of flesh and blood and recognize therein the countless functions which are possible only through the Spirit of God in him.

The one who – as I, Christ in Jesus – lives in the eternal Being needs no visible signs or miracles anymore. Already in the earthly garment, he perceives the reality of God, which radiates towards him through countless incidents and forms. Only the blind one wants to see without taking the blindfold of sin away from his eyes.

Therefore, watch your thoughts, words and senses, which close your eyes to the truth and open the gates for sin. For man allows himself to be tempted all too quickly and thus opens the way to the satan of the senses.

Soul and person are the house of God. When this house is defiled by thoughts of envy, hatred and animosity, when the person does recognize them but does not change them, and when the good principles and resolutions are not followed by the corresponding action then evil moves into the person, and becomes a yoke and a burden for him.

The one who does not recognize his way of thinking, speaking, and acting and does not turn back in time keeps his house open to more darklings. Then they enter into the house that has been decorated for them and compel the person to do what they want. The person thus loses control over his thinking and speaking. Then it is thought, spoken and acted through him. He is then no longer himself, but it is those, who think and speak through him, to whom he gave access through his behavior that was far from God.

Through his negative thinking, speaking and acting, the person attracts the corresponding powers which then influence him. For like attracts like.

Every arrogance, too, is dangerous, for it is the ornament of the dark one.

That is how it was and is for people in many generations and so it will be for many who refuse to admit the Spirit of God.

7. For I say to you, whoever blasphemes the Son of Man shall be forgiven. But whoever blasphemes the Holy Spirit shall not be forgiven, neither in this life nor in the next life; for he resists the light of God because of the false traditions of man." (Chap. 45:7)

I, Christ, explain, correct
and deepen the word:

I explain the following statement: "But whoever blasphemes the Holy Spirit shall not be forgiven, neither in this life nor in the next life."

The sin against the Holy Spirit is the gravest of sins. When the truth, the law of God, is revealed to the person – be it through the Ten Commandments or through the Sermon on the Mount or through My revelations in today's time [in the years around 1989] – and he nevertheless consciously thinks, speaks and acts against the law of God, he thus sins against the Holy Spirit. A sin against the Holy Spirit, depending on its intensity, cannot be atoned for in only one earthly existence. Depending on the circumstances, several incarnations could be necessary in order to expiate and atone for what the person has caused.

Even though a person has taught untruths that were handed down, he is bound to these untruths and thus to those people and souls whom he wrongly taught. Nevertheless, the opportunity is given to him day after day to change his way of thinking and to find in himself what truth and life mean.

8. While He was still speaking to the people, behold, His parents and His brothers and sisters were standing outside and wanted to talk to Him. Then one said to Him, "Behold, Your father and Your mother and Your brothers and sisters are standing outside and want to talk to you."

9. But He answered and said to him, "Who is My father and who is My mother? And who are My brothers and sisters?"

10. And He pointed with His hand towards His disciples, saying, "Behold My father and My mother, My brothers and sisters and My children. The one who does the will of My Father in heaven is My father and My mother, My brother and My sister, My son and My daughter." (Chap. 45:8-10)

I, Christ, explain, correct
and deepen the word:

Every child of God – whether he lives in heaven, or on Earth as a human being, or as a soul in the spheres of purification – is a member of the great family of God. The one who fulfills the will of God is drawn from within to where people live in and with God, for these belong to the family of God.

The one who does the will of men turns away from those who strive to fulfill the will of God. He becomes a loner and an advocate of his human ego.

The measure for each person is his way of living and thinking. He recognizes himself in the following:

The one who truly strives to fulfill the will of God in his way of feeling, thinking and acting is also drawn to where those people live who do the will of God. This is also where the work of God, the love, will then grow.

11. And some Pharisees were there who were proud of their wealth, and He said to them, "Take heed and beware of greed, for a man's life does not consist of the abundance of things which he possesses."

12. And He spoke in a parable to them: "The land of a rich man brought forth plentifully, and he thought to himself, saying: What shall I do? For I have no place where I can store my harvest.

13. And he said: This is what I will do; I will tear down my barns and build larger ones. And there I will store all my fruits and goods.

14. And I will say to my soul: You have laid up many goods for many years, take your ease, eat, drink and be merry.

15. But God said to him: You fool, this night your life will be demanded of you. To whom shall these things which you have hoarded now belong?

16. This is how it is for those who lay up treasures for themselves, but are not rich in good works towards those who suffer need and want." (Chap. 45:11-16)

I, Christ, explain, correct
and deepen the word:

What is related here happened and happens in all generations: The rich increase their wealth. Many of them were taken from the midst of their material wealth and stood as poor souls before their material garment, which they now could no longer use, and had to recognize that they were poor in light and power. At the same time, they experienced and learned in themselves how many souls and men they could have helped with their earthly wealth. The need of those whom they did not help because of their hoarding, then became the need of their own poor soul.

For the people of the New Era, I, Christ, explain:
During the sinful time, many people were very rich externally, but their hearts were cold and calculating. The rich strove for ever more wealth and the poor were envious of their worldly goods. Many had to work hard for them in order to be able to eke out their earthly living.

In the countries of so-called affluence, a middle class between the poor and the rich also existed. Many people of the middle class, too, strove towards wealth and prestige, and worked solely to become rich.

Much envy and grief came into this world because of the wealthy; even wars were instigated by the power-hungry rich who wanted to demonstrate their power and increase their prestige. Whole nations often had to suffer from such lust for power and tyranny; for through wars, famine, grief, illness and epidemics came to the nations which suffered under their rulers and leaders. Even in times of need, many of the wealthy enriched themselves, whereas the poor became even poorer. Through armament and war, some became even richer, while a great part of the people lived on under the constraint of the yoke and of oppression. Despite the external struggle, the middle class survived.

In proportion to the number of people on this Earth, only a few strove to fulfill the will of God. However, many spoke about the laws of God and about Me, the Christ of God, yet their speeches were empty. Mankind was not filled with the spirit of love which enters the words and deeds of people solely through actualization.

In the course of generations, more and more men and souls sought the light of truth and also lived accordingly. And so, the radical change from the sinful time to the Era of Light came about very gradually. It was a long process of fermentation of all that is dark, which went on over many centuries.

CHAPTER 46

The Transfiguration of Jesus –
The Twelve Commandments

*His path of suffering, His further mission as Christ
and the future of mankind and of the Earth were revealed to
Jesus in His transfiguration (1-6). The New Israel (7-21).
The new law of love – No soul is lost (22-24). The purging of
the soul (25). All true prophets are not recognized (26-28)*

1. *After six days, when the feast of the tabernacles
was near at hand, Jesus took the twelve with Him and
led them up a high mountain. And as He was praying
there, the appearance of His figure changed, and He
was transfigured before them, and His face shone like
the sun, and His raiment was as white as the light.*

2. *And behold, Moses and Elijah appeared to them
and talked with Him, speaking of the law and of His
passing, which should take place in Jerusalem.*

3. *And Moses said, "This is the One of whom I foretold: From the midst of your brothers, the Eternal will
send you a prophet who is similar to me, and what the
Eternal tells Him, He will tell you, and you should listen to Him, and those who do not want to obey Him
prepare their own destruction."*

4. *Peter said to Jesus, "Lord, it is good to be here; if
You want, we will build three tabernacles here: One for
you, one for Moses and one for Elijah."*

5. And while he was still speaking, behold, a bright cloud overshadowed them, and twelve rays as of the sun broke forth from behind the clouds, and a voice came out of the cloud, saying, "This is My beloved Son with whom I am well pleased. Listen to Him."

6. As the disciples heard this, they fell on their faces and were very frightened. Jesus came to them and touched them, saying, "Arise and be not afraid!" But as they lifted their eyes, they saw no one but Jesus. And the six rays were to be seen upon Him. (Chap. 46:1-6)

I, Christ, explain, correct
and deepen the word:

The cherubs of the natures of God announced to Me, Jesus of Nazareth, My death in Jerusalem, and revealed My further path as the Christ of God. At the same time, in images, I saw My path of suffering and what it means for all souls and men. I also saw My work as the Christ of God in heaven and on Earth. I also saw the further sufferings of man, despite the Redeemer-deed. I saw the light of the Earth, how it takes on form and shape very gradually, and saw the many people fulfilling the will of God more and more. I saw the entire mission and also the lineage of David – of which I, Jesus, was a descendant in the flesh – and its activities with Me, the Christ of God, on this Earth and in the spheres of purification.

I also saw the end of the Earth and of all material forms. Everything was revealed to Me.

The twelve rays mean, among other things, the twelve gates of the eternal Being, which descend to the Earth more and more and from which the radiation for the Kingdom of Peace of Jesus Christ comes forth.

The six rays mean the six basic powers of the heavens, whereby the seventh basic ray, the mercy, was dwelling among the people. The rays are to be understood as symbols. They are active in Me, the Christ of God, and become visible in the world: the law of life and the activity of the light among the people in the Kingdom of Peace of Jesus Christ.

7. *And Jesus said to them, "Behold, I give you a new law which, however, is not new, but old. Just as Moses gave the Ten Commandments to the people of Israel, according to the flesh, so will I give you the twelve commandments for the kingdom of Israel, according to the Holy Spirit.*

8. *Who is this Israel of God? All those, from every nation and every tribe, who practice righteousness, love and mercy and follow My commandments are the true Israel of God." And standing up, Jesus said:*

9. *"Hear, O Israel, Jehovah, your God, is the only One. I have many seers and prophets. All live and move and have their existence in Me.*

10. You shall not take away the life of any creature for your pleasure or your profit, nor torment it.

11. You shall not steal the goods of another one, nor gather for yourselves more land and riches than you need.

12. You shall not eat the flesh, nor drink the blood of a slaughtered creature, nor anything else that harms your health or your consciousness.

13. You shall not make impure marriages, where there is no love and purity, nor corrupt yourself or any creature that has been created pure by the holy One.

14. You shall not bear false witness against your neighbor, nor willfully deceive someone with a lie in order to harm him.

15. You shall not do to anyone what you do not want to have done to you.

16. You shall worship the One, the Father in heaven, from whom all things come, and honor His holy name.

17. You shall honor your fathers and mothers, who care for you, as well as all righteous teachers.

18. You shall love and protect the weak and oppressed ones and all creatures that suffer wrong.

19. You shall work all that is good and necessary with your hands. You shall eat the fruits of the earth, so that you live long in the land.

20. You shall cleanse yourselves every day, and on the seventh day, rest from your work, keeping holy the Sabbath and the feasts of your God.

21. You shall do to others what you want them to do to you." (Chap. 46:7-21)

I, Christ, explain, correct
and deepen the word:

The one who keeps these commandments becomes
an inhabitant of the Kingdom of Peace of Jesus Christ,
which has its laws that the Eternal revealed.* For My
Kingdom of Peace is the New Israel – no longer the old
Israel. The New Israel emerges in another country on
this Earth and with those people who have made and
also keep the covenant with God for the Kingdom of
Peace of Jesus Christ. The old Israel remained in sin.

And so, David became the progenitor, in the flesh,
for the Kingdom of Peace of Jesus Christ; the divine
wisdom became the progenitress, in the Spirit, for the
Kingdom of Peace of Jesus Christ. The lineage of
David is, at the same time, the lineage and the tribe for
My kingdom on earth: The Kingdom of Peace.

From the ruins of the old sinful world, the New Era,
the New Israel with the New Jerusalem, is arising: first
as the Covenant Community in God, My Father, and in
Me, the Christ of God, then as the city of Jerusalem,
and, in the Era of Light – when all that is materialistic
draws to an end – as the state of Christ, the Christ State
for the World Kingdom of Jesus Christ.

Meanings of words change. And so the following
correction holds true:

---

* *The text of this revelation may be found on page 1057.*

Replace the word "honor" in the commandment "You shall honor your fathers and mothers who care for you, and all righteous teachers, as well" with the word "respect." To God alone is due honor. Among themselves, people should respect their life from God.

22. *And when the disciples heard these words, they beat their breasts, saying, "Forgive us, O God, if we have done wrong, and may Your wisdom, Your love and truth within us incline our hearts to love and follow Your holy commandments."*

23. *And Jesus said to them, "My yoke is equal and My burden is light and, if you want to carry it, it will become easy for you. Lay no other burden but those which are necessary on those who enter the Kingdom of God.*

24. *That is the new law for the Israel of God, and the law is in Him; for it is the law of love and is not new, but old. Take heed not to add anything new to this law nor to take anything away from it. Verily, I say to you, all those who believe and who follow this law will be saved, and those who know it and do not follow it will be lost. (Chap. 46:22-24)*

I, Christ, explain, correct
and deepen the word:

From the commandments of God for the kingdom of Israel, the law, that is in Him, emerged for the New Israel of God. It is the law of love. It may be new for many people who are taking the first steps towards the law for the New Israel. However, it is given from the eternal law of life for the people of the New Era. The eternal law is described in the word [in the text of the "Gospel of Jesus"] as "old;" in this context it means "eternal."

I correct: Replace the words "be lost" with the words "lose their way," because this is how it is meant. Verily, I say to you: All those who believe and who follow this law will be the saved ones. And those who know it and do not follow it will lose their way in the world and will have to endure what they have sown, until they find themselves again as children of God in Me, the Christ of God.

No soul is lost. In every soul is the Redeemer-spark; it is its beacon into the inner homeland, into the inner peace, whence it came as a being of light and where it goes, again as a pure being of light, as a child of God.

25. *But just as all die in Adam, so will all be made alive in Christ. And the disobedient will be purged through many fires; and those who persist will descend and be lost for an eon." (Chap. 46:25)*

I, Christ, explain, correct
and deepen the word:

"But just as all die in Adam, so will all be made alive in Christ" means that the shell of the soul, the material body, which gradually developed through the Fall and which is of this Earth, will die. But the soul which is not of this Earth, but came from the heavens as a pure being, as a spirit being from God, will recognize the light of its homeland again through Me, Christ, and will return there as a pure being.

"And the disobedient will be purged through many fires; and those who persist will descend and be lost for an eon" means that the fire is the process of purging. It is the torments of those souls which have sinned against their fellow men, against animals, plants and minerals. All that is not atoned requires purging. The torments of the soul are the images of all that has not been atoned. What people, animals, yes, all of nature had to endure because of man, then comes up as images in the soul of the originator. The soul experiences on its own spirit body the grief, the pain and the anguish – all that it, as a human being, inflicted, on people, animals, plants, stones and minerals. This is then the fire, the purging of the soul.

The stubborn and unreasonable ones "will descend" means that they will go into incarnations which are poor in light and, alternating between being born and dying, will expiate what they have caused. This may take not only one eon but many eons. Eons can also be described as cosmic light cycles.

26. *And as they came down from the mountain, Jesus commanded them, saying, "You shall not speak to any-*

one about this vision until the Son of Man has risen again from the dead."

27. And His disciples asked Him, "Then why do the scribes say that Elijah has to come first?" And Jesus answered, saying to them, "Elijah shall truly come first and restore everything.

28. But I say to you that Elijah has already come and they have not recognized him, but have done whatever they pleased to him. In the same way, the Son of Man will also have to suffer at their hands." Then the disciples understood that He had spoken to them of John the Baptist. (Chap. 46:26-28)

I, Christ, explain, correct
and deepen the word:

At all times, the true prophets announced the great spirit beings, God's messengers of light in earthly garment, and people waited for them. However, as long as the true proclaimers, the prophets, were among men, they were not recognized, but doubted, discriminated against, persecuted or even killed. The people did not believe in their message; for the prophets were men among men, even though they had a high divine consciousness, which the worldly person could not perceive or grasp. Only when these great proclaimers of God were no longer in the temporal, were their words alive again in many an ear. Only then, after their discrimination, persecution and after their death, were many of them acknowledged as true prophets and proclaimers of God and were entered in the history of mankind.

When the great spirit beings in earthly garment who had been announced and then expected by the people appeared before the people, they, too, were not recognized, but were likewise mocked, ridiculed or even killed. When they no longer were in the temporal, then they were remembered and were spoken about as the true prophets and great beings from God who were in earthly garment. Because man looks only to the person, to the external, and hears only the word of the person – and does not endeavor to understand the meaning of the words – the majority of people considered all great spirit beings in the earthly garment as agitators, impostors, false prophets or teachers, who just wanted to distinguish themselves, and so figuratively called out: Crucify them!

And so, the people recognized neither John – in whom was not Elijah, but over whom the spirit of Elijah radiated – nor their Redeemer and, just as little, the righteous prophets and enlightened men and women. Only when the great spirit beings were no longer among them as human beings were many recognized and praised with words. The people recorded the words of some of them in the book of the institutions, too, which they called and call the Bible. However, the actualization of what the great spirit beings taught was and is yet to be accomplished; for to this day [1989], many have forgotten to live what the messengers of light of the heavens brought to mankind: the laws of selfless love.

What good is fame if the people do not fulfill what has been announced by those whom they praised? The divine souls in earthly garment, the true prophets, the great spirit beings, returned to the Kingdom of God and received their reward from God. Of what use is it to mankind when they are made famous in a book, which tells of their greatness and in which their prophecies are written down – when, however, these hardly find an echo in man, that is, when they are hardly taken seriously and actualized?

CHAPTER 47

A Correct Understanding of the Commandments –
The Parable of the Rich Man
and the Beggar, Lazarus

About the correct understanding of the written laws, for example, killing (1-3). Envy is theft – Begetting sick children – Adultery (4-5). Respect for all forms of life (6). Speaking the truth, but not exposing – Respecting the free will of one's neighbor (7). Living in God (8-9). Differences between the rich and the poor: causes and effects (10-17)

1. And when they had come down from the mountain, one of His disciples asked Him, "Master, will a person enter into life if he does not keep all the commandments?" And He said, "The law is good according to the letter, but it is even better according to the spirit. For the letter without the spirit is dead, but the spirit makes the letter alive.

2. Take heed that you follow all the commandments which I have given to you in your heart and in the spirit of love.

3. It is written, you shall not kill. But I say to you, those who hate and wish to kill are guilty before the law. Yes, if they cause pain and torment to innocent creatures, they are guilty. But when they kill only to put an end to the suffering which cannot be healed, they are not guilty, if they do it quickly and in love.
(Chap. 47:1-3)

I, Christ, explain, correct
and deepen the word:

"The law is good according to the letter, but it is even better according to the spirit" means that the law of God is the truth. The truth is eternal, because God is the law, the truth.

The one who acknowledges the law of God according to the letter believes in the law of God. However, he himself has not yet become the law of God. The one who penetrates the law of God with his alert soul, that is, with the spirit of truth, does not cling to the letter anymore. In this person, the letter comes alive because he fulfills what the letter expresses: the law of God. As you have read, "For the letter without the spirit is dead, but the spirit makes the letter alive."

The letter comes alive only when the person begins to fulfill the commandments. Through this, he gradually matures into the all-encompassing law of love and life. Only the one who fulfills the laws with his heart and in the spirit of love will recognize the all-encompassing law and will thus find his way to the truth, which is within, in the soul of man.

Recognize that the truth, the divine law, makes man free – the letter alone, in which the law is contained, does not.

"You shall not kill" – neither people nor shall you willfully kill animals. About this, I say to you: Even the one who hates and wishes to kill his neighbors and second neighbors, be it human beings or animals, is guilty before the law of God. The one who causes torment to human beings and animals is guilty before the law of God as well.

"But when they kill only to put an end to the suffering which cannot be healed, they are not guilty, if they do it quickly and in love" holds true only for the animal world.

Recognize that the animals have no soul guilt, that is, they have created no causes. When they suffer, they suffer only because man has no regard for their habits. Therefore, beware of killing animals with the motivation that they are suffering. In the present time [1989], many animals suffer because of the results of technology and because of agonizing animal experiments. So examine the reason why you kill animals. In this, too, the law is valid: What man sows he will reap, in his behavior towards people as well as towards animals and nature.

4. *It is said, you shall not steal. But I say to you, all those who are not content with what they have and desire and covet what others have, or who withhold from the worker what is due to him, have already stolen in their hearts, and their guilt is greater than that of a person who steals a loaf of bread out of need, in order to satisfy his hunger.*

5. *And I have told you, you shall not commit adultery. But I say to you, if a man and a woman join in marriage with sick bodies and beget sick offspring, they*

are guilty, even though they have not taken their neigh-bor's wife or husband. And those who have not taken a woman who belongs to someone else, but desire and covet her in their heart, have already committed adul-tery in spirit. (Chap. 47:4-5)

I, Christ, explain, correct
and deepen the word:

Recognize that the law of God is active in every de-tail of your earthly life, in every moment of this ex-istence. The ruling law of God is in all that you sense, think, speak and do. Depending on your behavior, it be-comes active.

When you turn against the law of God, you strengthen your human ego; this then enters your soul as guilt. When you let the law of God prevail in your feeling, thinking, speaking and acting, it helps you and prepares for you, in manifold ways, the path to selfless love, to inner happiness, to contentment and to moderation. Then your soul becomes more light-filled, your body more radiant and you will have what you need in this life and even more.

Remember the words, "... who are not content with what they have and desire and covet what others have," or the one who withholds from his neighbor what is due to the latter – has already stolen in his heart.

Thus, envy is already stealing and goes into the soul as such. Remember that this guilt is greater than that of a person who steals a loaf of bread out of need, in order to satisfy his hunger.

I explain the following statement: "But I say to you, if a man and a woman join in marriage with sick bodies and beget sick offspring, they are guilty, even though they have not taken their neighbor's wife or husband." The one who knows of his disease and knows that it is contagious and nevertheless marries and begets children who are then stricken with the same disease is guilty before the law of life and freedom.

This, too, is a law: The one who has not taken a woman because she belongs to another, but desires and covets her in his heart, has already committed adultery in spirit.

I repeat: The law of life permeates all fibres of material being. The soul is the book of life; the law of God writes all the "fors" and "againsts" into it. And so, nothing is lost, neither the good nor the less good, nor the evil. Everything is in the book of life, in the soul.

6. *And again I say to you: Anyone who seeks to possess the body of any creature for food, for pleasure or for profit thereby defiles himself. (Chap. 47:6)*

I, Christ, explain, correct
and deepen the word:

The burden of the soul is meant by the word "defiles." For the one who does violence to man or animal and disregards life sins against the life of the person or of the animal. The same holds true for plants, stones and minerals. All forms of life bear in themselves the life from God. They sense what their neighbors intend to do with them and feel it as joy or pain. What man does to his neighbor or to a form of life falls back on him.

7. *And if a person tells his neighbor the truth with the intention of hurting him, he is guilty even though it is literally true. (Chap. 47:7)*

I, Christ, explain, correct
and deepen the word:

If a person tells his neighbor the truth with the intention of humiliating him, exposing him or hurting him, that is, with the intention of harming him, he sins against the law of free will and harms himself by this. For everything that is done deliberately, out of egocentric reasons, is sin, even when what is said is literally the truth. This also applies to a lesser degree when it takes place unintentionally but out of egocentric motives, for many know the Ten Commandments of God.

Recognize that the truth should be told to your neighbor only when this is done selflessly, that is, without judgmental intention, and then, only if the one who conveys the truth is alone with his neighbor; for every person has free will and what he does concerns only God and His child.

You can selflessly draw the attention of your neighbor to his sinful behavior, but only if you can prove it. However, do not exert pressure on him to do or to leave this or that.

The one who discloses in public what his neighbor wanted to keep secret is also guilty before the law of free will. Everyone should be able to confess his faults freely and openly and to turn back, if this is necessary.

If, for example, you publicly label your neighbor as a thief, because you know of the theft, you violate the law of free will. Go to the thief and inform him that you know of his theft and ask him to openly confess to it and give back what he misappropriated. If he does not do this, you can then speak before the earthly guardians of the law in a general way, but never point to him and call him a thief. This is the explanation from the eternal law, but what a person does is, in turn, up to his free will.

8. *Walk in the Spirit and you will thus fulfill the law and become ripe for the Kingdom of God. Let the law be in your hearts rather than on your memorial plaques – which you should nevertheless do and not leave undone. For the law which I have given to you is holy, just and good, and blessed are all those who obey it and walk in it.*

9. *God is Spirit and those who worship God must worship Him in spirit and in truth, at all times and in all places." (Chap. 47:8-9)*

I, Christ, explain, correct
and deepen the word:

"Walk in the Spirit" means: Strive to fulfill the laws of God every day and you will grow into the eternal law more and more and will live in it.

So strive to live in the present and to selflessly fulfill what each day assigns you. Then you will be free from compelling desires and will live neither in the past nor in the future. Nor will you worry about tomorrow or want to secure your future, because you live in the present, in God. The one who walks with God through the day receives more and more strength from God, because he is obedient to God. He will then walk in Him, the great Spirit, God.

The one who walks in God also worships God in the spirit and in the truth, because he knows that God is Spirit. His light is in all places and at every moment of the day – just as in every situation, in all that comes toward him.

10. *And He spoke this parable to the rich, "There was a rich man who clad himself in purple and fine linen and lived every day sumptuously and in pleasures.*

11. *And there was also a beggar called Lazarus, who lay full of sores at his door. And he wanted to satisfy his hunger with the crumbs that fell from the rich man's table. And the dogs came and licked his sores.*

12. And so it happened that the beggar died and was carried by the angels into Abraham's bosom. The rich man also died and was buried with great pomp. When, in Hades, he raised his eyes in his torment, he saw Abraham far off and Lazarus in his bosom.

13. And he called, saying, 'Father Abraham, have mercy on me and send Lazarus that he may dip the tip of his finger in water and cool my tongue, for I suffer torment in this place.'

14. But Abraham said, 'Son, remember that you received good things in your life, whereas Lazarus received evil things. But now he is comforted and you are tormented. And so are the changes in life for the purging of souls. And besides, a great abyss is placed between us and you, so that those who wanted to go down to you from here cannot; and likewise, only a few of you can come here to us from there until their time is fulfilled.'

15. Then he said, 'Therefore, I ask you, father, that you send him to my father's house, for I still have five brothers, so that he bear witness to them, lest they also come into this place of torment.'

16. Abraham said to him, 'They have Moses and the prophets. Let them hear these.' But he said, 'No, father Abraham; but if one of the dead went to them, they would repent.'

17. Abraham said to him, 'If they hear not Moses or the prophets, neither will they believe, though someone rose from the dead.'" (Chap. 47:10-17)

I, Christ, explain, correct
and deepen the word:

Every human being is a child of God and should not walk over the Earth in beggar's clothing. On the other hand, nor should he revel in luxury and riches, by letting his fellow man work, so that he alone may prosper. For every person should fulfill the commandment "pray and work."

Every laborer is worthy of his hire. The one who works honestly is also fair to his neighbor. He will not hoard money and goods solely for himself, nor acquire earthly riches or great possessions. His effort will be that all people can live like children of God: in harmony and order, in their inner lives as well as in their external ones.

The one who thinks only of himself, who has others work only for him and pays the honest worker unfairly, will live a life of ease until what he has caused comes upon him either in this incarnation or in further ones or, as soul, in the spheres of purification. This is what the parable of the rich man and poor Lazarus means: The one who lives a life of ease at the expense of his neighbor in this incarnation will – either as a soul in the spheres of purification or in one of his further incarnations – lie as a beggar at the door of those who wallow in riches, as he once did.

There will be the poor and the rich until souls and men turn to the light of God and receive from the light of truth, from the law of life. Then all will live in unity with one another and will have what they need – and beyond that.

When the soul is rich in inner light, the human being is not poor, either. When the soul is poor in the light and power of God, it may well be possible that the person is externally rich in this life – because, for example, he exploits people and puts the profit in his own pocket. Either in the soul realms or in another earthly incarnation, the soul or the person will recognize his inner poverty and will have to bear the sorrow and torment which he, as a human being, once caused to his neighbor. Then the soul in its earthly garment will live either in poverty or sickness or will have to bear both; and many a one will content himself with the crumbs that fall from the table of the rich – until he dines at the table of the Lord with the people who turn to the light.

The differences between the rich and the poor will exist until all live in Me, the Christ, in the law of love, which unifies all in the eternal Father.

The gap between the different degrees of consciousness exists only from the point of view of the lower consciousness. It cannot reach to higher spheres of consciousness.

On the other hand, the souls on higher planes of consciousness can go to the souls on lower planes of consciousness. However, they do so only when they realize that they can help their neighbor, who still has a low consciousness, because he is open for help.

CHAPTER 48

Jesus Feeds a Thousand People and Heals on the Sabbath

Having compassion (1-9). Healing the sick –
Slanderous talk against Jesus and against the followers
of Christ (10-13)

1. And it came to pass that as Jesus was teaching the multitudes and they had become hungry and suffered from the heat of the day, there passed by that way a woman with a camel laden with melons and other fruits.

2. And Jesus raised His voice and called, "O you who thirst, seek the living water which comes from heaven; for this is the water of life and the one who drinks it will never be thirsty again."

3. And He took five melons and distributed them among the people, and they ate and their thirst was quenched. And He said to them, "If God makes the sun to shine and the water to fill these fruits of the earth, shall He, Himself, not be the sun of your souls and fill you with the water of life?

4. Seek the truth and let your souls be satisfied. The truth of God is the water that comes from heaven, without money and without price, and those who drink it will be fed." And those whom He satisfied were a thousand people – men, women and children – and no one went home hungry or thirsty. And many who had fever were healed.

5. *At that time, Jesus went through the grain fields on the Sabbath day, and His disciples were hungry and began to pick the heads of grain and to eat.*

6. *But when the Pharisees saw this, they said to Him, "Behold, your disciples are doing something that is not proper to do on the Sabbath."*

7. *And Jesus answered and said to them, "Have you not read what David did when he and his companions were hungry? How he went into the house of God and ate the shewbread, which only the priests should eat, but not David and those with him?*

8. *Or have you not read in the law that, on the Sabbath days, the priests in the temple do their work without punishment? But I say to you that in this place there is One who is greater than the temple.*

9. *But if you had recognized what this means, 'I want pity and not sacrifice', you would not have condemned the guiltless. The Son of Man is the Lord, even of the Sabbath." (Chap. 48:1-9)*

I, Christ, explain, correct
and deepen the word:

The account about the "melons" means that the one who lives in God and gives from the eternal truth will also receive from the eternal truth. Neither the soul, which lives solely by the power of God, nor the human being, who receives his earthly food by the power of God, will hunger or thirst.

563

"To pity" is to feel sorry for someone. The one who only feels sorry for his neighbor increases the self-pity of the latter. This is why you should understand the words "to pity" as empathizing.

The one who is able to accept his neighbor just as he is and has taken within himself his neighbor's spiritual being, which is from God, will not look down on him, pitying and feeling sorry for him: He will empathize – that is, have compassion – and at the same time will recognize what his neighbor really needs. He will then help and give selflessly, just as it is given to him, that is, as it is possible for him. This is the most beautiful and fair sacrifice, which is pleasing to God.

But the one who raises himself to be a judge over his neighbor condemns his fellow man. The one who practices justice places justice before the worldly law; for justice is God. Worldly laws are made by man.

10. *He went further and came into their synagogue. And there was a man whose hand was withered. And the scribes and Pharisees asked Him, "According to the law, is it allowed to heal on the Sabbath?," so that they could accuse Him.*

11. *And He said to them, "Is there one among you who, owning but one sheep which falls into a pit on a Sabbath, would let it lie there and not lift it out? And if you help a sheep, why should you not help a man who is in need?*

12. Therefore, it is according to the law to do good on the Sabbath." Then He said to the man, "Stretch out your hand!" And he stretched it out and it became like the other one again.

13. And the Pharisees went out and held council against Him as to how they could destroy Him. But when Jesus noticed this, He went away with His disciples; and a great multitude followed Him and He healed their sick and infirm, and He charged them not to make it known. (Chap. 48:10-13)

I, Christ, explain, correct
and deepen the word:

As Jesus, I healed many people, but there were many whom I could not help. Many a one was helped in his hour of self-recognition. But when his everyday life returned to him and he lived his old vices again, illness broke forth anew. For in the one who again commits the same sins which led to the illness, what was already in the process of transformation in the soul – the old affliction or illness – breaks out again.

This is what the scribes and Pharisees heard and saw and used as grounds to incite the people against Me, claiming, I was a charlatan who deceived the people and was in alliance with Satan. Furthermore, they said that if this Jesus were divine, then those who were seemingly healed would remain healthy. And so, He has brought out only deceptions in order to bind the masses to Himself. He is the Satan, so they continued to say; He creates a healing hysteria among the people and lays invisible powers on the wounds. If the so-called healing hysteria – which they explained as hypnosis – then subsides, those who were seemingly healed have to then recognize that they still bear the old afflictions.

Such and other slanderous talk of the former Pharisees and scribes was repeated throughout all generations, right up until today's time [1989]. Today, too, in the great turn of time, similar things are happening as during My earthly existence. Pharisees and scribes – today they are the intellectual church authorities and those servile to them – again slander those who follow Me, the Christ, and who strive to lead a genuinely Christian life, in order to help their fellow man selflessly and to announce the good news that the Kingdom of God has drawn near.

14. And so was fulfilled what Isaiah had said, "Behold My servant, whom I have chosen, My beloved, in whom My soul* is well pleased. I will pour My Spirit over Him and He will bring justice to the unbelievers.

15. He shall not call nor cry out, nor shall any man hear His voice in the streets. He shall not break a bent reed nor quench the fire of a smoldering flax until He has spread justice and victory. And the heathens will trust His name." (Chap. 48:14-15)

---

* *When the gospels were written and also when "The Gospel of Jesus" was written down, the word "soul" was often used for the pure spirit body.*

CHAPTER 49

The True Temple of God

About the destruction of the temple (1-3). Every person is a temple of God, a temple of the Holy Spirit (4). The meaning of external forms (5-7). Bloodshed and blood sacrifice (8-10). Only the one who strives for a life in God each day recognizes Christ and understands the language of the law (11-12)

1. The Passover feast was near. And it came to pass that some of the disciples who were masons repaired the chambers of the temple. Jesus came by, and they said to Him, "Master, do You see these great buildings and what manner of stones are here and how beautiful the work of our forefathers is?"

2. And Jesus said, "Yes, it is beautiful, and the stones are well fitted, but the time will come when not one stone will remain upon another; for the enemy will conquer the city and the temple.

3. But the true temple is the body of man, in which God dwells by the Spirit. And when this temple is destroyed, God will build an even more beautiful temple in three days, which the eye of the normal man cannot recognize. (Chap. 49:1-3)

I, Christ, explain, correct
and deepen the word:

I Am the Christ of God, the Son of the eternal Father, who, through Isaiah and other righteous men and women, was announced by the eternal and just God. I came into this world as Jesus of Nazareth, not to break things but to erect them, not to erase what has not been cleared up, but to lead all out of sin and to lead them to the One who has sent Me, to the eternal Father. For all spirit beings, souls and men are His children. My name is inscribed in all souls, and all will accept and receive Me, the Christ, because I Am their Redeemer and their redemption. The heathens, too, will accept and receive Me; for no one comes to the Father but through Me, Christ, His Son.

All earthly things will pass away, even the work of the forefathers. For that which is matter, that is, coarse-material, does not last permanently, but only until the primordial substance of the Earth returns to the eternal Being which is pure and fine-material.

From generation to generation, the enemy of the good lays his hand upon the structures of man and destroys what man treasures as good and of value. This will happen until the enemy becomes a friend of the good. Then the transformation to the finer and higher life can take place according to the laws of God.

The true temple is the temple of flesh and bone, the body of the human being in whose soul and in whose cells the Spirit of God dwells.

"And when this temple is destroyed, God will build an even more beautiful temple in three days, which the eye of a normal man cannot recognize" means that when the soul is separated from the body, that is, when death visits the earthly body, then the light-filled soul will overcome its still existing ties to the Earth – the attraction to the Earth – within three days. It will then go through the veils which separate the planes of consciousness from one another, because the soul has already discarded these veils while in the earthly garment. According to its level of consciousness, it will then dwell where it is guided to, and from where it is attracted. In these three days, during which the light-filled soul severs its still existing ties to the Earth, its spiritual garment also changes accordingly, in color and form.

4. Do you not know that you are the temple of the Holy Spirit and that the one who destroys one of these temples shall be destroyed himself?" (Chap. 49:4)

I, Christ, explain, correct
and deepen the word:

Every human being is a temple of God, for the Spirit of God dwells in every soul and in each cell of the earthly body.

Therefore, the one who disrespects his neighbor, the temple of God, disrespects his own temple, too – and thereby, God. For as a person behaves toward his neighbor, he also behaves toward God. Every lack of respect toward one's neighbor, that is, towards a temple of God, is a sin against the Holy Spirit.

The one who kills his neighbor thereby destroys a temple of God. Then the soul of the one who was killed no longer has the possibility, in its earthly body, to expiate, or maybe to accomplish, that which was assigned to it for this earthly existence.

The one who kills his neighbor, the temple of God, or has him killed, will experience the same or like thing. The fears, the grief, the terror and death will come over him, too. In his hour of death, he will have no peace, for he will be confronted by the soul of the one whose earthly body he killed and which has not yet forgiven him. On his soul body he will then experience what his neighbor, whom he killed or had killed, had to suffer.

I repeat: Every human being is a temple of the Holy Spirit. And every person is commanded to keep his own temple pure and to respect the temple of his neighbor. The one who keeps this commandment will neither suffer nor will his temple be destroyed by sickness, need or violence.

5. *And some of the scribes who heard Him tried to set a trap for Him with His words, saying, "If you reject the sacrifice of sheep and cattle and of birds, then for what purpose was this temple built by Solomon for God, which is in the process of being restored now for forty-six years?"*

6. *And Jesus answered, saying, "It is written in the prophets: For all peoples, My house shall be a house of*

prayer for offering praise and thanks. But you have
made a slaughterhouse out of it and have filled it with
abominations.

7. And furthermore it is written: From the rising of
the sun to its setting, My name shall be great among the
heathens, and incense with a pure offering shall be
offered to Me. But you have made of it a place of deso-
lation with your offerings of blood, and you use the
sweet incense just to cover up the ill smell of blood.
I Am not come to destroy the law, but to fulfill it.
(Chap. 49:5-7)

I, Christ, explain, correct
and deepen the word:

As long as the person himself has not yet become the
temple of the inner life – into which he enters in order
to dedicate his thinking and acting to the great All-One
and to offer Him thanks for his earthly life – he needs
external forms. In mighty buildings, which he calls temples or churches, he offers sacrifices in keeping with
external customs. In former times, there were animal
sacrifices; in the present time [1989], there are rituals
and ceremonies, meaningless singing and processions.
In today's generation [1989], too, such external and, in
part, still pagan, customs have not yet been done away
with and are still carried out "in the name of the Lord."
All this is an abomination before the eternal Father and
before Me, the Christ.

The eternal God, the God of Isaac and Jacob, wants neither magnificent churches nor temples. He wants His children to be the temple of the Holy Spirit, that they cleanse and keep themselves pure, and sacrifice their sinful thoughts and actions to Him. They should come together in a house of prayer that is open to all people for prayer, not to just a few who have declared their solidarity with the keepers of a teaching which is no longer My teaching.

The one who teaches the truth and lives accordingly need not hide anything. Only the one closes the doors of his churches and temples who spreads his own teaching and not the eternal truth which is open for all; for the law, the truth itself, is in every soul, and the soul shall find its way to the truth in order to be the eternal law once more as a spirit being.

May the one hear, who has ears to hear!

May the one see, who has eyes to see!

The one who practices righteousness recognizes the darkling who adorns himself with My name, Christ, in order to deceive people and to lead them astray. The one who has learned to behold recognizes where the truth flows. He will profess to the truth and will be with those who strive to live according to the truth.

My name will remain great among the peoples; for from generation to generation, there will be more and more righteous men and women who will crush the head of the treacherous serpent that calls itself Christian. That which is given from the Spirit is the truth and will remain; all that is pagan will pass away.

Then, when another sun shines, I, the Christ of God, will be consciously raised; that is, I, the I Am, will have become the consciousness of men and will be the ruler of the Kingdom of God on Earth. Then there will be neither pagans nor rituals. All people are then united in selfless love, and their lives are consecrated, because they fulfill the laws of the Eternal.

The word "incense" means the consecrated life of the people who align themselves with God, the Eternal. Man should dedicate his earthly life, his human sensations, thoughts, words and deeds to God. Then he will live in God and be pure of heart.

8. *Do you not know what is written? Obedience is better than sacrifice, and to hearken is better than the fat of rams. I, the Lord, am weary of your burnt sacrifices and your vain offerings, for your hands are full of blood.*

9. *And is it not written: What is the true sacrifice? Wash and cleanse yourselves and remove the evil from before My eyes; stop doing evil and learn to do good. Do justice for the fatherless and the widows and to all those who are oppressed. And in this way, you will fulfill the law.*

10. *The day will come when everything that is in the outer court and is part of the blood sacrifices will be taken away, and the pure worshippers will worship the Eternal in purity and in truth." (Chap. 49:8-10)*

I, Christ, explain, correct and deepen the word:

As long as the souls of people are impure, their hands, too, are stained with blood. The evil, that is, the sinfulness, that a person has sown in his soul is his causes and his deeds also mark him accordingly. As he has sown, so will he behave in his earthly life, and likewise, as a soul in the spheres of purification after the death of his body: The blood-thirsty one remains blood-thirsty and seeks revenge and wants to continue to shed the blood of his neighbor. All those who want revenge are the quarrelsome who stop at nothing, not even the life of their neighbor. In their madness, they even consider shedding the blood of others to be honorable, and do not hesitate to offer animals, too, as burnt sacrifices to the Eternal. Every blood sacrifice is satanic and is a desecration of the life from God. Through such vengeful darklings, the darkness wants to ridicule God.

God, the Eternal, wants man to sacrifice his carnal base ego and to worship Him, the Eternal, in his heart through thoughts, words and deeds of selfless love.

The words, "in the outer court" mean, among other things, the externalization of man and all that he has brought about through his external life, including what is a part of the blood sacrifices. For all the outer courts, which symbolize the world, will dissolve, as there will be but one people: the people of the Christ of God.

The day is near when all that is carnal and passionate will be taken away; for that which has been promised is gradually taking on form and shape: The Earth will purify itself, and life on Earth will renew itself, and the Kingdom of God will come to the Earth, to the children of God who are of pure heart.

11. And they replied, "Who are you who want to do away with the sacrifices and despise the seed of Abraham? Have you learned this blasphemy from the Greeks and the Egyptians?"

12. And Jesus said, "Before Abraham was, I Am." And they refused to listen, and some said, "He is possessed by a demon." And others said, "He is mad." And they went their way and told everything to the priests and elders. And these became enraged and said, "He has blasphemed God." (Chap. 49:11-12)

I, Christ, explain, correct
and deepen the word:

The one who looks solely at the external world and speaks its language and lives in the world does not know the eternal law or the language of the law. The one who does not recognize Me does not recognize the Father either, who has sent Me to the people. The one who does not recognize Me does not understand My language either, the law, which I Am. So it was at all times and so it is also in today's time [1989]: Only the one who strives each day to return to the righteous life, to God, understands the language of the eternal law.

Only the one who still has something demonic in himself calls his neighbor demonic. So, all those who led an externalized life could not understand Me, the Christ in Jesus, and therefore were of the opinion that My speech was demonic. Yet, I Am the I Am in God, My Father, the One who was first-beheld by Him and firstborn of Him. Before Abraham, I was perceived in Him. I Am in God and omnipresent in the four nature powers of God. Thus, I Am a part of the heritage of all the children of God, who are from eternity to eternity.

CHAPTER 50

Christ, the Light of the World

Human judgment and condemnation;
the justice of God (1-4). The true self in everyone: God –
The one who does not love his neighbor does not love God,
either (5-8). The one who believes without actualizing will
not behold the eternal Father (9-15)

1. And Jesus spoke to them once more, saying, "I Am the light of the world; the one who follows Me will not walk in the darkness, but will have the light of life."

2. But the Pharisees said to Him, "You bear witness of Yourself; Your witness is not valid."

3. Jesus answered, saying to them, "Even though I bear witness of Myself, My witness is still valid. For I know from where I came and where I go; but you do not know where I come from and where I go.

4. You judge according to the flesh, I judge no one. And yet, if I judge, My judgment is valid. For I Am not alone, but I come from My Father who has sent Me. (Chap. 50:1-4)

I, Christ, explain, correct
and deepen the word:

With the words "... where I come from and where I go" is meant the being from God. For the one who is of

577

pure heart is aware that he comes from God and will return to God.

The person whose soul is enveloped in sin does not know where his true being came from and where it goes. He looks only to his perishable body, of which he can say that it came from the womb of his mother and will return to the womb of the Earth. But his knowledge does not reach any further. Yet those who live in Me, the Christ, know where they come from and where they are going.

The one who "judges according to the flesh" is a judge. The one who lets justice prevail is righteous and from God.

Only those judge who still bear in themselves their own judgment, their causes, according to which they live and according to which they condemn their neighbor. The words "And yet, if I judge, My judgment is valid" mean the justice of God. God is perfect. God is just.

Every soul and every human being receive what they are aligned with. When soul and person align with God, they will receive from the love and wisdom of God.

If a person aligns with external things, with the world, he will also receive from the world, thus receiving all that is in the world: grief, sickness and need. According to the law of sowing and reaping, every person takes his own life in his hands and shapes it according to his feeling, thinking, speaking and acting. And just as he shapes it according to his will, so will it come back to him.

5. *It is also written in your law that the testimony of two people is valid. It is I who bear witness of My self. John bore witness of Me, and he is a prophet. And the Spirit of truth who sent Me bears witness of Me."*

6. *Therefore, they said to Him, "Where is Your Father?" Jesus answered, "You know neither Me nor My Father. If you knew Me, you would know also My Father."*

7. *And one said, "Show us Your Father and we will believe You." And He answered, saying, "When you have recognized your brother and have felt his love, then you have seen the Father and, likewise, when you have recognized your sister and have felt her love.*

8. *The Most Holy knows His own far and wide; yes, in each one of you the fatherhood can be recognized, for the Father is the one God." (Chap. 50:5-8)*

I, Christ, explain, correct
and deepen the word:

The one who lives in the Father bears witness of the Father. He bears witness of God, in word and in deed.

The soul of the one who lives in God has entered the Sanctum of God, the innermost part of the temple; and through its human being, its shell, it bears witness of itself, because it is the Self, the image of God. Then it is not the human being, his base ego, who speaks, but it is God, the I Am, the eternal law, who speaks through the human being. Then the person can say, as I, Christ, said in the following sense:

"It is I who bear witness of My self." The "self" is the Self, God, because the soul has become divine again. The eternal Father is beheld only by those of pure heart who therefore also accept and receive in themselves their neighbor. For the Spirit of the eternal Father dwells in every soul and thus in every human being.

The one who does not accept and receive his neighbor because he is prejudiced against him, because he rejects, belittles or even hates him, neither perceives the eternal Father nor does he know Me, the Son of the Father, Christ, nor his neighbor, nor even himself. For the Spirit of the eternal Father, which, however, he neither accepts nor receives in his neighbor, also dwells in him.

Recognize that the one who does not love his neighbor selflessly – no matter how he is, what he says and does – does not love God, either.

The one who despises his neighbor despises God.

The one who rejects his neighbor, that is, who does not accept and receive him in his heart, does not accept and receive God, his Father, either. For whatever you do to the least of My brothers, you have done to Me, and thus to God, My Father, in whom I, Christ, live.

9. *Jesus spoke these words in the treasury, when He taught in the temple. And no one laid a hand on Him, for His hour had not yet come. Then Jesus spoke to them once more, "I go My way, and you will seek Me and will die in your sins. Where I go, you cannot come."*

10. Then the Jews said, "Does He kill Himself, since He says: Where I go, you cannot come?" And He said to them, "You are from below, I Am from above; you are of this world, I Am not of this world.

11. This is why I said to you that you will die in your sins; for if you do not believe that I Am of God, you will die in your sins."

12. Thereupon, they said to Him, "Who are You, then?" And Jesus said to them, "None other than what I have told you from the beginning.

13. I have many things to say to you which will judge you. The holy One who sent Me is true; and I tell the world what I have heard from above."

14. Then Jesus said to them, "When you have raised the Son of Man, you will recognize that I Am sent by God, and that I do nothing of Myself; but as the All-Holy has taught Me, so I speak. And the One who has sent Me is with Me: The All-Holy does not forsake Me. For at all times, I do what pleases the Eternal."

15. As He spoke thus, many believed in Him and said, "He is a prophet, whom God has sent. Let us hear Him." (Chap. 50:9-15)

I, Christ, explain, correct
and deepen the word:

The words "I go My way, and you will seek Me and will die in your sins" have the following meaning:

The one who walks the path of the Christ of God, the path to the Father, which I, Christ, as Jesus, lived as an example for mankind, will not die in sin. For he has cleansed his soul and receives the light of God, which comes from "above."

But the one who does not walk the path to the heart of God remains in his sins and will die in his sins. As a soul, he then takes them to the places and spheres which he has prepared for himself through his sins.

With the words "Where I go, you cannot come," I alluded to what then happened: After the execution of My body, I went to the eternal Father, because My soul, My spirit body, lives in the Father. The one whose soul does not live in the Father, but in sin, cannot go to the eternal Father, because sin keeps him from God.

"You are from below, I Am from above; you are of this world, I Am not of this world" means that the one who relies on the world lives with the world and will return to this world again and again and will take his path of incarnation from below, from the world, again and again.

The one who lives in this world, but is not with this world, lives in God – and when he returns to this world, he will come from God, from above, as I, Christ, came from above and incarnated in Jesus, in the human body.

"I have many things to say to you which will judge you" means that I will instruct you about the law of sowing and reaping, so that you may recognize that you are your own judges. They are your sensations, thoughts, words and deeds, which are directed against the eternal law of love. You will be measured by the standard with which you measure.

Recognize that faith alone does not lead to salvation.

Many people believed in Me, in Jesus of Nazareth. But when the hour of My execution came, many renounced this faith, they began to doubt Me and thus became betrayers.

The one who merely believes, but does not actualize what was recognized, cannot become what God has promised him: One who beholds, who beholds the eternal Father face to face.

Faith alone neither makes one blessed nor one who beholds. Faith is just the first step towards the inner life. The one who relies on faith alone and stops at that, without taking the steps of actualization towards God, will doubt the truth again and again, because he has not yet experienced the laws of love; for they must be lived in order for him to behold God, our eternal Father.

The one who does not put the faith in God into practice, through selfless love, can be influenced. Only the one who actualizes what was recognized, the faith in God, will become strong in the Spirit of the Lord and will withstand the attacks of the darkness.

The All-Holy, God, does not forsake any one of His children, no matter how he thinks and lives; for the Spirit of God dwells in every soul and in every human being. He is the good, which ignites when man strives to fulfill the will of God. The one who fulfills the will of God at all times – as I did, as Jesus, and as I live in the will of the Father, as Christ – will bear witness of himself, of the eternal Self, because he lives as the Self in God, the truth.

The Self is God, and the one who lives in God is divine; he is the divine law, the Self.

CHAPTER 51

The Truth Sets One Free –
About the Correct Understanding of
the Commandments

"Remain in My word" (1). The slave of sin is far from God and from the eternal home (2). Only the actualization of selfless love counts before God (3-6). Satan, the father of lies; the satan of the senses (7-8). No soul is lost (9). Only the one who strives for the truth understands the word of God (10). Moses did not consent to animal sacrifice – Disregarding and respecting life – The old and the new humanity (11-13). Spiritual authorities and those who adhere to the letter, who do not actualize what they teach – Concessions of the prophets to the people (14-18)

1. *Then Jesus said to the Jews who believed in Him, "If you remain in My word, then you are My true disciples, and you will recognize the truth, and the truth will set you free." (Chap. 51:1)*

I, Christ, explain, correct
and deepen the word:

"... remain in My word" means to fill the word of God with life, to actualize it. Only through the actualization of the word of God does the person find his way to the eternal truth which sets him free, irrespective of people and things.

2. *Then they answered Him, "We are the seed of Abraham, and we have never been in bondage to anyone. Why do you say: You shall become free?" Jesus answered them, "Verily, verily, I say to you: The one who sins is the servant of sin. The servant does not abide in the house forever, but the son and the daughter remain forever. (Chap. 51:2)*

I, Christ, explain, correct
and deepen the word:

"The one who sins is a servant of sin" means that the one who sins is bound to the flesh and serves the flesh – not God. The one who serves the flesh will live in servitude because he becomes dependent on the flesh, on people who likewise depend on the flesh, because they, too, live in sin.

Recognize, "the servant of sin" is the human ego which aspires to recognition and approval and, for this reason, subjugates itself to other sinners, in turn. The one who lives in sin lives in and with this world and also believes in this world. Therefore, his home is also this world. This is why he cannot enter the house of the eternal Father, the eternal home. The servant of sin cannot be in the house of the Father. Only the son and the daughter who fulfill the will of God abide in God, in the Father, who is the eternal home.

3. *When the Son makes you free, you are truly free. I know well that you are Abraham's seed after the flesh; but you seek to kill Me, for My word has no place in you.*

4. *I speak what I have seen of My Father; and you do what you have seen of your father." They answered and said to Him, "Abraham is our father." Jesus said to them, "If you were Abraham's children, you would do Abraham's works.*

5. *But now, you seek to kill Me, a man who has told you the truth which I have heard from God. Abraham did not do that. You do the deeds of your father." Then they said to Him, "We are no bastards; we have one Father, namely, God."*

6. *Jesus said to them, "If God were your Father, you would love Me: For I went forth and came from God. I did not come of Myself, but the All-Holy sent Me. Why can you not understand My language? Because you cannot bear My word. (Chap. 51:3-6)*

I, Christ, explain, correct
and deepen the word:

The Son, who I Am, came from the Father in order to liberate all souls and men. This is why only *one* is

587

given power and strength to lead souls and men to the inner light, to God, our eternal Father – the one who left heaven for this. It is the Christ of God, who I Am.

I have been commissioned by God, My Father, to lead all souls and men home into their inner being, where the Father's Spirit dwells. I Am the salvation of every soul and the way to the eternal Father. No one comes to the Father, the great All-One, the only One, except through Me, Christ, who I Am, the Redeemer of all souls and men and the way into the eternal house of the Father.

The Jews said that they were Abraham's seed – and yet did not do the good works of Abraham. They were and are from Abraham according to the flesh only, not according to the law which Abraham, too, strove to fulfill.

The new people in the generations of the Kingdom of Peace of Jesus Christ come, for the most part, from the seed of David. They are neither Jewish, nor Moslem, nor Hindu, nor Buddhist, nor Catholic, nor Protestant, nor Orthodox. They do not belong to any of the numerous external religions. They are true Christians; for they fulfill the law of God which I, as Jesus of Nazareth, brought to them and lived as an example – and, as the Christ of God, reveal again in all details, in all facets of the inner life, through the ray of divine wisdom. They follow Me, the only Shepherd, Christ.

The one whose words are not filled with the law of life speaks only from his human ego – even though he uses the words of truth. That which is not filled with the life, with God, is not imbued with God, the life. This also holds true for the words of truth which are not lived by the one from whose mouth they flow. They have no power. The one who does not live in the eternal law speaks out of his person and also bears witness, solely as a human being, possibly of his earthly parents, who likewise lived and thought according to the word of human beings.

The words "If God were your Father, you would love Me" mean that the one who loves God, his eternal Father, also loves his neighbor and all of life; for all life – whether human beings, animals, plants, stones or minerals – comes from God. The one who does not love his neighbor selflessly does not love God, either.

Recognize that only the one who lives the law of life and of love can understand the language of the law.

The law of love is hardly bearable for those who speak the language of the world and love themselves more than God. They understand love according to their ego, and they love according to their ego, which gives only to receive. The one who is not with God is against God, and thus, cannot understand the language of the law, the absolute love.

7. *You are of your father, the devil, and you will do as your father desires. He was a murderer from the very beginning and was not in the truth, for the truth is not in him.*

8. When he tells a lie, he speaks of his own, for he is a liar and the father of lies. And because I speak the truth, you do not believe Me. (Chap. 51:7-8)

I, Christ, explain, correct
and deepen the word:

The words "You are of your father, the devil, and you will do as your father desires" have the following meaning:

Here, with the word "father," is meant the breeder of evil, Satan, who was and is intent on leading all people astray. It is the satanic, the seed and the brood of Satan, which souls and men have adopted – even after My "It is finished." In the broadest sense, the law of sowing and reaping, the satanic law, once developed out of this. Every person who adopted the satanic, the evil, is now liable to his own law: What he sows he will reap.

The originator of evil passed himself off as male – and the demons do the same, as well – although the originator was a female principle and is eternally so in the spirit, a being from the divine stream. Through the eternal love and through the "It is finished," she, too, will return to the primordial stream as a spirit being from God.

The words "he was a murderer from the very beginning and was not in the truth, for the truth is not in him" have the following meaning: From the beginning of the Fall, Satan wanted the divine to submit to him. Since evil, the violation of the law of life, is not in the law of truth, it has no lasting power. Since evil has no place in the truth, I, the Redeemer, came and brought redemption to all souls and men, so that they could find their way back to the truth and into the truth. For all came from the truth, and everything that belongs to the Fall event will be transformed through the law of God and return again to the truth.

The lie does not come from the truth. The one who lies does it out of himself, out of his sin, because he bears the lie, the sin, in himself. The lie is the breeder of sin.

The one who lies deceives not only his neighbor, but also himself. The lie comes from the liar and enters into the liar again. It affects not only the deceived one, but also the liar.

Satan is the creator of the lie and thus, also of the senses that have been led astray. The people who give way to lies, to sin, are "those who have been led astray by the senses," for they let themselves be led astray by Satan. The evil in man is thus called "the satan of the senses."

Therefore, may everyone beware of lies. For its diabolical offspring are many. They spread out like the roots of a tree. Such a soul will return to the flesh, as long as it is still possible, until it has grasped every root, including the taproot: until it has repented, asked for forgiveness, forgiven and made amends. Then, step by step, the human aspects transform into the divine, and the soul returns to God.

9. Just as Moses lifted up the serpent in the desert, so must the Son of Man be lifted up, so that all who look to Him, believing, are not lost, but have eternal life. (Chap. 51:9)

I, Christ, explain, correct
and deepen the word:

The Son of Man is raised. My crucifixion as Jesus and My return as Christ mean that all will be raised through Me, for no sheep is lost. Through redemption, all souls will be raised again, that is, they will become divine. After the purging and purification of their sins, they will return to the land of light, of eternal love, as flawless beings of light.

10. Which one among you can convict Me because of a sin? But if I tell you the truth, why do you not believe Me? The one who is of God hears the words of God. You do not hear them because you are not of God." (Chap. 51:10)

I, Christ, explain, correct
and deepen the word:

Only the person does not believe in the truth, who does not live and think truthfully.

The one who lives in sin does not know the truth and condemns those who speak from the truth. The one who does not know the truth does not understand the words of truth, either. He will reject them as untrue, because he is not truthful and therefore, labels as untrue everything that does not correspond to his conception of the truth.

But the one who strives towards the eternal truth understands the word of God, because he knows the voice of God, the truth. The one who does not know it does not hear it. Nor are his words from God, but from his human ego which talks only about itself.

In the Kingdom of Peace of Jesus Christ, in the Kingdom of God on Earth, the inhabitants of the Kingdom of God will not only hear the voice of their Father and of their heavenly brother, Christ, but they will themselves be the word of God, the law of love.

11. Then the Jews answered, saying to Him, "Are we not right that you are a Samaritan and that you are possessed by the devil?" Jesus answered, "I am not possessed by any devil, but I honor the All-Holy, and you dishonor Me. I do not seek My own glory, but the glory of God. But here is One who judges."

12. And some of the elders and scribes of the temple came to Him, saying, "Why do your disciples instruct the people that it is against the law to eat the flesh of animals, even though they are offered as sacrifice according to the order of Moses?

13. For it is written that God said to Noah: Fear and dread of you shall come over every animal of the field, every bird of the air and every fish in the water, when they have fallen into your hands." (Chap. 51:11-13)

I, Christ, explain, correct
and deepen the word:

Moses neither ordered nor condoned the sacrifice of animals. However, he did not interfere in the satanic will of those who wanted to eat meat. He taught and instructed them that the consumption as well as the sacrificing of animals is sin. But since the stubborn Israelites insisted on doing it, Moses had to be silent; for the Israelites, too, were children of God and had their free will. They saw everything only out of their own sin and, for this reason, considered the silence of Moses as approval.

I correct:

Words are symbols and change their meaning from one generation to the next. What the people of a generation put into the word is the meaning to them.

And so, many words in that book which I explain, correct and deepen today for you, who live in this turn of time from the old to the New Era [1989], have another meaning, in turn, than in the past epochs. For example, the statement "God said to Noah: Fear and dread of you shall come over every animal of the field, every bird of the air and every fish in the water, when they have fallen into your hands" means: Fear and dread seizes every animal of the field, every bird of the air and every fish in the water which falls into your hands. With this are meant the hands of those people who disregard and kill life.

Recognize that every animal senses and feels what a person intends to do with it.

At the turn of time I explain, correct and deepen the contents of that book [1989], brutality against the animal world and the plant world has reached unimaginable proportions. The animals and the plants suffer from man's capriciousness. Many people not only lack respect for their own life, but also for the entire creation. As a result of human behavior, the magnetic currents, for example, have been disturbed. Because of this, many animals lack orientation, especially the migratory birds which fly into warmer countries. Because of the pollution of the rivers, lakes and oceans, as well as of the earth's atmosphere, many animal and plant species – in the water, in the air and on Earth – are becoming extinct.

Since a great part of mankind continues to live in sin, the old world is dying – and with it many people are dying in great pain, who considered the temporal to be the only reality and treated life irresponsibly.

Yet, I, Christ, make all things new. The new world is My world, the world of the Christ, who I Am. In the new world, people will live who are renewed, that is, cleansed, from within, and who populate and cultivate the Earth in a lawful way.

The one who will read My words in the New Era will thus learn about the shadows and the light-filled sides of the old world and about the radical change into the New Era. The old sinful world shall serve as a warning to the people in the New Era.

The one who then attentively reads this book, with the explanations, corrections and deepenings, receives insight into the law of sowing and reaping which was once valid on Earth. The new man should make himself aware of this again and again, since in the fine-material world, in which the burdened souls still live, the harvest, the effects of the created causes, is still going on. For, as soul, man will then reap what he has sown and has not cleared up in time or has not yet expiated. This is why it is good and important for the people of the New Era to know about what takes place in the spheres of purification. For after the death of the body, when the souls of the new people pass through the veils of consciousness, they will experience there those souls who still have to pay off what they have sown.

14. *And Jesus said to them, "You, hypocrites, Isaiah spoke well of you and of your forefathers: These people are close to Me with their mouth, and they honor Me with their lips, but their heart is far from Me; for they worship Me in vain and, in My name, teach the commandments of men as divine teachings, in order to gratify their own lusts.*

15. And in like manner, Jeremiah bears witness when he says about the blood sacrifices: I, your God, commanded none of this in those days when you came out of Egypt, but I commanded you only to be righteous, to adhere to the old customs, to do justice, and to walk humbly before your God.

16. But you did not listen to Me, who from the beginning gave you all kinds of seeds, and fruits of the trees, and grains for the nourishment and for the healing of men and animals." And they replied, "You speak against the law."

17. And He spoke once again about Moses, "Verily, I do not speak against the law, but against those who corrupted his law, which he allowed because of the hardness of your hearts.

18. But behold! A greater One than Moses is here!" And they flew into a rage, and picked up stones in order to throw them at Him. But Jesus passed through their midst and was hidden from their violence.
(Chap. 51:14-18)

I, Christ, explain, correct
and deepen the word:

Almost 2000 years ago, as Jesus of Nazareth I spoke to the Pharisees and scribes, who clung to the letter alone and had their hearts in the world, and I called them hypocrites. And the prophet Isaiah, who announced My coming, spoke similar words as I spoke as Jesus of Nazareth.

Now, in the time of radical change, I, Christ, speak to My own through My instrument and I have to use similar words once again for today's Pharisees and scribes [1989]. Today, many Pharisees and scribes, theologians, Bible experts and lay preachers still teach according to the letter of the Bible – and again, only their mouth speaks, and again, they honor Me only with their lips and with sanctimonious or intellectual prayers. Their hearts are just as far from God as at My time on Earth and before that, when the great prophets brought the word of God to man.

Many dignitaries still teach today in the name of the Most High and in My name; yet their words are not vivified by the eternal power, since they themselves are not imbued with the Spirit of truth.

The leaders of the official churches who teach in My name have set up a structure of dogma in which they hide themselves, so that they do not have to face the truth. They invite their faithful into this structure, impose these dogmatic doctrines upon them in My name and oblige them – under the threat of so-called eternal damnation – to adhere to them.

This structure of dogma is now rotting and collapsing; it is like a house of cards, which is still held together only by external power and external riches – but not by Me, Christ, who I Am, the kingdom of the inner being.

For thousands of years, the name of the Eternal was taken in vain for human wheelings and dealings in many power structures. Since My "It is finished," My name, Christ, is also taken in vain, in that My teaching, with which I make the call to follow Me, was woven into the structure of dogma.

Thus, it can be said that the satan of the senses takes the name of the One in vain, the holy One, the eternal One, and the name of His Son, in order to lead the people astray. Yet all illusory flourishing of human wheelings and dealings is withering away because I bring the inner life to man; it is the steps of the Inner Path, where neither dogma nor human laws are valid, but only the law which I, as Jesus of Nazareth, have already taught and lived: the universal, eternal law, God.

Since every person has free will, the great prophets had to practice restraint, even before My earthly existence, when the people wanted it otherwise than was the will of God which they proclaimed. Before My earthly existence, polytheism was still very alive among the people and therefore the blood sacrifice, too. This is why several prophets had to make concessions, on the one hand, to not break the free will of the people, and on the other, to guide them to the truth, through self-recognition. This often meant pain and grief, until people set out on the way to Him, who is from eternity to eternity.

However, every concession includes a period of grace. During that time, man receives the strength of God in order to be able to overcome what is still human in him within a short time. But if he does not make use of this and continues to sin, he will, after the period of grace is over, have to endure and suffer all the negativities he has sown and not yet atoned for.

The one whose behavior is against God, against the law of life, has to bear what he has sown.

The farmer harvests what he sows into his field, and man will also harvest what he puts into the field of his soul.

With the words "to adhere to the old customs," the following is meant:

Man should keep his hours of prayer and strive to let his prayers bear fruit every day, by actualizing what he has prayed for. Then he will also understand and fulfill the Ten Commandments, the excerpts from the eternal law, better and better, and will thus mature into the all-encompassing, universal law, God.

CHAPTER 52

Jesus Explains His Pre-existence –
To Believe Means To Understand

*Physical death and spiritual death (1). Only the
one who fulfills the commandments recognizes and experiences God in himself (2-3). The Kingdom of God is seven-
dimensional – The infinite crystal: All is in all things (9-11).
Understanding the truth only through actualization (12)*

*1. Another time Jesus said, "Verily, verily, I say to
you, if one keeps My words, he will never see death."
Then the Jews said to Him, "Now we recognize that
you are possessed by a devil. (Chap. 52:1)*

I, Christ, explain, correct
and deepen the word:

As Jesus of Nazareth, I spoke of the living word
which is vivified by the Spirit of God. The person who
lives the living word, the life from God, will never see
death, because he looks into eternal life and lays aside
only his physical shell, which is of the earth and will return to the earth.

Recognize that the earthly body belongs to the earth,
because it is from the earth. But the spiritual body belongs to God, because it is from God. The one who looks

only to the perishable body does not understand My words, because for him, only the earthly life is the life.

But the true life is God, and the spiritual body is from God, the eternal stream; it moves in Him and never dies.

However, the soul can linger in the darkness a long time, if the person has thought, spoken and acted in a dark way only. This is the spiritual death, because the burdened soul looks to the perishable alone and considers this to be the true life.

Yet, all those who devote their life to God – by thinking nobly, speaking purely and acting lawfully – bear the light in themselves and, after the death of their body, will enter the light, that is, they will not remain in the darkness, in spiritual death.

Therefore, the one who keeps the law of God, the word of God, will not taste spiritual death; for already in his earthly garment, he lives in God.

The physical body is only a covering for the spiritual body; however, it cannot live without the spiritual body, the soul, in which is the source of life, the stream that flows from the life, God.

The spiritual person, who looks to God alone, by keeping His word and fulfilling the law of life, will lay aside his shell, the physical body, when the time has come for it to become earth again.

Only the devil makes a devil of his neighbor. The one who himself is still caught in the satanic insinuates the same of his neighbor.

The one who stands in the light of truth always looks to the good essence in his neighbor, to the truth, and will serve him and help him selflessly. He will not overlook what is dark, but will consider it from the light of truth and, if appropriate, also address it.

2. *Abraham is dead, and so are the prophets, and You say: If one keeps My word, he will never experience death. Are You greater than our father Abraham, who is dead? And the prophets, too, are dead. Whom do You make of Yourself?"*

3. *Jesus answered, "If I honor Myself, then My honor is nothing. It is My Father, of whom you say that He is your God, who honors Me. And you do not know Him, but I know Him. If I would say: I do not know Him, I would be a liar, just like you. But I know the All-Holy and I Am known to the Eternal. (Chap. 52:2-3)*

I, Christ, explain, correct
and deepen the word:

The one who merely speaks of God and does not keep the commandments of God does not know God; for God is the universal, eternal, omnipresent law of love. He will not experience God, the law, in another way, either. The law of love and of life is in every soul and in every human being. This is why man can experience the laws of God only in himself and can draw closer to God in himself only by fulfilling His commandments.

Every person can come to know and experience God in himself, if he senses, thinks, speaks and acts according to the law of life – that is, selflessly.

God is active in all that selflessly comes from a person. The one who is selfless experiences God and also becomes aware of his God-sonship or God-daughtership.

You should replace the word "honor" with the word "respect." Honor is due to God alone.

In earlier times, the word "honor," too, had a different meaning than it has today [1989]. This is why you should endeavor to grasp the meaning in every statement, so that you find your way to the source of life, to the eternal law, which is deeply rooted in every statement. However, this is possible only for the person who strives to fulfill the commandments of God every day. The one who understands the word of God only literally will think and speak today just as the scribes and their adherents did at that time.

4. Abraham, your father, rejoiced to see My day. And he saw it and was glad." Then the Jews said to Him, "You are not yet forty-five years of age and You have seen Abraham?"

5. Jesus said to them, "Verily, verily, I say to you, before Abraham was, I Am."

6. And He said to them, "The All-Holy has sent many prophets to you, but you rose against them because they opposed your lusts, and you disparaged some of them and killed others."

7. Then they picked up stones in order to throw them at Him, but Jesus was hidden and went out of the temple, right through their midst, and left again without being seen by them.

8. When His disciples were again with Him in a solitary place, one asked Him about the Kingdom of God, and Jesus said to them,

9. "As it is above, so it is below. As it is within, so it is without. As to the right, so also to the left. As it is before, so it is behind. As with the great, so with the small. As with the man, so with the woman. When this is recognized, then you will see the Kingdom of God.

10. For in Me there is neither male nor female, but both are one, perfect in the universe. The woman is not without the man, nor is the man without the woman.

11. Wisdom is not without love, nor is love without wisdom. The head is not without the heart, nor is the heart without the head, in the Christ, who reconciles all things. For God created all things by number, weight and measure, one corresponding to the other.
(Chap. 52:4-11)

I, Christ, explain, correct
and deepen the word:

God is the all-unity. Eternity is an infinite crystal which shines in countless facets. The words "as it is above, so it is below. As it is within, so it is without. As to the right, so also to the left. As it is before, so it is behind. As with the great, so with the small" were given to people for their better understanding. However, the one who has entered the kingdom of the inner being knows and experiences in himself that the three dimensions mean nothing to the soul which is imbued with the light of God.

Recognize that the Kingdom of God is seven-dimensional. The three-dimensional forms exist only in matter, where there is the above and below, the within and without, the right and left, the before and behind, the great and the small. In God, life is a mighty crystal which sparkles in countless facets. It radiates and everything is manifest in its radiation. It knows no limits. Unlimited, it radiates, for eternity is unlimited.

In you, O man, is everything – the smallest and the greatest. Each divine impulse, each divine primordial sensation and each divine thought comes true in you. That which is before and behind, above and below, to the right and to the left, is in you. Thus, all that is, is manifest in you, yourself.

That which is, is eternal – and remains eternally manifest in the spirit being and in all of creation. Words are notions. So the inner life, too, has to be expressed with words for the human beings.

Infinity, all that radiates from the pure being, from God, takes on form and shape in the entire universe.

And when it says, "the great" and "the small," it means the steps of evolution of the spiritual forms in the pure Being. A spark of light takes on form and shape and gradually becomes the all-power, the active radiation; out of it emerges the spiritual body, which is one with the primordial radiation, the radiation of eternity.

The one who devotes his life to God and purifies his soul is again aware of all this, because he then lives again in the consciousness, in God.

God is the Father-Mother-Principle for all and in all spirit beings. The eternal Father, who is also Mother, gave and gives to each of His children the all-radiation, the essence of infinity, as heritage.

The word "give" implies all further powers of evolution, in which spirit beings are, in turn, spiritually begotten through the Father-Mother-Principle in the spirit beings. From the Eternal, they all receive the whole of infinity as heritage.

Recognize that the spiritual body is compressed, eternal law, God. It consists of the essence of the All, which contains all the facets of infinity.

In the law, God, there is no male and female sexes. God created the positive, the giving principle, from His Father-radiation and the negative, the receiving principle, from His Mother-radiation. The spirit beings are either positive or negative principles. In the All-radiation, as well as in the duality, there are two – and yet, they are one in the All, because both feel and live according to the stream of the eternal law.

Both the giving principle and the receiving principle are one forever. The receiving principle is not without the giving principle and the giving principle is not without the receiving one. Said in the words of the world: Man and woman are eternally one. In unity, they are active; in unity, the spiritual procreations develop from the principle of giving and receiving, from the Father-Mother-Principle, which is active in every spirit being.

The laws of God are contained in the great, that is, in the fully active radiation, and also in the smallest, in the first step of evolution. Everything is in all things:

The rays of will, wisdom, earnestness, patience, love and mercy are in the ray of order. Order, wisdom, earnestness, patience, love and mercy are in the ray of will. Order, will, earnestness, patience, love and mercy are in the ray of wisdom. And it is the same for the rays of earnestness, patience, love and mercy.

All powers are thus contained in each power. All things considered, these powers constitute the All-radiation, God, the mighty universal crystal of eternity.

The words "For God created all things by number, weight and measure, one corresponding to the other" express the All-radiation: All in one. Thus, everything is in all things.

12. *Those who understand these things can believe them. When they do not understand them, then these things are not for them. For to believe means to understand, and not to believe means not to understand."* (Chap. 52:12)

I, Christ, explain, correct
and deepen the word:

"Those who understand these things can believe them" means that the truth can be grasped, that is, understood, only by the one who strives for the truth. Faith alone does not grasp the truth, because faith is just a step towards the truth, but not yet the truth itself.

The one who believes first of all accepts the word of the truth. Only the one who then actualizes it will understand the truth, because through the actualization of the truth, he will find his way to the truth, to the law, God.

Faith thus means to accept the truth first of all. The actualization of faith then leads to the understanding of the truth.

CHAPTER 53

Healing the One Born Blind –
The Question of the Sadducees about Resurrection

*Do not ask about the sins of your neighbor – Use the
moments of the day (1-2). The outer physician and the Inner
Healer (3-6). To marry or to wed before God (7-11)*

1. *On another day, Jesus met a man who was blind
from birth. And His disciples asked Him, saying, "Master, who sinned, this one or his parents, that he was
born blind?"*

2. *Jesus answered, "What does it matter, whether
this one or his parents sinned, as long as the works of
God become manifest in him? I must do the works of
My Father, who has sent Me, as long as it is day; the
night comes, when no one can work. As long as I Am in
the world, I Am the light of the world." (Chap. 53:1-2)*

I, Christ, explain, correct
and deepen the word:

The words "What does it matter whether this one or
his parents sinned, as long as the works of God become
manifest in him?" mean that you should not look at the
sin nor ask who has sinned. No one can pay off the debt
of another, unless he came into this world as a soul
which chose to bear the suffering of another.

However, when people are bound to one another through sin, then all, for example, parents and child, share in the sin. They pay off together what they also caused together.

Recognize that each day is given to each person to recognize and to repent of parts of his sins and faults. That's why, no one should ask who committed the sin and when or where. The soul is now in the earthly existence, in order to clear up what is being conveyed to the human being today, through the signs of the day or through illness, grief, need, blindness or through gloomy thoughts, words and deeds.

I Am the light of the world. The one who recognizes, repents, gives his humanness over to Me and leaves it in Me, thus making use of the days, will live in Me and will resurrect through Me, for I Am the eternal day.

If the person has not used the days, then the night of the soul breaks in over him, and then soul and person will suffer. So, make use of the moments of the day, for I Am each moment, the eternity. The one who uses the moments lives in Me, and he will have peace and attain salvation.

3. When He had thus spoken, He spat on the ground and mixed clay with the spittle and anointed the eyes of the blind man with it. And He said to him, "Go and wash yourself in the pool of Siloam" (to be translated: Sent). Then he went and washed himself and came back, seeing.

4. *The neighbors and those who had seen before that he was blind said, "Is he not the one that sat there begging?" Some said, "It is he," but others said, "He is like him." But he himself said, "I am the one."*

5. *Therefore, they asked him, "How were your eyes opened?" He answered, "A man called Jesus made a paste and anointed my eyes and said: Go and wash yourself in the pool of Siloam. I went there and washed myself and received sight."*

6. *Then they asked him, "Where is He?" He said, "I do not know where the One who healed me is."*
(Chap. 53:3-6)

I, Christ, explain, correct
and deepen the word:

The statement about clay and spittle symbolizes external healing.

Recognize that much that was reported and written down about Me, as Jesus of Nazareth, did not occur the way it is literally written. Here too, the clay and spittle are symbols for the fact that the Earth and everything growing on the Earth – herbs and fruits, as well as water – heal and cleanse, if the cause of the illness is no longer flowing out of the soul, but merely marks the body.

When the soul has passed the cause as effect to the body and no further causes are flowing, then healing can take place from without, through the earth and through all that it yields, as well as through the cleansing water which contains many healing substances.

The question "Where is He?" shows that many people look only to the help that comes from the outside and do not grasp the powers of inner healing. Therefore, do not seek the true healer of soul and body among the people; do not seek Him in this or that place. If you want to find Him, go into your inner being. There Am I, the Christ of God, the Redeemer, the Inner Physician and Healer.

Pray, repent and atone, forgive and ask for forgiveness and, if you have harmed your neighbor, make amends. You will then experience and receive the same and similar things as people did at that time when I, as Jesus, was among them.

The Son of God, the Christ of God, is risen, and the power of the Christ of God has implanted itself into each soul, so that it may experience and attain the same or similar things as the people and souls did at the time of My activity as Jesus of Nazareth.

Recognize that I Am Christ, your Redeemer and the One who prepares your way to the eternal Being, to becoming one with the eternal Father. I Am also your Inner Physician and Healer – the power which can free you from illness, need, grief, anguish and misery.

7. *Then some Sadducees, who denied that there is a resurrection, came to Jesus and said to Him, "Master, Moses has written that when someone's brother dies,*

having a wife and leaving no children, his brother should take his wife and raise up seed to his brother.

8. Now there were six brothers, and the first took a wife, and he died childless. And the second took her as wife and also died childless. And the third up to the sixth all took her, leaving no children. Last of all, the woman also died.

9. To whom will she now belong at the resurrection? For six had her as wife."

10. Jesus answered and said to them, "Whether one wife with six husbands, or one husband with six wives, it is the same. For the children of this world marry and are given in marriage.

11. But those who are worthy to experience the resurrection from the dead will neither marry, nor be given in marriage, nor can they ever die, but they are like the angels and are the children of God, the children of resurrection. (Chap. 53:7-11)

I, Christ, explain, correct
and deepen the word:

Recognize that the children of this world seduce and let themselves be seduced and marry. To seduce and to let themselves be seduced and to marry means to be taken and to let oneself be taken and to live as the world lives: in sin.

Yet, those who not only observe the earthly laws of marriage, but wed before God, have put their trust in the Spirit and not in the flesh. They have made a covenant with God for their earthly marriage.

To wed means a union in and with God. It is thus a covenant with God.

In the eternal Being, all are brother and sister. To wed before God means brotherliness and sisterliness and inner fidelity. Even though they beget children on Earth, they remain brother and sister in the Spirit of the Lord. When the soul has been purified and is again free from its burden, it will enter the heavens again as a spirit being after the earthly death of the body; it will return to its dual and together they will personify the unity in the Spirit of God – as it is written in them from eternity to eternity.

12. But even Moses bore witness, by the bush, that the dead will rise, when he called God, and God said to him: I Am the God of Abraham, Isaac and Jacob. God is not the God of the dead, but of the living. For all live through Him." (Chap. 53:12)

CHAPTER 54

The Examination of the One Born Blind –
The Disciples as the Spiritual Body of Christ

*The blind and the seeing (1-16). In the cosmic Being, all
is contained in all things and is equally important (17-24)*

1. Then they led to the Pharisees the one who was
formerly blind. It was the Sabbath when Jesus mixed
the clay and opened his eyes.

2. Then the Pharisees, too, asked him how he had received his sight. But he said to them, "He spread the
paste on my eyes, and I washed myself and can now see."

3. Some Pharisees said, "This man is not of God, because he does not keep the Sabbath." But others said,
"How can a sinful man do such miracles?" And there
was disagreement among them.

4. They said again to the blind man, "What do you
say of Him who opened your eyes?" He said, "He is a
prophet."

5. But the Jews did not believe that he had been blind
and could now see, and they called the parents of the
one who could now see.

6. And they asked them, saying, "Is this your son of
whom you say that he was born blind? How is it that he
can now see?" His parents answered them, saying,
"We know that this is our son and that he was born
blind; but we don't know how it is that he now sees, nor

do we know who opened his eyes. He is of age; ask him, let him speak for himself."

7. *His parents said such things because they were afraid of the Jews; for the Jews had already agreed that if anyone confessed that He was the Christ, he would be cast out of the synagogue. This is why his parents said, "He is of age, ask him."*

8. *Then they called once more the man who was blind and said to him, "Give honor to God; we know that this man is a sinner." He answered, saying, "I do not know whether He is a sinner or not; but I know one thing, that I was blind and can now see."*

9. *Then they asked him again, "What did He do to you? How did He open your eyes?" He answered them, "I already told you, and you did not hear it. Why do you want to hear it again? Do you, too, want to become His disciples?"*

10. *Then they reviled him saying, "You are His disciple, but we are the disciples of Moses. We know that God spoke to Moses. But we do not know where this man is from."*

11. *The man answered and said to them, "So, it is amazing that you do not know where He is from, and yet He opened my eyes. Now we know that God does not hear the sinners.*

12. *But when someone is God-fearing and does His will, this is the one He hears. Since the beginning of the world, it has not yet been heard that the eyes of one born blind were opened. If this man were not of God, He could do nothing."*

13. They answered and said to him, "You were born altogether in sin, and you want to teach us?" And they cast him out.

14. Jesus heard that they had cast him out; and when He found him, He said to him, "Do you believe in the Son of God?" He answered, saying, "Lord, who is He, that I may believe in Him?"

15. Jesus said to him, "You have seen Him twice, and He is the One who is speaking to you." And he said, "Lord, I believe." And he worshipped Him.

16. And Jesus said, "I Am come into this world for judgment, so that those who do not see may see and those who see become blind." And some Pharisees who were there with Him heard these words and said to Him, "Are we also blind?" (Chap. 54:1-16)

I, Christ, explain, correct
and deepen the word:

Grasp the meaning of what is written, and you will recognize that the spiritually blind and their guides have reacted blindly at all times. Even during today's time [1989], the spiritually blind and their guides react as at the time of My earthly life: blindly.

They do not know the truth and therefore cannot apply the laws of God, either.

But the one who knows the laws of God, because he lives in the truth, can see and is able to do much out of the truth. But the one who is spiritually blind – because he lets himself be blinded by this world and therefore lives in sin – condemns, rejects and accuses of evil those who speak and act from the truth.

"I Am come into this world for judgment, so that those who do not see may see and those who see become blind" means that I Am come into this world in order to let the justice of God become manifest through the actualization of the eternal law. The one who does not fulfill the justice of God in his earthly life gives himself over to his own judgment and becomes his own judge – for he reaps what he has sown.

Christ shows people the way to God, because He is their Redeemer. The willing ones who strive to live the laws of God will behold the life, for everything takes place in the soul of man. The light and the shadow, that which it has inflicted upon itself, flow from the soul. Salvation becomes manifest to the one who dissolves the shadows through Me, the Redeemer. And nothing stays hidden to the one who draws nearer to the source of divinity.

However, those who believe they are seeing ones because they teach the gospel are the blind ones, because they do not live accordingly. They hold great speeches and talk about the law of God and the deeds of Moses. Yet, in reality, they know neither the law of God nor the instructions of God through Moses: The one who only speaks of God is not in God and is therefore spiritually blind. The one who beholds is the one filled with God, because he lives in God.

17. Jesus came to a place where seven palm trees grew and gathered His disciples around Him and gave to each a number and a name, which were known only to the one who received them. And He said to them, "Stand like pillars in the house of God and carry out the orders according to the numbers which you have received."

18. And they stood around Him, and they formed a square and counted the numbers; but they could not do it. And they said, "Lord we cannot do it." And Jesus said, "Let the one who is the greatest among you be as the least, and let the symbol of the first be as the symbol of the last."

19. And they did so, and there was equality in every way, and yet each bore a different number, and the one side was as the other, and the upper was as the lower, and the inner was as the outer. And the Lord said, "It is enough. Such is the house of the wise master builder. It is square and perfect. Many are the chambers, but it is only one house.

20. Consider again the body of man, which is a temple of the Spirit. For the body is one with the head, and it is one body. And it has many parts, yet all are together one body, and the Spirit controls and rules all. It is the same in the Kingdom of God.

21. And the head does not say to the bosom, I do not need you, nor does the right hand say to the left, I do not need you, nor the left foot to the right foot, I do not need you; neither do the eyes say to the ears, we do not need you, nor the mouth to the nose, I do not need you. For God has placed each part where it fits best.

22. If the head were the whole, where would the breast be? If the innards were the most important, where would the feet be? Yes, to these parts which some consider to be less honorable, God has given the most honor.

23. And those parts which some consider uncomely have been given much more comeliness, so that they may care, the one for the other; so, if only one part suffers, all of them suffer; and if one part is honored, all other parts rejoice in it.

24. Now, you are My body; and each one of you is a particular part of Me, and I give a fitting place to each one of you, one head over all and one heart the center of all, that there be no gap anywhere, so that, just as your bodies, your souls and your spirit, you, too, may praise the All-Father through the Holy Spirit, who is active in all and through all." (Chap. 54:17-24)

I, Christ, explain, correct
and deepen the word:

As Jesus of Nazareth, as the incarnated Christ of God, I always referred to the whole eternal law in My teachings, for all is contained in all things – the smallest in the great whole and the great whole as essence in the smallest. When the wise one speaks about one aspect of life, he also perceives the whole in the aspect, that is, all the laws of life.

The seven palm trees symbolize the seven basic powers of God from order to mercy. All basic powers are effective in one basic power. That is the great whole, the all-law, God, in which everything is contained in all things. Be it a number or a name – everything is contained in all things.

I repeat: The smallest, which lives and is effective in the cycle of evolution, is in the greatest, and the great, the fully mature, is already contained in the first steps of evolution.

Just as each organ and each smallest component of the body is significant, so is the smallest significant in the Kingdom of God, too, for it contains all aspects of infinity. There is nothing in the cosmic Being that would have no significance, because the great is in the smallest as all-encompassing law and the smallest, which develops to the great, to the fully active divine law, is already in this great, all-encompassing active law.

The one who addresses the smallest, which is in the process of evolution on the way to the great, addresses, at the same time, the great, the fully unfolded law, God. The house of the universal master builder is created in this wonderful, absolutely perfect way: the infinity. This is why there is no above and below, no behind and before, no right and no left, no poverty and no prosperity, neither a small and insignificant, nor a great which puts itself over it.

God is equality, freedom and unity. There are neither masters nor servants in the eternal Being. All beings of light are brothers and sisters, children of the one Father, who is the one Lord of life, the Creator of the heaven and the Earth.

CHAPTER 55

Christ, the Good Shepherd – One with the Father

Christ, the true Shepherd and the only way
to the Father's house – My sheep know My voice – I lead
the sheep into the eternal law – Reference to the usurpation
and abuse of the Shepherd's role (1-16)

1. *One day a shepherd passed by, driving his flock to the fold. And Jesus took one of the young lambs in His arms and spoke to it lovingly and pressed it to His bosom. And He said to His disciples:*

2. *"I Am the Good Shepherd and I know My sheep, and they know Me. Just as the Father of all knows Me, in the same way I know My sheep and give My life for the sheep. And I still have other sheep which are not of this fold; and I also have to bring them here, and they will hear My voice and there will be one flock and one Shepherd.*

3. *I lay down My life, that I may take it up again. No one takes it from Me, but I lay it down of Myself. I have the power to lay down My body and I have the power to take it up again.*

4. *I Am the Good Shepherd; the Good Shepherd tends His flock; He takes the lambs in His arms and carries them on His bosom and gently leads those which are with young. Yes, the Good Shepherd gives His life for the sheep.*

5. *But the hireling, who is not the shepherd, who does not own the sheep, sees the wolf coming and*

abandons the sheep and flees. And the wolf seizes and scatters the sheep. The hireling flees; for he is a hireling and does not take care of the sheep.

6. I Am the door: All those who enter through Me will be safe and will go in and out and find pasture. The evil one comes only to steal, to kill and to destroy. I Am come that they may have life and abundance.

7. But the one who enters through the door is a shepherd of sheep, to whom the doorkeeper opens, and the sheep hear His voice, and He calls His sheep by name and leads them out, and He knows their number.

8. And when He has let out His sheep, He goes before them and the sheep follow Him, for they know His voice. And they do not follow a stranger, but flee from him, for they do not know the voice of strangers."

9. Jesus told them this parable; but they did not understand what He spoke to them about. Then Jesus said to them again, "My sheep hear My voice, and I know them, and they follow Me. And I give them the eternal life. And they will never perish again, and no one will tear them out of My hand.

10. My Father, who gave them to Me, is greater than all; and no one can pluck them out of the hand of My Father. I and My Father are one."

11. Then the Jews took up stones again to stone Him. Jesus asked them, "I have done to you many good works from My Father, for which of these works do you stone Me?"

12. The Jews answered Him, "We do not stone You for a good work, but for blasphemy; and because, being a man, you make Yourself equal to God." Jesus answered them, "Have I said that I Am equal to God? No, but I Am one with God. Is it not written in the scriptures: I have said, you are gods?

13. If He calls them gods, those to whom the word of God came, and if the scripture cannot be broken, would you then say to Him whom the Father has sanctified and sent into the world, 'You blaspheme God,' because I say, 'I Am the Son of God and so one with the All-Father'?

14. If I do not do the works of My Father, then do not believe Me; but if I do them, then believe the works, even if you do not want to believe Me, so that you may recognize and believe that the Spirit of the great Father is in Me and I Am in My Father."

15. This is why they sought once more to capture Him; but He escaped their hands and went again beyond the Jordan, to the place where John first baptized; and He remained there.

16. And many came to Him, saying, "John did no miracles, but everything that John has said of this man is true. He is the prophet who should come." And many believed in Him. (Chap. 55:1-16)

I, Christ, explain, correct
and deepen the word:

The Good Shepherd knows all His sheep, for they are a part of Him. And the sheep which know the voice of the Shepherd follow Him.

The voice of the Good Shepherd, Christ, is the eternal law of love. The one who keeps the law of love knows this law and thus, the voice of the law, the voice of the Shepherd, Christ.

As Jesus of Nazareth, I gave My earthly life for all men. As the Christ of God, I surrendered My divine heritage to be the support and the way to the Father's house for all souls and men.

Since the Redeemer-spark, a light-ray of My spiritual heritage, now shines in all souls and men, all will find the way again to the eternal Father. When redemption has been completed in the soul and the spirit being has returned to the inner temple, then it brings the light-ray, the Redeemer-spark, back into the primordial substance in which My spiritual heritage builds itself up again.

The sheep which do not yet know My voice and still seek their salvation in the pastures of the world, thus being servile to the insinuations of the satanic, also bear the Redeemer-spark in themselves. They, too, will return to the Father's house and will bring the Redeemer-spark into the primordial substance again – if they awaken and turn back through the strength and power of Christ, by taking the path to the inner life and by finding their pastures in the law of life. They will then hear My voice, the law, and follow Me, the law.

I, the Christ of God, go after each sheep, for every sheep is a part of Me. No man and no soul is lost forever.

"I have the power to lay down My body and I have the power to take it up again" means that when the time has come for the man, Jesus, the Christ will lay down His earthly body and will again be in His divine body. The divine body is the immaculate body, which is without sin. After the passing of My earthly body, I walked once again as the Christ of God, the divine, immaculate body; for as Jesus, I fulfilled the will of My Father and was without sin.

The words "which are with young" mean those who are filled by fulfilling the eternal law.

The hireling is the person who wants to appropriate the sheep or wants to hire them or to take care of them. No matter how, the sheep do not belong to him; he cannot be the shepherd. Christ alone is the true Shepherd; He alone is the way into the Father's house – for He is the light and the lamp of the soul on the way to the eternal life.

The one who does not know the way into the eternal life cannot lead the sheep to Me, Christ, either. When the wolf, the satanic, breaks into the flock to lead the sheep astray and scatter them, the hireling gives up and flees, because he does not know the way to life, the law of life. However, the one who knows the law of life and of love knows the way there, because he has already walked it – since I, Christ, have led him within to the Father, and he lives in the law of God by fulfilling it selflessly every day.

Such a light-filled soul and such a light-filled person then become a guide who shows My sheep the way to Me, the Christ, and brings the Good Shepherd, the law of God, the voice of love, close to them. He himself will not be a shepherd nor will he lead the sheep to the Father's house, but only a guide who points towards Me, the Christ. He can accompany the sheep all the way to Me. Thus, he is only the companion, but not the shepherd.

Only those who place themselves above Me, the Christ, presume to be shepherds of My sheep, believing that I have entrusted them with the authority for this. Just as there is only *one* Holy Father, the Father in heaven, the Creator of life, there is only *one* Shepherd: Christ, the Redeemer of all souls and men. He is the only way to the heart of God.

I, Christ, the law of life, Am also the portal, the door and the doorkeeper to eternal life. The one who goes through the door into the Kingdom of God enters the eternal life through Me. For no one comes to the Father but through Me, the Christ of God, the Co-Regent of the heavens, who lives in the Father. I, the Christ of God, bring back My sheep into the eternal Being; for I know them all, because through redemption, I have received them in Myself.

I Am the door and the doorkeeper and the Shepherd. The one who truly follows Me knows My voice.

When the sheep follow Me by fulfilling the law of life and of love, they unfold the gift of discernment between the voice of the eternal law and the foreign voice, which entices them and wants to lead them astray with enticements. The evil one cannot lead My sheep astray any longer, because they recognize him. He may very well prowl around them and want to woo them away with his honey-sweet voice, but they actualize and fulfill the law of love. Thus, they are secure in Me.

So, the one who actualizes and fulfills the laws of God hears My voice and will himself become the voice of the law through Me, the Christ. For I lead the sheep to the eternal law. And when they have become the law, they are the voice of the law, of the life and of the love. Then, there is no need anymore to hear My voice; they have become My voice.

The one who does not know himself throws stones at his neighbor. Many Jews did not recognize Me, the Christ of God in Jesus, because they did not know themselves. Since they themselves did not know who they were, they had innumerable excuses for their faults, which I showed them in the mirror of their own thinking and acting. They sought only their physical well-being and their earthly prestige. Since they were concerned only about themselves, they therefore interpreted the law of God as it seemed right to them.

In today's time [1989], the Pharisees and many scribes who now call themselves theologians do the same. They interpret the book which they call the Bible, and which contains parts of the eternal truth, according to their own conceptions and at their own discretion. To them, the one who speaks against their theological fables is, still today, in league with Satan. In the present time, [1989] too, they take up stones and throw them at those who strive to fulfill the will of God: They slander, they distort the truth and ridicule the word of God. They despise and discriminate against those people who do not follow their doctrines, just as the Pharisees did in My time as Jesus of Nazareth.

Recognize that the word of God can never flow through the mouth of sinners. The one who is not a channel of love is a channel of evil. The one who is a channel of love, by being for his neighbor and not against him, hears the voice of love. But the one who is against his neighbor is for the evil and also hears the voice of evil, the various insinuations of the darkness which even takes My name, Christ, in vain.

Many speak about the gospels and do not keep the truth which is in them. They even take their gospel texts as a basis for deriving their own regulations from it. It is the church institutions which make regulations, but not God.

Thus, the pioneers for the New Era have to struggle with similar satanic methods as I did, as Jesus of Nazareth. And so, My word is again fulfilled: As they have persecuted Me, they will persecute you, too. The one who not only speaks about God but strives to do the will of God will suffer persecution, for he is a thorn in the eyes of the adversary.

As long as man lives in the morass of his human ego, he looks only at the morass and does not perceive the light behind matter. For this reason, many people do not know the works of the Lord. They see only their own morass and are therefore of the opinion that all have to wade through the same morass of the human ego. The truth is thus misunderstood, and God's work, the truth, is despised.

The one who does not respect himself as a being from God despises himself and despises his neighbor, too. But the one who fulfills the will of God respects his life, because it is from God. He lives consciously in the Father, and the Father lives and acts through him.

CHAPTER 56

The Raising of Lazarus

About the raising of the dead (1-18)

1. In Bethany, the town of Mary and her sister Martha, lay a sick man called Lazarus. Mary was the one who anointed the Lord and dried His feet with her hair.

2. For this reason, his sisters sent word to Jesus saying, "Lord, behold, the one that you love is ill." When Jesus heard this, He said, "The illness does not lead to death, but that the glory of God may become visible in him." Now Jesus loved Mary and her sister and Lazarus.

3. Although He heard that he was ill, He stayed two days more in the same place where He was. Afterwards, He said to His disciples, "Let us go back to Judea."

4. His disciples said to Him, "Master, last time the Jews wanted to stone You, and You want to go there again?" Jesus answered, "Has the day not twelve hours? The one who walks in the day does not stumble, for he sees the light of this world.

5. But the one who walks at night stumbles, for there is no light in him." He said such things, and afterwards He said to them, "Our friend Lazarus sleeps, but I go there to awaken him from his sleep."

6. Then His disciples said, "Lord, if he sleeps, he will get well." But a messenger came to Him, saying, "Lazarus has died."

7. *And when Jesus arrived, He learned that Lazarus had lain in the grave for four days already (Bethany was close to Jerusalem, approximately one hour's walk). And many Jews had come to Martha and Mary to comfort them for their brother.*

8. *As soon as Martha heard that Jesus was coming, she went to meet Him, but Mary stayed at home. Then Martha said to Jesus, "Lord, if You had been here, my brother would not have died. But I also know that what You ask of God, God will give You."*

9. *Jesus said to her, "Your brother sleeps, and he shall rise." Martha said to Him, "I know well that he will rise in the resurrection on the Day of Judgment."*

10. *Jesus said to her, "I Am the resurrection and the life; the one who believes in Me will live, even though he were dead. I Am the way, the truth and the life, and the one who lives and believes in Me will never die."*

11. *She said to Him, "Yes, Lord, I believe that You are Christ, the Son of God, who has come into this world." And when she had said this, she went and secretly called her sister Mary, saying, "The Master is there and calls for you." When she heard this, she stood up quickly and went to Him.*

12. *For Jesus was not yet in the town, but was still at the place where Martha had met Him. The Jews who were with her in the house and comforted her saw Mary getting up hastily and going out. They followed her saying, "She goes to the grave to weep."*

13. *Then, when Mary saw Jesus and came to Him, she fell at His feet and said to Him, "Lord, if You had*

been here, my brother would not have died." When Jesus saw her and the Jews who came with her weeping, He sighed in the spirit and was troubled. And He said, "Where did you lay him?" They said to Him, "Lord, come and see." And Jesus wept.

14. Then the Jews said, "Behold, how He loved him." But some of them said, "Couldn't He, who opened the eyes of the blind have caused that this man, too, did not have to die?" Then Jesus sighed once more and came to the grave. It was a cave and a stone lay before it.

15. Jesus said, "Take the stone away." Martha, his sister, considering him dead, said, "Lord, now he already stinks; for he has been dead four days now." Jesus said to her, "Did I not say to you that if you would believe, you shall see the glory of God?" Then they lifted away the stone from where Lazarus lay.

16. And Jesus raised His eyes and, chanting, invoked the great name, saying, "My Father, I thank You that You have heard Me. Yet, I know that You hear Me at all times, but, for the sake of the people who are here, I call You, that they may believe that You have sent Me." And when He had said this, He called with a loud voice, "Lazarus, come forth!"

17. And the deceased came forth, bound hand and foot with shrouds, and his face wrapped with a kerchief.

18. Jesus said to them, "Undo him and let him go. When the thread of life is cut through, life does not come again; but, when it is still whole, there is still hope." Then many of the Jews who had come to Mary and saw what Jesus did believed in Him. (Chap. 56:1-18)

I, Christ, explain, correct
and deepen the word:

I, Christ in Jesus, showed the people that God is capable of everything when man strives to do God's works of love and mercy. And so it was given to Me, the Christ in Jesus, to let the works of God become manifest, also by healing and raising those presumed dead. For the glory of the Father should have become manifest in the world through the Son and Co-Regent of the heavens.

The one who walks in the day, that is, in the light of God, does not stumble. But the one who is in the darkness stumbles, because he does not fulfill the works of love and, consequently, has not unfolded his Inner Light. The one who is in the darkness looks only at the shadow of the light. He also does not recognize in whose soul the light of God shines brightly. But the person who walks in the light of the truth is one with the light, and God, the light, acts through him. God irradiates the light-filled soul and raises again to life the person who fulfills the works of God.

As long as the soul is still connected to the earthly body by the silver cord – the spiritual information cord – it is still near the body that appears to be dead and, if it is the will of God, can be called back into the body.

In human life, there are stages of belief and stages of doubt. When a person consciously lives in the moment and in the belief in God who is the light, then all his aspirations are light-filled, because he is aligned with God.

The one who lives in God receives from God. He will maintain life and, if it is the will of God, he will awaken a person to the inner life. To awaken to the inner life does not mean just to awaken and maintain the earthly life – that is, to bring the soul back to the body that appears to be dead – but, above all, it is to make the person conscious of Christ, that is, to serve as a guide indicating the way to Me, the Redeemer of all souls and men, who I Am, the life. The one who finds the light of God through a light-filled person has also been raised to life.

I Am Christ, the life of all souls and men. I Am the resurrection of the soul to the eternal life. The one who believes in Me and fulfills God's works of love will live. When his earthly body passes away, his soul will not be spiritually dead, but will walk in the light of truth and will stand in the splendor of glory.

Recognize that I Am the way, the truth and the life. The one who believes in Me and fulfills the laws of life and of love will never die – that is, he will not fall prey to spiritual death.

When the heartbeat of a person cannot be heard anymore, the earthly physician declares the person to be dead. But as long as the soul is still connected to the person through the spiritual information cord, the life force flows to the body. This life force, which can barely be perceived anymore, keeps certain basic cells of the brain active, through which the life can then build itself up again in the body.

The Inner Physician and Helper, the Christ of God, is the life of the soul. He can bring back into the earthly life all those who will align their further earthly existence with God, by striving to remove the still existing burdens of the soul with Me, the Christ, and to sin no more. This inherent law also holds true for the suffering and the sick.

CHAPTER 57

About the Little Children –
The Parable of the Fishes – The Forgiveness of Sins

Bring the little ones to Me – Who is "the greatest in the Kingdom of God"? (1-2). Causing our neighbor anger and its consequences (3). The task of parents (4-5). The earthly eyes and the spiritual eye – God is the all-radiation, the all-streaming law (6-9). Clearing things up according to the commandment of peace – To bind and to release – Requests to God and their fulfillment (10-12). Each one is his own judge – Forgiving, worldly law and justice – Man and state (13-20)

1. At the same time, the disciples came to Jesus and asked Him, "Who is the greatest in the Kingdom of God?" And Jesus called a little child to Him and put him in the midst of them and said, "Verily, I say to you, if you do not change and become as innocent and teachable as this little child, you will not enter the Kingdom of Heaven.

2. But the one who becomes simple like this child is the greatest in the Kingdom of Heaven. And the one who receives such a child in My name receives Me. (Chap. 57:1-2)

I, Christ, explain, correct
and deepen the word:

Many souls come into this world with the intention of clearing up, in the earthly garment, what is still negative in them. They also come with the knowledge that they can be tested and led astray. In their earthly body, which is still developing, they feel very precisely the good and the less good. Souls which have consciously incarnated are very sensitive, for they came inspired with the wish to become divine again.

The one who neglects one of these little children or even leads it astray, by orienting it towards this world, sins against the Holy Spirit. It would have been better for him if he had not aspired to earthly birth. But the one who strives for a lawful life and takes care to guide to Me the little children, whose earthly bodies are still growing, is himself a light-filled being who strives for perfection, for the rebirth in the Spirit of God.

The meaning of the word "simple" is to be discerning, modest, merciful and kind.

The one who neither doubts in God nor is arrogant towards his neighbor nor wants to be a know-it-all, but actualizes the commandments of God, becomes wise. The wise one serves his neighbor selflessly. He does not ask for acknowledgment or reward. He gives of himself out of the life of God, which is the fullness. He is "the greatest" in the Kingdom of God, because he fulfills the laws of God.

The word "the greatest" refers to the all-law. "To be the greatest in the Kingdom of Heaven" means after physical death, to go into the Absolute Law, to the beings of light, who live in the all-law, in the Greatest, in the Eternal, in the All-One, God.

3. Woe to the world because of its offenses to others! It is impossible that offenses do not come, but woe to him through whom the offense occurs! Therefore, if your lusts and pleasures cause offense to others, cast them away from you. For it is better for you to enter into life without them, than to be cast with them into the everlasting fire. (Chap. 57:3)

I, Christ, explain, correct
and deepen the word:

Take care that nothing comes from your mouth that is not divine, and that you do nothing that harms your neighbor and the nature kingdoms. Do not exert pressure on your neighbor, so that you can indulge in your lusts and passions.

So do not cause anyone offense by your human behavior, by your inclinations and stirrings. For if your neighbor does not forgive you, you may have to endure for a long time the grief and torment which your neighbor had to bear and endure because of you.

The recognition of what you have done to your neighbor can be very painful in your soul – like fire – depending on the causes which were created by you.

The meaning of the expression "everlasting fire" is to suffer for eons.

4. Take heed that you do not neglect any of these little ones; for I say to you, their angels perpetually be-

hold the face of God. For the Son of Man has come to save what was lost. (Chap. 57:4)

I, Christ, explain, correct
and deepen the word:

"... their angels" means that the light-filled soul of a child still lives consciously in God and sees into the inner life, which is God.

5. *Likewise, it is not the will of your Father in heaven that one of these little ones should come to suffer harm." (Chap. 57:5)*

I, Christ, explain, correct
and deepen the word:

The words "Likewise, it is not the will of your Father in heaven that one of these little ones should come to suffer harm" mean that the children are the children of the Father-Mother-God and are only entrusted to their earthly parents for this earthly existence. At the conception of the earthly body and at the birth of the child, the Eternal assigns to the parents the task of caring for the body of the child in the right way, to accept and receive the child, to care for it and protect it, and to accompany it on its journey through life – by an exemplary life and by good deeds in the family and for their neighbor.

6. *And some who were full of doubt came to Jesus, saying, "You told us that our life and being are from God, but we have never seen God, nor do we know of any God. Can You show us the One whom You call the Father and the only God? We do not know whether there is a God."*

7. *Jesus answered them, saying, "Hear this parable about the fishes. The fishes of a river spoke with one another and said: They tell us that our life and being comes from water, but we have never seen water, we do not know what it is. Then some of them, who were wiser than the others, said: We have heard that a wise and learned fish who knows all things lives in the sea. Let us go to him and ask him to show us the water.*

8. *And so, some of them set out to search for the great and wise fish, and they finally came to the sea where the fish lived, and they asked him.*

9. *And when he heard them, he said to them: Oh, you foolish fish, that you do not think. Yet wise are the few of you who seek. You live and move in water and have your existence in the water; you have come from the water and you will return to the water. You live in the water, but you do not know it. In the same way, you live in God and yet you ask Me: Show us God. God is in all things and everything is in God."*
(Chap. 57:6-9)

I, Christ, explain, correct
and deepen the word:

The doubter sees things and events within the limitations of matter. The earthly eyes perceive only what is earthly, the condensed substance, matter. So it is only the things and events of this world that are perceived by the earthly eyes and registered by the cells of the brain.

The spiritual eye, the eye of the soul, looks behind the material; it looks right through matter and perceives the things and events of this world in the light of the eternal law. And the fine senses of the soul recognize the true and the untrue.

God is law – and the one who lives in the law of God draws and gives from the source of eternal life, from the truth. The human being in the ocean, God, perceives matter as a reflection, as a reflected image of the truth, which emerged through the negative workings of the darkness. The doubter, on the other hand, considers this coarse-materiality to be the true life and sees only the reflections of the human ego.

The one who considers matter to be the truth takes unlawful reflections as reality, because he lives in this illusionary light, in this world of thoughts.

The soul and person who live in God do not ask: "Who or what is God?" or "Is there a God?" They live in God, and God is active through them.

God is the cosmic ocean; God is radiation; God is light; God is energy; God is love and wisdom. God is nature, the animal world and the starry firmament. God is the alpha; He is the omega for coarse-materiality; for truth is eternity – and eternity is fine-material.

The Being – the primordial power – in which all pure creatures and beings live, is eternal, from eternity to eternity, because God is eternity.

Man lives and moves solely through God, the life, which is in him and everywhere – omnipresent. And all that lives, lives from God.

God is all-radiation, God is all in all things, the ocean, the life and the love. Everything pure consists of countless aspects of life and of love. The pure beings, too, the spirit beings, are – as images of the Father – the all-radiation, the law. God is the all-streaming law. The divine beings, the spirit beings, are compressed eternal law; they move in the all-stream, God.

The one who only swims in the riverbed of the temporal does not live consciously in the ocean, God; this is why he asks about the One who maintains and nourishes him and pulsates through him. There is no life without God, the all-ocean.

10. Once again, Jesus said to the disciples, "If your brother or your sister sins against you, go alone and make your brother or your sister aware of his or her fault; if they listen to you, you have gained them. But if they do not want to listen to you, then take two or more with you, so that every word may be confirmed by the mouth of two or three witnesses.

11. And if they do not want to listen to them, then tell the community; and if they do not want to listen to the community either, then consider them as those who are outside of the community. Verily, I say to you, whatever you justly bind on Earth shall be also bound in heaven, and whatever you justly release on Earth, shall be also released in heaven.

12. And once again I say to you: If seven or even only three of you on Earth are in agreement in what they ask, it will be done to them by My Father who is in heaven. For if only three are gathered in My name, so Am I in the midst of them; and if there is only one, so Am I in the heart of this one." (Chap. 57:10-12)

I, Christ, explain, correct
and deepen the word:

As long as there are coarse-materiality and human beings who do not yet live in the law, in God – the Being, the eternal love – the law of sowing and reaping is in effect.

To the people who live the law of sowing and reaping, God gave a commandment which contributes to peace and to maintaining peace, when the person follows it:

When your brother or your sister sins against you, go and make your brother or your sister aware of his or her fault without the presence of a second or third party. If they listen to you and accept what you have advised them without emotion, and then act according to the commandment of peace, then you have won them for God. But if they do not want to listen to you, even though the question at issue is of significance for your life or for that of your neighbor or for the world, then take two or several people with you, so that they can hear and confirm your words.

If, even then, your brother or your sister does not want to listen to you or accept what you present, then bring it before the community, in the presence of those involved. And if the one concerned does not want to listen to the community either, then he or she thereby puts him or herself outside of the community which is striving to fulfill the will of God. He or she should then live in the outer court outside of the community, in the world.

This commandment is important. If you have acted according to this commandment, but your concern is not heard or accepted, then, at the latest, in the spheres of purification it will become evident to the soul or the souls that have refused to follow this commandment. Then the witnesses will also appear again.

However, the one who does not want to change and keeps up his sinfulness and does not leave the community, in spite of the request and suggestion that he leave it, will be looked upon by the community as if he were no longer a member of the community. But if, through his negative radiation and his negative speech and action, he poisons members of the community, who then rebel with him against those who strive toward God, he then bears the main blame for the unrest within the community and will be called to account by the law of sowing and reaping. For when you are not with your neighbor, you are against him. Then you should also take the appropriate steps.

The words "to justly bind on earth" mean: When you think that what you have acquired lawfully is your property – that is, when you bind it to yourself – then this is against the heavenly law of freedom, of being free from every binding; and it is registered in the law of sowing and reaping. No binding – be it to people or things – has a place in heaven. The earthly word "binding" means that the person binds himself to what is dear and valuable to him in the world, to what he puts above the gifts of God.

To be bound is the opposite of freedom, of being released. The one who releases himself from what is earthly, by not considering it as his property and possession, will enter heaven as a spirit being and will live in the fullness that comes from God.

The following instructions from God, from the eternal law, are also commandments for the people, aids for opening the inner life:

When people, no matter how many, come together in My name and strive together to fulfill the laws of God, then what they ask of God is already fulfilled in their souls – if it is good for soul and person. Then it becomes manifest to them when the time has become ripe for it.

I, the Christ, Am in the midst of men and souls who honor the Most High in their thinking and acting. And even when it is only one who asks for the gifts of salvation and strives to fulfill the laws of God, the request is already fulfilled in his soul, too – before he asked for it. For the eternal Father beholds His children in the light of the eternal law and knows them; and He will give their honest hearts what is good for them.

Therefore, be comforted: God knows all His children. He sees in every heart. And if one of His children – out of love for Him – renders Him honor in everything, then I, the Christ, Am active in his heart.

13. *Then Peter came to Him and asked, "Lord, how often may my brother sin against me, that I forgive him? Seven times?" Jesus said to him, "I say to you, not seven times, but seventy times seven. For unrighteousness was also among the prophets, even after they had been anointed by the Holy Spirit."*

14. *And He told this parable, "There was once a king who wanted to settle accounts with his servants. And when he had begun to settle accounts, they brought him one who owed him a thousand talents. But as he could not pay, his lord commanded that he and his wife and his children and all that he possessed be sold, so that the debt could be paid.*

15. *Then the servant fell down at the feet of his lord and begged him, saying: Lord, have patience with me, and I will pay you everything. Then the lord was moved*

by compassion and he set him free and forgave him his debt.

16. But the same servant went out and met one of his fellow servants who owed him a hundred pence, and he grabbed him and took him by the throat, shouting: Pay me your debt.

17. And his fellow servant fell on his knees before him and implored him, saying: Have patience with me, and I will pay you everything. But he would not; he went and had him put in prison until he would pay his debt.

18. And when his fellow servants saw what he had done, they became very sad and told their lord all that had happened.

19. Then the lord sent for him and said to him: O you wicked servant, I forgave you your debt because you begged me; should you not also have pity on your fellow servant, just as I had pity on you? And his lord was angry and delivered him up to the torturers, until he would pay all that he owed.

20. Likewise will the heavenly Father judge you, if you do not forgive each one his debt from your heart, whether brother or sister. Nevertheless, let each one see to it that he pays what he owes, for God loves the just ones." (Chap. 57:13-20)

I, Christ, explain, correct
and deepen the word:

Forgiving and asking for forgiveness make the person free and the soul filled with light.

The one who forgives, no matter how often his neighbor has sinned and sins against him, does not burden his soul and also keeps his body free from burden. The one who forgives from his heart will forgive again and again – no matter how often one sins against him through sensations, thoughts, words, or deeds. The one who forgives his neighbor without thinking negatively about him is not tied to the sinner. But the one who thinks negatively about the sinner is tied to the debtor in proportion to the intensity of his thoughts.

The judgment reads: By the standards with which you measure, you, too, will be measured. This means that the measure of your negative sensations, thoughts, words and deeds is your judge – but not God.

Therefore, have no negative thoughts about those who sin against you. Forgive, and forgive over and over again – and you will remain free from the burden of sin and will not be tied to the sinner, either.

However, the sinner will be tied to you until he has become reasonable and no longer commits, against you or other fellow men, what you have already forgiven him long ago.

Forgive and ask for forgiveness. Do not let the causes remain pending. As soon as you recognize them, you should settle them.

"Likewise will the heavenly Father judge you, if you do not forgive each one his debt from your heart, whether brother or sister" means that likewise, the heavenly Father will not forgive you, if you do not forgive each one his debt from your heart.

Recognize that God is not the worldly law, but He is justice.

Man has his earthly laws; to him they are his rights. As long as man does not know the law of life, the justice, he often thinks he is acting in a correct way. But with this, he entangles himself over and over again in the law of sowing and reaping, because rights do not always correspond to justice. The rights of man is not by any means the justice of God.

The one who insists on his rights counts on the rights of human laws, but not on justice. What he demands, obtains and accomplishes by insisting on his rights cannot last before the law of God, the justice. It is not the heavenly Father who judges the person, but it is he, the person, who judges himself according to what he sows.

These inherent laws are valid between man and man and not between man and state, the "Caesar." For as long as the incarnated spirit being is a human being, he is subject to the laws and obligations of the earthly state, of the "Caesar," and, as a human being, should fulfill, vis-à-vis the state, the "Caesar," what is not against the law of God. This is why it is said: Render unto Caesar the things which are Caesar's and unto God the things which are God's.

If a person keeps the laws of the state, he can also lay claim to the laws of the state; and the state, the Caesar, is also obligated to give to the one who gives to it.

CHAPTER 58

Joy Over the Repentant Sinner –
The Parable of the Prodigal Son

*The true sons and daughters of God – The people of
God on Earth (1-2). God created and beholds His children
as perfect – Every child returns to Him through Christ (3-15)*

1. *Jesus said to His disciples and to the people
around Him, "Who is the son of God? Who is the
daughter of God? They are those people who turn away
from all evil and do right, who love mercy and walk full
of reverence with their God. Those are the sons and the
daughters of man who came out of Egypt and to whom
it is given that they shall be called the sons and
daughters of God.*

2. *And they will be gathered from all tribes, nations,
peoples and tongues, and they come from the east and
from the west and from the north and from the south,
and they live on the mountain of Zion, and they eat
bread and drink the fruit of the vine at the table of God,
and they see God face to face." (Chap. 58:1-2)*

I, Christ, explain, correct
and deepen the word:

All people and beings are sons and daughters of
God. For I have raised all people and souls again to the

sonship and daughterhood of God through My Re-deemer-deed.

However, many people do not know this, because they still live in the bondage of sin and still call themselves the sons and daughters of man.

But the one who strives to fulfill the will of God is conscious of his son or daughtership in God. He will also call himself the son or daughter of God, because he lives in God, through the actualization and fulfillment of the eternal laws.

The time is dawning [1989] in which I, Christ, gather from all tribes, nations and peoples those who strive to follow the laws of God and to live consciously in the son and daughtership of God, in the law of God, the law of life and of love.

They come from the east, from the west, from the north and from the south, and form *one* people: the people of God on Earth. And they live in the city of Zion which is built on the blessed heights, in the city of New Jerusalem and in the communities which resemble the radiation of the New Jerusalem. Only out of Me, the Christ, will then come the New Israel, the true promised land, which will encompass the globe after the purification of the Earth.

The people in God live with nature; and nature, which is from God, lays the table for them. They eat what nature offers them, the gifts from God.

After this life in God, in the Kingdom of Peace of Jesus Christ, the transformation and the dissolution of all the forms which are still dense will gradually take place. Then all beings in God will behold the eternal Father face to face, because they live in the eternal law, God.

3. Then all the tax collectors and sinners came nearer to Him in order to hear Him. But the Pharisees and scribes murmured, saying, "This man receives sinners and eats with them."

4. And He told this parable to them: "Which one among you who has a hundred sheep and, losing one, does not leave the ninety-nine in the wilderness and search for the lost one until he has found it? And when he has found it, he takes it on his shoulders and rejoices.

5. And when he comes home, he calls his neighbors and friends together and says to them, 'Rejoice with me, for I have found my sheep that was lost!' I say to you that more joy will likewise reign in heaven over one repentant sinner than over ninety-nine just ones who need no repentance.

6. And which woman, having ten pieces of silver and losing one, will not light a candle and search for it diligently until she has found it? And when she has found it, will she not call together her friends and neighbors and say, 'Rejoice with me, for I have found the piece of silver which I had lost'? Likewise, I say to you, joy will reign among the angels of God over one repentant sinner."

7. And He also told this parable: "A man had two sons, and the younger of them said to his parents, 'Give

me the share of the goods that falls to me.' And they shared their fortune with him. And a few days later, the younger son picked up his belongings and traveled to a far country where he squandered his fortune in a life of debauchery.

8. And when he had used up everything, a severe famine came over the country, and he came into want. And he moved away and entered the service of a citizen of this country. This one sent him into his pastures to guard the swine. And he would have been glad to still his hunger with the husks that the pigs ate, but no one gave them to him.

9. And when he came to his senses, he said, 'How many of my father's servants have bread enough to spare and I perish with hunger. I will set out and go to my father and my mother and will say to them: My father and my mother, I have sinned against heaven and before you and am no longer worthy to be called your son. Take me in as one of your servants.'

10. And he set out and came to his parents. But while he was still a long way from the house, his parents saw him and felt compassion for him and ran toward him and fell on his neck and kissed him. And the son said to them, 'My father and my mother, I have sinned against heaven and in your sight, and I am no longer worthy to be called your son.'

11. But the father said to his servants, 'Bring out the best robe and put it on him and put a ring on his hand and shoes on his feet and bring the most beautiful fruits and bread and oil and wine and let us eat and be merry. For this my son was dead and is alive again; he was lost and is found.' And they all began to be merry.

12. Now the older son was in the field and, as he returned and drew near the house, he heard music and dancing. And he called one of the servants and asked what this meant. And he said to him, 'Your brother who was lost has returned home, and your father and your mother have brought him bread and oil and wine and the most beautiful fruits, because they have him back safe and sound.'

13. And he was angry and did not want to go into the house. And his father came out and entreated him. And he said to his father, 'Behold, I have served you for many years and have never overstepped your commandments, but you have never given me such a lavish feast, so that I may be merry with my friends.

14. But as soon as your son, who has wasted his share of inheritance with whores, has returned, you prepare him a feast of the best you have.'

15. And his father said to him, 'My son, you are always with me and all that I have is yours. But it is proper now that we should be merry and glad, for your brother was dead and is alive again; he was lost and is found.'" (Chap. 58:3-15)

I, Christ, explain, correct
and deepen the word:

These parables are at the same time commandments. The one who keeps them by forgiving and by receiving his neighbor in his heart thereby follows the commandments which indicate to him the path to eternal life.

The one who keeps the commandments not only looks at the sinful, but also sees into the heart which shows true remorse – just as the heavenly Father, too, does not look at the shortcomings and sins of His children, but only at what He has created: the pure, noble and good. When, through His eternally radiating love, His child has removed all shortcomings and has expiated all sins, God will receive it in His glory. And God, the Eternal, will not ask about what was; it is finished. In the Eternal is the now, the eternity, and His child is the child of eternity. So has He, the great Spirit, created it, and so does He behold it eternally. Why should God ask about the past when He always beholds His child in the present as pure, noble and good?

Because God, the eternal Father, cherishes each of His children in His heart, they will also return as children of God, as sons and daughters of the Eternal, and I, the Shepherd of all souls and men, will lead them to Him.

CHAPTER 59

About Vigilance – The Tax Collector Zacchaeus

The treasure in heaven and earthly
possessions (1-3).Being prepared for the coming of Christ
(4-6). The good steward (7-8). Much is required of the one
who is given much (9-10). To sin despite knowing better is
to sin against the Holy Spirit (11-12). No soul and no human
being is lost (13-18)

1. Jesus went up on a mountain and sat there with His disciples and taught them. And He said to them, "Fear not, little flock, for it is your Father's kind will to give you the kingdom.

2. Sell everything you have, and do good to those who have nothing. Provide yourselves with a pouch which does not wear out, a treasure in heaven, which does not diminish, which no thief can reach and which no moth consumes.

3. Let your loins be girded and your lights burn. And be like men who wait for their master to return from the wedding; so that when he comes and knocks, they open right away for him. (Chap. 59:1-3)

I, Christ, explain, correct
and deepen the word:

The statement "Sell everything you have, and do good to those who have nothing. Provide yourselves with a pouch which does not wear out, a treasure in heaven, which does not diminish, which no thief can reach and which no moth consumes" means that you should have only what you need. You should not gather earthly treasures and call them your own. For if you gather earthly treasures and call them your own, there, too, is your heart. A narrow, egocentric heart constantly beats in the fear of having what is actually not his own taken from him.

How can the person receive the bridegroom, when his heart is closed to Him, the bridegroom who brings with Him the gifts of heaven for all who have opened their heart to God, the inner fullness, the inner wealth?

The one who keeps his heart open to God will not live in want in this world. He will receive what he needs – and beyond that. However, he will not cling to what he owns on Earth, because he recognizes that it is the gifts from God. Such people do not cut themselves off into a world of conceptions of mine and thine, but manage the gifts of God in such a way that they also bring fruits to their fellow man. They live in God, and, from God, they give to the one who works in a righteous way, according to the commandment "pray and work."

The one who has turned within is in Me, the Christ, and I Am in him, and between us there is nothing which separates us anymore.

4. *Blessed are the servants whom the master finds awake when he comes. Verily, I say to you, he will gird*

himself and invite them to his table and will come and will serve them.

5. *And if he comes in the second watch or in the third watch and finds them so, then blessed are these servants.*

6. *But you should know this: If the guardian of the house knew what hour the thief would come, he would watch and would not let his house be broken into. This is why you, too, should be prepared, for the Son of Man will come at an hour when you do not expect it."*
(Chap. 59:4-6)

I, Christ, explain, correct
and deepen the word:

Blessed are the people who are vigilant and deny the base aspects, the human ego, access into their inner being. They keep their inner being, their house, clean and open for the bridegroom. No matter when He comes, they are ready; for they watch over themselves and thus, their senses will be alert when I, Christ, appear.

In today's time [1989], many people are already awake and aligned with Me, and thus prepare themselves for My coming. Many souls and men have already set out to receive Me in their inner being, for the Kingdom of God is a kingdom of the inner being. It takes on form and shape externally through the people who live in the kingdom of the inner being.

Recognize that the Kingdom of God on Earth is at hand. I, Christ, enter many hearts; for more and more people are walking the path within, in order to unite with Me, the Christ of God. My spiritual coming announces itself not only in the firmament, but first in the hearts of those who have decided for Me and for the Kingdom of God on Earth.

7. *Then Peter said to Him, "Lord, do you give this parable to us or to all others, too?" And the Lord said, "Who, then, is that faithful and wise steward whom the master puts in charge of his servants, that he give them their portion in due time?*

8. *Blessed is the servant whom his master finds awake, when he comes. Verily, I say to you, he will put him in charge of all his properties. (Chap. 59:7-8)*

I, Christ, explain, correct
and deepen the word:

The one who is able to manage the gifts of God lawfully is the steward of many. He is the one who knows and keeps the law of God and, at the right time, says and gives to each person, from the law of life, what his soul can accept and fulfill. Often, a person still rejects the help from the law of God. Nevertheless, his alert soul has absorbed it and will reflect it to the shell, to the human being, at the right time. The Lord will reward the one whose soul is alert and ripe for the gifts of life. This one will manage the goods of life on Earth well, by looking after the well-being of all those who work righteously, by fulfilling the commandment "pray and work."

The one whose heart is alert is also of clear mind. He is in Me and I Am in him. And the one who lives in Me is the one through whom I act. He will possess the Earth.

9. But if this servant will say to himself, 'My master is delaying his coming', and then begins to beat the other servants and maids, and to eat and get drunk, then the master of that servant will come on a day when he does not expect him and at an hour that he does not know; and he will give him his portion in keeping with the unfaithful.

10. And the servant who knows the will of his master and has not prepared himself, nor acted according to his will, will have to suffer many blows. However, the one who did not know it but did things worthy of blows will receive few blows. For much will be required of the one who was given much; and little will be required of the one who was given little. (Chap. 59:9-10)

I, Christ, explain, correct
and deepen the word:

The one who knows the will of the Lord, that is, the laws of life, and does not keep them will also create many causes and will have to bear the corresponding effects; he will suffer many blows, for he has knowingly violated the law of God.

"For much will be required of the one who was given much" means that the soul which possesses inner strength and power and which has not become the slave of sin should be there for those who are still at the beginning of the spiritual path, whose souls are only beginning to purify themselves and who are opening themselves to God and His works giving to them and helping them. This is why those who are still at the beginning of the spiritual path to the heart of God will "receive fewer blows," because their souls are still weak, like a small plant, and need to be protected until they have attained inner maturity, through the actualization of the eternal law.

The eternal love protects the germinating life in soul and person so that it cannot be attacked by the adversary. Only when the soul has been strengthened will it be exposed to outer influences in order to prove itself. For when soul and person have received much of the divine, that is, when they have been given an understanding of the laws of inner life and have actualized them, then soul and person are strengthened and can withstand the storms and attacks of the darkness. Then they are also able to give to those who still need to be protected in order to grow stronger. And so, the still weak souls which are just at the beginning of the spiritual path are protected by the power of love, since they cannot yet bear the blows of the darkness. However, the one who receives from the law of inner life and accepts it, thereby makes it his duty to actualize the eternal law which he received.

The one who does not actualize or fulfill it despite knowing better will also be exposed to the storms one day. For his negligence, he will then reap what he has sown during the time of spiritual protection, when he could have actualized the spiritual knowledge.

11. This is why those who know the Godhead and have found the path of life and the mysteries of light and have nevertheless fallen into sin will be punished more severely than those who did not know the path of life.

12. These will return when their cycle is completed, and they will be given the time to consider and to improve their lives and to learn the mysteries and enter the kingdom of light." (Chap. 59:11-12)

I, Christ, explain, correct
and deepen the word:

The one who knows the laws of God and sins despite knowing better will burden himself even more – that is, will have to bear far more severe effects – than those who know less about the path to the inner life.

Recognize that everyone knows the commandments for life. Therefore, no one is unknowing. The one who fulfills the commandments also comes to know the path within, the steps of evolution to eternal bliss.

But the one who knows the inner path and has already taken some steps of evolution and then sins, despite knowing better, sins against the Holy Spirit. Like all other people who live in deep sin, he will adhere to the wheel of reincarnation once he has died – until that which binds the soul to this wheel is paid off.

For this reason, the words "These will return when their cycle is completed" mean that only when they have left the wheel of reincarnation will they gradually enter the light.

13. Jesus came through Jericho. And behold, there was a man called Zacchaeus who was the chief of the tax collectors and very rich.

14. And he wanted to see who in the crowd was Jesus and could not, for he was small of stature. And he ran ahead and climbed a mulberry tree to see Him, for He was to pass by that way.

15. And when Jesus came to the place, He looked up and saw him and said to him, "Zacchaeus, make haste, come down, for I must stay at your house today." And he climbed down hastily and received Him joyfully.

16. When they saw that, they all murmured that He stayed as a guest at a sinner's house.

17. But Zacchaeus stood there and said to the Lord, "Behold, Lord, I give the poor half of my goods; and if I have defrauded anyone, I restore it fourfold."

18. And Jesus said to him, "Today, salvation has come to your house; if you are a righteous man, you are also a son of Abraham. For the Son of Man is come to seek and to save what was lost." (Chap. 59:13-18)

I, Christ, explain, correct
and deepen the word:

"For the Son of Man is come to seek and to save what was lost" means that I, Christ, came in Jesus into this world to gather all men and souls and to unite them in My Redeemer-light.

All souls and men are now united in Me. For this reason, no soul and no man will be lost. I, Christ, bear them in Me. Through My Redeemer-deed, every soul and every human being has become a cell in My body. Every soul – even when it thinks it is lost – will one day behold the glory of the Father, once it has left the wheel of reincarnation; for then, it has consciously accepted and received Me, its Redeemer and divine brother. Every soul will one day develop the longing for its Father's house, for it is there that its spiritual land of birth and home is.

Recognize that even now, the Son is glorified in the sons and daughters of God who fulfill the will of the Father.

CHAPTER 60

Jesus Condemns the Scribes and Pharisees as Hypocrites

Taking the name of Christ in vain for un-christian purposes – There are no "saints" – The ravenous wolves in sheep's clothing – The Antichrist – Christ is victorious (1-18)

1. Then Jesus said to the people and to His disciples, "The scribes and Pharisees sit on the seat of Moses. Now all that they bid you to observe, observe and also do. However, do not act according to their works; for they talk, but do not do it. For they themselves bind heavy and unbearable burdens and lay them on the shoulders of men; but they themselves do not want to move these with even one finger.

2. But they do all their works to be seen by men. They make their phylacteries broad and enlarge the borders of their garments. They love the place of honor at feasts and the best seat in the synagogues. They like to be greeted at the market and to be called by men Rabbi, Rabbi.

3. But you shall not let yourselves be called Rabbi. For One is your Rabbi, Christ. But you are all brothers. And you shall call no man on Earth, father, for on Earth the fathers are fathers in the flesh only; but in heaven is the One who is your Father, who has the Spirit of truth, which the world cannot receive.

4. Nor shall you let yourselves be called master, for One is your Master, Christ. But the greatest among you shall be your servant. For the one who exalts himself will be humbled. And those who are humble in themselves will be exalted.

5. Woe to you, scribes and Pharisees, you hypocrites! For you lock the Kingdom of Heaven to man. You do not enter yourselves, nor let those who would enter go in.

6. Woe to you, scribes and Pharisees, you hypocrites! You, who devour widows' houses and, for pretense sake, speak long prayers! For this reason, you will receive all the more damnation.

7. Woe to you, scribes and Pharisees, you hypocrites! You, who travel through sea and land to make one proselyte; and when he has become one, you make of him twice as much a child of hell as you are!

8. Woe to you, you blind guides, who say: Whoever swears by the temple, it is nothing; but the one who swears by the gold of the temple is guilty. You fools and blind ones! What is greater, the gold or the temple that sanctifies the gold?

9. And: Whoever swears by the altar, it is nothing. But the one who swears by the offering that is on the altar is guilty. You fools and blind ones, what is greater? The offering or the altar that sanctifies the offering?

10. Therefore, the one who swears by the altar swears by it and by all things thereon. And the one who swears by the temple swears by it and by him who dwells therein. And the one who swears by heaven swears by the throne of God and by the One who sits thereon.

11. Woe to you, scribes and Pharisees, you hypocrites! You, who tithe mint and anise and cumin, and neglect the weightiest matters of the law, namely judgment, mercy and faith. One should do this and not neglect that. You blinded guides, who strain out a gnat and swallow a camel!

12. Woe to you, scribes and Pharisees, you hypocrites! You, who clean the outside of cups and bowls, but inside they are filled with extortion and excess! You blind Pharisees, clean first the inside of the cup and of the bowl, so that the outside may also become clean!

13. Woe to you, scribes and Pharisees, you hypocrites! You are like whitewashed tombs which appear beautiful on the outside, but are filled within with the bones of the dead and all filth. So you, too, appear outwardly righteous before the people, but within you are full of hypocrisy and pretense.

14. Woe to you, scribes and Pharisees, who build the tombs of the prophets and adorn the sepulchers of the righteous and say: If we had lived in the days of our forefathers, we would not have been to blame for the blood of the prophets with them!

15. Thus, you bear witness of yourselves, that you act as children of those who have killed the prophets. So you, too, fulfill the measure of your forefathers!

16. Therefore, the holy wisdom says: Behold, I send you prophets and wise ones and scribes; and you will kill and crucify some of them, and you will scourge some of them in your synagogues and will persecute them from city to city. And upon you will come all the righteous blood that has been shed on Earth, from the blood of the righteous Abel up to the blood of Zacharias, the son of Barachias, whom you killed between the temple and the altar. Verily, I say to you, all that will come upon this generation.

17. *O Jerusalem, Jerusalem, you that kill the prophets and stone those who are sent to you! How often have I wanted to gather your children, as a hen gathers her chicks under her wings, and you would not.*

18. *Behold, your house shall be left desolate to you! For I say to you: From now on, you will not see Me until you say: Holy, holy, holy! Praised be the one who comes in the name of the just One!"* (Chap. 60:1-18)

I, Christ, explain, correct
and deepen the word:

What I, as Jesus of Nazareth, said to the Pharisees and scribes and their adherents still holds true today [1989]. Just as they have accused Me, Christ, in Jesus of Nazareth, of being satanic, and persecuted and ridiculed Me, so will the theologians and so-called Bible experts and their adherents treat My own today [1989]. Many church authorities and also some of the worldly authorities are today's scribes and Pharisees again. Since they consider their dogmas and their canons as the basis for being Christian, they do not understand what true Christianity means.

Many representatives of the ecclesiastic and worldly authorities pursue politics and use the word "Christian" for un-christian purposes. They use My name to do honor to their name. They talk to the people about the gospel of love, but very few of them live accordingly. They issue several laws which are against the divine law, thus trampling underfoot the Most Holy, the law of love and of life. They allow animals to be killed. They eat a lot of meat and drink strong drinks. Many of them are responsible along with others for the violation, the exploitation and poisoning of the Earth, and many who call themselves Christian arm themselves for purposes of war.

So-called Christians who are blindly loyal to their authorities receive training in the use of weapons of war, in order to kill men when the call to war sounds out. Blind to the eternal truth, they act like slaves and do what they are commanded. Dazed and intoxicated by their base ego, many violate the great "earth-man," the Earth, and interfere in its lawful processes. Thus, they disturb and destroy the atmosphere and the magnetic fields of the Earth. All of this are satanic excesses – the base ego of men who consider themselves Christian.

Still today, the ecclesiastic authorities sit in the places of honor, at feasts as well as in their churches, and let their faithful address them by honorary titles. Even during the present time [1989], they still continue to honor a man with the title "Holy Father," even though, as Jesus of Nazareth, I taught, there is only *one* Holy Father: He is the Father in heaven, the Father-Mother-God of all beings and men. They also honor their "saints," even though I taught that there are no "saints" – only blessed beings who live in God.

On Earth, there is the father in the flesh, the male as the begetting principle. The man who begets a child gives the seed for the earthly body of an incarnating soul. In the flesh, he then calls himself father – just as the female – who receives the seed of the man for the developing physical shell and bears the child under her heart and gives birth – calls herself mother, in the flesh.

The Earth is the place of expiation for the souls in an earthly body. At this time now, many of the hypocrites from back then are again in a shell of flesh, in order to continue their intrigues against Me, the Christ, by again persecuting those people who strive to let the truth become manifest. My words still hold true today: If they have persecuted Me, they will persecute you, too.

Driven by ambition, power and vain illusion, these souls go into earthly bodies again and again, in order to begin where they left off when earthly death seized them. This will continue until incarnations are no longer possible for such base souls, or until the ambitious and power-hungry souls bow, in order to become the least among their brothers and sisters, in the time remaining for incarnation. For the one who exalts himself has to come to his senses by way of humiliation.

And so in many cases, they are again and again the same hypocrites as in My time, when I walked on Earth as Christ in Jesus. The same and similar crimes take place again and again, yet with other arguments and methods, according to the changing times. However, the purpose is the same: Eliminate all those who let the eternal truth become manifest and who actualize a true Christian life.

Recognize that those who actualize true Christianity are the greatest danger to the demons. For this reason, the satan of the senses has wrapped himself in the guise of Christianity, to instigate great confusion, so that not everyone will recognize right away what is truly Christian. For the true Christian life is the life according to the laws of God which I taught and lived as Jesus of Nazareth.

At all times, many righteous prophets and righteous men and women had to suffer in a similar way as I, Jesus.

The one who not only preaches the gospel of love and of life but also practices it and gives an understanding of the law of love and of life to many, out of his own actualization – that is, who shows them the path to Me, the Christ of God, in their inner being, so that they can follow Me – is a danger to those who have only draped themselves in the guise of "being Christian."

Because the woman in the earthly garment – the co-bearer of divine wisdom of whom I have already told you – is again bringing to mankind the eternal laws and the path into the eternal law, like Me and many prophets, she has to bear scorn, ridicule, contempt and slander. Despite everything, the eternal truth will gain acceptance, and Christ, linked with the divine wisdom, will emerge victorious.

The one who wants to recognize the ravenous wolves in sheep's clothing of the so-called Christians should examine the ecclesiastic authorities and their adherents – among them are also many rulers of this world who use My name as a means to an end:

Are these ecclesiastic and worldly office-bearers followers of the Nazarene?

Does the teaching of the church authorities bring people health and happiness?

Is the Mother Earth healthy, and does the atmosphere of the Earth offer protection to the Earth and the people?

Who are those who approve of killing?

Look for the wolves in the sheep's clothing of the sham Christians. Then you will find the Antichrist who comes towards you with My name – Christ – and deceives you, leading you astray.

Since My time as Jesus of Nazareth until today, it is always the same hypocrites – just in other earthly bodies – who have given themselves over to the demonic power and to the satan of the senses, to tempt the people with the guise of Christianity. The one who gives himself over to the darkness also serves the darkness. It will send its own into the world again and again, to deceive people and lead them astray.

As a flock, many peoples have followed human shepherds and were led by them into chaos. But even in the chaos, there is hope for the good, for the New Era, the era of Christ.

I Am the hope; I Am the truth and the life.

In spirit, I Am very close to My own and prepare My coming through them. This led and leads to battle. For the one does not give up easily, who, for centuries, had put on and still wears the guise of Christianity, in order to seduce still many with it.

I, Christ, Am the life; I do not destroy. I explain, so that those who see the serpent recognize it and crush its head. In this way, I expose the hypocrites and, at the same time, give them the opportunity to bow their head and become the least among their brothers and sisters.

Recognize that I am victorious through people who are with Me and prepare the New Era. Equipped with My strength, they are still fighting against their own faults and weaknesses and at the same time – with the power of love – against the hypocrites in Christian guise.

The battle in and with Me is a righteous battle. I, Christ, go before those who strive to do the will of the Father. The Earth will become cleansed and more light-filled, because I come, the Christ of God.

The word "swear" should be understood according to its meaning. It corresponds to the word "affirm."

CHAPTER 61

Jesus Prophesies the End of an Age

You will know them by their fruits (1).
Reincarnations of the power-hungry and of the messengers
of God in the course of time (2-3). The darklings fight with
all methods (4-5). Instructions for the time of horror (6-7).
The return of Christ: Learn to discern (8-9). Changes in the
solar system and on Earth (10). The impending end-time –
The path of evolution of mankind and of the Earth into light-
materiality – The Kingdom of Peace – The last rebellion of
Satan – The "Let there be" of God: Dissolution of all coarse-
material things – The preparation for the return of Christ
through the divine wisdom – The coming of Christ, the
greatest event (11). Recognize the signs of the times (12-14).
The one who is awake does not waste the hour (15-19)

1. And when Jesus sat on the Mount of Olives, the
disciples came alone to Him, saying, "Tell us, when
will this happen? And what shall the sign of Your coming be and that of the end of the world?" Jesus answered and said to them, "Take care that no one lead
you astray. For many will come in My name and say: I
am Christ, and they will lead many astray." (Chap. 61:1)

I, Christ, explain, correct
and deepen the word:

Do not believe anyone who lets his name be honored
and claims to be the greatest and lets himself be vener-

ated as such. And do not believe anyone who says that he is the reincarnated Christ; for I will not come into the flesh again, but I Am with My own in the spirit.

However, everyone who serves, who praises only the name of the Lord, who does good deeds, bringing them into the world so that the good fruits may be visible for many, is a righteous guide; I act through him. You should not recognize them by their words, but by their fruits.

The turn of time in which I am coming closer and closer to My own can be compared to late summer and to autumn, for the time of change from the old sinful world to the New Era is a time of harvest.

Those who live in Me bring good fruits; and those who have taken and take My name in vain for their purposes, now show their bad fruits. The turn of time shows very clearly the good fruits and the bad ones.

Recognize: Late summer and autumn have already dawned for the sinful time. The fruits are becoming visible – the harvest is underway.

2. *And you will hear of wars and rumors of war; see to it that you are not bewildered. For all this must come to pass, but it is not yet the end. For one nation will rise against the other and one kingdom against the other; and there will be famines and pestilences and earthquakes in various places. And this will be just the beginning of sorrow.*

3. *And in those days, those who have power will gather the lands and the riches of the Earth for their*

own pleasure and will oppress the many others who suffer need, they will subjugate them and keep them in bondage and use them to increase their riches; and they will oppress even the animals of the field, setting up the abominable. But God will send them His messengers, and these will proclaim His laws which people have hidden with their tradition, and those who transgress them will die. (Chap. 61:2-3)

I, Christ, explain, correct
and deepen the word:

What was foretold has already begun [1989] and is taking its course like clockwork. One disaster follows the other and one blow of fate comes after the other. By this, the change of times can be recognized.

The sinful world is passing away. In it, the birth of the new age is already dawning; and the spiritually awakened generations, from which the spiritual humanity of the New Era will emerge, are manifesting themselves.

The present time [1989] is like the time of Noah or that of the destruction of Pompeii. The majority of people seduce and let themselves be seduced. Even though they hear about the signs of the times, they remain sinful people. They perished and are perishing with their riches and their external might.

In the course of past epochs, many of these souls came into earthly bodies again and again, and many began to act again where they had left off before, at their hour of death – only in another time, with other means and other methods. Many held and hold the same offices again and again, be it as rulers of nations and states or as church leaders. Their hunger for power pushed and pushes them to Earth again and again, in order to assume these positions.

As human beings, they then tried and try, again and again, to keep the wheel of the world, the external structures, on its usual course. Thus, over the centuries, they enacted and enact similar laws for the people. And the nations have let and still let themselves be more or less subjugated by their authorities and obey the leaders over and over again, who did the same or similar things already in former incarnations. Because it is always the same ones who rule the countries and distinguish themselves as church leaders, the same processes are repeated again and again in many a country as in bygone times. Blows of fate, disasters, and chaotic situations merely have different names. However, in many cases, they are worse today than in the past.

In everything that is negative is also the positive: In this time of decline and emergence, the light of Christ breaks through, again and again. It is the time of the Spirit of God, the New Era, the era of Christ, who I Am.

Recognize that in the change from the old sinful world to the New Era, messengers of God came and also come, again and again. Many righteous men and women are now in My service for the New Era.

The whole truth will become manifest – even if it was covered up for many centuries, intentionally and unintentionally, by people who were far from God. The messengers of God are again proclaiming the laws of God and strive to carry the gospel of love around the Earth, from continent to continent, from city to city, from town to town, from village to village. They are preparing the Kingdom of God on this Earth. Many people will awaken through the activity of the messengers of God and take the path to inner life.

4. Then, they will deliver you up to be tortured and will kill you. And you will be hated by all peoples for My name's sake. And then, many will be attacked and will betray one another and hate one another. And many false prophets will rise and will lead many astray.

5. And because iniquity will prevail, the love in many will grow cold. But the one who endures until the end will be saved. And this gospel of the Kingdom of God will be preached in the whole world as witness to all nations, and then the end will come. (Chap. 61:4-5)

I, Christ, explain, correct
and deepen the word:

This is how it happened in the past centuries: My own were tortured and killed.

What was, continues. Again and again, it is the same wolves in sheep's clothing who come into the world with their hunger for power. They also want to extinguish the Christ-light, which is a thorn in their eye, and for this purpose they also take My name in vain. You can hear their howling when the messengers of God confront them with their satanic works, which they do – as they even say – in My name.

Recognize that the messengers of God were once tormented, tortured and killed. In today's time, [1989] they are slandered, ridiculed, mocked and scorned. The true Christians are now persecuted, but with other means and methods, through defamation in the media, which they call the press, radio and the like. Behind these are those who feel threatened by the truth, the representatives of the churches, the pastors, priests and the so-called "sect-commissioners" of the churches, as well as the so-called politicians, journalists and reporters – and all the others who believe in them. And in today's time [1989], many righteous men and women are hated by those who call themselves Christians, because these righteous ones follow Me, the Christ.

Recognize that as it was at all times, so it also is in the change from the old sinful world to the New Era. Many people speak about Me, the Christ. But if they are touched by a slight breeze, for example, a slanderous statement, they collapse and betray Me. Fearing for their earthly life, for their prestige and position, they betray and hate, even each other.

Using the most varied methods, the darkling interferes in the nations and incites one people against the other. This is possible because people are not in unity with one another. Nations consider each other as enemies and develop aggressions and fear for the future. All this is stirred up again and again by the darklings, for they want to keep the masses agitated. Then they come as false prophets and pretend to be bringers of salvation; they tie people to their "mission" and to their person – but do not orient them to Me, the Christ.

In the change from the old sinful world to the New Era, the Era of Light, the darkling attacks the light along a wide front. But who can withstand the light indefinitely? No man and no soul either, no dark power – not even when they take My name in vain and oppose the true Christians. The light, the I Am, is stronger.

Recognize that I Am the light of the world which is not bound to time. The light permeates space and time and will make everything new. The time is coming when there will be neither retreat nor advance for the darkling, but only capitulation and – as for every single person and every soul – the turnabout to the light, which I Am.

In this final battle, even though the iniquities prevail and love grows ever colder in the hearts of many men, the light is already visible: It is the Christ, who I Am, who brings the light onto the Earth through messengers, through the pioneers of the New Era. Many people will pass away. But many, who have withstood the battle with the forces of darkness, will also be rescued. Those who remain faithful to Me will keep the gospel of love and continue to proclaim the Kingdom of God all over the Earth and bear witness of the truth, which I Am, that dwells in them, that speaks and acts through them: Christ.

6. *Therefore, when you see the abomination of the desolation, spoken of by the prophet Daniel, at the holy place (may the one who reads this grasp it!), then may whoever is in Judea flee to the mountains. And may whoever is on the roof not come down to fetch anything from his house; and may whoever is in the field not turn back to fetch his clothes.*

7. *But woe to those who are with child and the nursing mothers in those days! Pray that your flight take place neither in winter nor on the Sabbath. For then, there will be a great tribulation, as has not been from the beginning of the world until this time, and will never be anymore. And if these days were not shortened, then no flesh would be saved. But for the sake of the chosen ones, those days will be shortened.*
(Chap. 61:6-7)

I, Christ, explain, correct
and deepen the word:

What was revealed at all times to man by the Eternal through the prophets is now imminent – even though the admonishments and indications of the Eternal through the prophets met no response from most people. This great turn of time is dawning.

The one who still worries about his external things and wants to hold onto and increase them, not only stays tied to them, but will also perish with all his belongings. To the same extent that the world draws to an end, the Kingdom of God on Earth emerges very gradually, despite affliction and misery.

When you recognize that the world is falling apart, do not turn back, and do not stop to fetch or put order in this or that. Go to God's dwelling place which is in you and let yourself be guided by Him who dwells in you.

It is written, "Woe to those who are with child and the nursing mothers in those days!" When the fruit in the womb of the mother is full of light and strength, because father and mother live in God, it will be protected. But when the fruit in the womb of the mother is of this old sinful world, that is, when it is poor in light, just as the father and mother are poor in light, then it can be taken from them, depending on the underlying causes. Many a body which bears a light-poor fruit will also be taken away in this time of horror, the likes of which the world has not yet experienced.

Pray that the trumpets of order do not sound on a Sabbath, when people indulge even more in their life of pleasure, instead of praying to God and thanking Him for His guidance and help. Many who could give external help will not be available then. Pray that the great clean-up on Earth does not happen in winter; for many will have hardly any belongings with them and much will be destroyed, so that often they will not find refuge in a house, but in the open air or in open shelters. Then many will be cold and freeze, also those with child.

Many have relied on this world and its governments and will lose overnight all that they believe to be their property and security. The eternal, kind God, your Father and Mine, has already shortened the time for His faithful ones and will shorten it once more, when the chaos has reached its climax. As a sign of victory, many who bear the seal of love on their forehead will continue to build and establish the Kingdom of Peace of Jesus Christ in the whole world, on its ruins and chaos.

8. *Then if anyone says to you: Behold, here is Christ, or there, believe not so hastily. For false Christs and false prophets will arise and show great signs and do great miracles, so that, if possible, even the chosen ones will be deceived. Behold, I have told you this before it happens.*

9. *Therefore, when they say to you: Behold, He is in the wilderness, do not go out; behold, He is in the secret chambers, do not believe so hastily. For just as the light comes out of the east and shines as far as the west, so will be the coming of the Son of Man. For the vultures gather wherever there is a carcass.*
(Chap. 61:8-9)

I, Christ, explain, correct
and deepen the word:

Know that I will come to My own in the spirit – but not in the shell of flesh anymore.

If someone says that Christ is here or there, then remember that I have told you before: I will not come into the flesh anymore. As Jesus, I took on the flesh for you and overcame it for you, so that you, too, can overcome it through Me, the Christ, and that you, too, will attain resurrection and spiritual rebirth and thereby the reunification with God, your Father and Mine.

When you actualize the eternal laws, you learn to discern, for there will not only be false prophets. Especially during this great turn of time, there are many righteous men and women – people whom I have sent to you, who strive honestly and uprightly to bring you the laws of God and to found the Kingdom of Peace in the middle of tribulation and the end of the world. They are those who fulfill the gospel of love and thus bring the Kingdom of God to this Earth.

You shall know them by their fruits.

10. Immediately after the tribulation of those days, the sun will be darkened, and the moon will lose its light, and the stars will fall from heaven, and the powers of the heavens will be shaken. (Chap. 61:10)

I, Christ, explain, correct
and deepen the word:

With mighty turbulences in the whole solar system, the planets will come out of their orbits and will, for the time being, group themselves in another course around the present sun. The moon, too, will be given another position, and will enter another gravitational relationship with the Earth. Thus, the rhythm of day and night, the seasons and the tides will change on the Earth. With these events, a temporary darkening of the sun will come about.

"The stars will fall from heaven" means that mighty meteors will fall to the Earth. Through this, too, the planet Earth will change accordingly. The seas will seek other basins.

The high mountains will pass away; new heights and valleys will come into being. The Earth will become more gentle in its overall appearance.

Recognize that I make everything new.

11. And then, the sign of the Son of Man will appear in heaven; and then, all the peoples on Earth will mourn and will see the Son of Man coming in the clouds of heaven with great power and glory. And He will send His angels with a loud voice as that of a trumpet, and they will gather His chosen ones from the four winds, from one end of heaven to the other. (Chap. 61:11)

I, Christ, explain, correct and deepen the word:

The sign of the Son of Man is the light of Christ, who I Am. In the spirit, I come to My own, who serve Me in the earthly garment and inhabit the Kingdom of God, whose ruler I Am.

Recognize that I will not come from one day to the next, nor all of a sudden. All great events send their light or their shadow ahead of them. I Am the light of the world. My coming in the spirit is the greatest event for the Earth and for mankind. I, the Christ, have already set out, for My light is already effective on the Earth and in the atmosphere, because prophets of God and faithful men and women are preparing the way for Me, more and more.

The prophets of God in the Old Covenant and all prophets of God and enlightened men and women during the past two thousand years warned mankind again and again of its own sowing and called for turning back. From many facets of the eternal truth, mankind was shown its satanic seed and its corresponding future, in case it does not turn back and fulfill the laws of God. The forthcoming end-time was and is talked about at ever shorter intervals. But the majority of people lived and continue to live in sin and danced and continue to dance around their golden calf: around their ego, which seeks the "mine and me," and the life of pleasure. The admonishments come true. Mankind is in the so-called end-time.

Recognize that the word "end-time" does not mean the end of matter, the end of the planet Earth, but the end of all that is against God. Materialism is coming to an end.

Just as the Kingdom of Peace is emerging very gradually on Earth, large parts of matter, too, will very gradually refine; for it is written: I make all things new. A new heaven and a new Earth will emerge, and man will grow into a new time, the Era of Light. On this path of evolution towards more light-filled and finer forms, everything will be spiritualized more and more – up to light-materiality, to finer matter. For the people of the New Era will increase the light in and on the Earth and, through their spiritual life, will continue to raise the vibration of the Earth and of the entire solar system. Once the Kingdom of Peace has risen on the finer matter, on the light-material Earth, another sun will also shine.

Recognize that after the Kingdom of Peace, the satanic, the demon, is once again allowed to try his strength against Me, the Christ, for even then, he still will have the intent to reconquer the Earth. However, then he will have to recognize that the "Let there be" of God is in full swing and that he has fully used up the time span, the period of grace, that was given to him once more by God, our Father.

After this earth-encompassing event, all highly condensed planets will gradually burst apart and the purely spiritual substances in the material planets will come out of their shells, just as the souls of people whose bodies have died. The abandoned material parts of planets will then disintegrate more and more. Then, all that is coarse-material will gradually become fine-material, for God is pure, fine-material energy. God is spirit, power, love and wisdom.

The divine Wisdom has assumed the great task of bearing My light of peace and of unity in advance, and of bringing it to all the peoples of this Earth, and thus, to all people of good will. Through her, My light radiates out in countless facets of life: It is My word, which is manifest and becomes manifest through the mouth of My prophetess who, at the same time, is the emissary of God, and through many righteous men and women. My light also brings to the people the Inner Path to the heart of God. It also proclaims the Kingdom of Peace and causes the sons and daughters of God who are in the Mission of Redemption – before all others, the lineage of David, as well as people from other lineages – to spread the Work of Redemption and found and build up the Kingdom of Peace.

I am drawing ever closer to My own. I Am ever closer, more and more directly with them, to the same degree in which they advance on the path within, thus continuing to build the Kingdom of Peace from generation to generation. Since My light is already radiating into this world and is announcing My coming through the divine Wisdom much has already been accomplished on Earth according to My will.

Recognize that even now [1989], the angels of heaven and the faithful ones in earthly garment herald, with a loud voice, the ruler of the Kingdom of Peace, and the Kingdom of Peace, itself. Even now, many men and women gather from the four winds, to live with one another and to prepare themselves for the greatest event in the atmosphere and on earth: My coming. Then, when the trumpets sound from the heavens, when from the Spirit of God the cherubs of the four Natures announce Me, I will appear with all might and glory and assume rulership. Then, the people will be *one* flock and I will be their Shepherd – Christ.

But before all this occurs, great lamentation will come over the Earth and all those who do not bear the seal on their forehead will be taken away. They will then continue their path as souls.

Recognize that the light of Christ is the light of the New Era. I announce My coming by radiating My light out ahead of Me.

12. *Learn a parable about the fig tree: When its branches are tender and full of sap and put forth leaves, you know that summer is near. Likewise, when you see all that, you will know that it is imminent. Verily, I say to you, this generation will not pass away until all this is fulfilled. Heaven and Earth will pass away, but My words will not pass away.*

13. *No one knows of the day and the hour, not even the angels in heaven, but only the All-Father. Just as it was in the days of Noah, so will the coming of the Son of Man be.*

14. For it is just as in the days before the deluge – they ate, they drank, they seduced and let themselves be seduced, until the day Noah entered the ark. And they took no heed of it, until the deluge came and took them all away; so will the coming of the Son of Man also be. (Chap. 61:12-14)

I, Christ, explain, correct
and deepen the word:

The one who watches the occurrences and events on this Earth and hears about the blows of fate of people all over the world realizes that the course of events of the end of the world are casting their shadow before them as a sign, and that mankind is in the midst of the disintegration of the old sinful world. The one who is alert also realizes that the sinful person cannot withstand the great upheavals.

Recognize that these upheavals are the effects of equally tremendous causes, through which the law of sowing and reaping removes sin from the Earth. People in deep sin will then no longer have a place to stay on Earth; for the New Era, the era of Christ, will rise from the ruins and will bring forth the new heaven and the new Earth.

The one who stands in the shadow will perish from the coldness of his own ego, of his base senses and drives.

15. *Then two will be in the field; one will be taken and the other will be left. Two women will be grinding at the mill; one will be taken, the other will be left. Watch, therefore, for you do not know the hour when your Lord will come.*

16. *But you should know this: If the caretaker of the house had known at which hour the thief comes, he would have watched and would not have let his house be broken into. Therefore, you, too, be ready; for the Son of Man will come at an hour when you do not expect Him.*

17. *Who then is a faithful and wise servant, whom his master has placed over his servants, that he may give them to eat at the right time? Blessed be this servant when his master comes and finds him so doing. Verily, I say to you: He will place him over all his possessions.*

18. *But if the bad servant says in his heart, 'My master will delay for long' and begins to beat his fellow servants, to eat with the glutton and drink with the drunken,*

19. *the master of this servant will come on a day and at an hour when he does not expect him. And he will give him his due with the hypocrites in the outer darkness, with the cruel ones and those who have no love and no pity: And there will be weeping and gnashing of teeth. (Chap. 61:15-19)*

I, Christ, explain, correct
and deepen the word:

Watch and pray! Remain in Me and know that I Am in and with you. For the one who is watchful and awaits the Lord will not miss the hour in which I come, and he will live to see the tribulation and cruelty only from afar, because he did not let himself be lulled to sleep by the world and be drawn into it.

Remain active in My Spirit and stand strong – I come.

CHAPTER 62

The Parable of the Ten Virgins

The one who fulfills the commandments of love
is the watchful one. He has the Inner Light,
the seal on his forehead (1-7)

1. *Then the Kingdom of Heaven will be like ten virgins who took their lamps and went forth to meet the bridegroom. And five of them were wise, and five were foolish.*

2. *The foolish took their lamps, but took no oil with them. But the wise ones took oil in their vessels with their lamps.*

3. *Since the bridegroom was a long time coming, they all became sleepy and fell asleep. But at midnight there was a loud cry, 'Behold, the bridegroom is coming. Go out to meet Him!' Then all those virgins rose and trimmed their lamps.*

4. *But the foolish ones said to the wise ones, 'Give us of your oil, for our lamps have gone out.' But the wise ones answered, saying, 'No, otherwise there will not be enough for us and for you. Go rather to the shopkeeper and buy for yourselves.'*

5. *And while they went to buy, the bridegroom came, and those who were ready went with Him to the wedding. And the door was locked.*

6. *Afterwards, the other virgins, too, came, saying, 'Lord, lord, open to us.' He answered, saying, 'Verily, I say to you, I do not know you.'*

7. Therefore watch, for you know neither the day nor the hour when the Son of Man will come. Keep your lamps burning." (Chap. 62:1-7)

I, Christ, explain, correct
and deepen the word:

The watchful person who awaits his Lord can be compared to the wise virgins. They also took along a reserve of oil in their vessels for their lamps. This means that they bore the light within themselves, through the actualization of the laws of God.

The watchful person who takes care that he fulfill the commandments of love will have the Inner Light: It is the seal on his forehead.

But if a person only realized that he does not bear any light within himself when the Christ of God has already drawn very close to His own, and it is only then that he sets out to walk the path to the heart of God, then his soul in the human garment will not behold Me, the Christ. For the one who, to the very end, is servile to the world will pass away in the time when I assume the rulership over this Earth. The light-poor soul will then set out on its path to higher forms of life in the spheres of purification and will walk it with much hardship and heartache.

The one who does not know Me has not received Me either, and for this reason, also bears little light in his soul. These people have indeed heard of My coming, they have indeed spoken of the bridegroom, but they did not array themselves with the adornment of inner life and with the virtue of selflessness, in order to come toward Me, the bridegroom. But the true brides, who arrayed themselves with the virtue of selfless love and with the adornment of inner life, and have thus kindled the inner light, will be with Me, the bridegroom.

The stronger the light grows on Earth, the more the door will be closed to those who only heard and spoke of Me, but did not accept and receive Me. The door then remains closed for the incarnation of souls which did not unfold their inner light.

The words "I do not know you" imply that you do not know Me because you do not know yourselves. And as long as you do not know Me, you cannot enter the light, either; for I Am the light of the world, the truth and the life.

CHAPTER 63

The Parable of the Talents

*The one to whom is given shall pass it on – God rewards
only the one who gives from the heart (1-12)*

1. And He continued, saying, "The Kingdom of Heaven is like a man traveling into a far country, who called his servants and entrusted them with his possessions. And to one he gave five talents, to another two, and to the third one, each one according to his abilities, and left straightaway.

2. Then the one who had received five talents went forth and traded with them and made five talents more. Likewise, the one who had received two talents made two talents more. But the one who had received one went forth and dug a hole and hid his master's money.

3. After a long time, the master of these servants came and settled accounts with them. And the one who had received five talents came forward and also brought the others, saying, 'Master, you gave me five talents; behold, with them, I gained five talents more.' His master said to him, 'Well done, you good and faithful servant, you have been faithful over a little, I will put you in charge of many things. Enter into the joy of your master.'

4. The one who had received two talents came forward as well, saying, 'Master, you have given me two

talents; behold, with them I gained two talents more.'
His master said to him, 'Well done, you good and faithful servant, you have been faithful over a little, I will
put you in charge of many things. Enter into the joy of
your master.'

5. The one who had received one talent also came
forward, saying, 'Master, I knew that you are a hard
man; you reap where you have not sown and gather
where you have not strewn. And I was afraid and went
forth and hid your talent in the earth; behold, you have
what is yours.'

6. But his master answered, saying to him, 'You
wicked and lazy servant, did you know that I reap
where I have not sown and gather where I have not
strewn? You should have taken my money to the money-
dealer, in order to gain interest and, on my return, I
would have taken what is mine with profit.'

7. For this reason, take the talent from him and give
it to the one who has two talents. For to the one who
has increased will be given and he will have in abundance; but from the one who did not increase, what he
has shall also be taken. And cast the useless servant out
into the outer darkness; for that is the portion which he
has chosen."

8. Jesus also said to His disciples, "Be true moneychangers of the Kingdom of God, discard the bad and
false and retain the good and true."

9. Jesus sat opposite the offering box and watched
how people cast money into the offering box, and many
rich ones cast in a lot.

10. And a poor widow came, and she threw in two mites which were hardly worth anything.

11. And He called His disciples to Him, saying, "Verily, I say to you, that this poor widow threw more into the offering box than all others.

12. For all others gave of their surplus, but of her poverty she gave all that she had, namely, her livelihood." (Chap. 63:1-12)

I, Christ, explain, correct
and deepen the word:

Take heed: The one to whom it is given should not keep what he has received for himself, but pass it on. For the law is selfless, giving love. Everyone has received the commandments from God. What he has actualized from the commandments, he should pass on. For then it multiplies in the world for the good of many.

The one who fulfills the commandments feels that he should selflessly make use of his talents and abilities for the divine. The one who does this for the good of his neighbor brings the life of God into this world. He will offer the bread of inner life to many; for with his abilities and talents, he selflessly prepares the hearts of his neighbors for the inner life, so that they no longer hunger and thirst.

However, the one who did not actualize the commandments of God is a slave to sin and will remain in servitude to it and suffer under this, until he awakens to the filiation in God through the actualization of the commandments.

The one whose heart is filled gives from his heart, that is, selflessly. God does not look at the external gifts, but at the selfless gifts of the heart, at what a person has actualized and passes on selflessly. For only the gifts of selfless love contain power and light. The one who is able to give of this is rich in his heart.

Recognize that the one who does not give from his heart also does not receive from the heart of God. Only the one who gives from his heart will also be rewarded from the heart, from God. God loves all of His children. He has given equally much to all. God does not reward what the human ego gives, the ego which flaunts itself and is self-satisfied, but rewards the sincerity and selflessness, that which comes from the depth of the soul – what is from God.

CHAPTER 64

About the Nature of God

The powers of the Father-Mother-Principle are in man and woman; therefore, both are equal (1-3). Recognize the invisible in the visible; perceive God, the life, in everything (4-5). About the law of attraction in all Being – The decision for Christ's Redeemer-work in the throne room of God – The Mission of Redemption – The bearers of divine wisdom carry with Christ the main responsibility for the Work of Redemption – The detachments of incarnations of the sons and daughters of God who are in the mission – The incarnation of Christ – The mission remains until it is fulfilled (6-11). The spiritually dead (12). The free will must never be influenced (13)

1. *Jesus came to a fountain near Bethany, around which grew twelve palm trees, where He often went with His disciples to teach them the mysteries of the Kingdom of God. There He sat beneath the shade of the trees, and His disciples with Him.*

2. *And one of them said, "Master, it is written of old, Elohim made man in His own image and created man and woman. Why then do you say that God is one?" And Jesus said to them, "Verily, I say to you, in God there is neither man nor woman and yet both are one, and God is both in one. He is She and She is He. Elohim – our God – is perfect, infinite and one.*

703

3. Thus, in the man, the father is personified and the mother hidden; and in the woman, the mother is personified and the father hidden. Therefore, the name of the father and the mother shall be equally hallowed; for they are the great powers of God, and the one is not without the other in the one God. (Chap. 64:1-3)

I, Christ, explain, correct
and deepen the word:

In the Spirit of God, the law of inner life, there are no sexes, but the giving and receiving powers. I call the giving power, the principle of the male, and the receiving power, the principle of the female.

Recognize that when I speak of the male or the female, I am speaking of the two poles, the two principles of life, the giving pole and the receiving pole, that is, the male principle and the female principle. The powers of the father are manifest in the man: the male pole or principle, the giving pole, also called the spiritually creating or begetting element; but hidden in it is also the female pole, the female principle, the mother, the receiving and maintaining life. Correspondingly, the powers of the mother are manifest in the woman, in the receiving pole, the female principle, who receives and maintains life; and hidden in her is also the male, the giving one, the father.

Both powers, the giving principle and the receiving principle, are matched with each other. As beings, they are two – and yet one: the giving principle and the receiving and maintaining principle. Just as the giving principle, the male, has a greater share of creative powers and a lesser share of female powers – that is, receiving powers – the female, the receiving principle, the receiving pole, has more female aspects – that is, motherly aspects – and fewer male, fatherly, that is, giving, powers.

Recognize that the Being is contained in every power, whether giving or receiving. Therefore, the woman should be respected, just as the man. For both powers are contained in both, the male as well as the female element, the father-principle and the mother-principle. Therefore, your Father, who is also My Father, is the Father-Mother-God. Both powers are united in Him and are active in all Being. This is the impersonal Spirit of the inner life, the selfless love, power and wisdom.

In the world, the one who considers the woman inferior and places the man above the woman violates the law of life, the Father-Mother-Principle which is the all-law.

4. *Adore God, who is above you, beneath you, on the right hand, on the left hand, before you, behind you, within you and around you. Verily, there is but one God. He is all things in the All, and all things exist in Him, the source of all life and of all substance, without beginning and without end.*

5. The things which are visible and pass away are manifestations of the invisible which is eternal, so that, from the visible things of nature, you may reach the invisible things of the Godhead; and through the natural, you reach the supernatural. (Chap. 64:4-5)

I, Christ, explain, correct
and deepen the word:

You have read that all things visible are manifestations of the invisible, the Eternal. Therefore, learn to recognize, in all visible things, the life, the invisible, which is hidden in everything.

Everything will become evident to the person who strives to fulfill the laws of God. He sees what is hidden to the one who has turned to the world: the life which is the power and the Being in all. It is the heritage of the soul, the Spirit, God, who is the life and the substance and the form of life – that is: the All in all things.

Recognize that every soul has to again come into its heritage, that which is invisible to man, the spiritually divine. For every pure being has its origin in the Spirit, in God, and every soul will purify itself and, as a pure being, will return to the origin, into the Spirit, God, to the life, into the Father-Mother-Principle.

6. Verily, Elohim created man in the image of God, male and female, and all of nature is an image of God;

therefore, God is both male and female, not divided, but both in one, undivided and eternal, in whom are all things, the visible and the invisible.

7. They came from the eternal and will return into the eternal: spirit to spirit, soul to soul, mind to mind, feeling to feeling, life to life, form to form, dust to dust.

8. In the beginning is the will of God and then came His Son, the divine love, and the beloved daughter, the holy wisdom, likewise from the one eternal source; and from it have come the generations of the spirit beings of God, the sons and daughters of the Eternal.

9. And these descend to Earth and dwell with men and teach them the ways of God, to love the laws of the Eternal and to obey them, so that they may find salvation in them.

10. Many nations have seen their days. They have revealed themselves to them under various names, and the peoples rejoiced in their light; and even now they come to you again, but Israel does not receive them.

11. Verily, I say to you, my twelve whom I have chosen: Everything which has been said by them of old time is true – but distorted through the false conceptions of men." (Chap. 64:6-11)

I, Christ, explain, correct
and deepen the word:

Everything pure is in God and everything pure comes from God.

Beings of light come to Earth from the Eternal and to the Eternal, they will return.

The law of attraction says that the one who lives in the Spirit of God also moves in the Spirit of God, because he has his home in Him.

In accordance with this law of attraction – like attracts like – a soul or a person comes together with those souls or people who bear the same or something similar in themselves, so that they may clear up together what is sinful. Thus, the intellectual will meet intellectuals who have stored and move the same or like things in their consciousness. In the same way, an emotional person meets emotional people. If they have something to clear up with each other, they will be given the opportunity for this, by being brought together.

In this way, the divine aspect, too, finds its way again to the divine aspect. This means that souls and people who have the same or similar tendencies of inner life find each other, in order to help and serve each other and to unfold the inner life, the life which unifies all, more and more. Thus, form finds its way to form. For each form radiates its level of consciousness and is irradiated by the inner life, so that substance and form may rise towards the next higher spiritual form.

Dust finds its way to the same substance, dust, and lives as power and consciousness in God, who also dwells in the speck of dust, who stimulates it to evolve and guides it to the next higher spiritual form.

Like joins with like. In the material world, people join together; in the realms of the souls, souls join together; and in the eternal Being, everything which is in spiritual evolution joins together: spiritual minerals, plants, animals and nature beings.

From the eternal Spirit, from the Father-Mother-Principle, God, the eternal Father, created and creates male and female principles, the sons and daughters of God, the spirit beings, which came and come forth from His love and wisdom, from the one source, God.

When the Fall event had almost reached its deepest point, I, the Son, the Co-Regent of the heavens, went to Earth in order to bring redemption to man. In the "It is finished" which I spoke on the cross through My earthly body, Jesus, salvation took place in all souls: My heritage, the part-power of the primordial power, divided into sparks and implanted itself in all souls. The Redeemer-spark began to shine in each soul and since then is its support and salvation.

Before I, Christ, left the heavens in order to be active as Jesus of Nazareth, My mighty, powerful Work of Redemption was decided in the throne room of the Eternal.

Many sons and daughters of God contributed part of their spiritual light-potential to the Redeemer-mission and thus take part in the Work of Redemption. The Redeemer-work leads all souls back, that is, takes them home into their inner being, so that after the death of the earthly body, the being from God will be able to again enter God, the law of life and love.

The sons and daughters of God incarnated into various lineages, above all, into the lineage of David, which leads the Work of Redemption. The divine Wisdom leads the way. It is the third nature of God, represented by the cherub of divine wisdom, the third law-angel.

As I have already revealed, the female principle of the bearer of divine wisdom is in the earthly garment [1989]; the male principle is in the spirit garment. Both – the female spirit-dual in the earthly garment and the male spirit-dual in the spirit – bear with Me, Christ, the main responsibility for the Work of Redemption and lead the way for the sons and daughters of God who are in the Mission of Redemption. They all have the task of teaching people the path to God, of instructing them to love and keep the laws of the Eternal and of obeying God in everything. With this, people find their way to the Redeemer-spark in their soul and make it shine more and more. Then it is a beacon for them on the path into the eternal Being. It is the Christ of God who lives in the Father.

So it happened and happens. In a lawful sequence, the sons and daughters of God who were and still are assigned to the Redeemer-work incarnated into the lineages of this Earth, with the dual-pair of divine wisdom leading the way.

In the Old Covenant, the first detachments – the first sons and daughters assigned to the Redeemer-work –

went from the heavens to Earth and incarnated. For Me, the Christ, they prepared the way to the people. First, the male principle, the cherub of divine wisdom, came to this Earth as a prophet and announced the coming of the Redeemer.

Unbeknown to the human being in earthly garment, some of the sons and daughters of God were placed at the side of the prophet, so that in the Old Covenant they could bring about, with him, what was intended for that time by the Spirit of God. When their earthly existence came to an end, some of these sons and daughters of God, from the first detachments, who had hardly burdened themselves, returned to the eternal Being before the throne of the Father, led by the male principle of divine wisdom, the cherub, who had served the Eternal as a prophet on Earth.

The task in the Redeemer-work, however, remained and remains as a seal for the New Era in the two principles of divine wisdom. This means that it is indelibly engraved in them until the fulfillment of the mission – just as in all the sons and daughters of God who are in the mission.

Some of them, who had laid aside their earthly garment, gathered again in the spheres of purification to form further detachments – along with those who then came from the heavens – in order to again go into the earthly garment. Again and again, detachments of sons and daughters of God incarnated, among whom were also many who had not fulfilled their task in the first incarnation-detachments.

Burdens arose in the succession of incarnations. Some fulfilled a part of their task, whereas others burdened themselves. They returned again to the soul realms and, as souls, then stayed in the respective spheres which corresponded to their level of consciousness.

Again and again, new detachments of sons and daughters of God formed up in order to prepare the way on Earth for Me, the Christ. Eventually, the decisive detachment for the Redeemer-work gathered: I, Christ, the Son of God, the Co-Regent of the heavens, came into the earthly garment, and with Me, many sons and daughters of God to serve and help Me. Many of them were among My followers; they had incarnated into Roman and Jewish families. Many of these sons and daughters of God were already burdened because of their previous incarnations and now, in their earthly garment, did not recognize the great event. Nevertheless, I brought a part of My divine heritage to the people. I was supported by the Father and by the messengers of light and by the few sons and daughters in earthly garment who recognized Me, their brother and Redeemer, the Redeemer of mankind.

After My return to the Father, as Co-Regent of the Heavens and Redeemer of mankind, the next spiritual detachment went into an earthly existence. Again, sons and daughters of God gathered in the spheres of purification with sons and daughters of God from the heavens, in order to incarnate together. Leading the way, the female principle of divine wisdom came with this detachment. After the death of their bodies, these souls, too, went again either into the soul realms or into more light-filled spheres.

Thus, in one detachment after the other, the sons and daughters of God came and come to the people in order to instruct them in the laws of life, so that they love and obey God and thus, in Christ, find their way home to God, their Father and ours. Each time, they also brought to Earth the thought of the Kingdom of God, and so it is gradually taking on form and shape on earth: It is the Kingdom of Peace of Jesus Christ. Leading the way, the female principle of divine wisdom came again and again in co-operation with her spirit-dual, the positive of divine wisdom who was and is in the spirit garment, in order to continue to prepare the way for the sons and daughters of God.

Almost two thousand years have now gone by since My life on Earth. The will of the Eternal is being carried out very gradually in and through the sons and daughters of God. More and more, they fulfill on Earth what is written in the Mission of Redemption: to teach with Me, Christ, all people to keep the laws of life and love, so that they may become free for the Kingdom of God. The sons and daughters of God who are in the Mission of Redemption come and go until what I, the Christ, have promised is fulfilled: *one* flock and *one* Shepherd, *one* people in Me, the Christ, *one* kingdom on Earth, the kingdom of the Eternal.

The mission of the Son, who I Am, is to bring home all that seemed to be lost. This mission is in the hearts of those who serve Me in the Work of Redemption.

Recognize that until the entire Redeemer-work is fulfilled on Earth as well as in the spheres of purification, all these sons and daughters of God are in the Redeemer-mission, with the divine wisdom leading the way.

In Me, the Christ, every soul finds its way to the Father.

"Many nations have seen their days. They have revealed themselves to them under various names, and the peoples rejoiced in their light; and even now they come to you again, but Israel does not receive them" means that the sons and daughters of God – divine wisdom leading the way – came in the Old Covenant as well as in the New Covenant, and, in the present time [1989], are again among the people, in order to work as pioneers for the New Era.

The turn of time from the old sinful world to the new age of light and of love has begun. Very gradually, the life in Me, the Christ of God, will blossom.

Since Israel did not receive Me, the Son of God, or the other sons and daughters of God who were and are in the Mission of Redemption, Israel now rises again in another country, as well as New Jerusalem.

12. *And then, Jesus said to Mary Magdalene, "It is written in the law, the one who leaves father and mother, let him die the death. But the law does not*

speak of the parents in this life, but of the indwelling
light which is in us until this very day. (Chap. 64:12)

I, Christ, explain, correct
and deepen the word:

The meaning of the words "... The one who leaves
father and mother, let him die the death" is the following: The Father-Mother-God is original Father and original Mother to each spirit being and each human being.
He is the indwelling light. When man forsakes it by
knowingly committing sin, then he is a spiritually dead
person. He will wander restlessly around in the shadows of his ego until his soul awakens and aspires to the
rebirth in the Spirit of God, in order to reunite with the
Father-Mother-God.

13. And so the one who renounces Christ, the Re-
deemer, the holy law, and the community of the elect,
let him die the death. Yes, let him be lost in the outer
darkness, for so he willed it and none can hinder him."
(Chap. 64:13)

I, Christ, explain, correct
and deepen the word:

These words mean that the one who renounces Me,
the Christ, renounces the eternal law, God, and the

715

community of those who do His will. He will remain in the darkness and be spiritually dead until he seeks the light of the world, which I Am in him.

Every soul and every person has the free will to fulfill the laws of God – or to walk in the darkness. Since the spiritual body – in its burdened state, called soul – is from God, for every soul the time will come when it will accept and fulfill what sets it free: the law of love and of life. If, however, soul and person want to walk in the darkness, then, according to the law of free will, they also have to bear what they caused in the darkness: the effects of their sowing.

The law of justice stipulates that everyone has the free will to accept or reject the divine. Yet each one has to bear what he has caused, himself.

The words "be lost" mean to leave the free will to your neighbor – and not force him to accept the divine which makes him free. The divine laws should be taught to the person; yet it should be left up to him whether to apply them or not and when to make use of them. The one who observes this fulfills the will of God that says: Each one should accept the divine freely. The one who forces his neighbor to do so acts against the justice, love and freedom of God.

CHAPTER 65

The Last Anointing by Mary Magdalene – Preparing the Betrayal

About true giving and helping the poor –
The shadows of the human ego prevent one from seeing the
light of God; man then speaks of the "mysteries
of God" (1-10)

1. And on the evening of the Sabbath before the Passover, Jesus was in Bethany and went to the house of Simon the leper, where a supper was prepared for Him. And Martha served, while Lazarus was one of those who sat at the table with Him.

2. And there came Mary called Magdalene, who had an alabaster flask containing a very precious and expensive ointment of spikenard. She opened the flask and poured it on the head of Jesus and anointed His feet and dried them with the hair of her head.

3. Then one of His disciples, Judas Iscariot, who was to betray Him, said, "Why this waste of ointment? It could have been sold at a good price, and the money given to the poor." But he did not say that because he cared for the poor, but because he was filled with jealousy and greed and had the purse and was in charge of the money. And they murmured about Magdalene.

4. But Jesus said, "Leave her in peace! Why do you trouble her? She has done all she could. She has done a

717

good deed to Me. You always have the poor with you, but you do not always have Me. She has anointed My body for My burial.

5. *Verily, I say to you, wherever this Gospel is preached in the whole world, what she has done will also be told there, in memory of her."*

6. *Then Satan entered into the heart of Judas Iscariot, and he went his way and conferred with the high priests and elders as to how he could betray Him. And they were glad and agreed with him on thirty pieces of silver, the price of a slave. He promised it to them and sought an opportunity to betray Him.*

7. *And at that moment, Jesus said to His disciples, "Preach to all people in the world, saying: Strive to receive the mysteries of light and to enter the kingdom of light; for now the time has come for this and now is the day of salvation.*

8. *Do not postpone it from one day to the next, from one cycle (of the wheel of reincarnation) to the next and from eon to eon, thinking that when you return to this world, you will then succeed in gaining the mysteries and entering the kingdom of light.*

9. *For you do not know when the number of perfected souls will be complete. For then, the gates of the kingdom of light will be shut and henceforth none will be able to enter, nor will anyone go out.*

10. *Strive so that you may enter as long as the call sounds, before the number of the perfect ones is sealed and complete, and the gate is shut."*
(Chap. 65:1-10)

I, Christ, explain, correct
and deepen the word:

How often do you hear in this world that "It could have been sold at a good price and the money given to the poor." Everyone who uses these words should ask himself just how sincerely he means them, how much he himself has contributed to help the poor.

It is not enough to give alms to the poor as the Pharisees do, in order to be seen by the people.

True giving consists in fulfilling the law of love and of life. Then, a gift is not the giving of alms, but a true help. Through it, the poor soul in the poor body finds its way to the law of "pray and work" and becomes rich in heart. Then the human being, too, will receive all that he needs to live as a child of God.

Thus, where the gospel of love and of life is first lived and then taught, the poor one who accepts and fulfills it becomes rich in his heart, and the poor person will also receive what he needs to live as a child of God. The fulfillment of the gospel is what brings about the truly good deeds.

The words "Strive to receive the mysteries of light" mean that the shadows of the human ego veil the light and prevent man from seeing the light of God. That is why, man speaks of the mysteries of the light, for he is not able to see it yet. The one who wants to see behind the mysteries must first look at his shadows and eliminate what he has recognized and what led to the shadows, so that he can find his way to the light of God and enter the Kingdom of God.

Therefore, do not put off what you have recognized to be human, from one day to the next, from one "cycle" to the next, from one eon to the next, believing that you can still clear it up in one of your next earthly lives. For who of you knows when the wheel of reincarnation will stand still for heavily burdened souls, and the gates for such incarnations will be shut?

Recognize that in this earthly existence you should strive to fulfill the laws of God. Therefore, do not postpone the actualization of the holy life from one day to the next, by saying that in a further incarnation after this earthly life you would be more successful in fulfilling the laws of God and in penetrating the veils which prevent you from seeing the light and the life.

Recognize that a person speaks about the mysteries of God as long as he himself has secrets from his fellow man. However, the one who aspires to perfection has no secrets from his fellow man, because the law of God which he fulfills harbors no secret.

The one who fulfills the laws of love and of life is an open book, and everything is also evident to him.

The grace of God is more intensely effective in this world today [1989]. He, the Almighty, has once again given a span of time to all souls and people and with it the possibility to make amends for everything that is impure.

CHAPTER 66

Teachings about Perfection

The true life is a life in God (1-3).
The pure beings live in the all-unity; they are one – Polarity as the unity in God – Mary Magdalene, an example of the receiving principle – All Being is based on polarity (4-11). The tri-unity: spirit, soul and man – When will the Kingdom of God come to earth? (12-13)

1. And Jesus taught them once more, saying, "God has awakened witnesses to the truth in every people and every age, that all may hear the will of the Eternal and do it, in order to afterwards enter the Kingdom of God as rulers and co-workers.

2. God is power, love and wisdom, and these three are one. God is truth, goodness and beauty, and these three are one.

3. God is justice, knowledge and purity, and these three are one. God is magnificence, compassion and holiness, and these three are one. (Chap. 66:1-3)

I, Christ, explain, correct
and deepen the word:

All substance is in God, and all powers of the All are in the One, God.

At all times, the Eternal sent messengers into this world who bore witness of the truth and brought evidence to the people that the truth, when lived, bestows life. For the true life is the life in God.

In God's law of love and of life, the word "compassion" means to suffer with, to feel with and to have understanding for all men and souls and for every creature.

4. *And these four tri-unities are one in the hidden divinity, the perfect, the infinite, the only One.*

5. *Likewise in every man who is complete, there are three persons, the son, the spouse and the father, and these three are one.*

6. *Likewise in every woman who is complete, there are three persons, the daughter, the spouse and the mother, and these three are one. And the man and the woman are one, just as God is one.*

7. *So it is also with God, the Father, in whom is neither male nor female and in whom are both, and each is threefold, and all are one in the hidden unity.*

8. *Do not marvel at that, for as it is above so it is below, and as it is below so it is above, and that which is on Earth is so, because it is so in heaven.*

9. *And I say to you once more: I and My bride are one, just as Mary Magdalene, whom I have chosen and sanctified to Myself as an example, is one with Me; I and My community are one. And the community is the elect of mankind for the salvation of all.*

10. The community of the Firstborn is the Mary of God. Thus speaks the Eternal. She is My mother and she has always conceived Me from the beginning and has given birth to Me as her Son in every age and clime. She is My bride, eternally one in holy communion with Me, her bridegroom. She is My daughter, for she has eternally issued and proceeded from Me, her Father, and rejoices in Me.

11. And these two tri-unities are one in the Eternal and are evident in each man and each woman who has become perfect and is eternally born of God, rejoicing in the light, and being ever more lifted up and made one with God, ever conceiving and bringing forth God for the salvation of many. (Chap. 66:4-11)

I, Christ, explain, correct
and deepen the word:

The words of men are symbols. With the words "man" and "woman" people primarily refer to the sexes. However, they should also be understood here as the principle of duality of the heavens, where there are no sexes.

Just as God is the power of all powers of the All, in the same way all beings from God bear the powers of the All. It is not the earthly body that bears these powers, but the pure spirit body in the innermost recesses of the incarnated soul.

In the spirit, "man" and "woman" mean the giving principle and the receiving principle. At the same time, they are son or daughter of God, and father or mother. Both are one in their giving and receiving radiation and are also one in God, in the law of life.

Perfection knows neither thine nor mine. For each pure being, all Being is its own, too, for it knows no personal possession. What one pure being possesses, the other one possesses, as well. They are not only at one in everything – they *are* one. From the all-unity, flow the fullness and the inner wealth.

Each soul and each person who is one with Me, the Christ, is also one with Me in the eternal Father. He is a chosen one and, with many chosen ones, forms the community which consists of those selected from the mankind of this Earth, for the redemption of all. From all four winds, I gathered and gather those who are one with Me or walk the path of becoming one with Me.

My union with Mary Magdalene is a symbol that all Being is based on polarity, also in the union of man and woman. I chose for Myself the bride of My soul as a sign that the giving and the receiving is a unity in God, molten into one another in the Eternal. With this, I bore witness that, in the sight of God, woman and man are equal, as unity and polarity in Him.

The soul of Mary Magdalene came very close to the radiation of My soul. She lived in Me, as a living example of the spiritual woman, of the receiving principle, and I – as the living, giving principle – in her. So, in

Me, she is the hallowed aspect of God, the receiving principle. In Jesus of Nazareth she was in Me, and she is in Me, the Christ – and we are in God. For the women of this Earth, she is the living example of a receiving principle which also bears the aspects of the giving principle in itself.

Mary Magdalene expected nothing. She was in Me, the Jesus, and is with Me and in Me, eternally. For all heavenly powers, giving and receiving, unite in all Being, in every spirit being, in the heavenly bodies and in the nature kingdoms, because all Being is based on polarity. All Being is substantial life, it is God in all things.

Recognize that everything which the Earth bears as light and power from God is given by God for the redemption of the souls, of the human beings and of the Earth.

God, the all-unity, the love and wisdom, breathes His I Am in each eon, in every new act of creation. And what the Eternal has breathed into this world is, in turn, He, Himself, All in all things. The pure powers of the Earth are also the pure powers of the heavens. Just as the pure powers, the pure Being, are effective on the Earth as substance, they are also effective in an all-encompassing way in the eternal Being.

12. *This is the mystery of the tri-unity in mankind and, moreover, the mystery of God must be fulfilled in every child of man, beholding the light, enduring suffer-*

*ing for the truth, ascending into heaven, and sending
forth the Spirit of truth. This is the path of salvation, for
the Kingdom of God is within."*

13. *And one said to Him, "Master, when will the
Kingdom of God come?" And He answered, saying,
"When that which is without will be as that which is
within, and that which is within will be as that which is
without, and the male and the female neither male nor
female, but the two in one. Those who have ears to
hear, let them hear." (Chap. 66:12-13)*

I, Christ, explain, correct
and deepen the word:

The tri-unity in mankind is the spirit, the soul and
the human being. The human being cannot breathe without the spirit and without the soul. Breath is life. God is
the breath, the life, the Spirit, which breathes through
soul and person, thus maintaining all mankind.

So that a person may change and find his way to his
true being, I teach the path of love. The one who walks
this path to inner enlightenment very gradually lays
aside his passions and desires and his reprehensible
earthly thoughts. Then he speaks words of life and acts
just as he has again become: divine. For only then, has
the person changed. His outer being has become his
true being, his inner being.

Only when mankind has changed in the light of the
truth will the Kingdom of God come to this Earth. For

when the outer has become like the inner and the inner like the outer, the person fulfills the works of God; and life on Earth is then the life in God. Then woman and man, the male and the female, are one and are the polarity in God. The positive and the negative principles – that is, the giving and the receiving beings – then live consciously as children of God.

CHAPTER 67

Entry into Jerusalem – The Last Judgment

Hosanna – Crucify Him: The one who thinks only of his own welfare is inconsistent – For the past 2000 years, the Jews have been reaping their sowing – Man should respect God in every created form and, therefore, in his neighbor, too; otherwise he will stand to the left of Christ (1-10). The expiation and purification of the most heavily burdened souls (11). What you have not done to one of the least of My own you have not done to Me, either (12-14). The path of evolution of the most heavily burdened souls (15)

1. And on the first day of the week, when they came near Jerusalem to the Mount of Olives by Bethphage and Bethany, He sent out two of His disciples and said to them, "Go into the village that lies before you and, as soon as you have entered, you will find a colt tied, on which no man has ever sat; untie him and bring him.

2. And if anyone says to you, 'Why do you do this?' Say that the Lord needs him. And they will let him come here."

3. And they went their way and found the colt tied in a place where two ways met, and they untied him. And some of those who stood there said to them, "What are you doing, that you untie the colt?" And they said to them as Jesus had commanded, and they let them go.

4. And they brought the colt to Jesus and laid their garments on the animal, and He sat on him. And many spread their garments on the way, and others cut down branches from the trees and strewed them on the way.

5. And those who went before and those who followed, cried, saying, "Hosanna, blessed be You who come in the name of Jehovah, blessed be the kingdom of our ancestor David and blessed be You who come in the name of the Highest! Hosanna in the highest!"

6. And Jesus entered Jerusalem and the temple, and after He had seen everything around, He told this parable to them, saying:

7. "When the Son of Man will come in His glory and all the holy angels with Him, He will sit upon the throne of His glory. And before Him all people will be gathered, and He will separate them from each other, as a shepherd divides His sheep from the goats. And He will place the sheep to His right, but the goats to His left.

8. Then the King will say to those at His right, 'Come here, you blessed of My Father, inherit the kingdom which has been prepared for you from the beginning of the world. For I was hungry and you gave Me food. I was thirsty and you gave Me to drink. I was a stranger and you took Me in. I was naked and you clothed Me. I was sick and you visited Me. I was captive and you came to Me.'

9. Then the righteous will respond, saying, 'Lord, when did we see You hungry and fed You, or thirsty and gave You to drink? When did we see You a stranger and took You in, or naked and clothed You? When did we see You sick, or captive and came to You?'

10. *And the King will answer and say to them, 'Behold, I show Myself to you in all created forms; and verily, I say to you: What you have done to one of the least among these My brothers, you have done to Me.'*
(Chap. 67:1-10)

I, Christ, explain, correct
and deepen the word:

The word "colt" refers to the female donkey that carried Me through the loudly shouting crowd of Jews who wanted to have their earthly king.

As long as man is concerned only with his material welfare, he will think, speak and act like the Jews who praised Me with their lips, hoping that, in Me, God would send to them – the sinful people – a man who would even confirm their vices and do what would help them lead a corrupt life of earthly pleasures and excesses, gluttony and drunkenness – in other words, who would make possible all they desired.

The same Jews who cried "Hosanna, blessed be the kingdom of our ancestor David and blessed be You who come in the name of the Highest" cried a few days later, "Crucify Him, set Barabbas free."

Recognize people by their language: The one who thinks only of his own welfare will today honor the one who could make it possible for him and will curse the same one tomorrow, because he did not make it possible for him.

Examine yourselves and your life, whether – in smaller or larger issues – you do not think, speak and act like the Jews of that time. In this way, many a one becomes a Judas. They will have to suffer for this – if not in this present incarnation, then in the realm of the souls or in one of the following incarnations; for what man sows, he will reap.

For nearly 2000 years now, and from one incarnation to the next, the Jews have been reaping what they have sown at that time and also in their further incarnations – until they accept and receive their Redeemer and repent of what they have caused.

Grasp in your hearts: Everything which bears life has the power, love and wisdom of God; and everything that lives, lives because God dwells in it.

God is the totality in all things. His power is undivided in all things. Therefore, God is everything in all things. In each created form, is God, is the All-in-all things. All that lives on Earth, every material form, bears in itself the spiritual form, that which is created by God, thus bearing everything that is in God, that is, the All in all things.

The one who does not respect this does not honor God, nor respect his neighbor. Therefore, he did not feed him, he did not give him to drink, he did not take him in, did not clothe him, and did not serve him. The one who has not respected God in each form has not recognized God in his neighbor, either, and thus, has neither accepted nor received God. His place will be to My left.

11. Then He will also say to those on his left, 'Depart from Me, you evil souls, into the eon-long fire which you have prepared for yourselves, until you are purified seven times and freed from your sins. (Chap. 67:11)

I, Christ, explain, correct
and deepen the word:

The word "evil" means the corruptness of the soul which has covered all seven basic powers of God with grave sins.

The expiation of grave sins takes place in the cycle of eons*, for a deeply fallen soul often cannot expiate its burdens in shorter periods of time. In many cases, the soul in the spheres of purification as well as the human being would not be able to bear this. Furthermore, such a soul is bound to several or even many souls and human beings and becomes free only when all of them have forgiven it. It will also feel on its own soul-body the various afflictions which, as a human being, it caused to its neighbor. This expiation and purification can be the so-called hell, the fire, for such a soul.

---

* *The word "eons" means light-cycles or energy-cycles.*

12. For I was hungry and you did not feed Me. I was thirsty and you did not give Me to drink. I was a stranger and you did not take Me in, naked and you did not clothe Me, ill and captive and you did not visit Me.'

13. Then they will also respond, saying, 'Lord, when did we see You hungry or thirsty or a stranger or naked or ill and did not serve You?'

14. Then He will answer them, saying, 'Behold, I manifest Myself to you in all created forms, and verily, I say to you: What you have not done to one of the least among these, My brothers, you have not done to Me either. (Chap. 67:12-14)

I, Christ, explain, correct
and deepen the word:

Selfless love is the law of life. Only when his deeds are selfless, will man live consciously in God. Everything else relates to the human being, to his own person, and has no relationship to God, who is the all-unity and the selflessness. The one who serves his neighbor just to receive a reward from him already has his reward and will receive no further reward from God.

All forms of life live through the eternally streaming law, God, who is love, life and wisdom. The one who violates any form of life in sensations, thoughts, words or actions violates the law, God. Every human being is form created out of God. All stars and planets, every stone, every plant and every animal are forms created out of God.

God, the life, thus manifests Himself in all created forms. The one who does not selflessly serve all the powers of God that have taken on form sins against them and will have to bear and expiate what he has thereby inflicted upon himself. Thus, what you have not done selflessly to one of the least of My brothers, your neighbors, you have not done to Me, either.

Recognize that the one who inflicts sorrow upon his neighbor, exploits him and makes him work for little pay, thus accumulating riches, will feel on his own body all that he has caused to his neighbor.

I meet people in manifold shapes and forms. The one who does not accept and receive the life, which I Am in shape and form, repudiates his own life and often regains it only after eons of suffering. For no soul is lost – because I, Christ, the life, Am in each soul.

15. *And the cruel and loveless ones will go into severe punishment for eons, and if they do not repent, they will be utterly destroyed. But the righteous and merciful ones will enter into eternal life and eternal peace."* (Chap. 67:15)

I, Christ, explain, correct
and deepen the word:

The expression "be utterly destroyed" is to be understood as follows: Souls which have inflicted upon them-

734

selves the heaviest of burdens, which are the sins against the Holy Spirit – in other words, which have sinned against the eternal, holy life, despite knowing better – and do not repent, but continue to sin knowingly, will suffer harm on their soul body. Since each soul has eternal life, these souls will have to regenerate in the spiritual planes of evolution, that is, they will have to perfect their spiritual body again.

This also applies to the demons who will fight against Me until the dissolution of all material forms and even beyond that. As Fall beings, they are responsible for the entire potential of burdens and will also expiate accordingly, until the end of the Fall. On the other hand, individual souls and human beings expiate what they are guilty of.

All these heavily burdened souls will be integrated into the spiritual process of evolution, in order to build up again their spiritual life-buds, the particles of their spiritual body, and to align the spiritual types of atoms again with Me. Similar to the process of evolution in the eternal Being – from stone to plant, from plant to animal, and from animal to nature being – it will happen in these soul-bodies. In this way, such souls build their spiritual body up again and then enter the filiation of God again consciously – as children of selfless love. That which has been given to them, the filiation of God, has not been and will not be taken from them.

I repeat:

Such most heavily burdened souls, which have damaged parts of their spiritual body, go into the spiritual fields of evolution in order to restore what they have damaged by continuously burdening themselves. However, the filiation in God remains theirs.

CHAPTER 68

Parables
of Divine Judgment

"The Kingdom of God will be taken from you and given to another people which brings forth its fruits" (1-7). The fight against the messengers of God who also live what they teach (8-10). I came in Jesus and come as Christ (11). Inner and outer dignity – The earthly rulers will be broken on the cornerstone, Christ, who will become the capstone (12-14). Turn back in time, before fate takes its course – Human words, terms, standards and their meaning are but guides to the truth (15-20)

1. And Jesus told another parable, "There was a householder who planted a vineyard and hedged it in and dug a wine-press in it and built a tower and gave it over to the care of vine-dressers and went to a far country.

2. And when the time of the ripe fruits drew near, he sent his servants to the vine-dressers to collect the fruits from them. But the vine-dressers took the servants and beat the first one and stoned the second and killed the third.

3. Once again he sent to them other servants, of higher standing than the first ones, and they did the same to them. Finally, he sent to them his son, saying, 'They will acknowledge my son.'

4. But when the vine-dressers saw the son, they said among themselves, 'This is the heir, come, let us kill him and take possession of his inheritance.' And they took him, cast him out of the vineyard and slew him.

5. Now when the master of the vineyard comes, what will he do to those vine-dressers?" They said to Him, "He will kill these wicked men in a dreadful way and will give his vineyard into the care of other vine-dressers, who will deliver the fruits to him when they are ripe."

6. Jesus said to them, "Did you not read in the scripture: The stone which the builders rejected became the copingstone of the pyramid? This is the Lord's doing and it is marvelous in our eyes.

7. Therefore I say to you: The Kingdom of God will be taken from you and given to a people who bring forth its fruits. And the one who falls on this stone will be broken, but the one on whom it falls will be ground into dust." (Chap. 68:1-7)

I, Christ, explain, correct
and deepen the word:

Many parables which I, as Jesus of Nazareth, gave to My apostles, My disciples and the people still hold true for the present time [1989].

The statement "The Kingdom of God will be taken from you and given to a people who bring forth its fruits" was and is meant for the Jews and also for the so-called "representatives of Christ."

Even today, God is calling through His faithful and His prophets, and even today, is admonishing through them the "representatives of Christ" to bring forth the fruits of inner life. They may have wanted to spread My teaching, but it remained at that. Since they cannot show any fruits of inner life, but have spiritually empty hearts, they were and are driven by the lust for power and by greed, and they killed those sent by God, deriding and mocking them even today.

Now I gather from all four winds another chosen people who obey God and bring forth its spiritual fruits; and, with it, I will accomplish what I revealed through many righteous prophets: the Kingdom of God on this Earth.

8. *And when the high priests and Pharisees had heard these parables, they understood that He was speaking of them. But when they wanted to lay hands on Him, they feared the multitude, because the multitude took Him for a prophet.*

9. *The disciples asked Him afterwards about the meaning of this parable, and He said to them, "The vineyard is the world, the vine-dressers are your priests, and the servants are those who serve the good law and the prophets.*

10. *When the fruits of their labor are demanded of the priests, none are given. But they ill-treat the messengers who teach the truth of God, just as they have done from the beginning. (Chap. 68:8-10)*

I, Christ, explain, correct
and deepen the word:

What once was is still present today [1989]. The vineyard is the world; in it, the priests still think they can determine things. However, the time has come when the true servants and maids and the true prophets are active and teach the people the life from God, living it as an example to them so that the vines bring forth to Me, the Christ, the true fruits: themselves.

Recognize that time and again they are the same – the godless, the priests, the scribes and Pharisees – who condemn those men and women whom God has sent. The whole striving of the godless is to silence the truth. Yet, let it be said to the one who thinks he can obliterate the truth that even the stones speak.

At all times, the godless undertook the first steps against the righteous men and women. Those who are servile to the churchmen then dance to the same tune, destroying and annihilating what opposes their craving for prestige and wealth.

People who gather into their own barns alone can show no fruits of selflessness. Therefore, through His servants and maids, through prophets and enlightened men and women, God addresses egocentricity, selfishness, ambition for power and greed. Then, when they denounce the satan of the senses in man, he rebels and takes a position against the messengers of God.

11. And when the Son of Man comes, the Christ of God, Himself, they gather against the holy One and beat Him and cast Him out of the vineyard; for they have not wrought the things of the Spirit, but sought their own pleasure and gain, by rejecting the holy law. (Chap. 68:11)

I, Christ, explain, correct
and deepen the word:

I, the Christ of God, came to them in Jesus and come to them as Christ. They could have perceived and experienced Me in manifold forms; for, in the Father-Mother-God, I Am the life in all forms of life.

I also came and come to them with My holy word, which is the eternal truth. Through prophets of God, I admonished and admonish them to keep the laws of God. But they listened and listen only to the insinuations of the one to whom they have sold themselves. He tempts and leads them; and thus, they were and are concerned solely with their own pleasure and gain. In this way, they have rejected the law, God, and have continued to reject it until this very generation [1989].

12. Had they accepted the anointed One, who is the cornerstone and the head, things would have gone well with them, and the building would have stood just like the temple of God in which the Spirit dwells.

13. But the day will come when the law which they reject will become the headstone, seen by all; and those who stumble on it will be broken, but those who persist in disobedience will be ground to pieces.

14. For God gave dominion over the course of this world to some of the angels, charging them to rule in wisdom, justice and love. But they ignored the commandments of the Almighty and acted against the good orders of God. Thus, cruelty and suffering and sorrow have come into the world until the Master returns takes possession of all things, and calls His servants to account." (Chap. 68:12-14)

I, Christ, explain, correct
and deepen the word:

What has been announced here is now taking place [1989]. The New Era will disrupt the sinful world and bring to light everything, which thus far was hidden – be it in the governments of this world, among the rulers who want to maintain their power structures to subjugate the people, be it the power structures of the church institutions, which take My name, Christ, in vain, in order to bind their believers to their dogmas and doctrines.

Had they accepted and received Me, Christ, people would be consciously in Me, the Christ, and each person would consciously be a temple of God. Their churches would then be houses of prayer for all people, without splendid furnishings. Yet, these in power in the church institutions have turned the houses of prayer into palatial buildings, in which they exhibit their wealth. That is where they lead their submissive sheep to worship in external pomp and splendor, which is characteristic of the mammon, the satanic.

The one who grows cold in his innermost being, who is poor, who therefore has not adorned his temple with the ornament of inner love and virtue, needs the external extravagance of large, sumptuously decorated church buildings. He is then also eager to attain outer dignity and prestige, and to shine like a dignitary in such a setting.

The one who lacks inner dignity acquires outer dignity.

The law says that the one who is poor within seeks to adorn himself externally. The one who is rich within bears the ornament of selfless love, virtue, kindness and humility; his eye is clear and not blinded by vain delusion.

If the rulers of all nations as well as the rulers of the church institutions had accepted and received Me, the cornerstone and the head, they would be servants of the living salvation; they would be of equal standing with their neighbor and would not be superior. The one who fancies himself above his neighbor will fall. Thus, all superiors will be shattered on the cornerstone which becomes the capstone. Everything will be made manifest. This is the law of justice, which unveils everything.

God, the Eternal, has again and again called people to be selfless servants of all His children, so that all people may become selfless and unite in selfless love. God, the Eternal, has proclaimed the laws of inner salvation to them, so that they may lead an angel-like life in order to do on Earth as the angels do in heaven. They only accepted these laws, but did not actualize them in their life. They abused the truth for their purposes and, in the name of the Most Holy, created a hell of vices in which many people are kept in My name. Blindly believing in the good, they contribute their money as an offering which, however, is then mostly used for selfish purposes by those responsible.

The law of God – the justice, the love and the wisdom – brings to light all this and much more. By this, those who have kept the people blind will shatter. The people should recognize their false leaders and, in their recognition, voluntarily turn back. For every man has been given free will.

Because the cornerstone is becoming the capstone, the eyes of many will be opened, and they will recognize whom they have followed. Then many will abandon and tear down the external pomp and wealth. In this way, the power structures which twined up around deception and external wealth will vanish.

Since this book is a historic work, I want to repeatedly address the people in the Kingdom of God, in the Kingdom of Peace of Jesus Christ:

Recognize that in the mighty turn of time, the pioneers struggled with themselves to become free from all the humanness that still clung to them. At the same time, they fought against the power structures which emerged from the human ego. They knew that I was with them, just as I Am with you in the Kingdom of Peace. They fought against everything institutional, because they knew that God is freedom and leaves freedom to all men.

Within the Covenant Community New Jerusalem as well, a process of purification took place again and again: Either for or against Christ. Each one had the free will to remain in the Covenant Community New Jerusalem or to leave it. No one was bound to a statement or to a promise. Each one, however, has to answer for what he does to God alone, and not to people.

The pioneers for the Kingdom of Peace of Jesus Christ fought for the new world, the world of the Christ, in which only the laws of the heavens are valid. They knew this and relied on this: that I, Christ, make all things new.

They knew that I will erect those temples which will accept and receive Me. These temples will be shining torches of the true Christian life. They are the temples of flesh and bone in which light-filled souls will dwell, where the altar of God – on which the fire of selfless love, wisdom and goodness burns – has been raised. This is then what I, Christ, Am in My own.

15. And He spoke another parable, saying: "A man had two sons, and he came to the first and said, 'My son, go work today in my vineyard,' and the latter answered, saying, 'I will not.' But afterwards, he repented and went. And he came to the second and said the same. And the latter answered, saying, 'I will go, father.' But he did not go. Which one of the two did the will of his father?"

16. They said to Him, "The first." And Jesus said to them, "Verily, I say to you that the tax collectors and harlots will enter the Kingdom of God before you. For John came to you in the way of righteousness and you did not believe him; but the tax collectors and the harlots believed him, and you, when you had seen it, did not repent afterwards, so that you may believe him."

17. And the Lord gathered all His disciples around Him in a certain place. And He said to them, "Can you give perfection to what is imperfect? Can you make order out of disorder?" And they answered, "No, Lord."

18. And He placed them in a square, each according to his number, on each side one less than twelve; He did this, since He knew who would betray Him (who should be counted as one of His own, but was not).

19. The first in the seventh rank from above in the middle, and the last in the seventh rank from below, and the one who was neither the first nor the last, He made the center of all, and He placed the rest according to a divine order, and each found his place, so that those who were above were even as those who were below, and those who were below as those who were above, and the left side was equal to the right side, and the right side to the left, according to the sum of their numbers.

20. *And He said, "Do you see how you stand? I say to you, in like manner is the order in the Kingdom of God, and the One who rules everything is in your midst, and He is the center, and with Him are the hundred twenty, the elect of Israel, and after Him come the hundred forty-four thousand, the elect of the heathens, who are their brothers." (Chap. 68:15-20)*

I, Christ, explain, correct
and deepen the word:

Recognize that the one who recognizes and repents in time can also receive in time, before fate takes its course. Therefore, turn back before you enter the wheel of suffering and before what you have caused through your sensations, thoughts, words and deeds comes upon you.

The days are given to you so that you may read from the course of the day what the day wants to convey to you. If you live in the day consciously and have learned to interpret the language of the day, you will also recognize yourselves in it; and you will clear up what comes toward you as an admonition, before fate takes its course.

As Jesus of Nazareth, I spoke in many parables. Aside from this, I used numbers and measures to explain the kingdom of the inner life to My faithful.

The word of man has several meanings, and every person perceives only the meaning that he is capable of grasping according to his state of consciousness at the moment. Therefore, you should neither stick to words nor to meanings, nor to numbers or measures, but recognize all of these as aids, as guides, which lead you to the inner life, to the truth, which has neither words nor terms, nor numbers nor measures, but is the power, itself, the love and the wisdom – the All-consciousness.

Once the soul has found its way back to the All-Father-Consciousness, this means, once it is pure, then the person is conscious of many things and makes use of the aids only as long as he lives in the world of words, terms, numbers and measures.

Since everything is vibration, everything has a meaning. However, the meaning of things can also be understood only according to its sense; the meaning is not the truth itself – the latter is consciousness which reveals itself without words, terms, numbers or measures.

CHAPTER 69

About Death, Rebirth and Life

The rebirth in the Spirit of God
liberates from reincarnation (1-2). About the wheel of re-
incarnation – The souls of the shadows – The soul finds rest
only when all sins are expiated – The expiation of sins is
easier and faster on Earth than in the soul realms (3-4). The
word of man is the word of error (5-6). The working of the
Father-Mother-Principle in the duals (7-10). The one who is of
good will understands and fulfills the law of life and becomes
free from error (11-13)

1. As Jesus sat at the west side of the temple with His
disciples, behold, a dead person was being carried on a
stretcher to be buried, and one said to Him, "Master,
when a man has died, will he live again?"

2. And He answered, saying, "I Am the resurrection
and the life; I Am the good, the beautiful, the true, and
the one who believes in Me will not die, but live eternally. As in Adam all die, so will all come to life again
in Christ. Blessed be those who die in Me and have
become perfect in My likeness; for they rest from their
labor and their works follow them. They have overcome
evil and have been made pillars in the temple of My
God; and they go out no more, for they will abide in
eternity. (Chap. 69:1-2)

749

I, Christ, explain, correct
and deepen the word:

"... to die in Adam" means to die in sin. To be resurrected in Christ means to be released from sin by repenting, forgiving, asking for forgiveness, making amends and no longer committing the same or similar sins.

The one who strives for the purity of the soul and the one who believes in Me, Christ, the Redeemer of all men and souls, will live in Me consciously and attain rebirth in the Spirit of God. He will enter the Sanctum, God, and will also abide in God. The being which has consciously become the image of the Father again remains in the eternal heavens and will no longer return to reincarnation in the flesh – except to serve the Eternal, in the earthly garment.

3. But for those who have done evil, there is no rest; for they will go out and in, and, for their betterment, will have to endure sorrow for many ages, until they have become perfect. But those who have done good and attained perfection have eternal rest and enter eternal life. They rest in eternity.

4. Repeated death and birth have no more power over them; the wheel of the Eternal no longer revolves for them, for they have reached the center where eternal rest prevails; and the center of all things is God."
(Chap. 69:3-4)

I, Christ, explain, correct
and deepen the word:

The one who dies in sin will have no rest, because, in the spheres of purification at the latest, the sin becomes a piercing pain.

If, in this incarnation, the soul has not expiated the sins which it brought with it, but continued to add to them, then it continues to be bound to the wheel of reincarnation and will be drawn by it into another incarnation, since it could not rise because of the burden, the sin. Every sin matures according to predetermined laws, and then pushes to be expiated. As long as the soul clings to the wheel of reincarnation, it continues to be drawn to the Earth, because there, it has the opportunity to clear up, in a short time, what is still earth-heavy, that is, earth-rooted.

A soul can have several or even many incarnations behind it. This can continue until all the sins have been expiated, which repeatedly draw the soul to Earth because the soul is still rooted in the Earth.

When a soul debt bursts open in the spheres of purification, this can be a "fiery furnace" for the soul in which it languishes. In the heat of the sin, which has burst open and which hurts the soul just as wounds on the physical body hurt the person, many souls recognize that as human beings on Earth they could have the opportunity again to expiate this debt and other still latent sins as well. They learn from teaching angels that in another incarnation there is a chance to expiate the burdens of the soul more quickly and easily and to free themselves more quickly from the suffering which arose from the sin.

Still other souls go through many periods of time; they come into the earthly garment and go again – they come and go again. Many of them repeatedly burden themselves anew, because they are not willing – neither in the planes of purification nor in the earthly existence – to recognize their sins, to acknowledge them as being their debt, to repent and to sin no more. They are often the ones who speak ill of those people who strive to fulfill the will of God.

The one who lives in sin over long periods of time is far from the light – and is ultimately against the light, since for him the shadow is his home. These then, are those souls which, in the earthly garment, time and again go after the people to whom they already did bad things in times gone by. Through their correspondences, the persecutors can also recognize those who endeavor to clear up the shadows – their sins – with Christ.

Recognize that on this side of life many incarnated souls – that is, human beings – encounter their victims from past times in other human beings. With this, they are given the opportunity to recognize themselves and turn back.

The one recognizes, repents and, as a soul, gradually enters life and does not come back again. The other soul comes back into an earthly existence, because it has not made use of its former incarnations and has again sinned.

Recognize that, in the realm of the souls, the souls experience their sins as a fire within the soul-body when the causes, that is, the sins, become active; it is similar to the earthly existence when the causes come into effect and the person has to endure blows of fate and illness.

But in the spheres of purification, the soul experiences the effects of the sins much more painfully than if it has to expiate and endure them as a human being in the earthly garment. For the one who, in the earthly garment, repents and endeavors to give his sins over to Me, the Christ, and to leave them in Me, the one who lives in Me and sins no more – enters the eternal, pure, spiritual life. The wheel of reincarnation no longer revolves for him. He is released from death and birth, because the soul has again become the being from God and lives in the center, in God.

5. *And one of His disciples asked Him, "How shall one enter the Kingdom of God?" And He answered, saying, "If you do not make the below as the above, and the left as the right, and the behind as the before, and if you do not enter into the center and into the Spirit, you will not enter into the Kingdom of God."*

6. *And He said, "Do not believe that any man is without error, for the word of error is found even among the prophets and the initiates of the Christhood. But there are many errors which are covered by love."*
(Chap. 69:5-6)

I, Christ, explain, correct
and deepen the word:

The word of man is the word of error. For words are but symbols and can be interpreted in manifold ways. The word of man is understood by people only to the degree that their respective consciousness has matured. Spiritually alert people grasp the meaning of the word, because they have immersed in the truth. People whose consciousness is still in the embryonic state get caught up in the letter and see contradictions in everything.

The word of true prophets, of the initiates and of enlightened men and women is often wrongly interpreted because it is wrongly understood. People of different grades of consciousness live on Earth, and each one hears according to his level of consciousness, and each one interprets accordingly for himself and his neighbor.

The statement "... for the word of error is found even among the prophets and the initiates of the Christhood. But there are many errors which are covered by love" means the following:

The so-called prophets and initiates who use Me, the Christ, just as a means to an end, to promote their own interests, take My name in vain in order to bring error into this world. These unenlightened ones with their human conceptions – which they represent as the truth and yet are errors – quote the word of the true prophets and initiates which they wrongly understand and interpret, in order to legitimize themselves. The Eternal does not let these errors which are attributed to the true prophets and initiates fall upon them. However, He covers the errors, so to speak, until the time is ripe to uncover the error which came into this world.

7. *And when it was evening, He went out to Bethany with the twelve; for there lived Lazarus and Mary and Martha whom He loved.*

8. *And Salome came to Him and asked Him, "Lord, how long shall death hold sway?" And He answered, saying, "As long as you men inflict burdens and you women give birth. For this reason, I Am come to end the works of the heedless."*

9. *And Salome said to Him, "Then I have done well by not giving birth." And the Lord answered, saying, "Eat of every pasture which is good, but do not eat of that which has the bitterness of death."*

10. *And when Salome asked when those things about which she asked Him will be understood, the Lord said, "When you have worn out the garment of shame and have risen above lusts, when the two become one, and the male with the female will be neither male nor female." (Chap. 69:7-10)*

I, Christ, explain, correct
and deepen the word:

In God, the male and the female principles are called the positive and the negative principles. They are the

755

two poles which act in absolute unity. They are the giving and the receiving poles. In their unity, they form the Father-Mother-Principle.

Both poles, the giving and the receiving principles, also act in the children of God. Among other things, they bring together two beings, the giving and the receiving principles. In the duality, they melt into one another, thus activating the Father-Mother-Principle, the spiritually begetting and conceiving powers.

Beings in the light of God do not seduce, nor are they seduced. They love each other in God and from God and, in the union of the Father-Mother-Power, they beget spiritual beings, children of the light.

The dual-pair is the duality. They are the two powers that are melted into one another, the giving and the receiving powers. The duals are two beings – and yet, are merged in unity forever. They offer their spiritual children to the Eternal and raise them in the filiation of God in the all-family which forms the great family of God.

11. And once more, to another disciple who asked Him, "When will all obey the law?" "When the Spirit of God will fill the whole Earth and the heart of every man and of every woman.

12. I strewed the law into the Earth, and it took root and bore in due time twelve fruits for the nourishment of all. I cast the law into the water, and it was cleansed of all evil. I cast the law into the fire, and the gold was purged from all dross. I cast the law into the air, and it

received life from the Spirit of the living One, who fills
all things and dwells in the heart of each one."

13. And He told many other similar parables to those
who had ears to hear and an understanding soul. But to
the multitude they were obscure words.
(Chap. 69:11-13)

I, Christ, explain, correct
and deepen the word:

These words mean that the eternal Father in Me, His
Son, brought the law of life into this world. The deliberate and unintentional errors of man entwine the law of
love and of life. I will take these errors away, so that the
eternal law will be recognized and understood by every
person of good will, so that he may actualize the eternal
law and fulfill it in daily life.

When all people fulfill the law of God, they see their
own words and those of their neighbors; then error has
no place any longer. The one who lives in God lives as
a child of God in the all-embracing ocean, God. The
child of God knows the law of the Earth, of water, of
fire and of air, because it lives in the law. Thus, it also
has the power to move the four elements.

CHAPTER 70

Jesus Rebukes Peter for His Impetuosity

Respect life on each level of development; each form of life is on its path of evolution towards perfection (1-5). The one who lives in Me is a witness in this world (6-7). Those who pave the way for Christ from the old sinful world to the New Era (8). Christ is crucified again and again in the fight between light and darkness (9-10). In the turn of time, the all-embracing light becomes visible; the darkness wants to extinguish it (11). In the turn of time, the divine wisdom builds the original communities through which Christ, the light of the world, radiates towards all peoples – The Covenant Community New Jerusalem is the priestess (12-14)

1. And on the morrow, as they were coming from Bethany, Peter was hungry and spotted from afar a fig tree with leaves. In happy expectation, he ran to it, hoping to find fruit. But he found nothing except leaves, for the time of figs was not due for a long time.

2. And Peter became angry and said, "Accursed tree, nevermore shall man eat fruit from you!" And some of the disciples heard this.

3. And the next day, as Jesus and his disciples were passing by, Peter said to Jesus, "Master, behold, the fig tree which I cursed is green and flourishing. Why did my word not come true?"

4. Jesus said to Peter, "You do not know of what spirit you are. Why did you curse what God has not

cursed?" And Peter said, "Behold, Lord, I was hungry, and finding leaves and no fruit, I became angry and cursed the tree."

5. And Jesus said, "Son of Jonas, did you not know that the time of figs had not yet come? See the grain on the field; it grows according to its nature – first the green shoot, then the stalk and then the ear – would you also be angry if you came at the time of the tender shoots or stalks and did not find any grain in the ear? And would you curse the tree which, full of buds and blossoms, did not yet bear ripe fruit? (Chap. 70:1-5)

I, Christ, explain, correct
and deepen the word:

The fig tree is a parable for the evolution of life. All forms of life bear the life, which is evolution, in themselves – including soul and person. Each soul will again attain full maturity through Me, the Christ. Yet all souls and all men will mature differently – according to their level of consciousness and their thinking, speaking and acting. Therefore, respect life, no matter how far it has unfolded. For God, the life, is on all levels of development, leading the soul to perfection.

Each curse which passes the lips of a person or which is in his thoughts will be his doom. This is what the impetuous Peter, too, had to experience. He had to recognize that though he had much knowledge, he had but little wisdom.

The wise one knows the ways of the soul. If in these moments Peter had been filled with the wisdom of God, he would have known about the law of the inner ripening of life-forms, the path of evolution, which I pointed out to the apostles and disciples in many parables.

Few who wanted to follow Me understood the meaning of My explanations, for the majority of them were still far too much concerned with themselves and with their old habits. Therefore, they remained in error, as they heard the word alone and could not grasp the meaning of My explanations.

6. *Verily, Peter, I say to you, one of My twelve will deny Me thrice in his fear and anger with curses, and will swear that he does not know Me, and the rest will forsake Me for some time.*

7. *But you will repent and grieve bitterly; for you love Me in your hearts, and you shall be as an altar of twelve hewn stones and a witness to My name, and you shall be the servants of the servants, and I will give you the keys of the community, and you shall tend My sheep and My lambs, and you shall be My representatives on Earth. (Chap. 70:6-7)*

I, Christ, explain, correct
and deepen the word:

My words were meant not only for the apostles and disciples and for the people of Israel of that time. My

760

word was and is the word of the Father. From generation to generation, it is meant for all peoples of this Earth and for all souls in the spheres of purification.

The altar of God shall be formed by those men and women whose life rests in Me, the Christ. The one who lives in Me will be a witness for Christ in this world. In My name, he will be a guide to the members of the communities who live in Me. In Me, he will be a key which opens more and more hearts for Me, the Christ.

Those who live in Me and through whom I live shall be the servants of all. Through them, I show the members of My communities, My sheep and lambs, the way to the eternal pastures of inner life.

Time is ripening. As the maturity of people and of the Earth progresses, more and more sheep will find the one Shepherd – Me, the Christ, who dwells in all souls and men.

8. *But there will arise men amongst those who will succeed you, of whom some will indeed love Me just as you do and, being hot-headed and unwise and impatient, will curse those whom God has not cursed and, in their ignorance, will persecute them, because they cannot yet find in them the fruits they seek. (Chap. 70:8)*

I, Christ, explain, correct
and deepen the word:

All men and souls are fruits on the tree of life. Each fruit gradually ripens towards Me, the Christ. When the

761

fruit has reached its full ripeness, I carry it to the eternal Father who takes it in and leaves it where it has its place in the Kingdom of God eternally.

However, it often takes several earthly lives until a fruit has attained its inner ripeness. This is why many souls came and come into the earthly existence again and again. They slip into the earthly body and out again, upon physical death, until they have reached the maturity which liberates them from the wheel of reincarnation.

Only when the soul in man matures can man selflessly pass on the gifts of inner life to those people who thirst for them, so that they, too, may attain inner maturity.

Therefore, according to the law of eternal life, only a person who has become the truth to a great extent can pass on the gospel of love and carry it into all countries. Then he can touch many hearts, because he gives from the eternal truth.

Recognize that since My earthly existence as Jesus of Nazareth, the New Era, the era of Christ, has been growing to maturity from generation to generation – through the apostles, the disciples and all righteous prophets and enlightened ones. Again and again, from generation to generation, souls came which let their fruits of inner life continue to ripen in the earthly existence. The actualization which they respectively brought into this side of life they also shared by teaching and serving. Upon their physical death, they laid aside their earthly garment. They came back into a new earthly garment in another generation and brought along the inner maturity, the light of Christ, and gave of it to those who seriously strove to take the steps of inner maturity.

Many who came and come back bear within a mostly ripe fruit, the life in Me, the Christ. It is they who now prepare the way for Me from the old sinful world to the New Era which blossoms in Me, the Christ.

Recognize that only the one who has little maturity of the soul curses his fellow man. The one who still lives in sin cannot recognize the ripe fruits in his fellow man, because he looks only at his own shadows and is therefore of the opinion that his neighbors should be as he is, rich in shadows.

9. *And others who love themselves will ally with the kings and rulers of the world and will seek earthly power, riches and domination, and they will put to death by fire and sword those who seek the truth and are therefore truly My disciples.*

10. *And in those days I, Jesus, will be crucified anew and openly mocked, for they will profess to do all this in My name." And Peter said, "Be it far from You, Lord." (Chap. 70:9-10)*

I, Christ, explain, correct
and deepen the word:

The fight between light and darkness will last until the gates to incarnation are closed for the heavily burdened souls. This fight between light and darkness also takes place at this great turn of time [1989]. The demonic forces summon everything once again and mobilize all those servile to them, whether souls or men, in order to extinguish the light which is growing stronger and stronger on Earth.

It is similar today [1989] as it was during the time I, in Jesus, walked over this Earth. Those who love themselves and cling to their earthly belongings ally with the rulers of this world and with the ecclesiastic authorities, in order to eliminate with earthly power those who have devoted themselves to Me, the Christ, and who carry My gospel of love into the world. For those who carry forth the gospel of love and of life not only with words, but with selfless love, and who become active through My power, are a threat to the selfish one.

In earlier centuries, the power-hungry, the rulers, the ecclesiastic authorities and those servile to them set out in My name with fire and sword to bring the gospel of love to the people of other countries. Thus, they did to their neighbors what was in and on themselves: cruelty and murder.

In the present time [1989], the same ones again – only in different earthly bodies – move from place to place with slanderous talk. Through the media of the present generation, they spread their untruth among the people, in order to again act in this way against those who now mark the start of the turn of time and are helping My light to break through. Thus, from generation to generation, I Am crucified anew by those who call on My name and take it in vain for their purposes.

The pioneers for the New Era, for the era of the Christ, are the Christ-friends all over the world. He or she who abides in Me is My disciple in the present and in the future.

11. And Jesus answered, "Just as I will be nailed to the cross, so will My community in those days, too; for she is My bride and one with Me. But the day will come when the darkness will retreat and the true light will shine. (Chap. 70:11)

I, Christ, explain, correct
and deepen the word:

The first original communities were destroyed by the darkness. However, it was only the outer establishments that it was able to destroy. The life in Me was propagated from generation to generation. For the many souls which became ever more light-filled came into earthly bodies again and again and, visibly and invisibly, put into practice what they had brought with them. They began to found small original communities and taught the law of truth. In this way, more and more people found their way to Me, the Christ, who dwells in all souls and people.

During the present turn of time [1989], the all-embracing light is becoming visible. The Covenant Community New Jerusalem came into being and is expanding more and more – as do the other original communities in Universal Life. It is the Covenant Community for the Kingdom of Peace of Jesus Christ. She is My bride and I Am her bridegroom. More and more members of the Covenant Community New Jerusalem fulfill My will, the will of the Eternal.

The wolves continue to prowl, even around the Covenant Community New Jerusalem and, in My name, they spread untruth about the members of the community. And I Am crucified again, since My name is taken in vain. With My name, Christ, they want to extinguish the light of the world, that is, Me.

But the darkness will yield, for its days are numbered. The Earth opens up and devours the night, and the waters come and flood what is dark. Then the light, which I Am, will shine upon the whole earth: Christ.

12. And one will sit on My throne, who will be a man of truth and goodness and power, and he will be filled with love and wisdom beyond all others, and he will guide My community through fourfold twelve and seventy-two as of old. He will teach only what is true.

13. And My community will be filled with light and will give light to all peoples of the earth; and a high priest will sit on the throne as king and priest.

14. And My Spirit will be in him and his throne will endure and will not be shaken; for it will be founded on love, truth and justice, and light will come to it and radiate from it to all the peoples of the Earth, and the truth will set them free." (Chap. 70:12-14)

I, Christ, explain, correct
and deepen the word:

The statement "And one will sit on My throne, who will be a man of truth and goodness and power, and he will be filled with love and wisdom beyond all others, and he will guide My community through fourfold twelve and seventy-two as of old. He will teach only what is true. And My community will be filled with light and will give light to all peoples of the earth; and a high priest will sit on the throne as a king and a priest" has the following meaning:

The words are coded. What the turn of time will bring is stated in code.

These coded words mean that the divine wisdom will sit on My throne until I return in spirit. For I have placed the throne in this world for My coming. I Am the light of the world. The divine wisdom, called by the Father and Me, the Christ, to be in charge of My Work of Redemption and to prepare My coming, is the truth, goodness and power. The divine wisdom, created from the love of the Father, will build up the original communities in the turn of time and fill them with life and power. She will teach the whole truth and give to all people what they are able to grasp.

The numbers are symbols and were given as signs to those who could read from numbers. But the people of the New Era receive My word which is also the word of the eternal Father.

The light of the truth fills the Covenant Community New Jerusalem and its original communities with strength and power to do selfless deeds in My Spirit. The original communities in My Spirit in the Work of Redemption of Jesus Christ, in Universal Life, will provide all peoples on Earth with light and power for the New Era.

The Covenant Community New Jerusalem is, in Me, the instrument of life for this Earth. It reigns in Me and will gradually bring all nations together into *one* people in Me, the Christ. The Covenant Community New Jerusalem, joined with the divine wisdom, is the priestess who gives light, love and life to all people who come to her. She, the priestess, will be in Me, the Christ, and I will be active through her and through further original communities which are in Me. They all are founded on love, truth and wisdom, on the justice of God.

The light of the world which I Am will radiate through the communities which are in Me, and I will radiate to all peoples of the Earth through them. The truth will set more and more people free; they will then form *one* flock, which is in Me, the Christ. The one flock refers to the original communities in Me, Christ, which build themselves up by way of the Covenant Community New Jerusalem in the Work of Redemption of Universal Life. I will be their Shepherd.

CHAPTER 71

The Cleaning of the Temple

Whiplashes for soul and body (1-2).
The true divine service (3-4). Only the meaning of the word
vivifies (5-7). Every person marks himself (8-11)

1. *The Passover of the Jews was at hand, and Jesus went up again from Bethany to Jerusalem. And He found sitting in the temple those who sold oxen, sheep and doves, as well as the moneychangers.*

2. *Then He made a scourge of seven cords and drove them all out of the temple. He released the sheep and the oxen and the doves, poured out the changers' money and overturned the tables.(Chap. 71:1-2)*

I, Christ, explain, correct
and deepen the word:

The scourge of seven cords symbolized the seven basic powers of God, the law of life.

The one who acts against the law of God violates the seven basic powers of God and thus creates his causes. Every cause which is not repented and made good in time is a whiplash for soul and body.

The one who violates all seven basic powers will receive the corresponding whiplashes. They are the effects which he will feel on his body.

3. And He said to them, "Take these things out and do not make of My Father's house a house of merchandise. Is it not written: My house shall be called a house of prayer for all peoples? But you have made of it a den of thieves and filled it with all kinds of abominations."

4. And He did not tolerate that anyone carry a vessel of blood through the temple, or that animals be slain. And His disciples remembered that it was written, "Zeal for your house has eaten me up." (Chap. 71:3-4)

I, Christ, explain, correct
and deepen the word:

"My house shall be called a house of prayer for all peoples" means that it shall be a house or large room where all people gather – no matter from which denomination or race they are, no matter from which people or country or position they come. They come together there to pray and to praise and honor God – and to learn the laws of God and then keep them.

God is the One, the only One, the Father-Mother-God of all beings and men – there is no other God. Therefore, there shall be *one* people which worships the One and only One without rites, cults, dogmas or doctrines.

One shall not argue or exchange opinions about God.

God is in the hearts of all beings and men. He is the life in all Being. The one who respects himself, by holding his life sacred, also respects his neighbor and will become pleasing to God. He does not seek to fathom God, for he lives in the stream of life and does not ask about the stream.

Therefore, he needs no cults or ceremonies, nor any arguments. The one who is detached from these outer appearances is consciously liberated and is one with the life which lasts eternally.

God wants no blood sacrifices. This is an abomination to Him. He wants the pure and honest heart of His children who fulfill the laws of God, who remain faithful to God in all things and are devoted to each other in love.

5. *Then the Jews responded to Him, "What sign do You show us, seeing that You do these things?" Jesus answered and said to them, "I say to you once more: Destroy this temple, and in three days I will raise it up."*

6. *Then the Jews replied, "Forty-six years was this temple in the building, and You will raise it up in three days?" But He was speaking of the temple of His body.*

7. *When He was risen from the dead, His disciples remembered that He had said this to them; and they believed the scripture and the word which Jesus had said. (Chap. 71:5-7)*

I, Christ, explain, correct
and deepen the word:

It is much better not to take the scripture and the word literally and not to believe literally, that is, not to cling to the letter, but to understand the meaning of what is written and spoken. A person learns this through the actualization of the divine commandments; they are the first steps toward the fulfillment of the eternal laws. If a person is able to grasp the meaning of the word in its depth, he can no longer be misled. The letter alone is dead and does not bring out the aliveness of inner life. This is brought out only by the meaning which lies in the letter, in the word. The meaning of the word brings soul and person to life.

The one who heeds solely the word often lives in error. But the one who understands the sense, the meaning of the word, lives in the word and also understands the word, because he recognizes the sign of God in it.

8. *But the scribes and priests saw and heard this and were frightened and sought how they could destroy Him; for they feared Him, seeing that the people listened to His teachings.*

9. *When evening came, He went out of the city. For by day He taught in the temple and at night He went out to the Mount of Olives. The people came early in the morning to hear Him in the temple courtyards.*

10. *Now when He was in Jerusalem for the Passover, many believed in Him, for they saw the miracles which He did.*

11. *But Jesus did not commit Himself to them, for He knew them all. And He did not need that anyone bear witness for another; for He knew well what was in a person. (Chap. 71:8-11)*

I, Christ, explain, correct
and deepen the word:

The words "... for He knew well what was in a person" have the following meaning: As long as a person only hears and only believes in what he heard, but does not fulfill it in his everyday life, he remains a sinful person who judges and condemns. Today he cries, "Hosanna" – and tomorrow, "Crucify Him."

Every person marks himself by his thinking, speaking and acting. His thinking and living is the drawing pencil with which he marks his body and shapes his countenance. What each person thinks is thus in his countenance. What a person thinks, he is.

The one who only believes and does not put his faith into practice remains, despite his faith, the old person who keeps his habits and vices. Such people are unreliable. For the one who does not fulfill the laws of God is a reed wavering in the wind.

12. *Since the Passover was near, He sent two of His disciples to prepare the upper room where He wanted to eat with His twelve, and to buy all that was needed for the feast which He wanted to celebrate with them. (Chap. 71:12)*

CHAPTER 72

Jesus' Words of Farewell

*The image of the Father (1-3). They will do greater
works than I as Jesus (4). I will grant the one who serves
selflessly what he asks for (5). The one who keeps the temple
sacred lives in Me (6-7). Selfless love is communication with God (8). The meaning of the words,
"The Father is greater than I" (9-11)*

1. Jesus sat with His disciples in the garden of
Gethsemane and said to them, "Do not let your heart
be troubled. You believe in God, so believe also in Me.
In My Father's house are many mansions. If it were not
so, I would have told you. I go to prepare a place for
you. And if I go and prepare a place for you, I will
come again and receive you unto Myself, so that where
I Am, there you, too, may be. And you know where I go
and you also know the way."

2. Thomas said to Him, "Lord, we do not know
where You go; how can we know the way?" And Jesus
said to them, "I Am the way, the truth and the life. No
one comes to the Father but through Me. If you had
known Me, you would have known My Father, too. But
now you know and have seen My Father."

3. Philip said to Him, "Lord, show us the Father and
it will suffice us." Jesus said to him, "Do you still not
know Me, Philip, though I have been with you so long?
The one who has seen Me has seen the Father; so why

then do you say: Show us the Father? Do you not be-
lieve that I Am in the Father, and the Father in Me?
The words that I speak to you I do not speak of Myself.
For the Father who dwells in Me does all works.
(Chap. 72:1-3)

I, Christ, explain, correct
and deepen the word:

The one who has become the temple of God is the image of the Father. And the one who beholds the image of the Father experiences the glory of the Father. The Father is the manifestation from the primordial energy, the streaming life which is also called God.

God is omnipresent life. All pure beings are manifestations out of God, the primordial energy, the streaming life. The one who beholds the image of the Father, the being in God, also beholds the light of the Father which irradiates the being in God.

The beings of light do not ask about the form of the Father. They are the manifestation, the form of the Father, and they radiate what He is: love, wisdom, power and life. All pure Being moves in the stream of life, in God.

The one who has accepted and received his neighbor in himself, who loves him from his heart and with his pure being, beholds the image of the Father who is the love, the wisdom and the power.

4. Believe Me, that I Am in the Father and the Father in Me or, at least, believe Me for the sake of the true works. Verily, verily, I say to you, those who believe in Me will do the same works that I do; and they will do greater works than these, because I go to My Father. (Chap. 72:4)

I, Christ, explain, correct
and deepen the word:

Merely believing in Me does not suffice. Many believe in Me, and yet they think, speak and act like unbelievers. The works of God arise from the belief in God only when soul and person rise to the life in God, by fulfilling the eternal life, which is the eternal law.

The one who just believes and does not fulfill does not have the power to do the works of God. But the one who actualizes and keeps the laws of God more and more also has thereby the power to do the works of God which I have done as Jesus of Nazareth. With My part-power, the Redeemer-power, together with the primordial power, he will do even greater works. For I, the Christ – who came from the Father into this world and returned to the Father, in order to be active in all souls as the Christ of God, as Comforter and Redeemer – Am now active through those who keep the law of life, so that they do far greater works than those I did as Jesus.

5. *And whatever you will ask in My name, that will I do, so that the Father may be glorified in the Son of Man. What you will ask in My name, that will I do. (Chap. 72:5)*

I, Christ, explain, correct
and deepen the word:

The words "And whatever you will ask in My name, that will I do, so that the Father may be glorified in the Son of Man" mean that for the one who lives in Me, the Christ, and who serves selflessly, I will fulfill all that he asks for. For the one who lives in Me asks only for the gifts of the Spirit, because he lives in the Spirit of God and does not strive to live with the world.

6. *If you love Me, keep My commandments. And I will ask the Father, and He will give you another Comforter who will abide with you forever, the Spirit of truth whom the world cannot receive. For it does not see nor know Him; but you know Him, for the Spirit dwells in you and will be in you.*

7. *I will not leave you without comfort. I will come to you. Yet a little while, and the world will see Me no longer, but you will see Me. Because I live, you, too, will live. On that day, you will know that I Am in My Father, and you in Me, and I in you. (Chap. 72:6-7)*

I, Christ, explain, correct
and deepen the word:

The human being is the temple of the Holy Spirit;
for the spiritual body from God dwells in him, in the
innermost part of his soul. Since My Redeemer-deed, I
Am in this temple, in person and soul, as the Comforter
and Redeemer, as the Spirit of life. The one who keeps
the temple sacred, by keeping the commandments, lives
in Me and I live and act through him.

8. *Those who have My commandments and keep them
love Me; and those who love Me will be loved by My
Father, and I will love them and will manifest Myself to
them." (Chap. 72:8)*

I, Christ, explain, correct
and deepen the word:

God's love is heavenly communication. The one who
loves God more than this world also loves his neighbor.
But the one who says, "I love God" and is against his
neighbor does not love God. His words are not filled
with the love for God. They are empty, selfish words
that have no impact. But the one who selflessly loves
his neighbor also loves God, and is thus in communication with the highest power, with love, with God.
Communication with God is revelation.

9. And Judas (not Iscariot) asked Him, "Lord, how is it that You will show Yourself to us and not to the world?" Jesus answered and said to them, "Those who love Me will keep My words. And the holy One will love them, and We will come to them and will abide with them.

10. Those who do not love Me do not keep My words; and the words which you hear are not My words, but the words of the Father who sent Me. I have said these things to you, while I Am still with you. But the Comforter, who is the Holy Spirit, whom the Father will send in My name, will teach you all things and will remind you of everything I have told you.

11. Peace I leave with you, My peace I give to you. I give to you not as the world gives. Do not let your heart be troubled, nor be afraid. You heard what I said to you, 'I go away and I will come again to you.' And if you loved Me, you would rejoice; because I said to you, 'I go to the Father, for the Father is greater than I.' (Chap. 72:9-11)

I, Christ, explain, correct
and deepen the word:

The Comforter and Redeemer is the Christ of God, who lives in the Spirit of the eternal Father. I Am one with the Father. The Father and I are the one law – the truth that sets free all souls and men who believe and fulfill the will of God.

"... for the Father is greater than I" means that the Spirit of the Father is the All-Spirit, the law, which consists of the seven basic powers of life. God is law.

The Christ of God lives and acts in God, the All-Spirit, in the four divine basic powers: order, will, wisdom and earnestness. However, the Father is the All-power. He is the eternal law which consists of the seven basic powers: order, will, wisdom, earnestness, goodness, love and gentleness. On Earth these seven basic powers are called order, will, wisdom, earnestness, patience, love and mercy.

Thus, the Father is greater than the Son. He is the All-power – I Am the part-power in the All-power.

12. *And I have told you this now before it comes to pass, so that you may believe when it comes to pass. Now I will not talk much with you, for the prince of this world will come and find nothing in Me.*

13. *But so that the world may know that I love the Father, I will do as the Father has commanded Me, even unto the end." (Chap. 72:12-13)*

CHAPTER 73

The True Vine

Each branch of vine in Me bears fruit (1-2). The one who does not abide in Me sins (3). To live in Christ (4). The clear eye of the soul attains the gift to discern between truth and error (5). The faithful bear good fruits in My name (6-8). The one who perceives is no longer blind (9). Why Christ reveals Himself again today (10-11). The knowledge of the laws obligates you to actualize (12). No man will be able to say, "I did not know anything about Christ" (13)

1. And then Jesus said to them, "I Am the true vine, and My Father is the vine-dresser. Each branch in Me that bears no fruit is taken away, and each branch that bears fruit is pruned, so that it may bear still more fruit.

2. Abide in Me, and I in you. Just as the branch can bear no fruit of itself unless it remains on the vine, you cannot either unless you abide in Me. I Am the vine and you are the branches. The one who abides in Me and I in him bears much fruit, for without Me you can do nothing. (Chap. 73:1-2)

I, Christ, explain, correct
and deepen the word:

The fruit can ripen only when it abides in Me, the Christ, that is, when man devotes all his aspirations to

781

Me by striving to fulfill the will of God in order to become the law of God. Every vine – that is, every soul and every person who actualizes his inner life through Me, thus purifying himself through My power – will become the fruit, which, in turn, brings forth fruit; for the good fruit gives of itself selflessly.

Recognize that every person radiates what is in him, the divine or the undivine.

3. *Those who do not abide in Me are cast away as useless shoots, and these wither away; they are gathered and cast into the fire, and are burned. But if you abide in Me and My words abide in you, you shall ask what you will, and it will be given to you. (Chap. 73:3)*

I, Christ, explain, correct
and deepen the word:

All those who live with the world and, through their sinful life, deny the Christ of God will suffer the fire of their own thoughts, words and deeds. For what man sows he will reap. Every undivine thought, every unlawful word and every selfish deed is useless because it is without power. It is human embellishment and will wither away.

The one who does not abide in Me sins. The soul and the person who has committed the sin will have to bear it. The fire of sin brings about the purging of the soul. However, the one who abides in Me, the Christ of God, abides in the Father, too, for the Father and I are one. His prayers will be fulfilled, for he asks only what is the will of God.

4. Verily, I Am the true bread that comes from heaven, the substance of God that is one with the life of God. And just as there are many grains in your bread, so are you who believe and do the will of My Father also one in Me. Not as your ancestors who ate manna and died, for the one who eats this bread will live eternally. (Chap. 73:4)

I, Christ, explain, correct
and deepen the word:

The life in God is the spiritual bread. It is the nourishment of the soul. The one who partakes of it will neither hunger nor be in need as a human being.

The one who fulfills the will of God and lives out of the truth receives the truth in all facets. Then his thinking and acting are filled with the power of God, and his earthly life, too, will also be a fulfilled life.

People in Me, the Christ, live; they do not vegetate. Only the one vegetates who wastes his life, because he aligns his thoughts and his aspirations with the earthly world, and thus belongs to it. After his earthly death, he will also be spiritually dead, because he clung only to the world and was not turned towards God; his soul does not know where it came from and where it is going.

The one who lives in God is the essence from God and knows the path of his soul because it lives in Me, the Christ; for I Am the way, the truth and the life.

5. *As the wheat is separated from the chaff, so must you part from the falsities of this world; yet you need not leave the world, but shall live apart in the world, for the life of the world. (Chap. 73:5)*

I, Christ, explain, correct
and deepen the word:

The one who wants to live in God will also separate himself from the falsities of this world, which he increasingly recognizes, the more the eye of his soul becomes clear.

Only the clear eye of the soul attains the gift of discernment between truth and error. The clear eye of the soul is attained by the person who brings clarity into his life by thinking and living in accordance with the will of God.

The one who strives for God will also live with those who likewise strive to do the will of God, for like attracts like. From this ensues the meaning of the following statement: Who is My mother, who are My brothers? Those who do the will of My Father.

The one who lives in God does not shun this world. He lives in this world, but is not with this world. The one who lives in God lives in this world for all those people who seek the life in God, in order to fulfill it.

6. Verily, verily, the wheat is parched by fire; so must you, too, My disciples, pass through tribulations. But rejoice; for, having suffered with Me as one body, you will reign with Me in one body and give life to the world.

7. In this, the Father is glorified, that you bear many fruits; so will you be My disciples. As the Father has loved Me, so have I loved you. Abide in My love. If you keep My commandments, you will abide in My love, even as I have kept My Father's commandments and abide in the Spirit of love.

8. I told you all this, that My joy may remain in you and that your joy be perfect. This is My commandment, that you love one another as I have loved you. No man has a greater love than to lay down his life for his friend. You are My friends if you do all that I command you. (Chap. 73:6-8)

I, Christ, explain, correct
and deepen the word:

These words of comfort and love were meant not only for the apostles and disciples, but they are meant

785

for all people in all generations who strive to follow Me.

Many who follow Me will come into tribulation, for the adversary pressures them to break with God, to conform to the world and to fawn upon it.

The one who suffers for the gospel's sake bears the cross with Me. He will stand at My right when I appear as ruler of the Kingdom of Peace. And all who die in sin will see those upon whom they have inflicted grief and torment.

The Eternal, in whom I, the Christ, Am, will be glorified by My faithful who bring many ripe fruits to Him in My name and through My power. The one who abides in Me keeps the commandment of selfless love and will lay down his life for the commandment of love. Those who abide in Me will love one another selflessly and radiate selfless love into the hearts of all seeking people. The one who abides in Me will be filled with true joy and will also bring joy to those who let their hearts be filled with selfless love.

9. *Henceforth, I do not call you servants, for the servant does not know what his master does. But I have called you friends, for I have taught you all the things that I have heard from My Father. You have not chosen Me, but I have chosen you and appointed you, that you should go and bear fruit and that your fruit should last. Whatever you will ask of the Father in My name, you shall receive. (Chap. 73:9)*

I, Christ, explain, correct
and deepen the word:

The true servant is the friend of the Christ of God. The one who serves selflessly and bears good fruits is no longer ignorant. He knows the laws of God because he lives in them. He will no longer blindly meet the blind, but will recognize the blind, because his spiritual eyes have opened through the actualization of the eternal laws.

The perceiving one is no longer a blind one. He beholds the blind one as he is – and as he presents himself. For the one who fulfills the will of God finds his way out of the wheel of reincarnation and attains spiritual rebirth. And then, I Am no longer Comforter and Redeemer to him, but brother and friend.

10. This is what I command you: That you love one another and also all creatures of God. When the world hates you, then know that it hated Me before it hated you. If you were of this world, the world would love you as its own; but because you are not of this world, since I have chosen you from the world, therefore, the world hates you.

11. Remember the word that I said to you: The servant is not greater than the master. If they have persecuted Me, so will they persecute you, too; as they have kept My words, so will they keep your words, too. But they will do all things to you for My name's sake, because they do not know the One who sent Me. (Chap. 73:10-11)

I, Christ, explain, correct
and deepen the word:

The one who has chosen Me, Christ, has chosen to be apart from this world. He will be hated by the world for My sake.

What happened to Me as Jesus will also happen to all those who love Me, for they do not love the intrigues of this world. The one who is of this world is also loved by this world and accepted as its own. Yet the one who turns to Me, the Christ, will be hated by the world, as I was and am hated by the world.

Recognize that the present generation [1989] is not much better than the preceding generations. What the people did not recognize in former incarnations they do not recognize in this generation either, namely, the works of love. What they have misinterpreted in former incarnations they also misinterpret in this generation.

Many speak of My earthly life, of My work as Jesus of Nazareth – and yet do not understand what I taught. Today, many still interpret the words of the Eternal, in the Old Testament as well as in the New Testament, at their own discretion, including the words of God through Moses. If the world had changed, I would not have given My revelations anymore. But since the world has not changed, the Eternal and I, Christ, spoke and speak again now to the people through the prophetic word, in order to rectify what is wrong, in order to lead the people out of the confusion of dogmas, conceptions and misunderstood words.

Many words from the eternal truth were and are quoted and misused for human intrigues. Many so-called Christians merely speak in a Christian manner, but think like the Antichrist. Thus, they only pretend to be Christians – inside, they are ravening wolves.

12. *If I had not come and had not spoken to them, they would have been without sin. But now they have no cloak for their sins. The one who hates Me hates My Father, too. If I had not done among them those works which no one else did, they would have no sins; but now they do; and they have seen and hated Me and My Father. But all this must come to pass, so that the word that is written in their law may be fulfilled: They hated Me without cause. (Chap. 73:12)*

I, Christ, explain, correct
and deepen the word:

"If I had not come and had not spoken to them, they would have been without sin" means that if I had not come and spoken to them, they would not have recognized their sins and would have imagined themselves to be without sin. Yet I came and spoke about the law of the Father and lived it as an example to them.

The one who quotes the eternal Father and Me, Christ, and the true prophets has also accepted the words of the Eternal, My words and those of the prophets. But the one who does not live accordingly – as he was commanded – sins against the law of God; he is a sinner. He no longer has a smokescreen, called ignorance, for what he does.

The Eternal gave His word at all times: All peoples heard Him through prophets and enlightened ones. Moses brought the Ten Commandments, the excerpts from the eternal law. As Jesus of Nazareth, I taught the law to people and lived it as an example to them.

The law which I brought to them says: Love God, your Father, with all your heart and with all your strength, and your neighbor as yourself. No person can say that he is unknowing!

Recognize that the one who does not love his neighbor selflessly does not love God, either. The one who hates his neighbor also hates God, his eternal Father. The one who spurns his neighbor also spurns God, his eternal Father.

"If I had not done among them those works which no one else did, they would have no sins; but now they do; and they have seen and hated Me and My Father" means that if I had not done the works of God, many people would not know the works in God and would think that they have no sin. Yet, because they have seen My works or were told about them, they have thus been shown how they should think, speak and act. And if they do not do so, they can recognize their sins in this. In My thinking, speaking and acting as Jesus, they have seen and heard My Father, and they hear Him, the Eternal, in Me, the Christ, in what was handed down of the works, which I did.

The one who does not think, speak and act out of selfless love and holds on to and does not destroy what he has done out of greed, stinginess and striving for power is a sinner. In many situations, he also sins against the Holy Spirit.

Therefore, the one who has seen Me or was told about My works has seen the Father and experienced Him in Me, the Christ.

The one who acknowledges the works of God through His prophets and the works of the Christ, thus also commits himself to think and live as I, Christ, have commanded the people.

13. But the Comforter will come, whom I will send to you from the Father, namely the Spirit of truth, which will proceed from the Father and will testify of Me: And all of you will bear witness, because you have been with Me from the beginning. (Chap. 73:13)

I, Christ, explain, correct
and deepen the word:

In all generations, many people bore and bear witness of Me; so it is in this generation [1989], too. No person will be able to say one day, "I did not know about Christ." For the pioneers for the New Era who are in My mission will carry the truth, which I Am, into all countries. And the gospel of love will be offered to many people. The Christ of God is Comforter and Redeemer, the truth and the life in the stream of the eternal law.

Time does its part: Just as the present time drives and rushes people, so are the causes coming into effect faster and faster. Many who still pursue materialism today will succumb to these effects. However, those people who are left at the end of the turn of time of the world will acknowledge the gospel of love, and many will also live accordingly.

CHAPTER 74

Jesus Prepares His Disciples for the Coming Events

The fight in the name of Christ against Christ (1).
The Work of Redemption is fulfilled (2-3). Today the truth
flows as a great stream (4-5)

1. *I have told you all this in order to warn you. They will cast you out of the synagogues; yea, the time will come when every one who kills you will think that he does it in honor of God. And they will do such things because they have recognized neither the Father nor Me. (Chap. 74:1)*

I, Christ, explain, correct
and deepen the word:

What I said to My apostles and disciples happened and happens in all generations – and, in a similar way, around the year 2000, as well: Since they do not know My Father and Me, they will banish you from their life and will not let you take part in their worship services, because you do not belong to their faith. They will kill many of you and slander others and expose them to the derision of the people. Recognize that the one who has no love or respect towards his neighbor loves neither the eternal Father nor Me, the Christ.

During the past centuries, the authorities repeatedly stirred up the people against the true followers of Christ. For fear of the consequences, the people were servile to them. Therefore, it was possible for atrocities to be committed in My name to people who followed Me or were of different conviction than that of the ecclesiastic authorities.

My name was taken in vain and sold in a shameful way. It was not only in the so-called crusades that people who called themselves Christians, yet did not live in a Christian way, tried to Christianize those of different faith with the sword in their hand. Ecclesiastic authorities took and take My name in vain, bound it and bind it to their dogmas and claimed and claim that they have the only saving grace because they think that I, Christ, am caught under the yoke of their dogmas.

Just as it happened to some apostles and disciples, it is happening around the year two-thousand to some Christ-friends, the true pioneers for the New Era. Again, it is the ecclesiastic authority that stirs up the people against them. Again, this is done using similar arguments, so that the people who have been incited would oppose My true followers. As in former times, the rights which are due to every citizen of the country are denied to the Christ-friends, the pioneers for the New Era. As in former times, those who stir up the people and carry these things out also call themselves Christian.

Many of My true followers are outcasts in the eyes of the state and of the churches and of all those who are servile to them. In many cases, the law is interpreted against them, so that it may seem as if the Christ-friends were at fault. Thus, they make life difficult for people who strive to be true Christians.

Recognize that even today [1989] the satanic occupies the highest ranks of the authorities and rules those who are under its spell – those people who are content with what is decreed "from above." Without examining it themselves, they adopt the authorities' judgment about their neighbors. However, these authorities will not rule mankind in the long run. It is true that a great period of time has been given by God to the satanic, as a grace period for changing its ways. Yet this period of time, too, has its end; and the darkness stands before this end. For I, Christ, the light of the world, the truth and the life, come.

2. *But I have told you all this so that, when the time has come, you may remember what I have told you about it. And I did not say this to you at the beginning because I was with you. But now I go My way to My Father who sent Me; and none of you asks Me, 'Where do You go?' But because I have said all this to you, you are sad.*

3. *Nevertheless, I tell you the truth; it is necessary for you that I go away. For if I do not go away, the Comforter will not come to you; but if I go away, I will send My Spirit to you. And when He has come, He will*

point out to the world the sin, the righteousness and the judgment. (Chap. 74:2-3)

I, Christ, explain, correct
and deepen the word:

The Comforter is the Spirit of Christ, who I Am, the life in God, My Father. The Spirit of the Christ of God is omnipresent in the four natures of God, the creating and executing powers – which every soul bears in itself as power and life.

The Comforter, My Spirit, is the Redeemer-spark where comfort and redemption are active. The redemption is My work, which I received from the Father for the homebringing of all souls and men.

Many people are active in My Redeemer-work and carry My light into the world. Through their selfless help, My work grew all over the Earth within a few earthly years. Many beings went and go into the earthly garment for the Work of Redemption, in order to teach people the truth and to live it as an example for them, just as I did in Jesus of Nazareth. Through the thinking, living and working of these pioneers, many hearts and many people are moved and encouraged to stop and think and to actualize the eternal laws.

It is the superhuman achievement of a woman who lives in the Father and in Me, the Christ, that within a few years, the Work of Redemption has become world-wide. She is in the divine mission, together with the pioneers for the New Era, to call and teach all people of good will so that they may find the inner light of love and the true life, the eternal law of the All. For the truth, the law of the All, is in every human being.

Recognize that the eternal law of the All is the true law that will defeat all the laws of matter and the causal law, because it is impersonal and absolute.

In this mighty turn of time [1989], many beings are active in the earthly garment. Tirelessly, they achieve great things for the Era of Light and thus for Me, the Christ of God, and for all the generations that will come after them.

The one who will read these words in the New Era, when peace dwells in people, will hardly be able to understand some things. However, My words will keep their significance, because many beings who will incarnate into the New Era will bear within themselves the memory of the old world which they overcame with much pain, torment and suffering.

This memory-potential will remain alive in the souls and people of the New Era until what was carried out on Earth, the stage of the old world, is also fulfilled in the spheres of purification. Though the satanic is bound for some time on Earth, it is not bound in the spheres of purification. There, the soul continues to expiate the sins which it inflicted upon itself in the earthly garment.

I come to man in many different ways in order to point out to him his sins, his judgment and the justice of God.

4. The sin, because they do not believe in Me; the righteousness, because I go to the Father, and henceforth you will not see Me; the judgment, because the prince of this world has been judged.

5. I have yet many things to say to you, but you cannot bear them now. But when that One, the Spirit of truth, has come, He will guide you into all truth; for He will not speak of Himself, but He will speak whatever He hears. And He will show you what will come. He will glorify Me. For He will receive it from Me and will reveal it to you. (Chap. 74:4-5)

I, Christ, explain, correct
and deepen the word:

The Spirit of truth is the Christ of God of whom I, as the Son of Man, spoke. I fulfilled these promises during these almost two thousand years. The Spirit of truth came in all generations, and His work in this world increased in light and power more and more, for many people heard and read about the law of life, the eternal truth, and many a person began to develop the life within himself.

Nevertheless, at this turn of time [1989], the light – I, the Christ, the eternal truth – is breaking through in a broad spectrum and radiating into the whole world. The law of truth flows through the prophetic word as a great stream; for I sent the divine wisdom to the people, so that the truth may be revealed and shake up the people who live within the constraints of the world and in sin.

The truth also reveals what is in the present and what will come. For the many souls and people, it refreshes and gives to drink, and strengthens them with love, power and wisdom. The one who clears up his sins will recognize Me, the Christ, for sin clouds the spiritual eye. The one who is able to see recognizes Me, the Christ, in himself and in those who truly follow Me. And those who live in Me glorify the Eternal in Me, for they receive from Me in order to pass this on to others.

6. *All that My Father has is Mine. Therefore, I said to you that the Comforter will take it from Me and show it to you. A little while and you will not see Me, and again a little while and you will see Me, because I go to the Father." Then some of His disciples said among themselves, "What is the meaning of what He said to us, 'A little while and you will not see Me, and again a little while and you will see Me' and, 'because I go to the Father'"?*

7. *Now Jesus noticed that they wanted to ask Him, and said to them, "You ask among yourselves about My words 'A little while and you will not see Me, and again a little while and you will see Me.' Verily, verily, I say to you, you will weep and lament, but the world will rejoice: You will be sorrowful, but your sorrow shall turn into joy.*

8. *When a woman is in labor, she has sorrow because her hour has come; but when she has given birth to a child, she no longer remembers the anguish, for the joy that a human being has come into the world. And you now likewise have sorrow; but I will see you again, and your heart shall rejoice, and no one shall take your joy from you.*

9. *And on that day you will ask Me nothing. Verily, verily, I say to you: If you ask My Father in My name, you will receive. Until now, you have asked for nothing in My name. Ask, and you will receive, so that your joy may be full. I have said all that to you in parables; but the time will come when I will no longer speak to you in mysteries, but will openly tell you of My Father.*

10. *On that day you will ask in My name: And I do not tell you that I will ask My Father for you; for He Himself loves you, because you love Me and believe that I came forth from God. I came forth from God and have come into the world; and I leave the world again and go to My God."*

11. *Then His disciples said to Him, "Behold, now You speak plainly and speak no mystery. Now we know that You know all things; and it is not necessary that anyone ask You, for we believe that You came forth from God."*

12. *Jesus asked them, "Do you now believe? Behold, the hour will come, yes, it is already here, when you will be scattered, and every one will go home and will leave Me alone. But I Am not alone, because the Father is with Me.*

13. I have said these things to you that you may have peace in Me. In the world you will have tribulation; but be of good cheer, I have overcome the world. Come, let us set out." (Chap. 74:6-13)

CHAPTER 75

The Last Passover Supper

*Become pure in heart (1-2). About the betrayal –
Tolerance and understanding towards the ignorant (3-6).
In the New Era of Christ, there is no more bloodshed (7-
9). The purified Earth gives in abundance (10). To live in
Christ leads to the nobility of the soul and to true freedom (11-12). The law of life, the commandment of love –
The one who scorns his neighbor does not find his way to
Christ, to the truth, into the eternal Being – Every person
judges himself (13-16). The New Israel and the New Jerusalem (17). From all nations and tribes, those who do the
works of God will join in brotherhood (18)*

1. *In the evening, He came to the house where the
twelve and their fellows gathered: Peter, Jacob, Thomas, John, Simon, Matthew, Andrew, Nathanael, James,
Thaddeus, Jude, Philip and their companions (and
there was also Judas Iscariot, whom people counted
among the twelve, until the time came when he was
unmasked).*

2. *And they were all clad in garments of pure white
linen, for linen is the righteousness of the saints. And
each had the color of his tribe. But the Master was clad
in His pure white robe, without seam or spot.*
(Chap. 75:1-2)

I, Christ, explain, correct
and deepen the word:

As the Son of Man, I left the people. As the Christ of God, their Redeemer, the Spirit of truth, I Am come again.

The one who gathers in My name does not scatter. Only he scatters who wants to gather in his own name, even when he uses My name for this – thus taking it in vain.

Become pure, then you will behold God, the life, in everything. For the pure one beholds the pure. But he also sees the impure, which needs to be addressed, so that it may be recognized and overcome.

Recognize that the pure whiteness of linen was considered at that time to be the symbol of inner purity. I say to you: You shall not adorn yourselves solely externally, and pretend the purity in God, but you shall become pure in your heart. Then you will also wear clean and light-filled clothing. When the heart is pure, this will also show its effects externally in the behavior and clothing of the person who strives towards God.

3. And they began to quarrel about which one of them should be considered the greatest; therefore, He said to them, "The kings of the heathens hold sway over them, and those who rule are called benefactors. But you shall not be so. The one among you who is the greatest shall be as the youngest, and the one who is the first shall serve."

4. *And Jesus said, "I have longed to celebrate this Passover supper with you before I suffer, and to establish the memory of My sacrifice for the service and salvation of all people. For behold, the hour comes when the Son of Man will be delivered into the hands of the sinners."*

5. *And one of the twelve asked Him, "Lord, is it I?" And He answered, "He to whom I give the morsel is the one."*

6. *And Judas Iscariot said to Him, "Behold the unleavened bread, the mingled wine, the oil and the herbs, but where is the lamb that Moses commanded?" (For Judas had bought the lamb, but Jesus had forbidden that it be slaughtered.) (Chap. 75:3-6)*

I, Christ, explain, correct
and deepen the word:

People betray people, their neighbors. But God does not betray His child. Nor does the person who lives in God betray his neighbor. Nor did I, as Jesus of Nazareth, betray Judas. I spoke in a general way about the betrayer who takes the first morsel without inner prayer.

Neither the apostles nor the disciples gave the order to slaughter a lamb. But as a gift of love, parts of a prepared lamb were offered to Me as well as to the apostles and disciples. With this, our neighbors wanted to make a gift for us, for they did not know better. I blessed the gift and began to partake of the meat. My apostles and disciples did the same. Afterwards, they asked Me in the following sense: We should refrain from consuming meat. This is what You have commanded of us. Now You, Yourself, have consumed meat.

I instructed My own that man should not willfully kill an animal nor should he consume the meat of animals which were killed for the consumption of their meat. However, when people who are still unknowing have prepared meat as nourishment and make of it a gift to the guest, offering it with the meal, then the guest should not reject the gift. For there is a difference whether a person consumes meat because he craves for meat or as a token of gratitude to the host for his effort.

However, when it is possible for him and outer circumstances and time permit, the knowing person should give general indications to the host, but should not want to set him right. When the time is ripe, the host, too, will understand these general indications.

In this world, understanding and tolerance, too, are aspects of selfless love. Leave to each person his free will whether or not he wants to understand and accept your general indications. If you think, speak and act selflessly at all times, you abide in love and love will bless you. What is then offered to you as a gift of love is blessed.

7. *And John prophesied from the Spirit, saying, "Behold the lamb of God, the Good Shepherd who gives His life for His sheep." Judas was troubled at*

these words, for he knew that he would betray Him. But Judas asked once more, "Master, is it not written in the law that a lamb must be slain within the gates for Passover?"

8. And Jesus answered, "When I will be lifted up on the cross, then indeed will the lamb be slain. But woe unto the one who delivers it into the hands of the slayers. It would have been better for him if he had never been born.

9. Verily, I say to you, I Am come into the world in order to put an end to all blood offerings and to the eating of the flesh of animals and birds that are slain by men. (Chap. 75:7-9)

I, Christ, explain, correct
and deepen the word:

The one who loves the life in God loves God and is one with the life from God.

I came to this world to teach the gospel of love, the law of the heavens, and to live it as an example. The one who actualizes the law of love of the heavens will find his way to a fulfilled life.

The life in God includes not only one's neighbor, but also all other forms of life like animals, plants, minerals and stones; for all Being bears the life, God. The one who is in unity with life neither kills animals nor destroys plants willfully. He also respects the life – the forces of consciousness – of the minerals and stones.

The one who respects life also respects his neighbor, because he respects himself. For the life, God, is in the soul as substance and power. The one who respects his neighbor thus lives in peace with all Being and with his neighbor, for all beings and men are children of the Father-Mother-God.

Recognize that the one who actualizes the law of love changes his way of thinking and living. He thereby refines his senses and gradually gives up killing animals deliberately and also slaughtering them to consume their meat.

The one who relies on the flesh also consumes flesh. The one who relies on the Spirit nourishes himself with what the Earth gives him, just as it was in former times.

Recognize that no change, whether in a person or in the world, takes place from one day to the next. It is a gradual process of transformation. The one who turns to God changes his way of thinking and living quite gradually, and thus ennobles his senses, even his whole person. In so doing, he will refrain more and more from eating meat and will keep peace with people and with the nature kingdoms.

In the course of generations, blood sacrifices will no longer exist; for people will recognize that they do not honor God with them and that their self-invented gods do not react to their way of thinking and acting.

Recognize that the one who no longer envies, no longer quarrels, no longer binds and no longer wants to dominate and to be the greatest is a man of true peace.

As long as there is no peace in man himself, there will be blood sacrifices – whether in wars or through disasters. When people have found their way to inner peace, there will be neither wars nor disasters and no more bloodshed either.

All this will come; however, it will still take some time, for not all causes have been atoned for and settled yet. They come back as effect to those who have sown them. Yet the time in which peace will enter the hearts of people is ripening; it will be when the New Era, the time of the Christ, rises more and more.

Mankind today [1989] lives in a great turn of time from the old sinful world to the New Era. Once this change has been accomplished for the most part, people will fulfill the laws of God more and more and it will be as I foretold as Jesus: There will be *one* Shepherd and *one* flock, and the nations will be *one* people. Then any kind of blood sacrifice will be abolished as well as the eating of the flesh of animals.

10. *In the beginning, God gave everyone the fruits of the trees and the seeds and the herbs for food; but those who loved themselves more than God or their neighbor corrupted their ways and brought diseases into their bodies and filled the Earth with lust and cruelty. (Chap. 75:10)*

I, Christ, explain, correct
and deepen the word:

That which is base, satanic, is coming to an end. For more and more people, the life in and with God is turning into a need. Therefore, the Earth, too, will purify itself and nourish the children of God as it was at the beginning of the human race: Mother Earth again gives in abundance to the inhabitants of the Earth what they require for their earthly body. This is then the pure, in turn, for the bodies which are mostly pure.

11. Not by shedding innocent blood, but by living a righteous life, will you find the peace of God. You call Me the Christ of God and you speak true; for I Am the way, the truth and the life.

12. Walk this way, and you will find God. Seek the truth, and the truth will make you free. Live in the life, and you will not see death. All things live in God, and the Spirit of God fills all things. (Chap. 75:11-12)

I, Christ, explain, correct
and deepen the word:

A righteous life is a life in God. The righteous person does not take advantage of his neighbor, nor condemns him or judges him. The one who strives for righteousness in all things finds his way onto the path of truthfulness. He is true to himself in noble thoughts, words and deeds. He also behaves towards his fellow men according to his own way of thinking and living: He does not take advantage of them, nor does he condemn or judge them, because he has ennobled himself.

Recognize that peace and true Christianity can come into this world only through people who have ennobled their souls with the adornment of virtue and humility, with peaceful thoughts, selfless words and deeds.

I Am the way, the truth and the life. The one who raises his soul to Me also finds his way to Me. And the one who lives in Me, the truth, is free from outer ties and from the trumpery of this world. The one who lives in the truth fills all words and things with life, because he is filled, himself, with the Spirit of God.

13. Keep the commandments. Love your God with all your heart, and your neighbor as yourself. The whole law and the prophets are based on these. And the sum of the law is this: Do not do unto others as you would not that others do to you. Do unto others, as you would that others do to you.

14. Blessed are they who keep this law, for God is manifest in all creatures. All creatures live in God, and God is hidden in them."

15. And afterwards, Jesus dipped the morsel, and gave it to Judas Iscariot, saying, "What you do, do it soon!" But after he had received the morsel, he went out immediately. And it was night.

16. After Judas Iscariot had gone out, Jesus said, "Now is the Son of Man glorified among His twelve, and God is glorified in Him. And verily, I say to you, those who receive you will receive Me, and those who receive Me, receive the Father who sent Me. And for you, who follow Me in the spiritual renewal as My chosen ones, I will set up a kingdom as one was established for Me. And you who have been faithful to the truth will sit on twelve thrones and judge the twelve tribes of Israel." (Chap. 75:13-16)

I, Christ, explain, correct
and deepen the word:

The heart of the one who fulfills the commandments of selfless love is filled with love and with the wisdom of God, with the truth which lasts eternally, because it is the law of life.

The one who fulfills the commandment "Love your God with all your heart and your neighbor as yourself" lives in the law of God; for selfless love encompasses all the powers of the All, from order to mercy.

At all times and in all generations, the true prophets and all righteous men and women have fulfilled the law of God. The one who fulfills the law of God entrusts himself to God and gives what the will of God is: love and wisdom.

May the person who wants to become the law of love heed the first step to inner life, to selfless love:

"Do not do unto others as you would not that others do to you. Do unto others, as you would that others do to you."

To the one who fulfills the law of life, the love, God is manifest in all people, animals, plants, minerals, stones and in all the powers of the All. Nothing remains hidden to the one who opens himself to God. But from the one who wants to hide from God because of his sin, the things and powers of the All are hidden.

Judas took the morsel. Since he had not sincerely prayed, he put part of it back and left the small group. Thus, he showed his true colors and then carried out what he had in mind.

What I said to the small group should serve you and all coming generations to recognize your way of thinking and living. With it, you have a criterion for recognizing your spiritual maturity.

The one who belittles and condemns his fellow men has accepted and received neither them nor Me. He thus rejects and condemns Me, too, the Christ of God, for I live in your neighbor. By this behavior, he cannot find his way to the truth either, for I, the Christ, Am the way, the truth and the life. The one who rejects his neighbor also rejects Me. Therefore, he cannot find his way to the eternal Father who acts through Me, the Christ.

And the one who does not live in Me is also not chosen – neither for the Kingdom of God on Earth nor for the eternal kingdom, the eternal heavens – because the eternal Being is the Father in Me. The one who scorns his neighbor does not know Him, the Father, either.

The one who has found his way to the truth will neither judge nor condemn.

The word "judge" means:

The tribes of Israel will judge themselves according to their thinking and acting.

Recognize that every person judges himself; for every dishonest sensation, every negative thought, every egocentric word and every selfish action bears the judgment in itself. The criterion by which man measures is his own judgment: It is the selfishness in his sensations, thoughts, words and actions.

I, the Christ of God in Jesus, abided in the Father. Thus, the Father was glorified through Me, the Christ.

17. And one asked Him, "Lord, will You re-establish the Kingdom of Israel?" But Jesus answered, "My kingdom is not of this world, nor are all people Israel who call themselves Israel. (Chap. 75:17)

I, Christ, explain, correct
and deepen the word:

My kingdom is not of this world.

The word "establish" means that I will establish the Israel – with Jerusalem in its midst – where people fulfill the will of God. My kingdom consists of people who do the will of God in Me, the Christ.

Recognize that Israel and Jerusalem do not refer to a particular place. They are where people work in the name of the Most High and fulfill the law of selfless love. With the love and wisdom of God, they will found and build up what is revealed: The Kingdom of God on Earth whose ruler I, Christ, will be.

The Kingdom of God on Earth will not be where egoism prevails – that of the stubborn Jewish people and of those who accept Me only literally. Those people who have accepted and received the Father and Me, the Son, who thus fulfill the laws of the love and wisdom of God, will found and build up the New Israel and the New Jerusalem. It is they who bring the spiritual renewal. They are in My mission to found, build up and accomplish what has been revealed: the Kingdom of God, the Kingdom of Peace of Jesus Christ on this Earth.

Recognize that Israel and Jerusalem will be where the wellspring of God flows, from which the truth penetrates the whole world as a stream.

Those souls and men who have condemned themselves by not fulfilling the eternal laws will judge themselves.

Many spirit beings came from the Sanctum of God into the earthly garment. They will set up and preserve the throne of God on Earth. Therefore, Israel and Jerusalem will be where the wellspring of God rises and flows most strongly – far from the old Israel. When the old Israel no longer exists, the New Israel will replace the old Israel because the Earth masses will shift, due to world-upheaving processes and to the change of the so-called axis of the Earth.

18. *Those in every people who do not defile them-selves with cruelty, who practice righteousness, who love mercy and revere the works of God, who give help to the weak and oppressed – these are the Israel of God." (Chap. 75:18)*

I, Christ, explain, correct
and deepen the word:

From all four winds, from all nations and tribes of the entire Earth, I Am gathering those people who did not and do not defile themselves with acts of cruelty, but practice righteousness and mercy, who selflessly help the weak and oppressed and do the works of God.

They will avow brotherliness and ally with those who are establishing the New Israel and the New Jeru-salem, the Kingdom of God on this Earth, the Kingdom of Peace of Jesus Christ which will encompass the whole Earth.

CHAPTER 76

Washing the Feet of the Disciples – The Last Supper

*The development of the seven basic powers
of the soul begins with order (1-3). The one who loves
selflessly fulfills the law and perceives God in everything (4-
5). The true fighters for Christ are pure in heart (6). The
goal and the task of the soul: to become the law again (7).
The meaning of incense (8). About the Last Supper – Not a
ceremony, but a symbol (9). The prayer of Jesus for His
own. Fulfill the word of God and the commandment of love;
let flow what God gives you (10-19). The prayer of unity
(20-21). Bread and wine (22). The spiritual substance in the
gifts of nature (23-25). Concessions by Moses became
unlawful customs and habits (26-28). The betrayal of Christ –
Why Jesus could be captured and was crucified – The deed
of Christ for the lineage of David (29-30)*

1. And when the Passover supper had ended, the
lights were kindled, for it was evening. And Jesus arose
from the table, laid aside His cloak and put on a towel.
Afterwards, He poured water into a basin, washed the
feet of all of the fourfold twelve and dried them with the
towel with which He was girded.

2. And one of them said, "Lord, You should not wash
my feet." And Jesus said, "If I do not wash you, you are
no part of Me." And he answered, "Lord, not only my
feet, but also my head and my hands."

3. And Jesus said to him, "The one who comes out of the bath has to wash but his feet, for he is quite clean." (Chap. 76:1-3)

I, Christ, explain, correct
and deepen the word:

Washing the feet was a symbol as well. It signifies the inner purification.

In order to reach perfection, soul and person have to begin by opening the "lowest" basic power, the order. That means to purify the sensations and thoughts and to ennoble them in such a way that the words of the person, too, are vivified with My life. Then the person gradually recognizes the will of God. At the same time, the person striving towards God will refine his human senses more and more, to attain inner nobility. This takes place from one step of evolution to another. The maturing soul and the awakened person become noble and good.

In this way, soul and person gradually open the seven basic powers of the soul which are the law of God. Once the soul has completely opened these seven basic powers from order to mercy, it is then the immaculate spiritual body once more, the drop in the ocean, God, in the law of life.

4. When He had put on His cloak of pure white linen without spot or seam, He sat again at the table and said to them, *"Do you know what I have done to you? You call Me Lord and Master, and you say it well, for so I Am. And as I have washed your feet, you, too, should wash one another's feet. For I have given you an example, so that you do what I have done to you.*

5. *I give to you a new commandment, that you love one another and all the creatures of God. Love is the fulfillment of the law. Love is from God, and God is love. The one who does not love does not know God.* (Chap. 76:4-5)

I, Christ, explain, correct
and deepen the word:

The one who is able to selflessly love all people and all forms of life, that is, who no longer rates, evaluates and judges, fulfills the law.

The law, God, is love, because God is love. The one who lives selfless love is pure. He perceives God, the law of love, in all people, in all forms of life and in all things, because he knows God, the law of love.

The one who does not know himself does not know the law, God, either, nor does he perceive the law of love, God, in all people, forms of life and things.

6. *Now you are pure through the word which I have spoken to you. By this shall all people recognize that you are My disciples, that you love one another and show mercy and love to all the creatures of God, espe-*

cially to those that are weak and oppressed and suffer innocently. For the whole Earth is filled with dark places of cruelty, with torment and fear, because of the selfishness and ignorance of man. (Chap. 76:6)

I, Christ, explain, correct
and deepen the word:

"... pure through the word" means that the one who actualizes My word, which is life and power, will become pure in soul and body. The one who is pure in heart also contributes in the world, so that all people who long for God find fulfillment, and the dark places of horror, where torment, fear and death prevail, become more light-filled. For then, there, too, the life in God awakens and blossoms and people find their way toward inner peace.

The one who lives in God becomes the true selfless fighter for the Kingdom of God which is peace. He fights with the weapons of love against the selfishness and ignorance of his fellow man, so that the Earth may be renewed by Me, the Christ.

7. *I say to you: Love your enemies, bless those who curse you, give them light in their darkness, and let the Spirit of love dwell in your heart and overflow to all people. And once more, I say to you: Love one another and all the creatures of God." And when He had finished, they all said, "Praised be God." (Chap. 76:7)*

I, Christ, explain, correct
and deepen the word:

What I said as Jesus of Nazareth was meant not only for My own who were with Me, the Jesus, and not only for the people of that time. It was and is meant for people of all nations and of all generations; for it is the word of God which was and is directed to all people. It will be given until many people have become the law of life and they then speak the word, the law, God, themselves. Then everything that was foretold by Me as Jesus and by the true prophets of God is fulfilled.

Then, when I come again in the spirit, the Earth will be purified to a great extent, so that it is able to receive My light, the light of the Christ. Then all people who live upon the purified Earth will fulfill the commandments of God and speak the word, the law, since they live the law.

It is the task of the soul to become again, in its various earthly lives of different eras, the law, God, the word of life. People who have attained higher degrees of purity will love one another and all creatures of God, as I have loved and love them.

8. *And then, He raised His voice, and they joined together, saying, "As the stag longs for flowing streams, so my soul longs for You, O God!" And when they had finished, one brought to Him a censer full of glowing coals, and He spread incense on it, the same incense*

which His mother had given Him on the day of His manifestation, and the sweetness of the scent filled the room. (Chap. 76:8)

I, Christ, explain, correct
and deepen the word:

The so-called censer stood in the rooms of distinguished citizens. Incense symbolizes the consecrated life. It was and is used by many people who were not and are not aware of this meaning. In the institution church as well, incense is still used in ceremonies. On the other hand, the consecrated life is not lived by many people, even in the institution church. And yet, what is not lived remains a symbol and is thus also meaningless.

9. *Then Jesus, placing before Himself the platter and behind it the chalice, and lifting up His eyes to heaven, gave thanks to God for His goodness in all things and unto all, and took the unleavened bread in His hands and blessed it. Then He mingled the wine with water and blessed it, chanting the invocation of the sevenfold holy name, calling upon the three-in-one to send down the Holy Spirit and make the bread to be His body, that is, the body of Christ, and the wine to be His blood, that is, the blood of Christ, for the remission of sins and for an eternal life to all who obey the gospel. (Chap. 76:9)*

I, Christ, explain, correct
and deepen the word:

In the world, the one who holds an office uses the vocabulary that is necessary for it. Translators, too, can interpret the texts only with their vocabulary, which corresponds to their level of consciousness. Furthermore, the translations could not and cannot always be made according to the meaning of the word, since the same words can have a different meaning for each person – according to his consciousness and his conception. Thus, in many cases, My word, too, was seen in light of the faith of those who interpreted it. Therefore, I explain, correct and deepen the word which has been written in the book, "The Gospel of Jesus."

As Jesus of Nazareth, I often prayed to God, My Father, and communed with Him. I prayed to Him, the Eternal, for the blessing of the Last Supper with My own.

I spoke to them as follows: Continue to do in My memory what I now do. The food is for the body. I offer it to you as a symbol of inner strengthening.

Recognize that My body is sacrificed, so that you may attain eternal life. Let your body become a temple of God, so that the Spirit may be active in and through you. Through the resurrection of My spiritual body, you, too, will resurrect; for the Christ of God, who goes to the Father, is the Spirit of truth in God. The Spirit of truth will purify your spiritual body, and the light of the world, which I Am, will shine in and through you. For through My resurrection, I Am the light in you and the purification of your soul. The one who believes in Me and fulfills the laws of the heavens will attain rebirth in the Spirit of My Father through Me, the Christ.

I took the wine, added some water to it and spoke as follows: What I tell you now is a symbol. Recognize the meaning and think of Me while you eat and drink; for in all things is the Spirit of life, who I Am.

The wine is the symbol of My blood, which I will shed for all souls and men. The Spirit of the soul must be awakened again by soul and man, that is, it must be brought into the earthly life. The soul of the one who does not accept and receive the Spirit of truth – as a symbol, it is My blood – cannot return to eternity, because it does not live in the absolute truth. The soul remains outside heaven until it has accepted and received Me, the light of the world, its Redeemer. Thus, the one who does not accept and receive Me, his Redeemer, the Co-Regent of the heavens, will not attain absolute perfection.

Recognize that the one who does not accept and receive Me does not accept and receive the Father, either, for the Father and I are one.

I, in Jesus of Nazareth, carried out this symbolic event among My own, in order to explain to them that the life, the Spirit of God, is in all forms of life as substance and power, in the food as well as in the drink. For I died for all souls and men, so that they attain resurrection. During the supper and in everything you do, you should do it in remembrance of Me alone. For what you truly do in My name is well done.

Many people will bleed to death in the mighty turn of time, because they have not accepted and received Me, thus remaining in their sins. But the person who strives for God will celebrate his meal with Me. So, ask for God's blessing for your meal and, while eating, think of the power and love of God, and you will also think of your Redeemer, the Christ of God, who is in the Father.

10. Then, lifting up the offering towards heaven, He said, "The Son of Man is lifted up from the Earth, and I will draw all men to Me. Then all will know that I Am sent by God."

11. And when this had been done, Jesus spoke these words, lifting His eyes to heaven, "Abba, the hour has come, glorify Your Son, that Your Son may be glorified in You.

12. Yes, You have glorified Me; You have filled My heart with fire; You have placed lights at My right and at My left, so that no part of Me would be without light. Your love is shining at My right hand and Your wisdom at My left. Your love, Your wisdom and Your power are manifest in Me.

13. I have glorified You on Earth, I have finished the work which You have given Me to do. Holy One, through Your name, keep the twelve and their fellows whom You have given Me, that they may be one just as We are one. While I was with them in the world, I guided them in Your name, and none of them is lost; for the one who left us was not of us, but I pray for him that he may be saved. Father, forgive him, for he knows not what he does.

14. And now I come to You, and I say this to the world, that My joy be fulfilled in them. I give them Your word; and the world hates them, for they are not of the world, just as I Am not of the world.

15. I do not pray that You take them from this world, but that You keep them from evil, as long as they are in the world. They are not of this world, just as I Am not of the world. Bless them through Your truth. Your word is truth. As You have sent Me into the world, so I send them into the world and, for their sake, I sanctify My-self, that they, too, may be sanctified through the truth.

16. I do not pray for them alone, but for all those who will join them and for the seventy-two whom I also sent out. And for all those who will believe in the truth through Your word, that they, too, may be one, as You, Most Holy, are in Me and I in You, that they, too, may be one in You and that the world may know that You have sent Me.

17. Holy Father, I also want that all those You have given Me, yes, all those who live, be with Me where I Am, so that they may partake of the glory which You give Me; for You love Me in all and all in Me, from before the world was created.

18. *The world has not known You in Your righteousness, but I know You, and these know that You have sent Me.*

19. *And I have declared Your name to them, that the love with which You have loved Me may be in them, and that from them it may abound to all Your creatures, yes, to all." And when He had spoken these words, they all raised their voices with Him and prayed as He had taught them: (Chap. 76:10-19)*

I, Christ, explain, correct
and deepen the word:

This prayer, which was passed on according to its meaning, was said not only for My apostles and disciples; it was and is meant for all people, for all Being.

Those who fulfill the will of God more and more will carry the word of God, which fills them, into the world. This will take place in the present and in the future until I return in the spirit.

In the divine era, in the Kingdom of God on Earth, the life of man is a lived prayer, a life that is the eternal law. For the love for God and one's neighbor is the fulfillment of the law.

I, Christ, will exalt the one who loves selflessly, just as the eternal Father has exalted Me. At the same time, I will draw him to Me, his brother, and we will live in God as children of God.

I have brought the Work of Redemption into the world – into all souls and men. Redemption is accomplished in those souls and men who have attained perfection, that is, purity. They have again become one with the Father and have attained the brothership in Me. They are in the brothership with Me – and, in the Father-Mother-God, in the son and daughtership.

Never let your neighbor out of your heart, even if he has betrayed you or delivered you up, as Judas did to Me. Keep him in your heart, even though he is not with you then but against you. He is and remains your neighbor. This is how it is written in heaven, in the eternal law.

Heed and fulfill the commandment of love: Love your Father with all your heart, with all your strength; love Him in every sensation, in every thought, in every word and in every action; and love your neighbor as you love yourself. And if the love for God prevails in your feeling, thinking, speaking and acting, you will respect yourselves as children of God and also your neighbors, who are likewise children of the eternal Father, and whom God, our Father, loves just as He loves you. For in God, your Father and Mine, all are His children. He loves all equally – without distinction. And if you recognize this and accept it, you, too, will make no differences.

The love for God includes forgiveness as well. The one who lives in the Father has the inner greatness which forgives without bearing a grudge.

To the one who fulfills the word of God it is given to proclaim and teach the word of God to the world. But may the one who himself has not actualized the word of God remain silent. For the one who only speaks about the word of God burdens his soul. He sins against the holy word, against God. The words of the one who only preaches and teaches the word of God, without having actualized it, do not enter the heart of his neighbor; they become a boomerang to the one who sends out the word. And so, the one who merely preaches and teaches the word of God, without having actualized it, cannot fill it with strength and power either, because he is, himself, without strength.

The one who fills My word with life and power through his own actualization and teaches this in the world is often not understood by the people of this world – and will be hated by many because of the gospel.

The one who fulfills the word of God is not of this world, just as I, too, was not of this world as Jesus of Nazareth. The one who fulfills the word of God is a living wellspring and a stream of inner salvation that streams to all creatures and flows through all things; for God is the power that flows through all things. Therefore, the one who lives in God passes on what God gives him: love, wisdom and power, the stream for all people and all things.

20. *"Our Father, You who are above us and in us, hallowed be Your name in the trinity. Your kingdom*

come to all in wisdom, love and justice. Your holy will be done always as in heaven, so on Earth. Let us partake daily of Your holy bread and the fruit of Your living vine. As You forgive us our trespasses, may we forgive others who trespass against us. As we seek to guide others to perfection, perfect us in Your Christ. Give us Your goodness, that we may do the same to others. In the hour of trial, deliver us from evil.

21. For Yours is the kingdom, the power and the glory: In the beginning, now, and forever and ever. Amen." (Chap. 76:20-21)

I, Christ, explain, correct
and deepen the word:

Epochs have passed since My work as Jesus of Nazareth. Generations have come and gone. People have prayed at all times. The contents of many of their prayers were the same, but these prayers were said with other words, according to the respective generation of that time. Therefore, man should not attach too much importance to the earthly word, as it has taken on and can take on another meaning from epoch to epoch, from generation to generation. Therefore, strive to grasp the meaning and also to give it the right meaning.

Through the inner word, through the incarnated part-ray of divine wisdom, I gave to the people [1986] the prayer of unity as a prayer of thanks and love to God. It can be prayed according to its meaning. It also refers to the approach of the Kingdom of God on Earth and to My spiritual return. It became the prayer of the Christ-friends:

> Our Father, who are in heaven,
> hallowed is Your name.
> Our kingdom comes, Your will is done
> on Earth as it is in heaven.
> You give us this day our daily bread
> and forgive us our trespasses,
> and we forgive those who trespass against us;
> You lead us in time of temptation
> and deliver us from evil.
> For ours is the kingdom and the power
> and the glory,
> from eternity to eternity.

22. Then our Master took the holy bread and broke it, and also the fruit of the vine, and mingled it and blessed both. And He let a fragment of the bread fall into the cup and blessed the holy union. (Chap. 76:22)

I, Christ, explain, correct
and deepen the word:

The words "And He let a fragment of the bread fall into the cup and blessed the holy union" show that the writer was influenced by thinking in terms of ceremonies.

Recognize that everything is one in God. Nothing can exist without the other, because God is the substance and the power in everything. The result of this is the union with life. Likewise, the bread and wine are in God and come from God for man, and they cannot be separated. The Earth is the provider, the mother of all human beings, who receive from it through the Spirit of God. His Spirit flows throughout the Earth and man and gives life to all Being on Earth.

23. *Then He gave the bread which He had blessed to His disciples, saying, "Eat, for this is My body, the body of the Christ, which is given to you for the salvation of the body and the soul."*

24. *Likewise, He gave them the fruit of the vine which He had blessed, saying to them, "Drink, for this is My blood, the blood of the Christ, which is shed for you and for many, for the salvation of the soul and the body."*

25. *And when all had partaken, He said to them, "Every time you gather in My name, make this offering in memory of Me, prepare the bread of eternal life and the wine of eternal salvation, and eat and drink of it with a pure heart, and you will receive the substance and the life of God which dwells in Me." (Chap. 76:23-25)*

I, Christ, explain, correct
and deepen the word:

Bread and wine served only as a symbol for the sacrifice of My life and My blood. However, you should not make a ceremony out of it, but remember Me at all times, in all your sensations, thoughts, words and actions.

Likewise, when you partake of the gifts of life that are given to you by God out of the bosom of mother Earth, remember the Eternal thankfully and remember My Redeemer-deed as well. And if you do so with a sincere heart, not only your earthly body will receive the spiritual substance, the spiritual life, but also your soul. For in all that nature gives to mankind is the life, God, the spiritual substance, the power.

26. *And when they had sung a hymn of praise, Jesus stood up in the midst of His apostles, and they walked round Him, who was their center, as in a solemn dance and rejoiced in Him. And then, He went out to the Mount of Olives, and His disciples followed Him.*

27. *Meanwhile, Judas Iscariot had gone to the house of Caiaphas and said to him, "Behold, He has celebrated the Passover meal within the gates with unleavened bread instead of lamb. I had bought a lamb, but He forbade that it be killed. See, the man from whom I bought it is witness."*

28. *And Caiaphas rent his clothes and said, "Truly, this is no Passover according to the law of Moses. He has committed a deed which is worthy of death, for it is a grave transgression of the law. For what do we need further witnesses? Yes, even now two robbers have broken into the temple and stolen the book of the law; this*

is the result of His teaching. Let us tell the people who follow Him what He has done, for they fear the authority of the law." (Chap. 76:26-28)

I, Christ, explain, correct
and deepen the word:

The words "... and they walked round Him, who was their center, as in a solemn dance ..." mean that My apostles and disciples moved close to Me and around Me; for in these moments I was the center for them, because they felt the grief of My heart and became fearful for their own earthly life.

Moses had to make some concessions to the Israelites; for, like all beings and men, they had and have their free will from God to keep or disregard the laws of life. Despite the admonishments and indications of Moses that their thinking and acting did not comply with the will of God, many Israelites remained in sin. Many of them did not keep the laws of God or only partly kept them.

For this reason, too, they spent many years in the desert, because their customs did not comply with the will of God, and the life of many was like a desert. The thinking and living of many Israelites repeatedly revolved round the golden calf. They partly brought into the so-called promised land their wicked, egocentric behavior and their stubbornness against the fulfillment of the laws of God, and they turned the concessions of

Moses into their laws – believing they had received them as such from God through Moses. The one who was against their customs in the temple and against their unlawful traditions – which God had allegedly revealed through Moses – was an enemy of what they considered right and just.

It is similar in the present time [1989]. The one who denounces the behavior of the representatives of the church institutions is called un-christian by them. The one who does not believe in the dogmas and rites – just as it was with the Israelites in their customs and traditions – is ridiculed, scorned and hated. Many representatives of the church institutions abuse My word – just as the Israelites have abused the word of God through Moses and the concessions of Moses.

It was like this at all times: Whoever is not for the prevailing views and opinions of the people, that is, who does not think or believe as they do, is a betrayer in their eyes. At all times, the authorities have incited people against righteous men and women.

29. *And one who was standing by when Judas came out asked him, "Do you think that they will kill Him?"*

30. *And Judas said, "No, for He will work a miracle to deliver Himself out of their hands. When those in the synagogue in Capernaum rose up against Him and brought Him to the top of the hill, in order to cast Him down, did He not then pass safely through their midst? So will He surely escape them again and proclaim Him-*

self openly and establish the kingdom of which He has spoken." (Chap. 76:29-30)

I, Christ, explain, correct
and deepen the word:

By betraying Me, Judas wanted to acquire pieces of silver dishonestly.

Take heed, you people, that the same thing does not happen to you, as to Judas. For in the almost 2000 years since then, there were Judases who betrayed their master for a few pieces of silver, again and again.

The betrayal of the Christ of God is also apparent today [1989] to those who strive to fulfill the law of God. Many of today's scribes, Pharisees and those who bear responsibility in church, in politics and economy use My name for their personal concerns and advantages. This is taking the holy name in vain, and is thus, a sin against the Holy Spirit.

Judas thought that I would evade capture just as I had done before in many situations. Again and again, those who were against Me wanted to bind, stone or cast Me off the walls – yet I always went on My way through them as if invisible, protected by the eternal power.

But now, what had to happen did happen. Those who were against Me could take Me captive and deliver Me to the high priest and have Me crucified.

Many people repeatedly asked and ask the question: Why did Jesus escape so often from His persecutors and why not on that night? Today [1989], I want to explain only essential aspects of what happened then, for it concerns the redemption which I brought to all souls and men:

The part-power of the primordial power – a part of My spiritual, omnipresent heritage – was therefore released, because the entire Jewish people had not accepted Me, nor had it received – that is, fulfilled – My teachings, the law of life.

I took over a part of the guilt of the lineage of David and a part of the guilt of some other lineages. Shortly before My capture, I enveloped My pure spirit body with these energy-filled powers from the law of sowing and reaping. This envelopment made Me visible and seizable to the darkness.

Recognize that the lineage of David is the bridge to incarnation for those spirit beings who integrated themselves into the plan of God for the Earth and came and come directly from the center of eternal Being, in order to lead back with Me all that seemed lost.

Since the time of David, they came again and again to pave the way for Me and to prepare the fulfillment of the Redeemer-plan, the plan of salvation. It was intended that, in the earthly garment, these spirit beings from the lineage of David should first of all fulfill the laws themselves. Thus, they should have given the Jewish people an understanding of the laws of life and have been good examples to them, so that these, too, would fulfill the laws in order to recognize Me, the Christ, when I came to them in Jesus.

However, from incarnation to incarnation, many spirit beings in the earthly garment entangled themselves as human beings more and more, that is, they sinned and burdened their souls, so that, because of sin, they no longer sensed what they had gone out for. Consequently, the incarnated spirit beings from other lineages, who should have been active for the plan of God, could not find support among the people from the lineage of David.

In the course of My work as Jesus of Nazareth, I had to realize that the spirit beings – as human beings, Jews from the lineage of David – did not stand by Me because their spirit bodies were too shadowed, that is, they had become entangled in the law of sowing and reaping. Besides, I had to realize that the Jews talked about the laws of inner life, but did not keep them, and even used them to subjugate their neighbor. They were blinded by sin, just like the people from the lineage of David.

I knew that I must suffer for the sake of the Work of Redemption. I knew – and it was also revealed to Me in the exaltation, the transfiguration, when the cherubim appeared to Me in the spirit garment – that the spirit beings, who were people from the lineage of David and from other lineages in the earthly garment, should carry out with Me the entire plan of God, the redemption and the founding and building of the Kingdom of God on

Earth. I knew that the lineage of David stood in first place for this.

So that the sons and daughters of God could and can continue to incarnate again by way of the tribe of David, to then be active on Earth, as well, for the plan of God, I enveloped Myself above all with a part of the guilt of the lineage of David. It was the guilt of those souls in the plan of God, which had burdened themselves in previous incarnations to such an extent that they wouldn't have been able to work for the plan of God over many incarnations. By enveloping My spirit body with a part of this guilt, I became visible and vulnerable to the darkness. This is why they could capture Me.

I endured what then followed – the trial, the lashing, the way of the cross on which I repeatedly fell down, until the crucifixion – for the sake of the lineage of David and also for all Jews, and ultimately for all people of all past, present and future generations until the Kingdom of Peace encompasses the Earth.

Had the lineage of David been light-filled and had the Jews, from the time of Moses on, complied with the laws of God, they would have lived the all-encompassing laws with the sons and daughters from the lineage of David. The deed on Golgotha for redemption would not have had to take place, because the Israel and Jerusalem of that time would have then been the true Israel and the true Jerusalem – the Kingdom of God, which could have been effective all over the Earth at that time.

Even before My time on Earth, opportunities for the establishment of the Kingdom of God were created again and again on Earth by the Spirit of My Father. Yet people fell into sin more and more.

Had the lineage of David stood firm, the crucifixion would not have had to take place. Had the Jewish people been the true people of God, the whole plan of redemption would have taken a different course and I would not have had to release a part of My heritage, the part-power of the primordial power. But now it has been accomplished, and the way to the heart of God is free to all souls and men.

The lineage of David and people from other lineages are now beginning to fulfill their mission in the Work of Redemption more and more, so that the Kingdom of God can come to Earth. It is accomplished. This is why I also call the cross the Christ-David-Cross.

CHAPTER 77

The Agony in the Garden of Gethsemane

The sleeping disciples in the garden of Gethsemane –
The one who just gathers spiritual knowledge without put-
ting it into practice cannot understand a situation and falls
asleep over the need of his neighbor – The will and plan of
God will be fulfilled (1-13)

1. When they went to the Mount of Olives, Jesus said
to them, "I will be an offense to all of you this night;
for it is written, 'I will smite the shepherd, and the
sheep of the flock will scatter.' But when I rise, I will go
before you into Galilee."

2. Simon answered and said to Him, "Even though
all men will be offended because of You, I will not be
offended by any means." And Jesus said to him,
"Simon, Simon, behold, Satan wanted to own you, so
that he may sift you like wheat. But I have prayed for
you that your faith will not fail. And when you are
steadfast, strengthen your brothers."

3. And he said to Him, "Lord, I am ready to go with
You, into prison and also to death." And Jesus said, "I
tell you, Simon, the cock will not crow this night, before
you have denied three times that you know Me."

4. After they had crossed the Kidron brook, Jesus
came with them into the garden of Gethsemane. And He
said to His disciples, "Sit here, while I go yonder and

pray." (Judas, too, who betrayed Him, knew this place, for Jesus often stayed there with His disciples.)

5. *Then He said to them, "My soul is sorrowful, even unto death; remain here and watch with Me."*

6. *And He went a little farther, fell on His face and prayed, saying, "O My Father, if it be possible, let this cup pass from Me; however, not as I will, but as You will."*

7. *And an angel from heaven appeared to Him and strengthened Him. And He came to His disciples and, when He found them sleeping, He said to Peter, "Could you not watch with Me one hour?*

8. *Watch and pray that you do not fall into temptation: The spirit is indeed willing, but the flesh is weak."*

9. *He went away again a second time and prayed, "O, My Father, if this is not possible, if this cup may not pass from Me, Your will be done."*

10. *And in deep agony, He prayed even more fervently. And His sweat fell on the ground like big drops of blood.*

11. *And He came again and found them sleeping, for their eyes were heavy.*

12. *And He left them and went away once more and prayed for the third time, saying, "O, My Father, not My will be done but Yours, on Earth as in heaven."*

13. *Then He came to His disciples and said to them, "Sleep on now and take your rest; behold, the hour is at hand when the Son of Man is delivered into the*

hands of sinners. Rise, let us be going: Behold, the one who betrays Me is here." (Chap. 77:1-13)

I, Christ, explain, correct
and deepen the word:

The apostles and disciples who were with Me in the garden of Gethsemane fell asleep again and again. This shows that their souls were not yet alert enough to be able to grasp the import of the event that I now had to face.

Many of My apostles and disciples could not understand Me and My teaching, the law of life, in its depths. Since they were often preoccupied with themselves, they could not comprehend the great whole, nor did they gain deeper insight. Again and again, I had to admonish them to not only speak about the law, God, which I taught and lived as an example, but to fulfill it in everyday life. Yet even they – as many people in all generations – only collected and collect spiritual knowledge. Some of My apostles and disciples were overcome by pride again and again, because they walked at My side and which tempted them into overestimating themselves.

In many a one, My repeated admonishments fell on barren ground; for they sowed again and again in the flesh, instead of in the Spirit, God. Since they were with Me or flocked around Me again and again to hear about the eternal truth, they gathered spiritual knowledge and could therefore answer many questions. Thus, they believed that the knowledge about the laws of God alone would be sufficient to fill the soul with life and power. They confused knowledge with wisdom and this drew many a one into a whirlpool of overestimating themselves.

In the garden of Gethsemane, too, I wanted to explain to them what it means to sleep in such a decisive situation. This is why I awoke them and made it clear to them that they were hardly able to grasp the situation of their neighbor. Their physical eyes were heavy because their spiritual eyes did not see what was about to happen. Thus, they faced the grave event which lay before Me with indifference – even though I had repeatedly talked about the aforesaid hour in which I would become visible and vulnerable to the darkness.

Recognize that spiritual knowledge does not awaken the soul to inner life, nor does it make it alert and aware of the things and events which lie before it and before its neighbors.

The person who is preoccupied with himself falls asleep over the grief of his neighbor because the soul is still weak, that is, it has too little spiritual power, since the person lacks actualization. The egocentric person also misses the impulses which are given to him day after day, because he sows in the flesh, alone, and not in the Spirit, God. Thus, he does not recognize himself, and also faces the sorrow of his neighbor with indifference.

Had My apostles and disciples carried Me consciously within themselves, that is, had they received Me in their hearts through the actualization of the eternal laws, they would not have fallen asleep and would have become aware of the event that was in the offing, for I had revealed it to them in parables, again and again.

Only after My physical death did the great awakening come in many people, and many a one became a faithful follower and began to fulfill what I, as Jesus, had commanded him. Yet, as long as they walked at My side, many did not understand what I said to them and who I was and Am.

The will of the Father, which was also My will in Jesus and is My will as Christ, was fulfilled. I accomplished what had to happen, because, as a result of the sins of the sons and daughters from the lineage of David and other lineages, and, because of the sins of the Jews, the law, God, was not acknowledged. Since they had not established the Kingdom of God on Earth with Me, the cross had to be set up. Despite all adversities, My kingdom, the Kingdom of Peace, will be established through the "It is finished."

So it is in the plan of God. The will of God is being fulfilled. God is boundless, without time or space. Even though His will was not fulfilled at the time when I walked over the Earth as Jesus, it will be fulfilled at a later time. The light, God, is the All-power. The All-power is the victor over the darkness.

God does not look at human time. What to man is today or tomorrow is the present to God. God gives free will to every soul and every person. When His plan is not fulfilled on the path of liberation through the fulfillment of the law of God, then it will be fulfilled through redemption. The latter is given to people and souls as support and help, and it helps them attain liberation from the bondage of sin.

CHAPTER 78

The Betrayal by Judas – The Denial by Peter

*The capture: The darkness received
the power to capture Jesus – The one who takes up
the sword will perish by the sword – The crowing cock,
the voice of conscience (1-18)*

1. While He was still speaking, behold, there came a multitude, and Judas, called Iscariot, went before them. For Judas had received a troop of soldiers and officers from the high priests and Pharisees. They came with lanterns, torches and weapons.

2. But Jesus knew all that should happen to Him. He stepped forth and said to them, "Whom do you seek?" They answered Him, "Jesus of Nazareth." Jesus said to them, "I Am He."

3. As soon as He had said to them 'I Am He,' they withdrew and fell to the ground. When they arose, He asked them once more, "Whom do you seek?" And they said, "Jesus of Nazareth." Jesus answered, "I Am He." And when they heard that, they again withdrew and fell to the ground. And when they arose, He asked again, "Whom do you seek?" And they said, "Jesus of Nazareth." And Jesus answered, "I have told you, I Am He. If you seek Me, let these go."

4. Now the betrayer gave them a sign, saying, "The one I will kiss is He; seize Him."

5. And he stepped up to Jesus, saying, "Hail, Master," and kissed Him. And Jesus said to him, "Friend, why did you come? Is it with a kiss that you betray the Son of Man?"

6. Then Jesus said to the high priests and captains of the temple and to the elders who had come along, "You are coming out with swords and staves as against a thief. When I was with you everyday in the temple, you did not stretch out your hands against Me; but now is your hour and the power of darkness."

7. Then they came and laid hands on Jesus. And Simon Peter stretched out his hand, drew his sword, struck a servant of the high priest and cut off his ear.

8. Then Jesus said to him, "Put your sword back into its place; those who take up the sword will perish by the sword." And Jesus touched his ear and healed him.

9. And He said to Peter, "Do you think that now I could not ask My Father that He send Me more than twelve legions of angels at once? But then how will the scripture be fulfilled, according to which this must happen?"

10. Then all the disciples forsook Him and fled. But those who had seized Jesus led Him away to Caiaphas, the high priest. But they brought Him first to Annas, the father-in-law of Caiaphas, who was the high priest for that year.

11. But it was Caiaphas who advised the Jews that it would be expedient that one man die for the sins of the people.

12. The scribes and the elders were assembled together, but Peter, John and Judas followed from afar until the palace of the high priest. They went in and sat with the servants to see how it would end.

13. And they had kindled a fire in the midst of the hall; and when they had sat down, Peter sat down among them and warmed himself.

14. But a maid beheld him as he sat by the fire and gazing at him, said, "This man was also with Him." But he denied Him, saying, "Woman, I know Him not."

15. And after a little while, another saw him and said, "You are also one of them." And Simon Peter said, "Man, I am not."

16. And before one hour had passed, another one affirmed confidently, saying, "Truly, that one there was with Jesus of Nazareth. His speech betrays him."

17. And Simon denied a third time with an oath, saying, "I do not know the man." And immediately, while he was still speaking, the cock crew.

18. And the Lord turned around and looked upon Simon. And Simon remembered the word of the Lord, how He had said to him, "Before the cock crows this day, you will have denied Me three times." And Simon went out and wept bitterly. (Chap. 78:1-18)

I, Christ, explain, correct
and deepen the word:

The withdrawal of the soldiers shows that they had not yet recognized Me. They withdrew before My light.

With the kiss, I was betrayed and could be apprehended. It symbolizes the betrayal by the whole Jewish people and the betrayal by the sons and daughters from the lineage of David and from other lineages. I carried the cross for all Jews and carry it for all souls and men – for My Redeemer-deed is effective in all souls and men who cling to the wheel of reincarnation.

"When I was with you everyday in the temple, you did not stretch out your hands against Me; but now is your hour and the power of darkness" means that until then the darkness had no power over Me, because My spiritual body was and is immaculate. They received the power to seize Me only after I had enveloped Myself with the guilt of the lineage of David and other lineages and thus became visible to the darkness.

Remember, you people, "Those who take up the sword will perish by the sword" means that the one who arms himself against his neighbor, be it only by affirming the unlawful, will die because of what he has affirmed, or will have to suffer from it. For he has contributed to the negativities which were and are thus brought about. But the one who recognizes this in time, who repents his wrong behavior and makes amends for it, receives salvation and, in certain cases, does not have to bear the effects – or has to bear only a part of them. Whether everything that is sinful or only a part of it has to be borne depends on the complex of guilt.

It is written: "But it was Caiaphas who advised the Jews that it would be expedient that one man die for the sins of the people."

Recognize that I died for the sins of the people.

It is written: "...while he was still speaking, the cock crew."

What happened then still happens even today: When a person deliberately violates the law of life, the cock crows in his inner being. It is his conscience that speaks to him. Happy the one who listens to his conscience and turns back in time.

CHAPTER 79

The Trial Before the High Priest Caiaphas

Behavior when being accused –
The meaning of the words: "I can destroy the temple of God
and erect it in three days" (1-10)

1. The high priest then asked Jesus about His disciples and His teachings, saying, "How old are you? Are you the One who said that He has seen our Father Abraham in His time?"

2. And Jesus answered, "Verily; before Abraham was, I Am." And the high priest said, "You are not yet fifty years old; why do You say that You have seen Abraham? Who are You? Who do You claim to be? What do You teach?"

3. And Jesus answered him, "I have spoken openly to the world, I have always taught in the synagogue and in the temple where all Jews gather and I have said nothing in secret. Why do you ask Me? Ask those who heard Me what I have said to them; behold, they know what I said."

4. And when He had said that, one of the officers who stood by struck Jesus with the palm of his hand, saying, "Is that the way you answer the high priest?" Jesus answered him, "If I have spoken evil, bear witness that it is evil; but if I have spoken well, why do you strike Me?"

5. *Now the high priests, the elders and the whole council sought false witnesses against Jesus, so that they could put Him to death, but found none. Yes, many false witnesses came, but did not agree with one another.*

6. *At last, two false witnesses came. And one of them said, "This one said, 'I can destroy the temple of God and erect it again in three days.'" And the other said, "This man said, 'I will destroy this temple and build up another.'"*

7. *And the high priest arose and said to Him, "Will You not answer anything? What is it that these witnesses are bringing up against You?" But Jesus kept silent. For it was against the law of the Jews to try a man by night.*

8. *And they asked Him, "Are You the Christ? Tell us." And He said to them, "If I tell you, you will not believe Me. And if I also ask you, you would neither answer Me, nor let Me go."*

9. *And they asked Him further, saying, "Do You deny the laws and forbid the eating of flesh, which Moses commanded?" And He answered, "Behold, a greater One than Moses is here."*

10. *And the high priest answered and said to Him, "I entreat You by the living God that You tell us whether You are the Christ, the Son of God." Jesus said to him, "You have said it; but I say to you: Soon you will see the Son of Man sitting on the right side of the power and coming in the clouds of heaven." (Chap. 79:1-10)*

I, Christ, explain, correct
and deepen the word:

The statement "If I have spoken evil, bear witness
that it is evil; but if I have spoken well, why do you
strike Me?" is meant to give indication of a lawful
behavior: When false things are said about you or hands
are laid on you, you should explain and set right the
situation. However, you should not fight for the sake of
the truth with fire, sword or slander. This is done only
by those who do not live in Me. I, the Christ, know how
to protect you and know how to vindicate you – if not
in this earthly life, then in the worlds beyond, in the
realms of the souls.

It is written: "Now the high priests, the elders and
the whole council sought false witnesses against Jesus,
so that they could put Him to death, but found none.
Yes, many false witnesses came, but did not agree with
one another."
Recognize that My spiritual body was and is immaculate. The debt which I took upon Myself from the
lineage of David and from some of the other lineages
was not engraved in My spiritual body, because I had
not committed it. The part-guilt which I took upon
Myself *enveloped* only My body.
It is written: "This one said, 'I can destroy the temple
of God and erect it again in three days.'"
Recognize that the one who looks at matter, alone,
sees only the stones of a temple building and does not

know the inner temple which is resurrected in God. When the silver cord which joins the soul to the body has been severed, the spiritual body returns to the Eternal, who created it. This is possible when the spirit body is immaculate.

It is written: "Soon you will see the Son of Man sitting on the right side of the power and coming in the clouds of heaven." Yes, I, Christ, will come. I have already set out. And, through My own and with My own, I will establish the Kingdom of God, which is in the plan of the Eternal.

11. *Then the high priest rent his clothes, saying, "He has blasphemed; why do we need further witness? Behold, now you have heard His blasphemy. What do you think?" They answered, saying, "He is worthy of death."*

12. *Then they spit in His face and struck Him with their hands, saying, "Prophesy to us, You Christ, who is the one who struck You?"*

13. *And when morning had come, all the high priests and the elders of the people and the whole council held a consultation about Jesus in order to be able to put Him to death.*

14. *And they passed sentence against Jesus that He was worthy of death and that He be bound and led away, and they delivered Him to Pilate.*
(Chap. 79:11-14)

CHAPTER 80

The Remorse of Judas

Injustice towards one's neighbor
can become one's doom – The sinning of the initiates is the
sinning against the Holy Spirit – The one who knowingly
violates the gospel of love crucifies Christ anew (1-10)

1. When Judas saw that Jesus had been sentenced to death, he felt remorse for having betrayed Him. Then he brought again the thirty pieces of silver to the high priests and elders, saying, "I have sinned by betraying innocent blood."

2. They said, "What is that to us? See to it yourself!" And he cast the pieces of silver in the temple, went out and hanged himself.

3. But the high priests took the pieces of silver, saying, "It is not lawful to put them into the treasury, for this is blood money."

4. And they took counsel and bought with them the potter's field, to bury strangers in. Therefore, to this day, that field has been called Aceldama, that is, the field of blood.

5. Thus was fulfilled what was told by the prophet Zachariah, "They weighed thirty pieces of silver as My price. And they took the thirty pieces of silver, the sum for which He was valued by the children of Israel, and gave them for the potter's field and cast them to the potter in the house of the Lord."

6. Now, Jesus had said to His disciples, "Woe to the one who receives the initiation and thereafter falls into sin!

7. Because for such people, there is no place of repentance in this cycle, seeing that they have once more crucified the heavenly Son of God and Man, and put the Christ in them to deep shame.

8. For such ones are worse than animals, which you ignorantly cause to perish; for in your scriptures, it is written: What happens to the animals also happens to the sons of men.

9. They all have one breath; just as the one dies, so dies the other, so that no man has priority over an animal; for all go to the same place – all come from dust and return to dust."

10. Jesus said these things for those who had not yet been regenerated, who had not yet received the Spirit of God, the Spirit of divine love, in their souls, who, after having once received the light, nevertheless crucified the Son of God anew, putting Him to deep shame. (Chap. 80:1-10)

I, Christ, explain, correct
and deepen the word:

It is written about Judas, "I have sinned by betraying innocent blood." Remember this when you are against your neighbor, when you want to judge and condemn him.

The one who betrays, judges or condemns his neighbor delivers himself up to the darkness, which drives him into death – if this is possible and serves its interests – in order to possess his soul for a longer period of time.

With the words, "See to it yourself!" they drove Judas to death. They no longer gave him the possibility to explain what he had done and to make amends for it.

Therefore, pay attention to your words and deeds. An injustice can very quickly lead to a disaster. The cause is borne by the originator, but also by those who approve of it, who derive benefit from it and who make it larger.

Know that you can recognize a symbolism in every situation that concerned Me and My life as Jesus. Thus, everything that happened to Me and was perpetrated on Me, as Jesus, is a symbol for many.

It is written: "Woe to the one who receives the initiation and thereafter falls into sin!" The one who hears and accepts the laws of life thus commits himself to fulfilling them. Thereupon, he receives the initiation, the blessing, so that he, as a messenger of God, may bring the laws of life to those who want to hear them.

When an initiate falls into sin again, he sins against the Holy Spirit. Depending on the intensity and extent, he often can no longer make amends for his guilt within one cycle. For the one who knowingly violates the gospel of life crucifies Me, the Christ, in himself, thus crucifying himself, too.

You people in all generations, keep the following in mind, "What happens to the animals happens also to the sons of men."

What man does to the animals he does to himself. For the life, God, is in all forms of life; God did not give man the right to put himself above the animal. He gave him the commandment to love life, regardless of the form in which it manifests itself.

The words "Jesus said these things for those who had not yet been regenerated" should indicate that soul and man are called upon to attain rebirth in the Spirit of God. The one who strives for it will consciously receive the Spirit of the Eternal in himself and will also give love, which he receives from God.

The one who sins again, despite knowing better, crucifies Me, the Christ, anew.

CHAPTER 81

The Trial Before Pilate

Those who live in the truth
are righteous in their thinking, speaking and acting (8-9).
The negative forces tried to prevent the Redeemer-deed –
"I find no guilt in Him" – At all times, the darkness is
allowed to test its strength against the light – The power of
sham Christianity is vanishing – The just One suffered for
injustice – The cross: a symbol of redemption and resurrection
or of defeat (10-32)

1. Then they led Jesus from Caiaphas to the hall of judgment, to Pontius Pilate, the governor. It was early, and they did not go into the judgment hall, lest they should be defiled, but so that they could celebrate the feast.

2. Pilate therefore went out to them, saying, "What accusation do you bring against this man?" They answered, saying to him, "If He were not a wrongdoer, we would not have delivered Him up to you. We have a law and, according to our law, He must die; because He wants to abolish the customs and habits which Moses commanded of us, yes, He makes of Himself the Son of God."

3. Then Pilate said to them, "So take Him and judge Him according to your law." For he knew that they had delivered Him out of envy.

4. To that the Jews said to him, "The law does not allow us to sentence anyone to death." Thus was fulfilled the word of Jesus, who had said what kind of death He would die.

5. And they accused Him further, saying, "We found this man inciting the people, forbidding them to give tribute to Caesar, saying that He, Himself, is Christ, a king."

6. Then Pilate entered again into the judgment hall and called Jesus and asked Him, "Are You the king of the Jews?" Jesus answered him, "Do you say this yourself, or did others say it to you about Me?"

7. Pilate answered, "Am I a Jew? Your own people and the high priests have delivered You up to me; what have You done?" Jesus answered, "My kingdom is not of this world. If My kingdom were of this world, My followers would fight, so that I would not be delivered to the Jews; but now My kingdom is not from here."

8. Then Pilate asked Him, "Are You a king then?" Jesus answered: "You say that I Am a king. I was born and came into this world, so that I should bear witness to the truth. Every one who is of the truth hears My voice."

9. Pilate said to Him, "What is truth?" Jesus said, "Truth comes from heaven." Pilate said, "Then truth is not on Earth." Jesus said to Pilate, "Believe it, the truth is on Earth among those who accept and obey it. Those who are in the truth judge justly."
(Chap. 81: 1-9)

I, Christ, explain, correct
and deepen the word:

Verily, "truth comes from heaven." It came to Earth through all God-filled prophets and through Me, as Jesus of Nazareth; and it comes through Me, the Christ, and through all those who live in the truth. The truth sets soul and person free. And those who strive for the truth know My voice, the truth.

The Kingdom of God, which I, as Jesus of Nazareth, proclaimed and wanted to set up with the Jewish people, is coming to Earth. So it is in the plan of God, as already revealed. Those who live in the truth bring the justice of God, thus rendering the condemnation void.

It is written, "Those who are in the truth judge justly." During this time [1989], the word "judge" no longer has the meaning which it had generations ago. See in the word "judge" here, the meaning: to be righteous, faithful and honest. For those who live in God will be righteous in their thinking, speaking and acting.

10. *And when he had heard this, he went out again to the Jews and said to them, "I do not find any guilt in Him." And when He was accused by the high priests and elders, He did not answer them.*

11. *Then Pilate said to Him, "Do You not hear, how much they bring forth against You?"*

12. *And He did not answer a single word anymore, so much so that the governor was very astonished. And he again said to them, "I do not find any guilt in this man."*

13. And they flew into a rage even more, crying, "He incites the people, teaching in the whole Jewish country, from Galilee to here." But when Pilate heard the name Galilee, he asked whether the man were a Galilean.

14. And when he heard that He belonged to Herod's jurisdiction, he sent Him to Herod, who was also in Jerusalem at that time.

15. When Herod saw Jesus, he was very glad; for he had wished to see Him for a long time, because he had heard much about Him and he hoped that he would see a miracle from Him.

16. Then he questioned Him with many words; but He did not answer him. The high priests and scribes stood by and vehemently accused Him, and many false witnesses rose up against Him and charged Him with many things which He did not know.

17. And with his warriors, Herod despised and mocked Him, arrayed Him in a splendid robe and sent Him again to Pilate. And on the same day, Pilate and Herod became friends, for before they were enemies.

18. And Pilate went again into the judgment hall and asked Jesus, "Where do You come from?" But Jesus gave him no answer. Then Pilate said to Him, "Do You not speak to me? Do You not know that I have the power to crucify You and the power to release You?"

19. Jesus answered, "You would have no power at all against Me, were it not given you from above; therefore, the one who has delivered Me to you has the greater sin."

20. From then on, Pilate tried to release Him; but the Jews cried out, shouting, "If you let this man go, you are not Caesar's friend; for the one who makes a king of himself speaks against Caesar."

21. And Pilate called together the high priests and the responsible ones of the people. When he had sat down on the judgment seat, his wife sent someone to tell him, "Have nothing to do with this just man; for because of Him I have suffered many things last night in a dream."

22. And Pilate said to them, "You have brought this man to me as being one who incites the people, and behold, I have examined Him before you and have found no guilt in Him about the things you accused Him of. Nor did Herod, to whom I have sent Him, find anything in Him worthy of death.

23. But you have a custom that I should release someone to you for the Passover. Do you now want that I release the king of the Jews to you?"

24. Then they cried again in one voice, "Not this man, but Barabbas!" But Barabbas was a robber who, because of incitement in the city and a murder, had been cast into prison.

25. But Pilate wanted to release Jesus, and asked them once more, "Which one of the two do you want me to release? Barabbas or Jesus, who is called Christ?" And they shouted, "Barabbas!"

26. Pilate said to them, "What then shall I do with Jesus who, they say, is Christ?" Then they all shouted to him, "Let Him be crucified!"

27. *And the governor asked, "What evil has He done?" But they cried out ever louder, "Crucify Him! Crucify Him!"*

28. *And Pilate stepped forward and said to them, "Behold, I bring Him to you again and say to you that I find no guilt in Him." But they cried out again, "Crucify Him, Crucify Him!"*

29. *And Pilate asked them for the third time, "Why? What evil has He done? I have not found in Him any guilt worthy of death. Instead of that, I will have Him lashed and let Him go."*

30. *But they cried incessantly with loud voices, requiring that He should be crucified. And their voices and those of the high priests were louder than all others.*

31. *When Pilate saw that he did not have the upper hand, but that a considerable tumult arose, he took water and washed his hands before the people, saying, "I am innocent of the blood of this just person. See to it yourselves!"*

32. *Then the whole people answered, crying, "His blood be on us and on our children!" And Pilate gave orders that everything should take place as they required. And he delivered Jesus up to them, according to their will. (Chap. 81:10-32)*

I, Christ, explain, correct
and deepen the word:

Pilate spoke as follows: "I find no guilt in Him." I was not guilty, neither according to the law of God nor according to the law of this world. My incarnated spirit body was immaculate, but was enveloped by a part-guilt of the lineage of David and by the guilt of some others. This moved the negative forces to make use of every opportunity and of every active correspondence in the high priests, scribes, elders and in the people, in order to convict Me. For if I had committed only *one* sin, for example, if I had spoken one unlawful word or had defended Myself in any way, then the Redeemer-deed could not have been accomplished.

The part-guilt of those who were and are in the Redeemer-mission – with which I enveloped Myself and which made My capture possible – could not prevent the Deed of Redemption. I, Myself, Christ, would have had to have sinned against My Father. To attain this, the negative forces summoned everything. Every Jew who was vulnerable to this was incited by the demonic forces to speak against Me. All the accusations were contrived to bring about Pilate's downfall and, above all, Mine.

With Pilate they were successful. Even though he washed his hands of it, he still fell into sin. Though he was convinced of My innocence, he delivered Me up, the innocent. Pilate failed the test, for he gave orders against his conviction.

The inner recognition is of little use when the person does not do what he has recognized.

At all times – including today [1989] – those who believe they have to administer the laws of God stir up the people. They admittedly literally preach the word of God, but without actualizing or fulfilling it.

The one who does not live what he proclaims constantly lives in fear of what he teaches to his neighbor without fulfilling it himself. Thus, such people are afraid of their own doctrine, because they feel that what they have not fulfilled turns against them. In this way, and even today, they twist the law of God and use it to their own advantage.

It was the satanic that cried through the scribes, Pharisees and elders, and also through the Jewish people. The negative forces influenced all the Jews who let themselves be led astray, in order to stir up hatred against Me and bear false witness.

At all times, the opportunity is given to the negative forces to take their measure against the light. It was also this way almost two thousand years ago. The darkness was allowed to try its strength against the light. It could make use of all possibilities to still prevent what was already indicated in the spheres of purification as well as in the atmospheric layer of the earth: redemption through Me, the Christ of God, who became man and, as man, accepted the challenge of the negative forces, so that they could measure themselves against the man Jesus – and thus against the Christ of God, the Co-Regent of the heavens, in the earthly garment.

The persecution of Jesus and turning Him in point to the following:

The one who follows Me will suffer persecution like I did, as Jesus of Nazareth. He will have to endure humiliation and suffering, as I did. For, as they persecuted Me as Jesus of Nazareth, in the almost two thousand years since then, they have repeatedly persecuted, slandered and even killed those who have followed in My footsteps.

The persecution of My true followers persists into the present time [1989]. Again and again, it is the same ones who persecute Me in My own; for, despite the "It is finished," I Am still the thorn in the heart of those who want to maintain and expand the Demons' State. During the present time [1989], it is again the scribes and those who are servile to them in the ecclesiastic and worldly authorities. They, too, incite the people with untruths against the followers of the Christ.

Yet, everything comes to an end. What took place during almost two thousand years is now bearing its effects and befalls those who, for two thousand years, have continued to behave as they did at My time, as Jesus of Nazareth. Today too, they are afraid of losing their position and their prestige. But their power is gradually coming to an end – the effects of their causes are breaking in over them.

The position of the negative forces is becoming weaker and weaker. The present scribes, Pharisees and authorities of the state and of the church are calling out like drowning people. They sense that the flood which will sweep them away is already on its way. What was wrongly built up in My name, over the course of two thousand years, is fading away: a power which indeed called and calls itself Christian, but neither was nor is Christian and which, in many ways, took and takes My name, Christ, in vain.

The New Era is awakening and will rise from the ruins of the past. Through their selfless work, My own will cause the devastated land to blossom again. What is being built up even now, during the time of change, and will be completed when the sinfulness on Earth is over, is the New Israel – in its center, the New Jerusalem, the covenant city with its communities in the Kingdom of Peace of Jesus Christ.

Recognize that the statement "You would have no power at all against Me, were it not given you from above; therefore, the one who has delivered Me to you has the greater sin" means that the darkness has power solely over those who have darkened the light of the Eternal and keep it darkened. My eternal Father allowed My capture because I interceded for the lineage of David and for others, and suffered for the many Jews who wanted to have a king of this world. In the end, it happened for all souls as well as for all human beings who have sinned and sin against the law of life: The just One suffered for the injustice and endured the fact that what was done to Him was what He Himself had not caused.

The powers of the heavens did not rush to My help as much as they could have done, if the lineage of

David and others had not slept as a result of their sin and if the Jewish people had accepted Me as their Messiah and the builder of the Kingdom of God on Earth. I would have been their king – however, not for this world, but for the Kingdom of God on Earth, for a world in which the laws of God would have been fulfilled.

"Not this man, but Barabbas!" means that the blind ones and the demons keep the blind ones blind. They can blind and incite only the spiritually blind even more, so that these blindly cry and rage and demand the just One instead of the unjust one.

They cried "Crucify Him! Crucify Him!"

Only the one who himself still hangs on the cross of his sins calls, "Crucify Him, crucify Him." The one who has crucified himself through sin sees only through the eye of sin and wants to see all people where he himself is: on the cross of sin.

The cross was raised with the body of Jesus, but the body was taken from the cross, and the resurrected One showed and revealed Himself. This means that I, Christ, Am the resurrected life in all souls and men.

The true Christian sees the cross without the crucified One as the symbol of redemption and as the resurrection in God. The cross without the body also symbolizes the path from Earth into heaven, to the heart of God. Only *that* person who has not yet crucified his ego and wants to hold on to his humanness looks to the cross with the crucified One.

The demons made the cross with the body. With that, they want to symbolize My defeat. Yet the cross and the crucified One became and are *their* cross and their defeat.

The true Christian remembers My resurrection, since he is resurrected in Me and through Me. Only the one who is not yet consciously resurrected in Me, the Christ, mourns My death as Jesus. The one who is not yet consciously resurrected in Me, that is, who still lives in sin, cries out again and again, "Crucify Him, crucify Him!" Therefore, those people who still cherish their sins, who treasure their base ego, hold up the cross with the body.

The person who loves his sin and this sinful world thinks of the crucified One and not of the resurrected One, since he himself is not yet resurrected in Me.

"His blood be on us and on our children!" means that every cause already bears the effect in itself. Each person who creates causes must himself bear the effect. Thus, the one who sows will harvest his seed – in this incarnation or in future ones. And so, the same ones come to Earth again and again as children, until what they have caused has been atoned for.

CHAPTER 82

The Crucifixion of Jesus

Jesus resisted
all attacks and became the Redeemer (1-2).
Pilate sacrificed an innocent One in order to keep his posi-
tion (3-4). Begetting and giving birth in sin or in selfless
love (5-7). The person determines the garment his soul will
wear in the spheres beyond (8-13). The repentant sinner
(14-16). The seeming triumph of the darkness became a
victory of the Christ for the glorification of the Father –
Only the pure spiritual body can enter heaven (17-19). "My
God, My God, why have You forsaken Me?" (20). The law
of love and unity (21-23). The earthquake, a sign of the
Christ-power (24-27). There is no right to sentence to death
or to kill (28)

1. *Then he released Barabbas to them. After he had*
Jesus lashed, he delivered Him to be crucified. Then the
soldiers of the governor took Him into the judgment
hall and the whole band of soldiers gathered around
Him.

2. *And they stripped Him and put a purple robe on*
Him. And they plaited a crown of thorns and put it on
His head and gave Him a reed in His right hand, bowed
their knee before Him and mocked Him, saying, "Hail,
king of the Jews!" (Chap. 82:1-2)

I, Christ, explain, correct
and deepen the word:

The demons mobilized all the means at their disposal to tempt Me, so that I would doubt My mission. For any doubt in God is sin.

I did not doubt and did not sin and thus the "It is finished" could be spoken so that the part-power of the primordial power, a part of My spiritual heritage, could flow as sparks into the souls. Neither the mockery nor the derision with the purple robe and the crown of thorns and the reed could move Me to sin. I remained in the Eternal, in whom I Am, Christ.

No one comes to the Father in the heavens but through Me, the Son of God and Co-Regent of the heavens, who became the Redeemer of all souls and men.

Had the Jewish people and the lineage of David stood by Me, I would not have had to suffer death on the cross. I would have ascended to the heavens before the eyes of all and heaven would have remained among My people, since people would have fulfilled the heavenly laws – and I would have returned to them as the ruler of the Kingdom of God on Earth.

Recognize that the person who merely hears the law of life without actualizing it remains as he is and is used by the one who believes himself to be ruling the world: the satan of the senses, the negative forces.

I remained in the eternal Father and, in the spirit, accomplished the Work of Redemption which had been decided in heaven: the leading of all souls and men home through the work of love.

3. *Then Jesus stepped forth, wearing the crown of thorns and the purple robe. And Pilate said to them, "Behold this man!"*

4. *When the high priests and the officers of the people saw Him, they cried out, "Crucify Him! Crucify Him." And Pilate said to them, "Take Him and crucify Him, for I find no guilt in Him." (Chap. 82:3-4)*

I, Christ, explain, correct
and deepen the word:

Even though Pilate spoke words as follows "Take Him and crucify Him, for I find no guilt in Him," he nevertheless became guilty. Had Pilate used his inner recognition and his outer position, he could have brought many a Jew to his senses.

Remember that it is not possible to move an entire people to turn back all at once. Every single person is a part of the people and is important for the people. Had Pilate thought in such a way and acted accordingly, he would have been for Me, Christ. But this way, he opposed Me.

Pilate showed his weakness. He feared the people, for he wanted to keep his position in the world. The behavior of Pilate, too, was and is a symbol for many. The world-oriented person depends on the masses to maintain his power and position in this world. For this, he sacrifices his neighbor, in order to maintain his prestige and preserve his outer power.

5. *And they spit upon Him and took the reed and struck Him on the head. And when they had mocked Him, they took off His robe and put His own raiment on Him and led Him away to crucify Him.*

6. *And when they led Him away, they stopped a man, Simon, a Cyrenian, who was just coming in from the country. They forced him to carry the cross after Jesus. A great multitude followed Him, together with many women who bewailed and lamented Him.*

7. *But Jesus, turning to them, said, "Daughters of Jerusalem, do not weep over Me, but weep over yourselves and your children. For behold, the days will come when they will say: Blessed are the barren and the wombs which have not borne and the breasts that have not nursed! (Chap. 82:5-7)*

I, Christ, explain, correct
and deepen the word:

Recognize that only those people who themselves are spit on and beaten by their sins are the ones who spit on their neighbor and beat him. Thus, as Jesus, I was a symbol to many. Simon, too, who helped Me carry My cross, was a symbol for many.

Many simple people, who keep their hearts free from the trumpery, the pomp and splendor of this world, will be true selfless helpers in the vineyard of the Lord. They will help many people carry their cross.

My life as Jesus of Nazareth will be a symbol for all people until the spiritual life, the life in Me, has awakened in everyone. And My words will have validity in the world until the light of the world has penetrated all souls and people. But as long as many people still let themselves be ruled by the darkness, they will also mislead over and over again, those who are a wavering reed in the wind, who turn one time to the Spirit of God, then again to the world. Many of them repeatedly create new causes and will give birth, also repeatedly, to children having the same or similar causes.

The meaning of the words "Blessed are the barren and the wombs which have not borne and the breasts that have not nursed!" is: All those who are a wavering reed in the wind and who beget and give birth to children like themselves should be saddened about themselves. For like always draws to like again and again. The words contain the law of attraction and the settlement of the causes which bind parents and children to one another and which they have to expiate and clear up together.

The words "Blessed are the barren and the wombs which have not borne and the breasts that have not nursed!" also mean that the one who begets and conceives in sin and immorality gives birth again to those who are the same and similar, and the sinner will have to suffer again under his sin. This holds true especially in the days when that which I revealed will happen: The materialistic world will collapse. Woe to those who live in sin!

However, not every so-called barrenness is to be attributed to a guilt as a cause. People of the light will give birth to light-filled souls, when it is time for light-filled souls to come to Earth.

Recognize: Blessed are those who have given and give birth to light-filled souls; for they did not nor do they beget in sin, desire and passion; and they did not nor do they give birth in sin. They begot and beget in selfless love and give birth in selfless love. Such breasts will also give selfless life.

8. *Then they will begin to say to the mountains: Fall on us. And to the hills: Cover us. For if this is done to the green wood, what shall be done to the dry?"*

9. *And two others, being wrongdoers, were also led with Him to be put to death. And when they came to the place called Calvary or Golgotha – that is, place of the skull – they crucified Him, and also the wrongdoers, one on the right side and one on the left.*

10. *And it was the third hour when they crucified Him; and they gave Him vinegar to drink, mingled with gall. And after He had tasted it, He did not want to drink. And Jesus said, "Father, forgive them, for they know not what they do!"*

11. After the soldiers had crucified Jesus, they took His raiment and made four parts, to every soldier a part, and also His vesture. Now the vesture was without seam, woven in one piece. They therefore said among themselves: Let us not rend it, but cast lots for it, for whose it shall be.

12. That the scripture be fulfilled, which says, "They divided My raiment among them and cast lots for My vesture." So, this is what the soldiers did. And sitting down, they kept watch.

13. And an inscription was fastened over Him in Greek, Latin and Hebrew letters, "This is the King of the Jews." (Chap. 82:8-13)

I, Christ, explain, correct
and deepen the word:

They divided My clothes among themselves and cast lots for them. The greed of man does not even stop at the clothes of someone sentenced to death. The greedy ego does not respect anything or anybody – not even itself. A person cannot enter the Kingdom of Heaven with all the possessions that he has acquired in an honest or dishonest way. He will have to give up even his last piece of clothing.

On the other hand, the soul – with its garments of sin or virtue – goes into the life beyond. Neither soul nor person can prevent this. The soul will bear what the person has sown. It cannot conceal it nor cast it off, except by forgiving, by asking for forgiveness, by making amends and by not committing the same sins again. Only then, can the garment of sin be taken from the soul.

It is not the dice that determine which garment you wear or want to cast off as soul, but you, yourself – in the way you behave towards the law of God.

The words "This is the King of the Jews" were spoken in mockery; but Pilate sensed that they meant more: This is the king, the ruler of the Kingdom of God on Earth, of the New Israel and the New Jerusalem.

14. Many Jews read this title, for the place where Jesus was crucified was near the city. Then the high priests of the Jews said to Pilate: "Do not write 'the King of the Jews,' but that 'He said, I am the King of the Jews.'" Pilate answered, "What I have written, I have written."

15. One of the wrongdoers who were hanged mocked Him, saying, "If You are Christ, save Yourself and us!" Then the other rebuked him, saying, "Do you not fear God, seeing that you are in the same condemnation? We are in it justly, for we receive the due reward of our deeds; but this man has done nothing wrong."

16. And he said to Jesus, "Lord, remember me when You come into Your kingdom." And Jesus said to him, "Verily, I say to you: Today you will be with Me in paradise." (Chap. 82:14-16)

I, Christ, explain, correct
and deepen the word:

The words "Verily I say to you: Today you will be with Me in paradise," which I spoke as Jesus to the repentant sinner, were words of forgiveness. He entered into higher spheres of life where he had to endure neither pain nor torment; for he had recognized himself, had repented and atoned, and thus, was received in Me, the Christ. He had stolen for his starving family.

The other one was a murderer and received his reward.

17. And they passed by the cross and reviled Him, shaking their heads and saying, "You wanted to destroy the temple and build it again in three days. Save Yourself now! If You are the Son of God, come down from the cross!"

18. And the high priests, too, mocking Him with the scribes and elders, said, "He saved a lamb, but He cannot save Himself. If He is the king of Israel, let Him now come down from the cross, and we will believe in Him. He trusted in God; let God deliver Him now, if God will have Him. For He said: I Am the Son of God."

19. The usurers and the dealers in animals expressed themselves likewise, saying, "You have driven out of the temple the traders in oxen, sheep and doves, but You Yourself are a sheep that is sacrificed." (Chap. 82:17-19)

I, Christ, explain, correct
and deepen the word:

I endured all that, so that redemption could come to all souls and people – to the spheres of purification and to this world. The darkness slandered, ridiculed and killed My earthly body; however, it did not achieve what it wanted through this, namely, to separate Me from God by doubting Him. I abided in My Father and the Father abided in Me.

In this way, I glorified the Father in Me. And so, the glory of the Father came into this world through Me, the Christ, as the light of redemption. And no one can extinguish this light of the world. It has implanted itself in all souls and men – even in the darkest demon. Whether he wants to admit this or not: he, too, has received the light of the Redeemer-light from Me. He, too, will be freed from his sins through it.

I stepped down from the cross, but not with My earthly body. It is not the earthly body that can enter the heavens, but the pure spiritual body alone. However, the one who sees the earthly body as the criterion for all things wants to keep the physical body. And if he lives in sin, he will also cast off his physical body through sin and in sin. This can be accompanied by much suffering, for it is his sin that he wants to keep. The sin ties itself to the physical body and thus, to this world.

All those who follow Me will have to endure the same or similar things as I did – until the end of this sinful world. The following holds true for them: If they have persecuted Me, they will persecute you, too. If they have slandered and ridiculed Me, they will slander and ridicule you, too. If they have spoken evil of Me, they will speak evil of you, too. If they have killed Me, they will kill and torment many of you, too – whether by words, deeds or both.

20. *And there was darkness over all the land from the sixth hour to the ninth hour. But some who were standing around lit their torches, for the darkness was very great. And about the sixth hour, Jesus cried with a loud voice, "Eli, Eli, lama sabachthani?" that is, "My God, My God, why have You forsaken Me?"*
(Chap. 82:20)

I, Christ, explain, correct
and deepen the word:

The heart of Jesus cried the words, "My God, My God, why have You forsaken Me?"

From the cross I saw many peoples – countless people, whose souls repeatedly came into the earthly garment and walked in darkness for many centuries. They had lost the inner path. In their ignorance, in their need, illness and loneliness, they called out to God. However, they were concerned only with their physical bodies, not with their souls. They let the latter waste away.

Thus, My call on the cross was the call of many generations that believed and believe they are lost. For My suffering and dying were and are a symbol for the suffering and dying of people. My words "My God, My God, why have You forsaken Me?" are the words of the people of all nations and generations which, in their unbelief, accused and accuse God for their sins. I did not speak these words for Myself, but as a symbol for many.

Even today, My words on the cross are still a symbol for many people. Even today, they still call in their outer need, "My God, My God, why have You forsaken me?" For even today [1989], they still do not understand that salvation, help and healing come solely from within. Even today, many struggle only for their earthly life, because their true being is still foreign to them.

So My call on the cross was the call of those who believed and still believe they are lost. Their call will be heard – when they open their heart to God and no longer cling to their earthly life with their senses. Then they will be heard, since they have found the path to the heart of God.

The Comforter and the Redeemer, the Christ of God, who I Am, I, the way, the truth and the life, brought and brings into this world once more the path of love which leads to the heart of God.

As the Father glorified Himself in Me, the Jesus, and glorifies Himself in Me, the Christ, I will glorify Myself in those who truly call to God; for they will find what their heart longs for: God, the love and the life, their true being.

21. *Some of them who stood there and heard this said, "This man calls for Elijah;" others said, "He calls upon the sun." The rest said, "Let us stay and see whether Elijah will come and rescue Him."*

22. *Now there stood by the cross of Jesus His mother and His mother's sister, Mary, the wife of Cleophas, and Mary Magdalene.*

23. *When Jesus saw His mother and the disciple whom he loved standing by, He said to His mother, "Woman, behold your son!" And He said to the disciple, "Behold your mother!" And from that hour, the disciple took her into his own home. (Chap. 82:21-23)*

I, Christ, explain, correct
and deepen the word:

The words to Mary, "Woman, behold your son!" and to the disciple, "Behold your mother!," symbolize the law of selfless love and unity. These words were understood by those for whom they were meant. The disciple fulfilled the law of love and unity and took Mary into his home. For a commandment from the law of God says: One for all – Christ; and all for One – Christ; each one for each one – in good thoughts and in the right love and care.

The one who keeps the law of love and unity is there for his neighbor. He receives his neighbor not only in his heart but also in his home, when his neighbor truly needs help.

The one who keeps the law of love and unity and who himself abides in the house of God, in the heart of God, also leads the people of good will to God's love and unity.

24. *Jesus now knew that everything had taken place and that the scripture was fulfilled. He said, "I Am thirsty." And from a vessel they filled a sponge with vinegar and put it on a hyssop and held it to His mouth.*

25. *And Jesus cried with a loud voice, "Father, into Your hands I commend My Spirit!"*

26. *When Jesus had received the vinegar, He cried aloud, "It is finished!" And He bowed His head and gave up the spirit. And it was the ninth hour.*

27. *And behold, there was great thunder and lightning, and the partition wall of the sanctum before which the veil hung fell down and was rent in two. The Earth quaked, and the rocks, too, burst apart.*
(Chap. 82:24-27)

I, Christ, explain, correct
and deepen the word:

The earthquake symbolizes not only the freedom of the souls but above all the power, the life, which all souls received, whether they were incarnate or discarnate:

It is the part-power of the primordial power, the Christ-power, which divided into sparks and entered all souls – also those of the demons.

Through the powerful cosmic irradiation, some people became temporarily clairvoyant and perceived souls which, through this power of redemption, went into higher spheres of inner life; for they had attained the inner maturity for higher levels of life and had longingly waited for the power of redemption, for the Redeemer-spark, which pointed and points the way for them to the heart of the Eternal.

28. *Now when the centurion and those who were with him, watching Jesus, saw the earthquake and all that happened, they feared greatly and said, "Truly this was a Son of God." (Chap. 82:28)*

I, Christ, explain, correct
and deepen the word:

It is written that they feared greatly and said, "Truly this was a Son of God."

When recognition frightens people, they should examine their conscience: How often have they already committed deeds which they now recognize as being unlawful? The fear and the recognition were, in the last analysis, pangs of conscience; they wanted to admonish the so-called centurion and those who were guarding Jesus with him and to tell them that a person is not allowed to kill someone himself, nor to become an accomplice in the death of his neighbor, for instance, by ordering the death of a person. For who has the right to condemn others to death or to kill them?

God, the Eternal, did not command such a thing. On the contrary, He, the great All-One, who is the law of life, has commanded man: You shall not kill. For He is the life, not death.

So-called death is the passing away of the earthly body, which is from the earth and returns to the earth. It is a lawful process, contingent upon the incarnation of the soul, and will take place according to the way the person thinks and lives and according to the condition of his soul.

God is the life. For this reason, man has no right to kill the earthly body of his neighbor or to cause its death. The one who consciously kills or consciously causes death will, according to the law of sowing and reaping, have to endure and suffer what he has caused during a life that was far from God.

29. *And many women were there, who followed from Galilee, ministering unto Him. Among them were Mary, the mother of James and Joses, and the mother of Zebedee's children, and they cried and lamented, saying,*

"The light of the world is hidden before our eyes, the Lord of our love is crucified!"

30. Because it was the day before Sabbath, the Jews asked Pilate that the legs of the bodies might be broken and that the bodies be taken away, so that they would not remain on the cross over the Sabbath (for it was the Passover Sabbath).

31. Then the soldiers came and broke the legs of the two who were crucified with Him. But when they came to Jesus and saw that He had already died, they did not break His legs, but one of the soldiers pierced His heart with his spear and immediately there flowed out blood and water.

32. And he that saw it bore witness and his witness is true. He knows that he speaks the truth, that you, too, may believe. For those things happened that the scriptures might be fulfilled: You shall not break any of His bones, and again: They shall look on Him whom they pierced. (Chap. 82:29-32)

CHAPTER 83

The Burial of Jesus

*About the burial of the dead (1-3). Honoring the
dead and the wake (4-10)*

*1. Now when the evening had come, Joseph of Ari-
mathaea, an honorable councilor who also waited for
the Kingdom of God, came and went in boldly to Pilate
and requested the body of Jesus. (He was a good and
just man, and had not consented to the decision of the
council).*

*2. And Pilate marveled that He was already dead
and, calling the centurion to him, asked him whether
He had been dead for long. And when he had heard it
from the centurion, he gave the body to Joseph who
came and took down the body of Jesus.*

*3. And there came Nicodemus, too, who had come
before to Jesus at night. He brought a mixture of myrrh
and aloe, about a hundred pounds in weight. Then they
took the body of Jesus and wound it in linen cloths with
the herbs, according to the Jewish burial custom.
(Chap. 83: 1-3)*

I, Christ, explain, correct
and deepen the word:

It is written, "Then they took the body of Jesus and
wound it in linen cloths with the herbs, according to the

Jewish burial custom." It was a Jewish burial custom – a custom as such, but not a commandment. Therefore, I, Christ, say:

If your still existing earthly law permits, wrap the dead earthly bodies in cloths and give them to the earth; or if you recognize that the soul of the deceased lives in God because the person has led a righteous, God-filled life, then give the perishable body over to the fire a few days after death. Thus, the substances can more quickly be given to the Earth, from which man comes.

4. *Now in the place where He was crucified, there was a garden and in the garden a new sepulcher, wherein no man was yet laid. There they laid Jesus, and it was at the beginning of the second watch when they buried Him, because of the Jews' preparation day, for the sepulcher was nigh at hand.*

5. *And Mary Magdalene and the other Mary, and Mary, the mother of Joses, looked at the sepulcher in which He had been laid.*

6. *And also the women who had come with Him from Galilee followed, bearing lamps in their hands, looked at the sepulcher and how His body was laid and began to cry and lament.*

7. *And they returned and prepared herbal mixtures and ointments and waited for the end of the Sabbath.*

8. *Now on the day following the day of preparation, the high priests and Pharisees went together to Pilate,*

saying, "Master, we remember that this deceiver said while still alive, 'After three days, I will rise again.'

9. Command therefore to have the sepulcher secured until the third day is over, lest His disciples come at night and steal Him and say to the people, 'He is risen from the dead,' and the last deceit is worse than the first."

10. Pilate said to them, "You have a guard, go your way and make it as secure as you can." So they went and secured the sepulcher, sealing the stone and setting guards in front of it, until the third day would be over. (Chap. 83:4-10)

I, Christ, explain, correct
and deepen the word:

Recognize that your earthly customs show you where you stand. Why do you watch over your dead? You might say, to honor the deceased. I, the Christ, ask you, Whom do you want to honor? In whose honor?

If a person has not paid nor pays honor to God, he is then anxious to be honored by people and will try everything to be honored, alive or dead. When people honor people, they do not give honor to God, who knows all things, who is the life of the soul.

The person who watches over the dead, worrying that the earthly garment of the soul might be stolen, as was the case with the guard at Jesus' sepulcher – is aware of his own misdeed, and thus, of his sin.

CHAPTER 84

The Resurrection of Jesus

The angel at the sepulcher (1-5). The light-filled, powerful soul is closer to God (6). Message and guidance by angels (7-8). The task of the earthly body and the spiritual body of Christ (9). The transformation of the physical body of Jesus – The cross with or without a body (10-13)

1. *At the end of the Sabbath, as it began to dawn in the early morning of the first day of the week, Mary Magdalene came to the sepulcher, bringing the spices which she had prepared; and others came with her.*

2. *And as they were going, they said among themselves, "Who will roll away the stone from the entrance of the sepulcher for us?" For it was big. And when they came to the place and looked, they saw that the stone had been rolled away.*

3. *For behold, there was a great earthquake. The angel of the Lord descended from heaven and rolled the stone away from the entrance and sat upon it. His countenance was like lightning and his raiment white as snow. The guards were so much frightened that they fell on the ground as if they were dead.*

4. *And the angel said to the women, "Do not be afraid! I know that you seek Jesus, who was crucified. He is not here; for He is risen, as He said.*

5. *Come, see the place where the Lord lay. And go quickly and tell His disciples that He is risen from the*

dead. And behold, He goes before you into Galilee; there you will see Him; behold, I have told you." (Chap. 84:1-5)

I, Christ, explain, correct
and deepen the word:

The guards saw no angel. The earthquake affected their bad conscience and the fear affected their blood circulation for a short time, causing them to fall unconscious to the ground.

Recognize that the angel of the Lord, too, – one of many angels who were with Me as Jesus – was perceived only by those women who, through their actualization of the law of love, had brought their souls to shine; their inner ear had opened, and they understood the language of love. These women communicated to their neighbors what they had perceived. And those who believed, followed.

The one who lives in God lives in the law of love and freedom and respects free will. Therefore, the angel respected the free will of the people and spoke as follows, "If you want, look into the sepulcher where the earthly body of the Lord lay. And if you want, go your way and tell His disciples that the Lord knows no death. The Son of the Eternal is risen and, if you remain in faith and adoration, He will meet you on the way that you will take."

6. And they entered and did not find the body of Jesus. Then they ran away and came to Simon Peter and the other disciple whom Jesus loved, and said to them, "They have taken away the Lord from the sepulcher, and we do not know where they have laid Him." (Chap. 84:6)

I, Christ, explain, correct
and deepen the word:

"... whom Jesus loved" means: who was nearest to Him in his way of living and thinking.

God loves all His children equally – but when a child has purified its soul and devoted its life to Him, it draws nearer to Him.

The one who sees God as the center of his earthly life and lives in a way that is devoted to God attains an ever greater purity of his soul. The purged soul then finds its way into a deep, intimate communication with God, its Father.

It was similar with the said disciple of whom it is written. He was nearer to God, because his soul was more light-filled and more powerful, through his constant devotion to God, the Eternal.

The union between the Eternal and a light-filled soul also brings about a deep communication between those people who strive toward the divine. Thus, My spiritual body and his light-filled soul were linked with God and consciously united in God. He thereby understood the sense of My words and could also grasp their true purport in few words.

Recognize that understanding towards one's neighbor and mutual understanding lead to nearness to God and to deeds that are done together in the Spirit of the Lord.

7. *And they ran and came to the sepulcher and, looking in, they saw the linen cloths lying; and the cloth that had been about Jesus' head was not with the linen cloths, but folded up in a separate place.*

8. *And it came to pass that they were much perplexed; for behold, two angels stood close to them in glistening white garments and said to them, "Why do you seek the living One among the dead? He is not here, He is risen; and behold, He goes before you into Galilee; there you will see Him. (Chap. 84:7-8)*

I, Christ, explain, correct
and deepen the word:

The sepulcher was examined by the Jews and the Romans. They were driven by fear; for they could not understand My words "after three days I will rise again."

The beings from God, the angels, about whom it is written, were perceived by just a few in their hearts. Not all who were present believed in the statement of those who perceived the beings from God in their hearts. Because of this, a tumult developed at the sepulcher. Some lost their self-control and also began to doubt. Thus, some believed, others doubted. The upset doubters did not take the way to Galilee.

Because very often there are disagreements among people, God and the beings from God guide the people indirectly. They guided the believers through their God-filled sensations, but did not mention the word "Galilee."

9. *Do you not remember how He spoke to you when He was still in Galilee, that He, the Son of Man, would be crucified and that He would rise again after the third day?" And they remembered His words. And they went out quickly and fled from the sepulcher, for they trembled and were confounded. They did not speak to anyone about it, for they were afraid. (Chap. 84:9)*

I, Christ, explain, correct
and deepen the word:

The fear and the flight from the empty sepulcher explain the doubts which many had. Many were also disappointed in Me and dismayed about Me, for they had hoped for a so-called miracle. They had hoped for the resurrection of My earthly body. However, the earthly body is merely the acting organ for the spiritual body. When the spiritual body is pure and in God, the human body, the organ, has fulfilled its function.

So it was. I had accomplished it: A part of My heritage, the part-power of the primordial power, could be withdrawn from the primordial substance and became the Redeemer-energy, because My spiritual body abided in God and was without sin.

10. But Mary stood before the sepulcher weeping. And as she wept, she stooped down and looked into the sepulcher and saw two angels in white garments, one at the head and the other at the foot, where the body of Jesus had lain. And they said to her, "Woman, why do you weep?"

11. She said to them, "Because they have taken away My Lord, and I do not know where they have laid Him." And as she said this, she turned around and saw Jesus standing and did not know that it was Jesus.

12. Jesus said to her, "Woman, why do you weep? Whom do you seek?" Supposing Him to be the gardener, she said to Him, "Sir, if you have carried Him away, tell me where you have laid Him, and I will take Him away." Jesus said to her, "Mary!" She turned around and said to Him, "Rabboni," that is, Master.

13. Jesus said to her, "Do not touch Me, for I Am not yet ascended to My Father. But go to My brethren and say to them: I ascend to My Father and your Father, to My God and your God." (Chap. 84:10-13)

I, Christ, explain, correct
and deepen the word:

The eyes of Mary were also held blind until, addressing her as "Mary," I opened the eyes of her soul. Thereupon, she beheld My fine-material body. "Do not touch Me" also means, among other things: Believe!

Man can touch only the material, earthly body, but not the fine-material one.

While I appeared to Mary and some apostles and disciples, My earthly body was in the process of transformation. This transformation of My physical body was invisible to man. It took place until the ascension. Because My spiritual body had totally irradiated My earthly body, the latter was gradually absorbed by the spiritual atoms. Thus, the eternal power of the Father, the primordial power, transformed My coarse-material body, so that the matter irradiated by Me was removed from coarse matter.

The one who erects and worships the cross with the dead body points to the physical body and thus portrays wrongly to mankind that I was defeated. He venerates the dead body instead of praying to the resurrected One, to the inner light, to the Father in Me, the Christ. The cross without the body is the symbol of the resurrection, of the ascension.

14. Mary Magdalene went and told the disciples that she had seen the Lord, and that He had said these things to her, and had charged her to tell of His resurrection from the dead. (Chap. 84:14)

CHAPTER 85

The Risen Jesus Appears to Two Disciples at Emmaus

The blindness of those who were against Me –
The change in the satanic hierarchies after the
ascension (14-16)

1. *The same day, two disciples went to the village called Emmaus, which was three hours away from Jerusalem. And they talked together of all that had happened.*

2. *And it came to pass that, while they spoke with one another, Jesus Himself drew near and went with them. But their eyes were held, so that they could not know Him.*

3. *And He said to them, "What are you speaking about with each other that you are going along so sadly?"*

4. *And one of them, called Cleopas, answered, "Are you the only stranger in Jerusalem and have not yet come to know the things that have happened here in these days?" And He said to them, "What things?"*

5. *And they spoke to Him about Jesus of Nazareth, who had been a prophet, mighty in deed and word before God and all the people, and how the high priests and their authorities delivered Him to be condemned to death, and how they then nailed Him to the cross. "But we trusted that He was the One who should have redeemed the land of Israel. And never-*

theless, all these things have happened here in these last three days.

6. Yes, and certain women, also of our company, astonished us. They were at the sepulcher early in the morning and did not find the body. And they came and told us that angels had appeared to them, saying that He was risen.

7. And some of our people went to the sepulcher and found everything as the women had said. But they did not see Him."

8. Then He said to them, "Oh, you are fools and slow of heart and do not believe what the prophets have said! Should not Christ suffer all these things, in order to enter then into His glory?"

9. And beginning with Moses and all the prophets, He taught them about all the scriptures which concerned Him.

10. And they drew near the village to which they were going. And He made as though He wanted to go further. But they pressed Him, saying, "Stay with us, for it is towards evening and the day is almost over." And He went in to tarry with them.

11. And it happened as He sat with them at the table: He took bread and the fruit of the vine, gave thanks, blessed, broke the bread and gave it to them. And their eyes were opened, and they knew Him. And He vanished from their sight.

12. And they said to one another, "Did not our hearts burn while He talked to us on the way and explained the scripture to us?" And they immediately rose and returned to Jerusalem, and there they found the eleven gathered with their followers. And they said, "The Lord is truly risen, and He appeared to Simon."

13. And they told what had happened to them on their way and how they had recognized Him in the breaking of the bread.

14. While they were going to Emmaus, some of the watch came to the city and informed Caiaphas of what had happened.

15. And they gathered with the elders and took council, saying, "Behold, while the soldiers slept, several of His apostles came and carried His body away. And is not Joseph of Arimathaea one of His disciples?

16. For this reason, he had asked Pilate for the body, so that he could bury Him in his own tomb in his garden. Let us give the soldiers money, so that they say that His disciples had come in the night and had stolen the body while they were sleeping. And when this news reaches the ears of the governor, we will persuade him and protect you." (Chap. 85:1-16)

I, Christ, explain, correct
and deepen the word:

This lie is like a betrayal. Thus, to the very end I was unrecognized and betrayed. For those who were against Me, for fear of Me, wanted to prevent the people from believing in My resurrection.

After the death on the cross and the disappearance of My earthly body, which they assumed had been taken away, they believed to have defeated Me, for their invisible leaders in the satanic hierarchies were not aware of My being there, either. Therefore, they believed Me to be still near the Earth, possibly even as an earth-bound soul still trying to hide from them.

They did not yet recognize what had happened and what took place unnoticed by their senses. Only after My ascension, after My going home to the Father, did the souls in all spheres of the Fall right up to the gates of the pure Being experience that everything changed suddenly: The satanic hierarchies became rungs on the ladder to heaven; they became planes of purification. These exist from the level of purification of order to the level of purification of earnestness. The other three planes – patience, love and mercy – became planes of development. They are the pre-heavens which are also a part of the ladder to heaven; on it, the light-filled soul which has become a spirit body learns to apply the eternal law again in all details.

CHAPTER 86

Jesus Appears in the Temple and the Blood Sacrifices Cease

*Spiritual incidents in Jerusalem
and its surroundings in the days following the
physical death of Jesus (1-8)*

1. It was on the same day at the time of the sacrifice in the temple. There appeared among the dealers in animals and birds One clad in white raiment, radiant as light; He had in His hand a whip with seven cords.

2. And at the sight of Him, the dealers and buyers fled in terror, and some fell to the ground as if dead; for they recalled how, before His death, Jesus had driven them away from the temple enclosure in like manner.

3. And some declared that they had seen a spirit, and others that they had seen the One who had been crucified and that He had risen from death.

4. And the sacrifices in the temple ceased that day, for all feared to sell or to buy, and let their captives go free.

5. And the priests and elders caused a rumor to spread that those who had told about it had been drunk and had not seen anything. But many affirmed that they had seen Him with their own eyes and had felt the whip on their backs, but were not able to offer resistance. But when some of the bolder ones among them reached out their hands, they could not seize the figure that they saw, nor catch the whip that beat them.

6. And from these days on, they believed in Jesus, that He was sent by God to deliver the oppressed and free those who were bound. And they turned from their ways and sinned no longer.

7. He also appeared to others in love and compassion and healed them by His touch and liberated them from the hands of the persecutor. And many similar things were reported of Him, and many said, "Verily, the Kingdom of God has come."

8. And some of those who had died and then risen when Jesus rose from the dead appeared and were seen by many in the holy city; and great fear fell among the evil ones, but light and joy filled the hearts of the righteous. (Chap. 86:1-8)

I, Christ, explain, correct
and deepen the word:

Much of what happened in the days before I went home to the Father and that was also passed down corresponds to the truth.

Some people perceived Me with their spiritual eyes, while others saw only the reflection which their aura could attract from the atmospheric chronicle.

My life as Jesus of Nazareth had entered not only the hearts of many people, but also the atmospheric chronicle. A part of the thinking and living of people is stored in it and still affects the Earth. My physical passing brought the earthly and astral forces into stronger motion. The atmospheric chronicle, too, came into action, so that some people saw Me through the reflection of the atmospheric chronicle, while others whose hearts were filled with My life saw Me with their spiritual eyes. Through the atmospheric chronicle, still others saw souls that had gone to those planes of purification that corresponded to their spiritual level of consciousness.

Through My suffering, My dying and My resurrection, Jerusalem and the surrounding places where I had been active as Jesus were raised in their radiation, so that many people could spiritually perceive and many could receive from the atmospheric chronicle.

May it be revealed in a general way: One should not strive to receive from the atmospheric chronicle, but to receive from the Spirit of God alone, which can be possible only through the actualization and fulfillment of the laws of God.

CHAPTER 87

Jesus Appears to His Disciples

Why could the disciples perceive the resurrected One? (1-2)The cross without a body, a symbol of resurrection and of victory over the darkness (3-6). Redemption by belief alone? (7) Baptized by the Holy Spirit (8). Selfless love encompasses all Being (9). Leading a life devoted to God (10). The Spirit of God uses the vocabulary and terms of human conveyers; their meaning is subject to the change of time –

The communities in Christ until the Era of Light (11-15)

1. On the evening of this day, the first day of the week, the disciples were gathered and had locked the doors for fear of the Jews. Then Jesus came and stood in their midst and said to them, "Peace be with you!" But they became frightened and thought they had seen a spirit.

2. And He said to them, "Behold, it is I, Myself, as you have formerly seen Me. A spirit can indeed appear in flesh and bone, as you see that I have. Behold My hands and feet, touch them and see." (Chap. 87:1-2)

I, Christ, explain, correct
and deepen the word:

I had no body of flesh and bone, but I adapted My spiritual body to the vibration of the Earth and, at the

same time, also raised the consciousness of the disciples, so that they could perceive and sense Me.

3. *And when He had said that, He showed them His
hands and His feet. Then the disciples rejoiced when
they saw the Lord.*

4. *But Thomas, called Didymus, one of the disciples,
said to them, "Unless I see the marks of the nails in His
hands and lay my finger in the marks of the nails and
thrust my hand into His heart, I will not believe." Then
He said to Thomas, "See My hands, My heart and My
feet; reach out your hand and put your finger in the
marks of the nails and put your hand in My heart, and
be not faithless, but believing."*

5. *And Thomas said to Him, "My Lord and My
God!" And Jesus said to him, "Thomas, because you
have seen Me, you have believed. Blessed are those
who do not see and yet believe."*

6. *Then Jesus said again to them, "Peace be with
you! Just as My Father has sent Me, I Am sending you."
And when He had said that, He breathed on them and
said to them, "Receive the Holy Spirit; preach the
gospel and announce to all peoples the resurrection of
the Son of God. (Chap. 87:3-6)*

I, Christ, explain, correct
and deepen the word:

Verily, "Blessed are those who do not see and yet
believe." The one who lives in and from God does not

906

require an outer proof of the inner life. Only *that* person who lives more externally, who values the visible course of events more than what takes place within wants proof about the life of the inner being.

The words "Receive the Holy Spirit" mean to receive the Holy Spirit, the power from the eternal law, in order to speak and act from the law of love and wisdom, to announce to the peoples the resurrection of the Son of God and to bring them the gospel of love and wisdom.

Verily, you should bear in your heart the resurrection of the Son of God and should rise from your sins through Me, the Christ, the resurrected One, so that you can enter the life that I Am in the Father.

I repeat: The one who thinks of the crucified One and worships the body hanging on the cross of resurrection still hangs on the cross of sin, himself. He has not yet accepted Me nor received Me in his heart. Therefore, the one who affirms the body on the cross and clings to the cross with the tortured body has not yet risen in Me, the Christ. He testifies to his own servitude to sin, letting himself be influenced by the sinful.

For the demons want to see the crucified One, the cross with the body. To them, it means the defeat of the Nazarene – not the victory of the Christ. With the dead body on the cross, they want to impress upon mankind the concept that the Son of God has succumbed to sin.

Yet I Am risen and have returned to the Eternal. I have brought you redemption. The cross without the dead body symbolizes the resurrection and victory over the darkness. Therefore, all people who live in Me and through whom I live will abide by the cross of victory, that is without a body. For just as I have won victory over the darkness, those men and souls who consciously believe in Me and do the will of the All-Holy more and more each day have also won victory over sin.

7. *Teach them the holy law of love which I have given you. Those who renounce their sins are forgiven, and those who continue to sin retain their sins.* (*Chap. 87:7*)

I, Christ, explain, correct
and deepen the word:

The words "Those who renounce their sins are forgiven, and those who continue to sin retain their sins" mean that the one who asks for forgiveness and forgives and, if still possible, makes amends for what he has caused, and no longer does things that are similar to what led to the sin, that is, he sins no more, he is the one who has renounced sin. But the one, who despite knowing better, forgiving and asking for forgiveness, commits the same sins again, cannot have his sin taken from him – not even when he has asked for forgiveness.

And if your neighbor against whom you sinned does not forgive you, your heavenly Father cannot take this sin from you, either. However, His grace and love will cause your neighbor to recognize himself and to forgive you more quickly – if he is ready to do this of his own free will.

No one should say that just by believing in Me, the Christ, his sins will be taken from him. The one who neither recognizes his sins nor repents, thus continuing to sin, remains a sinner. My Redeemer-deed will not take his sin away. For the one who does not recognize himself will not recognize his sins, either, nor will he repent of them or make amends for what he has done to his neighbor. Thus, the one who does not take these steps to self-recognition, to true repentance and forgiveness, to asking for forgiveness and to making amends will fall into the same sins, again and again.

Although the light of salvation, redemption, shines in all souls, nevertheless only the one who purifies his soul and also keeps it pure becomes perfect. My Redeemer-deed did not wipe out the sins of this world, the sins of all souls and men. It is the power and the source of power for all those who repent and no longer sin. Redemption is the support of the soul and protection from the dissolution of the soul. It is also the light on the path to the heart of God.

No person and no soul can avoid this process of recognizing, repenting and sinning no more. Only when soul and person fulfill the law of love more and more will they become pure. The redemption of the soul is accomplished only when it has again attained purity and has consciously become a child with a pure heart.

The mere belief in Me, the Redeemer of all souls and men, does not bring about the purity of soul and person.

Redemption cannot dissolve a sin, if recognition and repentance by the sinner do not precede it. Redemption means support, strength and light for the soul and then, it causes the dissolution of the sin, if the sinner recognizes, repents and no longer commits his sin – and makes amends for what he has caused, insofar as this is still possible. By doing so, he lets the Redeemer-light become the inner fire of love, which then liberates him and accompanies him on the way to the Father's house, to the heart of God.

8. *Baptize those who believe and repent, bless and anoint them and present the pure offering of the fruits of the Earth, which I have established in My memory. (Chap. 87:8)*

I, Christ, explain, correct
and deepen the word:

Recognize that only the spiritual baptism is valid. Anything else are symbols, and, as such, have no meaning or validity, because they are not part of the law of God. I did not institute the ritual blessing, anointing and offering of the fruits of the Earth as external ceremonies. It is spoken as a symbol for the inner life and not meant as an outer ceremony.

Only the one through whom the Spirit of God is active and who no longer sins is truly spiritually baptized. Therefore, teach your neighbor to keep the law of God.

When the person has renounced sin, thus becoming pure in heart, and keeps the law of God, he is also filled with the Spirit of truth. Then, he is also spiritually baptized.

Your task is to keep the laws of God – and then to teach them. The Holy Spirit will then baptize the one who is pure in heart. For I, the Christ in the Father, baptize with the fire of the inner life, with the Holy Spirit.

9. *Behold, I have sacrificed My body and My blood on the cross for the redemption of the world from sins against love and from the blood sacrifices and feasts of the past. (Chap. 87:9)*

I, Christ, explain, correct
and deepen the word:

In the present and in the future, those who honestly repent of their sins and no longer commit them will also refrain from blood offerings and feasts of debauchery. The one who no longer sins against selfless love is consciously in the love of God, and selflessly loves all people and all Being – all that is from God: animals, plants and also stones.

The ennobled person and the soul which is imbued with the love of God will no longer lay violent hands on life. The one who is for God is also for his neighbor, and for the world of animals, plants and minerals.

10. And you shall offer the bread of life and the wine of redemption in a pure gift with incense, as it is written about Me; and you shall eat and drink of them in remembrance that I have liberated all those who believe in Me from the old servitude of your forefathers. (Chap. 87:10)

I, Christ, explain, correct
and deepen the word:

"And you shall offer the bread of life and the wine of redemption in a pure gift with incense" means in its sense that the one who leads a devoted, that is, God-filled, life, who devotes his thinking, speaking and acting to the Eternal, will remember Me in everything. Each meal will be a meal with Me, because he accepts thankfully the gifts from the hand of God and partakes of them consciously.

And the one who believes in Me, his Redeemer, and accepts and actualizes what I have taught is free from the bondage of sin.

Everything that was deduced and externalized from My words does not belong to the inner life, nor to My teaching.

11. For they had made a god of their stomach and sacrificed the innocent creatures of the Earth to this god, instead of sacrificing the carnal nature within themselves.

12. And they ate the flesh and drank the blood to their own ruin, destroying their body and shortening their life, just like the Gentiles who did not know the truth, or who, knowing it, turned it into a lie.

13. As I send you, so shall you, too, send others, so that they may do these things in My name," and He laid His hands on them.

14. And in the same way as with the apostles, He also appointed prophets and evangelists and pastors, a holy priesthood; and He laid His hands on all those whom they chose as deacons, on each one of the four times twelve.

15. And they are meant to lead and guide the universal community, so that all may be irreproachable, each one at his place in the unity of the body of Christ. (Chap. 87:11-15)

I, Christ, explain, correct
and deepen the word:

Recognize that even the words in the book called "The Gospel of Jesus" should be understood according to their meaning.

My word is the eternal truth. But since the eternal truth does not have the language and words of man, I fill the words of God-filled people with the eternal truth, so that people may hear Me and may understand Me according to their opened consciousness.

The truth, the law of the All, is active in all things and is not the shell, the matter. All the life that the Earth brings forth, the nature and animal kingdoms, and man, too, are but reflections of the eternal truth, of the eternal law. So is the word of God, spoken through the mouth of a human being, also only a reflection of the truth. Therefore, if a person wants to understand Me, he has to feel into the word and grasp the meaning of the word, the truth, which I Am in the word of the God-filled person. The word of God, spoken through a human being, is the conveyer of the truth and it has to be understood according to its meaning.

Just as people are subject to change in their way of thinking, speaking and acting from one epoch to another, so do their terms and words change. In each epoch, the Spirit of truth, which I Am, uses the respective words and terms of the prophetic and enlightened people living then.

Today [1989], many words and terms have a different meaning than in former times. Hence, I explain and correct what has been written down when the terms of today [1989] differ from those of former times. The vocabulary of the conveyers who put the divine message into the respective words of their time has to be considered.

When the conveyer receives the divine message by inspiration, the Spirit of life then uses the vocabulary and terms of the receiver to convey the truth. Therefore, as previously revealed, the words should be understood according to their meaning only – that is, they should be received in a way that is faithful to the sense and not to the word. The one who adheres to the letter considers the material shell to be the truth and cannot understand the meaning of the living word. Therefore, it is said: First actualize what you can understand; then your spiritual consciousness will expand for further aspects from the eternal truth, and you will gradually be able to understand and actualize more.

For this reason, words like "evangelists," "pastors," "holy priesthood" and "deacons" also have to be understood according to their meaning. The conveyer who wrote down the message many earthly years ago took his vocabulary and terms which were familiar to him in relation to the groups and communities of people in the Spirit of God.

I repeat: The Spirit of life puts the truth into the word of God-filled people, and the person expresses the word in his mother tongue. The Spirit, God, can use only those words of a person that are familiar to the person himself. Therefore, the words of truth should be understood according to their meaning. This is why I have to explain and correct again and again. This held and holds true in all epochs.

I explain: I spoke to My followers that I will appoint prophets; and enlightened men and women will bear witness of the life in God. At all times, there will be a host of fulfilled people who strive towards God, who do the will of God more and more. And those who fulfill the will of God will live in community, in brotherhood with Me, the Christ. Many of those who are called will found communities in My Spirit.

Until all people live in Me, the Christ, elders, spiritual teachers, leaders and healers are needed in the communities. From the original communities in Me, the Christ, there will repeatedly emerge elders, teachers, leaders and healers who discuss and vote on everything with the members of the original communities, and then initiate and carry out what was decided together.

These communities are the original image of life in the community of people who are with Me. The elders, teachers, leaders and healers are on the same level as the members of the communities. Among each other, all are brothers and sisters in Me, the Christ. But until all human beings have become one people in Me, the Christ, and comply with the law of love and of life, and follow the Shepherd, Christ, alone, there is need for elders, teachers, leaders and healers, who, however, do not put themselves above the other members of the community.

Once the Era of Light has enveloped the Earth, there will no longer be teachers, leaders and healers, because the fine-material kingdom will embrace the Kingdom of God on Earth. There will be *one* community between the human beings and the beings of light, and there will be *one* ruler and leader – Christ. And as above, so will it be below, that is, on Earth in the Kingdom of God.

When My life has become the life of all the members of these communities, the so-called elders in the original communities will also assume other functions. They will then be the older ones and the wise ones who know about all the things of inner life and who also know about the evolution toward the Kingdom of Peace of Jesus Christ; they can also be consulted in many matters by the members of the original communities.

CHAPTER 88

The Eighth Day after the Resurrection

*Israel and Jerusalem are where people fulfill the will
of God – The sinful world does not recognize the true sons
and daughters of God, nor the exalted woman who prepares
the way for Christ (1-3). He radiates His light to the whole
Earth through her (4-7). Willing people find the path of the
inner being (8). The darkness will be defeated in the fight
against the light of the world (9-10). The Redeemer-deed of
Christ prevented the plan of the female angel: the regression of all forms of life and the dissolution of creation (11-12)*

1. And after seven days, His disciples were again in
the upper room. The doors were locked. Then Jesus
came and stood in their midst and said, "Peace be with
you!" And He was known to them in the holy memorial
supper.

2. And He said to them, "Love one another and all
the creatures of God. Yet I say to you: Not all are men
who are in the form of man. Are those who use violence, oppression and injustice and tell a lie rather than
the truth, men and women in the image of God?

3. No, verily, not before they are born again and receive in their heart the Spirit of love and of wisdom.
For only then are they sons and daughters of Israel;
and being of Israel, they are children of God. And this
is why I came into the world and suffered at the hands
of the sinners." (Chap. 88:1-3)

I, Christ, explain, correct
and deepen the word:

The one who does not keep the commandment of selfless love neither loves his fellow man nor the world of animals, plants and minerals.

Only selflessly loving people love their neighbor and all Being selflessly, as well as animals, plants and stones. The one who does not live in the love from God, also does not give from the stream of selfless love and is thus blind towards the truth. A blind person lashes out blindly – as he is. He thinks only about himself, thus becoming a son or a daughter of cruelty.

For this reason, not all who have the form of human beings are conscious images of God. Only those who strive for the selfless life and are one with their fellow men and with all forms of life will be truly called sons and daughters of God. And only those who live in the true Israel, in the true Jerusalem, and who fulfill the will of God in the true Israel and in the true Jerusalem will be truly called sons and daughters of Israel. For Israel and Jerusalem are where the people strive to fulfill the will of God. Israel and Jerusalem are where salvation flows over the Earth in a broad stream.

Whoever believes that Israel and Jerusalem – where I was active as Jesus of Nazareth two thousand years ago – will also be the Israel and the Jerusalem of the coming era of the Spirit, is mistaken: It is not a question of the place, but of the radiation of the Earth. From the Earth, the radiation for the Kingdom of God on Earth breaks forth. It will build up where there are people who are truly called sons and daughters of God.

Because the sons and daughters of the old Israel did not accept Me, I suffered at the hands of the sinners. The old Israel and the old Jerusalem remained in their sin and will perish.

From the ruins of the old sinful world, the New Israel and the New Jerusalem, the Kingdom of God on Earth, will emerge. The sons and daughters of God who help the New Israel and the New Jerusalem to emerge will be persecuted, mocked and slandered – like I, as Jesus of Nazareth. The sinful world, which is composed of the sons and daughters of cruelty, will not recognize the conscious sons and daughters of God – just as it did not recognize Me, the Son of God, its Redeemer, either.

Just as it was with Me as Jesus of Nazareth, the exalted woman, too – the spirit being in the earthly garment who lives among them to prepare the way for Me, the Christ – is recognized by just a few people, but is not recognized by the world, nor by all those within the inner circle. Many sons and daughters of the world are against her, because she is steadfast in her devotion to the gospel of love and lives in Me, the Christ – and with Me, in the Father, for the New Era, the era of the Christ, who I Am.

Just as the Jews are still waiting today for the Messiah and do not accept Me, the Christ, the Messiah, it is the same with the woman who precedes Me, the Christ, in order to prepare My coming.

When I abided among the people as Jesus of Nazareth, many people talked about the Messiah and did not recognize Me. Many people talk – as was conveyed a long time ago – about an exalted woman who precedes the Lord, in order to prepare the way for Him. She is among the people as a human being – yet they do not recognize her. Just as I went unrecognized from the Earth, she, too, will similarly leave the Earth unrecognized. Many will continue to wait for the exalted woman who prepares the way for Me, the Christ; and yet, she was already among them.

Only when the time is ripe, when the truth breaks through, will people recognize that the part-ray of divine wisdom in the earthly garment was among them: the exalted woman in Me, the Christ, and we in God, our eternal Father, for the New Era, the Kingdom of the Christ.

With the words "the exalted woman" is not meant the human being, but the being in God which abides in the earthly garment [1989].

4. *And Jesus said, "I stood in the midst of the world and was seen and heard in the flesh; and I found all people gorged with their own lusts and drunk with their own follies; and I found no one who hungered and thirsted for the wisdom of God. My soul grieves over the*

sons and daughters of man, for they are blind in their hearts and deaf in their souls and do not hear My voice.

5. *These are the words which I spoke to you when I was still with you, so that all that was written about Me in the law of Moses and in the prophets and in the Psalms may be fulfilled."*

6. *And He opened their understanding, so that they could understand the scriptures, and said to them, "Thus, it is written and thus it behooved Christ to suffer and resurrect from the dead on the third day. And atonement and forgiveness of sins shall be preached in My name among all peoples, beginning from Jerusalem. And you are witnesses to this.*

7. *And I send you the promise of My Father, whom you did not see on Earth. For verily, I say to you, just as the whole world was ruined by the sin and vanity of a woman, so will it be saved by the simplicity and truth of a woman, and even by you shall it be saved. (Chap. 88:4-7)*

I, Christ, explain, correct
and deepen the word:

It is written, "I stood in the midst of the world and was seen and heard in the flesh; and I found all people gorged with their own lusts and drunk with their own follies; and I found no one who hungered and thirsted for the wisdom of God."

Almost two thousand years have gone by. Many people are still gorged with their own lusts and drunk with their own follies. I truly stood in the midst of the world – and I found few people who hungered and thirsted for the wisdom of God.

It is similar for the woman who prepares the way for Me. She stands in the midst of the world. My word, the word of salvation, resounds through her as the prophetic word and permeates the whole world [1989]. Many hear My words through her – and yet remain sinners. But many turn back and strive to let go of the old sinful world, that is, to sin no more, in order to join the flock of those who establish the New Era, the era of the Christ, who I Am.

Because the old world remained sinful, it will also die in its sins – and with it all those people who pay homage to sin.

It is written, "... just as the whole world was ruined by the sin and vanity of a woman, so will it be saved by the simplicity and truth of a woman, and even by you shall it be saved."

Recognize that a woman, that is, a female spirit being, the manifestation of the female aspect of God, brought about the Fall. God, the Eternal, is male as well as female; this means that He is giving *and* receiving. The female principle, the manifested female aspect of God wanted to be like the male principle, like God in His omnipresence, male and female, giving and receiving, the All-stream, the Being.

The woman about whom it is written "... by the simplicity and truth of a woman, and even by you shall it be saved" is the part-ray, the seraph, of divine wisdom, the exalted spirit being before the throne of the Almighty – today [1989] in the earthly garment. With the sons and daughters of God, she contributes to the deliverance of many. Together with them, she establishes the new world, the Kingdom of God on Earth.

The word "simplicity" means being modest. Truly, she walks over the Earth modestly, without rank or prestige, without a great name – and I, Christ, radiate My light through her to the whole Earth, to all people who are willing to accept and fulfill My holy word. I bring the truth, the way and the life, which I Am, to those who believe in Me, who actualize and fulfill what I teach and give them through the prophetic word: the law of God – as I did before as Jesus of Nazareth.

What I taught as Jesus of Nazareth I teach again and deepen, as Christ, through her who precedes Me, the woman before the throne of God. She is the one who will remain unrecognized until the truth has been born into the hearts of the people. And those who will then be filled with the truth and will speak and give from the truth will recognize her, and they will bear witness of the woman who, while in earthly garment, was not recognized by the world, yet lived and worked for the truth and brought the truth in Me, the Christ, into the whole world.

Many beings of light are in My Mission of Redemption to bring the law of love into the world and have it become manifest: the Kingdom of God on Earth. The beings from God, invisible to man, prepare the way into the New Era for the beloved daughter of wisdom and for the sons and daughters of God.

The words which I spoke to My apostles and disciples as I sent them on their mission were not meant for them alone, but were also spoken for all people and for all the sons and daughters of God on Earth who fulfill the will of the Eternal more and more.

8. *Rejoice therefore and be glad, for you are more blessed than all those who are on earth; because you, My twelve thousand, are the ones who will save the whole world. (Chap. 88:8)*

I, Christ, explain, correct
and deepen the word:

The words "... because you, My twelve thousand, are the ones who will save the whole world" should be understood according to their meaning.

Numbers had a different meaning in those days than in today's fast-moving time [1989], which has already been shortened by the Eternal. Do not cling to numbers, but to Me alone, the Christ.

Recognize that it is not those who live in Me, the Christ, and work in My mission who will save the world; nevertheless, they help make it possible for willing people to recognize Me, their Redeemer, and find their way to the heart of God on the path of the inner being which I teach them.

9. And again I say to you, when the great tyrant and all the seven tyrants began to fight in vain against the light, they did not know with whom and against whom they fought.

10. For they saw nothing other than a dazzling light, and since they fought, they wasted their strength, one against the other, and so it is. (Chap. 88:9-10)

I, Christ, explain, correct
and deepen the word:

"The great tyrant" was the leader of the demons. The other seven tyrants formed with him the head of the darkness; for the darkness tried and still tries to establish its territory as the Kingdom of God is built up: the Eternal and the seven princes of heaven.

When I, the Co-Regent, left the heavens, My light was covered up. I went through the satanic hierarchies – which became the spheres of purification after the Redeemer-deed – and remained unrecognized. Only when I entered the garment of matter, that is, when I incarnated, was I recognized by the darkness. From that moment on, the power of darkness fought against Me in order to lay hands on Me.

Recognize that the one who fights against his neighbor wastes his spiritual and physical strength and thus becomes weaker and weaker. In this way, the darkness has been weakening itself since the Fall and will lose ground more and more. The light of the world, which I

926

Am, will triumph and will irradiate the whole world, and there will be peace in the people who live in the ray of light.

11. *And for this reason, I took one fourth of their strength, so that they would not have so much power and persist in their evil deeds.*

12. *For through involution and evolution, the salvation of the world will be accomplished: by the descent of the Spirit into matter and the ascent of matter into the Spirit, throughout the ages." (Chap. 88:11-12)*

I, Christ, explain, correct
and deepen the word:

I correct the following statement, "And for this reason, I took one fourth of their strength, so that they would not have so much power and persist in their evil deeds." It is not I who took and take people's strength. They, themselves, waste their life force with their unlawful thinking, speaking and acting and by fighting with their neighbor.

Recognize that if the souls had lost more and more of their life force in this way, then what the female, who wanted to be like God, tried to achieve would have happened: the dissolution of the divine creation, so that all forms of life would have dissolved and merged in the primordial stream, in the primordial energy. Every spirit being, every soul and every other form of life would have gradually dissolved. For the female principle, the female angel, the female manifestation of God, wanted the original state again: all-streaming, omnipresent primordial energy without spiritual forms of life. For then, she would have been again in the omnipresent stream and thus would have defeated the Father-Mother-God and would have created herself as omnipresent goddess and would have created all forms of life, out of her own self.

Therefore, it was her desire that all souls lose their life force more and more, so that the substance which took on form, the soul and the spirit body, would regress and enter the primordial stream again. She would then have drawn from the primordial stream and created anew.

With My Redeemer-deed and by implanting the Redeemer-light into all souls and men, I put a stop to this regression. Since My Redeemer-deed, it is no longer possible for the forms of life created by God to dissolve and enter the primordial energy, the flowing stream, the stream of creation. Each soul can indeed burden itself, but cannot dissolve. The evolution of the soul is inherent in the Redeemer-deed.

The Spirit of God in Me, the Christ, descended into matter; it is the part-power of the primordial power. This part-power of the primordial power in the souls will ascend again with the souls into the eternal Being. This will take place "throughout the ages," by way of transformation and evolution – until each soul has become pure spiritual form again, the spirit being in God, as it came from God.

The Father-Mother-God in His Son, who I Am, Christ, is the victory over matter and all that is dark.

CHAPTER 89

Jesus Appears at the Sea of Galilee

The resurrected One meets His disciples (1-5).
The true disciples: guides, not shepherds; rocks of faith and
of God-fulfillment – The original communities are the one
flock of the Shepherd, Christ (6-8). The keys of the Kingdom
of Heaven (9). "Girded" and guided by the human ego or by
the Eternal (10). What your neighbor does is of no concern
to you (11-12)

1. After this, Jesus showed Himself once again to the disciples at the sea of Tiberias in the following manner: Simon Peter and Thomas, named Didymus and Nathaniel from Cana in Galilee and James and John and two others of His disciples were together.

2. Peter said to them, "I will go fishing." They said to him, "We want to go with you." They went out and immediately stepped into a boat, and they caught nothing that night. And when morning came, Jesus stood on the shore; but the disciples did not know that it was Jesus.

3. And Jesus said to them, "Children, do you have anything to eat?" They answered Him, "Not enough for all. Only a small loaf of bread, a little oil and a few dried fruits." And He said to them, "That will do. Come and eat."

4. And He blessed them, and they ate and were satisfied. And there was also a pitcher full of water, and He blessed it as well; and lo, it became the fruit of the vine.

*5. And they were amazed and said, "It is the Lord."
And none of the disciples dared to ask Him, "Who are
you?" For they knew that it was the Lord.
(Chap. 89:1-5)*

I, Christ, explain, correct
and deepen the word:

By transforming down the vibration of My spirit body
and raising the vibration of their souls, I became visible
to My apostles and disciples. With this, I showed them
that I Am with them. And so, we met on a higher level
of vibration. However, they recognized Me only when I
spoke or acted in the same or like way as I did as Jesus
of Nazareth. I was able to call up in them what reminded them of Me; for these images had been im-
printed in their inner being, so that they recognized Me
in them.

However, I did not eat nor drink the material substance with them, for the spiritual body lives solely
from the pure substance, God.

*6. This is now the sixth time that Jesus showed Him-
self to His disciples, after He was risen from the dead.
Having eaten, Jesus said to Peter, "Son of Jonas, do
you love Me more than these?" He said to Him, "Yes,
Lord, You know that I love You." He said to him, "Feed
My lambs." For the second time He said to him, "Peter,
son of Jonas, do you love Me?" He said to Him, "Yes,*

Lord, You know that I love You." He said to him, "Feed My sheep."

7. *For the third time He said to him, "Peter, son of Jonas, do you love Me?" Peter was grieved that He had spoken to him for the third time: Do you love Me? And he said to Him, "Lord, You know everything, You know that I love You."*

8. *Jesus said to him, "Feed My flock. Verily, verily, I say to you: You are a rock from the great rock, and on this rock I will build My community, and I will raise you from among My twelve to be My governor on Earth, a center of unity for the twelve, and another one will be called and chosen to fill your place among the twelve, and you shall be the servant of servants and shall feed My rams, My sheep and My lambs. (Chap. 89:6-8)*

I, Christ, explain, correct
and deepen the word:

The question to Peter is directed to all men who fulfill the will of God more and more and become the law of love.

I, the resurrected One, did not speak with the voice of man, for I was no longer a human being. My spiritual garment, the spirit body, was and is the image of the Father. With the voice of the All, I spoke into the voice of the hearts of those who were able to perceive Me. My divine words "... do you love Me more than these" were not directed to Peter alone, but to the disciples present there and ultimately to all people. For the one who loves most is the one who fulfills the law of God for the most part and loves Me more than the world.

Such people are rocks in the surf, strong of faith and God-conscious. It is given to them to explain the gospel of love and to teach the laws of life – because they themselves draw from the Spirit of God and live in the Spirit of the Lord. Such people can, from the Spirit of the Eternal, tend My lambs on the pastures of eternal life and can lead them onto the meadows of the spiritual Being, since I live and act through those who live in the Spirit of love and in the law of God and know it. They are given the power to teach My sheep, to give them an understanding of the law of life, so that they, too, will find the way to the pastures of life and become lambs, in order to unite with the Eternal.

The one who lives in the law of life, in God, will lead the sheep to the one flock whose Shepherd I, Christ, Am. He will see to it that the sheep neither scatter nor separate. However, he himself will be only a guide – and not the Shepherd.

The universal communities in Me, the Christ, will emerge from the people who in Me have become a rock of faith and of God-fulfillment.

Today [1989], the words "governor" and "center" have a different meaning. Among the original communities, the first original community is the center, the Covenant Community New Jerusalem with its elders, teachers, leaders and healers; it is the governor for all original communities. It is the central light of all communities and personifies the unity.

The members of the original communities strive to keep among each other what I commanded them: to be devoted in selfless love to each other and to all the creatures of the Earth. And the person whose spiritual consciousness has matured the most shall be the servant of all in My original communities and shall serve the members of the communities. Together with all the members of the original communities, he shall lead the rams, the sheep and the lambs to the heights of life, so that they become one flock whose Shepherd I Am – Christ.

9. *And yet another will arise, and he will teach many things which I have already taught you, and he will spread the gospel among the Gentiles with great zeal. But I will give the keys of the Kingdom of Heaven to those who follow you in My Spirit and obey My law. (Chap. 89:9)*

I, Christ, explain, correct
and deepen the word:

"And yet another will arise, and he will teach many things which I have already taught you, and he will spread the gospel among the Gentiles with great zeal" means:

In the epochs following My resurrection, yet others will go out into the world and spread the gospel, the law of love, which I have taught. However, the keys of the Kingdom of Heaven are in Me and in those who do

My will. I will be active through the one who follows Me by complying with the laws of love and of life. Through him, I will open the heavens to many people for the salvation and the life of their soul.

These words were not meant for Peter alone, but for all the disciples who were present; and they are also meant for all people who, in further epochs, became and will become My true followers and lived and will live in brotherhood with Me. For the one who actualizes and fulfills the laws of God lives consciously in Me, and I live through him. He becomes the true guide to the inner life, who leads the sheep to Me, the one Shepherd, Christ.

For I, alone, Am the way, the truth and the life. And I, Christ, Am the key to the gates of heaven, the key to the door of life.

10. *And once again I say to you: When you were young, you girded yourself and went where you wanted; but when you become old, you will stretch out your hand, and another one will gird you and lead you where you do not want to go." But He said that to show by what kind of death he would glorify God. (Chap. 89:10)*

I, Christ, explain, correct
and deepen the word:

As long as man girds himself with his humanness, he will go where the human ego directs him. However, when he has become more mature and stretches out his hand to the Eternal, the Eternal will gird and guide him – not to where his human being wants, but to where his soul longs for.

He becomes the righteous person who spreads the gospel of love, the law of God, in the world and gathers more people around himself. Among them will again be those of pure heart who will also pass on the gospel of love and of life. These people are girded with the ornament of love, beauty, virtue and purity.

11. And when He said that, He spoke to him, "Follow Me." But Peter turned about and saw the disciple whom Jesus loved. And when he saw him, he said to Jesus, "Lord, and what shall this one do?" Jesus said to him, "If I want him to stay until I come, what is this to you? But you, follow Me!"

12. So a rumor went among the brethren that this disciple will not die. But Jesus did not say to him, "He will not die," but "If I want him to stay until I come, what is this to you?" (Chap. 89:11-12)

I, Christ, explain, correct
and deepen the word:

The words in the following sense, "If I want him to stay until I come, what is this to you?" mean that even if, in the coming times, he goes into the earthly garment to serve Me on Earth again and again – what is this to you?

The words "... what is this to you?" also mean: Do not worry about whether your neighbor wants to follow Me or not. But you follow Me! And by your actualization, help those who are still weaker, so that by your good example, they, too, may follow Me. When and how – leave that up to Me and to your neighbor. For your neighbor has to answer before God for what he does, and that concerns God alone and His child – not you.

CHAPTER 90

What Is the Truth?

About the ability
to understand the eternal truth (1-3).
Everything is consciousness (4-5). Man can understand only
the truth that is actualized – Attainment of perfection (6-11).
Who has the truth? (12). The one who has no selfless love
does not live in the truth and does not recognize it – Each per-
son is guided according to his level of
consciousness (13-16)

1. *And again the twelve were gathered in the circle of the palm trees, and one of them, namely, Thomas, said to the others, "What is truth? For the same things appear differently to different people and even to the same person at different times. What then is truth?"*

2. *And as they were speaking, Jesus appeared in their midst and said, "The truth, the one and the absolute, is in God alone; for no one, not a single person, knows what God alone, who is in all things, knows. The truth can be revealed to man according to his ability to understand and grasp it.*

3. *The one truth has many sides; and the one sees only one side, another sees another side; and some see more than others, as it is given to them. (Chap. 90:1-3)*

I, Christ, explain, correct
and deepen the word:

The eternal truth radiates in many facets into this world. However, each person can receive and understand only as much as he himself has actualized from the eternal truth, that is, as much as his spiritual consciousness has opened up.

The "ability to understand and grasp it" means to have opened one's spiritual consciousness – by actualizing and fulfilling the laws of God – to such an extent that he may correctly understand the law, God, the truth, as well as the many facets of the truth which radiate into this world.

The divine laws are taught and thereby revealed to the people. One facet of the truth after the other will reveal itself to the person who lives according to the divine laws. Thus, his spiritual consciousness unfolds, and he is able to receive and understand more and more from the truth.

"... as it is given to them" means that a person's spiritual consciousness is unfolded to the extent that he has actualized from the eternal truth, from the law of God. With the opened part of his spiritual consciousness, he perceives the facet of the truth which is revealed to him according to the extent of his actualization. The one who has actualized more facets of the eternal truth perceives more; the other who has opened fewer facets perceives less. And so, the person understands more or less of the eternal truth, according to what he has opened of his spiritual consciousness.

4. *Behold this crystal: How the one light is manifest in twelve faces, yes, in four times twelve, and each face reflects one ray of light, and the one looks at one face, and another at another, yet it is the one crystal and the one light which shines in all.*

5. *And behold, when one climbs a mountain and has reached a certain height, he says: The top of the mountain is there, let us reach it. And when he has reached this height, lo, there is another beyond it, until he comes to the height from which no other height is to be seen – if he can attain it. (Chap. 90:4-5)*

I, Christ, explain, correct
and deepen the word:

Infinity is to be compared to a mighty crystal which radiates the various aspects of the eternal truth. Everything is consciousness. For this reason, the whole truth is contained in everything, in each building block of infinity.

Each person looks at the truth from another side or from another level, that is, from another degree of maturity of the soul. The true wise one has opened up all the facets of the truth and perceives the eternal truth in all things.

The one who lives in the truth has the eye of truth. With this eye of truth, he also perceives the humanness. The one who lives in the truth addresses the humanness, but does not live in the humanness.

6. *So it is with the truth. I Am the truth, the way and the life, and I have given you the truth which I received from above. And what is seen and received by one is not seen and received by another. What appears true to some does not appear true to others. Those in the valley do not see what those on the hilltop see.*

7. *But to each, it is the truth as the individual mind sees it and until a higher truth is revealed to this one; the soul which can receive more light will be given more light. For this reason, do not condemn the others, so that you will not be condemned.*

8. *When you keep the holy law of love which I have given you, the truth shall be revealed to you more and more, and the Spirit of truth which comes from above will guide you into the whole truth, albeit through many wrong ways, as the fiery cloud guided the children of Israel through the desert.*

9. *Trust the light that you have until a higher light is given to you. Seek more light, and you will have abundance. Do not rest until you find.*

10. *God gives you all truth for the liberation and perfection of the soul, like a ladder with many rungs. You will leave today's truth for the higher truth of tomorrow. Strive for perfection.*

11. Those who keep the holy law that I have given will save their souls, however differently they may see the truth that I have given them. (Chap. 90:6-11)

I, Christ, explain, correct
and deepen the word:

The statement "And what is seen and received by one is not seen and received by another" has the following meaning: The eternal truth radiates into infinity in countless facets. The whole universe, all Being, lives from the eternal truth. The divine, fine-material universe, the pure Being, is thus, in turn, the truth. All aspects of consciousness live from the life which is the truth – and all divine aspects of consciousness are, in turn, the truth.

According to his thinking and living, each person has his spiritual consciousness either shadowed over by negative things, by egocentric things, or expanded by a positive life that is devoted to God.

According to his level of consciousness, a person recognizes many or only a few facets of the eternal truth or, if he is oriented solely to the world, none at all. Thus, what one person can receive from the eternal truth, the other person whose consciousness does not yet have the far-sightedness of the inner life cannot receive, and therefore, cannot understand either. His light of consciousness does not yet reach as far as that of his neighbor. What appears true to the one who has expanded his spiritual consciousness appears to be untrue to his neighbor, whose consciousness still bears little spiritual light. Hence the words, "Those who are in the valley do not see what those who are on the hilltop see."

The further statement, "But to each, it is the truth as the individual mind sees it and until a higher truth is revealed to this one; the soul which can receive more light will be given more light" has the following meaning: As long as the individual does not fulfill the facet from the eternal truth that was revealed to him, no further facet of the truth can be revealed to him. This means that he can indeed hear it, but cannot fulfill it because he has not yet taken the first step, the actualization of the first facet. With his intellect, a person will look at and judge those facets of the eternal truth revealed to him until, step by step, he actualizes what he recognizes each time. Only then, will he be able to receive a higher truth. Once the correlations of all the facets of the eternal truth are revealed to him, he immerses into the law of life, into the truth.

God, the eternal light, radiates Himself, the whole eternal truth, into infinity as countless facets of consciousness.

Only that person climbs the ladder to perfection who day after day endeavors to recognize and clear up what the day and the events of the day show him. The days show the person his own way of thinking and living, not that of his neighbor. For the person should first recognize and work on the beam in his own eye, before he looks for the splinter in the eye of his brother.

The one who does not live in the day wastes the days. Then he cannot climb any further rungs on the ladder to perfection. But the one who strives for the perfection of his spiritual life, by recognizing himself in the day and by clearing up what lies before him, will also reach it.

12. *Many will say to Me: Lord, Lord, we were zealous for Your truth. But I will say to them: No, you were zealous just that others would see it as you see it and no other truth beside. Faith without charity is dead. Love is the fulfillment of the law. (Chap. 90:12)*

I, Christ, explain, correct
and deepen the word:

The one who just speaks of the truth and is of the opinion that his neighbor should see it as he does has not yet stepped onto the ladder to the eternal truth. Further facets of the eternal truth will not be revealed to the person who does not actualize that facet of the truth which is apparent to him and that he acknowledges to be true.

Therefore, the one who just speaks of the truth cannot reveal the truth to his neighbor, because he does not know the path of actualization.

And the one who thinks that only what he says is the right thing and does not accept other facets of the truth is a fool and is blind to the truth.

Therefore, the one who believes only in what he himself is able to understand and insists on this in the opinion that he has the whole truth opposes those who actualize one facet of the eternal truth after the other in order to reach the eternal truth.

Recognize that the one who, for whatever reason, is against his neighbor is against God. The one who is against God is not in the truth, in the fulfillment of the law of God, the love.

13. *How shall the faith which they have accepted be of use to them when they do not practice it in righteousness? Those who have love have everything and without love there is nothing of value. Let each one hold in love what he recognizes to be the truth, knowing that the truth is a dead letter and useless where there is no love.*

14. *Goodness, truth and beauty abide; but the greatest of these is goodness. If some have hated their brothers and hardened their hearts towards the creatures of God's hand, how can they see the truth for their salvation, when their eyes are blind and their hearts hardened towards God's creation?*

15. *As I have received the truth, so have I given it to you. Let each one receive it according to his enlightenment and his ability to understand it; and do not per-*

*secute those who receive it according to a different in-
terpretation.*

16. *For the truth is the might of God and will prevail
in the end over all errors. But the holy law which I have
given is plain for all and just and good. Let all observe
it for the salvation of their souls." (Chap. 90:13-16)*

I, Christ, explain, correct
and deepen the word:

The belief in the truth is not the truth itself, the law of
life. The one who contents himself with merely believing
in the truth will never recognize the truth nor live in it.

True belief is the prerequisite for actualizing the
recognized facet from the eternal truth. However, the
one who does not expand his consciousness through
actualization cannot recognize the justice of God, and
thus cannot practice righteousness either.

Nor can he give selflessly, because he has not unveiled selfless love, the law of life, the truth, within
himself. Only those spiritual principles of God which
the person has actualized can he also give selflessly.
For it is only out of the actualization of the recognized
facets of the truth, that selfless love grows which, in
turn, gives itself selflessly. The one who has no selfless
love does not live in the truth, either. He is interested in
himself only; he loves himself but not the truth, for this
is free of the human ego.

What is not given out of selfless love is of no value. Even if the person talks a great deal about the eternal truth and wants to teach it to his neighbor, the words remain empty, like dead husks; for they are without spiritual life and thus, dead letters.

The person who does not give out of the fulfillment of the law, out of God, but only spreads what he has read and considers to be the truth, is not a teacher of the truth – whether he is a theologian, priest, pastor or a believer in the Bible, even when he bears a high title.

The one whose heart is hardened is blind to life. He has no love – neither towards people nor towards animals, plants or stones.

The one whose heart is hardened and whose eyes are blind speaks and acts against his neighbor and against creation.

Therefore, examine with the eyes of justice, then you will recognize the righteous and the false teachers by their fruits.

The one who lives in the truth perceives what others do not see and hears what others do not hear; and so, he will let everyone believe as he wants to.

People in the Spirit of the Lord will neither condemn nor persecute their neighbors who receive spiritual knowledge from different sources and expound on it accordingly.

Each person is guided according to his level of consciousness, often through several obstacles or through other sources, until he is able to recognize the source of truth.

The truth is the life, God, the love, the power of infinity. After the return of all fallen spirit beings, it will fully permeate everything. Then the souls will have come together again in God as pure beings out of God, and all that is coarse-material will be primordial substance, that is, divine essence. Then there will be neither human beings nor souls, neither matter nor partcondensation. Everything will be united in the Eternal. All Being will again become the Absolute Law, God, the love, the life. Until all souls have again attained the conscious filiation in God, I remain the Redeemer of all souls and people: Christ, the key to the door of life.

*Foreword to the Community Order**

I, Christ, explain:

The following order of the community will continue to be valid until the people who live on the Earth, which is renewing itself more and more, have become mostly pure in heart and fulfill the law of God. This will be in the Kingdom of Peace of Jesus Christ, in the Kingdom of God on Earth, which will then encompass the whole Earth.

The community order is valid for all original communities in Universal Life and for the Kingdom of Peace which is growing and perfecting itself more and more.**

Moreover, for the people in the light-filled Kingdom of Peace, in the Kingdom of God on Earth, the community order will be a document from which they can see that those people who were still sinful and yet strove more and more for purity used this community order as a standard. They will recognize that people in the emerging Kingdom of Peace still needed this order,

---

* *We received the explanations in the footnotes of chapters 91 to 94, in-cluding the foreword, by way of a revelation of Christ through our sister Gabriele and from her divine consciousness. The first footnote in chapter 91 is based on a decision of the founding members of the first Original Community in Universal Life, the Community New Jerusalem, which was founded on November 8, 1987 in Würzburg, Germany.*

** *As the responsible community in the Kingdom of Peace of Jesus Christ, the Covenant Community New Jerusalem can make further decisions which are also binding for further Original Communities.*

so that they could fulfill the laws of inner life more and more.

In the same way, the various community books, in which the "for" and "against" of the original communities and their members is recorded, give insight into the struggle of the individual members and of the original communities for the lawful life, the life in God.

CHAPTER 91

The Regulations for the Community (Part 1)

Language, which is vibration (1-4).
Naming and baptizing newborns – Raising children in righteousness (5-6). The education of the growing children (7). Fitting into the life principle of the community: Peace and harmony (8). Spiritual baptism – The commandment "pray and work" – The angel of the community – The elders – The council of elders – The community book (9). The anointed one (10)

1. After His resurrection from the dead, Jesus was ninety days with Mary, His mother, and Mary Magdalene who had anointed His body, and Mary Cleophas and the twelve and their followers, instructing them and answering their questions concerning the Kingdom of God.

2. And as they sat for supper, Mary Magdalene asked Him, "Master, will You now explain to us the order of the Kingdom of God?"

3. And Jesus answered, saying, "Verily, I say to you, O Mary, and to each of My disciples: The Kingdom of Heaven is within you. But the time will come when that which is within will become manifest externally, for the salvation of the world.

4. Order is indeed good and useful; but above all is love. Love one another and all the creatures of God,

951

and by this shall all men know that you are My disciples." (Chap. 91:1-4)

I, Christ, explain, correct
and deepen the word:

I appeared to My own again and again and taught them through the inner word, for the one who is no longer in the flesh no longer gives voice to the sounds of this world. He gives the language, which is vibration, into the inner being of the person, so that the one whose soul has been purified and has aligned with Me can perceive Me. In this way, My own perceived My word.

5. *And one asked Him, saying, "Master, is it Your will that infants be received into the community by circumcision, as Moses commanded?" And Jesus answered, "For those who are in Christ, there is neither circumcision nor shedding of blood.*

6. *After eight days, bring the infant with prayer and thanksgiving to the Father who is in heaven. Let the child be given a name by its parents; and let the elders sprinkle pure water upon the crown of its head, as it is written in the prophets. Let its parents see to it that it is brought up in the ways of righteousness, neither eating meat, nor drinking strong drinks, nor hurting the creatures which God has given into the hands of man to protect." (Chap. 91:5-6)*

I, Christ, explain, correct and deepen the word:

After a few days, the newborn infant should be consecrated to the eternal Father, the Father-Mother-God in heaven. The parents shall thank the Eternal for their child and give it the name which rises from their feelings and sensations. For the child is a part of the mother under whose heart it lay and a part of the father who begot it. The hereditary predisposition of the child is similar to that of the father and mother; thus the vibration of the child's soul is connected with the soul of the mother and of the father. If a name flows out of the world of sensations of the mother and the father and they agree on this name, then this can be the right name vibration of the newborn child, which also corresponds to the child's soul.

The customary functions for conveying the message of God – the positions like priests, high priests and church officers – do not correspond to the divine law. Therefore, replace the word "priest" by the word "elder," for in My community there are the elders who also preside over the community.

You may keep the external sign of inner strength – sprinkling water on the crown of the head. But it is not necessary.* If you do it, keep the following:

---

* *The first members of the community wanted to attach more importance to the spiritual than to the external ritual. Therefore, they decided to do without this external form.*

One of the elders will sprinkle water on the crown of the newborn's head, which means that God is the driving, eternal element, the life. Move, child, and know that the driving element, the streaming Spirit, flows through you. You are blessed, and received by God, who is Father and Mother to you.

And the elders speak to the parents as follows: If you live in righteousness, you will also bring up your child, who is the child of the Father-Mother-God, in the right way. You will teach it to neither eat meat nor drink strong drinks, nor hurt or kill the creatures of the sky, the Earth and the waters, to live in unity with stones and plants and to recognize the light-filled radiation of the stars as the light of God. If you are righteous, your child, too, will become wise.

7. *Again another asked Him, "Master, how do You want it to be when they grow up?" And Jesus said, "After seven years, or when they begin to distinguish evil from good and learn to look for the good, let them come to Me, receive the blessing, with thanksgiving and prayer, at the hands of the elder or the angel of the community; and admonish them to refrain from eating flesh, taking strong drinks and hunting the innocent creatures of God; for should they be lower than the horses or the sheep to whom these things are against nature?" (Chap. 91:7)*

I, Christ, explain, correct
and deepen the word:

If you have raised your children according to the law of selfless love and they have reached the age when they learn to distinguish good from evil, then do your best so that your children, who are the children of the Father-Mother-God, find the good in their fellow men. Bring your child or children to the Inner Church at the house of the community. Together with many who strive towards God, they shall receive My blessing through an elder of the community, whom the community has elected and whom I have consecrated.

A true elder radiates much spirituality and is thus just. He is a fulfilled person; his selflessness is the sign of consecration.

The community will bring Me its young brothers and sisters; and through the elder who has the confidence of the community, I will bless My children, thus giving them increased strength.

Then, the parents and the elder will entrust the children to God-filled educators and teachers, who will instruct them in the worldly duties and, in the course of the first school years, will explain to them the laws of God as far as they can understand them in their still childlike ways.

Teach them also to refrain from consuming the flesh of animals.

And let it be said to the parents: If your child feels the urge to eat meat, let it taste the meat, for you do not know how the soul lived in an earlier incarnation and what the person was used to eating. You, however, continue to be an example for your developing children. The teaching and actualization of the eternal laws will gradually refine the senses of the child, and it will then refrain from this.

In My community, animals shall be neither slaughtered nor eaten. If one or another is in the process of changing from eating meat to eating lawful food and now and then still feels the need for meat, then he shall partake of it – outside of the community. However, this applies only for eating meat, not for taking strong drinks.*

The one whose senses no longer crave meat lives the law "You shall not kill." He will not consume his second neighbor, the animal. The one whose senses are still dulled is called upon to let go of this.

In My community, there shall be neither strong drinks nor the meat of animals.

Teach the children not to hunt innocent creatures, the animals, and not to deliberately crush them underfoot. For the one who hunts the innocent creatures will be hunted by his senses and by all those who influence his senses. The one who deliberately crushes underfoot, torments or kills animals will be tormented by his senses and thoughts, and will vegetate as a spiritually

---

* *In principle, strong drinks are not allowed for community members. This means drinks that intoxicate the person and deprive him of his clear thinking. This means that alcohol shall not be used to dull the senses.*

dead person among the living, and in the realm of the souls, too, he will be spiritually dead.

Therefore, teach your children the law of life, namely that everything that lives feels and has the right to live, until the primordial substance, the Spirit, withdraws from the material form and enters into the law of the All-harmony.

And teach your children, who are also Mine, to love nature, to respect the plants and to stay in communication with the essence of life in them. In this way, they will receive the life of nature into their bodies and remain strengthened and healthy.

Also teach the children to gratefully accept the food which the All-Father gives them from His hands.

And teach them the right way to eat: to be quiet while eating and to link with the divine essence in the gifts, so that the body may digest them in the right way. And when they drink, they shall not gulp their drinks down, but take them sip by sip, so that the body can also assimilate them, in the right way.

Only in this way does the person attain the nobility of his soul and become a conscious, spiritually living person, whose home is the Kingdom of God within and around him.

8. *And he asked again, "If there comes to us one who eats meat and drinks strong drinks, shall we take him in?" And Jesus said to him, "Let such ones abide in the*

outer court until they have cleansed themselves from these grosser faults; for until they understand and repent of these, they will not be fit to receive the higher instructions." (Chap. 91:8)

I, Christ, explain, correct
and deepen the word:

The person who does not want to fit into the community life shall stay where he has lived thus far and read and actualize the regulations of the community which shall be handed over to him. According to the law, he is permitted to attend the community schooling from where he lives, until he has purified himself and acknowledges and actualizes the laws of life.

In the community, peace and harmony shall be the life principle that unites all My human children.

Anyone who causes trouble in the community for his fellow men, who quarrels and lives in discord with his neighbor – thus disturbing the community order, the peace and harmony – should leave the community and live outside of it, until he is one again with the laws of God for the community and also in harmony with his neighbor.*

---

* *This spiritual principle is valid for all original communities in Universal Life, but not for the Covenant Community New Jerusalem. Higher instructions are given to it.*

9. And another asked Him, "When is it Your will that they receive baptism?" And Jesus answered, "After another seven years, or when they know the teachings and do what is good and have learned a craft by which they may live and are steadfastly set on the right way. Then let them ask for initiation and let the angel or the elder of the community examine them and see whether they are worthy, and let the angel or the elder offer thanksgiving and prayer and immerse them in the purifying water, that they may rise to new life, confessing God as their Father and vowing to obey the holy law and to keep themselves apart from the evil of this world." (Chap. 91:9)

I, Christ, explain, correct
and deepen the word:

By baptism, spiritual baptism is meant. Only *that* person who is filled with the Spirit of life and is My word for the most part, having actualized the eternal law, is an initiate and is baptized with the Spirit of life.

The one who actualizes the spiritual laws will also keep the commandment, "pray and work," which the Father-Mother-God gave to His earthly children.

In order to keep this commandment, a proper profession is necessary, which the human child shall choose according to its abilities, talents and qualities.

The one who walks the path to the heart of God with firm steps and straightforwardness is the one who keeps the eternal laws and is baptized with the law of life.

Baptism by water is an old ritual. It need not be performed in My community.*

The *angel* of the community is a human being who has become My word, who proclaims it and keeps it. The one who has become the word of God is perfect to a great extent; he has become the law for the most part. These can be elders and other enlightened men and women.

The one who has the position of a teaching prophet** or a proclaiming prophet can be My word as well: God speaks through the prophet in order to communicate directly with the community. When the prophet has become the word, he is then the emissary of the Kingdom of God. But only the one who is in the divine mission, who descended from the heavens in order to bring and announce My word to the world, is prophet and emissary of the Kingdom of God.

The *elder* hears the word of God in himself, he knows the eternal law and is filled with it through the actualization of the eternal laws.

---

* *cf. note p. 932*

** *These words of the Lord are meant for the teaching prophetess of God, Gabriele of Würzburg, for the time of her teaching position. God said, "After her time of activity, I will not call again a teaching prophet who draws from Me, because My word was given to the world in a wide spectrum through her. After her time on earth, people will find their way to Me by themselves and will hear My word for themselves and, in the course of time, will be My word, the law. All this will happen in My community. This is where the development from man to God-man will take place."*

The angel of the community or the elder will examine the human child who says about himself, "I am spiritually baptized, because my life is the law of God," or about whom his neighbors say so. The angel or the elder will examine whether the community member is worthy to be accepted into the council of the elders or into the midst of the spiritually baptized ones.

Together with the community, the angel or the elder or both will praise, glorify and thank the Father-Mother-God, whose children we all are. The initiate whom the community has accepted vows to keep the laws, to devote his life to God in sensations, thoughts, words and deeds.

Not every one is meant for the council* of the elders. These are solely the men and women who have become wise because of their actualization of the eternal laws and their spiritual activities and abilities in the community, that is, who speak and give from the truth and work responsibly in the community.

Only those who are filled with the Spirit of love,** through the actualization of the eternal laws and

---

* *Council means the activity of the elders in cooperation with the community.*
** *All those who are selflessly active for the Kingdom of God on earth are filled with God's love. This means those who do not reflect their human ego in order to flaunt themselves, but who have become impersonal for the most part, that is, who have become the law of God.*

The one who gradually is becoming the law of God hears the voice of God and the one whose sensations, thoughts, words and actions are the law and are the word has become the law of God.

May the one who believes to possess these selfless gifts examine himself. If he believes that God speaks to him, that is, that God addresses him, he through selfless deeds, are accepted in the sanctum, in the midst of the spiritually baptized ones. They become elders, healers-by-faith and spiritual teachers.

The one who is on a high level of actualization can be a leader of various activities within the community. Only the one who, according to his aptitudes, has fulfilled the different degrees of selfless serving, that is, who was already active in the community in manifold ways, will gradually come into the circle of the angels and elders.

Everything that happens in the community – the blessing of the newborn infants and the spiritual baptism following the inner maturity, the weddings, the

---

should examine if he has already actualized what God says to him or has already fulfilled a large part of it.

To be addressed by God is given to the one who has filled with light the first four consciousness centers within himself. The one whom God addresses has not yet become the word of God. He can perceive God through his soul garments that have become more luminous, that is, through his light-filled shadows.

This being spoken to - that is, the perception of the word of God - is explicitly meant for the one whom God addresses, not for a second or third person.

As long as God addresses His word to the person, the soul is not yet pure for the most part, nor is the word of the Lord pure when it reaches the human being. This, in turn, means that God can indeed address His child, but because the human being still has to listen for it, some human aspects will reach the conscious mind with it. The word of God may be clear; but when it arrives in the consciousness of the still burdened person, it is mixed knowledge, thus meant for the individual. The one who has become the word of God has left the four planes of purification; he immerses into the Absolute Law.

If a person comes to the community and says of himself, "I am a prophet and am sent to you by God," then the elders shall tell him, "Be silent with the prophetic word. Come into the community, live in the community, work in the community and let yourself be examined by the community for some years."

birth of children and all essential events – shall be recorded in the *community book*, which the elders have in their keeping and which one elder keeps up to date.

10. And still another one asked Him, "Master, when shall they receive the anointing?" And Jesus answered, "When they have reached the age of maturity and have manifested in themselves the sevenfold gifts of the Spirit, let the angel offer prayer and thanksgiving for them and give them the seal of anointment. It is good that all be tried in each degree for seven years. Nevertheless, let it take place for each one according to his growth in the love and wisdom of God." (Chap. 91:10)

I, Christ, explain, correct
and deepen the word:

An *anointed* person is the one who perceives within himself the seven basic powers of the eternal life as a gift of love and is the one through whom I have become the word.

The one who has raised his consciousness to Me and whose sensations, thoughts and senses rest in Me is the *angel* of the community, about whom I have already spoken. This angel is My word and the word of the Father-Mother-God. For the one who has become the law – whose feeling, thinking, speaking and acting I Myself Am, the law – is an anointed person, that is, a person consecrated by God, the law, who can then become the angel of the community.

If there is among you such a one who has reached the stage of anointment, the angel of the community and an elder should thank God that He has awakened another angel for this or another community.

The one who is accepted by the community as an anointed one should first prove himself for some years and bring the seven basic powers of life into the community by his wise way of living.

The examination means that an anointed one is the law; and accordingly he has to know and live the seven basic powers of God, the eternal law, and bring them into the community. It is by this that the community recognizes his inner maturity and his being spiritually awakened in the love and in the wisdom of the Eternal.

If the community has accepted and received him, then it will commend him in praise and thanks to the Father-God and to Me, the Christ, and will see to it that he keep the laws of God for the community and also fulfill them in the community.

CHAPTER 92

The Regulations for the Community (Part 2)

Marriage and partnership,
a union according to the law of selfless love and fidelity –
Marriage in the community, a covenant with God (1-3).
Parents bear the responsibility for their children before God
– The Father-Mother-House – Children not considered as
one's own – About the spiritual dual-pairs and the emer-
gence of "spiritual children" (4). About the supper at the
Lord's table in the community – Weekly review – No cere-
monies (5). External forms and ceremonies are concessions
and not principles of the law (6-7)

1. And another asked Him, "Master, is it Your will that there be marriages among us as it is among the peoples of the Earth?" And Jesus answered, saying, "Among some, it is the custom that one woman may marry several men who say to her, 'Be our wife and take away our disgrace.' Among others, it is the custom that one man may marry several women who say to him, 'Be our husband and take away our disgrace.' For those who love feel that it is a fault not to be loved.

2. But I want to show you, My disciples, a better and more perfect way: A marriage should be between one man and one woman united in full freedom by perfect love and affection, and this, for so long as love and life last. But let them see to it that they have perfect health

*and that they truly love each other in all purity and not
only for worldly advantage. And then let them vow their
fidelity to one another before witnesses.*

*3. Then, when the time has come, let the angel or the
elder offer prayer and thanksgiving and tie them with
the scarlet cord, if you want, and crown them and lead
them three times round the altar and let them eat of one
bread and drink of one cup. Then, holding their hands
together, let him say: Be two in one, blessed be the holy
union. You whom God has joined together, let no man
put asunder, so long as life and love do last."*
(Chap. 92:1-3)

I, Christ, explain, correct
and deepen the word:

It is not in accordance with the eternal law that a
man has several wives and a woman several husbands.

It shall be on Earth as in heaven: The man chooses a
wife, and when the chosen woman consents to the union with the man, both shall ask themselves what connects them.

In heaven, two beings, the spiritual man – called the
positive – and the spiritual woman – called the negative –
unite through similar predispositions of mentality. This
means that they resemble each other in their character
traits. They complement each other in their work together because their abilities attuned to each other. For

the law of God says, "Like unites with like." This also refers to mentality. Love for God and all Being is the bond that eternally unites all pure beings. Therefore, when two beings resemble each other in some basic powers of life, for instance in the basic power of patience and of order, they can then enter into a dual union. The oneness in the love of God unites all beings with one another as brothers and sisters.

The unifying love is the expression of the polarity that unites two beings that are in tune with each other through their mentality. Like attracts like. That is the eternal law of attraction. From this ensues the dual union.

For My community on Earth, still more holds true:

When a woman or a man is lonely and not loved, she or he has violated the law of love.

This means that the lonely person who is not loved is himself incapable of loving. Consequently, he also radiates little love and can therefore attract few people who love selflessly. Either he stays alone or attracts, in turn, people with a similar vibration, who are likewise hardly capable of loving. Such people are then bound to one another by worldly desires, ideas and their orientation to the physical.

However, if two human beings, man and woman, are devoted to one another in selfless love and affection and in deep trust, then they will meet each other in freedom, without one forcing the other to fulfill his wishes. Such marriages and partnerships will last as long as the earthly life lasts and, in the spirit, the partners will be brother and sister in heaven as on Earth.

When two human beings enter a union, they should be enlightened about the law of selfless love and fidelity, by the angel – by the person who has become My word – and an elder. If there is not yet an angel in the community, a person who has become My word, then some elders should assume the task.

When two people unite in marriage* in the name of the Father-Mother-God – it can also be a partnership** – they enter into a covenant with God. The union should take place among witnesses within the community.

Then the community commits itself to act as God-parents, so to speak, to the couple. It sees to it that the vow before God to stay with each other in selfless love is adhered to.

If one of the partners leaves the other, because there is no agreement in their thinking and living anymore and the gap can no longer be bridged, and if they agree to keep the brother-sister bond, then both of them can enter another marriage or partnership, provided they

---

* *A partnership is a union before God without a civil ceremony. A marriage is a union before God which also takes place through a civil ceremony.*

** *This regulation is in accordance with the divine law. It will have full validity in the time when the Kingdom of Peace of Jesus Christ has taken form on earth. To enter into such a partnership within the community without a previous civil wedding is not allowed at present in some countries according to the worldly law. The members of the Original Christian communities in Universal Life comply, of course, also in this respect with state laws which require that a couple has had a civil ceremony before they make the covenant with God within the community.*

were both in their first marriage or partnership. A third marriage or partnership cannot be approved. The one who nevertheless undertakes this should leave the community. This rule does not hold true in the case of the death of one of the partners.[*]

The union of a couple in accordance with the laws of selfless love needs no ceremonies. The angel, who has become My word, the elders and the community pray to the eternal Father in heaven and thank Him for the love that He has placed in these two persons who love each other selflessly. They also pray for strength, so that the man can beget children out of selfless love for the woman, and that the woman can give birth to children out of selfless love for the man. Afterwards, the community prays that they may become members of the community life and participate in the great family of God.

---

[*] *When in the first marriage or partnership a spiritual development is no longer possible because the partners go different ways - the one longing for worldly things, the other for higher ideals and values - then a second marriage or partnership can be approved if it is entered into and led on a higher spiritual level, with the goal of a spiritual union and unity with all people and beings.*

The one who wants to live according to the principle of duality of the heavens can also enter into a divine union that is no longer physically oriented, after having dissolved a second marriage or partnership. A third physically-oriented marriage or partnership is not permitted according to the laws of God.

When a person decides to join the community, a new phase of life according to the eternal law begins for him. He will discuss his situation with the elders in this light, and will receive advice and support from them for his new way through life.

The person who wants to make use of the earthly laws as a criterion for marriage is not forbidden to do so. But may his word which he gave to God be his main criterion.

However, the one who enters a marriage or a partnership for the sake of worldly benefits should not do so before God, but before those who approve of such things. The couple, however, should not lead their private life within the community, but outside the community, so that the community not take offense to this and the couple not become a nuisance.

The one who enters into a marriage in order to gain advantage from it is not rejected. The community supports both partners in prayer, asking the Eternal to guide everything in such a way that they gradually learn to love each other selflessly and become a solid link in the chain of the great family.

4. *"And when they beget children, let them do so with prudence and reason, according to their ability to support them. Nevertheless, to those who want to be perfect and to whom it is given, I say: Let them be like the angels of God in heaven, who neither marry nor are married, nor have children, nor care for tomorrow, but are free from all ties, as I Am, and keep and store up the power of God within for their service and for works of healing, as I have done. But the multitude cannot grasp these words, only those to whom it is given."* (Chap. 92:4)

I, Christ, explain, correct
and deepen the word:

The one who begets children should bear the responsibility for them before God that they become God-filled people, who keep My laws and be a great support and strength to the community.

Many who begot and gave birth to children awaken to the service for their neighbor and consider this their task. They should not neglect their children, but should entrust them to a Father-Mother-House where they are brought up in the right way, according to the laws of selfless love.

However, the parents will remain linked with their children and will not leave them. The one who is in selfless service keeps the commandments of selfless love.

The parents will have the children at home with them as often as it is possible for them. They will support the Father-Mother-House and let positive energies flow into it, so that all children feel well in the Father-Mother-House and have their home there, too.

God takes cares of the souls and human beings who fulfill His will. The one who entrusts himself and his children to God and is active in selfless service for his neighbor is not bound to people and will neither bind himself to his child nor consider it to be his own. He will raise it according to the law of eternal love and will be a good advisor, helper and friend to the child.

But the one who makes of his children his property has to worry about tomorrow, because he relies solely on his human powers. He considers everything he owns to be his property, including the wife or husband and the children and, by his self-will, is bound to his property, to the wife or husband and the children.

A person who is bound cannot freely and selflessly live and work like the angels of God. He is married to matter, to the body of the wife or to that of the husband, and his children should fulfill his will. Thus, they are enslaved and bound to him. He keeps them as his property.

People whose home is this world – whose thoughts are oriented solely towards human institutions, possessions and earthly pleasures and to people who also think and live as they do – cannot understand the meaning of the following statement of "The Gospel of Jesus:"

"Let them be like the angels of God in heaven, who neither marry nor are married, nor have children, nor care for tomorrow, but are free from all ties, as I Am, and keep and store up the power of God within for their service and for works of healing, as I have done."

Only the one who has attained inner freedom, who actualizes the laws of infinity more and more, understands My word; heaven opens to him not only in the word, but also in the deeds. Those through whom I Am active on Earth understand My following words which I speak from the heavens:

The angels in heaven, the heavenly beings, do not marry in the sense of how human beings marry. They find one another through the eternal law of love that brings them together. They do not woo and are not wooed. They do not beget as man does. They are not sexual, but are two beings of polarity in the Spirit of the Father-Mother-God: the spiritual woman – the negative principle – and the spiritual man – the positive principle – two beings in the uniting powers of the polarities, positive and negative.[*]

For My human children's better understanding, again and again, I name the spiritual positive principle "man" and the spiritual negative principle "woman."

From the radiating love of the female and male principles, of the dual-pair, from the spiritual man and the spiritual woman, spiritual principles come forth again – for better understanding called "spiritual children." The duals, the spiritual man and the spiritual woman, dedicate the child to the Father-Mother-God; for God, the Father-Mother-Principle, has caused the spiritual body to come forth, out of one of His rays of love.

The dual-pair gave the power of their dual-love to the mature substance of the spirit body which was be-

---

[*] *The one who simply marries is bound to the body and therefore, to the human being. The one who enters matrimony is united with God and with the one he has chosen. Therefore, may everyone recognize the difference: being in a matrimony or being married. The one who is simply m a r r i e d cannot live like the angels in heaven, who find and love each other in God, our Father.*

stowed upon them by God, and raised it to filiation. For My earthly children's better understanding: The dual-pair raised a mature nature being to the filiation in God.

The dual-pair is the bearing and sustaining life for the spiritually exalted being, for the spiritual child, which is positive or negative – in human words: a boy or a girl. The dual-pair, which has raised a nature being to the filiation through and for the Father-Mother-God, is the spiritual parents. Through the spiritual parents, the Father-Mother-Spirit transfers the filiation attributes to the nature being.

5. *And another asked Him, "Master, in what manner shall we present the holy offering?" And Jesus answered, saying, "The offering which God loves in secret is a pure heart. But for a memorial and worship, offer unleavened bread, mingled wine, oil and incense. When you come together in one place to give the holy offering, the lamps being lighted, let the one who makes the offering, the angel of the community or the elder, have clean hands and a pure heart and take from the offered gifts, unleavened bread and mingled wine and the incense. (Chap. 92:5)*

I, Christ, explain, correct
and deepen the word:

In My community, there is no need for ceremonies. I conceded this to the Jews, because they did not yet

974

know the direct path to the heart of God, as you do in this time [1989], nor did they bear redemption in themselves yet.

However, My community shall come together once a week; it shall be on a Saturday evening. My own meet clad in clean – if possible, festive – clothes, in order to partake of the meal at a table that has been laid and has burning candles in honor of the One who nourishes them and keeps them healthy. The one who partakes of the food in My name, in the spirit of truth, has Me as his guest.

Before the meal, one or two of the elders lead the review of the week. Everything that is essential, the "for" and "against," should be openly expressed.

The elders who lead the community ask the community the question: What was in general positive and constructive in the last week and why? And who and what has contributed to that?

The community reports on the "for." The elders who lead the community will then enter the corresponding remarks into the community book. Also the noteworthy deeds of the community members for the Spirit of Christ, which have contributed to the welfare and to the growth of the community, shall be recorded in the community book.

The same takes place with the "against." Who or what was the cause of the negative aspects in the past week? Notes about this are also entered into the book of the week, which is one of the community books – also notes about those who caused it or participated in it and the reason they had or still have difficulties and problems.

After the meal at the Lord's Table, the appropriate elders should speak with those who may still be burdened with difficulties or problems. And if second or third parties are concerned, they should take part in the talk.[*]

The burning candles symbolize the inner light around which God-filled people gather.

This meal, like all meals, shall be taken silently, in the awareness that the human being is receiving and taking in the gifts of God.

One among you who is of honest heart, that is, who is filled with love for God, should say the prayer of thanksgiving before and after the meal and commend the community to the Lord, so that the following week will also be under the sign of selfless love and the still burdened brothers and sisters may recognize and acquire the strength to clear up what still needs attention. For the new week will again bring to each one what he needs to clear up.

---

[*] *Only serious problems which would require a longer time to be cleared up should be discussed after the meal at the Lord's Table with one or several of the elders. The simple problems and difficulties, however, which take a short time to be cleared up should be discussed with an elder b e f o r e the meal at the Lord's Table.*

In My community, each one should serve everyone.

Every week, different community members should take turns in setting the table for the meal, bringing in the food and selflessly serving their neighbor who is sitting at the table. The preparation of the food should also be done in turns, so that each one renders everyone a lesser or greater service.

The community of Christ, My community, should be filled with spiritual life. Therefore, each community member should devote himself to the Father-Mother-God at the beginning of each day by asking the Eternal to grant him the strength to become pure in heart; for those who are pure in heart will behold God and possess the Earth. Everyone should take the meaning of the following words with him into the day: The offering that God loves is the pure heart of His children.

The "offering" does not mean "sacrifice," but a heart-felt desire to joyfully devote oneself to the One who loves him and to be with those who love Him.

I repeat: Ceremonies were not needed in the past, nor are they needed in the present and in the future. The words that you read in the book "The Gospel of Jesus" are symbols for the life in the Spirit, symbols for the meal and the dining of those who have received God in their hearts.

The one who drinks consciously receives the essence of life, and the one who dines consciously receives the bread of the heavens. Therefore, do everything from the heart; thus you do it consciously and no further consecrations or ceremonies are needed.

The one who does everything consciously, aligned with Me, Christ, does it in My memory.

6. *And let him give thanks for all things and bless them and call upon the Father in heaven that He may send His Holy Spirit, so that it may come upon them and make them to be the body and the blood, the substance and the life of the Eternal, which is eternally being broken and shed for all.*

7. *And let him lift them up to heaven and pray for all, for those who have gone before, for those who are still alive, and for those who are yet to come. As I have taught you, so you pray, too, and let him break the bread and put a morsel in the cup and then bless the holy union, and then let him give it to the faithful, speaking in this manner: This is the body of Christ, the substance of God. This is the blood of Christ, the life of God, eternally being broken and shed for you and for all unto eternal life. And as you have seen Me doing, do likewise in the spirit of love, for the words which I speak to you are spirit and life." (Chap. 92:6-7)*

I, Christ, explain, correct
and deepen the word:

These statements are concessions as well, but not principles of the law. People of that time were looking for something external to hold on to and needed the outer

978

rituals. I accommodated their wishes according to their mentality. However, the inner temple opens to the one who seeks and finds the Spirit of life within himself. He will devote his life to God in reverence and thus, all that he accomplishes.

CHAPTER 93

The Regulations for the Community (Part 3)

About forgiving and asking for forgiveness (1-2).
Healing out of the Spirit of God (3-4). The responsible ones
in the community (5-10)

1. And another asked, "Master, if one has committed a sin, can a person forgive him his sin or not?" And Jesus said, "God forgives every sin to those who repent; but what you have sown you must also reap. Neither God nor man can forgive the sins of those who do not repent or renounce their sins; just as little as they can retain the sins of those who renounce them. But when one is in the Spirit and clearly recognizes that one repents of his sins and renounces them, he may truly say to the repentant sinner, 'You are forgiven your sins.' For every sin is forgiven by repenting and making amends; and those who renounce them are released therefrom, but those who continue to sin remain bound to their sin.

2. Nevertheless, the fruits of sin continue for some time; as we sow so must we reap. For God does not let Himself be mocked, and those who sow in the flesh will reap corruption, but those who sow in the Spirit will reap eternal life. To the one who renounces and confesses his sins, the elder shall speak in this way, 'May God forgive you your sins and lead you to eternal life.'

Every sin against God is forgiven by God, and every sin against man is forgiven by man." (Chap. 93:1-2)

I, Christ, explain, correct
and deepen the word:

Only the one against whom his neighbor has sinned can forgive his sin. No uninvolved person, a second or third party, can forgive him his sin.

What man sows he will also reap, unless he repents in time of his sins, the violations of the law, and asks his neighbor for forgiveness through Me, the Christ. If the latter forgives him, then his sin is taken away from him, for God wipes out everything that has been repented and forgiven, if the person endeavors not to do the same anymore.

But what is not repented and forgiven has to be expiated, either in this life or in one of the next earthly lives or in the spheres of purification, where the soul will go after it leaves its body.

And if one asks for forgiveness and is not forgiven his debt, not even God will take it from him. However, God's love and grace will increasingly irradiate the unforgiving one with His light, so that he, too, may recognize his wrong behavior, forgive his neighbor and also ask for forgiveness, himself. For it is not always one alone who is guilty. In many cases, both of them are guilty through their behavior.

Before the causes become effective in the body, the love and grace of God touch the heart of the sinner again and again and move it to clear up the sin in time, by forgiving and asking for forgiveness; for every sin is a guilt, that is, an offense against the divine law.

Only the one who has obtained forgiveness from his neighbor can enter the Kingdom of Heaven. Therefore, O man, pay attention to your thoughts and speech, so that both thought and speech may comply with My law.

Man can indeed forgive, but only God can dissolve the blemish of the soul. The elder can explain to those who ask for forgiveness and who forgive, according to the law of reparation, that only those sins are dissolved which are no longer committed in the future. Man cannot absolve sins, only God.

When two persons have a quarrel and cannot clear up their disagreement, because they do not know the divine laws, they can be advised, if they so wish, by a wise elder or by the angel of the community on what the eternal laws say, so that it may again be possible for both to think and act in a lawful way.

3. *And another asked Him, "When one among us is sick, will we have the power to heal as You do?" And Jesus answered, "This power comes from perfect chastity and faith. Those who are born of God keep their seed within them.*

4. *But if one among you is sick, let him send for the elder of the community, that he may anoint him with*

olive oil in the name of the Lord. The prayer of faith, the flowing out of power, together with a prayer of thanksgiving, will raise him up, if he is not held down by sin from this life or a former life." (Chap. 93:3-4)

I, Christ, explain, correct
and deepen the word:

In My community, there will be people who have the gift of healing. In order to be able to heal from the Spirit of God, their souls have to be purified for the most part, so that My healing stream can flow through them to the weak soul and to the suffering body.* But only the person who surrenders to Me the burden of his body – the sin which has its effect there – can recover. Then healing takes place by way of his soul, provided that this is good for the soul and the body. However, if the person continues to commit the same faults, then it is better for his soul that he bear his suffering and mature through it, even if it is in one of the next earthly lives, for the faults are likened to his suffering.

There are no ceremonies in heaven. In many cases, I conceded them to the unknowing people, who knew but

---

* *Healers-by-faith, also called Christ-healers or prayer-healers, must have served in the community for a longer time according to the law of life. Here, too, the community determines if the community member has developed the inner quality for this task.*
Healing-by-faith does not rule out the consultation of a physician or a naturopath.

a part of the laws of life, because they still clung to rituals and, through rituals, found their way to stillness and introspection.

My own, who know the law and live in My community, which is a building stone of the Kingdom of Peace, do not need ceremonies and thus, not even the anointing. Heaven is the law of love, and so shall it be on Earth among My own.

The person who asks Me for healing shall also, at the same time, give thanks for the healing; for the one who asks from the heart and does the works of selfless love – and no longer commits the same sins – has already obtained healing in his soul. Give thanks and be certain that the one who gives thanks from the heart and does not commit his faults anymore has already received.

5. *And another asked Him, "Master, how shall the holy community be ordered and who shall serve in it?" And Jesus answered, "When My disciples are gathered in My name, let them choose from among themselves true and faithful men and women who assume duties and advise in worldly matters, who provide for the necessities of the poor and of those who cannot work, and let them administer the possessions of the community and assist in the offering, and let them, through their help, be your deacons.*

6. *And when these have proved themselves in their service, let them choose from among themselves those who have spiritual gifts, whether of leadership, proph-*

ecy, preaching, teaching or healing, so that they may spiritually edify the flock, make the holy offering and celebrate the mysteries of God and let these be your elders and their helpers.

7. And from those who have served well in their position, let them choose one who is considered most worthy and let him preside over all and he shall be your angel. And let the angel appoint the deacons and consecrate the elders, by anointing them and laying hands upon them and breathing upon them, that they may receive the Holy Spirit for the service to which they are called. And as for the angel, let one of higher leadership from the supreme council anoint and consecrate him.

8. For as I have sent apostles and prophets, so I send evangelists and pastors, too – the eight and forty pillars of the temple – that by the service of the four I may build up and perfect My community. They shall sit in Jerusalem in a holy congregation, each with his helper and deacon, and to them shall the scattered congregations refer in all matters regarding the maintenance of the community. And just as the light comes, so shall they lead and guide and edify and teach My holy community. They shall receive light from all, and to all shall they give more light.

9. And do not forget, in your prayers and invocations, intercessions and thanksgiving, to offer the incense, as it is written in the last of your prophets: From the rising of the sun until its setting, incense shall be offered in My name in all places as a pure offering; for My name shall be great among the Gentiles.

10. For verily, I say to you, incense is the reminder of the hidden intercession of the saints with words that cannot be uttered." (Chap. 93:5-10)

I, Christ, explain, correct
and deepen the word:

All those who, on the Inner Path to the kingdom of the heart, have recognized and actualized the second level, the divine will, serve in My community. They are growing ripe for the deeds in My Spirit.

The ones who are in My service are the angel of the community, the elders, the healers-by-faith, the spiritual teachers, the leaders of the Inner Spirit-Christ Churches and those who selflessly work in serving their neighbors.

The community life does not have any rigid forms. A life in My Spirit is evolution. There are no superiors and subordinates.

Again and again, men and women who have grown in the Spirit are elected from the community, who preside over the growing community or build up further communities, so that the Earth may be populated with people who do the will of the Father-Mother-God.

At first, those elected are placed at the side of the spiritual teachers and leaders of the Inner Spirit-Christ Churches and those who carry out various tasks, like, for example, in education and social concerns and in the field of business and finance, as well as at the side of those who care for the poor and administer the community possessions. In this way, they grow into further tasks in My Spirit that require their self-reliance, so that the community – and in the broadest sense, the communities – may expand and the Kingdom of Peace may thus grow on Earth.

The elected men and women shall also increase the number of elders. Therefore, let a few gifted ones lead the community life under the supervision of an elder, be it at the community evenings, the prayer evenings, the Inner Spirit-Christ Churches and in everything that is incumbent on the elders.*

Some elected elders or the angel of the growing community will set up and keep the community book for further communities and will see to it that all essential occurrences within the community are recorded.

And if one among those elected stands out through good, selfless deeds, by keeping the eternal laws, give him the opportunity to become the angel of a community. He will be appointed by the elders and the community as an angel only when he has successfully gone through the years of probation and has truly completed the fourth level, the divine earnestness, and has become My word, the law.

Let it be said: I teach My law to My own, so that it will be on Earth as it is in heaven.

---

* The elders' duty is to serve and lead the community in all areas and see to it that the eternal laws are kept and lived.

My own, who know and keep My laws because they are walking the Inner Path to the kingdom of the inner being, to the law of life, do not need ceremonies – nor evangelists or pastors.

The one who does My will knows the law. The shepherd is then the law. This is the Christ within you through the person who is My word and hears My word within himself.

The one who is My word – the angel – and those who hear My word – the elders – and those who are close to My word – the healers-by-faith, the spiritual teachers and the leaders of the Inner Spirit-Christ Churches – and all those who selflessly serve My community are responsible for My community.

CHAPTER 94

The Regulations for the Community (Part 4)

*About the burial of the dead –
Conscious living – The spiritually dead – God does not
want repeated incarnations (1-4). The one who has found
his way to his inner God needs no earthly leaders – Criteria
for the genuineness of those responsible: Selfless service –
About clothing: Inner beauty becomes visible on the outside (5-7). Growth and livelihood of the community, a task
in common (8-10)*

1. And another asked Him, "Master, how is Your will
that we bury our dead?" And Jesus answered, "Seek
counsel from the deacons in this matter, for it concerns
only the body. Verily, I say to you, there is no death for
those who believe in the life to come. What you believe
to be death is the door to life, and the grave is the gate
to resurrection for those who believe and obey. Do not
mourn nor weep for those who have left you, but rather
rejoice for their entrance into life.

2. As all creatures come forth from the unseen into
this world, so do they return to the unseen and so will
they come again until they are purified. Let their bodies
be committed to the elements, and the Father, who renews all things, will charge the angels to look after
them. Let the elders pray that their bodies may rest in
peace and their souls awaken to a joyful resurrection.

3. *There is a resurrection from the body and there is a resurrection into the body. There is an ascent from the life of the flesh and a descent into the life of the flesh. Let prayers be spoken for those who have gone before and for those who are alive and for those who are yet to come, for all are one family in God. In God they live, move and have their being.*

4. *The body which you lay in the grave or which is consumed by fire is not the body that will be; for those who come will receive other bodies, but nevertheless their own, and as they have sown in one life, so will they reap in another. Blessed are those who suffer wrong in this life, for they will have greater joy in the life to come. Blessed are those who have practiced righteousness in this life, for they will receive the crown of life."* (Chap. 94:1-4)

I, Christ, explain, correct
and deepen the word:

There is only *one* decomposable body; it is the material body, which is from the earth and becomes earth again.

Therefore, I advise you to give the dead body, that which is from the earth, back to the earth. Just as the leaves of the trees that fall to the earth in autumn are given back to the earth, so is the decomposable body, too, given back to the earth.

Your graveyards should not be decorated with tomb-stones and all kinds of embellishments. The flowers which the earth brings forth are the most beautiful adornments. And if you wish, and if it is customary according to the earthly law, a small stone or a wooden board may bear the name of the decomposable body which was given to the earth.

If the decomposable body was given to the fire, put the ashes in a vessel which will be kept in a burial chamber until the time has come when it also falls apart and returns to what it is made of. Vessels of clay would be good for the remains of the body.

You can give the ashes of the body to the winds, the element air, if this is in accordance with the still existing worldly laws. The wind scatters the ashes of the former body and gives them back to the earth.

There is no death of the soul. Whatever comes from God lives eternally and whatever comes from the earth will become earth again.

Therefore, strive to fulfill the eternal law and to live in the law of love, so that your soul, while in the body, may attain the resurrection from spiritual death, namely the conscious life which the soul actualizes in word and deed, while in the person.

Conscious living means to actualize and fulfill the laws of love. In this way, man gains clarity and will think and act lawfully. Then, after the death of the body, the soul will immediately resurrect and go into more light-filled spheres, according to the life of the soul and body, or will ascend into the light, into the heavens.

As long as the earthly laws exist, these words hold true: Give to Caesar what is Caesar's and to God what is due to God. Therefore, strive to keep the laws of God and to fulfill the earthly laws, too, insofar as they do not violate the divine law. For the one who offends against God, the universal law, burdens himself.

The one who does not know the eternal law of life, nor wants to know it or experience it, is spiritually dead. Therefore, only spiritually dead people will mourn their dead, believing that these have left them. But these have just moved into the fine-material life which cannot be perceived with the eyes of the body.

Rejoice when a light-filled soul has risen from the grave of the human ego and, after the death of the body, enters the light-filled kingdom, the heavens – the life which is granted to those who have lived in the Spirit, in the true life, while still in the earthly garment.

It is the will of the Father-Mother-God and of the Son, who I Am, that the soul in the earthly garment purify itself to such a degree that it no longer returns to the flesh, into a new body of earth which was begotten by an earthly man and carried by an earthly woman. When the soul comes back to Earth, the new body again corresponds to the condition of the soul, to its characteristics. The light and shadowed sides of the soul thus shape the earthly body. The material body of the reincarnated soul is the house into which it has entered to clear away its shadows, on Earth, in the school of life of incarnated souls.

The light of the day shows to a person what he should accomplish each day. Thus, the moments and minutes are precious energies for self-recognition. The one who makes use of the moments, the minutes and the hours, and thus lives in the present, gains mastery over himself. He holds precious life energy in his soul and in his body.

A soul will keep on wanting to incarnate again until it bears more light than shadow.

Light-filled souls, too, strive to come to Earth in order to serve those who struggle with their shadows. As long as these souls stay in the light, they are not bound to the law of sowing and reaping. After their physical death, they go back into the light. So there is an ascent from the life of the flesh and a descent into the life of the flesh.

Pray to the Father-Mother-God that He may give you new life energies every day, so that you may recognize what you should accomplish this day – so that you return to more light-filled kingdoms after your physical death, in order to not descend into the life of the flesh anymore.

Pray for the departed, so that they may recognize their path and walk on the path to the divine, to the Kingdom of Peace. But pray also for those who will come, so that in the spheres of purification they may recognize what needs to be done in the earthly garment.

The one who lives in God moves in God and has his being in God.

The person who lives in and with the world will have his existence in the world again and again and will continue to live in the world until he uses the days to attain the spiritual, which, ultimately, is life.

The one who, as a human being, pulls through and remains in the light of the truth, in God, and suffers injustice in God, despite the temptations of the darkness, will have great joy in the eternal Being, because he did not have to forgive nor did he have to ask for forgiveness. He has lived and lives in God. And the one who remained righteous despite temptations, that is, who kept the eternal laws, will wear the crown of love in eternal life.

5. *And another asked Him, "Master, under the law, Moses clad the priests with splendid garments for their services in the temple. Shall we also likewise clothe those we have entrusted with the holy services which You have taught us?" And Jesus answered, "White linen is the righteousness of the saints; but verily, the time will come when Zion will be desolate and, when the time of her affliction is over, she will arise and put on her beautiful garments, as it is written.*

6. But seek first the kingdom of righteousness, and all these things will be added to you. Seek simplicity in all things and give no chance to vain glory. Seek first to be clad with mercy and with the garment of salvation and the cloak of righteousness.

7. For what does it profit if you have not these? You are like the sound of brass and the tinkling of cymbals, if you have not love. Seek righteousness, love and peace, and all things of beauty will be added to you." (Chap. 94:5-7)

I, Christ, explain, correct
and deepen the word:

Recognize that there is no castigation in the law of love. The law does not take anything from a person that he still wants to keep. The law leads a person out of his habits, traditions, opinions and egocentricities and allows many things, until the person has found himself in Me, the law. This is how Moses, too, acted.

However, the one who looks solely to Me and actualizes the laws needs no outer splendor nor human leaders. He has found his leader and Redeemer within himself. It is Christ, who I Am, the Good Shepherd of all faithful sheep.

Therefore, do not strive for outer prestige or human leaders. In God there is equality. For this reason, in My community, the angel and the elders should be neither more nor less important than the community. In Me, there is only *one* people that keeps the eternal laws of love.

Why do people elect their earthly leaders again and again? Because they have not placed the Spirit of Christ in the center of their life. Mankind will need its worldly idols until it has found the way to the inner truth. When a person has found his way to his inner God, to the Father-Mother-God, he does not look up to any human idol, but fulfills the eternal laws and is pleasing to God. With like-minded people, he will then form the family of God on Earth.

As long as people who form the community or the communities in Me, the Christ, are in the process of evolution, there will, again and again, be people who have already reached a higher spiritual maturity. These will then be the angels and the elders, the healers-by-faith, the spiritual teachers and the leaders of the Inner Spirit-Christ Churches in the community. The one who has matured in Spirit does not claim to be better than his neighbor.

A criterion for the genuineness of an angel and an elder and all the others who preside over the community is selflessness, serving selflessly without seeking reward or acknowledgment.

This does not concern the activities in Christian enterprises and social establishments. There, one fulfills the law of "pray and work" and will receive a salary, so that he may subsist in the material life. But here, too, it is said: Work selflessly, serving your neighbor. Then you, too, will receive.

Selflessness in serving the community, as angel and elder, should not fall under the law of "pray and work." It is the selfless service without reward.

Seek first to attain righteousness and selfless love, then you will receive and have everything you need and beyond that. The one who serves selflessly will also earn. For the will of God is with him and the Father-Mother-God will take care of him, so that he lack nothing.

Clothe yourself with the adornment of virtue, with the strength of love and mercy, and you will be delivered from what still clings to the worldly man – his human ego, which is reflected in many facets: in pomp and splendor, in external wealth, in wanting to be and in claims of possession, in envy, hatred and enmity.

Moses conceded splendid garments to the priests, because they had not yet developed mercy, and the people wanted it that way.

The one who is permeated with love, mercy and justice is saved. He will dress and behave according to his inner radiation.

The one who keeps the eternal laws will also dress in colors consistent with the harmony of the divine law. The basic powers of the Spirit are the seven basic colors of the heavens. They are like the colors of the rainbow.*

---

* *This includes, also for the three-dimensional world, harmonious intermediate shades (blended colors) – as it is in nature.*

The selfless person is tidy, clean and tastefully dressed in a color from the spectrum of the rainbow. However, he will not wrap himself in pomp and splendor.

The selfless person will not show off or be conspicuous. He will radiate what he has actualized – also by his clothing.

As a person senses, thinks, speaks and acts, so he is and so he behaves in his family and in public.

As he is, so he dines. And as he is and dines, so he behaves and clothes himself.

A person can hide his ego for a long time and deceive the unenlightened one. The time comes for each one when his ego becomes visible and he shows what he really is.

Each one recognizes in himself where he stands; each one is his own measure; in this, his neighbor is his mirror: For what he dislikes in his neighbor, what agitates him and what he thinks and speaks about in agitation is on and in him in the same or similar way. Every agitation about your neighbor is your own measure.

Find the way to inner beauty through selfless love, peace and righteousness – and everything will be given to you by the Father in heaven.

God does not want His children to live in need, but to be rich in spirit. Then, as human beings, they will have what they need and much more, so that they may share with those who are on the way, from external poverty and the burdening of the soul, to inner beauty and inner wealth.

Therefore, strive first for the Kingdom of God and His justice, and you will then receive everything you need and beyond that. But this does not mean that your hands shall be idle. The law for man is "pray and work."

8. And yet another asked Him, "Master, how many of the rich and mighty will enter into life and join us, who are poor and despised? How shall we carry on the work of God in the spiritual regeneration of mankind?" And Jesus said, "This is also a matter for the deacons and for the community in counsel with the elders.

9. But when My disciples come together on the Sabbath evening or in the morning of the first day of the week, let each one of them bring an offering of a tithe, be it only the smallest part of their belongings, as God gave them, and put it in the offering box for the maintenance of the community and the services and their works. For I say to you, it is more blessed to give than to receive.

10. So shall all things be done, properly and in order. And the rest will be put in order by the Spirit who goes forth from the Father in heaven. I have instructed you now in the first principles, and behold, I Am with you always, even unto the end of the ages." (Chap. 94:8-10)

I, Christ, explain, correct
and deepen the word:

No wealthy one who calls his possessions his own will enter the Kingdom of God and no powerful one who exerts power over My people will come into heaven.

Both the rich and the powerful are poor in the spirit of love and in the works of mercy. Only when they bow their heads, when they use their possessions in the right way for the common good, for the people, and are like those who love Me more than this world with its temptations, attractions and pleasures – will they grow in My Spirit and then be with you, who are to be rich in inner values.

The one who repents of his claim to power, of his intolerance, his domineering nature and arrogance, and makes amends for what he has caused – that is, where it is necessary and appropriate – thus submitting to the eternal laws, will be with My own, and My own will be with him.

So do not say that you are poor, you who have chosen the Kingdom of God. The truly rich are those who do the will of My Father and theirs.

The time is near when My own will possess the Earth. For in the time of Christ, there will be neither rich nor poor, neither powerful ones nor subordinates. All are equal in Me: My brothers and sisters – and all of us are the sons and daughters of God.

As long as the inner kingdom gradually grows outwards – that is, becomes visible on the Earth through those who do the will of the Father and also through those who have begun to walk the path to the kingdom of the inner being, in order to recognize and fulfill the will of the Father – My own will still need servants of their community: the angel, the elders, the healers-by-faith, the spiritual teachers, the leaders of the Inner Spirit-Christ Churches and the other selfless servants of God in the community buildings, schools, kindergartens, Christ-places (which you call "Christ-enterprises" and "farms for life") in the "houses for health" and in the "houses for the inner homeland" (homes for the elderly) and much more of what a person needs and is necessary to live in the temporal.

The help of each individual is needed, so that the community can be maintained and grow larger. Therefore, everyone should contribute a tithe every week or every month and thank God that he is healthy and strong and thus able to serve the eternal Father, the community and his neighbor.

The selfless person will contribute voluntarily, for he knows that all things come from God and all things go back to God.

Just as the sea feeds the lakes and rivers and brooks and these, in turn, feed the sea, just as the water becomes vapor and clouds and these, in turn, water the Earth, so shall My own also let the energies flow. Only a healthy circulation, a flowing of energy, ensures a healthy growth and an increase of energy. The one who is connected to this selfless circulation will never suffer want. He heeds the streaming eternal law of selfless love and keeps the commandment "pray and work."

The one who keeps the law and the commandments, which are excerpts from the eternal law, will belong to the Christ-people, which has only one leader and Redeemer, Christ, who I Am as the Son in the Father-Mother-God, from eternity to eternity.

These regulations of the community order shall be valid for the community life until all men and beings are one in God, My Father.

Do not despair. I Am with you until the end of time – and as a brother in all eternity.

Do not despair. The angels of the heavens are with My own and My own are with the angels of the heavens, with the divine beings, so that it may be on Earth as it is in heaven, where love and peace prevail.

The one who is with Me walks under the banner of Christ, which symbolizes the inner kingdom, the Kingdom of Peace: freedom, unity and brotherliness.

All people are one people in Me, the Christ.

CHAPTER 95

The Ascension

The resurrected One teaches His disciples about the fulfillment of the Redeemer-mission and about the influence of negative powers – In the mighty memory bank of the All, as well as in the atmospheric chronicle, the work of leading-back and the Kingdom of God on Earth are stored as positive energy and build up more and more (1). The earthly rule in the name of Christ through the tools of the demons (2-3). This mighty turn of time allows for all negativities to become visible – The darkness in its effects and self-created chains (4). The promise of the Holy Spirit (5). Bear Christ within you (6). I return in all glory (7). Selfless love is a bond that cannot be severed (8). As human being, Jesus experienced and suffered what it means to be a human being (9-10)

1. After His resurrection, Jesus showed Himself alive to His disciples and spent ninety days with them. He taught and spoke about the Kingdom of God and what pertains to it, and finished everything that He had to do. Then He let the twelve with Mary Magdalene and Joseph, His father, and Mary, His mother, and the other faithful women go to Bethany onto the Mount of Olives, which He had indicated to them.
(Chap. 95:1)

I, Christ, explain, correct
and deepen the word:

It is written, "After His resurrection, Jesus showed Himself alive to His disciples and spent ninety days with them. He taught and spoke about the Kingdom of God and what pertains to it, and finished everything that He had to do." These words, too, should be understood according to their meaning.

My disciples remained together for the whole time. They prayed and devoted themselves entirely to the One who had left them and yet was and is with them – the Christ of God in the eternal Father.

During these days of prayer and devotion, I, the resurrected One, appeared to the praying ones again and again. Through those who perceived the inner word, I taught My disciples to keep the laws of God, which I, as Jesus, had explained to them and had lived as an example. For they should have been able to fulfill what I, as Jesus, could no longer carry out, because the Jews were distant from God, as they did not want to see in Me anything but their king for this world.

That which I revealed to My disciples held true – and holds true – for all further generations, as well for God-filled people came and come again and again in order to actualize it. My thinking, living and working as Jesus of Nazareth also entered the great memory bank of the All and the atmospheric chronicle, in order to radiate from there onto the Earth again and again.

This mighty memory bank of the All and the atmospheric chronicle register all the energies that emanate from people, as well as what has been and is revealed from the pure Being. For nothing which is thought, spoken, revealed and done is lost.

I revealed the Kingdom of God, the eternal Being, to the disciples and spoke about the Kingdom of God on Earth. I revealed to them the "for" and "against," the influence and battles of the negative forces of this world, which will go on until what is pure, the law of life, finds access into the hearts of many people and is fulfilled by them. For if man is pure, noble and good, he will establish the Kingdom of God on this Earth, with Me, the Christ.

I could not fulfill this task as Jesus of Nazareth, because My own were not with Me. This is why, by way of revelation, I entered it into the memory bank of the All and into the atmospheric chronicle. There, invisible to man, the entire Redeemer-mission built itself up: the work of leading-back the children of God and the Kingdom of God on Earth. It is the mighty Work of Redemption, in which many pure spirit beings, together with spirit beings in the earthly garment – that is, human beings – are included.

At all times, beings went into the earthly garment – faithful to their mission – and began to bring parts of it into the world. Either they led a selfless life in the service of their neighbor or they repeatedly assumed smaller or greater parts of the spiritual mission, thus making it visible. In a life with each other and for their neighbor, they created establishments where they strove to live the true following of Christ. Yet the darkling came again and again to destroy the external establishments.

Over generations, dark souls incarnated to serve in the earthly garment as tools for the demons. As long as the demonic still had power, it was able to destroy the external aspect of the true Christian establishments – but not what was being built up more and more as positive energy in the memory bank of the All, in the atmospheric chronicle and in the earth: the Kingdom of God on Earth.

In the mighty turn of time [1989], many of these incarnated dark souls now experience the effects of their former deeds and are thus weakened. Therefore, the demons now have less and less access to the activities for the Kingdom of God on Earth. As a result, they are also divided among themselves and are hardly capable anymore of extensive negative deeds, of destroying and killing people who seem dangerous to them, because they strive for a life in Me, the Christ.

And so, the negative powers are losing ground more and more, and thus, their influence and power. At the same time, the light of the heavens increases in many people and through them on Earth, too. The dark power will recede.

It is written, "... let the twelve with Mary Magdalene and Joseph, His father, and Mary, His mother, and the other faithful women go to Bethany onto the Mount of Olives, which He had indicated to them."

I asked My faithful ones to witness My ascension, so that the event would enter their souls and they would recognize that all who truly accept and receive Me, the Christ, will journey towards heaven. They went up the mountain which I indicated.

Many spirit beings were present at My ascension. They accompanied Me to the eternal Father, to whom I returned as Son and Co-Regent of the heavens.

I correct: Among these spirit beings, there was also the spirit being which once had been, in the earthly garment, My foster-father Joseph, whose son was My earthly garment, Jesus. Joseph had already passed away. His spirit body, the being from God, was among the many messengers of God.

2. And Jesus said to them, "Behold, I have chosen you from among men and have given you the law and the word of truth.

3. I have placed you as the light of the world and as a city which cannot be hidden. But the time will come when darkness will cover the Earth and great darkness will cover the people. The enemies of truth and righteousness will rule in My name and establish a kingdom of this world. They will oppress the peoples and cause the enemy to blaspheme, replacing My teachings with the opinions of men and teaching in My name what I did not teach and darkening with their traditions what I did teach. (Chap. 95:2-3)

I, Christ, explain, correct
and deepen the word:

It is written, "Behold, I have chosen you from among men and have given you the law and the word of truth. I have placed you as the light of the world and as a city which cannot be hidden."

I said this not only to the faithful ones in the earthly garment, but also to the many messengers of God who were present, as well as to those who, in the realm of the souls, were preparing themselves for further incarnations to fulfill, throughout the ages and generations, their mission for the work of leading-home, of redemption, in order to announce it and establish the Kingdom of Peace on Earth. Today [1989], many beings from God are again incarnated in order to spread the message of love, which I revealed and reveal anew, and to establish the Kingdom of God on Earth.

What I revealed to My own before My ascension has come true:

"But the time will come when darkness will cover the Earth and great darkness will cover the people. The enemies of truth and righteousness will rule in My name and establish a kingdom of this world. They will oppress the peoples and cause the enemy to blaspheme, replacing My teachings with the opinions of men and teaching in My name what I did not teach and darkening with their traditions what I did teach."

The demons took their tools and established, with My name, Christ, a dominion in this world. With My name, Christ, they subjugated entire nations and still subjugate many people. In My name, they led crusades and killed many people. They forcibly Christianized others, so that these, too, would take My name in vain, just as the armies of darkness did and still do.

They took and take under their dominion and censorship the holy word, which holds true for the Earth and for mankind, and made of it their own book, their "Holy Scripture." They do teach in My name, in the name of Jesus and of the Christ and they refer to their book as the truth – but they themselves do not live what they proclaim to be the truth. In order to force people under their dominion, they lay down doctrines which are devised by people. These doctrines are not the law of life which I, as Jesus of Nazareth, taught and reveal again as the Christ of God. They established pagan customs, made up "traditions" and thus veiled and veil the truth.

With My name, they embellished and embellish, as "Christianity," this human world of conceptions, which has nothing in common with the world of God, and darken My teaching in order to thereby continue to bind the people to them and to keep them blind to the truth. In My name, Christ, the misguided ones even found political parties in order to induce, with My name,

Christ, the population to vote for their un-christian purposes.

Thus, My name is ridiculed in many ways, and all those who truly wish to follow Me are scorned, ridiculed and accused of false teaching. Of the true followers, they claim what they themselves are, namely, tools of the darkness who take My name in vain.

Thus, up to the present generation [1989], My words hold true: If they have persecuted Me, they will also persecute you. If they have mocked, scorned and ridiculed Me, they will also mock, scorn and ridicule you in public. If they have killed Me, they will also kill many of you.

4. *But be of good cheer; for the time will also come when the truth which they have hidden will become manifest; and the light will radiate, and the darkness will disappear and the true kingdom, which will be in the world but not of the world, will be established. The word of righteousness and love will go forth from the center, from the holy city on Mount Zion, and the mount which is in the land of Egypt will be known as an altar of witness to the Lord. (Chap. 95:4)*

I, Christ, explain, correct
and deepen the word:

The New Era, the era of the Christ, comes with power. Mankind is standing at a turn of time the equal of which has never been seen in matter. I, the Christ, come – and those who profess their faith in Me through their works of true and selfless love come with Me.

In this mighty turn of time, all negativities are becoming visible, so that all the people who have sinned against the law of life may recognize themselves, repent and make amends.

I Am the lord of love and life and I do not destroy. Only the spirit of the times destroys. I build up and raise all those who repent from their hearts and make amends for what they have caused. Thus, the chance for self-recognition, repentance and making amends is also given to those who have covered My holy word, the truth, with their satanic activities and their traditions. They are given the chance to confess in public before all peoples that they have taken My name, Christ, in vain for satanic purposes, in order to make a name for themselves in the world and to lead astray those who became servile to them.

The law of cause and effect interferes more and more in the church institutions where many who bear responsibility adorned and adorn themselves with My name, and took and take it in vain for the sake of their own prestige in the world.

The law of cause and effect interferes more and more in the so-called Christian parties, too, and seizes those people who have placed themselves under their banner without living and fulfilling what I taught as Jesus.

The one who repents, confesses and asks for forgiveness and tears down what he has built up by taking My name, Christ, in vain will also gain the grace and the help of the Eternal.

But the one who persists in building the structure of his human ego with My name, Christ, will be torn down – with everything he has built up and holds on to.

For behold: I, the Christ, make all things new. Rejoice and be of good cheer. The adversary ties himself up more and more. He has forged his own chains in the law of sowing and reaping, and all those who are and remain servile to him chain themselves up with him.

The one who quotes My name but does not fulfill My teachings, which are the law of life, is against Me; he is for the adversary and also binds himself to the chains of the adversary.

The one who quotes My name, Christ, thereby commits himself before the law of life to actualize and fulfill what I taught as Jesus and what I teach as the Christ of God. The one who does not do this is against Me and is an enemy of the truth.

While, through its effects, the darkness is shackling itself more and more to its chains, the light of God in Me, the Christ, radiates ever more strongly into this world. A new world, the world of the Christ, comes into being on the purified Earth.

Already now, before the Earth has been purified and the Kingdom of God, the Kingdom of Peace of Jesus Christ, has spanned the Earth, My kingdom is very gradually emerging in the declining, old sinful world – and yet it is not with this world.

It is written, "The word of righteousness and love will go forth from the center, from the holy city on Mount Zion, and the mount which is in the land of Egypt will be known as an altar of witness to the Lord."

I, Christ, say to you: The Israelites received a long time of grace from the Eternal, in order to reflect upon the law of love and justice and upon Me, their Redeemer. But since up to this mighty turn of time, the Israelites have not reflected on it and still hold on to their world of conceptions and their traditions and still wage battles with their neighbors instead of letting love and justice prevail, and still wait for the Messiah, who once lived among them as Jesus – the Eternal has taken salvation from Israel and has given it to another people. As a result, salvation will come from the New Jerusalem and from the emerging New Israel. And the mountain of the Lord will be where people live according to the message of salvation. And they will bear witness that the Kingdom of God can be lived on Earth, on matter, and that the laws of life can be fulfilled in all their details.

In the gradually expanding New Jerusalem – which includes all establishments for the life in God – people live and work according to the laws of the Sermon on the Mount. They fulfill the laws of selfless love more and more, thus letting the light of God in Me, the Christ, radiate into the world.

In this way, everything not founded in Me, the Christ, will become increasingly visible. And those who have taken My holy name in vain, who have not repented and have not cleared up what was clearly shown them by the light, will expose themselves and will bind themselves more and more to the chains of the darkness. The light shows them their base, egocentric life, which they embellished with My name in order to lead people astray, to bind them to themselves and to fill their churches – and it shows them that, in previous lives, they forcibly Christianized people in crusades or tortured them or had them killed in My name and with the cross of redemption. All this will become manifest before this sinful world perishes.

5. *And now I go to My Father and yours, to My God and yours. But you, remain in Jerusalem and abide in prayer, and after seven days you will receive power from on high, and the promise of the Holy Spirit will be fulfilled to you, and you will go forth from Jerusalem to all the tribes of Israel, and to the farthest parts of the Earth." (Chap. 95:5)*

I, Christ, explain, correct
and deepen the word:

These words "... and after seven days you will receive power from on high, and the promise of the Holy Spirit will be fulfilled to you, and you will go forth from

Jerusalem to all the tribes of Israel, and to the farthest parts of the earth" have the following meaning:

I, Christ, go to My Father and yours, to My God and yours; for I, the Christ, abided in God – without the blemish of sin.

I, Christ, Am in the Father, who is the love and the truth, the law of life. The law, God, consists of the seven basic powers of God. They are the all-stream, the law and the Spirit of life which permeates everything. I go through all seven basic powers of life to the Father of life and I send you the power, the Spirit, the life – the seven basic powers of the heavens. After the ascension, I act again in the seven basic powers in God, in the Spirit of life and in all forms of life, since all powers are contained in all powers, including the four powers of the natures of God, the creating and the creative powers in which I Am omnipresent.

The Holy Spirit, which I send to you, is the Father in Me, the Christ. He will let what I have said to you be fulfilled on you and in and through you – and in all those who faithfully follow Me. I will establish the Kingdom of God on Earth through you and through people in other generations who become My followers.

Through the word of the heart, I spoke this and more to those who were present in the earthly garment and in the spirit garment. For many who were present in the spirit garment had prepared themselves for incarnation in order to continue what I had taught as Jesus of Nazareth, as far as it is possible for them in the generation into which they incarnate.

This has been fulfilled:

The truth, which I Am, is being taught in all parts of the world. The one who accepts it and lives accordingly is the servant of all and the least among My own. For great in Spirit is that person who serves selflessly and is the servant of all, without honors, title or acknowledgment.

The one who is great in the Spirit, God, lives in God; and the one who lives in God lives in the truth, which is the law, God. The one who lives in the truth also lives in the fulfillment: He perceives what others do not see, and hears what others do not hear. He acts and gives from the law of life what others are not yet able to comprehend. He is rich in inner values because he lives in the kingdom of the inner being.

6. *And when He had said this, He lifted His pure and holy hands and blessed them. And it came to pass that, while He blessed them, He was parted from them, and a cloud which shone like the sun took Him away from before their eyes. And as He ascended, some held Him by the feet and others prayed, falling to the earth on their faces. (Chap. 95:6)*

I, Christ, explain, correct
and deepen the word:

The "cloud" of which is written that it shone like the sun was the radiation of the seven basic powers of God,

1016

of the eternal law which enveloped Me and which can be grasped only by the one who lives in the law, in God.

The statement "... some held Him by the feet" shows that man wants to hold on to and have visibly and tangibly with himself what he has not yet unfolded in himself. Yet the one who consciously bears Me, the Christ of God, within himself as the law of life and truth does not need to have Me close to him as a human being. He is one with Me in his heart. Therefore, pray and live the law and become the law of life which I Am in the Father. Then you are consciously one with Me, the Christ of God.

7. *While they gazed after Him towards heaven, behold, two stood by them in white apparel, saying, "You men of Israel, why do you stand gazing into heaven? This Jesus who was taken from you in a cloud will in like manner come again out of a cloud. And as you saw Him go to heaven, so will He come again to Earth."* (Chap. 95:7)

I, Christ, explain, correct
and deepen the word:

I, Christ, will come again on the seven rays, the seven basic powers of God, and will rule the Kingdom of God on Earth, which I have established with My own as the Christ of God, as their divine brother. This is what I promised to My Own. My word holds true.

I will come again in all glory to those who live in Me. They will be all the people who live on Earth after it has been purified and filled with light. I, Christ, will not come in the earthly garment to My own, but in the spirit garment. And yet, they will behold Me, because they have opened up the inner heavens through the fulfillment of the eternal law.

8. *Then they returned to Jerusalem from the Mount of Olives, which is a Sabbath day's journey away from the city. And as they returned, they missed Mary Magdalene, and they looked for her and did not find her. And some of the disciples said, "The Master has taken her with Him," and they marveled and were in great awe. (Chap. 95:8)*

I, Christ, explain, correct
and deepen the word:

Mary Magdalene went to that place to pray where I had been with some faithful men and women disciples and her, and had spoken about the law of love which the eternal Father in us is. She felt My inner nearness and wanted to be where she perceived the holiest sensations, the selfless love which unified us and eternally unifies us.

Selfless love is a brotherly-sisterly bond that cannot be severed and which joins all those who are with each other and for each other in purity. For the one who lives in his neighbor feels what his neighbor needs, and serves him selflessly.

Mary Magdalene felt a yen for distant travels. Yet when I dipped My rays of resurrection in her, the longing to be far away became a feeling of nearness, it became joy and the word of the heart, which I Am.

9. And it was midsummer when Jesus ascended into heaven, and He had not yet reached His fiftieth year; for it was necessary that seven times seven years be fulfilled in His life.

10. Yes, so that He would become perfect through the suffering of all experiences and become an example to all, to children and parents, to the married and the unmarried, to the young and the old, yes, in all times and in all conditions of earthly life. (Chap. 95:9-10)

I, Christ, explain, correct
and deepen the word:

The seven times seven years symbolize the seven basic rays. In each basic ray the other six rays are contained as power. They form the sub-regions in the basic rays. This is why there are seven times seven powers, rays, which emanate from the seven basic rays – also called the basic or primordial radiation.

As Jesus of Nazareth, I experienced and fulfilled what is significant for the redemption of all people: I experienced and suffered what it means to be a human being, and I suffered for the sake of man. Thus, I took, as memory, into the seven times seven rays what I had experienced and suffered, the "for" and "against" of mankind.

In the Redeemer-spark, I feel the joy and grief of every soul and of every person – be it the growing children or their parents, the married or the unmarried, the young or the old. I did not live through the number of earthly years of man; yet I felt his grief and how it continues if man keeps on sinning.

I have seen, perceived and sensed the people. I have experienced and come to know them. I have come to know the female principle and the male principle and have seen marriage as pressure and binding and, as a human being, I experienced matrimony – that is, a spiritual union. I have absorbed everything into the Redeemer-spark, so that I can provide each soul and person with the help, the salvation and the words, which for him can be comfort and direction on the path to the inner life, to the Kingdom of God of the inner being, if he accepts and fulfills the life in Me, the Christ.

CHAPTER 96

The Outpouring of the Holy Spirit

About the tasks and status of the disciples (1-3).
The one who is great in spirit serves and gives in humility
and gratitude (4-5). The beginning of the church hierarchy
through superiors and dignitaries – The selfless servants of
all give from their hearts (6-7). What happened during the
inflow of the Holy Spirit? (8-9). The true brotherhood of
Christ in the service of the common good (10). One for all,
Christ (11). Human aspects in the original communities –
The splintering of the early communities due to dissension
and an attitude of obedience to authorities (12-13). Cere-
monies and other works of man are not a part of the teach-
ing of the Nazarene (14-15). Harmony of mind brings about
freedom and unity (16). The explanation of the creed (17-23).
The one who follows Me becomes the temple of love (24-25).
I Am the truth (26). Through the work "This Is My Word,"
the life will flow out into the world.

1. And after the disciples had come down from the mountain, they gathered in the upper room and were all united in common prayer and supplication; and their number was about one hundred and twenty.

2. And on that day James stood up and said, "Men and brothers, you know how the Lord, before He left us, chose Peter to preside over us and watch over us in His name, and said that it is necessary that one among

those who were with us and witnessed His resurrection be chosen and appointed to take his place."

3. And they chose two, Barsabas and Matthias, and they prayed, saying, "O God, You who know the hearts of all men, show us which of the two you have chosen to take part in the apostleship from which You have raised Your servant Peter to preside over us." (Chap. 96:1-3)

I, Christ, explain, correct
and deepen the word:

I have raised no person to watch over My own. Look deeper into the words "...chose Peter to preside over us and watch over us in His name," and grasp their meaning.

To all who followed Me – including Peter, who asked Me who should preside – I spoke, among other things, in the following sense: The one who is the greatest among you shall be the least; and the one who can be given the most in light and power, through his life in the love of God, shall be a guide for many towards the love of God.

I have chosen all of you to be bearers of the light in order to fulfill – with those who will come after you and with whom you will possibly be together again – what I, the Christ of God, wanted to bring into the world as Jesus. Preside over the members of the growing communities only as it is suitable for a guide and never let yourselves be exalted and honored as the greatest.

For the one who lets himself be exalted and honored does not live in My Spirit; he will be humbled. And the inner schools which lead to the inner mystery of life and which I can no longer establish – but which will emerge – shall be built and inspired in My Spirit by those who live in Me, the Christ.

Thus, to all the men and women who are My disciples, the task is given now and in the future to fulfill what I, as Jesus of Nazareth, taught and fulfilled. For, in the course of time, you and many with you will return several times to prepare and establish what I, as Jesus, was not able to do – because of the unbelief and stubbornness and sin of the Jewish people and of those who should have stood by Me.

Yet when I, the Spirit of truth in God, your Father and Mine, return, everything that I have said to you and have prepared in the spirit will take place on Earth. For then I will be with My own in the spirit and will establish and build with them all that was not possible for Me as Jesus of Nazareth.

4. *And they cast their lots, and the lot fell upon Matthias, and the twelve received him, and he was counted among the apostles.*

5. *Then John and James separated Peter from their number by the laying on of hands, that he might preside over them in the name of the Lord, saying, "Brother, be like a hewn stone with six sides; you, Petros, are Petra, bearing witness to the truth on every side." (Chap. 96:4-5)*

I, Christ, explain, correct
and deepen the word:

Just as the disciples used the voting process, it also happened in the early communities that formed after My going home to the Father. And it also happens again in a similar way in the Covenant Community New Jerusalem and in all the original communities of My Work of Redemption, in Universal Life [1989].

The members of the communities did not and do not lay hands on the head of those whom they have elected into their community. They pray and commend the new members of the original communities to the Eternal and to Me, the Christ.

The one who lets himself be elected by the members of the original community commits himself to become the "hewn stone": a cut and polished stone, which radiates the truth of God into the world in many facets and brings the truth to all those who thirst for it. The one who has become the hewn stone has found in himself the "stone of the wise" and radiates into this world in humility and gratitude, without putting himself above others.

For the one who is great in the Spirit of the Eternal is the least among My own. Without putting himself above others, he gives what he has unfolded in himself: the truth from the source of truth – God. He will not be a superior, but will serve solely as evidence of the inner life to the developing members of the community. And he will teach them and give them what they still need for their inner maturity, so that the stone of the wise, the eternal consciousness, may fully unfold within them, too, and that they, too, may radiate what heaven is: the law of love.

6. *And the apostles were given staves to guide their steps on the way of truth, and crowns of glory as well; and to the prophets, burning lamps to spread light on the way, and incense holders with fire; and to the evangelists, the book and the holy law to remind the people of the first principles; and to the pastors were given the cup and the plate to feed and nourish the flock.*

7. *But nothing was given to anyone that was not given to all; for all were one priesthood under Christ as their master and high priest in the temple of God. And to the deacons were given baskets, that they might put therein the things necessary for the holy offering. And their number was one hundred and twenty, and Peter presided over them. (Chap. 96:6-7)*

I, Christ, explain, correct
and deepen the word:

What is stated here does not correspond to My teaching as Jesus of Nazareth.

After My ascension, so-called head officials developed in the course of time, who asserted their official power; for the many people who came to the apostles and disciples and, in the course of time, formed the communities were in need of leadership. Some of the disciples remembered from their youth the customs which were considered lawful in the religious institutions of that time, but which came from paganism. In the course of time, they introduced these heathen aspects into the emerging Christian communities.

Thus, a so-called Christianity with outer rituals and ceremonies, developed more and more, a hierarchy of so-called officeholders, that is, superiors and dignitaries. I did not teach this as Jesus of Nazareth nor as the Christ of God.

Recognize that the greatest among My own is the one who has opened up the "stone of the wise" – the hallowed consciousness in the depths of the soul. He is the selfless servant of all. He is not a shepherd, but only a guide to the inner life, which he himself has opened up through the actualization of the eternal laws. As Jesus of Nazareth, I spoke neither of crowns nor of titles nor of dignitaries. These are terms for individuals who wanted to stand out from the people.

What I spoke as Jesus is the law. This is also what I speak as Christ. I did not appoint evangelists, deacons or priests. I wanted and want *one* flock, whose Shepherd I, Christ, Am.

I spoke to Peter and with this was meant all those who faithfully follow Me. They should have been and should be guides to the inner life, but should not put themselves above others in order to influence the people in a determining way.

That which is written here from the so-called "Gospel of Jesus" was added only later on. It was brought into the emerging communities by some disciples who wanted to put themselves above others.

I also did not call into being a so-called priesthood, but a large number of selfless servants, who are the servants of all. The righteous prophets carry no lamps; they themselves are lamps, lights of the truth which they carry into the world, for the salvation of all who long for the truth, for the inner life.

I taught them to bring the gospel of the heart – it is what the individual has actualized – but never the letter.

Those who truly wanted to follow Me were equipped for their journey – what they needed as human beings. For they went far away to teach what I had taught and had lived as an example to them. They had no books. The true followers carried in their hearts what I had taught. This is what they passed on selflessly. For only what flows out of the heart gains access again to the heart – not what comes from intellectual thinking and from book knowledge.

The truth which is recorded in the word can show the way to those who long for the truth. The letter alone is not the truth, but only the reflection of the truth.

8. *And when the seventh day had come, they were all of one mind in the same house and, as they were pray-*

ing, there came a sound from heaven like the roar of a mighty wind, and the room in which they were gathered was shaken, and it filled the whole house.

9. And there appeared cloven tongues like flames of fire and hovered over the head of each of them. And they were all filled with the Holy Spirit and began to speak in tongues as the Spirit caused them to utter. Then Peter stood up and preached the law of Christ to the multitude of all nations and tongues who were gathered there. As reported by those who had seen and heard this, each man heard the word in his own tongue with which he was born. (Chap. 96:8-9)

I, Christ, explain, correct
and deepen the word:

When many were united in prayer, the holy power, the Holy Spirit, increased in the souls which were lifted towards God. Many believed to be hearing a "sound from heaven like the roar of a mighty wind" which filled the whole room, the whole house.

Recognize that the eternal Spirit, the Holy Spirit, has no human sound which reaches the human ear. The inflow of the Holy Spirit into many righteous men and women caused a surge of blood in them, for the hearts of the fulfilled ones beat loudly. Then they heard the voice of truth within their hearts – each one in his mother tongue. In this state of being touched in their inner being and in their outer emotion, they believed to see tongues of fire. Those who truly saw them perceived the inflow of the Holy Spirit into their souls and hearts. And those who heard the word of God through the mouth of man felt it in their hearts as if it had been spoken in their language. Yet what they understood was what they could understand according to the maturity of their spiritual consciousness. Because they could understand the word of God in their innermost being through the mouth of man, they believed it was their language.

Recognize that with many statements some things were added, some left out, always according to the understanding of the writer and the translator. And in the translations, those words were used which were familiar to the translators and corresponded to their understanding of the truth.

10. And of those who listened, three thousand souls were gathered in the community on that day; and they received the holy law, repented of their sins and were baptized and continued their life in the brotherhood of the apostles, in constant offering and prayer.
(Chap. 96:10)

I, Christ, explain, correct
and deepen the word:

Recognize that not all who were gathered on the aforesaid day honestly repented of their sins, forgave and asked for forgiveness and sinned no more. Many only thought to have done so. They fell back into their old sins and became again who they were before the divine event.

None of them was baptized; however, all were blessed by the Spirit of truth. And all those who remained faithful to the truth, by living according to their prayers day by day and actualizing the laws of life more and more, gradually became the law of life. This is how they attained spiritual baptism; for they immersed into the eternal law, God, thus becoming the law of love.

All those who strove for the life in Me and conscientiously perfected themselves entered the brotherhood of Christ, the life in the Spirit of God. It is the fulfillment of the eternal law for your own inner development, as well as through the commandment "pray and work." "Pray and work" did and does not apply just to one's personal interests, it also includes true, selfless service for one's neighbor.

As it was at that time, so it continued in the course of the centuries. Time and again, people stepped into My following – into the true brotherhood of Christ, which does not isolate itself in monasteries but grows in the midst of the world – among those people who strive to live in Me, the Christ, for all people of good will. The true brotherhood in and with Me, the Christ, is the fulfillment of the eternal laws in the midst of the world.

11. And those who believed gave up all their posses-
sions, had everything in common and lived together in
the same place and showed the love and kindness of
God to their brothers and sisters and to all creatures.
They worked with their hands for the common good.
(Chap. 96:11)

I, Christ, explain, correct
and deepen the word:

All those who fulfilled the law of God – equality,
freedom, unity, brotherliness and justice – put their belongings together and administered everything together,
thus fulfilling the law of life: One for all – Christ; all
for One – Christ. And all with Christ – for all people of
good will. They lived – like the beings of light – with
one another in selfless love, as brothers and sisters, and
served the common good.

This brotherhood in My Spirit which, after My ascension, developed among those who truly followed Me
also took place in all the following epochs. Again and
again, people came together in My name to live in Me
and with Me in the true brotherhood – in service of the
common good for their neighbor. For only this is the
true and absolute following of Christ.

What once was, is now again [1989]:
More and more people strive to follow Me, in order
to live in Me and to come into the brotherhood with Me
and, as a unit, to promote the common good, thus bring-

ing heaven to Earth, the Kingdom of Peace of Jesus Christ.

The basis for the brotherhood in Me is selfless love in working together for the common good; for as it is in heaven, likewise will it be on Earth – on matter, within the three dimensions.

The one who lives in Me, the Christ, lives in peace with his neighbor and with the nature kingdoms, with animals, plants and stones.

12. And from these, twelve were called to be prophets with the twelve evangelists and twelve pastors and their helpers were added to them and deacons of the universal community, and they numbered one hundred and twenty. And thus was the temple of David set up, with living men filled with goodness, just as the Master had shown them.

13. And James, the brother of the Lord, was given to the community in Jerusalem as its head and angel, and additionally twenty-four priests in a fourfold ministry, and also deacons and their helpers. And after six days, many came together and were joined by six thousand men and women who received the holy law of love, and they received the word with gladness. (Chap. 96:12-13)

I, Christ, explain, correct
and deepen the word:

As Jesus of Nazareth, I spoke indeed about the universal communities – which are the universal life, the life out of the Spirit of God – but not about evangelists, pastors, deacons or other officeholders. Human conceptions are twined around what I brought into this world as teaching and power.

What I, as Jesus, wanted to establish with those who were and are in the mission – mainly with people from the lineage of David and, beyond that, with those from other lineages, too – should have been established after My resurrection in all simplicity and modesty by My own with Me – with Me who was with them in spirit after the resurrection.

Many of those who let themselves be blessed, but did not fulfill what I commanded of everyone, brought *their* conceptions into the simple inner structure which should have become visible, also externally, in the world. They adulterated My teaching with their tradition-bound thinking, which was still caught up in the hierarchy of superiors and subordinates. They appointed officials and articulate people and assigned the emerging communities to them. They left the leadership up to them and listened less and less to the word of God and to the angel of the respective community. The subordinate mindset toward authority took the upper hand, which resulted in disunity and quarrels.

Through this subordinate mindset, human behavioral patterns began to flourish, for each one wanted to be the greatest. The result was discord and division among the members of the first early communities, which then resulted in schisms. It was My concern that My own would establish the inner temple and carry out what the lineage of David and some people from other lineages were and are called to do: Found and build the Kingdom of God, the Kingdom of Peace of Jesus Christ.

And so disagreements arose. However, all who became true followers and remained faithful to My teaching received the word of justice, the law of life. Those who were able to grasp it received it with inner joy and gratitude.

A certain order is required until people fulfill the eternal law of God. Therefore, elders, teachers, leaders and healers should still be active in the original communities until all the members of the original communities are in the law of inner life for the most part. However, no one should distinguish himself as someone special. The greatest among them should be the least. The elders, teachers, leaders and healers should be people who are deeply immersed in My following. They should be only guides, not authorities.

As it should have been then, so shall it be again now [1989] in the original communities of Universal Life, in those original communities in the center of which is the Covenant Community New Jerusalem in the emerging New Israel.

14. And as they gathered together on the Lord's day after the Sabbath was past and were making the holy offering, they missed Mary and Joseph, the parents of Jesus. And they looked for them, but did not find them.

15. And some among them said, "Surely, the Lord has taken them away, as He did with Magdalene." And they were filled with awe and sang praises to God. (Chap. 96:14-15)

I, Christ, explain, correct
and deepen the word:

My foster-father was at that time a being in God and no longer a human being. He was among the many invisible ones who were preparing for the fulfillment of the mission. Some remained in the spirit, they served Me in the spirit and invisibly served those who were in the earthly garment. Others prepared for incarnation, in order to serve Me, the Christ, as human beings.

I had entrusted Mary to John. In a quiet place, she was united in prayer with Me and with all those who surrounded her in the spirit.

Soon after My resurrection and ascension, also after the inflowing of the Holy Spirit, there was much insecurity among the apostles and disciples and among those who had joined them; this led to dissension.

Every dissension has its voices. Some understood the meaning of My teachings and My parables as they were able to grasp them according to their spiritual consciousness; the others held on to their concepts and believed that the truth should be as they had grasped My teachings and My parables with their mind.

From My ascension on, this dissension remained until the first early communities broke up. This led to the emergence of authorities. They decided on what should be right and made of My teaching – the content of which is the law of life and the freedom of will – a binding religious doctrine. Thus, the words, which at first were symbols that made the inner life understandable, were fitted into a human world of thought. Under the guise of My name, Christ, they elected authorities such as pastors, priests and still others. In the course of time, they built up a denominational hierarchy in My name, with splendid houses of God and cathedrals and palaces in which they resided. Thus, Christianity grew rigid and became an institution with dogmas, doctrines, cults, worldly rule, church fees and taxes and much more.

Since their hearts were impoverished, they included in their denominational system of doctrines more and more pagan cults so that they could offer the people external celebrations, which they embellished with much ceremonial, in order to stimulate their faithful. They called them Christian celebrations, which should be held in honor of God. In reality they were – and still partly are today [1989] – snares with which they bound and bind their faithful to themselves. The ecclesiastic laws, the dogmas, doctrines, structures and customs became, for many, prisons from which it is difficult to escape.

They did not and do not keep the commandment of freedom; they decided and decide, for example, that people should first be baptized while they are children, before they are instructed and can receive the blessing of the church.

But the commandment of freedom says: Teach first. This means to teach your children the laws of life – and if they keep them and fulfill them in their daily life, they will be baptized by Me, the Spirit of Christ, with the Spirit of truth, for they will have immersed in the truth, in the law of life. However, the one who himself can no longer distinguish between truth and customs and looks at the veils of traditions, sees only the church commandments and doctrines, ceremonies and cults and believes that all this work of man is part of the teaching of the Nazarene, because everything was and is [1989] still embellished with My name.

In Me, the Christ, there is *one* flock, and I Am the *one* Shepherd.

In Me, the Christ, there are no authorities and no thinking in terms of rank – and therefore no servility, either. In Me, the Christ, there are only brothers and sisters who live in the eternal Father and in Me, and who are of one spirit.

Even though in the universal, original communities [1989] there are still elders, teachers, leaders and healers, these are merely designations for the respective tasks of the members of the original communities. These members distinguish themselves in the communities by their true following of Me. The elders, teachers, leaders and healers are brothers and sisters in *one* spirit with all the members of the community.

Terms such as elders, teachers, leaders and healers must not be seen as titles of authorities. The one who considers those who fulfill these tasks to be authorities is guilty before the law of freedom – just as those became guilty who, after My ascension, broke up the emerging early communities by appointing authorities.

In the eternal Being, there are the seven cherubs and seraphs, the princes of the heavens and the elders. Yet they are equal with all spirit beings: They all are children of the Father – without exception. Names like cherubs, seraphs and elders are names that indicate the corresponding tasks determined by creation.

16. *And the Spirit of the Lord came upon the apostles and the prophets among them, and when they remembered what the Lord had taught them, they confessed and praised God all with one voice, saying:*
(Chap. 96:16)

I, Christ, explain, correct
and deepen the word:

"... with one voice" means: They were of one mind. Harmony of mind gradually brings about freedom and unity in Me, the Christ.

17. *"We believe in One God: the Infinite, the secret source, the eternal Father, from whom all things come – the invisible and the visible – the All-in-all through all and around all. The holy One in whom all things exist – what was, what is and what will be.*

18. *We believe in one Lord, our Lady, the perfect holy Christ: God of God, light of light begotten. Our Lord, the Father, Bridegroom and Son. Our Lady, the Mother, the Bride and the Daughter. Three manifestations in one indivisible essence. A twofold trinity. That God may become manifest as the Father, Bridegroom and Son of every soul, and that every soul may become perfect as the Mother, the Bride and the Daughter of God.*

19. *And this by the ascent of the soul into the Spirit and the descent of the Spirit into the soul. The Spirit comes from heaven and is incarnate, from the eternally blessed virgin in Jesus and every Christ of God *, and was born and taught the path of life and suffered under the worldly rulers and was crucified and buried and descended into hell. And He rises again and ascends into glory, from where He gives light and life to all.*

20. *We believe in the sevenfold Spirit of God, the giver of life, which came forth from the holy twain, which came upon Jesus and upon all who are faithful to*

---

* *According to the meaning, this should read: in Jesus, the Christ of God.*

the inner light; which dwells in the community, in the Israel elected by God; which comes again and again into the world and enlightens every soul which seeks; which gives the law, which judges the living and the dead; which speaks through the prophets of all times and all countries.

21. We believe in the one holy, all-encompassing and apostolic community: the witness to all truth, the receiver and giver of the same. Created of the Spirit and the fire of God; nourished by the waters, seeds and fruits of the Earth. Which – through the Spirit of life, its twelve books and sacraments, its holy words and works – links together the chosen ones in one mystical union and unites mankind with God, making us partakers of the divine life and substance, attesting this in holy symbols.

22. And we await the return of the all-encompassing Christ and of the Kingdom of God, wherein righteousness dwells. And the holy city which has twelve gates: Therein are the temple and the altar of God. From where proceed three orders in fourfold ministry, to teach all truth and to make the daily offering of praise.

23. As in the inner so in the outer. As in the great so in the small. As above so below, as in heaven so on Earth. We believe in the purification of the soul through many births and experiences, the resurrection from the dead, in the eternal life of the just, from eternity to eternity, and rest in God forever. – Amen."
(Chap. 96:17-23)

I, Christ, explain, correct
and deepen this confession of faith
according to the laws of life:

(Verse 17) "...the secret source" means: the hallowed source. For in God there are no secrets.

(Verse 18) The words "our Lady" mean the mother-principle in the Father-Mother-God.

"God of God, light of light begotten" means: the Christ is the Son of God who came forth from the Father-Mother-God, the beheld One, who, in some aspects of inner life, is created and in other aspects of inner life is spiritually begotten, the Son from the holy, eternal Father and the Mother.

In the Father-Mother-Principle is also the daughter, the female principle, which has more aspects of the Mother.

The bridegroom and the bride symbolize the union – also called matrimony – of the two powers, positive and negative, male and female, Father and Mother.

"Three manifestations" means: Three powers: the positive power, the positive pole, the giving principle, the Father-power – the negative power, the negative pole, the receiving principle, the Mother-power. Both powers together, the Father-Mother-Principle, are also called the primordial power or the Holy Spirit, in which the part-power, the omnipresent power of the Co-Regent, the Christ of God, is active. Since all powers are contained in everything, the three powers – the Father-

Mother-powers and the part-power in the primordial power, the Christ-of-God-power – are contained undivided in each being.

Since all powers are contained in all beings from God, the Father-principle personifies the Son, and the Son, the Father. The Mother-principle personifies the daughter, and the daughter, the Mother.

The bridegroom and the bride symbolize the inner union, the matrimony.

(Verse 19) "And this by the ascent of the soul into the Spirit and the descent of the Spirit into the soul" means that the one who takes the first step towards the Spirit of life will also be met by the Spirit. The soul on the path to perfection rises to the Spirit of life, to the Father-Mother-God; and the Spirit, the Father-Mother-God, comes toward it.

The Spirit, God, the Father-Mother-Principle, flows into the soul to the same degree as it accepts again its heritage, the powers of infinity; whereby it attains again the perfection in God, the Father-Mother-Principle.

"The Spirit comes from heaven and is incarnate from the eternally blessed virgin" means that the Spirit of the Christ of God came into this world in the Son of God. He was and is the Co-Regent of the heavens, the Son who in Jesus became the Christ, the Redeemer.

The laws of nature are noble laws, if man keeps them pure. By way of the pure begetting, I, the Son of God, was born into the young woman who became the mother of Jesus. "Virgin" means: young woman.

As Jesus of Nazareth, I taught the holy laws of God and lived them as an example to the people. With My teachings and with My life, I showed them the way into the eternal life. I suffered under the worldly rulers and was crucified, because My own, to whom I came, did not accept or receive Me.

The body of Jesus was laid in the grave and was then made divine through the transformation of matter into divine substance.

As the Christ of God, the Redeemer, I descended into hell by irradiating all the realms of the Fall, making them planes of purification.

The resurrected One, who ascended to God, the eternal Father, and lives again in God as Co-Regent of the heavens, will return in all glory when the Kingdom of God on Earth has been established.

My Spirit, the redeeming power, is in all souls and human beings. The one who turns to Me, the Christ of God, the Redeemer, by fulfilling the laws receives more and more light and power and will enter into the life, which I Am.

(Verse 20) "... sevenfold Spirit of God" means that it is the seven basic powers of God which give life to all Being. These seven basic powers of God are the omnipresent law, God, the life in all that is.

The "holy twain" means the two primordial powers; the giving and the receiving power – the male, the Father; and the female, the Mother.

The two primordial powers form the core of the Primordial Central Sun, which is the life-power-station of creation, from where the life – the seven basic powers – streams into the seven prism suns. In the seven prism suns the primordial light – the seven basic powers, the primordial power – is split and radiates into the All in seven times seven powers. The seven times seven powers are also called the consciousness radiation. For they radiate throughout all the consciousness aspects of infinity, including matter.

It is the Spirit, God, in Me, the Christ, who dwells and is active in the true Christian communities and in the members of the communities who fulfill the will of the Eternal in Me, the Christ.

The Spirit, God, in Me, the Christ, has chosen and founded the New Jerusalem in the New Israel. From there, the life radiates over the whole Earth, and from the light-filled people and the purified Earth into the planes of purification to all souls.

The Spirit, God, the truth, radiates into this world in Me, the Christ. The one who seeks, by striving for the commandments of inner life, will find his way to the law, God, and become the eternal law which I Am, Christ, in God, My Father and yours.

"... who gives the law which judges the living and the dead" means that the one who lives the law, God, enters the law, God, the eternal truth.

The law of inner life does not stop, neither before human beings nor before the deceased, the so-called "dead," the souls in the realms beyond the veils of consciousness which are between this life and the life beyond.

The one who violates the law, God, judges himself to the same extent that he has violated the law of life, the eternal truth.

Verily, at all times – in the past and in the present – the Spirit, God, spoke and speaks through true prophets.

My word, the word of the Spirit, is without limit. It streams through all times and into all countries. And the person who has awakened in the Spirit of life knows My voice. Yes, My sheep know My voice, no matter in which country they live as human beings.

(Verse 21) "We believe in one holy all-encompassing and apostolic community" means:

The foundation pillars of inner life on which My true apostles and disciples founded the early communities shall be built upon. The spirit of the community is the only holy One. When the members of the community fulfill the law of life by living in the truth, then they are the blessed ones. These blessed ones, the brothers and sisters who live in My Spirit, form the true community.

They are the witnesses of the truth, and the community which is formed by them is the maintainer and giver of the truth. Everything else is human conceptions and also intrigues, which have nothing in common with Me, the Christ.

The one who lives in Me, the Christ, lives in God and accomplishes the works of God – in this world, as well.

In the true communities in Me, the Christ, there are no superiors and subordinates. The true communities in Me, the Christ, consist of brothers and sisters who strive to fulfill the will of God and who already fulfill it. These communities in Me, the Christ, are created by the Spirit of life and imbued with the fire of God.

The one who is aglow with the fire of God fulfills the laws of God. He is for all people and also for the nature kingdoms. And so, he lives with all people in his heart. He treasures and respects the life in nature and is sustained and nourished by God by means of the earth, the waters, the seeds and the fruits.

The following statement, "Which through the Spirit of life, its twelve books and sacraments, its holy words and works links together the chosen ones in one mystical union and unites mankind with God, making us partakers of the divine life and substance, attesting this in the holy symbols" was brought into the early communities by *people*. It does not correspond to the eternal law.

The one who truly lives according to the law of God is a pure temple of God. He does not need books, sacraments or symbols. He has become the holy word, the law, God.

Nothing remains a mystery to the one who has become the law of God. The life in God is the law, God, and the one who lives in the eternal law also knows all the laws of God – for he is irradiated by the primordial light, by the seven basic powers of life, which reveal everything to him. He draws and gives from this.

These are the people who come together truly in My name and are true partakers of the divine life. They are beings in the earthly garment who have founded and maintain the Inner Religion and who know no superiors and subordinates, no ceremonies, rites, cults and dogmas. The Inner Spirit-Christ Church, the Inner Religion, in which all people are brothers and sisters, and which unites, accepts and receives all people in God. The true followers, who are in Me in their inner being, came and come from it. They founded and found the original communities of inner life in which only I, Christ, Am the Shepherd, because in the Father I Am their life.

Mystical life means inner union in the temple of the inner being with all those who strive toward God. This was My wish as Jesus of Nazareth; this is also My wish as the Christ of God. With people who strive to fulfill the will of God and who already live in the fulfillment, I will bring to My own an understanding of the inner life, in the developing Kingdom of God on Earth, in the emerging Kingdom of Peace of Jesus Christ. When the Kingdom of God, the Kingdom of Peace of Jesus Christ, has spanned the Earth, then people who need neither religious books for their life nor ceremonies, cults, rites, sacraments and the like, will live in the Kingdom of God on Earth. They are united in God, because they live in Me, the Christ. They fulfill the eternal law and thus know about all things of life.

For them, the book "This Is My Word" will be a historic work of reference which serves them for understanding the past events, from which they recognize the "for" and "against" of mankind, which continues in and among the souls – in the realm of the souls.

(Verse 22) The return of the Christ of God, who I Am, is imminent. In the present time [1989] and in future epochs, I gradually establish the Kingdom of God on Earth, in which peace, unity and justice prevail.

"And the holy city which has twelve gates" is the New Jerusalem on Earth. It forms the inner altar for all universal original communities all over the Earth. For it is from there that the light of the Eternal in Me, the Christ, radiates the laws of inner life to all communities. The inhabitants of the Kingdom of God on Earth will recognize, acknowledge and keep these laws, and there will be order. The task of every single member of the community is selfless service, through which all members of the communities praise and glorify God.

Those who are given the ability to teach will teach the laws of God to the children who come forth from the mystical unions – from the matrimony of two people, man and woman in God – and will guide them in such a way that they keep these laws in the brotherhood with Me, which unites all people in the Kingdom of God on Earth.

(Verse 23) "As in the inner so in the outer. As in the great so in the small. As above so below, as in heaven so on Earth" means:

God is omnipresent. As it is in the innermost, in what is pure, so it is also in the outer existence. As it is above, that is, in heaven, so will it be on Earth, too: pure.

In its earthly structure, the Earth is only the reflection of the heavens, but not heaven itself. However, through the power of love, heaven, too, will come to Earth, the pure, to the pure. For the souls will purify themselves through the power of the Christ, which I Am – even though they may have to go through many earthly births and experiences, until they recognize themselves and repent of their human aspects, the sins, which they have recognized, ask for forgiveness and forgive and make amends for what they have caused and then sin no more. They will awaken from spiritual death and resurrect into eternal life and, as pure beings from God, will again return to God, their Father, from whom they came forth as pure beings. In the eternal Being, they will then live and work with all pure beings in love, wisdom and justice, and the love and glory will have no end. For the eternal light, God, in whom they live, *is* – as they all *are* – from eternity to eternity.

The one who lives in Me needs no confession of faith, for he lives the law – just as the beings of heaven are and live the law.

24. And as the clouds of incense rose, the sound of many bells was heard and also a multitude of the heavenly host praising God and saying:

25. "Glory, honor, praise and laud be to God, the Father, Bridegroom and Son, one with the Mother, Bride and Daughter, from whom the eternal Spirit goes forth, through whom all beings are created. From all eternity, now and in all eternity – Amen – Alleluia, Alleluia, Alleluia." (Chap. 96:24-25)

I, Christ, explain, correct
and deepen the word:

The person in God needs no external forms and rites. The sound of the so-called bells are then the melodies of the heavens which flow through a light-filled soul, a pure heart, because the being from the Father-Mother-God lives again in God, the Father and the Mother. This is the path of each soul in which I, Christ, Am. I Am the way, the truth and the life.

The one who follows Me becomes the temple of love. This temple has no external customs. All people and beings and all of creation are received in it. With the beings from God, the one who lives in this temple, in his innermost being, the Sanctum of God, will glorify, honor, laud and praise the Eternal, by fulfilling the holy law, which is God, the Father-Mother-God. The Eternal beheld and beholds all beings and gave and gives heaven, in which they live eternally.

26. And if anyone takes from or adds to the words of this gospel or hides the light thereof, as under a bushel, the light which is given by the Holy Spirit to us, the twelve witnesses, chosen by God for the enlightenment of the world, for its redemption: Let him be Anathema Maranatha until the apparition of the Christ Jesus, our Redeemer, with all the Saints. Amen. (Chap. 96:26)

I, Christ, explain, correct
and deepen the word:

I Am the Christ of God, the way, the truth and the life.

I Am the truth, and the truth which I Am shines in countless facets into this world.

The so-called "Gospel of Jesus" is one of the many facets of the truth. Not just any person, but I, the Christ of God, took, explained, corrected and deepened it and added further light to it, that is, further facets of the truth, so that the people of the present generation [1989] and of future generations may see the eternal truth – Me, the Christ of God – shining from many facets of the truth.

I Am the truth, and the truth gives to the children of the truth – and thus it is the truth.

I, the Christ, do not curse or wish any person ill. This is what those people do to themselves who abuse Me, the Christ, the truth, for their human ends.

I Am the gospel of truth, and the truth, which I Am, gives to the generations in such a way that they can understand the gospel in the light of the truth, today and in the future.

Here ends the holy gospel of the perfect life of Jesus, the Christ, the son of David, in the flesh, the Son of God, in the Spirit.

Here ends also the gospel of Jesus, as originally recorded by the apostles and later handed over to the true followers of the Master in the early days of the community of Jerusalem.

Glory be to God, through whose power this has been written.

I, Christ, explain, correct
and deepen the word:

"Here ends the holy gospel of the perfect life of Jesus, the Christ, the son of David, in the flesh, the Son of God, in the Spirit" means: Here ends the book "The Gospel of Jesus," which was taken into the work "This Is My Word," the latter being given from the truth.

Only what is external can have an end, but not what is divine. It streams and streams and always has something to say. It is the law of life, which is continuous revelation.

Therefore, let life stream out through the work "This Is My Word" which is, at the same time, a historic work of reference. If you do not seek the letter but grasp the meaning, the heavens will open up for you – the heavens which I let become manifest in My words, given through a human mouth for all those who strive toward heaven by truly following Me.

The blessed sensations of Jesus – the son of David in the flesh, the Son of God in the Spirit – never end. They were pure in Me, Jesus, and, in Me, the Christ, they are one with all who feel as Jesus did.

Through the Covenant Community New Jerusalem and through all universal original communities, this work "This Is My Word" goes into this world to the children of God and to the children of the world. As children of God, all will become one in Me, the Christ. That is the truth. For no sheep will be lost. The children of the world, too, will consciously become children of the light, because they, too, bear the light of the Eternal, the eternal life, within themselves.

I Am the Christ of God, who came into this world as Jesus and accomplished what leads to the unification of all peoples, to the purification of the Earth and to the refinement and assimilation of all coarse-material forms. For God is Spirit, He is fine-material, pure life. Everything will be guided back into the pure Being through the primordial power, God, the Father-Mother-Principle, and through the part-power of the primordial power, through the Son and Co-Regent of the heavens who comes to His own in the Kingdom of Peace of

Jesus Christ as Jehovah, as brother to the brothers and sisters who are in the earthly garment.

I Am Christ in God, your Father and Mine,
the life from eternity to eternity.

Epilogue

This is, this was, and this will be:
the life in the Spirit of God.

My word has been given for yesterday, for today and for tomorrow.
In Me, the Christ, everything is present for I Am everlasting.
In Me everything is concluded and is manifest to My own.
That which is still the future for man is the present in Me.
My word is the word of the present. What will be is in Me and has also already been completed in Me.

Any fight against your neighbor is already your end.
The one who fights against his neighbor has already perished.
Therefore, according to the law of inner life, the world has already perished,
and the I Am is already effective:
the peace.

I Am the peace.

The Laws of God
for the Kingdom of Peace of Jesus Christ

**I Am the Lord, your God, the One and Only
from eternity to eternity.
From the eternal law, I reveal to mankind
the laws of life
for the Kingdom of Peace of Jesus Christ**

The Kingdom of God on Earth is in Me, your Father, and in Christ, the ruler of the Kingdom of Peace.

I Am the Lord, your God, the Eternal, the One, the law of life. Your God, who I Am, is with you.

My Son, the Christ of God, is the ruler of the Kingdom of God on this Earth. As Jesus of Nazareth, He brought the laws of life to the people and lived them as an example. As Christ, the Redeemer of all men and souls, He has revealed them again through the incarnated part-ray of divine wisdom.

The ruler is with His own and His own keep the eternal laws.

The laws of the Kingdom of Peace of Jesus Christ are excerpts from the eternal laws. These excerpts hold true for the three-dimensional world, where My children live in the earthly garment, that is, in the garment of matter. Human beings will exist for as long as the Earth brings forth fruit to nourish man and animal.

Recognize that infinity is absolute order. It consists of countless suns, repository planets and dwelling planets. On every dwelling planet of the heavens there are pure beings; on every dwelling planet in the planes of purification there are souls – and on the material dwelling planet, the Earth, there are human beings.

My Absolute Law is the giving and receiving life. Every planet that is pure primordial substance vibrates in My Absolute Law. The beings of light that inhabit the pure, fine-material planets form, with their dwelling-planets, an absolute unity within the unity of the great whole, within the law of radiation, God. To explain this to you in human words, this means: One for all, all for One.

The process of evolution takes place in the planes of purification and in the planes of preparation, as well as in the material stars and planets, including the dwelling planet Earth. This process flows into the law of unity, into the divine law of radiation.

All material stars, starting with the planet Earth and its inhabitants, will gradually become so spiritualized that the pure parts of the planets, the "souls of the planets," can be released without great difficulties when the time is ripe for this, so that they again integrate into the law of radiation, into the eternal law.

This mighty transformation of matter into finer substances of higher vibration begins on Earth. This means that first, the vibration of the soul and body of the human being refines itself and then – starting with the human being – the transformation of the coarsest structure, the Earth, takes place. As a result of the refinement of man and earth, the matter of all material stars then becomes lucent step by step. The refinement takes place through the purification of man and Earth – through people who turn to Me, the Spirit of truth, and keep what I have commanded them: to recognize their faults and sins, to ask for forgiveness, to forgive their neighbor and, if necessary, to make amends for what led to the sin, and then, no longer commit the same or like sins. Only then, is it possible for Me to act through them, because they fulfill My will: the law of love, of life and of freedom.

The one who fits into this process of evolution contributes towards the renewal of the entire radiation law of the Earth and to raising the vibration of the Earth, so that it may increase in light and power. For the one who purifies himself in My Spirit, renews himself and gradually again becomes the eternal law itself – and thus, divine. He will then also take part in this great process of evolution, so that in all spheres outside of the eternal heavens, of the pure Being, redemption will be completed in a shorter cycle.

The Earth is about to cleanse itself by first shaking off all that prevents it from having a higher vibration. Thus, it gives man the chance to live on it in accordance with My will, My law. This mighty turn of time has begun. I, the Spirit of truth, make all things new.

In this time of radical change from the old world to the Age of Light, a radical change is also taking place in many of My human children. They sense the movement of My Spirit in themselves and strive to put My powers, the laws of life, into practice in everyday life. However, the causal energies, too, are still active in them, so that many waver between Me, the Spirit of eternity, and matter: between fulfilling the eternal laws and following their humanness, their human desires and passions. This back and forth causes My human children to waver.

The phase of transformation of My human children's nature and of the transformations in and on the Earth will come to an end. During the time of radical change, the darkness will attack again and again in order to save its territory, the Earth, for itself. In accordance with this, again and again, there will be invasions of the darkness, fighting and peace, a back and forth, a "for" and "against" in and among all nations.

The invasions of the demonic forces will keep increasing, because the people are not yet sufficiently firm in Me, the Spirit. Again and again, nations will rise and be against each other. Fighting, need, illness, suffering and infirmity will carry off people. Many will flee from the centers of concentration of negative energies – that is, from *those* nations where wars, riots, disasters, diseases and epidemics have their effects. The New Age, the Age of Light, will rise from this chaos of causes and effects. This age will take on form and shape more and more clearly and extensively on the Earth, which is increasingly purifying itself.

To the same extent as the Earth purifies itself and the Age of Light rises, those people who seriously and consistently walk the path to Me, the Eternal, will spiritualize themselves. A new human race in and with Christ, the human race of Christ – will rise from the ruins of the human ego.

The human race of Christ, which has its roots in the lineage of David, will form the race of the God-men, which is characterized by its adherence to the eternal laws. The ruler of the God-men, of the human race of Christ, is the Christ, My first-beheld and firstborn Son, the Co-Regent of the heavens. He is the ruler of the Kingdom of God on Earth, of the Kingdom of Peace. The ruler of the Kingdom of God, My Son, is, at the same time, brother and friend to the God-men. They will call Him Jaehowea, the divine One.

I, your Lord and God, now reveal from My eternal law the excerpts for the Kingdom of Peace of Jesus Christ in the three-dimensional world.

Even now, people who strive for the race of God-men can orient themselves by these aspects of the law for the Kingdom of God on Earth.

God-men rest in themselves, in their purified temple. They remain faithful to Me, God, their Lord, by keeping the eternal laws. Faithfulness towards Me also includes faithfulness in thinking, speaking and acting towards one's neighbor.

There is a commandment that says: Maintain openness in every situation of life, then you will also remain faithful to your neighbor in God.

Heaven is open and accessible to the God-man, because it is active and effective in him – it is the law of purity, of justice, of absolute selfless love. Therefore, there should be no malice in your heart, nor should it be closed.

God-men love each other selflessly as I, their Lord and God, love them. Every thought, every word and also every deed of the God-men is a divine action.

Every lawful action already bears in itself the lawful reaction, the eternally streaming life, the I Am.

In the Kingdom of Peace of Jesus Christ, My own waste no energy with impure sensations, thoughts, words and deeds. They let the eternal law flow; for their sensations, thoughts, words and deeds are the Absolute Law – even when they speak about things and events, when they talk with each other in their free time or before or after the meal at the Lord's Table. They rest in Me and I, the eternal law, flow through them, through every sensation, through every thought, through every word, through every deed.

God-men in the Kingdom of Peace of Jesus Christ live in time and space. Therefore, they have their fixed times, their working hours and their leisure time.

At work, too, they activate the eternal law flowing through them with lawful sensations, thoughts, words and deeds. Through them and the work of their hands, this then begins to increasingly bring forth and accomplish what they have entered into the flowing stream, into the law. Their life is a giving and receiving.

God-men fulfill the law that says: Every sensation, every thought, every word and every deed is lawful, and is thus, prayer. And so, God-men will no longer "earn their bread by the sweat of their brow."

Work is active prayer.

God-men live together, they are active and work together, because One is for all and all are for One: Christ. Therefore, they do not cut themselves off from each other and also arrange their leisure time together in a lawful way.

They will also live in their living communities, too, in accordance with these high ethics and morals, so that they may always appear before My face as noble, pure beings.

God-men live in unity with the nature kingdoms, and the animals and plants serve them. Therefore, they will lawfully possess the Earth.

God-men in the Kingdom of Peace of Jesus Christ work with their developed spiritual talents and abilities *on* the Earth and *for* the Earth, the three-dimensional world. The entire Earth – the planet of God, of the Creator – will be one great garden of God, where the dwelling places of the God-men blend harmoniously into the landscape. Their workplaces fit into the landscape in the same way. There, they work and are active in serving their neighbor.

The creative powers of serving, of giving and receiving are thus developed within the divine person: The God-man has a sense of community. He is in unity with God and his neighbor and cultivates the community with all brothers and sisters. His life is a giving and receiving. The God-man has no claims of possession, for he lives in the fullness; everything belongs to him.

He does not work for so-called money, but for the community, for the great whole.

The God-man owns infinity, because the fullness from God is alive in him and he thus knows the great whole, infinity, to be his own. He calls everything his own and maintains and tends it according to the eternal laws of unity and community. He knows that possession obligates.

The God-man is kind and radiates love. In all matters of his life, he represents his divine brother, the ruler of the Kingdom of Peace, Christ, through lawful feeling, thinking, living and acting.

The thoughts of God-men are thoughts of light and have no limitation. Accordingly, their dwelling places are not separated by fences or walls. Just as they are one with God, the Eternal, who I Am, and with the ruler of the Kingdom of Peace, their brother Jaehowea, the divine One, they are united among each other, too, in selfless love.

They feel they are one great unit in God, as the family of God on Earth, in which individual families live. There is no wooing among them.

The divine people find each other in accordance with the eternal laws; that is, they find each other as man and woman according to their radiation, which consists of mutual energies of like vibration and are based on the vibration of their mentality. These like-vibrating energies have their effect as positive radiation, as the giving element, in the male principle, and as negative radiation, as the receiving element in the female principle. Both are poles attuned to each other; their basic tendency is of like vibration.

They find each other through the contact of the vibration of their mentality. They join in matrimony in My Spirit and, in the solemn promise of faithfulness, they enter into the covenant with Me, the Eternal, and with each other. They enter into the great family of God, in order to live and be active in the law of unity, within the great whole.

The union of man and woman takes place only when they wish to have a child. The wish for a child is simultaneously stirred in both man and woman solely by the pure law of radiation. Procreation occurs according to the laws of nature for human bodies; it is pure and takes place in the pure radiation of the law in which they live and in which they move.

Both the man and the woman are in the service of their neighbor; they contribute their abilities and talents to the common good.

They live in Me, the Father-Mother-God. Whatever they do, they do thoroughly. They put the energy of God into everything they do and accomplish.

Everything is energy. I, your Lord and God, use your words and speak about energy with your words. Accordingly, the energy of an article of clothing is not less in value than the energy of a bowl of fruit, for all energy is vivified with My life, with My power. Everyone gives according to the amount of energy that he has received.

The God-man feels the energy-potential which radiates from the goods and services. He gives a corresponding energy-potential in return. For building a house, for example, he will give the corresponding energy-potential in service or goods. Said with your human words, the energy-potential can also be measured in amount or extent. The amount of energy-potential flows again in proportion to its extent.

When a person lives in Me, the Spirit of God, then he is wise and gives from Me, from the intelligence of God. Then he will no longer appraise and weigh, in a human manner, what is of lower or higher value. He knows it from within, from Me, the intelligence, God, and draws from it. This is not bartering, but a giving and receiving of energy. He achieves the just compensation in all things. There is no "mine" or "thine."

The gifts of the God-men are highly vibrating energy-potentials. God-men perform high-quality work, because their spiritual consciousness penetrates everything. Their goods and services are gifts of the Spirit of God. They know from their opened consciousness that eternal energies must flow; for the Earth and everything on it and in the more light-filled material cosmos can increase in light and power only when like energies unite. They know that, through the eternally streaming energy, they themselves and also the layers of the Earth reach an ever higher energetic vibration and that matter is thereby refined more and more, in order to finally enter again into the primordial substance, the seven-dimensional eternal creation.

The one who serves, for example, in the care of children or as a teacher in the educational field receives corresponding gifts, goods or coupons from the families whose children he, as teacher or helper, takes care of and guides into a lawful life. While teaching the use of language and numbers and helping the young people to unfold their abilities and talents, a teacher also introduces them to the laws of God.

The help and care of elderly people is also included in the service of helping others. The elderly remain in the family of God, which also guides them on their way into the fine-material life. Whether the soul is in a younger or older body – people of the Spirit help each other.

In this way, God-men fulfill the law of spiritual evolution, of higher development. Their thinking, living and working takes place in the stream of the eternal law. Thus, they cause the Earth – and moreover, the entire material universe – to become spiritualized more and more.

In the Kingdom of Peace, in the Kingdom of God on Earth, the radiation law of the Earth is the spiritual life of the children of God. They are thus united with the whole of infinity, because they are one with Me, the Eternal. The atmosphere of the Earth, which is the mirror of the Earth, will also be clear and receptive for higher energies and forms of life.

Just as the pure heavenly messengers will be among the people, so will the part-material beings from higher light-sources, who serve in the Redeemer-work of Christ, also unite again with the human brothers and sisters. For they and their human brothers and sisters are of one spirit in Christ, their divine brother – called Jaehowea, the divine One – the ruler of the Kingdom of Peace of God on Earth.

At the end of the Kingdom of Peace of Jesus Christ, the demons will be allowed to try their strength once more against man and the Earth. It is still their aim to reconquer the Earth, their former base. This is conceded to them by Me, so that they may recognize themselves and accept Me, the eternal God, in Christ, My Son, and bow to the might and power and love. This invasion of the demonic forces into those regions of the Earth and of the atmosphere where centers of concentration of negative energies still exist will be merely a deplorable attempt – like outbursts of the human ego – and will no longer extend over the whole Earth. Every venture to possess the whole Earth will fail, because the God-men will have imbued the Earth with light and power.

After this invasion, the further transformation will follow: Since I have transformed layers of the coarse-material substance into energies of higher vibration through the activities of the spiritual people, the earth-mantle has become more permeable. It will expand and burst apart, and the soul of the Earth, the spiritual part-planet from the eternal Jerusalem, will be assimilated into the pure Being. The bursting earth-mantle will continue to refine in the universe and be led to the eternally streaming energy.

At the same time, other material suns and stars will also be shaken. Their spiritual part-aspects, too, will gradually be led to the eternal Being. This is how the dissolution of all material forms and energies will take place.

The one who hears and reads these words of Mine is initiated into the coming events and into the Being. Each one of My children is free to believe in it or to reject Me, the truth of life, God, his Lord, for I have given free will to them. Therefore, each one is responsible for himself – for his belief or his unbelief, for the "for" or "against" Me.

May the one who has eyes, see; may the one who has ears, hear. The one whose soul feels the light of the Eternal knows that these laws for the Kingdom of Peace of Jesus Christ are given from Me, God, the eternal truth, which I Am from eternity to eternity – the primordial Father of all My children from eternity to eternity.

Appendix

Universal Life Worldwide

Jesus, the Christ, the prophetic Spirit of Original Christianity, has drawn a mighty bow by way of the prophetic word in our time. Universal Life worldwide means that the universal, eternal Spirit, God in Jesus, the Christ, brought an all-encompassing work into the world. His radiation is strengthened in the people who are of good will. The great bow can be compared to a mighty rainbow, which stretches around the Earth in all facets of inner life.

Jesus of Nazareth, the Son of God, was not a clergyman. His teaching was and is the highest spiritual standard, which He taught us from the eternal Being. The highest Being has no churches. For this reason, He did not found any churches. Because Jesus of Nazareth was Spirit of the eternal Spirit, of perfection, He had neither titles nor means, nor did He introduce any "high clergy."

Jesus, the Christ, spoke of His following. He wanted His teaching to be actualized. The Kingdom of Peace of Jesus Christ, which He announced, will develop solely from actualization.

Every external church is an institution filled with traditions, which are rites, dogmas, creeds and the like. Where tradition exists there is not only a standstill but also regression. We experience this today in the institutional churches founded by human beings.

The Spirit of God cannot be pressed into templates, which the caste of priests at the time of Jesus and the present-day caste of priests wants to impose on the great all-encompassing Spirit through institutional proclamations.

Where people follow Christ, by doing what Jesus taught, they are directly in the Original Christian stream, which already after Christ moved in the prophetic Spirit. It is reported of the Early Christians that one had the gift of healing and the other the gift of prophecy. At all times, there were enlightened people and mystics, Christian movements, which liberated themselves from the pressures of dogmatic and ritual church leadership, in order to solely follow the Nazarene, which means to fulfill His teachings step by step, not the teachings of the institutional "high clergy." For example, the Bogumils, Cathars, Waldesians, and others, followed the great Spirit and strove to honor Jesus, the Christ, and no institution. That is why many of them were tortured to death during the church Inquisition.

And today there are again people who directly link up with the teachings of Jesus of Nazareth; and the prophetic Spirit speaks again today – through a woman with the earthly name Gabriele, through whom a mighty work of revelation has developed, which is distributed worldwide through countless books, cassettes, CDs and DVDs and hundreds of radio and television programs.

The prophetic Spirit, the Christ of God, gave insight into the almighty, eternally prevailing laws of eternal life. For 33 years, He has been teaching this great cosmic Being, which comes to the Earth and brings the Kingdom of Peace to people who are on the path toward peaceableness.

Jesus, the Christ, taught and teaches the eternal, all-encompassing law. He instructed and instructs every person in the law of cause and effect. Jesus, the Christ, and the heavenly messengers taught the Inner Path, in order to open up the seven basic powers of the Being in the soul, which bring freedom, happiness, inner success, peace and peaceableness to those people who develop love for the all-encompassing eternal Spirit. Through this, the person becomes healthy, happy and peaceable, in order to found the Kingdom of Peace, which the prophets of the Old Testament and Jesus, the Christ, have announced.

In this mighty bow that is spanned worldwide, comparable to a rainbow, and which was announced already at the time of Noah, the mighty Spirit founded, via people who move in the following of Jesus, the Christ, nonprofit social and medical facilities and an agriculture that is in accord with nature and keeps no livestock, that produces natural foodstuffs in peaceable farming, marketing them at marketplaces and via a mail order house.

Jesus, the Christ, still teaches the Inner Path today through His prophetess. Via radio and television, it goes out into the whole world, and all over the Earth people are walking this path. His word, which flows over the Earth in the mighty bow of the I AM THE I AM, embraces all people who are of good will.

The teaching of Jesus of Nazareth was and is an absolutely free teaching. This lies in the words "Follow Me." Jesus did not coerce people to believe God's word. He taught the path to the eternal Father and teaches it today as the Christ of God. However, He does not exert pressure on anyone, neither as Jesus, nor today, as Christ. Today, as then, it is: The one who wants to accept His teaching walks the path of the Sermon on the Mount and the Ten Commandments, that is, he follows Jesus, the Christ. The cornerstone of the Kingdom of Peace lies in the teaching of Jesus, the Christ. Whoever lives the peaceable teaching of Jesus, the Christ, step by step, that is, fulfills it, is a fellow builder of the Kingdom of God on Earth.

Many of today's Original Christians strive to follow Jesus, the Christ, so that His Kingdom of Peace can open up, which first announces itself in the hearts of those who fulfill His teaching step by step. As Original Christians in the following of the Nazarene, we have neither dogmas nor rites: we are not bound to ceremonies or creeds. We feel free in the one Spirit, in the Spirit of the Nazarene, of Jesus, the Christ, who is the Redeemer of all men and souls.

Jesus, the Christ, taught His followers ethical-moral principles – the highest values of the Inner Being, so that they may live and work in His Spirit. The all-encompassing teaching work and aid organization of Jesus, the Christ, finds completion in the Gabriele Foundation, the Saamlinic Work of Neighborly Love for Nature and Animals, for in this foundation the law of life, love, is in first place.

If you would like more information or are interested in the gathering places of events near you, call or write us. We will gladly send you information free of charge.

Universal Life
Haugerring 7
97070 Würzburg, Germany

P.O. Box 3549
Woodbridge, CT 06525, USA
www.universal-life.cc
1-800-846-2691

Christ, the Key
to the Door of Life
Universal Life

His Word Comes True
Gabriele Foundation
The Saamlinic Work of Neighborly Love
For Nature and Animals
Your Kingdom Comes – Your Will Is Done
Pray and Work

For nearly 3000 years, it has been said that a Kingdom of Peace will emerge on this Earth. The first to speak about this was the prophet Isaiah: "They shall beat their swords into plowshares and their spears into pruning hooks ... The wolf shall dwell with the lamb, the leopard shall lie down with the kid, the calf and the lion and the fatling together ... and a little child shall lead them ..." Seven hundred years later Jesus of Nazareth walked on this Earth and spoke about the Kingdom of God that was near. He did not mean an external kingdom, but an inner change through the fulfillment of the commandment of love for God and for neighbor. The Early Christians lived in this certainty, up until the influential church teacher Augustine announced at the beginning of the 5th century that the expected Kingdom of God had already emerged in the shape of the church. What became of this heinous distortion of the teachings of the Nazarene, has been experienced and endured by mankind during the past 2000 years.

Human beings have not only warred against each other and torn each other apart, but have even destroyed the Earth with its plants and animals more and more, which God, the Eternal, had given into their care. His will was that the people would preserve the Earth in love and unity, thus bringing about the Kingdom of Peace and of selfless, that is, giving, love on the Earth. But the opposite is what happened: The brutality of humans toward animals has reach proportions never before known; millions of cows and pigs lead a sad, dreary life in the dark barns of factory farms; millions of monkeys, dogs, cats and mice are brutalized to death in experimental laboratories; millions of wild animals fall victim to a primitive, merciless hunting, which ever more people are rejecting.

During this time of human hard-heartedness toward plants and animals, God, the eternal Spirit, has again sent a great prophet to us. Through Gabriele, the Spirit of God has given us countless revelations. From these one can deduce that this materialistic age is coming to an end and that the Kingdom of Peace is emerging through people, who – in the fulfillment of the divine will, which was expressed in the Ten Commandments of God and deepened in the true teachings of Jesus, the Christ – preserve the Earth in love and unity, so that the Kingdom of Peace can emerge. The Gabriele Foundation, the Saamlinic Work of Neighborly Love for Nature and Animals, was developed on an external level for this purpose. The foundation, which bears the name of its founder, creates habitats from the fields and *woods, where animals can lead a life that is worthy of the free creatures of God, where they can move freely and in peace, according to their species, without fear, of being chased and tormented. A positive communication is developing there, between the animals and humans, who go toward them with help and care, showing them respect, esteem and friendship in their feelings, thoughts and selfless deeds. The Gabriele Foundation builds shelters and nesting boxes, as well as watering places and sees to the maintenance of food sources for the animals. It cares for the biotopes on the developing isle of peace, it frees the woods of people's trash and protects the meadows, fields and groundwater from poison and slurry, so that natural growth flourishes on the fields. It appoints trained hunters as forest rangers, to do justice to the interests of the woods and the animals – through care and attention and through a peaceable way of forestry that considers the animals' natural requirements for life. The animals accept this help thankfully. Through this daily care, they overcome their fear of people bit by bit and gradually gain trust.*

Many people feel addressed by this task; they want to grow into an awareness of the unity of life, which encompasses the animals and all of creation. Peaceable farming is also part of neighborly love for nature and animals; it neither keeps livestock nor slaughters animals, and it protects the soil from environmental poisons. The collaboration of people, nature and animals takes place (on Earth as it is in heaven) in a great, creative unity, which brings forth life.

A team of scientists is associated with the foundation, which, via field tests, analyzes how much nature and animals suffer under the aggressive behavior of people – not only through herbicides and pesticides or manure and slurry; hunting also has an invisible negative effect on the harmony and unity of nature that goes beyond the measurable damage. Shots not only frighten animals, but also impair the life in plants and soil. The first measurements have already been taken. The study of the effects of human aggression toward the animal world will also include the repercussions on human beings and will explore to what extent the animal flesh consumed by them contains harmful substances and, for example, the vibration potential of fear and suffering.

Through Gabriele, the Spirit of God pointed out that mankind is gradually reaching the pinnacle of its negative doings. People believe that animals are a commodity and that the Earth may be exploited, to satisfy every pursuit of profit. The effects of this wrong behavior are coming toward mankind ever more rapidly – above all, in the form of epidemics and natural disasters.

Man, to whom the care of the Earth was given, has lost his dominion over it. This is why the Spirit of God revealed the following through the prophetic word for this time: When spiritually cosmic, peaceable people inhabit the Earth, I will again give the Earth to the people, just as Jesus, the Christ, said in the Sermon on the Mount: "Blessed are the meek, for they shall inherit the Earth." The animals, the plants, the elemental forces, the Earth, all of nature are a part of life; via them, the Kingdom of Peace of God will emerge, in which it will be on Earth as it is in heaven.

The Gabriele Foundation vouches for the fact that the work of neighborly love is carried out in the spirit of the teachings of Jesus, the Christ, and in fulfillment of God's will. Those responsible in the foundation stand for this before God and the authorities of this world. Friends and supporters of the foundation are aware that peace among people and peace between humans and animals belong together. They act in the awareness that all life comes from God and that nature and animals, just as humans, are imbued by His power. What now becomes visible externally emerged from the spiritual foundation, from the great work of revelation of God through Gabriele: the first foundations for the Kingdom of Peace.

Gabriele Foundation
The Saamlinic Work of
Neighborly Love for Nature and Animals
Max-Braun-Str. 2
97828 Marktheidenfeld, Germany
Tel. +49(0)9391/504-427, Fax +49(0)9391/504-430

www.Gabriele-Foundation.org

For a better understanding of this work:

God-Prophecy

What is a prophet? –
His calling and his task – The prophetic word of the Christ
of God in our time

"This Is My Word" is the book whose contents come directly from the primordial source, God. Christ, the Redeemer of all men and souls, reveals Himself through the prophetic word of a human being, Gabriele – through our sister, the prophetess and emissary of God in this mighty turn of time.

Even though God spoke and communicated with people at all times through prophets, enlightening, admonishing, comforting and guiding them – thus being with His children – many people in our time no longer know of this nearness of the speaking God; prophecy hardly has any more place in this world-oriented, materialistic way of thinking and living. This is why these explanatory words about prophecy are necessary. However, these explanations are also important for people in the coming epochs, as well as for those who will live on Earth after the mighty turn of time, the inhabitants of the Kingdom of Peace of Jesus Christ. These explanations serve as a reminder; for the prophetic word will no longer exist in the Era of Light. The people will have become the word itself, since they live the law of God.

God spoke to mankind in the Old Covenant. Through the mouth of prophets, He addressed people in His "I Am." Some of the most renown prophets were Isaiah, Elijah, Jeremiah, Daniel and Job. The greatest of all prophets was Jesus of Nazareth, the incarnated Son of God. And in the two thousand years that followed, prophets of God appeared again and again in Christianity. Light-filled beings from heaven, whose mission was to be the speaking instruments of God, were incarnated in the human bodies of these prophets.

The prophet is like a trumpet through which God, the eternal Spirit, blows. So that the people can hear and understand the eternal truth, God, the language of light of God is translated into the mother-tongue of His instrument, the human being. True prophets of God remain fully conscious while the Spirit of God speaks through them. Jesus of Nazareth, the greatest prophet, is also an example of this. While Jesus was fully conscious, God, the Eternal, spoke through Him as through all true prophets – in the Old Covenant as well as after the time of Jesus. A person falls into a trance solely when he takes in forces from the beyond which are not the direct radiation of God. This is not the case with a genuine prophet of God.

The soul of the prophet is prepared for the approaching task in its human body over a long period of time, often over several incarnations. Finally, the human being is reminded by God at a certain moment of the mission lying in his soul; this is the so-called "call-ing."

The path of the prophet of God is a path of suffering. He has an absolute obligation to God and has to express what God inspires him with. The earnest and admonishing words of God, which call for changing one's ways, are always disagreeable to the people of this world. This is why the prophets usually had to suffer mockery, slander, persecution and often death.

There are two categories of prophets: the proclaiming prophets – generally called prophets – and the teaching prophets. Through the proclaiming prophets, God gave and gives mankind the spiritual knowledge and the basic spiritual laws which the people need to orient their life to the divine and to gradually attain a lawful life. He admonished and admonishes people to fulfill the will of God. Proclaiming prophets make people aware that they are children of God; they give them an understanding of His love and wisdom and show them the way home to Him.

Through teaching prophets, who appear during great turns of time, the eternal Spirit not only anchors the spiritual wealth that had been revealed before in the consciousness of people, but conveys further and higher spiritual laws as well as aspects of the holy primordial law. The teaching prophet thus brings to mankind the laws of God in detail and interprets them. Through him, the Spirit of God teaches people the Inner Path back to the eternal homeland, where every soul once came from. Through the teaching prophet, God has always taught a spiritual wealth that exceeds what was known thus far.

The teaching prophet has first to work on himself, to develop and to actualize everything that God, the Lord, wants to teach through him. He has to walk the Inner Path, the path of self-recognition and purification, himself, ahead of all people. After some time, this person, who is instructed and schooled directly by the Spirit of God, reaches the peak of mystical development, the goal of the seven-level path to God, thus becoming one with the consciousness, God. Such a person then recognizes, perceives and knows instantly those things and events that are concealed to the person who still lives in the world of the senses.

Through this, the teaching prophet becomes the emissary of God, drawing from his opened consciousness that has become one with the divine. He no longer sees things or people as they seem to be, but perceives things, events and people as they are. He sees to the very bottom of everything that exists.

In the Old Testament, God sent to the Earth mainly proclaiming prophets, through whom He sought to bring mankind out of its bondage to matter and onto the right path to higher spiritual development.

After this, Christ, the part-power of the primordial power, the Co-Regent of the heavens, was active as Redeemer and teaching prophet among the people. They did not recognize Him nor accept Him as Jesus of Nazareth – like many of the true prophets – and brought His life to an early end. With the words "It is finished" on Golgotha, He was able to accomplish Redemption, implanting into every soul a spark of the redeeming part-power of the primordial power as supporting power that leads back to God.

Now, God has sent again into this world a being, incarnated in the person called Gabriele. She serves the Eternal in this world as His teaching prophetess. Her opened spiritual consciousness, that rests in the Almighty and is imbued with the power of the Almighty, knows the eternal laws and the path to the eternal law, God. Our sister, Gabriele, thus perceives in her divine consciousness and receives from the Eternal, via her divine consciousness, the all-encompassing path to the heart of God. Using simple words, she is able to explain the all-encompassing Inner Path, to lead a person to his causes, to help him eliminate them and, if he is willing, to guide him to Christ. She has insight into the depths of a person, into the state of his soul. Her other task as teaching prophetess is to now bring into this world the details of the eternal law of God for all spheres of life: for living together in the family and at work, in business and society, for raising children and for social services, as well as for the well-being of soul and body. She also teaches the step by step application of the eternal laws in all spheres of life.

Teaching prophets thus have – in addition to the mission of being God's direct trumpet – the task of instructing their fellow men in all the laws of spiritual life and helping them in all questions concerning the inner life.

This is why our sister Gabriele had to go through, experience, suffer and overcome a great deal herself – over several lives on Earth – in order to be able to understand people and show them the right path.

In this great turn of time in which we now live, Christ founded His Kingdom of Peace on Earth through His prophetic word and through the Covenant Community New Jerusalem.

To prepare mankind for the Kingdom of God on Earth, the Eternal is now giving explanations and teachings for all the basic questions of man at this time. And so, Christ gave a revelation through the prophetic word in 1989 on His way of living, thinking and working as Jesus of Nazareth; at the same time, He explained for the present and coming times the correlations and significance of His life on Earth. The explanations, corrections and deepenings in this book "This Is My Word" are the authentic word of Christ. The statements in the already existing book, "The Gospel of Jesus," and what is now additionally explained, corrected and deepened by Christ, significantly highlight His way of living, thinking and working as Jesus of Nazareth. They serve the people's understanding and are an example for them at this time, as well as for the inhabitants of the

Kingdom of Peace, the Kingdom of Light of Christ on Earth.

Moreover, during this mighty turn of time, Christ leads us into the whole truth: He now reveals – as already mentioned – the laws of God for all spheres of life on this Earth, thus building up the all-encompassing Kingdom of God on Earth.

*The Original Christians
in Universal Life*

Books in Universal Life

*To order any of these books
or to obtain a complete catalog of all our books,
please contact:*

*THE WORD
P. O. Box 5643
97006 Wuerzburg
GERMANY*

*The Word – The Universal Spirit
P. O. Box 3549
Woodbridge, CT 06525
U S A*
1-800-846-2691

www.universal-spirit.org
E-mail: info@universal-spirit.org

*or:
Order our books at amazon.com*